BLOOM'S PERIOD STUDIES

BLOOM'S PERIOD STUDIES

Modern American Poetry

Edited and with an introduction by

Harold Bloom
Sterling Professor of the Humanities
Yale University

CHELSEA HOUSE
P U B L I S H E R S
A Haights Cross Communications ⚡ Company ®

P h i l a d e l p h i a

Library of Congress Cataloging-in-Publication Data

Modern American poetry / [edited by] Harold Bloom.
    p. cm. — (Bloom's period studies)
  Includes bibliographical references and index.
  ISBN 0-7910-8237-7 (alk. paper)
  1. American poetry—20th century—History and criticism. 2. Modernism (Literature)–
United States. I. Bloom, Harold. II. Series.
  PS374.M535M63 2005
  811'.508—dc22
                                      2005000754

Contributing editor: Jesse Zuba

Cover design by Keith Trego

Cover:

Layout by EJB Publishing Services

All links and web addresses were checked and verified to be correct at the time of
publication. Because of the dynamic nature of the web, some addresses and links may
have changed since publication and may no longer be valid.

Every effort has been made to trace the owners of copyrighted material and secure
copyright permission. Articles appearing in this volume generally appear much as they di
in their original publication with little to no editorial changes. Those interested in
locating the original source will find bibliographic information on the first page of each
article as well as in the bibliography and acknowledgments sections of this volume.

Contents

Editor's Note

My Introduction comments upon eight poets: E.A. Robinson, Robert Frost, Wallace Stevens, William Carlos Williams, Ezra Pound, Marianne Moore, T.S. Eliot, and Hart Crane, who can be regarded as the major modern American poets who were born in the nineteenth century. Except for Moore, they are connected by the influence, sometimes concealed, of Emerson or Whitman, or both.

Moore is the subject of the greatest American critic since Emerson, the great theorist of rhetoric, Kenneth Burke, who finds in her a radiant sensitivity, after which the late Huge Kenner, supreme antiquarian Modernist, celebrates Pound's *Mauberley* sequence.

Alan Trachtenberg balances redemption and evil in Hart Crane's majestic myth of *The Bridge*, after which Thomas Whitaker praises an early group of the poems of W.C. Williams.

Wallace Stevens, our strongest poet since Whitman and Dickinson, is read as an ironic pastoralist by Helen Vendler, while Robert Langbaum examines *The Waste Land* as a blend of dramatic monologues.

Richard Poirier, Frost's canonical critic, contrasts his poet with Stevens, preferring Frost for his realistic vision of limitations, after which James E. Miller, Jr. contemplates the epic of W.C. Williams, *Paterson*.

The later poems of Stevens are regarded as those of his "whole being" by his best critic, Eleanor Cook, while the poet Edward Hirsch gives an overview of our poetry of the 1920s: Eliot, Millay, Cummings, Pound, Ransom, Williams, Moore, Stevens, Hart Crane, and a group including Bogan, Adams, Wylie, and Teasdale.

The most gifted of all American poets, ever, was Hart Crane, but his suicide at thirty-two deprived us of what should have been his major phases.

Langdon Hammer traces the antithetical influences of William Blake and T.S. Eliot on the young Hart Crane.

Katherine Kearns, in a brilliant feminist reading of Frost, shows us Frost's obsession with visionary, mythical maidens, after which David Bromwich accurately depicts Hart Crane's struggle with Eliot's influence.

Hilda Doolittle (H.D.) is praised by L.L. Martz as a prophet who proclaimed a curious new religion that blended lesbianism and Sigmund Freud.

The Harlem jazz poet, Langston Hughes, is realistically hailed by Anita Patterson for his authentic sense of the aesthetic achievement of jazz, while Bonnie Costello concludes this volume with an apotheosis of Marianne Moore as a poet of the American landscape.

HAROLD BLOOM

Introduction

EDWIN ARLINGTON ROBINSON

Emerson himself was a product of New England and a man of strong moral habits.... He gave to American romanticism, in spite of its irresponsible doctrine, a religious tone which it has not yet lost and which has often proved disastrous.... there is a good deal of this intellectual laziness in Robinson; and as a result of the laziness, there is a certain admixture of Emersonian doctrine, which runs counter to the principles governing most of his work and the best of it.

—YVOR WINTERS

The Torrent and the Night Before (published late in 1896 by Robinson himself) remains one of the best first volumes in our poetry. Three of its shorter poems—"George Crabbe," "Luke Havergal," "The Clerks"—Robinson hardly surpassed, and three more—"Credo," "Walt Whitman" (which Robinson unfortunately abandoned), and "The Children of the Night" (reprinted as title-poem in his next volume)—are memorable works, all in the earlier Emersonian mode that culminates in "Bacchus." The stronger "Luke Havergal" stems from the darker Emersonianism of "Experience" and "Fate," and has a relation to the singular principles of *Merlin*. It prophesies Robinson's finest later lyrics, such as "Eros Turannos" and "For a Dead Lady," and suggests the affinity between Robinson and Frost that is due to their common Emersonian tradition.

In *Captain Craig* (1902) Robinson published "The Sage," a direct hymn of homage to Emerson, whose *The Conduct of Life* had moved him profoundly at a first reading in August 1899. Robinson had read the earlier

1

Emerson well before, but it is fascinating that he came to essays like "Fate" and "Power" only after writing "Luke Havergal" and some similar poems, for his deeper nature then discovered itself anew. He called "Luke Havergal" "a piece of deliberate degeneration," which I take to mean what an early letter calls "sympathy for failure where fate has been abused and self demoralized." Browning, the other great influence upon Robinson, is obsessed with "deliberate degeneration" in this sense; Childe Roland's and Andrea del Sarto's failures are wilful abuses of fate and demoralizations of self. "The Sage" praises Emerson's "fierce wisdom," emphasizes Asia's influence upon him, and hardly touches his dialectical optimism. This Emerson is "previsioned of the madness and the mean," fit seer for "the fiery night" of "Luke Havergal":

> But there, where western glooms are gathering,
> The dark will end the dark, if anything:
> God slays Himself with every leaf that flies,
> And hell is more than half of paradise.

These are the laws of Compensation, "or that nothing is got for nothing," as Emerson says in "Power." At the depth of Robinson is this Emersonian fatalism, as it is in Frost, and even in Henry James. "The world is mathematical," Emerson says, "and has no casualty in all its vast and flowing curve." Robinson, brooding on the end of "Power," confessed: "He really gets after one," and spoke of Emerson as walloping one "with a big New England shingle," the cudgel of Fate. But Robinson was walloped too well, by which I do not mean what Winters means, since I cannot locate any "intellectual laziness" in Emerson. Unlike Browning and Hardy, Robinson yielded too much to Necessity.... Circumstances and temperament share in Robinson's obsession with Nemesis, but poetic misprision is part of the story also, for Robinson's *tessera* in regard to Emerson relies on completing the sage's fatalism. From Emerson's categories of power and circumstance, Robinson fashions a more complete single category, in a personal idealism that is a "philosophy of desperation," as he feared it might be called. The persuasive desperation of "Luke Havergal" and "Eros Turannos" is his best expression of this nameless idealism that is also a fatalism, but "The Children of the Night," for all its obtrusive echoes of Tennyson and even Longfellow, shows more clearly what Robinson found to be a possible stance:

> It is the crimson, not the gray,
>   That charms the twilight of all time;

It is the promise of the day
That makes the starry sky sublime;

It is the faith within the fear
That holds us to the life we curse;
So let us in ourselves revere
The Self which is the Universe!

The bitter charm of this is that it qualifies so severely its too-hopeful and borrowed music. Even so early, Robinson has "completed" Emersonian Self-Reliance and made it his own by emphasizing its Stoic as against its Transcendental or Bacchic aspect. When, in "Credo," Robinson feels "the coming glory of the Light!" the light nevertheless emanates from unaware angels who wove "dead leaves to garlands where no roses are." It is not that Robinson believed, with Melville, that the invisible spheres were formed in fright, but he shrewdly suspected that the ultimate world, though existent, was nearly as destitute as this one. He is an Emersonian incapable of transport, an ascetic of the Transcendental spirit, contrary to an inspired saint like Jones Very or to the Emerson of "The Poet," but a contrary, not a negation, to use Blake's distinction. Not less gifted than Frost, he achieves so much less because he gave himself away to Necessity so soon in his poetic life. Frost's Job quotes "Uriel" to suggest that confusion is "the form of forms," the way all things return upon themselves, like rays:

Though I hold rays deteriorate to nothing,
First white, then red, then ultra red, then out.

This is cunning and deep in Frost, the conviction that "all things come round," even the mental confusions of God as He morally blunders. What we miss in Robinson is this quality of savagery, the strength that can end "Directive" by saying:

Here are your waters and your watering place.
Drink and be whole again beyond confusion.

To be beyond confusion is to be beyond the form of forms that is Fate's, and to be whole beyond Fate suggests an end to circlings, a resolution to all the Emersonian turnings that see unity, and yet behold divisions. Frost will play at [yielding to Necessity], many times, but his wariness saved him from Robinson's self-exhaustions.

There is a fine passage in "Captain Craig" where the talkative captain asks: "Is it better to be blinded by the lights, / Or by the shadows?" This supposes grandly that we are to be blinded in any case, but Robinson was not blinded by his shadows. Yet he was ill-served by American Romanticism, though not for the reasons Winters offers. It demands the exuberance of a Whitman in his fury of poetic incarnation, lest the temptation to join Ananke come too soon and too urgently to be resisted. Robinson was nearly a great poet, and would have prospered more if he had been chosen by a less drastic tradition.

ROBERT FROST

"Directive" is Frost's poem of poems or form of forms, a meditation whose rays perpetually return upon themselves. "All things come round," even our mental confusion as we blunder morally, since the Demiurge is nothing but a moral blunderer. Frost shares the fine Emersonian wildness or freedom, the savage strength of the essay "Power" that suggests a way of being whole beyond Fate, of arriving at an end to circlings, at a resolution to all the Emersonian turnings that see unity, and yet behold divisions: "The world is mathematical, and has no casualty, in all its vast and flowing curve." "Directive" appears to be the poem in which Frost measures the lot, and forgives himself the lot, and perhaps even casts out remorse. In some sense, it was the poem he always wrote and rewrote, in a revisionary process present already in *A Boy's Will* (1913) but not fully worked out until *Steeple Bush* (1947), where "Directive" was published when Frost was seventy-three. "The Demiurge's Laugh" in *A Boy's Will* features a mocking demonic derision at the self-realization that "what I hunted was no true god."

North of Boston (1914) has its most memorable poem in the famous "After Apple-Picking," a gracious hymn to the necessity of yielding up the quest, of clambering down from one's "long two-pointed ladder's sticking through a tree / Toward heaven still." Frost's subtlest of perspectivizings is the true center of the poem:

> I cannot rub the strangeness from my sight
> I got from looking through a pane of glass
> I skimmed this morning from the drinking trough
> And held against the world of hoary grass.
> It melted, and I let it fall and break.

The sheet of ice is a lens upon irreality, but so are Frost's own eyes, or anyone's, in his cosmos. This supposed nature-poet represents his harsh landscapes as a full version of the Gnostic *kenoma*, the cosmological emptiness into which we have been thrown by the mocking Demiurge. This is the world of *Mountain Interval* (1916), where "the broken moon" is preferred to the dimmed sun, where the oven bird sings of "that other fall we name the fall," and where the birches:

> shed crystal shells
> Shattering and avalanching on the snow crust—
> Such heaps of broken glass to sweep away
> You'd think the inner dome of heaven had fallen.

Mountain Interval abounds in images of the shattering of human ties, and of humans, as in the horrifying "Out, Out—." But it would be redundant to conduct an overview of all Frost's volumes in pursuit of an experiential darkness that never is dispelled. A measurer of stone walls, as Frost names himself in the remarkable "A Star in a Stoneboat," is never going to be surprised that life is a sensible emptiness. The demiurgic pattern of "Design," with its "assorted characters of death and blight," is the rule in Frost. There are a few exceptions, but they give Frost parodies rather than poems.

Frost wrote the concluding and conclusive Emersonian irony for all his work in the allegorical "A Cabin in the Clearing," the set-piece of *In the Clearing* (1962), published for his eighty-eighth birthday, less than a year before his death. Mist and Smoke, guardian wraiths and counterparts, eavesdrop on the unrest of a human couple, murmuring in their sleep. These guardians haunt us because we are their kindred spirits, for we do not know where we are, since who we are "is too much to believe." We are "too sudden to be credible," and so the accurate image for us is "an inner haze," full kindred to mist and smoke. For all the genial tone, the spirit of "A Cabin in the Clearing" is negative even for Frost. His final letter, dictated just before his death, states an unanswerable question as though it were not a question: "How can we be just in a world that needs mercy and merciful in a world that needs justice." The Demiurge's laugh lurks behind the sentence, though Frost was then in no frame of spirit to indulge a demiurgic imagination.

Frost would have been well content to give his mentor Emerson the last word, though "content" is necessarily an inadequate word in this dark context. Each time I reread the magnificent essay "Illusions," which concludes and crowns *The Conduct of Life*, I am reminded of the poetry of Robert Frost. The reminder is strongest in two paragraphs near the end that seem to be "Directive" writ large, as though Emerson had been brooding upon his descendant:

> We cannot write the order of the variable winds. How can we penetrate the law of our shifting moods and susceptibility? Yet they differ as all and nothing. Instead of the firmament of yesterday, which our eyes require, it is to-day an eggshell which coops us in; we cannot even see what or where our stars of destiny are. From day to day, the capital facts of human life are hidden from our eyes. Suddenly the mist rolls up, and reveals them, and we think how much good time is gone, that might have been saved, had any hint of these things been shown. A sudden rise in the road shows us the system of mountains, and all the summits, which have been just as near us all the year, but quite out of mind. But these alternations are not without their order, and we are parties to our various fortune. If life seem a succession of dreams, yet poetic justice is done in dreams also. The visions of good men are good; it is the undisciplined will that is whipped with bad thoughts and bad fortunes. When we break the laws, we lose our hold on the central reality. Like sick men in hospitals, we change only from bed to bed, from one folly to another; and it cannot signify much what becomes of such castaways, wailing, stupid, comatose creatures, lifted from bed to bed, from the nothing of life to the nothing of death.
>
> In this kingdom of illusions we grope eagerly for stays and foundations. There is none but a strict and faithful dealing at home, and a severe barring out of all duplicity or illusion there. Whatever games are played with us, we must play no games with ourselves, but deal in our privacy with the last honesty and truth. I look upon the simple and childish virtues of veracity and honesty as the root of all that is sublime in character. Speak as you think, be what you are, pay your debts of all kinds. I prefer to be owned as sound and solvent, and my word as good as my bond, and to be what cannot be skipped, or dissipated, or undermined, to all the *éclat* in the universe. This reality is the foundation of friendship, religion, poetry, and art. At the top or at the bottom of all illusions, I set the cheat which still leads us to work and live for appearances, in spite of our conviction, in all sane hours, that it is what we really are that avails with friends, with strangers, and with fate or fortune.

WALLACE STEVENS

"Leave the many and hold the few," Emerson advises in his late poem "Terminus," thus sanctioning the democratic poet, like Whitman, in the pragmatic address to an actual elite. Stevens needed little sanctioning as to audience, but he was rather anxious about his own constant emphasis upon the self as solitary "scholar," and his recourse was to plead "poverty." He cannot have been unaware that both "scholar" and "poverty" in his rather precise senses were Emersonian usages. A great coverer of traces, Stevens may be judged nevertheless to have turned more to a tradition than to a man. American Romanticism found its last giant in Stevens, who defines the tradition quite as strongly as it informs him.

"The prologues are over.... It is time to choose," and the Stevens I think we must choose writes the poems not of an empty spirit in vacant space, but of a spirit so full of itself that there is room for nothing else. This description hardly appears to flatter Stevens, yet I render it in his praise. Another of his still neglected poems, for which my own love is intense, is entitled simply "Poem with Rhythms":

The hand between the candle and the wall
Grows large on the wall.

The mind between this light or that and space,
(This man in a room with an image of the world,
That woman waiting for the man she loves,)
Grows large against space:

There the man sees the image clearly at last.
There the woman receives her lover into her heart
And weeps on his breast, though he never comes.

It must be that the hand
Has a will to grow larger on the wall,
To grow larger and heavier and stronger than
The wall; and that the mind
Turns to its own figurations and declares,
"This image, this love, I compose myself
Of these. In these, I come forth outwardly.
In these, I wear a vital cleanliness,

Not as in air, bright-blue-resembling air,
But as in the powerful mirror of my wish and will."

The principal difference between Stevens and Whitman appears to be that Stevens admits his mind is alone with its own figurations, while Whitman keeps inaccurately but movingly insisting he wants "contact" with other selves. His "contact" is an Emersonian term, and we know, as Whitman's readers, that he actually cannot bear "contact," any more than Emerson, Dickinson, Frost, or Stevens can tolerate it. "Poem with Rhythms," like so much of Stevens, has a hidden origin in Whitman's "The Sleepers," particularly in a great passage apparently describing a woman's disappointment in love:

I am she who adorn'd herself and folded her hair expectantly,
My truant lover has come, and it is dark.

Double yourself and receive me darkness,
Receive me and my lover too, he will not let me go without him.
I roll myself upon you as upon a bed, I resign myself to the dusk.

He whom I call answers me and takes the place of my lover,
He rises with me silently from the bed.

Darkness, you are gentler than my lover, his flesh was
     sweaty and panting,
I feel the hot moisture yet that he left me.

My hands are spread forth, I pass them in all directions.
I would sound up the shadowy shore to which you are journeying.

Be careful, darkness! already, what was it touch'd me?
I thought my lover had gone, else darkness and he are one,
I hear the heart-beat, I follow, I fade away.

This juxtaposition of major Whitman to relatively minor Stevens is not altogether fair, but then I don't think I hurt Stevens by granting that Whitman, upon his heights, is likely to make his descendant seem only a dwarf of disintegration. Whitman-as-Woman invokes the darkness of birth, and blends himself into the mingled Sublimity of death and the Native Strain. Stevens-as-Interior-Paramour invokes only his mind's own figurations, but he sees himself cleansed in the vitalizing mirror of will as he could never hope to see himself in the mere outwardness of air. Whitman oddly but beautifully persuades us of a dramatic poignance that his actual solipsism does not earn, while Stevens rather less beautifully knows only the non-dramatic truth of his own fine desperation.

What then is Stevens giving us? What do we celebrate with and in him when he leads us to celebrate? His vigorous affirmation, "The Well Dressed Man with a Beard," centers on "a speech / Of the self that must sustain itself on speech." Is eloquence enough? I turn again to the fountain of our will, Emerson, who had the courage to insist that eloquence was enough, because he identified eloquence with "something unlimited and boundless," in the manner of Cicero. Here is Stevens mounting through eloquence to his individual sense of "something unlimited and boundless," a "something" not beyond our apprehension:

> Last night at the end of night his starry head,
> Like the head of fate, looked out in darkness, part
> Thereof and part desire and part the sense
> Of what men are. The collective being knew
> There were others like him safely under roof:
>
> The captain squalid on his pillow, the great
> Cardinal, saying the prayers of earliest day;
> The stone, the categorical effigy;
> And the mother, the music, the name; the scholar,
> Whose green mind bulges with complicated hues:
>
> True transfigurers fetched out of the human mountain,
> True genii for the diminished, spheres,
> Gigantic embryos of populations,
> Blue friends in shadows, rich conspirators,
> Confiders and comforters and lofty kin.
>
> To say more than human things with human voice,
> That cannot be; to say human things with more
> Than human voice, that, also, cannot be;
> To speak humanly from the height or from the depth
> Of human things, that is acutest speech.

A critic who has learned, ruefully, to accept the reductive view that the imagination is only decaying sense, must ask himself: Why is he so moved by this transfiguration of language into acutest speech? He may remember, in this connection, the prose statement by Stevens that moves him most:

> Why should a poem not change in sense when there is a fluctuation of the whole of appearance? Or why should it not change when we realize that the indifferent experience of life is the unique experience, the item of ecstasy which we have been isolating and reserving for another time and place, loftier and more secluded.

The doctrinal voice of Walter Pater, another unacknowledged ancestor, is heard in this passage, as perhaps it must be heard in any modern Epicureanism. Stevens, I suggest, is the Lucretius of our modern poetry, and like Lucretius seeks his truth in mere appearances, seeks his spirit in things of the weather. Both poets are beyond illusions, yet both invest their knowing of the way things are with a certain grim ecstasy. But an American Lucretius, coming after the double alienation of European Romanticism and domestic Transcendentalism, will have lost all sense of the communal in his ecstasy. Stevens fulfilled the unique enterprise of a specifically American poetry by exposing the essential solipsism of our Native Strain. No American feels free when he is not alone, and every American's passion for Yes affirms a hidden belief that his soul's substance is no part of the creation. We are mortal gods, the central strain in our poetry keeps saying, and our aboriginal selves are forbidden to find companionship in one another. Our ecstasy comes only from self-recognition, yet cannot be complete if we reduce wholly to "the evilly compounded, vital I ... made ... fresh in a world of white." We need "The Poems of Our Climate" because we are, happily, imperfect solipsists, unhappy in a happily imperfect and still external world—which is to say, we need Stevens:

> There would still remain the never-resting mind,
> So that one would want to escape, come back
> To what had been so long composed.
> The imperfect is our paradise.
> Note that, in this bitterness, delight,
> Since the imperfect is so hot in us,
> Lies in flawed words and stubborn sounds.

WILLIAM CARLOS WILLIAMS

Poetic influence, an intensely problematical process, normally brings
together a strong poet's earliest and final phases. Williams's true precursor,
necessarily composite and in some sense imaginary, was a figure that fused
Keats with Walt Whitman. Such a figure has in it the potential for a serious
splitting of the poetic ego in its defense against the poetic past. The
"negative capability" of Keats sorts oddly with Whitman's rather positive
capability for conveying the powerful press of himself. "Memory is a kind /
of accomplishment," Williams wrote in "The Descent," a crucial poem in his
The Desert Music (1954). The descent to dying beckons to a return of the
dead precursors in one's own colors, even as Keats and Whitman beckoned
Williams to ascend into his own poetry. But the poem "The Descent"
Williams shrewdly quarried from book 2 of his own major long poem,
Paterson, a quarrying that suggests his pride in his own continuities.

Those continuities are massive throughout Williams's best work, which
can be cataloged (against the numerous Williams idolators) as a limited yet
still remarkably diverse canon: *Paterson* (book 1), *Kora in Hell, Spring and All*,
"The Widow's Lament in Springtime," "To Waken an Old Lady," "The
Trees," "The Yachts," "A Coronal," "These," "The Poor," "A Marriage
Ritual," "Raleigh Was Right," "Burning the Christmas Greens," "A Unison,"
and the grand return of Keats-as-Williams in *Asphodel, That Greeny Flower*.

The best lyrics and book 1 of *Paterson* are of a higher order, though
they also betray darker anxieties of influence than even Williams"s defiances
dared to confront. They display also another kind of agon, the anxiety as to
contemporary rivals, not so much Pound and Eliot as Wallace Stevens and
Hart Crane, heirs to Keats and to Whitman, even as Williams was. No two
readers are likely to agree upon just which shorter poems by Williams are his
strongest, but the one that impresses and moves me most is "A Unison,"
where the title seems to comprehend most of the dictionary meanings of
"unison": an identity of pitch in music; the same words spoken
simultaneously by two or more speakers; musical parts combined in octaves;
a concord, agreement, harmony. Thomas R. Whitaker, one of Williams's
best and most sympathetic critics but no idolator, gives the best introduction
to "A Unison":

It is like an improvisation from *Kora in Hell*—but one with the
quiet maturity of vision and movement that some three decades
have brought.... As the implicit analogies and contrasts
accumulate, we discover (long before the speaker tells us) that we

are attending a "unison and a dance." This "death's festival"—
memento mori and celebration of the "Undying"—evades neither
the mystery of transience nor that of organic continuance,
though neither can be "parsed" by the analytical mind.... In this
composed testament of acceptance, Williams's saxifrage
("through metaphor to reconcile / the people and the stones")
quietly does its work.... Not since Wordsworth has this natural
piety been rendered so freshly and poignantly.

I would not wish to quarrel with Whitaker's judgment, yet there is very
little Wordsworth and (inevitably) much Whitman and considerable Keats in
"A Unison." Indeed; the poem opens with what must be called an echo from
Whitman, in what I assume was a controlled allusion:

The grass is very green, my friend,
And tousled, like the head of—
your grandson, yes?

We hear one of the uncanniest passages in Whitman, from "Song of
Myself" 6:

This grass is very dark to be from the white heads of old mothers,
Darker than the colorless beards of old men,
Dark to come from under the faint red roofs of mouths.

Whitman's great fantasia answers a child's question: *"What is the grass?"*
As an Epicurean materialist, Whitman believed that the *what* was
unknowable, but his remarkable troping on the grass takes a grand turn after
his Homeric line: "And now it seems to me the beautiful uncut hair of
graves." Williams simply borrows the trope, and even his "very green"
merely follows Whitman's hint that a "very green" becomes a "very dark"
color, in the shadow of mortality. "A Unison" insists upon

—what cannot be escaped: the
mountain riding the afternoon as
it does, the grass matted green,
green underfoot and the air—
rotten wood. *Hear! Hear them!*
the Undying. The hill slopes away,
then rises in the middleground,

you remember, with a grove of gnarled
maples centering the bare pasture,
sacred, surely—for what reason?

Williams does not know whether he can or cannot say the reason, but
the allusion is to Keats's characteristic, Saturnian shrine in *Hyperion*. For
Williams it is "a shrine cinctured there by / the trees," the girdling effect
suggested by the natural sculpture of Keats's shrine. Where Keats as the
quester in *The Fall of Hyperion* pledges "all the mortals of the world, / And all
the dead whose names are in our lips," and where Whitman insists, "The
smallest sprout shows there is really no death," Williams neither salutes the
living and the dead nor folds the two into a single figuration. Rather, he *hears*
and urges us to: "*Hear the unison of their voices.*" How are we to interpret such
an imaginative gesture? Are we hearing more, or enough more, than the
unison of the voices of John Keats and Walt Whitman? Devoted Williamsites
doubtless would reject the question, but it always retains its force
nevertheless. It is not less true of *The Waste Land* than it is of Williams. Eliot
revises Whitman's "When Lilacs Last in the Dooryard Bloom'd" by fusing it
with Tennyson (among others, but prime among those others). Image of voice
or the trope of poetic identity then becomes a central problem.

Whitman once contrasted himself to Keats by rejecting "negative
capability" and insisting instead that the great poet gave us the "powerful
press of himself." Admirable as *Paterson* is (particularly its first book), does
even it resolve the antithesis in Williams between his "objectivism" or
negative capability, and his own, agonistic, powerful press of himself? Paul
Mariani ends his vast, idealizing biography by asserting that Williams
established "an American poetic based on a new measure and a primary
regard for the living, protean shape of the language as it was actually used."
J. Hillis Miller, even more generously, tells us that Williams gave us a
concept of poetry transcending both Homer and Wordsworth, both Aristotle
and Coleridge:

> The word is given reality by the fact it names, but the
> independence of the fact from the word frees the word to be a
> fact in its own right and at the same time "dynamizes" it with
> meaning. The word can then carry the facts named in a new form
> into the realm of imagination.

Mariani and Miller are quite sober compared to more apocalyptic
Williamsites. Not even Whitman gave us "a new measure," and not

Shakespeare himself freed a single word "to be a fact in its own right."
William Carlos Williams was, at his best, a strong American poet, far better
than his hordes of imitators. Like Ezra Pound's, Williams's remains a fairly
problematical achievement in the traditions of American poetry. Some
generations hence, it will become clear whether his critics have canonized
him permanently or subverted him by taking him too much at his own
intentions. For now he abides, a live influence, and perhaps with even more
fame to come.

EZRA POUND

I have brought the great ball of crystal; who can lift it?
—Canto 116

I do not know many readers who have an equal affection for the *Cantos* and
for, say, Wallace Stevens's *An Ordinary Evening in New Haven* or his *The
Auroras of Autumn*. Doubtless, such differences in poetic taste belong to the
accidents of sensibility, or to irreconcilable attitudes concerning the relation
of poetry to belief. They may indeed belong to more profound distinctions;
in judgments as to value that transcend literary preferences. I do not desire
to address myself to such matters here. Nor will I consider Pound's politics.
The *Cantos* contain material that is not humanly acceptable to me, and if that
material is acceptable to others, then they themselves are thereby less
acceptable, at least to me.

My subject here, in necessarily curtailed terms, is Pound's relation to
poetic tradition in his own language, and to Whitman in particular. Pound's
critics have taken him at his word in this regard, but no poet whatsoever can
be trusted in his or her own story of poetic origins, even as no man or woman
can be relied on to speak with dispassionate accuracy of his or her parents.
Perhaps Pound triumphed in his agon with poetic tradition, which is the
invariable assertion of all of his critical partisans. But the triumph, if it
occurred, was a very qualified one. My own experience as a reader of the
Cantos, across many years, is that the long poem or sequence is marred
throughout by Pound's relative failure to transume or transcend his
precursors. Their ancestral voices abound, and indeed become more rather
than less evident as the sequence continues. Nor is this invariably a
controlled allusiveness. Collage, which is handled as metaphor by Marianne
Moore and by the Eliot of *The Waste Land*, is a much more literal process in
Pound, is more scheme than trope, as it were. The allusive triumph over
tradition in Moore's "Marriage" or *The Waste Land* is fairly problematical, yet

nowhere near so dubious as it is in the *Cantos*. Confronted by a past poetic wealth in figuration, Pound tends to resort to baroque elaborations of the anterior metaphors. What he almost never manages is to achieve an ellipsis of further troping by his own inventiveness at metaphor. He cannot make the voices of Whitman and Browning seem belated, while his own voice manifests what Stevens called an "ever early candor."

I am aware that I am in apparent defiance of the proud Poundian dictum: *Make It New*. Whitman made it new in one way, and Browning in another, but Pound's strength was elsewhere. Anglo-American Poetic "Modernism" was Ezra Pound's revolution, but it seems now only another continuity in the long history of Romanticism. Literary history may or may not someday regard Pound as it now regards Abraham Cowley, John Cleveland, and Edmund Waller, luminaries of one era who faded into the common light of another age. But, as a manneristic poet, master of a period style, Pound has his deep affinities to Cowley, Cleveland, and above all Waller. He has affinities also though to Dante Gabriel Rossetti, a permanent poet who suffered from belatedness in a mode strikingly akin to that of Pound. Poundian critics tend to regard Rossetti as a kind of embarrassing prelude to their hero, but I certainly intend only a tribute to Pound in comparing him to Rossetti. It is, after all, far better to be called the Dante Gabriel Rossetti than the Edmund Waller of your era.

Pound, brash and natural child of Whitman and Browning, found his idealized forerunners in Arnaut Daniel and Cavalcanti, Villon and Landor. Oedipal ambivalence, which marks Pound's stance towards Whitman, never surfaces in his observations on Cavalcanti and Villon, safely remote not only in time and language, but more crucially isolated from the realities of Pound's equivocal relation to his country and compatriots.

I find Whitman quite unrecognizable in nearly every reference Pound makes to him. Our greatest poet and our most elusive, because most figurative, Whitman consistently is literalized by Pound, as though the Whitmanian self could be accepted as a machine rather than as a metaphor.

Many Poundians have quoted as evidence of their hero's esteem of Whitman a bad little poem of 1913:

A PACT

I make a pact with you, Walt Whitman—
I have detested you long enough.
I come to you as a grown child
Who has had a pig-headed father;
I am old enough now to make friends.

It was you that broke the new wood,
Now is a time for carving.
We have one sap and one root—
Let there be commerce between us.

"Truce," the original word in the first line, is more accurate than
"pact," because truly there was a failure in commerce between Whitman and
Pound. Whether Pound remembered that Whitman's father was a carpenter,
and that Whitman himself had worked, with his father, at the trade, is
beyond surmise. The root, as Pound perhaps knew, was Emerson. It is no
accident that Whitman and Emerson return to Pound together in *The Pisan
Cantos*, with Whitman central in the eighty-second and Emerson in the
eighty-third of the *Cantos*. Emerson, I think, returns in his own trope of self-
identification, the Transparent Eyeball, yet in Pound's voice, since Emerson
was at most Pound's American grandfather. But Whitman returns in
Whitman's own voice, and even in his own image of voice, the "tally,"
because the obstinate old father's voice remains strong enough to insist upon
itself:

"Fvy! in Tdaenmarck efen dh' beasantz gnow him,"
        meaning Whitman, exotic, still suspect
    four miles from Camden
        "O troubled reflection
        "O Throat, O throbbing heart"
    How drawn, O GEA TERRA,
        what draws as thou drawest
            till one sink into thee by an arm's width
        embracing thee. Drawest,
            truly thou drawest.
    Wisdom lies next thee,
        simply, past metaphor.
    Where I lie let the thyme rise ...
    · · · · · · · · · · · · · · · · · ·
                fluid ΧΘΟΝΟΣ, strong as the undertow
        of the wave receding
    but that a man should live in that further terror, and live

    the loneliness of death came upon me
        (at 3 P.M., for an instant)   δακρύων
                                                ἐντεῦθεν

three solemn half notes
   their white downy chests black-rimmed
on the middle wire
   periplum

Pound begins by recalling his German teacher at the University of
Pennsylvania, forty years before, one Richard Henry Riethmuller,
author of *Walt Whitman and the Germans* (1966), an identification I owe
to Roy Harvey Pearce. Riethmuller (Pound got the spelling wrong) had
contrasted Whitman's fame in the professor's native Denmark to the
bard's supposed obscurity in the America of 1905, a contrast that leads
Pound to a recall of Whitman's "Out of the Cradle Endlessly Rocking."
Whitman's poem is an elegy for the poetic self so powerful that any other
poet ought to be wary of invoking so great a hymn of poetic incarnation
and disincarnation. Whitman's "O troubled reflection in the sea! / O
throat! O throbbing heart!" is revised by Pound into "O troubled
reflection / O throat, O throbbing heart," with "in the sea" omitted.
These are the last two lines of the penultimate stanza of the song of the
bird lamenting his lost mate:

O darkness! O in vain!
O I am very sick and sorrowful.
O brown halo in the sky near the moon, drooping upon the sea!
O throat! O throbbing heart!
And I singing uselessly, uselessly all the night.

Canto 82 rather movingly has shown the incarcerated poet studying
the nostalgias of his early literary life, while meditating upon the
unrighteousness of all wars. A vision of the earth now comes to him, in
response to his partly repressed recall of Whitman's vision of the sea.
Marrying the earth is Pound's counterpart to Whitman's marrying the sea,
both in "Out of the Cradle Endlessly Rocking" and in "When Lilacs Last in
the Dooryard Bloom'd," and both brides are at once death and the mother.
"Where I lie let the thyme rise," perhaps repeating William Blake's similar
grand pun on "thyme" and "time," is a profound acceptance of the reality
principle, with no more idealizations of a timeless order. Whitman returns
from the dead even more strongly in the closing lines of Canto 82, where
Pound lies down in a fluid time "strong as the undertow / of the wave
receding," which invokes another great elegiac triumph of Whitman's, "As
I Ebb'd with the Ocean of Life." The two song-birds of "Out of the

Cradle," with Whitman their brother making a third, utter "three solemn half notes" even as the loneliness of death came, for an instant, upon Whitman's son, Pound. Most powerful, to me, is Pound's recall of Whitman's great image of voice, the tally, from "Lilacs," "Song of Myself," and other contexts in the poet of night, death, the mother, and the sea. In Whitman, the tally counts up the poet's songs as so many wounds, so many auto-erotic gratifications that yet, somehow, do not exclude otherness. Pound, marrying the earth, realizes his terrible solitude: "man, earth: two halves of the tally / but I will come out of this knowing no one / neither they me."

Kenner is able to read this as commerce between Whitman and Pound, and insists that "the resources in the Canto are Pound's, as are those of Canto 1." But Homer, ultimate ancestor in Canto 1, was safely distant. Whitman is very close in Canto 82, and the resources are clearly his. Pound does better at converting Emerson to his own purposes, a canto later, than he is able to do with Whitman here. Would the following judgment seem valid to a fully informed and dispassionate reader?

> Pound's faults are superficial, he does convey an image of his time, he has written *histoire morale*, as Montaigne wrote the history of his epoch. You can learn more of 20th century America from Pound than from any of the writers who either refrained from perceiving, or limited their record to what they had been taught to consider suitable literary expression. The only way to enjoy Pound thoroughly is to concentrate on his fundamental meaning.

This is Pound on Whitman from the *ABC of Reading* (1934), with Pound substituted for Whitman, and the twentieth for the nineteenth century. Pound was half right about Whitman; Whitman does teach us his country in his century, but his form and his content are not so split as Pound says, and his fundamental meaning resides in nuance, beautifully shaped in figurative language. Pound's faults are not superficial, and absolutely nothing about our country in this century can be learned from him. He conveys an image only of himself, and the only way to enjoy him is not to seek a fundamental meaning that is not there, but to take his drafts and fragments one by one, shattered crystals, but crystalline nevertheless. He had brought the great ball of crystal, of poetic tradition, but it proved too heavy for him to lift.

MARIANNE MOORE

For Plato the only reality that mattered is exemplified best for us in the principles of mathematics. The aim of our lives should be to draw ourselves away as much as possible from the unsubstantial, fluctuating facts of the world about us and establish some communion with the objects which are apprehended by thought and not sense. This was the source of Plato's asceticism. To the extent that Miss Moore finds only allusion tolerable she shares that asceticism. While she shares it she does so only as it may be necessary for her to do so in order to establish a particular reality or, better, a reality of her own particulars.

—WALLACE STEVENS

Allusion was Marianne Moore's method, a method that was her self. One of the most American of all poets, she was fecund in her progeny; Elizabeth Bishop, May Swenson, and Richard Wilbur being the most gifted among them. Her own American precursors were not Emily Dickinson and Walt Whitman—still our two greatest poets—but the much slighter Stephen Crane, who is echoed in her earliest poems, and in an oblique way Edgar Poe, whom she parodied. I suspect that her nearest poetic father, in English, was Thomas Hardy, who seems to have taught her lessons in the mastery of incongruity, and whose secularized version of Biblical irony is not far from her own. If we compare her with her major poetic contemporaries—Frost, Stevens, Eliot, Pound, Williams, Aiken, Ransom, Cummings, H.D., Hart Crane—she is clearly the most original American poet of her era, though not quite of the eminence of Frost, Stevens, or Crane. A curious kind of devotional poet, with some authentic affinities to George Herbert, she reminds us implicitly but constantly that any distinction between sacred and secular poetry is only a shibboleth of cultural politics. Some day she will remind us also of what current cultural politics obscure: that any distinction between poetry written by women and poetry by men is a mere polemic, unless it follows upon an initial distinction between good and bad poetry. Moore, like Bishop and Swenson, is an extraordinary poet-as-poet. The issue of how gender enters into her vision should arise only after the aesthetic achievement is judged as such.

Moore, as all her readers know, to their lasting delight, is the visionary of natural creatures: the jerboa, frigate pelican, buffalo, monkeys, fish, snakes, mongooses, the octopus (actually a trope for a mountain), snail, peacock, whale, pangolin, wood-weasel, elephants, race horses, chameleon, jellyfish, arctic ox (or goat), giraffe, blue bug (another trope, this time for a pony), all of La Fontaine's bestiary, not to mention sea and land unicorns, basilisks, and all the weird fabulous roster that perhaps only Borges also, among crucial modern writers, celebrates so consistently. There is something of Blake and of the Christopher Smart of *Jubilate Agno* in Moore, though the affinity does not result from influence, but rather is the consequence of election. Moore's famous eye, like that of Bishop after her, is not so much a visual gift as it is visionary, for the beasts in her poems are charged with a spiritual intensity that doubtless they possess, but which I myself cannot see without the aid of Blake, Smart, and Moore.

I remember always in reading Moore again that her favorite poem was the Book of Job. Just as I cannot read Ecclesiastes without thinking of Dr. Johnson, I cannot read certain passages in Job without recalling Marianne Moore:

> But ask now the beasts, and they shall teach thee; and the fowls of the air, and they shall tell thee:
> Or speak to the earth, and it shall teach thee: and the fishes of the sea shall declare unto thee.
> Who knoweth not in all these that the hand of the Lord hath wrought this?
> In whose hand is the soul of every living thing ...

This, from chapter 12, is the prelude to the great chant of Yahweh, the Voice out of the whirlwind that sounds forth in the frightening magnificence of chapters 38 through 41, where the grand procession of beasts comprehends lions, ravens, wild goats, the wild ass, the unicorn, peacocks, the ostrich, the sublime battle-horse who "saith among the trumpets, Ha, ha," the hawk, the eagle, and at last behemoth and leviathan. Gorgeously celebrating his own creation, Yahweh through the poet of Job engendered another strong poet in Marianne Moore. Of the Book of job, she remarked that its agony was veracious and its fidelity of a force "that contrives glory for ashes."

"Glory for ashes" might be called Moore's ethical motto, the basis for the drive of her poetic will towards a reality of her own particulars. Her poetry, as befitted the translator of La Fontaine and the heir of George Herbert, would be in some danger of dwindling into moral essays, an impossible form for our time, were it not for her wild allusiveness, her zest for quotations, and her essentially anarchic stance, the American and Emersonian insistence upon seeing everything in her own way, with "conscientious inconsistency." When her wildness or freedom subsided, she produced an occasional poetic disaster like the patriotic war poems, "In Distrust of Merits," and "'Keeping Their World Large.'" But her greatest poems are at just the opposite edge of consciousness: "A Grave," "Novices," "Marriage," "An Octopus," "He 'Digesteth Harde Yron,'" "Elephants," the deceptively light "Tom Fool at Jamaica."

Those seven poems by themselves have an idiosyncratic splendor that restores my faith, as a critic, in what the language of the poets truly is: diction, or choice of words, playing endlessly upon the dialectic of denotation and connotation, a dialectic that simply vanishes in all Structuralist and post-Structuralist ruminations upon the supposed priority of "language" over meaning. "The arbitrariness of the signifier" loses its charm when one asks a Gallic psycholinguistifier whether denotation or connotation belongs to the signifier, as opposed to the signified, and one beholds blank incredulity as one's only answer. Moore's best poems give the adequate reply: the play of the signifier is answered always by the play of the signified, because the play of diction, or the poet's will over language, is itself constituted by the endless interchanges of denotation and connotation. Moore, with her rage to order allusion, echo, and quotation in ghostlier demarcations, keener sounds, helps us to realize that the belated Modernism of the Gallic proclamation of the death of the author was no less premature than it was, always already, belated.

T.S. ELIOT

Thomas Stearns Eliot is a central figure in the Western literary culture of this century. His undoubted achievement as a lyric and elegiac poet in itself would suffice to establish him in the main Romantic tradition of British and American poetry that moves from Wordsworth and Whitman on to Geoffrey Hill and John Ashbery, poets of our moment. There is an obvious irony in such a judgment. Eliot's professed sense of *the* tradition, his tradition, was rather different, tracing as it did the true line of poetry in English from its origins in medieval Provence and Italy through its later developments in France (I borrow that remark from Northrop Frye). Eliot's polemical stance as a literary critic can be distinguished from his rhetorical stance as a poet, and both postures of the spirit are fortunately quite distinct from his cultural position, self-proclaimed as Anglo-Catholic, Royalist and Classical.

An obsessive reader of poetry growing up in the 1930s and 1940s entered a critical world dominated by the opinions and example of Eliot. To speak out of even narrower personal experience, anyone adopting the profession of teaching literature in the early 1950s entered a discipline virtually enslaved not only by Eliot's insights but by the entire span of his preferences and prejudices. If one's cultural position was Jewish, Liberal, and Romantic, one was likely to start out with a certain lack of affection for Eliot's predominance, however much (against the will) the subtle force of the poetry was felt. If a young critic particularly loved Shelley, Milton, Emerson, Pater, and if that same critic did not believe that Blake was a naive and eccentric genius, then regard for Eliot seemed unnecessary. Whatever he actually represented, a neochristian and neoclassic Academy had exalted him, by merit raised, to what was pragmatically rather a bad eminence. In *that* critical climate, Hopkins was considered the only valid Victorian poet, greatly superior to Browning and Tennyson, while Whitman seemed an American nightmare and Wallace Stevens, if he passed at all, had to be salvaged as a Late Augustan. Thirty years on, these views have a kind of antique charm, but in 1954 they were at least annoying, and if one cared enough, they had some capacity for infuriating.

I resume these matters not to stir up waning rancors, but to explain why, for some critics of my own generation, Eliot only recently has ceased to represent the spiritual enemy. His disdain for Freud, his flair for demonstrating the authenticity of his Christianity by exhibiting a judicious anti-Semitism, his refined contempt for human sexuality—somehow these did not seem to be the inevitable foundations for contemporary culture. Granted that he refrained from the rhetorical excesses of his ally Ezra Pound; there is nothing in him resembling the Poundian apothegm: "All the jew part of the Bible is black evil." Still, an Academy that found its ideology in Eliot was not a place where one could teach comfortably, or where one could have remained, had the Age of Eliot not begun to wane. The ascendancy of Eliot, as a fact of cultural politics, is something many among us could not wish to see return.

Eliot asserted for his poetry a seventeenth-century ancestry, out of Jacobean dramatists and Metaphysical lyricists. Its actual forerunners are Whitman and Tennyson, and Eliot's strength is felt now when we read "When Lilacs Last in the Dooryard Bloom'd" and "Maud: A Monodrama," and find ourselves believing that they are influenced by *The Waste Land*. It is a neglected truth of American poetic history that Eliot and Stevens are more Whitmanian than Hart Crane, whose allegiance to Whitman was overt. Though Eliot and Stevens consciously did not feel or know it, their poetry is obsessed with Whitman's poetry. By this I mean Whitman's tropes and Whitman's curious transitions between topics, and not at all the example of Whitman, far more crucial for Crane and many others.

It is the pattern of Eliot's figurations that is most High Romantic, a pattern that I suspect he learned from Tennyson and Whitman, who derived it from Keats and Shelley, who in turn had been instructed by Wordsworth's crisis lyrics and odes, which go back yet further to Spenserian and Miltonic models. Consider Eliot's *Ash-Wednesday*, his conversion-sequence of 1930. The poem's six movements are not a Dantesque *Vita Nuova*, despite Eliot's desires, but a rather strict reenactment of the Wordsworthian drama of experiential loss and compensatory imaginative gain:

(I) This is an ironic movement that says "I rejoice" but means "I despair," which is the limited irony that Freud terms a "reaction formation," or an emotion masking ambivalently as its opposite. Despite the deliberate allusions to Cavalcanti and Dante, Ezekiel and the Mass, that throng the poem, the presumably unintended echoes of Wordsworth's Intimations of Immortality Ode carry the reader closer to the center of the poet's partially repressed anxieties and to his poetic anxieties in particular. "The infirm glory" and the "one veritable transitory power" are stigmata of the visionary gleam in its flight from the poet, and if what is lost here is more-than-natural, we remember that the loss in Wordsworth also transcends nature. Though Eliot employs the language of mysticism and Wordsworth the language of nature, the crisis for each is poetic rather than mystical or natural. Eliot's renunciation of voice, however ironical, leads directly to what for many readers has been the most memorable and poignant realization in the sequence: "Consequently I rejoice, having to construct something / Upon which to rejoice." No more illuminating epigraph could be assigned to Wordsworth's Intimations Ode, or to "Tintern Abbey" or "Resolution and Independence." The absence lamented in the first part of *Ash-Wednesday* is a once-present poetic strength, whatever else it represented experientially. In the Shakespearean rejection of the desire for "this man's gift and that man's scope," we need not doubt that the men are precursor poets, nor ought we to forget that not hoping to turn again is also an ironic farewell to troping, and so to one's own quest for poetic voice.

(II) The question that haunts the transition between the first two sections, pragmatically considered, is, "Am I, Eliot, still a poet?" "Shall these bones live?" is a synecdochal question, whole for part, since the immortality involved is the figurative survival of one's poetry: "As I am forgotten / And would be forgotten, so I would forget." Turning around against himself, this poet, in the mode of Browning's Childe Roland, asks only to be numbered among the scattered precursors, to fail as they have failed: "We have our inheritance."

(III) After such self-wounding, the poet seeks a kind of Pauline *kenosis*, akin to Christ's emptying himself of his own Divinity, which here can only mean the undoing of one's poetic gift. As inspiration fades away willfully, the gift wonderfully declares itself nevertheless, in that enchanted lyricism Eliot never ceased to share with the elegiac Whitman and the Virgilian Tennyson: "Lilac and brown hair; / Distraction, music of the flute, stops and steps of the mind over the third stair." The figurative movement is metonymic, as in the displacement of poetic power from the speaker to the curiously Pre-Raphaelite "broadbacked figure drest in blue and green," who is anything but a possible representation of Eliot's own poetic self.

(IV) This is the daemonic vision proper, allowing a sequence that denies sublimity, to reattain a Romantic Sublime. In the transition between sections 3 and 4, Eliot appears to surmount the temptations of solipsism, so as to ask and answer the question, "Am I capable of loving another?" The unnamed other or "silent sister" is akin to shadowy images of desire in Tennyson and Whitman, narcissistic emblems certainly, but pointing beyond the self's passion for the self. Hugh Kenner, indubitably Eliot's best and most Eliotic critic, suggestively compares *Ash-Wednesday* to Tennyson's "The Holy Grail," and particularly to the fearful death-march of Percivale's quest in that most ornate portion of *The Idylls of the King*. Kenner of course awards the palm to Eliot over what he dismisses as a crude "Victorian ceremony of iterations" as compared to Eliot's "austere gestures of withdrawal and submission." A quarter of a century after he made them, Kenner's judgments seem eminently reversible, since Tennyson's gestures are, in this case, palpably more austere than his inheritor's. Tennyson has, after all, nothing quite so gaudy as "Redeem / The unread vision in the higher dream / While jewelled unicorns draw by the gilded hearse."

(V) Percivale's desert and the wasteland of Browning's Childe Roland join the Biblical wildernesses in this extraordinary *askesis*, a self-curtailing rhapsody that truncates Romantic tradition as much as it does Eliot's individual talent. One could assert that this section affirms all the possibilities of sublimation, from Plato through Nietzsche to Freud, except that the inside/outside metaphor of dualism confines itself here only to "The Word without a word, the Word within." Eliot, like all his Romantic ancestors from Wordsworth to Pater, seeks a crossing to a subtle identification with an innocent earliness, while fearing to introject instead the belatedness of a world without imagination, the death-in-life of the poet who has outlasted his gift.

(VI) This is one of Eliot's triumphs, as an earliness is recovered under the sign of contrition. The "unbroken wings" still flying seaward are a beautiful metalepsis of the wings of section I, which were "merely vans to beat the air." A characteristic pattern of the Romantic crisis lyric is extended as the precursors return from the dead, but in Eliot's own colors, the "lost lilac" of Whitman and the "lost sea voices" of Tennyson joining Eliot's "lost heart" in the labor of rejoicing, having indeed constructed something upon which to rejoice.

That Eliot, in retrospect, will seem the Matthew Arnold rather than the Abraham Cowley of his age, is the sympathetic judgment of A. Walton Litz. For motives admitted already, one might prefer to see Eliot as the Cowley, and some celebrated passages in *Four Quartets* are worthy of comparison with long-ago-admired Pindarics of that forgotten wit, but Arnold's burden as involuntary belated Romantic is indeed close to Eliot's. A direct comparison of Eliot's elegiac achievement to Whitman's or Tennyson's seems to me both more problematical and more inevitable. "Gerontion" contrasts unfavorably to "Tithonus" or "Ulysses," while *The Waste Land*, despite its critical high priests, lacks the coherence, maturity, and experiential authenticity of "When Lilacs Last in the Dooryard Bloom'd." And yet it must be admitted that Eliot is what the closing lines of *The Waste Land* assert him to be: a shorer of fragments against his (and our) ruins. The phantasmagoric intensity of his best poems and passages can be matched only in the greatest visionaries and poets of Western literature. It is another paradox that the Anglo-Catholic, Royalist, Classical spokesperson should excel in the mode of fictive hallucination and lyric derangement, in the fashioning of nightmare images perfectly expressive of his age.

Eliot's influence as a poet is by no means spent, yet it seems likely that Robert Penn Warren's later poetry, the most distinguished now being written among us, will be the final stand of Eliot's extraordinary effort to establish an anti-Romantic counter-Sublime sense of *the* tradition to replace the continuity of Romantic tradition. That the continuity now has absorbed him is hardly a defeat; absorption is not rejection, and Eliot's poetry is securely in the canon. Eliot's strength, manifested in the many poets indebted to him, is probably most authentically commemorated by the poetry of Hart Crane, which engages Eliot's poetry in an agon without which Crane could not have achieved his difficult greatness. One can prefer Crane to Eliot, as I do, and yet be forced to concede that Eliot, more than Whitman, made Crane possible.

HART CRANE

Again the traffic lights that skim thy swift
Unfractioned idiom, immaculate sigh of stars,
Beading thy path—condense eternity:
And we have seen night lifted in thine arms.

Under thy shadow by the piers I waited;
Only in darkness is thy shadow clear.
The City's fiery parcels all undone,
Already snow submerges an iron year ...

O Sleepless as the river under thee,
Vaulting the sea, the prairies' dreaming sod,
Unto us lowliest sometime sweep, descend
And of the curveship lend a myth to God.

—"Proem" to *The Bridge*

Hart Crane in *White Buildings* is wholly Orphic, in that his concern is his relation, as poet, to his own vision, rather than *with* the content of poetic vision, to utilize a general distinction inaugurated by Northrop Frye, following after Ruskin. The peculiar power of *The Bridge* at its strongest is that Crane succeeds in becoming what Pater and Nietzsche urged the future poet to be: ascetic of the spirit, which is an accurate definition of a purified Gnosis. Directly before these three final quatrains of "To Brooklyn Bridge," Crane had saluted the bridge first as Orphic emblem, both harp and altar, but then as the threshold of the full triad of the Orphic destiny: Dionysus or prophet's pledge, Ananke or prayer of pariah, and Eros, the lover's cry. It is after the range of relations to his own vision has been acknowledged and accepted that a stronger Crane achieves the Gnosis of those three last quatrains. There the poet remains present, but only as a knowing Abyss, contemplating the content of that knowing, which is a fullness or presence he can invoke but scarcely share. He sees "night lifted in thine arms"; he waits, for a shadow to clarify in darkness; he knows, yet what he knows is a vaulting, a sweep, a descent, above all a curveship, a realization of an angle of vision not yet his own.

This peculiarly effective stance has a precursor in Shelley's visionary skepticism, particularly in his final phase of *Adonais* and *The Triumph of Life*. Crane's achievement of this stance is the still-unexplored origin of *The Bridge*, but the textual evolution of "Atlantis," the first section of the visionary epic to be composed, is the probable area that should be considered. Lacking space here, I point instead to the achieved stance of "Voyages" 6 as the earliest full instance of Crane's mature Orphism, after which I will conclude with a reading of "Atlantis" and a brief glance at Crane's testament, "The Broken Tower."

The governing deities of the "Voyages" sequence are Eros and Ananke, or Emil Oppfer and the Caribbean as a Whitmanian fierce old mother moaning for her castaways. But the Orphic Dionysus, rent apart by Titanic forces, dominates the sixth lyric, which like Stevens's "The Paltry Nude Starts on a Spring Voyage" partly derives from Pater's description of Botticelli's Venus in *The Renaissance*. Pater's sado-masochistic maternal love-goddess, with her eyes smiling "unsearchable repose," becomes Crane's overtly destructive muse whose seer is no longer at home in his own vision:

> My eyes pressed black against the prow,
> —Thy derelict and blinded guest
>
> Waiting, afire, what name, unspoke,
> I cannot claim: let thy waves rear
> More savage than the death of kings,
> Some splintered garland for the seer.

The unspoken, unclaimed name is that of Orpheus, in his terrible final phase of "floating singer." Crane's highly deliberate echo of Shakespeare's Richard II at his most self-destructively masochistic is assimilated to the poetic equivalent, which is the splintering of the garland of laurel. Yet the final stanza returns to the central image of poetic incarnation in Crane, "Repose of Rivers" and its "hushed willows":

> The imaged Word, it is, that holds
> Hushed willows anchored in its glow.
> It is the unbetrayable reply
> Whose accent no farewell can know.

This is the achieved and curiously firm balance of a visionary skepticism, or the Orphic stance of *The Bridge*. It can be contrasted to Lawrence, in the "Orphic farewell" of "Medlars and Sorb Apples" in *Birds, Beasts and Flowers*. For Lawrence, Orphic assurance is the solipsism of an "intoxication of perfect loneliness." Crane crosses that intoxication by transuming his own and tradition's trope of the hushed willows as signifying an end to solitary mourning and a renewal of poetic divination. "Voyages" 6 turns its "imaged Word" against Eliot's neo-orthodox Word, or Christ, and Whitman's Word out of the Sea, or death, death that is the Oedipal merging back into the mother. Crane ends upon "know" because knowledge, and not faith, is his religious mode, a Gnosis that is more fully developed in *The Bridge*.

The dozen octaves of the final version of "Atlantis" show Crane in his mastery of the traditional Sublime, and are wholly comparable to the final seventeen stanzas of Shelley's *Adonais*. Crane's absolute music, like Plato's, "is then the knowledge of that which relates to love in harmony and system," but Crane's love is rather more like Shelley's desperate and skeptical outleaping than it is like Diotima's vision. For six stanzas, Crane drives upward, in a hyperbolic arc whose burden is agonistic, struggling to break beyond every achieved Sublime in the language. This agon belongs to the Sublime, and perhaps in America it is the Sublime. But such an agon requires particular contestants, and "Atlantis" finds them in *The Waste Land* and, yet more repressedly, in Whitman's "Crossing Brooklyn Ferry," the great addition to the second, 1856, *Leaves of Grass*, and Thoreau's favorite poem by Whitman.

Much of Crane's struggle with Eliot was revised out of the final "Atlantis," but only as overt textual traces; the deep inwardness of the battle is recoverable. Two modes of phantasmagoria clash:

> Through the bound cable strands, the arching path
> Upward, veering with light, the flight of strings,—
> Taut miles of shuttling moonlight syncopate
> The whispered rush, telepathy of wires.
> Up the index of night, granite and steel—
> Transparent meshes—fleckless the gleaming staves—
> Sibylline voices flicker, waveringly stream
>
> . . . .
>
> As though a god were issue of the strings.
> A woman drew her long black hair out tight
> And fiddled whisper music on those strings
> And bats with baby faces in the violet light
> Whistled, and beat their wings
> And crawled head downward down a blackened wall
> And upside down in air were towers
> Tolling reminiscent bells, that kept the hours
>   And voices singing out of empty cisterns and exhausted wells.

The latter hallucination might be called an amalgam of *Dracula* and the Gospels, as rendered in the high style of Tennyson's *Idylls of the King*, and obviously is in no sense a source or cause of Crane's transcendental opening octave. Nevertheless, no clearer contrast could be afforded, for Crane's lines answer Eliot's, in every meaning of "answer." "Music is then the knowledge of that which relates to love in harmony and system," and one knowledge answers another in these competing and marvelous musics of poetry, and of visionary history. Crane's bridge is to Atlantis, in fulfillment of the Platonic quest of Crane's Columbus. Eliot's bridge is to the Inferno, in fulfillment of the neo-Christian condemnation of Romantic, Transcendentalist, Gnostic quest. Crane's Sibylline voices stream upward; his night-illuminated bridge becomes a transparent musical score, until Orpheus is born out of the flight of strings. Eliot's Sibyl wishes to die; her counterpart plays a vampiric score upon her own hair, until instead of Orphic birth upwards we have an impotent triumph of time.

This contrast, and others equally sharp, constitutes the context of Crane's aspiration in "Atlantis." But this aspiration, which is for knowledge, in the particular sense of Gnosis, yields to Eliot, as it must, much of the world of things-as-they-are. The closing images of "The Tunnel," the section of *The Bridge* preceding "Atlantis," combine *The Waste Land*'s accounts of loss with Whitman's darker visions of those losses in "Crossing Brooklyn Ferry":

> And this thy harbor, O my City, I have driven under,
> Tossed from the coil of ticking towers.... Tomorrow,
> And to be.... Here by the River that is East—
> Here at the waters' edge the hands drop memory;
> Shadowless in that abyss they unaccounting he.
> How far away the star has pooled the sea—
> Or shall the hands be drawn away, to die?
> Kiss of our agony Thou gatherest,
>   O Hand of Fire
>   gatherest—

Emerson's was a Gnosis without Gnosticism; Crane's religion, at its darkest, shades from Orphism into Gnosticism, in a negative transcendence even of the Whitman who proclaimed, "It is not upon you alone the dark patches fall, / The dark threw its patches upon me also." The negative transcendence of "Atlantis" surmounts the world, history, and even precursors as knowing, in their rival ways, as Eliot and Whitman. Crane condenses the upward intensities of his first six octaves by a deliberate recall of his own Columbus triumphantly but delusively chanting: "I bring you back Cathay!" But Crane's Columbus invoked the Demiurge under Emily Dickinson's name for him, "Inquisitor! incognizable Word / Of Eden." This beautiful pathos of defeat, in "Ave Maria," was consonant with Whitman's "Prayer of Columbus," where the battered, wrecked old mariner denied all knowledge: "I know not even my own word past or present." Crane's American burden, in the second half of "Atlantis," is to start again where Dickinson and Whitman ended, and where Eliot had sought to show no fresh start was possible. Knowledge in precisely the Gnostic sense—a knowing that knows the knower and is, *in itself,* the form of salvation—becomes Crane's formidable hymn addressed directly to itself, to poem and to bridge, until they become momentarily "—One Song, one Bridge of Fire!" But is this persuasively different from the "Hand of Fire" that gathers the kiss of our agony?

The dialectic of Gnosticism is a triad of negation, evasion, and extravagance. Lurianic Kabbalah renders these as contraction, breaking-of-the-vessels, and restitution. Fate, freedom, power is the Emersonian or American equivalent. All of these triads translate aesthetically into a dialectic of limitation, substitution, and representation, as I have shown in several critical books starting with *A Map of Misreading.* Crane's negation or limitation, his contraction into Fate, is scarcely different from Eliot's, but then such rival negative theologies as Valentinian Gnosticism and Johannine Christianity are difficult to distinguish in their accounts of how to express divinity. Gnostic evasion, like Crane's notorious freedom and range in troping, is dearly more inventive than authorized Christian modes of substitution, just as Gnostic extravagance, again like Crane's hyperbolical Sublime, easily surpasses orthodox expressions of power.

Crane's elaborate evasiveness is crucial in the seventh stanza of "Atlantis," where the upward movement of the tropology has ended, and a westward lateral sweep of vision is substituted, with the bridge no longer confronted and addressed, but seen now as binding the continent:

We left the haven hanging in the night—
Sheened harbor lanterns backward fled the keel.
Pacific here at time's end, bearing corn,—
Eyes stammer through the pangs of dust and steel.
And still the circular, indubitable frieze
Of heaven's meditation, yoking wave
To kneeling wave, one song devoutly binds—
The vernal strophe chimes from deathless strings!

The third line implies not merely a circuit of the earth, but an achieved peace at the end of days, a millennial harvest. When the bridge returns in this stanza's last four lines, it has become heaven's own meditation, the known knowing the human knower. And such a knowing leads Crane on to the single most central stanza of his life and work:

O Thou steeled Cognizance whose leap commits
The agile precincts of the lark's return,
Within whose lariat sweep encinctured sing
In single chrysalis the many twain,—
Of stars Thou art the stitch and stallion glow
And like an organ, Thou, with sound of doom—
Sight, sound and flesh Thou leadest from time's realm
As love strikes clear direction for the helm.

Contrast the precise Shelleyan equivalent:

The One remains, the many change and pass;
Heaven's light forever shines, Earth's shadows fly;
Life, like a dome of many-colored glass,
Stains the white radiance of Eternity,
Until Death tramples it to fragments.—Die,
If thou wouldst be with that which thou dost seek!
Follow where all is fled!—Rome's azure sky,
Flowers, ruins, statues, music, words, are weak
The glory they transfuse with fitting truth to speak.

Superficially, the two stanzas are much at variance, with Crane's tone apparently triumphal, Shelley's apparently despairing. But the pragmatic or merely natural burden of both stanzas is quite suicidal. The bridge, as "steeled Cognizance," resolves the many into One, but this music of unity is a "sound of doom" for all flesh and its senses living in time's realm. Love's "clear direction," as in Shelley's climactic stanza, is towards death. But Shelley is very much involved in his own relation, as poet, to his own vision. Crane's role, as known to the bridge's knower, forsakes that relation, and a terrifyingly free concentration on the content of poetic vision is the reward. "Of stars Thou art the stitch and stallion glow" Marlowe himself would have envied, but since both terms of the trope, bridge and stars, exclude the human, Crane is impelled on to extraordinary achievements in hyperbole. When the bridge is "iridescently upborne / Through the bright drench and fabric of our veins," then the human price of Gnosticism begins to mount also. Crane insists that all this is "to our joy," but that joy is as dialectical as Shelley's despair. And Crane, supremely intelligent, counts the cost, foreknowing all criticism:

Migrations that must needs void memory,
Inventions that cobblestone the heart,—

Unspeakable Thou Bridge to Thee, O Love.
Thy pardon for this history, whitest Flower,
O Answerer of all,—Anemone,—
Now while thy petals spend the suns about us, hold—
(O Thou whose radiance doth inherit me)
Atlantis, hold thy floating singer late!

Would it make a difference if this read: "Cathay, hold thy floating
singer late!" so that the prayer of pariah would belong to Columbus and not
to Orpheus? Yes, for the final stanza then would have the Orphic strings leap
and converge to a question clearly different:

—One Song, one Bridge of Fire! Is it Atlantis,
Now pity steeps the grass and rainbows ring
The serpent with the eagle in the leaves ...?

Crane's revision of the Orphic stance of *White Buildings* here allows
him a difference that is a triumph. His serpent and eagle are likelier to be
Shelley's than Nietzsche's, for they remain at strife *within* their border of
covenant, the ring of rainbows. Atlantis is urged to hold its Orpheus late, as
a kind of newly fused Platonic myth of reconcilement to a higher world of
forms, a myth of which Gnosticism was a direct heir. "Is it Cathay?,"
repeating the noble delusion of Columbus, is not a question hinting defeat,
but foreboding victory. Yet Orphic victories are dialectical, as Crane well
knew. Knowledge indeed is the kernel, for Crane astutely shows awareness of
what the greatest poets always know, which is that their figurations intend
the will's revenge against time's "it was," but actually achieve the will's limits,
in the bewilderments of the Abyss of troping and of tropes.
　　The coda to Crane's poetry, and his life, is "The Broken Tower," where
the transumption of the Orphic quest does allow a final triumph:

And so it was I entered the broken world
To trace the visionary company of love, its voice
An instant in the wind (I know not whither hurled)
But not for long to hold each desperate choice.

Crane mentions reading other books by Pater, but not the unfinished
novel *Gaston de Latour*. Its first few chapters, at least, would have fascinated
him, and perhaps he did look into the opening pages, where the young
Gaston undergoes a ceremony bridging the spirit and nature:

Gaston alone, with all his mystic preoccupations, by the privilege of youth, seemed to belong to both, and link the visionary company about him to the external scene.

The "privilege of youth" was still Crane's when he died, and "The Broken Tower" remains as one of those links. Such a link, finally, is not to be judged as what Freud called "a false connection" or as another irony to be ironically recognized, but rather as a noble synecdoche, self-mutilating perhaps as is a steeled Cognizance, but by its very turning against the self, endlessly reconstituting the American poetic self, the *pneuma* or spark of an American Gnosis.

KENNETH BURKE

Motives and Motifs in
the Poetry of Marianne Moore

In this essay we would characterize the substance of Miss Moore's work as a specific poetic strategy. And we would watch it for insights which the contemplation of it may give us into the ways of poetic and linguistic action generally. For this purpose we shall use both her recently published book, *What Are Years*, and her *Selected Poems*, published in 1935 with an introduction by T.S. Eliot (and including some work reprinted from an earlier volume, *Observations*).

On page 8 of the new book, Miss Moore writes:

> The power of the visible
> is the invisible;

and in keeping with the pattern, when recalling her former title, *Observations*, we might even have been justified in reading it as a deceptively technical synonym for "visions." One observes the visibles—but of the corresponding invisibles, one must be visionary. And while dealing much in things that can be empirically here, the poet reminds us that they may

> dramatize a
> meaning always missed
> by the externalist.

From *A Grammar of Motives*. © 1969 by the University of California Press.

It is, then, a relation between external and internal, or visible and invisible, or background and personality, that her poems characteristically establish. Though her names for things are representative of attitudes, we could not say that the method is Symbolist. The objects exist too fully in their own right for us to treat them merely as objective words for subjects. T.S. Eliot says that her poetry "might be classified as 'descriptive' rather than 'lyrical' or 'dramatic.'" He cites an early poem that "suggests a slight influence of H.D., certainly of H.D. rather than of any other 'Imagist.'" And though asserting that "Miss Moore has no immediate poetic derivations," he seems to locate her work in the general vicinity of imagism, as when he writes:

> The aim of 'imagism,' so far as I understand it, or so far as it had any, was to introduce a peculiar concentration upon something visual, and to set in motion an expanding succession of concentric feelings. Some of Miss Moore's poems—for instance with animal or bird subjects—have a very good spread of association.

I think of William Carlos Williams. For though Williams differs much from Miss Moore in temperament and method, there is an important quality common to their modes of perception. It is what Williams has chosen to call by the trade name of "objectivist."

Symbolism, imagism, and objectivism would obviously merge into one another, since they are recipes all having the same ingredients but in different proportions. In symbolism, the subject is much stronger than the object as an organizing motive. That is, it is *what the images are symbolic of* that shapes their treatment. In imagism, there would ideally be an equality of the two motives, the subjective and objective. But in objectivism, though an object may be chosen for treatment because of its symbolic or subjective reference, once it has been chosen it is to be studied in its own right.

A man might become an electrician, for instance, because of some deep response to electricity as a symbol of power. Yet, once he had become an electrician and thus had converted his response to this subject into an objective knowledge of its laws and properties, he would thereafter treat electricity as he did, not because each of his acts as an electrician would be symbolic like his original choice of occupation, but because such acts were required by the peculiar nature of electricity. Similarly, a poet writing in an "objectivist" idiom might select his subject because of some secret reference or personal significance it has had for him; yet having selected it, he would find that its corresponding object had qualities to be featured and appraised for themselves. And he might pay so much attention to such appraisal that the treatment of the object would in effect "transcend" the motive behind its original singling-out.

Thus, the poem "Four Quartz Crystal Clocks" (in *What Are Years*) begins:

> There are four vibrators, the world's exactest clocks;
>   and these quartz time-pieces that tell
> time intervals to other clocks,
>   these worksless clocks work well;
> and all four, independently the
>   same, are there in the cool Bell
>   Laboratory time
> vault. Checked by a comparator with Arlington
>   they punctualize ... (Etc.)

I think there would be no use in looking for "symbolist" or "imagist" motives behind the reference to the fact that precisely *four* clocks are mentioned here. It is an "objectivist" observation. We read of four, not because the number corresponds, for instance, to the Horsemen of the Apocalypse, but simply because there actually are four of them in the time vault. Similarly, "cool Bell Laboratory time vault" might have outlying suggestions of something like the coolness of a tomb—but primarily one feels that the description is there for purposes of objective statement; and had the nature of the scene itself dictated it, we should be reading of a "hot Bell Laboratory time tower." Though not journalism, it is reporting.

Yet any reader of Miss Moore's verse will quickly acknowledge that this theme, which provides an "objective" opportunity for the insertion of transitions between such words as "exactest," "punctualize," "careful timing," "clear ice," "instruments of truth," and "accuracy," is quite representative of her (and thus "symbolic" in the proportions of imagism). And the secondary level of the theme (its quality as being not the theme of clocks that tell the time, but of clocks that tell the time to clocks that tell the time)—I should consider thoroughly symbolic, as signalizing a concern not merely for the withinness of motives, but for the withinness-of-withinness of motives, the motives behind motives.[1]

We can call Miss Moore "objectivist," then, only by taking away the epithet in part. For though many details in her work seem to get there purely out of her attempt to report and judge of a thing's intrinsic qualities, to make us feel its properties as accurately as possible, the fact remains that, after you have read several of her poems, you begin to discern a strict principle of selection motivating her appraisals.

In *Selected Poems*, for instance, consider the poem, "People's Surroundings," that gives us a catalogue of correspondence between various kinds of agents and the scenes related to their roles. The poet is concerned to feature, in a background, the details that are an objective portrait of the person to whose kind of action this background belongs. "A setting must not have the air of being one"—a proscription one can observe if he makes the setting the extension of those in it. Here are relationships among act, scene, and agent (I use the three terms central to the philosophy of drama embodied in Henry James's prefaces). And among these people who move "in their respective places," we read of

> ... the acacia-like lady shivering at the touch of a hand,
> lost in a small collision of orchids—
> dyed quicksilver let fall
> to disappear like an obedient chameleon in fifty shades of mauve
>   and amethyst.

Here, with person and ground merged as indistinguishably as in a pontillist painting by Seurat, the items objectify a tentative mood we encounter throughout Miss Moore's verses. The lines are like a miniature impression of her work in its entirety. And when, contemplating a game of bowls, she writes, "I learn that we are precisians, not citizens of Pompeii arrested in action / as a cross-section of one's correspondence would seem to imply," she here "learns" what she is forever learning, in her contemplation of animals and natural and fabricated things, as she seeks to isolate, for her appreciation and our own, the "great amount of poetry in unconscious fastidiousness."

I think appreciation is as strong a motive in her work as it was in the work of Henry James. "The thing is to lodge somewhere at the heart of one's complexity an irrepressible *appreciation*," he says in his preface to *The Spoils of Poynton*. And: "To criticise is to appreciate, to appropriate, to take intellectual possession, to establish in fine a relation with the criticised thing and make it one's own." It is a kind of private property available to everyone—and is perhaps the closest secular equivalent to the religious motive of glorification. It is a form of gratitude. And following out its possibilities, where one might otherwise be querulous he can instead choose to be precise. This redemption or transformation of complaint is, I think, essential to the quality of perception in Miss Moore's verse. (Rather, it is an anticipation of complaint: getting there first, it takes up all the room.)

In "Spenser's Ireland" (*What Are Years*), we may glimpse somewhat how this redemption can take place. Beginning in a mood of appreciation almost studious, the poem ends

> The Irish say your trouble is their
> trouble and your
>   joy their joy? I wish
> I could believe it;
> I am troubled, I'm dissat-
> isfied, I'm Irish.

Since it is towards this end that the poem is directed, we may assume that from this end it derives the logic of its progression.

Note the general tenor of the other observations: on family, on marriage, on independence and yielding, on the freedom of those "made captive by supreme belief." There is talk of enchantments, of transformations, of a coat "like Venus' mantle lined with stars ... the sleeves new from disuse," of such discriminations as we get

> when large dainty
> fingers tremblingly divide the wings
>   of the fly.

And there are lines naming birds, and having a verbal music most lovely in its flutter of internal rhymes:

> the guillemot
>   so neat and the hen
> of the heath and the
> linnet spinet-sweet.

All these details could be thought of as contextual to the poem's ending (for, if you single out one moment of a poem, all the other moments automatically become its context). If, then, we think of the final assertion as the act, we may think of the preceding contextual material as the scene, or background, of this act (a background that somehow contains the same quality as the act, saying implicitly what the act of the final assertion says explicitly). Viewed thus we see, as the underlying structure of this "description," a poem that, if treated as a lyric, would have somewhat the following argument:

"Surrounded with details appropriate to my present mood, with a background of such items as go with matters to do with family, union, independence, I, an Irish girl (while the birds are about—and sweetly) am dissatisfied."

I won't insist that I'm not wrong. But in any case, that's the way I read it. And I would discern, behind her "objectivist" study and editorializing, what are essentially the lineaments of a lyric. But where the lyrist might set about to write, "In the moonlight, by the river, on a night like this in Spain," I can think of Miss Moore's distributing these items (discreetly and discretely) among conversational observations about the quality of light in general and moonlight in particular, about rivers mighty and tiny, in mountains, across plains, and emptying into the desert or the sea, about the various qualifications that apply to the transformation from twilight to darkness, in suburbs, or over bays, etc.; and from travel books of Spain we might get some bits that, pieced together, gave us all those elements into which, in her opinion, the given night in Spain should be "broken down."

We might try from another angle by suggesting that Miss Moore makes "because" look like "and." That is, the orthodox lyrist might say, in effect, "I am sad *because* the birds are singing thus." A translation into Miss Moore's objectivist idiom would say in effect: "There are such and such birds—*and* birds sing thus and so—*and* I am sad." The scenic material would presumably be chosen because of its quality as objective replica of the subjective (as observed moments in the scene that correspond to observing moments in the agent). But even where they had been selected because of their bearing upon the plaint, her subsequent attention to them, with appreciation as a motive, would transform the result from a purely psychologistic rhetoric (the traditional romantic device of simply using scenic terms as a vocabulary for the sympathetic naming of personal moods). And the result would be, instead, an appraisal or judgment of many things in and for themselves. They would be encouraged to disclose their traits, not simply that they might exist through the vicarage of words, but that they might reveal their properties as workmanship (workmanship being a trait in which the ethical and the esthetic are one).

What are years? That is, if we were to assemble a thesaurus of all the important qualifications of the term "years" as Miss Moore uses it, what would these qualifications be? I suppose a title is always an assertion because it is a thing—and every thing is positive. Years, we learn by her opening poem of that title, are at least a quality of observation (vision), involving the obligation of courage, of commands laid upon the self to be strong, to see deep and be glad. And years possess the quality of one

> ... who
> accedes to mortality
> and in his imprisonment, rises
> upon himself as
> the sea in a chasm ...

Who does this, we are told, "sees deep and is glad." Years are also, by the nature of the case, steps from something to something. And to indicate a curve of development from the earlier volume, we might recall this same theme (of the rising water) as it was treated previously. I refer to a poem, "Sojourn in the Whale," which, beginning on the theme, "Trying to open locked doors with a sword," had likewise talked of Ireland. It is addressed to "you," a "you" who has heard men say: "she will become wise and will be forced to give / in. Compelled by experience, she / will turn back; water seeks its own level." Whereat

> ... you
> have smiled. 'Water in motion is far
> from level.' You have seen it, when obstacles happened to bar
> the path, rise automatically.

In the earlier poem, the figure was used defensively, even oppositionally. It is a tactic not common in Miss Moore's verse; as against the dialectician's morality of eristic, she shows a more feminine preference for the sheer ostracizing of the enemy, refuting by silence—disagreement implying the respect of intimacy, as in her poem on "Marriage," wittily appraising the "fight to be affectionate," she quotes, "No truth can be fully known until it has been tried by the tooth of disputation."

(When Miss Moore was editor of *The Dial*, her ideal number, as regards the reviews and articles of criticism, would I think have been one in which all good books got long favorable reviews, all middling books got short favorable reviews, and all books deserving of attack were allowed to go without mention. One can imagine how such a norm could be reached either charitably, through stress upon appreciation as motive, or not so charitably, by way of punishment, as when Miss Moore observes in "Spenser's Ireland": "Denunciations do not affect the culprit: nor blows, but it / is torture to him not to be spoken to." We need not decide between these motives in all cases, since they can comfortably work in unison.)

In contrast with the "oppositional" context qualifying the figure of the rising water in the earlier poem, "Sojourn in the Whale," its later variant has a context almost exaltedly positive. And repeating the same pattern (of affirmation in imprisonment) in another figure, the later poem widens the connotations of the years thus:

> ... The very bird
> grown taller as he sings, steels
> his form straight up. Though he is captive
> his mighty singing
> says satisfaction is a lowly
> thing, how pure a thing is joy.
> This is mortality,
> this is eternity.

The pattern appears more conversationally (*What Are Years*, p. 12) in the suggestion that it must have been a "humorous" workman who made

> this greenish Waterford
> glass weight with the summit curled down toward
> itself as the
> grass grew,

and in "The Monkey Puzzle" (*Selected Poems*) we read

> its tail superimposed upon itself in a complacent half spiral,
> incidentally so witty.

Still, then, trying to discover what are years (or rather, what all are years), we might also recall, in *Selected Poems*, the poem on "The Fish," where the one fish featured as representative of its tribe is observed "opening and shutting itself like / an / injured fan"—in quality not unlike "The Student" of *What Are Years* who

> ... is too reclusive for
> some things to seem to touch
> him, not because he
> has no feeling but because he has so much.

As the poem of "The Fish" develops, we might say that the theme is transferred "from the organism to the environment"; for we next read of a chasm through which the water has driven a wedge—and injury is here too, since

> All
> external
>   marks of abuse are present on this
>   defiant edifice.—

And finally

> Repeated
>   evidence has proved that it can live
>   on what cannot revive
>   its youth. The sea grows old in it.

A chasm in the sea, then, becomes rather the sea in a chasm. And this notable reversal, that takes place in the areas of the "submerged," would also seem to be an aspect of "years." Which would mean that "years" subsume the synecdochic possibilities whereby those elements that cluster together can represent one another: here the active can become passive, the environed can become the environment, the container can be interchangeable with the contained. In possessing such attributes, "years" are poetry.

We may at this point recall our beginning—the citation concerning visible and invisible. In "The Plumet Basilisk" (*Selected Poems*) we read of this particular lizard that, "king with king,"

> He leaps and meets his
>   likeness in the stream.

He is (in the poem it is a quotation)

> 'the ruler of Rivers, Lakes, and Seas,
>   invisible or visible'—

and as scene appropriate to the agent, this basilisk is said to live in a basilica. (Another lizard, in the same poem, is said to be "conferring wings on what it grasps, as the airplant does"; and in "The Jerboa," we are told of "this small desert rat" that it "honours the sand by assuming its colour.") Likewise

> the plumet portrays
> mythology's wish
> to be interchangeably man and fish.

What I am trying to do, in reaching out for these various associations, is to get some comprehensive glimpse of the ways in which the one pervasive quality of motivation is modified and ramified. I am trying, in necessarily tenuous material, to indicate how the avowed relation between the visible and the invisible finds variants, or sophistications, in "objectivist" appreciation; how this appreciation, in an age of much querulousness, serves rather to transcend the querulous (*Selected Poems*, p. 34: "The staff, the bag, the feigned inconsequence / of manner, best bespeak that weapon, self-protectiveness"); and how this same pattern takes form in the theme of submergence, with its interchange-abilities, and so in the theme of water rising on itself. At another point the motive takes as its object the motif of the spinster ("You have been compelled by hags to spin / gold thread from straw," with incidental suggestions of esthetic alchemy, lines that appear in "Sojourn in the Whale," and so link with submergence, Ireland, and the theme of spirited feminine independence, thus relating to kindred subjects in the later poem, "Spenser's Ireland"). I have also suggested that a like quality of imagination is to be found in the intellectual ways of one who selects as his subject not clocks, but clocks for clocks. (To appreciate just what goes on here, one might contrast these contemplative clocks—serene in their role as the motives behind motives—with the ominous clock-faces of Verhaeren, or in the grotesque plays of Edmund Wilson, which no one seems to have read but me.) From these crystal clocks, I could then advance to another variant, as revealed in the treatment of ice and glass. These would, I think, be animated by the same spirit. See for instance (in *Selected Poems*) the study of the glacier as "an octopus of ice":

> this fossil flower concise without a shiver,
> intact when it is cut,
> damned for its sacrosanct remoteness.

"Relentless accuracy is the nature of this octopus / with its capacity for fact"—which would make it a glacier with an objectivist esthetic. And two levels of motive are figured in the splendid concluding vista of

> ... the hard mountain 'planed by ice and polished by the wind'—the
> white volcano with no weather side;

the lightning flashing at its base,
rain falling in the valleys, and snow falling on the peak—.[2]

We might have managed more easily by simply demarcating several themes, like naming the different ingredients that go to make up a dish. Or as with the planks that are brought together, to make a campaign platform, regardless of their fit with one another. But the relation among the themes of a genuine poetry is not of this sort. It is *substantial*—which is to say that all the branches spread from a single trunk.

I am trying to suggest that, without this initial substantiality, "objectivism" would lead not to the "feigned inconsequence of manner" that Miss Moore has mastered, but to inconsequence pure and simple. But because of this substantiality, the surfaces are derived from depth; indeed, the strict lawfulness in their choice of surfaces is depth. And the objects treated have the property not simply of things, but of volitions. They derive their poignancy as motifs from their relation to the sources of motive. And the relation between observer and observed is not that of news and reporter, but of "conversities" (her word).

In the earlier volume there is a poem, "Black Earth," wherein surprisingly the poet establishes so close an identification with her theme as not merely to "observe" it with sympathy and appreciation, but to speak for it. This is one of her rare "I" poems—and in it the elephant sometimes speaks with the challenge and confidence of an Invictus. Beginning on the theme of emergence (coupled with delight in the thought of submergence at will), there is first a celebration of the sturdy skin; then talk of power ("my back is full of the history of power"); and then: "My soul shall never be cut into / by a wooden spear." Next comes mention of the trunk, and of poise. And interwoven with the vigor of assertion, the focal theme is there likewise:

> that tree-trunk without
> roots, accustomed to shout
>   its own thoughts to itself ...

and:

> ... The I of each is to
> the I of each
> a kind of fretful speech
>   which sets a limit on itself; the elephant is
>   black earth preceded by a tendril?

I think we can make a point by recalling this earlier poem when, in
"Smooth Gnarled Crape Myrtle" (*What Are Years*), the theme of the
elephant's trunk appears again, this time but in passing, contextual and
"tangential" to the themes of birds, union, loneliness:

> ... 'joined in
> friendship, crowned by love.'
> An aspect may deceive; as the
> elephant's columbine-tubed trunk
> held waveringly out—
> an at will heavy thing—is
> delicate.

Surely, "an at will heavy thing" is a remarkable find. But one does not make
such observation by merely looking at an elephant's trunk. There must have
been much to discard. In this instance, we can know something about the
omissions, quite as though we had inspected earlier drafts of the poem with
their record of revisions. For though a usage in any given poem is a finished
thing, and thus brilliant with surface, it becomes in effect but "work in
progress" when we align it with kindred usages (emergent, fully developed,
or retrospectively condensed) in other poems. And here, by referring to
"Black Earth," we can find what lies behind the reference to the elephant's
trunk in "Smooth Gnarled Crape Myrtle." We can know it for a fact what
kind of connotations must, for the poet, have been implicit in the second,
condensed usage. Hence we can appreciate the motives that enabled this
trunk to be seen not merely as a *thing*, but as an *act*, representative of the
assertion in "Black Earth." And by reviewing the earlier usage we can know
the kind of volitional material which, implicit in the later usage, led beyond
the perception of the trunk as a thing to this perception of it as an act. At
such moments, I should say, out of our idealistic trammels we get a glimpse
of realism in its purity.

Or let us look at another instance. Sensitivity in the selection of words
resides in the ability, or necessity, to feel behind the given word a history—
not a past history, but a future one. Within the word, collapsed into its
simultaneous oneness, there is implicit a sequence, a complexity of possible
narratives that could be drawn from it. If you would remember what words
are in this respect, and how in the simultaneity of a word histories are
implicit, recall the old pleasantry of asking someone, "What's an accordion,"
whereat invariably as he explains he will start pumping a bellows.

Well, among Miss Moore's many poems enunciating aspects of her esthetic credo, or commenting on literary doctrines and methods, there is one, "To a Snail," beginning:

> If 'compression is the first grace of style,'
> you have it. Contractility is a virtue
> as modesty is a virtue.

And this equating of an esthetic value with a moral one is summed up by locating the principle of style "in the curious phenomenon of your occipital horn."

In her poem on the butterfly (*What Are Years*, p. 17), the mood of tentativeness that had been compressed within the term "contractility" reveals its significant narrative equivalents. As befits the tentative, or contractile, it is a poem of jeopardy, tracing a tenuous relationship between a butterfly ("half deity half worm," "last of the elves") and a nymph ("dressed in Wedgewood blue"), with light winds (even a "zephyr") to figure the motives of passion. Were not the course of a butterfly so intrinsically akin to the "inconsequential ease" and "drover-like tenacity" of Miss Moore's own versa-tilities, one might not have much hope for a poem built about this theme (reminiscent of many musical Papillons—perhaps more than a theme, perhaps a set idiom, almost a form). Here, with the minute accuracy of sheerly "objectivist" description, there is a subtle dialectic of giving and receiving, of fascinations and releases—an interchange of delicately shaded attitudes. In this realm, things reached for will evade, but will follow the hand as it recedes.

Through the tracery of flight, there are two striking moments of stasis, each the termination of a course: one when "the butterfly's tobacco-brown unglazed / china eyes and furry countenance confront / the nymph's large eyes"—and the second when, having broken contact with the nymph's "controlled agitated glance," the "fiery tiger-horse" (at rest, but poised against the wind, "chest arching / bravely out") is motivated purely by relation to the zephyr alone. The poem concludes by observing that this "talk" between the animal and the zephyr "was as strange as my grandmother's muff."

I have called it a poem of jeopardy. (When butterfly and nymph confront each other, "It is Goya's scene of the tame magpie faced / by crouching cats.") It is also a poem of coquetry (perhaps our last poem of coquetry, quite as this butterfly was the last of the elves—coquetry now usually being understood as something that comes down like a ton of brick).[3]

The tentativeness, contractility, acquires more purely the theme of jeopardy in "Bird-Witted" (*What Are Years*), reciting the incident of the "three large fledgling mocking-birds," awaiting "their no longer larger mother," while there approaches

> the
> intellectual cautious-
> ly c r e e p ing cat.

If her animals are selected for their "fastidiousness," their fastidiousness itself is an aspect of contractility, of jeopardy. "The Pangolin" (*What Are Years*), a poem which takes us through odd nocturnal journeys to the joyous saluting of the dawn, begins: "Another armoured animal"—and of a sudden you realize that Miss Moore's recondite menagerie is almost a thesaurus of protectivenesses. Thus also, the poem in which occur the lines anent visible and invisible, has as its conclusion:

> unsolicitude having swallowed up
> all giant birds but an
> alert gargantuan
> little-winged, magnificently
> speedy running-bird. This one
> remaining rebel
> is the sparrow-camel.

The tentativeness also manifests itself at times in a cult of rarity, a collector's or antiquarian interest in the present, a kind of stylistic tourism. And it may lead to a sheer word play, of graduated sort (a Laforguian delight in showing how the pedantries can be reclaimed for poetry):

> The lemur-student can see
> that the aye-aye is not
>
> an angwan-tíbo, potto, or loris.

Yet mention of the "aepyornis" may suggest the answer we might have given, were we up on such matters, to one who, pencil in hand and with the newspaper folded to make it firmer, had asked, "What's a gigantic bird, found fossil in Madagascar in nine letters?" As for her invention, "invisible," I can't see it.

Tonally, the "contractility" reveals itself in the great agility, even restlessness, which Miss Moore imparts to her poetry by assonance, internal rhyme, and her many variants of the run-over line. We should also note those sudden nodules of sound which are scattered throughout her verses, such quick concentrations as "rude root cudgel," "the raised device reversed," "trim trio on the tree-stem," "furled fringed frill," or tonal episodes more sustained and complex, as the lines on the birds in Ireland (already quoted), or the title, "Walking-Sticks and Paper-Weights and Water-Marks," or

> ... the redbird
> the red-coated musketeer,
> the trumpet-flower, the cavalier,
> the parson, and the
> wild parishioner. A deer-
> track in a church-floor
> brick ...

One noticeable difference between the later selection and the earlier one is omission of poems on method. In *Selected Poems* there were a great many such. I think for instance of: "Poetry," containing her ingenious conceit, "imaginary gardens with real toads in them"; "Critics and Connoisseurs"; "The Monkeys"; "In the Days of Prismatic Colour"; "Picking and Choosing"; "When I Buy Pictures"; "Novices" (on action in language, and developed in imagery of the sea); "The Past is the Present" ("ecstasy affords / the occasion and expediency determines the form"); and one which propounds a doctrine as its title: "In This Age of Hard Trying, Nonchalance is Good and."

But though methodological pronouncements of this sort have dropped away, in the closing poem on "The Paper Nautilus," the theme does reappear. Yet in an almost startlingly deepened transformation. Here, proclaiming the poet's attachment to the poem, there are likenesses to the maternal attachment to the young. And the themes of bondage and freedom (as with one "hindered to succeed") are fiercely and flashingly merged.

NOTES

1. In passing we might consider a whole series of literary ways from this point of view. Allegory would deal with correspondences on a purely dogmatic, or conceptual basis. In the article on "Vestments," for instance, in the *Encyclopædia Britannica*, we read of various "symbolical interpretations": "(1) the *moralizing school*, the oldest, by which—as in the case of St. Jerome's treatment of the Jewish vestments—the vestments are explained as typical of the virtues proper to those who wear them; (2) the *Christological school*, *i.e.* that which

considered the minister as the representative of Christ and his garments as typical of some aspects of Christ's person or office—*e.g.* the stole is his obedience and servitude for our sakes; (3) the *allegorical school*, which treats the priest as a warrior or champion, who puts on the amice as a helmet, the alb as a breastplate, and so on." A work constructed about the systematic use of any such theories of correspondence would, to our way of thinking, be allegorical. The symbolic would use an objective vocabulary for its suggestion of the subjective, with the subjective motive being organizationally more important than the objective one. The specific literary movement called Symbolism would exemplify this stress to a large extent, but would also gravitate towards Surrealism, which stresses the incongruous and contradictory nature of motives by the use of gargoyles as motifs. Imagism would be "personalistic," in the idealistic sense, in using scenic material as the reflection, or extension of human characters. The "objectivist," though rooted in symbolic and imagist concerns, would move into a plane where the object, originally selected by reason of its subjective reference, is studied in its own right. (The result will be "descriptive" poetry. And it will be "scientific" in the sense that, whereas poetry is a kind of act, the descriptiveness of science is rather the *preparation* for an act, the delayed action of a Hamletic reconnaissance in search of the accurate knowledge necessary for the, act. And descriptive poetry falls across the two categories in that it acts by describing the scene preparatory to an act.) Naturalism has a greater stress upon the scenic from the polemic or depreciatory point of view (its quasi-scientific quality as delayed action, or preparation for action, often being revealed in that such literature generally either calls for action in the non-esthetic field or makes one very conscious of the fact that a "solution" is needed but is not being offered). True realism is difficult for us to conceive of, after so long a stretch of monetary idealism (accentuated as surrealism) and its counterpart, technological materialism (accentuated as behaviorism and operationalism), while pragmatic philosophies stress *making* and *doing* and *getting* in a localized way that obscures the realistic stress upon the *act*. The German term, *Realpolitik*, for instance, exemplifies a crude brand of pragmatism that completely misrepresents the realistic motive. The communicative nature of art gives all art a realistic ingredient, but the esthetic philosophies which the modern artist consciously or unconsciously absorbs continually serve to obscure this ingredient rather than to cultivate it.

2. This is cited from the poem that follows the one on "Marriage," and is in turn followed by "Sea Unicorns and Land Unicorns." The three could be taken together as a triptych that superbly illustrates three stages in the development of one idea. First, we have the subtly averse poem on marriage (done in a spirit of high comedy that portrays marital quarrelings as interrelated somewhat like the steps of a minuet). Then comes the precise yet exalted contemplation of the glacier. And finally a discussion of the unicorn, a legendary solitaire:

> Thus this strange animal with its miraculous elusiveness,
> has come to be unique,
> 'impossible to take alive',
> tamed only by a lady inoffensive like itself—
> as curiously wild and gentle.

And typically, she cites of it that, since lions and unicorns are arch enemies, and "where the one is the other cannot be missing," Sir John Hawkins deduced an abundance of lions in Florida from the presence of unicorns there.

The theme of the lightning that flashes at the base of the glacier is varied in the unicorn poem (in a reference to "the dogs / which are dismayed by the chain lightning / playing at them from its horn"). And it is varied also in a poem on the elephant (still to be discussed) that

> has looked at the electricity and at the earth-
> quake and is still
> here; ...

3. In the earlier volume there is an epigram-like poem, "To a Steam Roller," that I have always thought very entertaining. It excoriates this sorry, ungainly mechanism as a bungling kind of fellow that, when confronting such discriminations as are the vital purpose of Miss Moore's lines, would "crush all the particles down / into close conformity, and then walk back and forth / on them." We also read there:

> As for butterflies, I can hardly conceive
> of one's attending upon you, but to question
> the congruence of the complement is vain, if it exists.

Heretofore I had been content to think of this reference to a butterfly simply as a device for suggesting weight by a contrasting image of lightness. But the role of butterfly as elf conversant to nymph might also suggest the presence of such overtones as contrasting types of masculinity. (This would give us a perfect instance of what Coleridge meant by fancy, which occurs when we discern behind the contrast an element that the contrasted images share in common.)

As for the later poem, where the theme of the butterfly is fully developed, I might now try to make more clearly the point I had in mind with reference to the two moments of stasis. In the opening words ("half deity half worm" and "We all, infant and adult, have / stopped to watch the butterfly") the poem clearly suggests the possibility that it will figure two levels of motivation, a deity being in a different realm of motives than a worm, and the child's quality of perception being critically distinct from the adult's. Examining the two moments of stasis, we find here too the indications of an important difference between them. At the first stasis, elf and nymph confront each other, while "all's a-quiver with significance." But at the final stasis, the conversity is between butterfly and west wind, a directer colloquy (its greater inwardness linking it, in my opinion, with the motive-behind-motive figuration in the theme of clocks-for-clocks). At this second stage, the butterfly is called "historic metamorphoser / and saintly animal"; hence we may take it that the "deity" level of motive prevails at this second stage. The quality of the image in the closing line ("their talk was as strange as my grandmother's muff") would suggest that the deified level is equated with the quality of perception as a child. (The grandmother theme also appears in "Spenser's Ireland," where we are told that "Hindered characters ... in Irish stories ... all have grandmothers." Another reason for believing that the second stage of the butterfly poem is also the "motives-behind-motives" stage is offered tenuously by this tie-up with the word "hindered," since the final poem in the book, as we shall know when we come to it, does well by this word in proclaiming a morality of art.)

Another poem, "Virginia Britannia" (*What Are Years*), that seems on the surface almost exclusively descriptive (though there is passing reference to a "fritillary" that "zig-zags") is found to be progressing through scenic details to a similar transcendence. At the last, against sunset, two levels are figured, while the intermediate trees "become with lost identity, part of the ground." The clouds, thus marked off, are then heralded in words suggestive of Wordworth's ode as "to the child an intimation of / what glory is."

HUGH KENNER

Mauberley

Firmness,
Not the full smile,
His art, but an art
In profile.

With the partial exception of the *Cathay* sequence, the *Personae* volume up to page 183 may be said to be implicit in the *Cantos*. The early poems are deficient in finality; they supplement and correct one another; they stand up individually as renderings of moods, but not as manifestations of mature self-knowledge; they try out poses. They are leading their author somewhere; the reader may be excused if his interests are not wholly engaged, if he finds himself separating the technique from the value of the presented state. This may be said without unsaying anything in the preceding survey, the object of which has been to suggest considerable profit in what may not appear of compelling interest at first glance in 1951. Not only is the history of the purification of our post-Victorian speech contained in those pages, but a right perception of the kinds of achievement there contained will make the *Cantos* easier reading. And in isolating principles of apprehension it has been an advantage to have relatively uncomplicated texts to explicate.

The volume ends, however, with two great self-justifying poems. *Homage to Sextus Propertius* (1917) and *Hugh Selwyn Mauberley* (1920) would,

From *The Poetry of Ezra Pound*. © 1968 by New Directions Publishing Corp.

had not a single Canto been finished, dispel any doubt of Pound's being a major poet.

It will be convenient to shorten our discussion by referring the reader to Dr. Leavis' tributes to *Mauberley* in *New Bearings in English Poetry*. That the poem moves him as it does, and that he registers his admiration so adequately and with such economical power of inciting others to comprehension, may, considering the intrinsic resistance of the Bloomsbury-Cambridge milieu to all but certain types of subtly-discriminated moral fervours, be taken as some gauge of the emotional weight, the momentum of essential seriousness, massed in these seventeen pages of disrupted quatrains.

Yet the reader will infer correctly from this way of describing Dr. Leavis' dealings with *Mauberley* that the highly selective vision of that honest and irascible critic has screened out certain essential elements. Pound emerges from his account as a man of one poem; the early work is uninteresting, the *Cantos* a monument of elegant dilettantism. In *Mauberley*, for a few pages, under urgent and unhappily transient personal pressures, he found himself with precision and sincerity. Dr. Leavis' view of Pound's career is introduced here as representative of the most respectable critical thought. Setting aside journalistic opportunism of the kind that has no real concern for letters, attacks on Pound are generally attacks on the *Cantos*. The isolated success of *Mauberley* is generally conceded. The dispraise even of Mr. Winters is qualified somewhat at this point.

Mauberley, that is, is a tricky poem. It is difficult for men of a certain training not to misread it subtly, to select from its elements certain strings that reverberate to an Eliotic tuning fork. A taste for contemporary poetry that has shaped itself almost entirely on Mr. Eliot's resonant introspections has no difficulty in catching what it has come to regard as the sole note of contemporary poetic sincerity in:

> For three years, out of key with his time,
> He strove to resuscitate the dead art
> Of poetry: to maintain 'the sublime'
> In the old sense. Wrong from the start—

It is easy to see how this chimes with such passages as:

> So here I am, in the middle way, having had twenty years—
> Twenty years largely wasted, the years of *l'entre deux guerres*—
> Trying to learn to use words, and every attempt
> Is a wholly new start, and a different kind of failure

Because one has only learnt to get the better of words
For the thing one no longer has to say, or the way in which
One is no longer disposed to say it ...

East Coker, V.

It may briefly be said that there has been a muddle about 'impersonality'. Mr. Eliot's impersonality is Augustinian; a dispassionate contemplation of the self which permits without romantic impurities a poetic corpus of metamorphosed personae. Pound's impersonality is Flaubertian: an effacement of the personal accidents of the perceiving medium in the interests of accurate registration of *mœurs contemporaines*. As we have said, the adoption of various personae is for such an artist merely a means to ultimate depersonalization, ancillary and not substantial to his major work. J. Alfred Prufrock is not Mr. Eliot, but he speaks with Mr. Eliot's voice and bears intricate analogical relations with the later Eliot persona who is the speaker of *Four Quartets*. Hugh Selwyn Mauberley, on the other hand, does not speak with Mr. Pound's voice, and is more antithetically than intimately related to the poet of the *Cantos*. It would be misleading to say that he is a portion of Mr. Pound's self whom Mr. Pound is externalizing in order to get rid of him (like Stephen Dedalus); it would be a more accurate exaggeration to say that he is a parody of Pound the poet with whom Mr. Pound is anxious not to be confounded.

The sort of critic we have been mentioning, the one who finds the note of sincerity in *Mauberley* as nowhere else in Pound, pays unconscious tribute to the accuracy with which Pound, in quest of devices for articulating this quasi-Prufrockian figure, has echoed the intonations and gestures of a characteristic Eliot poem.[1] Such a critic has been known to quote in confirmation of his view of Pound Mr. Eliot's remark, 'I am sure of *Mauberley*, whatever else I am sure of.' Mr. Eliot has not, however, the perceptive limitations of his disciples; in the same essay he insists that the entire *Personae* collection is to be read as a process of exploration leading up to the *Cantos*, 'which are wholly himself.'

It may be helpful to remark that Joyce is in this respect like Pound, an artist of the Flaubertian kind; his Stephen Dedalus is a parody of himself, not an artist but an aesthete, at length mercilessly ridiculed in *Finnegans Wake*. The analogy is reasonably exact; Stephen is partly an aspect of Joyce himself which Joyce is trying to purify; his horror of bourgeois civilization echoes Joyce's much as *Mauberley's* 'sense of graduations',

Quite out of place amid
Resistance of current exacerbations,

echoes Pound's. But Joyce refrains from unambiguous sympathy with Stephen's desire for Shelleyan sunward flight; he involves Stephen in an Icarian fall into the sea of matter just as Pound reduces Mauberley to

> Nothing, in brief, but maudlin confession,
> Irresponse to human aggression,
> Amid the precipitation, down-float
> Of insubstantial manna,
> Lifting the faint susurrus
> Of his subjective hosannah.

This cannot be taken as an account of the poet of the *Cantos* any more than Stephen's fastidious shrinking away from common noises can be regarded as characteristic of the author of *Ulysses*. Both men channelled their disgust into patient sifting of immense sottisiers; Pound has been, significantly, almost alone in perceiving the continuity between *Ulysses* and *Bouvard et Pécuchet*. In *Ulysses* Stephen is the focus of spectacular technical sonorities, sympathized with and rejected; the same is true of the Lotus-eaters in the *Cantos*.

It may be remarked that the critic who thinks of *Mauberley* as Pound's one successful poem commonly sees Stephen Dedalus as the hero of *Ulysses*, perceives in both figures elements of failure, and takes as dim a view of Joyce as of the author of the *Cantos*.

Against what may be mistaken for the drift of the above paragraphs, it should be insisted that the process of creating and disowning Hugh Selwyn Mauberley had not the personal importance for Pound that the purgation of the Dedalian aspects of himself had for Joyce. No such trauma was involved in the Idaho poet's flight from America as in the Irish novelist's disentanglement from Church and Motherland. It is not true, on the other hand, to say that Joyce could do nothing until he had focused and gotten rid of Stephen: the bulk of *Dubliners* was written in 1904, in Joyce's twenty-third year. But even when we have balanced *Dubliners* with the social observations in *Lustra*, and *Chamber Music* with the first volume of *Personae*, the excernment of Stephen Dedalus remains of crucial importance to Joyce's future achievement in a way that the writing of *Mauberley* probably was not to Pound. It was probably necessary that he focus in some such oblique way the tension between popular demands and his earlier poetic activities before embarking on the *Cantos*; but the process need not be thought to have coincided with a spiritual crisis from which, as it suits the critic, he emerged either crippled or annealed.

Mauberley does not mark in that way a hurt awakening from aesthetic playgrounds into thin cruel daylight. Its postures and conflicts continue, as we have indicated, those of *Propertius*, the *robustezza* of which could scarcely be confounded with hurt awakening.[2] If a decisive point of maturation must be found, it is to be found in *Propertius*, the earlier poem, it is not always remembered, by some three years. It is easy, for that matter, to over-estimate the reorientation there involved *vis-à-vis* the earlier work. There need be nothing traumatic about supervening maturity; the bulk of *Personae* is the work of a young man in his twenties. Pound was born in 1885. The earliest *Personae*, dated 1908, belong therefore to *ætat.* 23. He published the *Seafarer* translation at 27; *Lustra* at 30, *Cathay* at 31. The next year saw *Propertius* and the first drafts of the earliest *Cantos*. He published *Mauberley* at 35. The *Pisan Cantos* are the work of a man of 60. Emotional maturation may be seen going on in the *Lustra* volume; and there is enough difference between the monolinear intensity of 'The Needle' (*Ripostes*, 1912):

> Come, or the stellar tide will slip away,
> Eastward avoid the hour of its decline,
> Now! for the needle trembles in my soul! ...

and the calm detached emotion of. 'Gentildonna' (*Lustra*, 1915):

> She passed and left no quiver in the veins, who now
> Moving among the trees, and clinging in the air she severed,
> Fanning the grass she walked on then, endures:
> Grey olive leaves beneath a rain-cold sky.

to preclude any suggestion of a cataclysmic reorientation a few years later.

These pages will have performed their function if they can arm the reader against the too-easy supposition that Pound found in *Mauberley* an eloquence of disillusion. The subtle balance of diverse strong emotions in that poem will be utterly destroyed by too ready a response to one or two elements. We may now look, belatedly, at the text.

The subtitle ('Life and Contacts') and the title-page footnote ('... distinctly a farewell to London') furnish a perspective on the title of the first of the eighteen poems: 'E.P. Ode Pour L'Election de son Sepulchre.[3]' This is largely Pound's career in London seen through the eyes of uncomprehending but not unsympathetic conservers of the 'better tradition': a strenuous but ineffectual angel, his subtleties of passion 'wrong from the start', accorded the patronizing excuse of having been born 'in a half savage country, out of date', and given to Yankee intensities ('bent resolutely on

wringing lilies from the acorn') of an unclubbable sort. The epitaph modulates
into grudging admiration for the pertinacity of this dedicated spirit—

> His true Penelope was Flaubert,
> He fished by obstinate isles;
> Observed the elegance of Circe's hair
> Rather than the mottoes on sun-dials.

The first line of this stanza renders with astonishing concision an intricate set
of cultural perspectives. Pound's voyages to China, to Tuscany, to Provence,
his battles with Polyphemic editors and his dallyings with pre-Raphaelite
Sirens, are transformed, as in the *Cantos*, into an Odyssey of discovery and
frustration, imposed, for jealous and irrelevant reasons, by the ruler of the
seas (a neat fusion of the chaotic state of letters with English mercantile
smugness; the 'obstinate isles' are both the British Isles and recalcitrant
aesthetic objectives.) The irony with which the British mortician of
reputations is made to utter unambiguous truths about artistic effort (cf. the
'Beauty is difficult' motif of the *Pisan Cantos*) at the same time as he vaunts
his national obstinacy and imperception, is carried on with the mention of
Flaubert, the 'true Penelope' of this voyage. For Pound, Flaubert is the true
(=faithful) counterpart, entangling crowds of suitors (superficial 'realists') in
their own self-deceit while she awaits the dedicated partner whose arm can
bend the hard bow of the 'mot juste'. Flaubert represents the ideal of
disciplined self-immolation from which English poetry has been too long
estranged, only to be rejoined by apparently circuitous voyaging. For the
writer of the epitaph, on the other hand, Flaubert is conceded to be E.P.'s
'true' (=equivalent) Penelope only in deprecation: Flaubert being for the
English literary mind of the first quarter of the present century a foreign,
feminine, rather comically earnest indulger in quite un-British preciosity;
'wrong from the start,' surrounded by mistaken admirers, and very possibly
a whore; a suitable Penelope for this energetic American. England was at that
time preparing to burn and ban *Ulysses* exactly as France had sixty years
before subjected *Madame Bovary* to juridical process; it was the complaint of
the tribunal against Flaubert that he had spent pains on the elegance of his
Circe's hair that might better have been diverted to honester causes.

   The implications of line after line, irony upon irony, might be
expanded in this way; the epitaph concludes with a superbly categorical
dismissal of this *impetuus juventus* from the cadres of responsible literary
position:

Unaffected by 'the march of events',
He passed from men's memory in *l'an trentiesme*
De son eage; the case presents
No adjunct to the Muse's diadem.

The echo of Villon is of course the crowning irony. *His* passage from the memory of his contemporaries has if anything augmented his place in the history of poetry.

As soon as we see that this epitaph is not (except at the level at which it transposes Corbière) being written by Pound, the entire sequence falls into focus. The eleven succeeding poems (II–XII) present an ideogrammic survey of the cultural state of post-war England: of the culture which we have just heard pronouncing upon the futility of Pound's effort to 'resuscitate the dead art of poetry'. The artist who was 'unaffected by the march of events' offers his version of this criterion:

The age demanded an image
Of its accelerated grimace;

the third poem, with its audacious closing counterpoint from Pindar's *Second Olympic* (of which there is a readily accessible translation in the *Biographia Literaria*, ch. xviii), generalizes with a more austere bitterness:

All things are a flowing,
Sage Heracleitus says;
But a tawdry cheapness
Shall outlast our days.

Poems IV and V are similarly paired. IV surveys with compassion the moral dilemmas of the war:

These fought in any case,
and some believing,
        pro domo, in any case ...

poises sacrifice against domestic cheapness:

walked eye-deep in hell
believing in old men's lies, then unbelieving
came home, home to a lie,

home to many deceits,
home to old lies and new infamy;
usury age-old and age-thick
and liars in public places.

and closes with a quick evocation of the pullulating new artistic soil,
entrapping the artist in an opportunity for defined and significant passions
that all but swamp his Flaubertian criteria:

frankness as never before,
disillusions as never told in the old days,
hysterias, trench confessions,
laughter out of dead bellies.

Poem V intensifies the antithesis between sacrifice and gain:

Charm, smiling at the good mouth,
Quick eyes gone under earth's lid,

For two gross of broken statues,
For a few thousand battered books.

The cultural heritage has been reduced to the status of a junkman's inventory
by the conservators of tradition mobilized behind the epitaph of poem I; the
superimposed tension of the apparent incommensurability, at best, of human
lives and civilized achievements brings the sequence to a preliminary climax
that prepares for the change of the next six sections into a retrospective key.
    'Yeux Glauques' poises the pre-Raphaelite purity,

Thin like brook water,
With a vacant gaze

against the bustle of Gladstone and Buchanan (whose attack on 'The Fleshly
School of Poetry' was answered by Rossetti and Swinburne). The painted
woman of the poem contains in her 'questing and passive' gaze the complex
qualities of passion, between the poles of Swinburne and Burne-Jones, which
the aesthetic movement of the nineteenth century mobilized against a world
in which 'The English Rubaiyat was still-born'. The picturesque
reminiscences of the nineties in the next poem intensify the personal
tragedies of the inheritors of that movement; 'Dowson found harlots cheaper

than hotels.' This struggle and rebuttal is, we see, still being carried on; a new dimension of tradition and conflict is added to the efforts of the epitaphed E.P. of the first poem. The success of official literary history in discrediting the vitality of the century of Rossetti, Swinburne, and Fitzgerald and turning it instead into the century of Ruskin, Carlyle, and Tennyson is epitomized in the final stanza:

> M. Verog, out of step with the decade,
> Detached from his contemporaries,
> Neglected by the young,
> Because of these reveries.

M. Verog, 'author of *The Dorian Mood*', is a pseudonym for Victor Plarr, who appears in Canto LXXIV 'talking of mathematics'.

The next three poems are vignettes of three contrasting literary careers. 'Brennbaum' (? Max Beerbohm) embodies what passes for the cult of 'style':

> The stiffness from spats to collar
> Never relaxing into grace.

This style is neo-classical, not that of the leaping arch; Brennbaum's motive is simply to prepare a face to meet the faces that he meets; such emotional intensity as he knows is not only repressed almost to imperceptibility, its dynamic is private, alien, and accidental to the traditions of Latin Europe: 'The heavy memories of Horeb, Sinai, and the forty years.'

Mr. Nixon, exhibit number two, is the successful public man of letters (? Arnold Bennett). The forced rhymes (reviewer/you are) enact his hearty grimaces; his drawled climactic maxim,

> ... as for literature
> It gives no man a sinecure,

unites the pretentious popular philosophy of a Wells, a Shaw, a Bennett with the smug generalizations of commercial success and the hard-boiled saws of *Poor Richard's Almanac*.

> 'And give up verse, my boy,
> 'There's nothing in it.'

The third exhibit is the genuine stylist in hiding, an anticlimactic redaction of the Lake Isle of Innisfree:

The haven from sophistications and contentions
Leaks through its thatch;
He offers succulent cooking;
The door has a creaking latch.

These are not *poèmes à clef*; but the post-war fortunes of Ford Madox Ford are entirely apropos. Ford, the collaborator of Conrad and in the decade pre-war the lone enunciator of the Flaubertian gospel in England, on his discharge from the army retired in disgust to Sussex to raise pigs, and ultimately, at about the same time as Pound, left England. His detailed account of the cultural state of post-war London in the first third of *It Was the Nightingale* can be made to document *Mauberley* line by line. The reviewing synod hastened to write his epitaph, so effectively that his reputation is only beginning to quicken a quarter of a century after the publication of his best work. Pound has never made a secret of his respect for Ford, and Ford has testified that Pound alone of the young writers he could claim to have 'discovered' about 1908 did not amid his later misfortunes disown and castigate him. It pleases at least one reader to suppose that it is the spectacle of Ford's disillusion that animates these three extraordinary stanzas.

Poems XI and XII present a post-war contrast to the intricate contemplative passion of 'Yeux Glauques'. The twelfth closes the survey of the London situation with an image of grotesquely effusive aristocratic patronage; 'Daphne with her thighs in bark' dwindles to the Lady Valentine in her stuffed-satin drawing-room, dispensing 'well-gowned approbation of literary effort' in sublime assurance of her vocation for a career of taste and discrimination:

Poetry, her border of ideas,
The edge, uncertain, but a means of blending
With other strata
Where the lower and higher have ending;

A hook to catch the Lady Jane's attention,
A modulation toward the theatre,
Also, in the case of revolution,
A possible friend and comforter.

Dr. Johnson's letter to Lord Chesterfield stands as the archtypal repudiation of the vague, vain, and irrelevant claims of patronage; but the street of literary commerce to which Johnson turned has also lost its power to support the artist:

> Beside this thoroughfare
> The sale of half-hose has
> Long since superseded the cultivation
> Of Pierian roses.

The *Envoi* which follows is a consummate ironic climax; against these squalors is asserted the audacious Shakespearean vocation of preserving transient beauty against the tooth of time (cf. the end of the first *Propertius* poem); against the halting and adroitly short-winded quatrains of the 'dumb-born book' is set a magnificently sustained melodic line:

> Go, dumb-born book,
> Tell her that sang me once that song of Lawes:
> Hadst thou but song
> As thou hast subjects known,
> Then were there cause in thee that should condone
> Even my faults that heavy upon me lie,
> And build her glories their longevity....

Seventeenth-century music, the union of poetry with song, immortal beauty, vocalic melody, treasure shed on the air, transcend for a single page the fogs and squabbles of the preceding sections in a poem that ironically yearns for the freedom and power which it displays in every turn of phrase, in triumphant vindication of those years of fishing by obstinate isles. The poet who was buried in the first section amid such deprecation rises a Phoenix to confront his immolators, asserting the survival of at least this song

> When our two dusts with Waller's shall be laid,
> Siftings on siftings in oblivion,
> Till change hath broken down
> All things save Beauty alone.

There follows a five-part coda in which the Mauberley *persona* comes to the fore; gathering up the motifs of the earlier sections, the enigmatic stanzas mount from-intensity to intensity to chronicle the death of the

Jamesian hero who might have been Pound. Part two is practically a précis of the flirtation with passionate illusion of Lambert Strether in *The Ambassadors*. 'Of course I moved among miracles,' said Strether. 'It was all phantasmagoric.' The third part contains the essential action; having postulated Mauberley's 'fundamental passion':

> This urge to convey the relation
> Of eye-lid and cheek-bone
> By verbal manifestations;
>
> To present the series
> Of curious heads in medallion,

and implied a context of opportunities missed—

> Which anaesthesis, noted a year late,
> And weighed, revealed his great affect,
> (Orchid), mandate
> Of Eros, a retrospect.

—Pound particularizes on the Propertian conflict between the aesthetic martyr and the demands of the age.

Contemplation is weighed against Shavian strenuousness:

> The glow of porcelain
> Brought no reforming sense
> To his perception
> Of the social inconsequence.
>
> Thus if her colour
> Came against his gaze,
> Tempered as if
> It were through a perfect glaze
>
> He made no immediate application
> Of this to relation of the state
> To the individual, the month was more temperate
> Because this beauty had been.

In Canto XIII Confucius provides a cross-light:

And Kung raised his cane against Yuan Jang,
    Yuan Jang being his elder,
For Yuan Jang sat by the roadside pretending to
    be receiving wisdom.
And Kung said
    'You old fool, come out of it,
Get up and do something useful.'

The serious artist does not 'pretend to be receiving wisdom'; we have heard Pound dilating on his quasi-automatic social functions. It is the essence of the artist's cruel dilemma that his just reaction against politicians' and journalists' canons of usefulness drives him so perilously close to

    ... an Olympian *apathein*
In the presence of selected perceptions.[4]

The descent into this Nirvana of the fastidious moth with the preciously-cadenced name is chronicled with elaborate subtlety. The validity of his perceptions is played off against 'neo-Nietzschean clatter'; but meanwhile the directness of the opening images, the red-beaked steeds, the glow of porcelain, is being gradually overlaid by a crescendo of abstractions: 'isolation,' 'examination,' 'elimination,' 'consternation,' 'undulation,' 'concentration.' The tone shifts from the sympathetic to the clinical:

Invitation, mere invitation to perceptivity
Gradually led him to the isolation
Which these presents place
Under a more tolerant, perhaps, examination.

The preservation of a critical distance both from the inadequacies of Mauberley and from the irrelevantly active world of Mr. Nixon, Nietzsche, and Bishop Bloughram, with its 'discouraging doctrine of chances', the realization of an impersonality that extracts strength from both of the antithetical cadres of the first twelve poems, is the major achievement of these final pages. Mauberley's disappearance into his dream-world is related without approbation and without scorn:

A pale gold, in the aforesaid pattern,
The unexpected palms
Destroying, certainly, the artist's urge,

Left him delighted with the imaginary
Audition of the phantasmal sea-surge,

and we are warned by inverted commas in the next stanza against adopting
too readily the standpoint of pontifical criticism:

Incapable of the least utterance or composition,
Emendation, conservation of the 'better tradition',
Refinement of medium, elimination of superfluities,
August attraction or concentration.

That 'better tradition' interjects the accent of a Buchanan or an Edmund
Gosse; the other canons are Flaubertian. Mauberley is not simply a failure by
Mr. Nixon's standards of success, he is a failure *tout court*; he is the man to
whom that initial epitaph might with justice be applied; the man for whom
the writer of the epitaph has mistaken 'E.P.' It is the focusing of this that
guarantees the closing irony:

Ultimate affronts to
Human redundancies;

Non-esteem of self-styled 'his betters'
Leading, as he well knew,
To his final
Exclusion from the world of letters.

The irrelevancy of the canons of 'the world of letters', for once right but
from utterly wrong reasons, very efficient in guillotining the already defunct,
could not be more subtly indicated.

As a technical marvel this poem cannot be too highly praised. Only
Pound's economical means were sufficiently delicate for the discriminations
he sought to effect: 'perhaps' and 'we admit' belong to one mode of
perception, 'the month was more temperate because this beauty had been' to
another, the concessive 'certainly' and the clinical 'incapable' and 'in brief' to
a third. The technique of distinguishing motivations and qualities of insight
solely by scrupulous groupings of notes on the connotative or etymological
keyboard has never been brought to greater refinement. One cannot think of
another poet who could have brought it off.

The sequence is re-focused by a vignette of hedonistic drift protracting
the coral island imagery that had troubled Mauberley's reverie, ending with

an epitaph scrawled on an oar,

> 'I was
> And I no more exist;
> Here drifted
> An hedonist.'

pathetic echo of the elaborate opening 'Ode Pour L'Election de son Sepulchre'. The final 'Medallion', to be balanced against the 'Envoi' of the first part, recurs in witty disenchantment to the singing lady. Neither the Envoi's passion:

> Tell her that sheds
> Such treasure on the air,
> Recking naught else but that her graces give
> Life to the moment ...

nor Mauberley's 'porcelain reverie':

> Thus if her colour
> Came against his gaze,
> Tempered as if
> It were through a perfect glaze

is denied by the paradoxical dispassion of the final picture:

> Luini in porcelain!
> The grand piano
> Utters a profane
> Protest with her clear soprano.

But the tone is 'objective' in a way that detaches the 'Medal lion' from the claims of the various worlds of perception projected in earlier parts of the poem. There are witty echoes of those worlds: the 'profane protest' of heavy-fingered clubbably professional letters;[5] an ambrosial Mauberleian dream of braids

> Spun in King Minos' hall
> From metal, or intractable amber;

but the closing stanza is pitched to a key of quasi-scientific meticulousness that delivers with Flaubertian inscrutability a last voiceless verdict of inadequacy on all the human squinting, interpreting, and colouring that has preceded: fact revenging itself on art and the artists—

> The face-oval beneath the glaze,
> Bright in its suave bounding-line, as,
> Beneath half-watt rays,
> The eyes turn topaz.

Beauty? Irony? Geometrical and optical fact?

And this last poem yields a final irony. 'To present the series / Of curious heads in medallion' was, we remember, Mauberley's ambition, and this sample Medallion in its very scrupulousness exemplifies his sterility. His imagination falls back upon precedents; his visual particularity comes out of an art-gallery and his Venus Anadyomene out of a book. The 'true Penelope' of both poets was Flaubert, but Pound's contrasting Envoi moves with authority of another order. Mauberley cringed before the age's demands; he wrote one poem and collapsed. Pound with sardonic compliance presents the age with its desiderated 'image' (poems 3–12); then proves he was *right* from the start by offering as indisputable climax the 'sculpture of rhyme' and the 'sublime in the old sense' which the epitaph-writer had dismissed as a foolish quest. And he adds a sympathetic obituary and epitaph of his own for the *alter ego*.

This thin-line tracing of the action of *Mauberley* is offered with no pretence to fulness. It is possible, as we have seen, to spend a page meditating on a line. The writer professes two objectives in proceeding as above. First, it seemed profitable to trace the 'intaglio method' through an entire work, with a detail which will be impossible when we come to the *Cantos*. Secondly, it seemed important to guide the reader towards an apprehension of *Mauberley* in terms that will not falsify his notion of Pound's later or earlier work. The poem has commended itself too readily as a memorable confession of failure to those whom it comforts to decide that Pound has failed. Anyone to whom the above pages are persuasive will perhaps agree that a less obvious perspective augments, if anything, the stature of this astonishing poem.

NOTES

1. The primary echo is as a matter of fact with Corbière.
2. Since writing this I find in Pound's recently published *Letters* a reference to

Mauberley as essentially a popularization of *Propertius*; though the context indicates Pound's awareness that this is not the whole story.

3. A line of Ronsard, connected by Pound with the *Epitaphe* of Corbière, to whose procedures *Mauberley* is related as early Eliot is related to Laforgue. At the time when *Mauberley* was written, Eliot was getting rid of Laforgue and in collaboration with Pound assimilating Corbière and Gautier. The Corbière reverberations are functional in Pound's poem, relating it to still more complex modes of self-knowledge than we have opportunity to go into here. At its deepest levels the poem is still virtually unread.

4. It should be noted that the *Pisan Cantos* derive their extraordinary vitality from the fact that an *apathein*, among memorably-rendered 'selected perceptions' is not being crudely opposed, in H.S. Mauberley's fashion, to the 'current exacerbations' of the prison-camp. The moon-nymph, the lynxes, the Chinese sages, the healing rain, unite with the gun-roosts and the dialogue of murderers to form new-perceptive wholes. Pound's 'armor against utter consternation' is not gotten 'by constant elimination' but by vigorous fusion. *The Pisan Cantos* comment on *Mauberley* in a way Pound furthered by incorporating plangent scraps of the earlier poem into Canto LXXIV.

5. Cf. 'as the young horse whinnies against the tubas' (Canto LXXIX) and the comments in chapter 28 below.

ALAN TRACHTENBERG

The Shadow of a Myth

Oh, grassy glades! oh, ever vernal endless landscapes in the soul; in ye,—
men yet may roll, like young horses in new morning clover; and for some
few fleeting moments, feel the cool dew of the life immortal on them.
Would to God these blessed calms would last.

—HERMAN MELVILLE, Moby Dick (1851)

In the winter of 1923, Hart Crane, a twenty-four-year-old poet living
in Cleveland, announced plans to write a long poem called *The Bridge*. It was
to be an epic, a "mystical synthesis of America."[1] Crane had just completed
For the Marriage of Faustus and Helen, a poem which sought to infuse modern
Faustian culture (the term was Spengler's, designating science and restless
searching) with love of beauty and religious devotion. Now, confirmed in his
commitment to visionary poetry and feeling "directly connected with
Whitman," Crane prepared for an even greater effort: to compose the myth
of America. The poem would answer "the complete renunciation symbolized
in *The Waste Land*," published the year before. Eliot had used London Bridge
as a passageway for the dead, on which "each man fixed his eyes before his
feet." Crane replied by projecting his myth of affirmation upon Brooklyn
Bridge.

In the spring of 1923, Hart Crane left his father's home in Cleveland,
and from then until his suicide in 1932, lived frequently in Brooklyn Heights,

From *Brooklyn Bridge: Fact and Symbol*. © 1965 by Alan Trachtenberg.

close to "the most beautiful Bridge of the world." He crossed the bridge often, alone and with friends, sometimes with lovers: "the cables enclosing us and pulling us upward in such a dance as I have never walked and never can walk with another." Part III of *Faustus and Helen* had been set in the shadow of the bridge, "where," Crane wrote, "the edge of the bridge leaps over the edge of the street." In the poem the bridge is the "Capped arbiter of beauty in this street," "the ominous lifted arm/ That lowers down the arc of Helen's brow." Its "curve" of "memory" transcends "all stubble streets."

Crane tried to keep Brooklyn Bridge always before him, in eye as well as in mind. In April 1924 he wrote: "I am now living in the shadow of the bridge." He had moved to 110 Columbia Heights, into the very house, and later, the very room occupied fifty years earlier by Roebling. Like the crippled engineer, the poet was to devote his most creative years to the vision across the harbor. In his imagination the shadow of the bridge deepened into the shadow of a myth.

I

The Bridge, Crane wrote, "carries further the tendencies manifest in 'F and H.'" These tendencies included a neo-Platonic conception of a "reality" beyond the evidence of the senses. The blind chaos of sensation in the modern city apparently denies this transcendent reality, but a glimpse of it is available, through ecstasy, to the properly devout poet. Helen represents the eternal, the unchanging; Faustus, the poet's aspiration; and the "religious gunman" of Part III, spirit of the Dionysian surrender (sexual as well as aesthetic) necessary for a vision of the eternal. The threefold image constitutes what Kenneth Burke has called an "aesthetic myth"—a modern substitute for "religious myth."[2] The poet's impulse toward beauty is a mark of divinity. A part of the myth, and another "tendency" of the poem, is what Crane called its "fusion of our time with the past." The past is represented by the names Faustus and Helen; the present by the data of the poem: the "memoranda," the "baseball scores," and "stock quotations" of Part I; the jazz dance of Part II; the warplanes of Part III. The present fails to live up to the past. But the poet, a "bent axle of devotion," keeps his "lone eye" riveted upon Helen; he offers her "one inconspicuous, glowing orb of praise." At the end, in communion with the "religious gunman," he accepts and affirms past and present, the "years" whose "hands" are bloody; he has attained "the height/ The imagination spans beyond despair."

The idea of a bridge is explicit in the closing image; earlier, as I have indicated, it had appeared in fact, leaping over the street. In the projected poem, it will leap far beyond the street, but its function will be similar: an emblem of the eternal, providing a passage between the Ideal and the transitory sensations of history, a way to unify them.

In the earliest lines written for the new poem, the bridge was the location of an experience like that which ends *Faustus and Helen:* the imagination spanning beyond despair.

> And midway on that structure I would stand
> One moment, not as diver, but with arms
>
> That open to project a disk's resilience
> Winding the sun and planets in its face.
>
>   *   *   *
>
> Expansive center, pure moment and electron
> That guards like eyes that must look always down
> In reconcilement of our chains and ecstasy
>
> Crashing manifoldly on us as we hear
> The looms, the wheels, the whistles in concord
> Tethered and welded as the hills of dawn ...[3]

Somewhat like Wordsworth on Westminster Bridge, here the poet experiences harmony, his troubled self annihilated in a moment of worship. Subsequently Crane developed a narrative to precede this experience. In the narrative, or myth, the poet, like Faustus, was to be the hero, and his task a quest—not for Helen but her modern equivalent: Brooklyn Bridge.

Although the bridge lay at the end of quest, it was not, like the grail in *The Waste Land,* simply a magical object occupying a given location: It does not wait to be found, but to be created. That is, it represents not an external "thing," but an internal process, an act of consciousness. The bridge is not "found" in "Atlantis," the final section of the poem, but "made" throughout the poem. In "Atlantis" what has been "made" is at last recognized and named: "O Thou steeled Cognizance." Its properties are not magical but conceptual: it is a "Paradigm" of love and beauty, the eternal ideas which lie behind and inform human experience.

If we follow the poet's Platonic idea, to "think" the bridge is to perceive the unity and wholeness of history. In the poem, history is not chronological nor economic nor political. Crane wrote: "History, and fact, location, etc., all have to be transfigured into abstract form that would almost function independently of its subject matter." Crane intended to re-create American history according to a pattern he derived from its facts. His version of American history has nothing in common with the ceremonial parade of Founding Fathers and bearded generals of popular culture. The poet's idea, and especially his distinction between history and "abstract form," is closer to what the anthropologist Mircea Eliade describes as the predominant ontology of archaic man—the myth of "eternal return." According to Eliade, the mind of archaic man sought to resist history—the line of "irreversible events"—by recreating, in his rituals, the pre-temporal events of his mythology, such as the creation of the world. Unable to abide a feeling of uniqueness, early men identified, in their rituals, the present with the mythic past, thus abolishing the present as an autonomous moment of time. All events and actions "acquire a value," writes Eliade, "and in so doing become real, because they participate, after one fashion or another, in a reality that transcends them." The only "real" events are those recorded in mythology, which in turn become models for imitation, "paradigmatic gestures." All precious stones are precious because of thunder from heaven; all sacred buildings are sacred because they are built over the divine Center of the world; all sexual acts repeat the primordial act of creation. A non-precious stone, a non-sacred building, a non-sanctified act of sex—these are not real. History, as distinct from myth, consists of such random acts and events, underived from an archetype; therefore history is not real and must be periodically "annulled." By imitating the "paradigmatic gesture" in ritual, archaic men transported themselves out of the realm of the random, of "irreversible events," and "re-actualized" the mythic epoch in which the original archetypal act occurred. Hence for the primitive as for the mystic, time has no lasting influence: "events repeat themselves because they imitate an archetype." Like the mystic, the primitive lives in a "continual present."[4]

The Bridge is a sophisticated and well-wrought version of the archaic myth of return. The subject matter of the poem is drawn from legends about American history: Columbus, Pocahontas, Cortez, De Soto, Rip Van Winkel, the gold-rush, the whalers; and from contemporary reality: railroads, subways, warplanes, office buildings, cinemas, burlesque queens. Woven among these strands are allusions to world literature: the Bible, Plato, Marlowe, Shakespeare, Blake; and most important, to American artists: Whitman, Melville, Poe, Dickinson, Isadora Duncan. The action of the poem comprises through its fifteen sections, one waking day, from dawn in "Harbor Dawn," to midnight in "Atlantis." Through the device of dream, that single day includes vast stretches of time and space: a subway ride in the morning extends to a railroad journey to the Mississippi, then back in time, beyond De Soto, to the primeval world of the Indians,[5] then forward to the

West of the pioneers. In a sense, the entire day is a dream; the poet journeys through his own consciousness toward an awakening. He seeks to learn the meaning of American history which, in so far as the history is inseparable from his own memories, is the meaning of himself: Cathay, which designates the end of the journey, or the discovery of a new world, Crane wrote, is "an attitude of spirit," a self-discovery.

Thus in no sense of the word is *The Bridge* a historical poem. Its mode is myth. Its aim is to overcome history, to abolish time and the autonomy of events, and to show that all meaningful events partake of an archetype: the quest for a new world. In this regard the importance of Walt Whitman requires special notice. For among the many influences that worked upon Crane, few were as persuasive as Whitman's.[6]

In "Passage to India," we have seen, Whitman identified the quest for wholeness—the "rondure"—as the chief theme and motive of American life. In Whitman's version of history, man was expelled from Eden into time: "Wandering, yearning, curious, with restless explorations,/ With questions, baffled, formless, feverish." Divided into separate and warring nations, at odds with nature, historical man was a sufferer. Now, however, in modern America, the end of suffering was in sight. The connecting works of engineers—the Suez Canal, the Atlantic Cable, the Union Pacific Railroad— had introduced a new stage; the separate geographical parts of the world were now linked into one system. The physical labors of engineers, moreover, were spiritual food for the poet; the "true son of God" recognized that by uniting East and West such works completed Columbus's voyage. Now it was clear: The "hidden" purpose of history was the brotherhood of races that would follow the bridges and canals of modern technology.

Crane was not interested principally in Whitman's social vision, but in his conception of poetry as the final step in the restoration of man's wholeness. Not the engineer nor the statesman nor the captain of industry, but the poet was the true civilizer. Translating engineering accomplishments into ideas, the poet completed the work of history, and prepared for the ultimate journey to "more than India," the journey to the Soul: "thou actual Me." Thus the poet recognized that all of history culminated in self-discovery; and he would lead the race out of its bondage in time and space to that moment of consciousness in which all would seem one. That moment of "return" would redeem history by abolishing it. In short, Crane inherited from Whitman the belief in the poet's function to judge history from the point of view of myth.

Whitman himself appears in "Cape Hatteras," which represents a critical phase of the action of *The Bridge*. In the preceding sections, the poet had set out to find Pocahontas, the spirit of the land. With Rip Van Winkle his Muse of Memory, and the Twentieth Century Limited his vehicle, he moved westward out of the city to the Mississippi, the river of time. Borne backward on the stream, he found the goddess, joined her dance of union with nature and thus entered the archetype. Now he must return to the present, to bridge the personal vision of the goddess and the actuality of modern America. An older sailor (possibly Melville) in a South Street bar and an apparition of old clipper ships from Brooklyn Bridge in "Cutty Sark," are reminders of the quest. But the old has lost its direction; the age requires a renewal.

"Cape Hatteras" is the center of the span that leaps from Columbus to Brooklyn Bridge. The sea voyages are now done, the rondure accomplished. Now, a complacent age of stocks, traffic, and radios has lost sight of its goal; instead of a bridge, the age has created "a labyrinth submersed/ Where each sees only his dim past reversed." War, not peace and brotherhood, has succeeded the engineers, and flights into space are undertaken, not by poets but by war planes. "Cape Hatteras" poses the key questions of the poem: "What are the grounds for hope that modern history will not destroy itself?" "Where lies redemption?" "Is there an alternative to the chaos of the City?"

The answers are in Whitman's "sea eyes," "bright with myth." He alone has kept sight of the abstract form, the vision of ultimate integration. His perspective is geological; he stands apart, with "something green/ Beyond all sesames of science." Whitman envisioned the highest human possibilities within the facts of chaos. It was he who "stood up and flung the span on even wing/ Of that great Bridge, our Myth, whereof I sing." He is a presence: "Familiar, thou, as mendicants in public places." He has kept faith, even among the most disastrous circumstances of betrayal. With his help, the flight into space might yet become "that span of consciousness thou'st named/ The Open Road."

"Cape Hatteras" introduces the violence and the promise, the despair and the hope, of modern life. It argues for the effectiveness of ideals, for the power of Utopia over history. The poet places his hand in Whitman's, and proceeds upon his quest. Returning from the sea in "Southern Cross," he searches for love in "National Winter Garden" and "Virginia," for community and friendship in "Quaker Hill," and for art in "The Tunnel." He finds nothing but betrayal: the strip tease dancer burlesques Pocahontas, the office girl is a pallid Mary, the New Avalon Hotel and golf course mock the New England tradition, and the tunnel crucifies Poe. But throughout, the poet's hand is in Whitman's, and at last, having survived the terrors of "The Tunnel," he arrives at the bridge.

II

Brooklyn Bridge lay at the end of the poet's journey, the pledge of a "cognizance" that would explain and redeem history. To reach the bridge, to attain its understanding, the poet suffered the travail of hell. But he emerges unscathed, and ascends the span. In "Atlantis" he reaches Cathay, the symbol of sublime consciousness. The entire action implies a steady optimism that no matter how bad history may be, the bridge will reward the struggle richly. Such is its promise in the opening section of the poem, "Proem: To Brooklyn Bridge."

How many dawns, chill from his rippling rest
The seagull's wings shall dip and pivot him,
Shedding white rings of tumult, building high
Over the chained bay waters Liberty—

Then, with inviolate curve, forsake our eyes
As apparitional as sails that cross
Some page of figures to be filed away;
—Till elevators drop us from our day ...

I think of cinemas, panoramic sleights
With multitudes bent toward some flashing scene
Never disclosed, but hastened to again,
Foretold to other eyes on the same screen;

And Thee, across the harbor, silver-paced
As though the sun took step of thee, yet left
Some motion ever unspent in thy stride,—
Implicitly thy freedom staying thee!

Out of some subway scuttle, cell or loft
A bedlamite speeds to thy parapets,
Tilting there momently, shrill shirt ballooning,
A jest falls from the speechless caravan.

Down Wall, from girder into street noon leaks,
A rip-tooth of the sky's acetylene;
All afternoon the cloud-flown derricks turn ...
Thy cables breathe the North Atlantic still.

And obscure as that heaven of the Jews,
Thy guerdon ... Accolade thou dost bestow
Of anonymity time cannot raise:
Vibrant reprieve and pardon thou dost show.

O harp and altar, of the fury fused,
(How could mere toil align thy choiring strings!)
Terrific threshold of the prophet's pledge,
Prayer of pariah, and the lover's cry,—

Again the traffic lights that skim thy swift
Unfractioned idiom, immaculate sigh of stars,
Beading thy path—condense eternity:
And we have seen night lifted in thine arms.

Under thy shadow by the piers I waited;
Only in darkness is thy shadow clear.
The City's fiery parcels all undone,
Already snow submerges an iron year ...

O Sleepless as the river under thee,
Vaulting the sea, the prairies' dreaming sod,
Unto us lowliest sometime sweep, descend
And of the curveship lend a myth to God.

The setting of "Proem" in the harbor and lower Manhattan area is distinct, though the point of view shifts a good deal within this area, from a long view of the Bay and the Statue of Liberty, to an office in a skyscraper, down an elevator into the street, into a dark movie house, and then to the sun-bathed bridge. The view of the bridge also changes, from "across the harbor," in which the sun appears to be walking up the diagonal stays, to the promenade and towers as the bedlamite "speeds to thy parapets." Later the point of view is under the bridge, in its shadow. The shifting perspectives secure the object in space; there is no question that it is a bridge across a river between two concretely realized cities.

At the same time, the bridge stands apart from its setting, a world of its own. A series of transformations in the opening stanzas bring us to it. We begin with a seagull at dawn—a specific occurrence, yet eternal ("How many dawns"). The bird's wings leave our eyes as an "inviolate curve" (meaning unprofaned as well as unbroken) to become "apparitional as sails" (apparitional implies "epiphanal" as well as spectral and subjective). Then, in a further transmutation, they become a "page of figures." As the wings leave our eyes, so does the page: "filed away." Then, elevators "drop us" from the bird to the street. In the shift from bird to page to elevator, we have witnessed the transformation of a curve into a perpendicular, of an organism into a mechanism—wings into a list of numbers. "Filed away," the vision of the curve, identified with "sails" and voyages, has been forgotten ("How many" times?), like a page of reckonings. The quest for a vision of bird and sails resumes in the cinema, but, as in Plato's cave, the "flashing scene" is "never disclosed." Then, the eye finds a permanent vision of the curve in the "silver-paced" bridge.

The bridge has emerged from a counterpoint of motions (bird vs. elevator; sails vs. "multitudes bent") as an image of self-containment. Surrounded by a frantic energy ("some flashing scene ... hastened to again"; "A bedlamite speeds ...") the bridge is aloof; its motions express the sun. Verbs like drop, tilt, leak, submerge describe the city; the bridge is rendered by verbs like turn, breathe, lift, sweep. Established in its own visual plane, with a motion of its own, the bridge is prepared, by stanza seven, to receive the epithets of divinity addressed to it. Like Mary, it embraces, reprieves, and pardons. Its cables and towers are "harp and altar." The lights of traffic along its roadway, its "unfractioned idiom," seem to "condense eternity." Finally, as night has extinguished the cities and thereby clarified the shadow of the bridge, its true meaning becomes clear: its "curveship" represents an epiphany, a myth to manifest the divine. Such at least is what the poet implores the bridge to be.

In "Proem," Brooklyn Bridge achieves its status in direct opposition to the way of life embodied in the cities. Bridge and city are opposing and apparently irreconcilable forms of energy. This opposition, which is equivalent to that between myth and history, continues through the remainder of the poem; it creates the local tensions of each section, and the major tension of the entire work.

This tension is best illustrated in "The Tunnel," the penultimate section of the poem. After a fruitless search for reality in a Times Square theater, the protagonist boards a subway as "the quickest promise home." The short ride to Brooklyn Bridge is a nightmare of banal conversations and advertisements: "To brush some new presentiment of pain." The images are bizarre: "and love/ A burnt match skating in a urinal." Poe appears, his head "swinging from the swollen strap," his eyes "Below the toothpaste and the dandruff ads." The crucified poet, dragged to his death through the streets of Baltimore, "That last night on the ballot rounds," represents how society uses its visionary devotees of beauty.[7]

If the "Proem" promised deliverance, "The Tunnel" seems to deliver damnation; its chief character is a Daemon, whose "hideous laughter" is "the muffled slaughter of a day in birth." The Daemon's joke is that he has inverted the highest hopes and brightest prophecies: "O cruelly to inoculate the brinking dawn/ With antennae toward worlds that glow and sink." The presiding spirit in the tunnel, he represents the transvaluation of ideals in modern America.

At the end of "The Tunnel," the protagonist leaves the subway and prepares, at the water's edge, to ascend the bridge. His faith, like Job's, is unimpaired. Job endured the assault of Satan, uttered no complaints, and in the end profited by an enlightened understanding, albeit an irrational one, of the power of his God. It is revealing—although it has been largely unnoticed—that Crane's epigraph to *The Bridge* is taken from Satan's reply to God in Job, 1.7: "From going to and fro in the earth, and from walking up and down in it." The words might be read to indicate the theme of voyage, but their source suggests a richer interpretation: the omnipresence of evil, of the Daemon of "The Tunnel." Job's only defense is unremitting faith in his own righteousness and God's justice. And the same holds for the poet: faith in Whitman, his own powers, and in his bridge.

III

To keep the faith but not close his eyes to reality was Hart Crane's chief struggle in composing *The Bridge*. Reality in the 1920's—the age of jazz, inflated money, and Prohibition—did not seem to support any faith let alone one like Crane's. It was a period of frantic construction, of competition for the title of "Tallest Building in the World," won in 1930 by the Empire State Building. That tower had climbed the sky at the rate of a story a day to the height of a hundred and two floors. Elsewhere, Florida experienced a hysterical real-estate boom. In 1927 the first cross-country highway announced the age of the automobile. The same year, Lindbergh crossed the Atlantic. And in the same decade, the movie palace spread into neighborhoods.

In certain moods, Crane was possessed by the fever of the period: "Time and space is the myth of the modern world," he wrote about Lindbergh, "and it is interesting to see how any victory in the field is heralded by the mass of humanity. In a way my Bridge is a manifestation of the same general subject. Maybe I'm just a little jealous of Lindy!"[8] But the over-all effect of the direction of American life did not accord with his myth. From 1926 to 1929, years during which his own physical and emotional life deteriorated noticeably,[9] Crane searched for a way to acknowledge the unhappy reality of America without surrendering his faith. The changes he made in the final poem of the sequence—the poem he had begun in 1923 and altered time and again—disclose the accommodation he reached.

At first, as I have indicated, the finale projected an intense experience of harmony. As his conception of the bridge took shape, he changed the ending accordingly, weaving into it the major images developed earlier, which are mainly nautical and musical. He reorganized the section into a walk across the bridge, and incorporated many structural details of the cables and towers. "I have attempted to induce the same feelings of elation, etc.— like being carried forward and upward simultaneously—both in imagery, rhythm and repetition, that one experiences in walking across my beloved Brooklyn Bridge."

> Through the bound cable strands, the arching path
> Upward, veering with light, the flight of strings,—
> Taut miles of shuttling moonlight syncopate
> The whispered rush, telepathy of wires.
> Up the index of night, granite and steel—
> Transparent meshes—fleckless the gleaming staves—
> Sibylline voices flicker, waveringly stream
> As though a god were issue of the strings....
>
>   *   *   *
>
> Sheerly the eyes, like seagulls strung with rime—
> Slit and propelled by glistening fins of light—
> Pick biting way up towering looms that press
> Sidelong with flight of blade on tendon blade
> —Tomorrows into yesteryear—and link
> What cipher-script of time no traveller reads

Rhythm and imagery convey a real bridge as well as an "arc synoptic": the walk across the span recapitulates the experience of the concluding day.

In stanza six, at the center of the roadway, the poet attains his vision. It is midnight; night is lifted "to cycloramic crest/ Of deepest day." Now, as "Tall Vision-of-the-Voyage," the bridge becomes a "Choir, translating time/ Into what multitudinous Verb": it is "Psalm of Cathay!/ O Love, thy white pervasive Paradigm ...!" This moment is the climax of the poem. In the six stanzas which follow, Crane interprets the "multitudinous Verb" as the explicit action of reaching Cathay. He achieves this through predominant images of voyage; the bridge becomes a ship which, in stanza seven, "left the haven hanging in the night." The past tense modulates the tone of the entire section, for we are now "Pacific here at time's end, bearing corn." We have left the physical bridge, and are transported to another realm, a realm which fuses land ("corn") and water ("Pacific")—or Pocahontas and Columbus. The implied image is clearly that of an island, much like the "insular Tahiti" of the soul which Ishmael discovers to his salvation in Melville's *Moby Dick*. The *Pequod* too had rushed ahead "from all havens astern." In stanza eleven, the poet, like the lone survivor of Ahab's madness, finds himself "floating" on the waters, his visionary Belle Isle (Atlantis) sustaining him. In the last stanza, still addressing the bridge, he floats onward toward Cathay. The passage has been made "from time's realm" to "time's end" to "thine Everpresence, beyond time." Like Melville, Crane began his spiritual voyage in the North Atlantic, plunged into older waters, and nearing Cathay, recovered the even older shores of Atlantis. East and West have merged in a single chrysalis.

The language of the closing six stanzas of the section has the resonance of a hymn; it includes some of Crane's most quoted epithets: "Unspeakable Thou Bridge to Thee, O Love." But the oracular tone is bought at an expense. The opening six stanzas were dominated by the physical presence of the bridge and the kinetic sense of moving across it; the last six, having left the "sheened harbor lanterns" behind, remove to a watery element. And as the bridge becomes a symbolic ship, we sense an underlying relaxation. It is true that the language remains rich, even rugged ("Of thy white seizure springs the prophecy"). But the hyperbolic imagery itself seems an effort to substitute verbal energy for genuine tension. The original tension, between the poet-hero and history, seems to be replaced by an unformulated struggle *within* the poet, a struggle to maintain a pitch of language unsupported by a concrete action. For the climactic action of the entire poem had already occurred, when, at the center of the span, the poet names the bridge as "Paradigm." The rest is an effort, bound to prove inadequate in the nature of the case, to say what it is a paradigm of. Thus the poet, full of ponderous (and, we sense, conflicting) emotions, sails away from the harbor, detaching the myth from its concreteness. And the bridge achieves its final transmutation, into a floating and lonely abstraction.

IV

The dissolution of the bridge as fact—and the subsequent drop in the poem's intensity—was perhaps an inevitable outcome of the poet's conflict between his faith and reality. In the summer of 1926, suffering an attack of skepticism about his "myth of America," Crane stated the problem in his own terms. "Intellectually judged," he wrote to Waldo Frank, "the whole theme and project seems more and more absurd." He felt his materials were not authentic, that "these forms, materials, dynamics are simply nonexistent in the world." As for Brooklyn Bridge: "The bridge today has no significance beyond an economical approach to shorter hours, quicker lunches behaviorism and toothpicks." A month later he had recovered his faith. "I feel an absolute music in the air again," he wrote to Frank, "and some tremendous rondure floating somewhere." He had composed the "Proem," in which the bridge stands firmly opposed to the cities. He had beaten back the nightmarish view of the bridge, and could now proceed with his aim of translating a mechanical structure into a threshold of life.[10]

But Crane could not dismiss the nightmare. He had to account for it, and he did so in a subtle fashion. Later in 1926 he arrived at the title for his last section: "Atlantis." Until then, it had been "Bridge Finale." The destination of the protagonist's journey, like Columbus's, had been called Cathay, the traditional symbol of the East. Atlantis was the sunken island of the West—older even than the Orient. What does Crane intend by his new title? Does he mean to identify East and West? Or to introduce the idea of the decline of greatness at the very moment his hero's journey is accomplished? What precisely does Atlantis add to our "cognizance" of the bridge?[11]

The fable of Atlantis had been as important as Cathay to the discovery of the New World. Originally, it was a somewhat mystical legend told by Plato in *Timaeus* and *Critias*, concerning a land in the western ocean (the Atlantic), founded by Poseidon, god of the sea. Once all-powerful, the nation had grown lustful, and was punished for its pride with earthquakes and floods; in a single day it sunk forever. But the legend remained, and during the fifteenth century, was popular among sailors. The island was believed to be the place where seven Portuguese bishops, fleeing the Moors, had founded seven golden cities. Sailors hoped to rediscover this land, where Christians still lived in piety and wealth. To discover Atlantis, or to reach Cathay—these were the leading motifs among the navigators who sailed westward in the fifteenth century. No one, not even Columbus, dreamed that an entirely new world lay between the sunken world and the legendary riches of the Orient.[12]

Crane thus had historical grounds for identifying Atlantis and Cathay. As it turned out, the discovery of America proved both legends to be illusions: neither had the geographical position attributed to it by Renaissance navigators. Both, however, remained active myths—Cathay inspiring the revived theme of the Northwest Passage in the nineteenth century, and Atlantis even yet arousing speculation. Crane had indicated early in the composition of his poem that Cathay would stand for "consciousness, knowledge, spiritual unity"—material conquest transmuted into "an attitude of spirit." What does Atlantis stand for?

The answer is complex. When we learn from Plato that the Atlanteans possessed a land with a great central plain, "said to have been the fairest of all plains, and very fertile," the resemblance to America is striking. Further, we learn that they were a race of highly inventive builders, who intersected the island with a vast system of inland canals. They had invented basic tools, farming, and the alphabet. Their proudest creations, however, were bridges—a series of bridges, in fact, which led over the canals toward the exact center of the island. There, a monumental bridge opened upon the gate to a temple, the shrine of Poseidon.

This was Atlantis in its glory. But, Plato revealed, the glory did not last. The "divine portion" faded away, and human nature "got the upper hand." The people grew prideful, avaricious, imperialistic. And most of all, they grew blind to their own failings—blind to the loss of their true powers.

Crane wove references to the sunken island throughout the fabric of the poem. They appear in "Cutty Sark" as the old sailor's memory of "the skeletons of cities." They recur forcefully in "The Tunnel" in two echoes of Poe's "The City in the Sea"; "And Death, aloft,—gigantically down," and "worlds that glow and sink." And they emerge explicitly in stanza eleven of the finale:

> Now while thy petals spend the suns about us, hold—
> (O Thou whose radiance doth inherit me)
> Atlantis,—hold thy floating singer late!

In the preceding line, the bridge was addressed as a sea creature—"Anemone." Here, the poet invokes the floating form, now called Atlantis, to sustain his faith. In the following stanza, the last of the poem, the poet passes "to thine Everpresence, beyond time," as the "orphic strings ... leap and converge." Then:

> —One Song, one Bridge of Fire! Is it Cathay,
> Now pity steeps the grass and rainbows ring
> The serpent with the eagle in the leaves ...?
> Whispers antiphonal in azure swing.

The question *may* indicate doubt that the bridge does in fact represent the "mystic consummation" of Cathay; more likely, it indicates wonder. The antiphonal whispers through the cables of the disembodied bridge could hardly be negative. Atlantis, the bridge-anemone, had answered the prayer and held the "floating singer late."

How did the sunken island earn such a high function? Where did it get the "radiance" to bestow upon the poet? The answer lies once more in Plato's account. The people of Atlantis had indeed become blind in their pride and materialism—but not all of them. "To those who had no eye to see the true happiness, they still appeared glorious and blessed at the very time when they were filled with unrighteous avarice and power." Some, however, retained "an eye to see," and these few recognized baseness as baseness. The still radiant ones kept their "precious gift" of the "divine portion."[13]

It is now clear what Crane meant. His Cathay, his moment of supreme awareness, was a moment of Atlantean "radiance." With an "eye to see," he perceived the bridge as more than stone and steel, as a "mystic consummation." He perceived the gift embodied in the bridge. The inhabitants of the Daemon's dark tunnels could no longer see—no longer make out the shape of the future within the chaos of the present. These are the people for whom the bridge was nothing but "an economical approach." They represented the loss of radiance, the sinking of Atlantis.

Crane used the Atlantis legend, like the epigraph from Job, to maintain a double insight: the promise of redemption and the actuality of evil. As long as he held the double view, as long as he was able to affirm the myth while condemning the actuality of his culture, he would not sink. To this end he required a bridge to rise above the wreckage of history—to rise above itself— and be a pure curveship. The purity was essential; the bridge could harbor no ambiguities. Hence its symbolic radiance became the only enduring fact of Hart Crane's Brooklyn Bridge.

NOTES

1. *The Bridge* was first published by The Black Sun Press, Paris, 1930; this edition included three photographs by Walker Evans. The lines quoted throughout this chapter are from *The Complete Poems of Hart Crane* (New York, 1933), ed., Waldo Frank; references in the chapter are to *The Letters of Hart Crane* (New York, 1952), ed., Brom Weber. The critical works I have profited from most in my reading of *The Bridge* are, Allen Tate, "Hart Crane," *Reactionary Essays* (New York, 1936); Yvor Winters, "The Significance of *The Bridge,*" *In Defense of Reason* (New York, 1947), 575–605; R.P. Blackmur, "New Thresholds, New Anatomies: Notes on a Text of Hart Crane," *Language of Gesture* (New York, 1952) [See this book, p. 49].

Brom Weber, *Hart Crane: A Biographical and Critical Study* (New York, 1948); L.S. Dembo, *Hart Crane's Sanskrit Charge: A Study of The Bridge* (Ithaca, 1960); Sister M. Bernetta Quinn, *The Metamorphic Tradition in Modern Poetry* (New Brunswick, 1955), 130–68; Stanley K. Coffman, "Symbolism in *The Bridge*," *PMLA*, Vol. LXVI (March 1951), 65–77; John Unterecker, "The Architecture of The Bridge," *Wisconsin Studies in Contemporary Literature*, Vol. III (Spring–Summer 1962),5–20 [See this book, p. 80].

2. *A Rhetoric of Motives* (New York, 1950), 203.

3. The first four lines are from "Lines sent to Wilbur Underwood, February, 1923," and the remainder from "Worksheets, Spring, 1923," in Brom Weber, *Hart Crane*, 425–6.

4. *Cosmos and History: The Myth of the Eternal Return* ([New York,] 1959), 4, 90.

5. Crane's conception of the Indian in "The Dance"—in the "Powhatan's Daughter" section of *The Bridge*—seems to owe something to Waldo Frank's *Our America* (1919). In his personal copy, Crane had underlined the following passage: "His [the Indian's] magic is not, as in most religions, the tricky power of men over their gods. It lies in the power of Nature herself to yield corn from irrigation, to yield meat in game. The Indian therefore does not pray to his God for direct favors. He prays for harmony between himself and the mysterious forces that surround him: of which he is one. For he has learned that from this harmony comes health." Hart Crane Collection, Columbia University Library.

6. A word should be said about the powerful influence upon Crane's sensibility—and his plans for *The Bridge*—of the Russian mystic, P.D. Ouspensky, and his work, *Tertium Organum: The Third Canon of Thought, A Key to the Enigmas of the World*, tr. Nicholas Bessaraboff and Claude Bragdon (New York, 1922). Crane read this book early in his creative life—possibly in 1920 (an earlier edition had been published that year). It seems very likely that he derived most of his philosophical idealism, and a good deal of his language and imagery, from Ouspensky. A case could be made for the fact that he interpreted Whitman in Ouspenskian terms—as a mystic who saw through the world to a higher reality. "Higher consciousness" was a typical Ouspenskian term. So was "vision," in its literal and metaphoric senses. Plato's parable of the cave, in which most men sit in darkness, hidden from the truth, is the unstated assumption of Ouspensky's book. The book attempts to place the mystical experience of light and oneness on accountable grounds; its method is to prove by analogies that the true or noumenal world lies beyond space and time, beyond the capacity of the normal mind to perceive. Limited to a three-dimensional view of the world (a consequence of education and bad science), the mind normally interprets what are really flashes from the true world as things moving in time. In truth, however, the "whole" is motionless and self-contained; time itself is man's illusion: "The idea of time recedes with the expansion of consciousness." The true world being "invisible" to normal sight, it is necessary to cultivate the inner eye. This can be accomplished only by exercising the outer eye to its fullest capacities—to strain vision until familiar things seem unfamiliar, new, and exciting. Then we might penetrate the "hidden meaning in everything." Then we will see the "invisible threads" which bind all things together—"with the entire world, with all the past and all the future." It should be noted that an idea of a bridge is implicit here—a metaphoric bridge which represents the true unity of all things. Moreover, Ouspensky held that art, especially poetry, was a means to attain this metaphoric bridge. To do so, however, poetry must develop a new language: "New parts of speech are necessary, an infinite number of new words." The function of poetry is to reveal the "invisible threads," to translate them into language which will

"bind" the reader to the new perceptions. It is quite easy to see how attractive these ideas were to Hart Crane's poetic program. See Weber, 150–63.

7. It is wrong to assume that Poe and Whitman oppose each other in this work—one gloomy, the other cheerful. Poe in the tunnel does indeed represent the actuality of art in modern life, but the image is not meant to contradict Whitman's vision—perhaps to countervail it, and by so doing, to reinforce its strength. According to his friends—especially Samuel Loveman—Crane loved both poets, although he derived more substance for his art from Whitman (and Melville). To make this point may also be a good occasion to recall that Whitman himself was powerfully drawn to Poe. There is some evidence they knew each other as newspaper men in New York in the 1840s. Whitman was the only major American writer to attend the dedication of a Poe memorial in Baltimore in 1875, and sat on the platform as Mallarmé's famous poem was being read. In *Specimen Days*, Whitman wrote that Poe's verse expressed the "sub-currents" of the age; his poems were "lurid dreams." Thus, Poe presented an "entire contrast and contradiction" to the image of "perfect and noble life" which Whitman himself had tried to realize. But it is significant that Whitman concedes morbidity to be as true of the times as health. He tells of a dream he once had of a "superb little schooner" yacht, with "torn sails and broken spars," tossed in a stormy sea at midnight. "On the deck was a slender, slight, beautiful figure, a dim man, apparently enjoying all the terror, the murk, and the dislocation of which he was the center and the victim. That figure of my lurid dream might stand for Edgar Poe" (*Complete Prose Works*, 150). Whitman's "lurid dream" may very well be a source for Crane's nightmare in "The Tunnel"—where once more Poe is "the center and the victim."

8. Hart Crane to his father, June 21, 1927. Yale American Literature Collection.

9. See Philip Horton, *Hart Crane: The Life of an American Poet* (New York: W.W. Norton and Company, Inc., 1937).

10. In light of Crane's efforts to sustain belief in his cultural symbol, Henry Miller's treatment of the bridge is significant. For Miller, Brooklyn Bridge was an intensely private experience—a means of release from his culture. It served him as it did John Marin, as a perspective upon the city. Only Miller found nothing in modern New York to celebrate. "Way up there," he wrote in *Tropic of Capricorn* (Paris, 1939), he seemed to be "hanging over a void": "up there everything that had ever happened to me seemed unreal ... unnecessary" (p. 72). The bridge, he felt, disconnected him from the "howling chaos" of the shores. See also "The 14th Ward," *Black Spring* (Paris, 1936). In "The Brooklyn Bridge," the concluding essay in *The Cosmological Eye* (New York, 1939), he writes that the bridge had appeared to him with "splendour and illumination" in "violent dreams and visions." He recalled that he took to the bridge "only in moments of extreme anguish," and that he "dreamt very violently" at its center. In these dreams "the whole past would click"; he felt himself annihilated as an ego in space and time, but reborn in a "new realm of consciousness." Thus, he now realizes, the bridge was no longer "a thing of stone and steel" but "incorporated in my consciousness as a symbol." And as a symbol it was a "harp of death," "a means of reinstating myself in the universal stream." Through it he felt "securely situated in my time, yet above it and beyond it." Crane's conception is similar, with this crucial difference: Miller stripped the bridge altogether of its ties with American life, but Crane wished to restore a meaningful relation between bridge and city, and to fuse the personal and the cultural. Moreover, Crane wished to incorporate the stone and steel into the symbol—to join meaning to fact.

Other treatments of the bridge versus the city theme appear in John Dos Passos,

Manhattan Transfer (New York, 1925); Thomas Wolfe, *The Web and the Rock* (New York, 1938); Vladimir Mayakovsky, "Brooklyn Bridge" (1925), reprinted in *Atlantic* (June 1960); Federico Garcia Lorca, "Unsleeping City (Brooklyn Bridge Nocturne)" (1932), *Poet in New York* (New York, 1955). On May 26, 1923, the Sunday Brooklyn *Eagle* celebrated the fortieth birthday of the bridge with a poem by Martin H. Weyrauch, "The Bridge Speaks," in which the structure argues against modernization of itself in these words: "I think we ought to have/ At least one personality In this City of Wild Motion/ That stands for the solid,/ The poised,/ The quiet/ things of Life." It is likely that Hart Crane; already at work on his poem and living in Brooklyn Heights, read these lines.

11. In May 1926 Crane recorded in a letter that he had been reading *Atlantis in America* by Lewis Spence. Spence, a leading student of mythology (he died in 1955), devoted much of his time and numerous books to "the Atlantean question." Crane found convincing his argument that there are traces of Atlantean civilization in American Indian culture: "it's easy to believe that a continent existed in mid-Atlantic waters and that the Antilles and West Indies are but salient peaks of its surface" (*Letters*, 255–6). It is, unfortunately, impossible to learn whether Crane knew *Atlantis: The Antediluvian World* (1882)—a remarkable work by Ignatius Donnelly, the fascinating Minnesotan, who tried to found a city in the 1850s, served many years in Congress, was an out-spoken Populist, a Baconian in the controversy over the identity of Shakespeare (he produced a massive argument in 1885, *The Great Cryptogram*), and something of an embittered prophet (*Caesar's Column*, 1890). His book on Atlantis was widely influential among students of the problem; Lewis Spence linked his name with Plato as the most prominent in "Atlantean science." Among the propositions Donnelly tried to prove were that Atlantis was "the true Antediluvian world; the Garden of Eden," and therefore, "the region where man first rose from a state of barbarism to civilization." To establish these—and other—"facts," would, he wrote, "aid us to rehabilitate the fathers of our civilization, our blood, and our fundamental ideas—the men who lived, loved, and labored ages before the Aryans descended upon India, or the Phoenicians had settled in Syria, or the Goths had reached the shores of the Baltic." Atlantis, in other words, provided mankind—and Americans in particular—with a historical tradition far older than any yet imagined. Donnelly's book was reissued, with revisions by Egerton Sykes, in 1949.

12. See Boies Penrose, *Travel and Discovery in the Renaissance, 1420–1620* (Cambridge, 1952), 5, 19, 25; also, J.H. Parry, *The Age of Reconnaissance* (New York, 1964), 165.

13. It should be noted that Crane's epigraph to "Atlantis" is from *The Symposium:* "Music is then the knowledge of that which relates to love in harmony and system." This reinforces my view of his reliance upon the Platonic version of Atlantis—and the Platonism of *The Bridge*. Harmony and system were central features of the island civilization—as they are of the Platonic cosmology. Love and music, moreover, had been identified with the poet's quest throughout, and with the bridge in "Proem." The image of Atlantis, then, helps Crane draw these threads together in the finale.

THOMAS R. WHITAKER

Open to the Weather

Moral
   the tree moving diversely
   in all parts—

During the decade and a half that followed *Kora in Hell,* Williams engaged in a variety of poetic descents, explorations, and refinements. Their rather confusing history of publication—especially the long delay before some poems appeared in collected volumes—has laid some traps for critics and has thus indirectly given rise to a number of misunderstandings concerning Williams' chronological development.[1] However, the combination of expediency and design that produced this history also laid bare (as Williams knew) the heart of the matter: the unity-in-diversity of his field of attention. For that reason, any gain in biographical understanding that might result here from a strictly chronological account, poem by poem, would be more than offset by the distortions that a single linear pattern would impose.

   Considering the poems published between 1918 and 1934, I shall therefore focus primarily upon the new developments in Williams' art. There are first-person utterances of tougher and more delicate fiber; flower-poems, weather-poems, and portraits of yet subtler emergent symbolism; musical pieces that further explore quantity and temporal measure; and studies of local culture that are more probing and inclusive. There are also

From William Carlos Williams. © 1968 by Twayne Publishers.

new Cubist constructions that enact the swift transit of the attention or raise the disorder of the moment to the plane of abstract design. And there are other experiments with large forms—loose seasonal sequence that render the open imagination's response to inner and outer weather.

I *"TRANSITIONAL" POEMS AND* SOUR GRAPES

Something of the range and balance of consciousness rendered in the work of 1918 through 1921 may be suggested by certain poems which focus upon the author himself. Perhaps the most notable quality of "Le Médecin Malgré Lui" is its deft casualness. The ostensible conflict in this poem, treated with engagingly light irony, is a matter of career; but the real conflict concerns the deeper question of vocation. Should one really devote oneself to the cleaning, ordering, keeping up, adding (debts), growing ("a decent beard"), and cultivating ("a look / of importance") that mean "credit" according to the socially defined norms of "my Lady Happiness"?

In the poem's ironic plot, such respectable ambition leads to an ambiguous nullity: "and never think anything / but a white thought!" (*CEP,* 36). The implicit alternative is enacted by the poem itself: to let be—and thereby to attend to one's present "chaos." In the rhythmic vitality of its itemizing, the attention in this poem (as in the earlier "Pastoral" on a similar theme) does its own ordering. When ambition and acquisition drop away, what emerges (as "Thursday" states) is openness to the present field of contact: rather than an empty order possessed, a fruitful disorder to be contemplated and grown with.

The delicate balance implicit in such contemplation appears in "Lighthearted William," twirlingly poised between light and dark, Yang and Ying. After dancing through its contrasts—fall and spring, sighs and gaiety, "up and down," "heavy sunlight" and "blue shadows," out and in—the poem pirouettes to a close on a surprising instance of a color-word that balances "November": "quietly / twirling his green moustaches" (*CEP,* 226). That transfiguration of the appropriately "half dressed" William springs from an inner, quite as much as, an outer weather.

"Portrait of a Lady," which is really another paradoxical self-portrait, amusingly renders the descending movements of that fiber of swift attention with which *Kora in Hell* was primarily concerned:

> Your thighs are appletrees
> whose blossoms touch the sky.
> Which sky? The sky

where Watteau hung a lady's
slipper. Your knees
are a southern breeze—or
a gust of snow. Agh! what
sort of man was Fragonard?
—as if that answered
anything. Ah, yes—below
the knees, since the tune
drops that way, it is
one of those white summer days ...

The descent, of course, is not merely visual. The poem moves, through interior dialogue, from an easy formalized tribute toward a more disturbing contact. The witty and sentimental style of Watteau or of Fragonard (whose "The Swing" does leave a slipper hanging in the sky) defines that delightful art which is yet a means of fending off immediacy. The sequence of initial composition and sardonic question or retort carries the speaker beneath such decorative surfaces toward an inarticulate contact from which he attempts (with half a mind) to defend himself: "Which shore?— / the sand clings to my lips—" And, in the poem's final line, the tribute has lost the simplicity of its formal distance: "I said petals from an appletree" (*CEP*, 40). As a whimsically protective mask, the tribute becomes an accurate figure of the speaker's relation to himself and to his lady.

When this central consciousness, with its appetite for the novel and its candid self-observation, turns to the world at large, it may discover or become a variety of figures of contact. Some of the resulting poems are, in structure, little forays out into the banal or the random which neatly conclude with the discovery of a gestalt. Two such, firmly realized, are "The Nightingales" and "Complete Destruction." Each focuses the fullness and the emptiness of the world: the first, by its deft reversal of perspective upon substance and shadow, or solid object and artistic plane; the second, by its arrival (in a flat statement that includes the particular and the universal, the whimsical and the terrible) at the full stop that was implicit in its beginning.

Elsewhere the indirections and discontinuities become more complex. The poem may be a montage or a multifaceted construction that points to an experience not directly presentable in an outworn language. Such is the montage of "To Mark Anthony in Heaven," which joins the speaker's "quiet morning light" (reflected from, and in turn reflecting, a world of loved particulars) with what Anthony apprehended through attention to the particulars of "that beloved body" (*CEP*, 33). Such too is the ABA movement of a "A Coronal," which frames in repeated motifs of "new books of poetry," postal delivery of "other men's business," and autumn leaves, a glimpse of something quite different:

> But we ran ahead of it all.
> One coming after
> could have seen her footprints
> in the wet and followed us
> among the stark chestnuts.
> Anemones spring where she pressed
> and cresses
> stood green in the slender source— (*CEP,* 38)

As a love poem that delicately moves toward personal mythology, "A Coronal" evokes that immediate contact with the "source" which poetry may freshly record but which it too often merely falsifies by means of an autumnal ritual. As Williams said of Marianne Moore's work: "If from such a flight a ritual results it is more the care of those who follow than of the one who leads. 'Ritual' connotes a stereotyped mode of procedure from which the pleasure has passed, whereas the poetry to which my attention clings, if it ever knew those conditions, is distinguished only as it leaves them behind" (*SE,* 127).

In "Queen-Ann's-Lace" the montage may seem at first an ordinary analogy:

> Her body is not so white as
> anemone petals nor so smooth—nor
> so remote a thing. It is a field
> of the wild carrot taking
> the field by force; the grass
> does not raise above it.

But the introductory negations, which give the speaker's meditative distance, have yielded quickly to the pseudoredundancy of "field ... taking / the field by force," which suggests passionate involvement. As the passion described and felt increases, the speaker's analogy gains in points of reference. Finally—

> Each part
> is a blossom under his touch

        to which the fibres of her being
        stem one by one, each to its end,
        until the whole field is a
        white desire, empty, a single stem,
        a cluster, flower by flower,
        a pious wish to whiteness gone over—
        or nothing. (*CEP*, 210)

To describe the poem as an account of sexual arousal presented through a sustained metaphysical conceit would be to ignore the peculiar poise that makes the wild carrot as real a presence as the woman's body. The consciousness eddies between the two images; as it does so, it enacts the process whereby the field of "white desire" takes by force (and by touch) the field of the ordinary discriminative consciousness.

Such poise—eddying or twirling between fields of contact—produces much of the freshness in *Sour Grapes*. This process of thinking *with* things, rather than of them to illustrate, thought, prepares for the more sustained composition of "homologues" in *Paterson* itself. Here it enters such weather-poems as "The Hunter," with its static midsummer violence, a locked embrace of love-or-hate that may seem timeless but that means a hidden drain of vitality; or "Arrival," with its casual and surprising descent into a "tawdry" winter of experience; or "Blizzard," where focus on outer solitude widens to include the inner.

Although beginning with a deceptively simple equivalence, "To Waken an Old Lady" is of the same order. This poem is no prepared definition but an observation in the moving present, which leads the speaker to his shared discovery:

        Old age is
        a flight of small
        cheeping birds
        skimming
        bare trees
        above a snow glaze.
        Gaining and failing
        they are buffeted
        by a dark wind—
        But what?
        On harsh weedstalks
        the flock has rested,

> the snow
> is covered with broken
> seedhusks
> and the wind tempered
> by a shrill
> piping of plenty. (*CEP,* 200)

As the short lines imply, each word is to be carefully weighed. Step by step, the poem makes its precarious affirmation. The connotations "gain" and "fail" ("flight," "small"), fail and gain ("cheeping," "birds"), or momentarily hover ("skimming," "snow glaze"). The poem then moves through a more ominously falling section to an enigmatic rise ("But what?"), to other balancings ("harsh" and "rested," "covered" and "broken," "seed-" and "-husks"), and then on to its paradoxical assertion ("tempered" by something "shrill"!) of plenitude in poverty. With its delicate balance, the poem might be set beside Keats's "To Autumn" as a later and more thinly resonant phase of the organic cycle.

A similar definition of the abstract, one disarming yet surprising in its flat colloquialism, opens "The Widow's Lament in Springtime": "Sorrow is my own yard ..." But that bare phrasing of the familiar, possessed, and limited is at once given a paradoxical development:

> where the new grass
> flames as it has flamed
> often before but not
> with the cold fire
> that closes round me this year. (*CEP,* 223)

All freshness now means only the intense continuity of deprivation. The speaker then moves toward her own heavily weighted climax of white desire, in which a freshness beyond the edge of the known may image a final deprivation and so a release.

In a very different poem of isolation and desire, "The Lonely Street," the concrete indirections are the observable data of local culture.

> School is over. It is too hot
> to walk at ease. At ease
> in light frocks they walk the streets
> to while the time away.
> They have grown tall. They hold

> pink flames in their right hands.
> In white from head to foot,
> with sidelong, idle look—
> in yellow, floating stuff,
> black sash and stockings—
> touching their avid mouths
> with pink sugar on a stick—
> like a carnation each holds in her hand—
> they mount the lonely street. (*CEP,* 227)

Aside from one overt metaphor ("flames"), another hidden in a simile ("carnation"), and the final attribution of loneliness to the street itself, the statements are uncompromisingly literal. But each conveys more than its literal meaning. We are urged to pay close attention almost at once by the repeated "at ease" and by the seeming contradiction between the second sentence and the third. What has happened to that heat? We find it again in "flames"—by which time the end of schooling, the walking of streets, the expectation, and the growth have begun to form their significant pattern. The insubstantiality of the white—its sweeping innocence immediately modified by "sidelong, idle look"; the frothiness of the yellow—given point, with a rhythmic shift, by "black sash and stockings"; and, most intensely, the bare physicality of the next line, with its key word "avid": these details complete a situation in which the "pink sugar on a stick" reveals itself as the substitute satisfaction of a desire that may not have become fully conscious.

The last two lines distance and formalize this hidden seasonal restlessness, the flower of flesh, and generalize its urban meaning. Yet that fresh word, "mount," focuses with immediacy the rising effort under their "ease"—even as it signals the entry into a new phase of life. Surely it is a drastic reduction of this poem to find its main notes to be "adolescent silliness and girlish charm, ... foolish pleasures and their grey setting."[2] Of other poets writing in English or American in 1921, only D.H. Lawrence would have been able to render this scene with comparable realism, sympathetic detachment, and penetration.

II SPRING AND ALL

The diversity of Williams' art is further evident in two poems of 1922: "The Jungle," with its "Jamesian perception"[3] of non-Jamesian material (obliquely presented through a negated analogy and a quoted phrase), and "The Bull," which symbolically diagnoses a temptation for the Jamesian artist: remote probing may degenerate into an unproductive self-refinement. This poem is carefully balanced, from its opening antithesis ("in captivity" and "godlike") to the delicate oppositions in the closing lines:

> he nods
> the hair between his horns
> and eyes matted
> with hyacinthine curls (*CEP*, 336f)

Though the bull is an "Olympian commentary" on the "bright pasage of days," the poem itself acts as implicit comment on that beautifully aloof, half-blind, and "milkless" self-concern. It is in such negative ways that these two poems point toward Williams' next movement of growth, which had little in common with the subtly Olympian academicism that he saw in Eliot's *The Waste Land*, published in this same year (*Au*, 174).

    Spring and All (1923), in its prose chapters, argues for a yet more radical immediacy. If the imagination is to refine, clarify, and intensify "that eternal moment in which we alone live," we must destroy the barriers with which we usually fend off "consciousness of immediate contact with the world" (*S&A*, 3, 1). We must reject all "beautiful illusion" in art, all "crude symbolism" (*S&A*, 3, 20), and even all "realism"—which is the mere copying of selected surfaces from a conventionally given (and therefore subtly protective and self-blinding) point of view. Any "conscious recording of the day's experiences 'freshly and with the appearance of reality'" will make "nature an accessory to the particular theory" the writer is following; it therefore "blinds him to his world" (*S&A*, 49). Because the realist is clinging to the past (as source of material and method), he cannot freely attend to the present. The resulting "reflection of nature" is not nature but "only a sham nature, a 'lie.'" The true work of the imagination is "not 'like' anything but transfused with the same forces which transfuse the earth." The maker of such a work does not "copy" nature but becomes it, "continuing its marvels" (*S&A*, 51).

    But what then is a *present* process of composition? Williams offers some suggestive notes: "Not to attempt, at that time, to set values on the word being used, according to presupposed measures, but to write down that which happens at that time—" Or again: "To perfect the ability to record at the moment when the consciousness is enlarged by the sympathies and the unity of understanding which the imagination gives...." This recording of what is *now* is "not 'fit' but a unification of experience" (*S&A*, 48, 49). It is not "realism" but "reality itself"; it means the abandonment of "acquisitive understanding" and a satisfaction of the "sense of inclusiveness without redundancy" (*S&A*, 45, 42). All this, of course, is anterior to technique, which can have "only a sequent value" (*S&A*, 27).

The imagination exists as an integrating and liberating force, Williams said, "to free the world of fact from the impositions of 'art'"—that is, from all past stylized apprehensions of experience—and thereby to free "the man to act in whatever direction his disposition leads" (*S&A*, 92). Understanding that purpose, he found himself extending the values discovered in the *Improvisations* (*S&A*, 44). Specific clues to technique were at hand in analytic and synthetic Cubism—especially in the work of Juan Gris, where Williams saw "forms common to experience" caught up in a design which "the onlooker is not for a moment permitted to witness as an 'illusion'" (*S&A*, 11). That design not only adds to nature but also refreshes, the onlooker's attention to natural forms. Its disjunctions and overlappings, translated into the modes of poetry, might render the swift movement of the mind from point to point. However, the argument of *Spring and All* is not a firm commitment to a new mode of art; it is rather an important beginning in that continual "beginning" which constitutes Williams' esthetic. Certainly the poems in this volume are not in any single new style.

"The Rose," like "To a Solitary Disciple," both states and enacts a somewhat Cubist position; but the sentimentalism of the image is now more radically abandoned for a novel geometric construction:

> The rose is obsolete
> but each petal ends in
> an edge, the double facet
> cementing the grooved
> columns of air ...

This is not mere imitation of analytic Cubism. In the play on "ends," one level of statement wittily modulates into another. The first—abstract assertion—reappears thereafter in disguise ("meets—nothing—renews / itself") or openly ("love is at an end—of roses")—where another punning modulation prepares for:

> It is at the edge of the
> petal that love waits

The dissolve after "waits," like a more emphatic dissolve later on, renders on a yet more immediate level the poem's major theme: a renewal (of image, of flowering, of love) manifests itself whenever an ending is genuinely ("neither hanging / nor pushing") enacted.

> The fragility of the flower
> unbruised
> penetrates space. (*CEP*, 249f)

Closer to synthetic Cubism, as in the Gris construction entitled "The Open Window"—"a shutter, a bunch of grapes, a sheet of music, a picture of sea and mountains" (*S&A*, 34)—is "At the Faucet of June." It has been suggested that here the "writing problem is considered from another angle: How to reconcile the poetic and the anti-poetic?"[4] But "consideration," in the usual sense, is foreign to this poem's non-discursive mode; and "poetic" and "anti-poetic" are categories (suggested by Wallace Stevens) that Williams' work generally repudiates. However, this construction does draw its parts from a world that has brutalized itself by such categories.

The artist as a man is in that world, and his words are "a dance over the body of his condition accurately accompanying it" (*S&A*, 91). As dance, it communicates release from the fixities in that condition. The first three stanzas catch up increasingly disparate matters, each line requiring a yet more agile imaginative leap, before the contemporary rape of Persephone by that gloomy Dis, "J.P.M.," is ever in question. The "Gordian knot" of the relation between the classical and an era of finance capitalism is therefore dissolved before it is named as matter for the dance. Though a Morgan might cut that knot with a purchase of "a Veronese or / perhaps a Rubens," this poem knows with Gris that the "only way to resemble the classics is to have no part in what we do come of them but to have it our own" (*SE*, 132). The poem dances past the June sunlight, the rape and maiming of song by the market mentality, into a destructive autumn in which sudden emergence of refreshing detail is still possible:

> wind, earthquakes in
>
> Manchuria, a
> partridge
> from dry leaves. (*CEP*, 251f)

As Williams said of Marianne Moore's "Marriage," this poem is "an anthology of transit," a "pleasure that can be held firm only by moving rapidly from one thing to the next" (*SE*, 123).

Less difficult poems are "The Eyeglasses" and "The Right of Way,"
where imaginative disjunction is subdued by the ordinary mode of prose
discourse. In "The Eyeglasses" the potential relatedness in the field of
constructive vision—the "swiftness that passes without repugnance from
thing to thing" (*SE*, 124)—is itself the theme. "It takes writing such as
unrelated passing on the street," Williams said later, when exploring this
vision in *January: A Novelette*, "to rescue us for a design that alone affords
conversation" (*Nov*, 28). In "The Right of Way" he has lightly combined a
realistic narrative frame of "passing on the street" with the dynamics of rapid
transit. The opening lines may seem at first to be banal:

> In passing with my mind
> on nothing in the world
>
> but the right of way
> I enjoy on the road by
>
> virtue of the law—
> I saw

—but, after tracing the interrelated and interrupted figures in the snapshots
that follow, we realize that we have already been given quite accurately the
poem's esthetic: the law of its vision. It relates a transit unblurred by concern
for before and after; the eye is fixed concretely on emptiness. A later passage
gives the self-sustaining dynamism of that essentially non-verbal vision:

> The supreme importance
> of this nameless spectacle
>
> sped me by them
> without a word—(*CEP*, 258f)

In its humorous realism this poem is close to Pieter Brueghel, whose
paintings Williams would later use as bases for just such constructions, or to
a photographer (say, Jacques Henri Lartigue) who may capture the transient
relationships of "unrelated" life in flux. But the weakness of the poem results
from its very realism: focusing with self-indulgence upon the speaker as
possessor of this vision, it subtly negates *now* the past experience which he
can merely relate.

Closer to the immediate is "The Red Wheelbarrow"—a poem that recalls Emerson's statement in "The Poet" about the possibility of using words with "a terrible simplicity": "It does not need that a poem should be long. Every word was once a poem. Every new relation is a new word."

> so much depends
> upon
>
> a red wheel
> barrow
>
> glazed with rain
> water
>
> beside the white
> chickens (*CEP*, 277)

The opening assertion of importance is free of gratifying reference to the speaker as poet or self. The poem's vitality is no one's possession but a possibility for any mind that traces the lines. Line units, stress, quantity, echoing sounds—are all adjusted to render the delicate movement of apprehending a "new world."

As Louis Zukofsky has noted, it takes "only four words to shift the level at which emotion is held from neatness of surface to comprehension which includes surface and what is under it."[5] Each quantitatively long "holding" of the surface lifts it into esthetic abstraction ("a red wheel," "glazed with rain," "beside the white"). The descent into short, trochaic rendering of "substance" then gives a more inclusive comprehension, which in turn leads to a related "surface." Each pattern refreshes without becoming final; and at the central climax, the momentary abstraction becomes a metaphorical transformation, "glazed," which is followed by a more complex descent. To add that this poem was "written in 2 minutes"[6] does not diminish its importance. It testifies to the ability to record at the moment of enlarged and focused consciousness. Writing as revelation, Williams later said, consists of "the most complicated formulas worked out ... in a few seconds and set down" (*SE*, 268f).

The first poem of *Spring and All* (itself later entitled "Spring and All") introduces this new world of present attention by rendering the triumph of awakening sensibility. From the very beginning its words are charged with the emergence of life amid the stasis of disease or death:

By the road to the contagious hospital
under the surge of the blue
mottled clouds driven from the
northeast—a cold wind. Beyond, the
waste of broad, muddy fields
brown with dried weeds, standing and fallen

patches of standing water
the scattering of tall trees

The "road" already establishes the theme of transit and arrival; and the structure of the first sentence fragment, proceeding through modifiers to the spondaically weighted subject, begins the pattern of emergence. Ironically, what there emerges as a living force is the adverse (yet bracing) element. The texture—rising from the connotations of "contagious hospital" to the vital "surge of the blue," lapsing back into the passivity of "mottled clouds driven," and rising again to the active force now defined, "a cold wind"— enacts in little the larger texture of the poem. For there is now a lapse into "waste," "standing and fallen," and the yet more fragmentary notation of inert or passively moved "standing water" and "scattering of tall trees."

Yet endurance and vitality lurk in those verbal forms, which will lead to the next upsurge of movement toward clear definition (through "reddish / purplish, forked, upstanding, twiggy"), only to relapse again into the indeterminate "stuff" and the specification of objects dead or dormant. After these preliminary movements the pattern itself can emerge into explicit statement—

Lifeless in appearance, sluggish
dazed spring approaches—

only to relapse into a less bold personification:

They enter the new world naked,
cold, uncertain of all
save that they enter.

However, the connotations of "hospital" have now shifted from disease to birth; and the proleptic "they" fits the pattern of syntactical emergence established by the first sentence fragment. We now look forward in more intense anticipation; yet, even after the "objects are defined" (first the generic "grass," then *tomorrow* the more specific "stiff curl of wildcarrot leaf"), there will be a little relapse into: "It quickens: clarity, outline of leaf." The poem is on the *edge* of clear definition:

> But now the stark dignity of
> entrance—Still, the profound change
> has come upon them: rooted, they
> grip down and begin to awaken (*CEP*, 241f)

The kinesthetic mode implicit in the earlier visual imagery fully emerges in that "grip." The conclusion renders the mysterious edge of quickening: movement in stillness, interior action arising from being acted upon, an awakening that implies descent into the sustaining ground.

Other poems in *Spring and All* extend Williams' study of local culture, sometimes with fresh economy. There is "To an Old Jaundiced Woman," for example, with its spare and metaphorically heightened details—or "Shoot it Jimmy!" in which the line is a unit of musical measure, with regular beat and syncopated verbal stress. But most important of these is "To Elsie," which focuses three of Williams' main concerns: a despoiled America, the alienated and self-alienating human condition, and the ravished Eden of the imagination.

The considerable power of this poem resides neither in the summary image of Elsie herself, which occupies so few lines, nor in any texture of precise particulars. The diction is often general and seemingly flaccid: "devil-may-care men who have taken / to railroading / out of sheer lust of adventure," or "young slatterns, bathed / in filth." As a dramatic monologue, however, the poem surmounts such language. Its major focus is the speaker himself, who sums up—in swift, passionate, and broken utterance—the human condition in which he participates. The well-worn counters give the speed and immediacy of actual speech; but, through the careful disposition of those words, Williams presents the speaker's fresh awareness:

> The pure products of America
> go crazy—
> mountain folk from Kentucky
>
> or the ribbed north end of
> Jersey
> with its isolate lakes and

> valleys, its deaf-mutes, thieves
> old names
> and promiscuity between ...

Here a fresh juxtaposition of clichés ("pure products ... go crazy") leads into precise, natural description that is symbolically resonant ("ribbed north end" and "isolate lakes"), and on into parallelism that pulls together seemingly disparate elements in the syndrome of degradation ("lakes and / valleys, ... deaf-mutes, thieves / old names / and promiscuity"). And later the emptiness of

> succumbing without
> emotion
> save numbed terror

is sharpened by a sudden movement into more specific (and suggestive) naming, the two sequences bound together by sound-pattern:

> under some hedge of choke-cherry
> or viburnum—
> which they cannot express—

However, this texture could not sustain a mounting intensity for 66 lines without the poem's major syntactical and prosodic devices. Syntactically, most of the poem is one long sequence of progressive subordination—a sequence that is not anticlimactic because it renders the proliferation of the speaker's thought. He does not set forth a position; instead, he discovers and seeks to express the increasingly immediate and stifling implications of his first brief intuition. Hence the poem's forward thrust; and hence the fact that every phrase comes as a *present* apprehension. It is as though the techniques of "Tract" and "Dedication for a Plot of Ground" were now combined. But that flow of commonplace diction and progressive subordination plays against a quite regular prosodic structure. By means of the long-short-long triplets (a more rigorous scheme than the later triadic line), with each line a unit of attention, Williams renders the varying pace of the concerned mind, as it feels its way among the data of experience, rushes on, revises, pauses to give a phrase deliberate weight or ironic point, searches again, shifts the angle of vision, or suddenly hits upon a new meaning.

After that sustained and intense sequence of subordination, the following brief assertions (with unexpected shorter lines and a final sentence fragment) carry unusual weight:

> Somehow
> it seems to destroy us
>
> It is only in isolate flecks that
> something
> is given off
>
> No one
> to witness
> and adjust, no one to drive the car (*CEP,* 270–72)

The vague phrases render the speaker's own straining to perceive and articulate. He too "cannot express." But "isolate flecks"—with its reminders of "isolate lakes," "desolate," "voluptuous water / expressing," and the distant image of deer—transcends that in-articulateness. And so does the final colloquial metaphor. The imagination in this poem does not merely strain after deer; it confronts our chronic and devastating blindness and inflexibility.

In doing so, the imagination composes an utterance that exemplifies Williams' own definition of "style": "There is something to say and one says it. That's writing. But to say it one must have it alive with the overtones which give not a type of statement but an actual statement that is alive, marked with a gait and appearance which show it to be the motion of an individual who has suffered it and brought it into fact. This is style."[7] Such style is itself a witnessing and an adjustment.

III COLLECTED POEMS 1921–1931

During the next decade or so—through the publication of *Collected Poems 1921–1931* (1934)—Williams was seeking a more inclusive structure that might render his sense of community and history, and also a new loosening and a new precision of measure. These inquiries led him to devote much of his energy to experiment with prose fictions, but his poetic accomplishment during this period was considerable. The poems include further oblique portraiture with social implications ("New England," "All the Fancy Things," "The Dead Baby," "Hemmed-in Males"), delicate patternings of perception ("On Gay Wallpaper," "The Lily," "Nantucket"), and such diversely fresh things as the implicit image of "Young Sycamore," the descent through woods in "The Source," the vitreous marine descent in "The Cod Head," the sardonic "scaleless / jumble" of "It is a Living Coral," and the brief transits of "Poem" and "Between Walls."

Because such poems involve no very new structural principle or law of vision, they do not require extended comment here. There are also, however, three important steps toward more sustained sequence: the fragmentary "Paterson" of 1927, a good deal of which would be incorporated in the later *Paterson*; "The Descent of Winter," a verse-and-prose sequence that emerged from a diary-script of late 1927; and the poetic sequence that followed, "Della Primavera Trasportata Al Morale." In each of these poems appear new lines of growth.

The texture of "Paterson" renders with meditative detachment that central consciousness which is both man and city, one and many, self and non-self, ideas and things. Its leisurely pace accommodates remarkably swift changes of perspective, and its potential wholeness of vision consorts with an honest ignorance. Williams here occupied the multidimensional position that would make his later epic possible. However, "Paterson" contains no really immediate voices. We hear no living people in this somnambulistic city—not even the poet as actual man, suffering this condition and bringing it to articulation.

In "The Descent of Winter" the diary organization gives us that actual man. *The Great American Novel* had already explored the possibilities of a fiction in which the author would seem an immediate and improvisatory presence, and *Kora in Hell* and *Spring and All* had used seasonal frameworks. Now Williams combined verse and prose in a sequence that locates us in the day-by-day consciousness of the writer as one engaged in an actual descent into local and therefore universal ground. We need not regard the unity given by the entry-dates as "spurious" and merely criticize the poems as separate pieces, even though Williams' own later dismantling of the script leaves the way open for such a procedure.[8]

The structure of the whole, though quite imperfect, does give support to its parts. There are frequent cross-references and illuminating juxtapositions: the poems of 10/22, 10/28, and 10/29, for example, gain from their prose context; and 11/2 ("A Morning Imagination of Russia") is in the following prose related to Charles Sheeler, Shakespeare, and the local Fairfield.[9] The entire sequence may be seen as enacting a descent from auto-erotic and barren isolation (9/27, 9/29) through expansive and fructifying movements toward a new discovery of community, the past, love, and the writer's vocation as earlier known by the "fluid" and "accessible"

Shakespeare, "who had that mean ability to fuse himself with everyone which nobody's have, to be anything at any time."[10]

As a total construct—a series of shots through the material, with a self-revising dramatic movement of descent into contact—this script complements "Paterson." Putting the two together and adding the projected fiction about Dolores Marie Pischak and Fairfield, we can see that Williams was approaching the mode of the later *Paterson*. An unpublished note of October 29 makes clear that larger intent: "ALL that I am doing (dated) will go in it. Poems. Talk of poetry. sequently IS it—from the way I look, it is THIS I want. I shall use her [Dolores Marie Pischak], picking up *all I can*, to the best of my power, but all the rest goes in strainlessly, without exclusion.... Paterson is really—part of it."

And a note of November 13 relates that intent to the Shakespearean vocation: "... and so I become her and everyone. My rocks, my trees, my people, my self imagined part of everything. The name of everything, every kind of grass, every kind of grimace speaking to me. And when that is—Then roses will have cheap jewelry."[11] That was the inclusiveness without redundancy which now beckoned.

"Della Primavera Trasportata Al Morale," the spring loosening of 1928 that followed the descent into winter, focuses on the natural and the human with some of that inclusiveness. Its first poem, "April," includes responses to inner and outer weather, direct transcriptions of urban sights and sounds (like those Williams had probably found in Louis Aragon's *Le Paysan de Paris*)—and also little vignettes, rhythmic studies of the language, and semi-ironic translations of things into ideas. The most comprehensive "moral" of this piece is "love, bred of / the mind and eyes and hands" (*CEP*, 60)—a love that is starved and deformed, imperfectly in touch. The poem's multifaceted structure results from the insight that "The forms / of the emotions are crystalline" (*CEP*, 64). But the larger structure and whiter heat of *Paterson* would be required adequately to support and fuse such disparate elements.

More successful in this sequence are the shorter pieces, which present what Marianne Moore has called "the breathless budding of thought from thought."[12] Three poems that emerged after "April" from the same long first draft—"The Trees," "The Wind Increases," and "The Bird's Companion"— dissolve and reconstitute the poetic line as they seek immediacy. Here, as Zukofsky said, we do not think of line-ends but of "essential rhythm, each cadence emphasized, the rhythm breaking and beginning again, an action, each action deserving a line."[13]

> The harried
> earth is swept
> > The trees
> the tulip's bright
> > tips
> > > sidle and
> toss— (*CEP*, 68)

And here nouns are "acts as much as verbs."[14] The last half of "The Wind Increases" gives in statement and structure that understanding of "actual" words:

> having the form
> > of motion
>
> At each twigtip
>
> new
>
> upon the tortured
> body of thought
>
> > gripping
> the ground
>
> a way
> > to the last leaftip (*CEP*, 68f)

Williams considered giving "Della Primavera Trasportata Al Morale" the subtitle "Words Sans Lines,"[15] as a way of pointing to such structure. But in "The Bird's Companion" the loosening (in the first draft) led to a reconstitution of the line in a new stanza pattern. The tortured body of thought—the tree discerned in and through the diverse movements of the leaves—may then appear more clearly in its total rhythm.

"The Sea-Elephant" was in a rough four-line stanza in its earlier drafts. Revision of this poem meant substantial cutting, reorganizing of details to produce a symbolic *progression d'effet*, and counterpointing of syntactical and line units to give the dynamic structure of advancing perception. The pruning of this stanza was characteristic:

I am sick	Sick
of the smallness of April	of April's smallness
the leaves the	the little
yellow flowers—[16]	leaves—(*CEP*, 71)

In another poem, "Rain," much of the meaning of this sequence is summarized: on the one hand, our chronic psychological cramp, which closes, shapes, possesses, and defends from the weather; on the other, that opening which may discover the healing wash of love.

> As the rain falls
> so does
>   your love
>
> bathe every
>   open
> object of the world— (*CEP*, 74)

> It is this recognition that then
>   so spreads
>   the words
>   far apart to let in
>   her love (*CEP*, 75)

Though necessarily discerned in and through forms, love transcends those forms and is negated by any form that would capture and hold rather than reveal. Love is not, therefore, consonant with the desire for perfect formal or practical attainment. In the wordly sense (as *Kora in Hell* had said of the imagination) "nothing will come of it" (*K*, 17). That is why the poem's opening analogy leads to a contrast. From the "liquid clearness" of the rain "flowers / come / perfectly / into form"—

> But love is
> unworldly
>
>   and nothing
> comes of it but love
>
> following
> and falling endlessly

from
                    her thoughts (*CEP*, 76f)

Form must constantly be opened, reshaped, transcended—so that the
attention or imagination or love (which are essentially a single creative force)
may be allowed re-entry and dance or song may be quickened. Perhaps the
most remarkable rendering of that process in the first half of Williams' work
is the concluding poem in this sequence, "The Botticellian Trees":

           The alphabet of
           the trees

           is fading in the
           song of the leaves ...

The single conceit that the poem at first seems to develop with unusual
metaphysical rigor gradually dissolves—in accord with its own meaning.
Moving to its formal close, the poem enacts that opening which transcends
the formal without denying it:

           In summer the song
           sings itself

           above the muffled words— (*CEP*, 80f)

NOTES

1. In addition to the erroneous dating of the "Transitional" poems, other mistakes
have resulted from reliance upon published volumes or longer sequences. Vivienne Koch,
for example, judged that the period between *Spring and All* (1923) and "The Descent of
Winter" (1928) had been a "stalemate in Williams' otherwise clear line of progress"
(*William Carlos Williams*, p. 60). But both the "stalemate" and the "clear line of progress"
must be questioned. Poems published in magazines before 1928 but not collected until
1934 (*Collected Poems 1921–1931*) include—aside from the "Transitional" group—such
pieces as: "The Bull," *Dial*, LXXII (February, 1922), 156; "The Jungle," *Dial*, LXXII
(February, 1922), 157; "New England," *Contact* V (June, 1923); "Paterson," *Dial*, LXXXII
(February, 1927), 91–93; "Young Sycamore," *Dial*, LXXXII (March, 1927), 210; "All the
Fancy Things," *Dial*, LXXXII (June, 1927), 476; and "Brilliant Sad Sun," *Dial*, LXXXII
(June, 1927), 478. Other poems remained uncollected still longer. "The Dead Baby,"
transition, No. 2 (May, 1927), 118, was not republished until *An Early Martyr* (1935); and
"St. Francis Einstein of the Daffodils," *Contact* IV (1921), after much pruning and
rearranging, finally reappeared in *Adam & Eve & The City* (1936). If it should prove

possible to date the manuscript versions of other poems published in the 1930s, many other revisions of chronology might have to be made.

2. Babette Deutsch, *Poetry in Our Time* (New York, 1952), p. 102.

3. Louis Zukofsky, "An Old Note on WCW," *Massachusetts Review*, III (Winter, 1962), 302.

4. Koch, *William Carlos Williams*, p. 50.

5. Louis Zukofsky, *A Test of Poetry* (New York, 1948), p. 101.

6. MS.

7. "The Somnambulists," *transition*, No. 18 (November, 1929), 148.

8. See Koch, *William Carlos Williams*, p. 58. With a few deletions (and with the inaccurate heading *"Not previously published"*) the prose passages from "The Descent of Winter" are now included in *Selected Essays*, pp. 62–74, as "Notes in Diary Form."

9. "The Descent of Winter," *Exile*, No. 4 (Autumn, 1928), 52–53. In MS, "Fairfield" is specified as Garfield, New Jersey.

10. "The Descent of Winter," *Exile*, No. 4, p. 53.

11. MS.

12. *Predilections*, p. 136.

13. Zukofsky, "American Poetry 1920–1930," *Symposium*, II (January, 1931), 83.

14. *Idem.*

15. MS.

16. MS.

HELEN HENNESSY VENDLER

Douceurs, Tristesses

A blaze of summer straw, in winter's nick.

Wallace Stevens' late version of pastoral is a double one, embodied in two difficult poems—*Credences of Summer* (1947) and *The Auroras of Autumn* (1948).[1] The two poems are in effect the same day seen from two perspectives, Stevens' Allegro and his Penseroso, a day piece matched with a night piece (a night piece nonetheless auroral), his innocent Eden confronted by his true Paradise, where he finds the serpent. They are two, or rather twenty, ways (since each has ten cantos) of looking at middle age, when all moments of life are potentially overcast by memory or fear. A poem takes us, as Stevens said, from its "ever-early candor to its late plural," and *Credences of Summer* describes for us that late plural in all its harvest magnitude, while the chill that falls across *The Auroras of Autumn* springs, in contrast, from an austerity of mind not far from Keats's when he saw the Grecian urn as a cold pastoral. Though the scene of middle age remains unchanged, "the Eye altering, alters all."

No previous long poem in Stevens' collections had ever placed a lyric speaker firmly in a landscape of the present moment: all had used the haziness of a past distancing or the impersonality of an invented persona, whether a woman, a shearsman, or a comedian. In contrast, the

---

From *On Extended Wings: Wallace Stevens' Longer Poems.* © 1969 by the President and Fellows of Harvard College.

confrontation of the present is insisted on over and over in these two poems; the eye is not allowed to stray, but is kept tightly bound by the repetitive "this" and "here" of successive lines:

> This is the last day of a certain year.
>
> This, this is the centre that I seek.
>
> This is where the serpent lives, the bodiless.
>
> Here, being visible is being white.

The scrutiny represented by the insistence on the demonstrative adjective and pronoun is a new mode for an expansive poem in Stevens. Though it is more evenly sustained in *The Auroras of Autumn* it is best described in *Credences of Summer*:

> Three times the concentred self takes hold, three times
> The thrice concentred self, having possessed
>
> The object, grips it in savage scrutiny,
> Once to make captive, once to subjugate
> Or yield to subjugation, once to proclaim
> The meaning of the capture, this hard prize,
> Fully made, fully apparent, fully found. (vii)

This hard prize, so grasped and so exhibited, over and over, is the ever elusive present, so likely, like the ghost of Anchises, to evade embrace. These poems represent the wresting of Stevens' naturally elegiac style into a temporarily topographical poetry. Again, the result is happier in *The Auroras of Autumn*, where elegy and description are kept in a dissolving equilibrium, and present and past remain in a fluid focus. But in both poems, Stevens calls the present internal moment "this," and everything outside it in space and time "that," and the purpose of these two seasonal pastorals of inner weather is to find a relation between "this" and "that," a relation shadowed forth in an earlier poem, "This as Including That" (1944–45):

> This rock and the dry birds
> Fluttering in blue leaves,

This rock and the priest,
The priest of nothingness who intones—

It is true that you live on this rock
And in it. It is wholly you.

It is true that there are thoughts
That move in the air as large as air,

That are almost not our own, but thoughts
To which we are related,

In an association like yours
With the rock and mine with you.

But the assertion of relation, undermined by the same bitterness we have seen in the rejection of Cinderella in *Notes*, collapses in the final couplet:

The iron settee is cold.
A fly crawls on the balustrades. (*OP*, 88)

"This" clearly does not include the complete "that," as the settee and the fly stand outside the harmonious relation of thoughts, the rock, and the poet with his interior paramour.

The attempt to make "this" (the present moment) include "that" is the soul of *Credences of Summer*, and is expressed in the intellectual pivot of the poem: "One day enriches a year ... / Or do the other days enrich the one?" "The indifferent experience of life," as Stevens said in *Two or Three Ideas* (1951), "is the unique experience, the item of ecstasy which we have been isolating and reserving for another time and place, loftier and more secluded." (*OP*, 213). Or, as he put it programmatically in *Notes*, the function of poetry is "forthwith,/ On the image of what we see, to catch from that/ Irrational moment its unreasoning." Stevens stands in the perfection of an August day in harvest, and asks whether this day in Oley, in its uniqueness, includes all others in the year, or whether it stands extrinsic to them. To fix the attention on the present is not at all a new idea in Stevens' verse; what is new is the expression of the idea in the present tense, in the actual scene, in the poetry of "this" and "here" and "now." *Notes toward a Supreme Fiction*, by its nature, had been a program for action, a Utopian poem, and had about it a marvelous note of expectancy, confidence, and buoyancy. *Credences of*

Summer, as its title betrays, is the creed of the believer rather than the certain projection of the prophet or the divided commentary of the skeptic, but its intention cannot all command the strings. Its initial impetus of praise and involvement, resolutely kept in the original moment, is maintained through the first three cantos, but from then on the oneness with the here and now diminishes, until by the end of the poem Stevens is at an inhuman distance from his starting point.

Stevens is fully conscious of his wish to bask in the present and of the forces working against it, chiefly his natural asceticism and his equally natural intellectuality. As always, his protagonists represent aspects of himself, and so the vanishing present object is not only gripped in savage scrutiny by one Stevens, but also avoided by another:

> It was difficult to sing in face
> Of the object. The singers had to avert themselves
> Or else avert the object.

It is no longer enough to be an onlooker, as it was for the shears-man with the blue guitar, who wanted "to be the lion in the lute/ Before the lion locked in stone," his life spent in an eternal mirroring of the world. That spectatorship has turned into an immersion in the scene, a scene which is at once fully made by the poet, fully apparent of itself, and fully found, as if left, like Whitman's grass, designedly dropped. This mode of the this, the here, and the now, so remarkably difficult to maintain at any length, gives a suspense to the progress of both poems, as the tenuous identity of man and environmental moment is sought, precariously supported, and, finally, lost.

The identity dissolves, of course, with the entrance of the analytic mind, with the change from description to interrogation. This questioning occurs halfway through the ten cantos of *Credences of Summer*, and entirely pervades *The Auroras of Autumn*: in both cases the central question forces its way to the surface, almost against the speaker's will. In *Credences of Summer* the question, already quoted, asks the relation of the present to its context in time:

> One day enriches a year ...
> Or do the other days enrich the one?

In *The Auroras of Autumn* the question looks for the relation of insight to sight, or the envisaged to the now:

Is there an imagination that sits enthroned
As grim as it is benevolent, the just
And the unjust, which in the midst of summer stops

To imagine winter?

After the question is put, a simple ease of landscape is never regained. The
analytic is in the ascendant, as detachment, generalization, and removal from
the scene take precedence over receptivity. The poems do not fail, but the
human effort to rest in the present is predestined to collapse, at least for
Stevens, who never was a poet formed to chant in orgy to the summer sun.
Fifteen lines after he has asserted that the summer land is too ripe for
enigmas, the central enigma of moment and context rises in him, and the
hope of serenity is lost. But the end was foreshadowed in the elegiac and
brutal claims for the land's ripeness with which the poem had begun:

> Now in midsummer come and all fools slaughtered
> And spring's infuriations over and a long way
> To the first autumnal inhalations, young broods
> Are in the grass, the roses are heavy with a weight
> Of fragrance and the mind lays by its trouble.
>
> Now the mind lays by its trouble and considers.
> The fidgets of remembrance come to this.
> This is the last day of a certain year
> Beyond which there is nothing left of time.
> It comes to this and the imagination's life.

All of Stevens' praise of summer is put in negative terms. There is "nothing
left of time," and

> There is nothing more inscribed nor thought nor felt
> And this must comfort the heart's core against
> Its false disasters—these fathers standing round,
> These mothers touching, speaking, being near,
> These lovers waiting in the soft dry grass.

The scene is composed of details of warmth and feeling—the young broods,
the fragrant roses, the mythical fathers, mothers, and lovers—but they
emerge from the heavy toll of the mind's trouble, the disasters (even if false)

of the heart's core, the fidgets of remembrance, the slaughtering, even of fools, and the repetitive knell of negative phrases. It is with all our memories of negative phrasing used pejoratively that we hear Stevens say "There is nothing more inscribed nor thought nor felt," and we feel the truth of deprivation in his paradoxes to come, when he will speak of "the barrenness of the fertile thing that can attain no more," and of "a feeling capable of nothing more."[2]

Credences of Summer, as I have said, turns on the difficult relation between the moment of satisfaction and "the waste sad time stretching before and after." Stevens attempts a Hegelian synthesis of the two in a triple invoking of a day, a woman, and a man, all raised above the norm into an embellishment, a queen, and a hero. He asks how they are related to that matrix which they resemble and from which they rise, and his answer falls into a logical scheme:

	One day enriches a year.
Thesis:	One woman makes the rest look down.
	One man becomes a race, lofty like him, like him perpetual.
	Or do the other days enrich the one?
Antithesis:	And is the queen humble as she seems to be, the charitable majesty of her whole kin?
	The bristling soldier ... who looms in the sunshine is a filial form.
	The more than casual blue contains the year and other years and hymns and people, without souvenir.
Synthesis:	The day enriches the year, not as embellishment.
	Stripped of remembrance, it displays its strength— the youth, the vital son, the heroic power.

The extreme neatness of this processional resolution, in which the day, at the end, has metaphorically absorbed the queen (in the word "embellishment") and the soldier (in the word "heroic"), is not particularly convincing, since the permutations seem summoned not by feeling but by a too avid logic. After suggesting that a day in Oley can enrich a year as embellishment, Stevens makes the counterassertion that routine provides the necessary backdrop for the effect of this day: the other days, then, enrich the one, perhaps, if we are to speak justly. The final resolution—that this midsummer day *contains* all the rest, but without souvenir (rather as a concept contains, virtually, all its instances)—is an ingenious but frigid appropriation from logical abstraction. Its weakness is betrayed as Stevens has to buttress it by his gaudy language, always produced in moments of strain: the soldier who bristles and looms comes in phrases not flesh but fustian.

Because this blustering solution is a false one, the poem will have to begin all over again, resorting in turn to both self-enhancement and self-parody. Earlier, in the third canto, a visionary exaltation had been sketched in a tableau of height attained in the here and now:

> This is the barrenness
> Of the fertile thing that can attain no more.
>
> It is the natural tower of all the world,
> The point of survey, green's green apogee,
> But a tower more precious than the view beyond,
> A point of survey squatting like a throne,
> Axis of everything, green's apogee
>
> And happiest folk-land, mostly marriage-hymns.
> It is the mountain on which the tower stands,
> It is the final mountain ...
> It is the old man standing on the tower,
> Who reads no book.

The tower, the mountain underneath it, and the old man above it, though drawn from Stevens' walks to the tower on Mount Penn,[3] are all emblems of the perfect day "in Oley when the hay,/ Baked through long days, is piled in mows." After the analytic questions about the day arise in the fifth canto, however, a different stance is needed: the tower and the old man are dispensed with, and the mountain is made to do duty for all three. The day had first been construed in pure greenness as green's green apogee, with its natural mountain base, its prolongation into the man-made tower, and its coronation with the human;[4] now in its self-enhancement it becomes at once purely "natural" without tower or man, and at the same time purely mythical and celestial, with only the most minor concessions to the original green. Metaphysics surmounts the physical:

> It is a mountain half way green and then,

>   The other immeasurable half, such rock
>   As placid air becomes.

Stevens had once admitted "This is the pit of torment, that placid end/
Should be illusion" (292), but here, for this brief moment of idealization, he
sustains the immobility of his myth:

>   It is the rock of summer, the extreme,
>   A mountain luminous half way in bloom
>   And then half way in the extremest light
>   Of sapphires flashing from the central sky,
>   As if twelve princes sat before a king.

The earlier old man has been enhanced into the sun-king, a Charlemagne
surrounded by twelve peers; and the tower has been metamorphosed into the
airy half of the mountain, previously seen in the "green" passage as a
squatting throne, but here as a flashing beacon. It is a radiation upward of the
entire original scene, and of course brings about its own downfall, or in
literary terms its own parody. When we next see the tower, in the ninth
canto, it has turned into a beanpole; the green mountain has been dwarfed to
a weedy garden in decay, and the old man has degenerated into a cock robin
perched on the beanpole, no longer garbed in a "ruddy ancientness" which
"absorbs the ruddy summer" but instead huddled, waiting for warmth.

   The imperatives with which Stevens will begin the scene in the
salacious garden parody the confident imperatives of the second canto.
There, action was paramount and insistent:

>   Postpone the anatomy of summer ...
>   Burn everything not part of it to ash.
>
>   Trace the gold sun about the whitened sky ...
>   And fill the foliage with arrested peace.

But like a fabliau coexisting with a miracle tale, the beast fable of the robin corrects
this energetic and idealized perspective with a low and slackened demand:

>   Fly low, cock bright, and stop on a bean pole. Let
>   Your brown breast redden, while you wait for warmth.
>   With one eye watch the willow, motionless.

That stopping, waiting, and watching while a complex of emotions falls apart into a soft decay is a psychological alternative to the active purging and redecorating of the second canto, just as the scarcely perceived sound made by the bird is an alternative to the marriage hymns of the natural greenery, and as the salacious weeds are an alternative to the fragrant roses of the opening. And both these "natural" extremes (of greenery or of weeds) are alternatives to the celestial possible: the luminous, the princely, the flashing sapphire stations before the king. Next to that aristocratic Round Table, the low primitiveness of the robin's utterance stands in a sinister guttural:

> This complex falls apart.
> And on your bean pole, it may be, you detect
>
> Another complex of other emotions, not
> So soft, so civil, and you make a sound,
> Which is not part of the listener's own sense.

Stevens has prepared us for this scrawny bird sound by the "green" marriage hymns and by two other passages in the poem—the choirs of the fourth canto and the trumpet of the eighth. These two are also mutual parodies, or, to speak more gently, sideglances at each other, mutual forms of critical reference. The choirs express final achieved polyphony, a primary which is not primitive but superbly complex, a primary free from doubt, as it was defined earlier in "Man Carrying Thing" (350). Things uncertain, indistinct, dubious, were there defined as secondary:

> Accept them, then,
> As secondary (parts not quite perceived
>
> Of the obvious whole, uncertain particles
> of the certain solid, the primary free from doubt ...) (350–351)

But here, in *Credences of Summer*, we are, in theory, confronted with "the obvious whole," "the certain solid," as Stevens assures us that the normally secondary senses of the ear, less immediate than the eye, swarm

> Not with secondary sounds, but choirs,
> Not evocations but last choirs, last sounds

With nothing else compounded, carried full,
Pure rhetoric of a language without words.

The earlier current of paradoxical negatives eddies through this fourth canto, as the thing that can attain no more, and the old man capable of nothing more, produce the music compounded with nothing else, full but without words. Stevens' aim is to disappoint us subtly as he pairs each word of potential, like "full" or "capable," with a negation of potential. All of *Credences of Summer*, in fact, may be seen as a meditation on that Keatsian moment in which the bees find that summer has o'erbrimm'd their clammy cells. Direction must either stop at the plenary season, or it imperceptibly conveys excess and decay, and Stevens' response is exactly that of the humanized bees: to think that warm days will never cease, or to follow a devious logic of wish.

Things stop in that direction and since they stop
The direction stops and we accept what is
As good. The utmost must be good and is
And is our fortune and honey hived in the trees
And mingling of colors at a festival.

In the explicit critique of this passage in *The Auroras of Autumn*, Stevens will question his harvest credences:

We stand in the tumult of a festival.

What festival? This loud, disordered mooch?

But Stevens expresses perceptible dualities even within *Credences of Summer*, and can follow his celebratory polyphony with a single sharpened analytic clarion, forsaking the seductive lingerings of the last choirs for the peremptory fiats of the trumpet:

It is the visible announced,
It is the more than visible, the more
Than sharp, illustrious scene. The trumpet cries
This is the successor of the invisible.

And unlike those last choirs, which suppose nothing as they rise in the land "too serene" for enigmas, the trumpet is fully conscious. It knows that

A mind exists, aware of division, aware
Of its cry as clarion ...
Man's mind grown venerable in the unreal.

That venerable mind belongs to what Stevens will call the Omega in man, peering forever into distances. Credences of summer are only possible when that aspect of the mind is suspended by an effort, so that for a moment the present can suffice and the distant can "fail" the normally clairvoyant eye.

As Stevens has moved further and further away from the original gifted moment when the scene subdues the intellect and the mind lays by its troubles, he has approached a vantage point in which the mind, in a new ascendancy, more than half creates what it perceives. The final canto in *Credences of Summer* begins very coldly indeed, with the poet as a deliberate and distant manipulator of marionettes:

> The personae of summer play the characters
> Of an inhuman author, who meditates
> With the gold bugs, in blue meadows, late at night.
> He does not hear his characters talk.

The poem has passed from noon to night, and the gold bugs and blue meadows are the nighttime imitation of the gold sun and the blue sky of earlier stanzas. But as the puppet master sets his characters in motion, they achieve some life of their own: they bulge beyond his control, and they wear mottled costumes, wanting to take on the ideal self-forgetful ripeness of summer, but remaining personae nevertheless. To the end they remain fictions, and their costumes are moody, and they are free only for a moment. Even so, Stevens risks sentimentality in the ending,

> In which the characters speak because they want
> To speak, the fat, the roseate characters,
> Free, for a moment, from malice and sudden cry,
> Complete in a completed scene, speaking
> Their parts as in a youthful happiness.

No criticism of this passage, or of the entire stance of *Credences of Summer*, could be more pointed than Stevens' own later backward glance in "The Ultimate Poem Is Abstract," written about a day which also seems plenary, full of revelations, placid, blue, roseate, ripe, complete:

This day writhes with what? The lecturer
On This Beautiful World Of Ours composes himself
And hems the planet rose and haws it ripe ...

If the day writhes, it is not with revelations.
One goes on asking questions. That, then, is one
Of the categories. So said, this placid space

Is changed. It is not so blue as we thought. To be blue
There must be no questions ...

                                    It would be enough
If we were ever, just once, at the middle, fixed
In This Beautiful World Of Ours and not as now,

Helplessly at the edge, enough to be
Complete, because at the middle, if only in sense,
And in that enormous sense, merely enjoy. (429)

Credences of Summer, which begins "at the middle," is undermined by the difficulties made so bald in this later poem. To be blue, there must be no questions. Stevens' desperate, if truthful, expedient with which to end the poem is the creation of the inhuman author whose characters undergo spontaneous generation for a flicker of feeling. This inhuman author is the hermit in the hermitage at the center, and he, not the senses, controls the ending of the poem. Earlier, Stevens had denied that the natural mountain depended in any way on the hermit:

                    It is not
A hermit's truth nor symbol in hermitage.
It is the visible rock, the audible.

But if the personae of summer are the author's creations, so perhaps is the rock of summer, and the poem, by posing what are for Stevens the false poles of reality on the one hand and imagination on the other, diverts him from his truer subject: the variety of several imaginative modes playing on any one thing. He is never more uneasy than when he is trying to claim some autonomy for haymows in Oley, as he does earlier in the poem; it forces him into his concluding evocation of a disembodied and inhuman author as proper counterpart to the irremediably obdurate hay.

In *The Auroras of Autumn*, Stevens more suitably fixes his shape-changing eye, not on the land, but on the huge cloudy symbols of the night's starred face. In this wholly individual poem there is nevertheless scarcely a line not reminiscent of earlier volumes. Stevens' density of internal reference to earlier leitmotivs is greater here than in any other poem, so much so that almost nothing is unfamiliar in the images except the superb aurora borealis which dominates the whole. Stevens may have had Wordsworth's northern lights in mind, that manifestation which is "Here, nowhere, there, and everywhere at once" (*Prelude* V, 533). Wherever he found the symbol, whether in literature or in nature,[5] it corresponds perfectly to the bravura of his imagination, even more so than the slower transformations of "Sea-Surface Full of Clouds." And certainly these changing auroras match his solemn fantasia better than the effort, so marked in *Credences of Summer*, to hold the imagination still. Stevens' restless modulations need an equally restless symbol, and the lights (with their lord, the flashing serpent) are, like his poetry, "always enlarging the change."

For all its lingering glances at other poems, *The Auroras of Autumn* remains essentially the partner to its antithesis, *Credences of Summer*. Like the earlier poem, it begins, so unusually for Stevens in the long poems, by placing its speaker in the lyric present, declaring by that emphasis on the here and now a firm attempt to center the mind on the present, not to drift elegiacally back or press wishfully forward. But whereas Summer represented repose, immobility, static piled haymows and monolithic mountains, Autumn is compounded of Stevens' most congenial subjects—flux, rapidity, flickerings, and winds. For all the difference in state between the two seasons, it is characteristic of Stevens at this period to place himself in the same relation to each, as the poet attempting total absorption in the scene, refusing to distance himself from it until the poem is well advanced. The ostentation of the first canto of *The Auroras of Autumn* lies in its insistence on the formula "This is," repeated with different predicates, recalling the similar demonstrative beginning of *Credences of Summer*. And although Stevens begins at once his parable of father, mother, children, and scholar, the speaker's voice interpolates again and again references to "this" throne, "this" thing, "these" heavens, "these" lights, "this" imminence, and so on. The "thisness" of *The Auroras of Autumn*, in other words, is never allowed to lapse entirely, and in this way it is a poem more consistent than *Credences of Summer*. The narrator remains discreetly present in these recurrent demonstrative phrases.

The boreal serpent in his nest at the zenith, marking the north pole raised to the tip of the heavens, is clearly another variation on the old man on the tower or the robin on the beanpole, but where the old man reads no book and the robin takes no flight, the serpent is engaged in perpetual rapacious motion, wriggling out of its egg, sloughing its skin, gulping objects into itself, moving in the grass. There are at first two serpents, one on the earth and one in the sky, and the motion of the canto is a nervous ascent and descent and reascent and redescent, a vertiginous uncertainty expressed in antiphonal rhetoric:

This is where the serpent lives, the bodiless. This is his nest.	Or is this another wriggling out of the egg? These lights may finally attain a pole In the midmost midnight and find the serpent there, In another nest.
This is his poison: that we should disbelieve even that.	

Unlike *Credences of Summer,* which staved off interrogation as long as it could, *The Auroras of Autumn* encourages the anatomy of the season, and the analytic questions which form so strong a thread in the construction of the poem begin in the fourth line of the first canto. Stevens' demanding intellectuality stops in the midst of summer to imagine winter because it is natural to him to be reflective and abstract, even idly metaphysical, because he "likes magnificence/ And the solemn pleasures of magnificent space" (vi). But there are two manners of the analytic moment. One rests in the metaphor, say, of the serpent, and keeping the vehicle intact asks whether this moment is "another wriggling out of the egg"; the other sort departs from the original metaphor, and inventing surrogate poet-selves (like the inhuman author in *Credences of Summer* or his counterpart the spectre of the spheres in *The Auroras of Autumn*) uses these supplementary selves to pose the questions.

By the time Stevens reaches out to his disembodied spectre he has stepped considerably beyond the autumnal moment, and at the end, he converses with the rabbi in speculative and generalizing terms, juggling his combinations of happiness and unhappiness. With a wrench, at the end of the last canto, he returns to his original autumnal and auroral metaphors, and only retrieves his balance in the final tercet, where the spectre is violently set down to live all lives,

That he might know

In hall harridan, not hushful paradise,
To a haggling of wind and weather, by these lights
Like a blaze of summer straw, in winter's nick. (x)

The energy of repudiation directed toward *Credence of Summer* in *The Auroras of Autumn* is nowhere clearer than in this igniting of the Oley hay mows. As they go up in flame, in a blaze of summer straw, they produce the streamers of the auroras, and the hushful paradise of August gives way to the hall harridan, a fit locale for "the harridan self and ever maladive fate" that went crying through the autumn leaves in *Owl's Clover.* Like the inhuman author of *Credences of Summer* who meditates with the gold bugs, and like the serpent who meditates in the ferns, the spectre meditates a whole as he lives all lives, and the whole that he envisages is to be, in some season, relentlessly in possession of happiness by being relentless in knowledge. Someday, Stevens hopes, we may find

The possible nest in the invisible tree,
Which in a composite season, now unknown,
Denied, dismissed, may hold a serpent, loud
In our captious hymns, erect and sinuous,
Whose venom and whose wisdom will be one. (437)

But that new composite androgynous stability of serpent and nest, described in "St. John and the Backache," is not attained in *The Auroras of Autumn*, which remains bound in its glittering motion, a brilliant reproduction of Stevens' apprehensive compulsion in change.

To the extent that *The Auroras of Autumn* remains a poem of the sky and motion, it is a dazzling performance. Indoors, it weakens, and it falters in its regressive motion toward childhood, before the serpent entered Eden. The first canto summons up three manifestations of the Fate-serpent, which are rapidly reduced to two, as the visionary image of the serpent transcendent, relentless in happiness, belonging purely to an airy nest, is dismissed. The other two levels of being remain. One is the simple animal nature of the serpent as he lives in the ferns, on the rock, in the grass, like an Indian in a glade, native and hidden; in this nature his head is wholly zoological—flecked, black-beaded, visible. The serpent's pure bestiality makes us disbelieve in his possible transcendence; we are sure of his naturalness as he moves to make sure of sun. But in contrast, there is the changeable serpent, whose head has become air, whose tip is higher than the stars, whose nest is not the low grass but yet is still the earth, this time the earth in total panorama:

> This is his nest,
> These fields, these hills, these tinted distances,
> And the pines above and along and beside the sea.

This changeable serpent lives in present participles, gulping, wriggling, flashing, and emerging, and he is the true genius of the poem. The wholly natural beast, at ease in the glade, is the presiding spirit of Stevens' willful wish, even here, to be entirely at home in the world, to be an Indian in America, an aborigine indigenous to the place. The children who appear in the poem are the regressive human embodiment of the Indian-serpent, which in its pristine innocence is a biological serpent native to Eden, not an interloping malice. This serpent is dismissed in favor of the grimmer changing one, and the epigraph to *The Auroras of Autumn* could well be Donne's harsh couplet from "Twicknam Garden":

> And that this place may thoroughly be thought
> True paradise, I have the serpent brought.

Like Donne, "blasted with sighs" in spite of the garden, Stevens here bids farewell to the idea which engendered *Credences of Summer*—the idea that one could give credence to summer, that the mind could lay by its trouble, that honey could be hived and a festival held. "As the Eye altering, alters all," the luxuriant haymows bleach to an expanse of desolate sand.

The four cantos that follow the appearance of the serpent are like the scenes following an overture. The overture is the warning—hard-surfaced, intellectual, abstract—but the scenes are elegiac, subtle, personal, "toned" as the overture was not. In the last canto of the four (canto v), the elegiac tone is routed in disorder, and the cause of the rout seems to be a surge of violent disgust for the mythologized father of the poem, who is a mixture of Prospero and Caliban. In his Prospero-role, the father "fetches tellers of tales/ And musicians;" he "fetches pageants out of air,/ Scenes of the theatre, vistas and blocks of woods/ And curtains like a naive pretence of sleep." But as Caliban, the father grossly fetches negresses and "unherded herds,/ Of barbarous tongue, slavered and panting halves of breath." The second perspective wins, finally, as the speaker brutalizes the pageant:

We stand in the tumult of a festival.

What festival? This loud, disordered mooch?
These hospitaliers? These brute-like guests?
These musicians dubbing at a tragedy

A-dub, a-dub, which is made up of this:
That there are no lines to speak? There is no play.
Or, the persons act one merely by being here. (v)

With this dismissal of the characters of the inhuman author Stevens turns the
puppet theater into a happening with no script. The central figure of the
father is rendered barbarous by the iterative sentence pattern into which he
is confined. Whereas the mother "invites humanity to her house/ And table"
the father "fetches" things and people, and the phrase "the father fetches" is
four times repeated in identical form, three times repeated in identical line
position, till the father is made an automatic robot. Under this manipulation,
the natural ripeness of *Credences of Summer* becomes the decadent and self-
involved ripeness of the negresses who "dance/ Among the children, like
curious ripenesses/ Of pattern in the dance's ripening." The marriage hymns
of Oley are replaced by the "insidious tones" of the musicians who are
"clawing the sing-song of their instruments" at the father's behest. The
source of the disgust for the father-impresario seems to be Stevens' revulsion
against that deliberate primitivism of his own which wants summer, not
winter, and which sets itself to conjure up negresses, guitarists, and the
"unherded herds" of oxlike freed men, all in a vain attempt to reproduce on
an ignorant and one-stringed instrument the sophisticated chaos of the self.

But before he arrives at this recoil against his harmonium's cruder
subterfuges, Stevens gives us the beautiful triad of poems each beginning
"Farewell to an idea," where his elegy reaches a perfection of naturalness and
subdued restraint hardly possible in earlier long poems. These three cantos
are an elegy written before the fact, an anticipatory mourning in which "a
darkness gathers though it does not fall." The first (canto ii) is a brilliant
exercise in more and less—a little more in one place, a little less somewhere
else—but in this season even more is less, since the positive comparatives are
mostly pejorative: the white of the flowers grows duller, and the lines of the
beach grow longer and emptier. Some equivocation remains in the
comparisons, but the direction of atrophy is clear.

Stevens' tendency in the first elegiac canto is to match unequivocal
notations of skeletal whiteness against extremely conjectural modifiers of

that whiteness: his mind, in other words, must admit the phenomenon, but will not for a long time admit its significance. Instead, it casts around for ways of explaining this whiteness, or ways of softening its harshness. The scene develops brilliantly by slow increments, beginning with a sketched line:

> Farewell to an idea ... A cabin stands,
> Deserted, on a beach. It is white.

The mind immediately skitters off into harmless explanations of that whiteness:

> It is white,
> As by a custom or according to
> An ancestral theme or as a consequence
> Of an infinite course.

As soon as Stevens begins on a multiplicity of "or's" we sense his uneasiness. The deadly observant eye returns, and notes that

> The flowers against the wall
> Are white.

But again the qualifiers multiply in haste and confuse the issue beyond any possible clarity: the flowers

> Are white, a little dried, a kind of mark
>
> Reminding, trying to remind, of a white
> That was different, something else, last year
> Or before, not the white of an aging afternoon.
>
> Whether fresher or duller, whether of winter cloud
> Or of winter sky, from horizon to horizon.

Every means is used to distract the attention from the adamant dry whiteness of the flowers, including the rephrasing of "reminding," the evasiveness about time, the unwillingness to decide between fresher and duller, and the uncertainty about cloud or sky. But the relentless eye is not to be put off, and now it is joined in its infallible perception by the whole body, which senses, in the same flat sentence-form used for the eye's notations, that

The wind is blowing the sand across the floor.

With that union of the white sand to the white cabin and the white flowers, the joining is made between the total atmosphere, dominated by the wind, and the deserted cabin, its floors tenanted only by sand. The totality of whiteness is at last admitted wholly:

Here, being visible is being white.

The scene becomes a white-on-white bas-relief, "the solid of white, the accomplishment/ Of an extremist in an exercise."
    With this submission to the truth, the mind has left its deceits, and the declarative statements become dominant and unequivocal:

The season changes. A cold wind chills the beach.
The long lines of it grow longer, emptier,
A darkness gathers though it does not fall

And the whiteness grows less vivid on the wall.

The severity of the language justifies a daring play on words:

The man who is walking turns blankly on the sand.

The man, to use Milton's words, has been presented with a universal blank, and becomes himself blanched and blank, like the scene. But because he has finally granted the desolate whiteness in the landscape, he can give up looking to it for sustenance, and can turn his fixed gaze away from the beach and to the sky. What he sees, inhuman though it is, repays his glance: he sees, but only after he has abjured land-flowerings, the great gusts and colored sweeps of the Northern lights, and they are exhilarating:

He observes how the north is always enlarging the change

With its frigid brilliances, its blue-red sweeps
And gusts of great enkindlings, its polar green,
The color of ice and fire and solitude.

The verbal parallels between the celestial aurora and the chilling earthly wind make us realize that the one does not exist without the other, that they are two manifestations of the same force. The identification is made first syntactically: "the wind is blowing" and "the north is ... enlarging the change" are the canto's only independent clauses in the continuous present. Later, the parallel is made metaphorically, as Stevens borrows the vocabulary of wind in composing his auroras of "sweeps" and "gusts." For the moment, the enkindling fire of the auroras is not metaphorically reinforced, but the fiery color later gives rise to other burnings in the poem, ending in the wonderful invention of "the blaze of summer straw," when Oley goes up in flames.

The splendor of desolation in the sight of Crispin's deserted cabin is not matched again in the poem until the final cantos regather their energies after the repudiation of the father. But there are gentler moments, in which Stevens surmounts the dangers of pathos by having his "observant" eye, not his rhapsodic one, note his fading tableaux. As he watches the dissolving mother (iii), he phrases the scene in short empty sentences, the fatal notation of necessity:[6]

> Farewell to an idea ...
> The mother's face, the purpose of the poem, fills the room.
> They are together, here, and it is warm, with none of the
>   prescience of oncoming dreams.
> It is evening.
> The house is evening, half-dissolved.
> Only the half they can never possess remains, still-starred.
> It is the mother they possess, who gives transparence to
>   their present peace.
> She makes that gentler that can gentle be.
> And yet she too is dissolved, she is destroyed.
> She gives transparence.
> But she has grown old.
> The necklace is a carving not a kiss.
> The soft hands are a motion not a touch.
> The house will crumble and the books will burn.

This canto depends on the continuing antithesis of the beauty and the dissolution of the mother, an antithesis which reaches its strictest point in the two rigid sentences at the center of the poem: "She gives transparence. But she has grown old." The images of this canto and of the next are quarried from the early ode "To the One of Fictive Music," but the imposition of the stern syntactic form on the yielding lyric material makes for a new sort of nostalgia. The modulation from statement to prophecy is made so unobtrusively that we scarcely notice it until it has happened:

> She gives transparence. But she has grown old.
> The necklace is a carving not a kiss.
>
> The soft hands are a motion not a touch.
> The house will crumble and the books will burn.

These four symmetrical lines are so tonelessly uttered that the fourth seems as unarguable, as much a natural fact, as the preceding three. But the effect of the intensification into prophecy is to send the mind rapidly back to the lulling present of the unsuspecting family:

> They are at ease in a shelter of the mind
>
> And the house is of the mind and they and time,
> Together, all together.

The prophecy reappears, but in a softened rephrasing, first in the deceptive appearance of the approaching consuming fire:

> Boreal night
> Will look like frost as it approaches them
>
> And to the mother as she falls asleep
> And as they say good-night, good-night.

And the inevitable extinction of the family is announced in a sinister but understated mention of the extinguished lights in the bedchambers, lit now only by the flaring auroras outside:

> Upstairs
> The windows will be lighted, not the rooms.

Finally, though, these mitigations and evasions give way to the peremptory doom:

> The wind will spread its windy grandeurs round
> And knock like a rifle-butt against the door.
> The wind will command them with invincible sound.

Stevens' simplicity of response to the mythological mother is replaced in the next canto (iv) by his ambivalent attentions to the father. On the one hand, the father is descended from the outmoded Jehovah figures, giants, mythy Joves, and so on, of earlier poems, but on the other hand, he has agreeable qualities in common with both Canon Aspirin and the angel of *Notes toward a Supreme Fiction*, those acrobatic seraphic figures who leap through space. Stevens' language becomes archaic, as the father is said to sit "as one that is strong in the bushes of his eyes," with a pun on bushy eyebrows and the burning bush. He sits in "green-a-day" (another reminiscence of *Credences of Summer*), but is also perpetually in motion, just as "green-a-day" is also "bleak regard"; he stops in summer to imagine winter, and his rapid oscillations from saying no to no and yes to yes and yes to no are imitated in the poem by the oscillations between the moving and the motionless. Like the girl at Key West who "measured to the hour its solitude" he "measures the velocities of change," and by his motion establishes a norm of nature; but unlike the singing girl, the father is sometimes comic, as "he leaps from heaven to heaven more rapidly/ Than bad angels leap from heaven to hell in flames." The tension of attitudes mounts as Stevens constructs an apotheosis of the father, moving fully into the regressive diction of "To the One of Fictive Music":

> Master O master seated by the fire
> And yet in space and motionless and yet
> Of motion the ever-brightening origin,
>
> Profound, and yet the king and yet the crown—

The sentimental effort breaks here, as Stevens brusquely forsakes his celebratory incantation-weaving and says dismissively:

> Look at this present throne. What company,
> In masks, can choir it with the naked wind?

Exit the whole shebang, as Stevens had said earlier about Crispin's fiction, and with this dismissal we leave, not only this scene, but the throne and the motley company of *Credences of Summer.* The autumnal wind has blown pretenses away, and the creator-father becomes, in consequence, the object of contempt, the "fetcher" of negresses and clawing musicians and slavering herds, the hospitalier of a disorderly riot.[7] With this denial of meaning to poetic gesture, the first half of the poem comes to a close, in a cynicism that touches both the events and their poems: "There are no lines to speak. There is no play."

One could hardly have guessed where the poem might go from here. *Credences of Summer*, too, had come to a halt halfway through, and had had to rephrase itself, first in celestial and then in "low" terms, in order to deal with its original tableau of mountain, tower, and man. Here, Stevens saves himself by forsaking for a moment his family myth and looking again at the auroras. Earlier, they had only been sketched for us; we saw them once directly in the view of the man on the sand, in a vivid blur of motion and color; and later we saw them obliquely, in their sinister approach, when "boreal light/ Will look like frost" as it lights the windows. But now, two great cantos (vi and vii) are devoted to a panorama of the auroras, the first giving a physical account, the second a metaphysical one. We have finally arrived at that anatomy of summer that Stevens had so hoped to postpone, since summer, anatomized, turns immediately to winter.

The first canto (vi) is exquisitely undemanding, as Stevens is content to imagine no revelatory function for the auroras, no purpose to their activity, simply change for the sake of change, transformation idly done "to no end." The absolute parity of all forms is established, emergence equals collapse in interest and beauty, and activity exists for the time being without dénouement. The mountain of *Credences of Summer* is no longer half green, half rocklike air—nothing so stolid as that. In the boreal night the mountain is now rock, water, light, and clouds, all at once, as Stevens describes the aurora:

It is a theatre floating through the clouds,
Itself a cloud, although of misted rock
And mountains running like water, wave on wave,

Through waves of light.

These transformations of the sky occur as an enormous relief to Stevens, as he feels momentarily that he can give up the difficult labor of willed imaginative transformation: the sky will do it all for him. In the past, he had usually represented nature as the fixed principle, and the interpreting mind as the chief source of change: even in "Sea Surface full of Clouds" the variable surface is pressed into doctrinal service, and the changes have to be seen as symbolic and ordered. In more violently willed transformations, the mind plants in the sky a converse to the monotony of time and place, rather as it placed the jar in Tennessee:

Human Arrangement

Place-bound and time-bound in evening rain
And bound by a sound which does not change,

Except that it begins and ends,
Begins again and ends again—

Rain without change within or from
Without. In this place and in this time

And in this sound, which do not change,
In which the rain is all one thing,

In the sky, an imagined, wooden chair
Is the clear-point of an edifice,

Forced up from nothing, evening's chair,
Blue-strutted curule, true—unreal,

The centre of transformations that
Transform for transformation's self,

In a glitter that is a life, a gold
That is a being, a will, a fate.   (363)

This forced transformation, set up in defiance of the monotonous scene, reminds us of Stevens' apocalyptic transformations, nowhere more baldly put than in *Owl's Clover*, where the porcelain muses are to repeat *To Be Itself*,

Until the sharply colored glass transforms
Itself into the speech of the spirit.

Such transformations are one-directional, lifting the subject up a notch from the real to the unreal. But the beautiful transformations of the aurora are directionless:

          ... It is of cloud transformed
To cloud transformed again, idly, the way
A season changes color to no end.

Except the lavishing of itself in change,
As light changes yellow into gold and gold
To its opal elements and fire's delight,

Splashed wide-wise because it likes magnificence
And the solemn pleasures of magnificent space.
The cloud drifts idly through half-thought-of forms.

In these childlike phrases, we sense the "innocence" Stevens will later claim for the aurora: it is "splashed wide-wise," it "likes magnificence," it likes the "solemn pleasures" of its playground, magnificent space.

This will to change of the aurora is rather like the will to change of the west wind (in *Notes*, It Must Change, x), in which metaphor is seen as something we imitate from nature, from this "volatile world." The will of *Notes* was directed, human, urgent, "A will to change, a necessitous/ And present way"; the aurora's will is idle, purposeless, lavish, purely pleasurable, and inhuman. Against the aurora there suddenly appear terrified birds, surrogates for the poet as he recoils from the aurora's meaningless if gorgeous will-to-change:

The theatre is filled with flying birds,
Wild wedges, as of a volcano's smoke, palm-eyed
And vanishing, a web in a corridor

Or massive portico.

This matches Tennyson's recoil from the perception of a purposeless universe, as Sorrow speaks to him in *In Memoriam:*

"The stars," she whispered, "blindly run,
A web is woven about the sky."

The surrealism of the birds, dehumanized into wedges, made fluid in form like the auroras themselves, startling and evanescent as spurting smoke, tenuous as a web, and mysteriously palm-eyed, is the surrealism of the poet's terrified response as he feels himself momentarily caught up into the metamorphoses of the lights, absorbed into a nature constantly shifting shape. With an effort of mind he rejects the temptation to be drawn into the undertow of these waves, and sets his scholar of one candle against "the earth's whole amplitude and Nature's multiform power consign'd for once to colors," as Whitman once said of a prairie sunset. It is up to the scholar to destroy the aurora, this named thing, and render it nameless by seeing it as a new phenomenon. The intellectual formulation here is suspect and should not be scrutinized, but the confrontation that follows, as the single man opens the door of his house on flames, is a worthy climax to the poem:

> The scholar of one candle sees
> An Arctic effulgence flaring on the frame
> Of everything he is. And he feels afraid.

As changeful light, the aurora is innocent; as flame, it is dangerous; as cold fire, Arctic effulgence, it is the intimidating unknown. Stevens, in this version of "the multiform beauty" (*OP*, 12), has found the final correlative for his reflections on middle age and for the fear and fascination of ongoing process.

When Stevens passes from these illustrations of the aurora to an analysis of it, the advance on *Credences of Summer* is most visible. Instead of the rather sterile playing-off of the day against the year, the queen against her kin, and the soldier against the land, those social and communal questions always less than urgent to Stevens, we encounter a question more immediate to him, as it was to Keats: why it is, and how it is, that the dreamer venoms all his days, and cannot know, as other men do, the pain alone, the joy alone, distinct. Stevens advances in fact (in canto vii) to three questions—his last great interrogation of the world, since he will come, in *An Ordinary Evening in New Haven*, to pure declaration. The first question examines the necessary passage from the pastoral to the tragic:

> Is there an imagination that sits enthroned
> As grim as it is benevolent, the just
> And the unjust, which in the midst of summer stops
>
> To imagine winter?

The summer throne of "quiet and green-a-day" has stiffened itself into the throne of Rhadamanthus, and the father's motion from heaven to heaven now becomes more like a leap from heaven to hell. Stevens' second question personifies the leaper, now robed and composed in the deathly magnificence of the auroras:

> When the leaves are dead,
> Does it take its place in the north and enfold itself,
> Goat-leaper, crystalled and luminous, sitting
>
> In highest night?

The third question asks, in a cold horror, and with an echo of the Psalms, what indeed these heavens proclaim: what is the source of the aurora's splendid contrast of black sky with white light; is it true that it adorns itself in black by extinguishing planets in its snowy radiance, and does it leave unextinguished only those planets it decides to retain for its own starry crown?

> And do these heavens adorn
> And proclaim it, the white creator of black, jetted
> By extinguishings, even of planets as may be,
>
> Even of earth, even of sight, in snow,
> Except as needed by way of majesty,
> In the sky, as crown and diamond cabala?

The absolute accuracy of these suspicions is confirmed as Stevens answers his own questions in precisely the fated terms of his previous formulation, repeating the leaps and the extinguishings; but putting them, this time, not as nouns, but as instant verbs:

> It leaps through us, through all our heavens leaps,
> Extinguishing our planets, one by one,
> Leaving, of where we were and looked, of where
>
> We knew each other and of each other thought,
> A shivering residue, chilled and foregone,
> Except for that crown and mystical cabala.

We remain finally only as an adjunct to that diadem which has so swallowed up the known. "To see the gods dispelled in midair ... is one of the great human experiences ... We shared likewise this experience of annihilation. It was their annihilation, not ours, and yet it left us feeling that in a measure, we, too, had been annihilated. It left us feeling dispossessed and alone in a solitude, like children without parents, in a home that seemed deserted." These sentences from "Two or Three Ideas" (*OP,* 206–207) are not the only possible gloss on *The Auroras of Autumn*, but they are a partial one: on the one hand the great experience of extinction, leaving a hard brilliance like the diamond crown in the impersonal universe, and on the other hand, the dispossessed children, a shivering residue. A superb and unyielding glitter surmounts everything else in these lines, as it dwarfs with its energy and regality the pathos of the disinherited spectators.

But Sevens will not rest in the sublime. True to its nature, the tragic imagination must beget its opposite. As we went from untroubled summer to winter fatality, we now reverse direction, and go "from destiny to slight caprice." The only force regulating the leaper is its necessary polarity: "it dare not leap by chance," but it moves to unmake itself in comic flippancy—or so Stevens says. *The Auroras of Autumn* itself does not rediscover summer in winter after having discovered winter in summer. It is hard to imagine what might undo the aurora borealis, as the aurora "undid" summer. Stevens becomes purely referential:

> And thus its jetted tragedy, its stele
>
> And shape and mournful making move to find
> What must unmake it and, at last, what can,
> Say, a flippant communication under the moon.

This seems an imposed order, not a discovered one, and Stevens' uneasiness with it is visible in his inference from "must" to "can." In later poems, Stevens will "unmake" tragedy, not through flippancy but through a withdrawal from the theatrical mode in which the tragic perception voices itself. From questions, dramas, theaters, histrionics, brilliancies, we pass in Stevens' work to a sober declarativeness. Here, and for the moment, in canto viii, all that Stevens can summon up are gestures of willed assertion:

> But [innocence] exists,
> It exists, it is visible, it is, it is.

In this wish, the mother is replaced by a dream-vision of her absent self, no longer old but rejuvenated, and the imaginary quality of the vision is reinforced by the fictive "as if":

> So then, these lights are not a spell of light,
> A saying out of a cloud, but innocence.
> An innocence of the earth and no false sign

Or symbol of malice. That we partake thereof,
Lie down like children in this holiness,
As if, awake, we lay in the quiet of sleep,

As if the innocent mother sang in the dark
Of the room and on an accordion, half-heard,
Created the time and place in which we breathed ...

We have already seen the wintry fear "unmade" by an imagined comedy or
flippancy; now we are offered a resolution by a pure ethereality. But this
moving ending, attached to a stanza that began in the arid vein of *Description
without Place*, in a toying with the philosophical mode, makes a centaurlike
poem, half abstract discussion, half wish-fantasy, with no middle term of the
real to join these two detached poles of the unreal. The ninth canto makes a
lulling effort to assimilate terror and innocence, affirming simply that disaster

May come tomorrow in the simplest word,
Almost as part of innocence, almost,
Almost as the tenderest and the truest part.

But what is remembered of this poem is not that assumed naïveté, but the
etched anticipation of a secularized doomsday:

Shall we be found hanging in the trees next spring?
Of what disaster is this the imminence:
Bare limbs, bare trees and a wind as sharp as salt?

As before, Stevens answers his own question, this time pairing the earthly
wasteland with its wonderfully burnished cause, a mustering of the heavenly
army:

The stars are putting on their glittering belts.
They throw around their shoulders cloaks that flash
Like a great shadow's last embellishment.

Here, as in the last lines of *The Auroras*, Stevens is remembering a passage in
Owl's Clover on evening, where the old woman spoils the being of the night:

Without her, evening like a budding yew,
Would soon be brilliant, as it was, before

The harridan self and ever-maladive fate
Went crying their desolate syllables, before
Their voice and the voice of the tortured wind were one ...

That uninhabited evening would have a sky "thick with stars/ Of a lunar light, dark belted sorcerers," and Stevens would wish to be free of the old woman so that he could "flourish the great cloak we wear/ At night, to turn away from the abominable/ Farewells" (*OP*, 45, 46, 71), those farewells that begin *The Auroras of Autumn*. Our disaster (and Stevens would have been conscious of the etymology of the word) is in fact the gathering of the stars, and the green-queen-like embellishments of summer yield to a different kind of jewels. To see the stars in this way is to awake from the stolid sensual drowse of the Danes in Denmark, "for whom the outlandish was [only] another day/ Of the week, [just slightly] queerer than Sunday." Exposed to the auroras, Stevens, like Melville's dying soldier, has been "enlightened by the glare," and the final flippancy of the last canto, juggling discrepant phases of man's feelings and the world's landscapes, still yields, at the end, to the total reign of the auroras, "these lights/ Like a blaze of summer straw, in winter's nick." It is these flaring lights, and the apprehensive questions they raise, that are the radiant center of the poem: Stevens' theatrical auroras and his repeated interrogations of them create his most ravishing lines. From this, the most economical and yet the most brilliant of his long poems, he will pass on to the looser and quieter recapitulations of *An Ordinary Evening in New Haven*.

NOTES

1. *Credences of Summer* was first published in *Transport to Summer* (Knopf, 1947). *The Auroras of Autumn* followed the next year in *The Kenyon Review*, 10 (Winter 1948): 1–10, and was republished in the volume of which it was the title poem (Knopf, 1950).

2. Frank Kermode's simplistic account of Stevens' "tone of rapture" in his "total satisfaction, the moment of total summer ... the paradise of living as and where one lives," in this "passionate celebration of this August heat" (*Wallace Stevens*, pp. 106–107) has been somewhat corrected by later readers. Joseph Riddel, for instance, sees a "lingering nostalgia" but concludes that "it is a time for marriages, for balances" (*The Clairvoyant Eye*, pp. 218, 223), a phrase which scants Stevens' own uneasiness that will find full voice in *The Auroras of Autumn*.

3. See "Wallace Stevens" by Michael Lafferty, *Historical Review of Berks County*, 24 (Fall 1959): 108: "The whole series, 'Credences of Summer,' seems written in reminiscence of a hike over Mount Penn, from whose Tower Stevens could see 'Oley, too rich for enigmas.'"

4. It seems possible that Stevens' central construct in *Credences of Summer*—the mountain, the throne, the old man—may owe something to Wordsworth's *Excursion* (IX, 48ff):

Rightly it is said
That man descends into the VALE of years.
Yet have I thought that we might also speak,
And not presumptuously, I trust, of Age,
As of a final EMINENCE; though bare
In aspect and forbidding, yet a point
On which 'tis not impossible to sit
In awful sovereignty; a place of power,
A throne, that may be likened unto his,
Who, in some placid day of summer, looks
Down from a mountain-top,—say one of those
High peaks, that bound the vale where now we are.
Faint, and diminished to the gazing eye,
Forest and field, and hill and dale appear,
With all the shapes over their surface spread.

5. Harold Bloom in "The Central Man," *Massachusetts Review*, 7 (Winter 1966): 38, cites Emerson and Dickinson as other users of the image of the auroras.

6. I adopt here the punctuation of the first printing of *The Auroras of Autumn* in the *Kenyon Review*. The sense and cadence of this passage seem to require a period, not a comma, after "dreams," and the *Collected Poems* has no absolute authority. There is no punctuation at all, for instance, in the *Collected Poems* following the word "base" (*Auroras* i, l.13) though something is clearly needed. The *KR* version has Stevens' familiar three periods. In vi, the *KR* does not have the hyphens in "half-thought-of," and it has a simple period instead of three periods after l.18. There is also a simple period closing viii. The next edition of Stevens will doubtless be a variorum.

7. I have been told by Harold Bloom that Chatillon is the proper name of a Renaissance translator of the Bible from Hebrew into Latin and French, one Sebastián Castellio (1515–1563), or Castalion, as he is sometimes called (see *Enciclopedia Universal Illustrada*, Madrid, *s.v. Castalion*). The passage remains obscure, and perhaps the choice of name may rather be dictated by Stevens' recurrent châteaux, built by his figures resembling, in their desire for a *mise-en-scène*, the father of *Auroras*. See, for instance, "Architecture," an early poem later dropped from *Harmonium*:

Architecture

What manner of building shall we build?
Let us design a chastel de chasteté.
De pensée ...

In this house, what manner of utterance shall there be?
What heavenly dithyramb
And cantilene?
What niggling forms of gargoyle patter?

And how shall those come vested that come there?
In their ugly reminders?

Or gaudy as tulips? ...
As they climb the flights
To the closes
Overlooking whole seasons?

Let us build the building of light.
Push up the towers to the cock-tops.
These are the pointings of our edifice,
Which, like a gorgeous palm,
Shall tuft the commonplace.

                                        ...

How [shall we] carve the violet moon
To set in nicks? (*OP*, 16–17)

This sketchy poem reads like a first draft of the idea for *Credences of Summer* and *The Auroras of Autumn*, both poems composed in "the closes/ Overlooking whole seasons." The tower, the company of actors, their speech, their garments, even the word nick (though perhaps in a different sense) are all points in common, as is the prescribing of a ritual.

ROBERT LANGBAUM

New Modes of Characterization in
The Waste Land

One sign of a great poem is that it continues to grow in meaning. A new generation of readers can find in the poem their own preoccupations, and can use those preoccupations to illuminate the poem, to find new meanings in it. Presumably the poem contains the germ of all these accrued meanings; that is why it is great and endures. Certainly no poem ever seemed more of its time than *The Waste Land*, which expressed, as we used to hear, the despair and disillusion of the twenties. Yet a survey of *Waste Land* criticism illustrates perfectly the reciprocal relationship between poem and criticism in the growth, indeed transformation, of a poem's meaning.

The first stunned, admiring critics—Conrad Aiken in 1923, I.A. Richards in 1926—saw the poem as completely incoherent and completely negative in meaning. Richards saw Eliot as "accurately describing the contemporary state of mind ... by effecting a complete severance between his poetry and *all* beliefs," and remarked "the absence of any coherent intellectual thread upon which the items of the poem are strung." F.R. Leavis (1932) saw in the note on Tiresias a clue to the poem's unity as the unity of "an inclusive consciousness," but saw no progression: "the poem ends where it began." Really constructive criticism begins with F.O. Matthiessen (1935) and continues with such critics as Cleanth Brooks (1939) and George Williamson (1953), who, taking Eliot's notes seriously, find progression, unity, and positive meaning through the built-in analogy with the Grail and

From *Eliot in His Time: Essays on the Occasion of the Fiftieth Anniversary of The Waste Land.* © 1973 by Princeton University Press.

vegetation myths. Hugh Kenner (1959) is therefore retrograde in taking off from Pound's later recollection of the original draft as "a series of poems," and in considering that Eliot, dismayed by what he and Pound had wrought through cutting, added the note on Tiresias as an afterthought "to supply the poem with a nameable, point of view" that was not really there.[1]

Yet Eliot himself insisted in 1923 that *"The Waste Land* is intended to form a whole."[2] Pound, in his letters of 1921–1922, always referred to *the* poem and showed his sense of its unity by advising Eliot not to omit Phlebas, because "Phlebas is an integral part of the poem; the card pack introduces him, the drowned phoen. sailor."[3] The original draft, now that it has been published, shows Tiresias as we now have him and shows the same organization as the final version.[4] Eliot tried to combine even more disparate fragments than in the final version; Pound cut out the fragments that were at once least successful and most disparate in tone. Even Mr. Kenner refers more than once to "the protagonist," without specifying who he is or how he happens to exist at all in "a series of poems."

The protagonist, Tiresias, and the relation between them present the next problem for *Waste Land* criticism; even the constructive critics have fallen short here. In building upon the work of these critics, I have the advantage of Mr. Kenner's suggestions as to the importance of Bradley and Eliot's doctoral dissertation on Bradley for understanding Eliot's modes of characterization. I have the advantage of the recently published dissertation[5] and of the newly published original draft of *The Waste Land* with Pound's annotations. But my main advantage is the preoccupation of the last decade with problems of identity—a preoccupation that has caused me to single out this question and to try to show that the next step in understanding the structure and meaning of *The Waste Land*, in understanding its continuing greatness and relevance, is to understand that the poem is organized around new concepts of identity and new modes of characterization, concepts and modes that Eliot had been working toward in the poems preceding *The Waste Land*.

Prufrock, as we all know by now, takes two aspects of his conscious self ("Let us go then, you and I") to that party where he ought to, but does not, make the sexual proposal that could have saved him. Prufrock's sensuous apprehension reveals also a buried libidinal self that he cannot make operative in the social world, cannot reconcile with the constructed self seen by "The eyes that fix you in a formulated phrase." In the end he makes the split complete by constructing for the regard of his other conscious self a Prufrock as removed as possible from the libidinal self.

> I grow old ... I grow old ...
> I shall wear the bottoms of my trousers rolled.
>
> Shall I part my hair behind? Do I dare to eat
>   a peach?
> I shall wear white flannel trousers, and walk upon
>   the beach.[6]

The timid, sexless old man does, however, walk upon the beach, where—in the final passage that brings to a climax the imagery of ocean (yellow fog, "restaurants with oyster shells") as suggesting sex and unconsciousness—he hears in the sounds of the waves mermaids singing, not to him, but to each other. By relegating his libidinal self to fantasy, Prufrock makes the split wider than ever. He thus avoids sex; he sings his love song to his other conscious self, while the girls sing to each other.

This is Eliot's way of handling character in the early poems. The conscious self is mechanical, constructed, dead; but it has, as its one last sign of vitality, sudden, momentary accesses to a buried libidinal life—accesses that only deepen the split between unconsciousness and self-regarding consciousness. Even the utterly blank young man in the satirical "Portrait of a Lady"—who puts on "faces" to cover his lack of response to the lady's advances, just as he keeps his "countenance" before the miscellaneous, spectacular happenings in the newspapers—even this emotionally dead young man has momentary access to a libidinal life recalling at least things *other* people have desired:

> I keep my countenance,
> I remain self-possessed
> Except when a street-piano, mechanical and tired
> Reiterates some worn-out common song
> With the smell of hyacinths across the garden
> Recalling things that other people have desired.
> Are these ideas right or wrong?

The pattern, distinctively post-romantic, is to be found in a poem like Arnold's "The Buried Life." The romanticists portray the conscious self as connected with the unconscious and suffused with its vitality. In "The Buried Life," however, Arnold portrays our conscious existence as an unenergetic "Eddying at large in blind uncertainty." "Tricked in disguises, alien to the rest/ Of men, and alien to themselves," men are cut off from their unconscious self—except for an inexplicable nostalgia:

But often, in the world's most crowded streets,
But often, in the din of strife,
There rises an unspeakable desire
After the knowledge of our buried life.

And sometimes, in rare erotic moments, we have access to our buried self:

A bolt is shot back somewhere in our breast,
And a lost pulse of feeling stirs again.
The eye sinks inward, and the heart lies plain,
And what we mean, we say, and what we would, we
    know.
A man becomes aware of his life's flow,
And hears its winding murmur; and he sees
The meadows where it glides, the sun, the breeze.

The buried self is non-individual; it is the life force. It is well that it is buried,
for man would with his meddling intellect "well-nigh change his own
identity," but is in spite of himself carried, by the unregarded river in his
breast, to the fulfillment of his biological destiny and "genuine self."

In Eliot, the self is buried even deeper than in Arnold and is even less
individual. The buried self is, in *The Waste Land*, extended in time through
unconscious racial memory. When the upper-class lady, aware of inner
vacancy, asks: "'What shall I do now? What shall I do?/ ... What shall we do
tomorrow?/ What shall we ever do?'"—the protagonist answers by
describing the routine of their life:

The hot water at ten.
And if it rains, a closed car at four.
And we shall play a game of chess,
Pressing lidless eyes and waiting for a knock upon
    the door.

On the surface, his answer confirms her sense of vacancy; we shall fill our
lives, he is saying, with meaningless routines. But there is also a positive
implication, deriving from the poem's underlying patterns, that these
routines are unconscious repetitions of ancient rituals. The morning bath
recalls rituals of purification and rebirth through water. The game of chess
recalls not only the game played in Middleton's *Women Beware Women* while
destiny works itself out behind the door, but also all the games, including the

Tarot cards, by which men have tried to foresee and manipulate destiny while waiting for its inevitable arrival. It is the consciousness of the poem blending imperceptibly with the protagonist's consciousness that makes us aware of what the protagonist can only know unconsciously.

As in Arnold's poem, the characters are, in spite of themselves, living their buried life; but they do this not only through personal, but also through racial memory, through unconsciously making rituals even when they think they have abolished all rituals. Similarly, the personal libidinal associations of music and hyacinths in "Portrait of a Lady" become in *The Waste Land* unconscious memories of ancient rituals and myths. The poem's awareness makes us remember consciously what the protagonist, in recalling the Hyacinth garden, remembers unconsciously—that Hyacinth was a fertility god.

When Eliot, in reviewing *Ulysses* for *The Dial* of November 1923, said that Joyce had discovered in the "continuous parallel between contemporaneity and antiquity" a way of giving shape and significance to modern "futility and anarchy," he surely had in mind his own method in *The Waste Land*, published like *Ulysses* the year before and possibly influenced by it since Eliot read the latter part in manuscript in 1921 when he was just beginning *The Waste Land*.[7] This "mythical method," as Eliot called it, allows the writer to be naturalistic, to portray modern chaos, while suggesting through psychological naturalism a continuing buried life that rises irrepressibly into those shapes which express the primal meeting of mind with nature. Since the parallel with antiquity appears as unconscious memory, it is psychologically justified and cannot be dismissed as mere literary *appliqué*. The parallel is grounded in that conception of mind as shading off into unconsciousness which, having come from romantic literature, was articulated by Freud and Jung and remains still our conception, indeed our experience, of mind. The mythical method gives a doubleness of language to parallel our doubleness (doubleness between the apparent and buried) of consciousness and selfhood.

This doubleness of language reaches a climax at the end of Part I, "The Burial of the Dead," which deals with the sprouting of seed and tubers in spring. In one of the poem's most powerful passages, the protagonist recognizes an old acquaintance; and just as in "Prufrock" we are to infer the small talk at the party, so here we are to infer an ordinary conversation about gardening. But the language tells us what is unconsciously transpiring.

> There I saw one I knew, and stopped him, crying:
> "Stetson!

"You who were with me in the ships at Mylae!
"That corpse you planted last year in your garden,
"Has it begun to sprout? Will it bloom this year?
"Or has the sudden frost disturbed its bed?"

The shocking substitution of "corpse" for "seed" reminds us that corpses are
a kind of seed, and that this truth was symbolized in the old vegetation
rituals. We find gardening satisfying because we unconsciously repeat the
ritual by which gods were killed and buried in order that they might sprout
anew as vegetation. Even more surprising is the connection of Stetson with
the ships at Mylae—the naval battle where the Carthaginians or Phoenicians
were defeated by the Romans. The passage is a haunting recognition scene
in which conscious recognition derives from unconscious recognition of
another life. The protagonist unconsciously recognizes his fellow gardener
as also a fellow sailor and Phoenician; for they are devotees of rebirth, and it
was the Phoenician sailors who carried the Mysteries or vegetation cults
around the Mediterranean.
    The heavily ironic final lines return us to the modern situation:

"Oh keep the Dog far hence, that's friend to men,
"Or with his nails he'll dig it up again!
"You! hypocrite lecteur!—mon semblable,—
    mon frère!"

Instead of Webster's "keep the wolf far thence that's foe to men" (*White
Devil*, V, iv, 113), the friendly Dog (perhaps, as Cleanth Brooks has
suggested, modern humanitarianism) is the more likely animal and the more
likely danger. Webster's dirge says it is good for the dead to be buried, and
Eliot tells why—by digging up the corpse, the Dog would prevent rebirth.
But we are all, protagonist and hypocrite readers, with our advanced ideas
that cut us off from the natural cycle, engaged in a conspiracy against fertility
and rebirth. So we return to the theme with which Part I began: "April is the
cruellest month, breeding/ Lilacs out of the dead land"—the fear of sex, of
burying the seed that will sprout.
    In *The Waste Land*, the buried life manifests itself through the
unconscious memory of characters from the past. There is already some
reaching toward this method in "Prufrock," where Prufrock *consciously* thinks
he might have been John the Baptist, Lazarus, Hamlet. But the emphasis is
on the ironical disparity between these legendary figures and Prufrock's
actual character or lack of character. Prufrock does not in fact fulfill the

destinies of these legendary figures. In *The Waste Land*, however, the speakers do in spite of themselves unconsciously fulfill destinies laid out in myth; and their unconscious identification with the legendary figures who have already walked through these destinies gives them the only substantial identity they have.

Compared to the characters in *The Waste Land*, Prufrock, for all his lack of vitality, has the sharp external delineation of characters in, say, Henry James. He has a name (a characterizing one), a social milieu to which he genuinely belongs, a face (we all have our idea of what he looks like, probably like Eliot). Prufrock has—his deliberate trying on of masks is a sign of this— a clear idea of himself. The characters in *The Waste Land*, however, are nameless, faceless, isolated, and have no clear idea of themselves. All they have is a sense of loss and a neural itch, a restless, inchoate desire to recover what has been lost. But in this very minimum of restless aliveness, they repeat the pattern of the Quest. And it is the archetypal Quest pattern, as manifested in the Grail legend, that gives whatever form there is to the protagonist's movement through the poem.

We would not know what to make of the characters were it not for the intrusion of a central consciousness that assimilates them to characters of the past. This is done through the double language of the Stetson passage. The same purpose is accomplished in Part II through shifting references. Part II opens with an opulently old-fashioned blank-verse-style description, not so much of a lady as of her luxurious surroundings. The chair she sits in reminds us of Cleopatra's "burnished throne" and the stately room of Dido's palace, while a picture recalls the rape of Philomela. The shifting references suggest that the lady is seductive, but that she is also, like Cleopatra with Anthony and Dido with Aeneas, one of those who is in the end violated and abandoned by a man. The theme of violation takes over; for the picture shows Philomela's change, after her rape, into a nightingale whose wordless cry rings down through the ages:

> So rudely forced; yet there the nightingale
> Filled all the desert with inviolable voice
> And still she cried, and still the world pursues,
> "Jug Jug" to dirty ears.

The nightingale's *voice*, the story's meaning, is inviolable; but the violation of innocence in the waste land goes on.

When the lady finally speaks, she utters twentieth-century words that her prototypes of the past would not have understood: "'My nerves are bad to-night. Yes, bad. Stay with me.'" We gather from the passage that the lady is rich, that her house is filled with mementoes of the past which she understands only as frightening ghosts, that the protagonist to whom she speaks is her lover, and that he has in some special modern sense violated her. The violation would seem to lie in his inability to communicate with her:

> "Speak to me. Why do you never speak. Speak.
> "What are you thinking of? What thinking? What?
> "I never know what you are thinking. Think."

The modern situation is unprecedented and meaningless; therein lies the poem's negative impulse. But, deep down, these people are repeating an ancient drama with ancient meanings; therein lies the poem's positive impulse. The shifting references to various ladies of the past evoke the archetype that subsumes them—the archetype already revealed in Part I, where the protagonist has his fortune told by Madame Sosostris. "Here," she said pulling a card from the ancient Tarot deck, "is Belladonna, the Lady of the Rocks,/ The lady of situations." Because all the ladies referred to are Belladonnas, we understand the character of our modern rich lady and the character—in the abrupt shift to a London pub—of the working-class Belladonna who tells a friend of her efforts to steal away the husband of another friend, another Belladonna, who has ruined her health and looks with abortion pills. Beneath the meaningless surface, the underlying tale tells again of violation in the desert—violation of innocence, sex, fertility.

The protagonist's card is "the drowned Phoenician Sailor." This explains not only the Stetson passage, but also the protagonist's reflection after his card has been drawn: "Those are pearls that were his eyes." The line is from Ariel's song in *The Tempest*, addressed to Prince Ferdinand, who thinks his father, the King of Naples, has been drowned. Lines from *The Tempest* keep running through the protagonist's head, because *The Tempest* is a water poem in which all the human characters are sailors, having sailed to the island. Drowning and metamorphosis, the consolation in Ariel's song, relate to drowning and resurrection in the cult of the Phoenician fertility god Adonis (an effigy of the dead Adonis was cast upon the waves, where resurrection was assumed to take place).[8]

Among the other Tarot cards named is "the one-eyed merchant"; he turns up in Part III as the Smyrna merchant who makes the protagonist a homosexual proposition. Eliot in a note (III, 218) explains his method of characterization: "Just as the one-eyed merchant, seller of currants, melts into the Phoenician Sailor, and the latter is not wholly distinct from

Ferdinand Prince of Naples, so all the women are one woman, and the two sexes meet in Tiresias. What Tiresias *sees*, in fact, is the substance of the poem." The figures either on the Tarot cards, or in some cases frankly imagined by Eliot to be on them, provide the archetypes from which the nameless, faceless modern characters derive identity. Tiresias, not a Tarot figure but the blind hermaphroditic prophet of Greek mythology, appears only once—in the Part III episode about another violated Belladonna, the typist whose mechanical fornication with a clerk leaves her neither a sense of sin nor a memory of pleasure.

The central consciousness, which intruded through the double language of the Stetson passage and the cultural memory of Part II's introductory passage, now takes on the name of Tiresias: "I Tiresias, old man with wrinkled dugs/ Perceived the scene, and foretold the rest." After the scene has been enacted, Tiresias interjects:

> (And I Tiresias have foresuffered all
> Enacted on this same divan or bed;
> I who have sat by Thebes below the wall
> And walked among the lowest of the dead.)

Again we are enabled to understand the contrast between the passionate auspicious fornications of the past and this modern perfunctory performance. Again we are reminded that this scene is nevertheless a reenactment. Sexual union was used in the fertility ceremonies to promote by sympathetic magic the fertility of the soil. But modern sexuality is sterile.

Through the Tiresias consciousness in him, the protagonist repeatedly finds an underlying ancient pattern but also sees that in the modern situation the pattern does not come to the preordained conclusion. This gives a direction to his Quest—to complete the pattern by restoring fertility. It is a sign of their connection that Tiresias appears as a stand-in for the protagonist in just the scene the protagonist can only have imagined.

To say that all the characters meet in Tiresias is to suggest that archetypal identities emerge from larger archetypes, in the way smaller Chinese boxes emerge from larger. The Smyrna merchant, identified with the Tarot one-eyed merchant, propositions the protagonist, who is identified with the Phoenician Sailor. Yet we are told that the one-eyed merchant melts into the Phoenician Sailor; so that the protagonist really stands on both sides of the proposition. In the same way the protagonist is identified with the Quester of the Grail legend, who sets out to find the Grail and thus cure the ailing Fisher King and restore fertility to the waste land. The protagonist is the Quester inasmuch as he moves through the episodes of the poem to arrive at the Perilous Chapel. But in the following lines from Part III, he is the Fisher King, whose illness is in some Grail romances assigned to the King's brother or father:

> While I was fishing in the dull canal
> On a winter evening round behind the gashouse
> Musing upon the king my brother's wreck
> And on the king my father's death before him.

He is also—according to the method of shifting references—Prince Ferdinand (from whom, in *Tempest*, I, ii, 390–91, the last two lines derive), Hamlet, Claudius: all of whom have to do with dead kings who in turn recall the murdered kings of vegetation ritual. All this combines with the modern industrial setting to portray the modern moment with modern voices and collapse them into timeless archetypes. At the end of the poem, the protagonist is both Quester and Fisher King; he is the Fisher King questing for a cure: "I sat upon the shore/ Fishing, with the arid plain behind me."

Since the protagonist plays at one and the same time both active and passive roles, we must understand all the characters as aspects or projections of his consciousness—that the poem is essentially a monodrama. It is difficult to say just where the various characters melt into the protagonist and where the protagonist melts into the poet. We have to distinguish the scenes in which the protagonist himself plays a part—the recollection of the Hyacinth garden, the visit to Madame Sosostris, the meeting with Stetson, the scene with the rich Belladonna—from the scenes in the pub and at the typist's. We can either consider that the protagonist overhears the first and imagines the second, or that at these points the poet's consciousness takes leave of the protagonist to portray parallel instances. I prefer the first line of interpretation because it yields a more consistent structure on the model of romantic monodrama. In *Faust* and *Manfred*, the other characters do not have the same order of existence as the protagonists' just because the protagonists' consciousnesses blend with the poets'. We must understand the other characters, therefore, as ambiguously objective, as only partly themselves and partly the projection of forces within the protagonist and ultimately within the poet. If we take the line that Eliot's poem is what the protagonist *sees*, then Tiresias becomes the figure in which the protagonist's consciousness blends perfectly with the poet's so that the protagonist can *see* imaginatively more than he could physically. (Pound in one of his annotations calls Eliot Tiresias.)[9]

But the poet's consciousness is itself an aspect of the age's. We get the overheard scraps of conversation, miscellaneous literary tags, and incoherent cultural recollections that would stock a modern cultivated cosmopolitan mind of 1920. This is where Western culture has come to, the poem is telling us, as of 1920. The protagonist's consciousness emerges from the collective consciousness of the time, as another nameless, faceless modern voice. The protagonist has no character in the old-fashioned sense; for he acquires delineation or identity not through individualization, but through making connection with ancient archetypes.

The point is that Eliot introduces a new method of characterization deriving from the reaction against the nineteenth-century belief in the individual as the one reality you could be sure of. Eliot's nameless, faceless voices derive from the twentieth-century sense that the self, if it exists at all, is changing and discontinuous, and that its unity is as problematical as its freedom from external conditions. In *The Waste Land*, and in his earlier poems, Eliot is preoccupied with the mechanical, automatic quality of existence. In "Rhapsody on a Windy Night," he had written:

> I could see nothing behind that child's eye.
> I have seen eyes in the street
> Trying to peer through lighted shutters,
> And a crab one afternoon in a pool,
> An old crab with barnacles on his back,
> Gripped the end of a stick which I held him.

In *The Waste Land*, he says of the clerk: "Exploring hands encounter no defence"; and of the typist afterward: "She smoothes her hair with automatic hand,/ And puts a record on the gramophone." The solution, toward which he had been finding his way through the early poems, is the breaking out from and enlargement of self through archetypalization. Behind the solution lie the demonstrations by Freud and Jung that when we delve deep into the psyche we find an archetypal self and a desire to repeat the patterns laid out in the sort of myths described by Frazer and Jessie Weston.

The Waste Land opens with scraps of cosmopolitan conversations that the protagonist might be understood to overhear, but which have enough in common to project an upper-class tourist mentality, out of touch with and afraid of life's rhythms: "I read, much of the night, and go south in the winter"—yet still feeding on recollected moments of genuine experience:

> And when we were children, staying at the arch-duke's,
> My cousin's, he took me out on a sled,
> And I was frightened. He said, Marie,
> Marie, hold on tight. And down we went.
> In the mountains, there you feel free.

There follow cultural recollections, mainly from the Bible—"I will show you fear in a handful of dust"—that establish in the image of the dry waste land the spiritual habitat of the previous speakers. This is a new prophetic voice, the Tiresias consciousness, which goes on through a recollection of the Sailor's song that opens Wagner's *Tristan* to establish also the opposite Sailor theme of water and hope for redemption. There follows a personal memory of love; and only here, in the lines introduced by a dash, can we single out a voice that we come to recognize as the protagonist's.

> "You gave me hyacinths first a year ago;
> "They called me the hyacinth girl."
> —Yet when we came back, late, from the
>   Hyacinth garden,
> Your arms full, and your hair wet, I could not
> Speak, and my eyes failed, I was neither
> Living nor dead, and I knew nothing,
> Looking into the heart of light, the silence.
> *Oed' und leer das Meer.*

The protagonist had in the past his chance for love; he had like Marie his perfect moment, his vision of fulfillment. But he was unable to reach out and take what the moment offered, and thus break through to fertility, creativity. We know he failed only through the last line from the opening of Wagner's tragic Third Act: "Desolate and empty the sea."

This way of rendering the protagonist's failure makes it also collective; as does the reference to the Hyacinth garden, since Hyacinth was a fertility god. (Eliot capitalized the small *h* of the original draft; but restored it for the final edition of 1963, having presumably lost interest by then in vegetation myths.) It is the vision and loss of vision that sets the protagonist in motion; insofar as *The Waste Land* has a plot, it tells the story of the protagonist's attempt to recover his lost vision. All his subsequent memories are transformations of the scene in the Hyacinth garden. This observation is confirmed by the words, which I have bracketed, that Eliot deleted from the original draft. When in Part II the rich lady asks: "'Do you remember/

Nothing?'"—the protagonist answers: "I remember/ [The hyacinth garden.] Those are pearls that were his eyes [, yes!]" The Hyacinth garden (love) and Ariel's song (drowning) are related as forms of natural salvation (love is a kind of drowning). This attempt at recovery is the pattern of the Grail Quest; in most versions, a vision or fleeting sight of the Grail leads to the Quest to recover the Grail.

The Waste Land is about sexual failure as a sign of spiritual failure. This is made especially clear by the deleted opening passage about a rowdy Irishman, on an all-night binge, who lands in a brothel but is too drunk to have intercourse. The original draft then shifts to "April is the cruellest month"—about upper-class people who, like the Irishman, fail in sex not because they are practicing Christian abstinence but because of spiritual torpor. The vegetation myths are better than Christianity for diagnosing modern sexual failure; for the myths make clear that sex and religion spring from the same impulse and that sexual and religious fulfillment are related.

To understand how far Eliot has come in his treatment of sex and in his concepts of character and identity, we have only to compare the memory of the Hyacinth garden with a corresponding memory in the early poem, written in French, "Dans le Restaurant." In the French poem, a dirty broken-down waiter recalls an amorous experience under a tree in the rain when he was only seven and the little girl was even younger. She was soaking wet, he gave her primroses and tickled her to make her laugh. He experienced a moment of power and ecstasy. But he too lost his vision, for a big dog came along and he became scared and deserted her; he has never fulfilled the promise of that moment. The customer to whom he has insisted on telling this story remarks on his physical filthiness as a way of separating the waiter from himself: "What right have you to experiences like mine?" The customer gives the waiter ten sous for a bath.

The poem escapes from this sordid situation by taking a quite unprepared-for leap to the cleansing by drowning of Phlebas the Phoenician, a character for whom we have not been in the least prepared.

> Phlébas, le Phénicien, pendant quinze jours noyé,
> Oubliait les cris des mouettes et la houle de Cornouaille,
> Et les profits et les pertes....

The sudden contrast affords welcome relief. Since Part IV of *The Waste Land* is an English revision of this passage:

> Phlebas the Phoenician, a fortnight dead,

> Forgot the cry of gulls, and the deep sea swell
> And the profit and loss,

we are justified in connecting certain details preceding this passage with "Dans le Restaurant." The dog may stand behind "'Oh keep the Dog far hence,'" and the customer who wants to separate himself from the waiter may stand behind "'You! hypocrite lecteur!—mon semblable,—mon frère!'" But most important, the connection with the waiter's memory suggests that the protagonist betrayed the hyacinth girl through non-consummation. The experience took place *after* "we came back, late, from the Hyacinth garden," presumably in the rooms of one or the other. In both scenes, sexuality is associated with rain and flowers; the hyacinth girl came back with her arms full of flowers and her hair wet.

Having failed to consummate a union that would have combined love with sex, the protagonist turns to the fortune-teller and then proceeds to live out his fortune by experiencing dry, sterile lust. He fails the rich Belladonna, overhears the dialogue in the pub, is propositioned by the Smyrna merchant, conceives the typist's fornication and the lament of the girl seduced on the Thames:

> "Highbury bore me. Richmond and Kew
> Undid me. By Richmond I raised my knees
> Supine on the floor of a narrow canoe."

Finally the imagery of dryness and burning comes to a climax: "Burning burning burning burning," and we are afforded the welcome relief of Phlebas's "Death By Water."

>   A current under sea
> Picked his bones in whispers. As he rose and fell
> He passed the stages of his age and youth
> Entering the whirlpool.

The passage holds out to the protagonist the possibility of a natural or pagan salvation, the kind suggested by the song from *The Tempest* in which Ariel makes drowning seem so desirable because it is "a sea change/ Into something rich and strange" (I, ii, 401–02).

"Fear death by water," said Madame Sosostris. "Here, said she,/ Is your card, the drowned Phoenician Sailor"; at which point the protagonist recalled "Those are pearls that were his eyes," another line from this same song of

Ariel's. Thus Eliot does in *The Waste Land* what he has not done in "Dans le Restaurant": he prepares for the drowning of Phlebas. He retains on the surface the vacant characters of the earlier poem, but he prepares beneath the surface archetypal identities that give the characters positive force. We must read the protagonist's development in self-understanding through the shift in the archetypes with which he identifies himself. In identifying himself with Phlebas, the protagonist fulfills in Part IV his natural fortune. Part V, "What the Thunder Said," moves beyond Madame Sosostris, who could not find the "Hanged Man." Part V explores the possibility of a supernatural answer through the unpredictable miracle of revelation.

The drowning of Phlebas must be understood as the equivalent of a psychological experience—as a *rite de passage* or psychic dying through which the protagonist can be reborn into the identity that enables him to continue his Quest. The protagonist has after Part IV outgrown pagan archetypes; the references now are to Christianity and the higher ethical Hinduism of the Upanishads. The Hyacinth garden turns into the garden of Gethsemane: "After the torchlight red on sweaty faces/ After the frosty silence in the gardens." The missing "Hanged Man" of the Tarot deck turns into the hooded figure whom the disciples on the journey to Emmaus saw but did not recognize as the risen Christ:

> Who is the third who walks always beside you?
> When I count, there are only you and I together
> But when I look ahead up the white road
> There is always another one walking beside you
> Gliding wrapt in a brown mantle, hooded
> I do not know whether a man or a woman
> —But who is that on the other side of you?

Eliot so suggestively avoids specification that he eludes an exclusively Christian reading and turns the personages and situation archetypal. He makes the passage refer also to an account he read of an Antarctic expedition where the explorers, as he says in his note to these lines, "at the extremity of their strength, had the constant delusion that there was *one more member* than could actually be counted." Because of the new concept of identity advanced in *The Waste Land*, we have had to learn how to read a passage in which the twentieth-century London protagonist exhibits his character by melting into other quite remote characters—a disciple of Christ, an Antarctic explorer. We are to understand by the identifications that the protagonist has reached the point where he has intimations of Godhead.

It is in Part V that the Grail legend becomes most explicit, and explicit in its Christian interpretation. The protagonist might be said to repeat in his own progress the evolution of the Grail legend, as described by Jessie Weston, from pagan ritual to Christian romance.[10] Even those female lamentations which precede the protagonist's arrival at the empty chapel—and which refer, as Eliot's note explains, to "the present decay of eastern Europe"—recall the lamenting voices of unseen women that, in certain versions described by Miss Weston, the Grail knight hears amid the desolation of the Perilous Chapel. When in the final passage the protagonist becomes both Quester and Fisher King, there is a powerful recapitulation of the disorder that has been the poem's main theme. We are given a most poignant sense of the incoherent fragments that stock the cultural memory of Europe.

> I sat upon the shore
> Fishing, with the arid plain behind me
> Shall I at least set my lands in order?
> London Bridge is falling down falling down falling down
> *Poi s'ascose nel foco che gli affina*
> *Quando fiam uti chelidon*—O swallow swallow
> *Le Prince d'Aquitaine à la tour abolie*
> These fragments I have shored against my ruins
> Why then Ile fit you. Hieronymo's mad againe.
> Datta.   Dayadhvam.   Damyata.
>   Shantih   shantih   shantih.

Yet all these apparently miscellaneous fragments speak of purgation—whether through the refining fire of Dante's line, or the melancholy of Nerval's ghostly Prince, or the purposeful madness of Kyd's Hieronymo—or else they speak of desire for salvation, as in the line from the Latin *Pervigilium Veneris*: "When shall I become as the swallow?"

"These fragments I have shored against my ruins." The line turns to a positive purpose the fragmentation upon which the poem has been built. They point to a tradition which, though in disarray, is all we have to draw on for salvation. The fragments are in many languages because all European culture is being tapped, going back to its earliest origins in the Sanskrit Upanishads. As the protagonist, through association and memory, makes his identity, he is able to give the fragments a new order. They are made to issue in the three Sanskrit precepts—give, sympathize, control—upon which the protagonist has already meditated, and which are to guide him toward that peace, signified by *shantih*, which passes understanding.

Once we see that *The Waste Land* dramatizes the making of an identity, that the Quest is for personal order that leads to cultural order and cultural order that leads to personal order, then the poem turns out more positive than we used to think it. The deadness and disorder that made the biggest, indeed the only, impression on the poem's first readers are seen as a phase through which the poem passes to point toward the Christian poems that are to follow Eliot's conversion in 1927. We can now see from *The Waste Land* that Eliot was by 1922 farther along toward conversion than we had thought. Eliot—"Fishing, with the arid plain behind me," and wanting to set "my lands in order"—has by now put behind him all liberal humanitarian modern answers: he is fishing, waiting for revelation. He has by now seen the need for Christianity, though he still cannot believe.

To understand the modern problem of identity that Eliot is trying to solve in *The Waste Land*, we have to look back not to "Prufrock" or "Portrait of a Lady," whose speakers are still, as I have suggested, Jamesian in their delineation, but to "Preludes" and "Rhapsody on a Windy Night," which were written during those same years, 1909–1911. The characters of these poems are not, like Prufrock and the lady, separated from external reality by an unspoken ideal; they are, on the contrary, undistinguishable from the images of external reality that make up their consciousness.

II
The morning comes to consciousness
Of faint stale smells of beer ...

III
You dozed, and watched the night revealing
The thousand sordid images
Of which your soul was constituted;
They flickered against the ceiling.
And when all the world came back
And the light crept up between the shutters
And you heard the sparrows in the gutters,
You had such a vision of the street
As the street hardly understands; ...

IV
His soul stretched tight across the skies
That fade behind a city block,
Or trampled by insistent feet
At four and five and six o'clock.

In all these instances from "Preludes," there is a minimum of that distinction between perceiver and perceived, and hence of that will and organizing power, which constitute an identity. Yet the validity of the sensations and the vision of the street suggest some minimal awareness.

"Rhapsody on a Windy Night" parodies the Wordsworth tradition in that it opens up, under the transforming influence of moonlight, the flow of memory and association. But moonlight in an urban setting does not yield beauty. Reinforced by the light of a street lamp, it transforms the streetwalker into a grotesque:

> "Regard that woman
> Who hesitates toward you in the light of the door
> Which opens on her like a grin.
> You see the border of her dress
> Is torn and stained with sand,
> And you see the corner of her eye
> Twists like a crooked pin."

The twisted eye recalls the memory of twisted things:

> The memory throws up high and dry
> A crowd of twisted things;
> A twisted branch upon the beach ...
> A broken spring in a factory yard,
> Rust that clings to the form that the strength has left
> Hard and curled and ready to snap.

Perception again stirs memory when the sight of a cat slipping out its tongue to devour butter recalls, in the passage I have quoted earlier, the equally automatic reach of a child's hand for a toy: "I could see nothing behind that child's eye."

This vacancy, this automatic action without reserve of thought and feeling, fascinates Eliot in his early view of character. Prufrock, who is paralyzed by too much reserve of thought and feeling, longs for such automatism: "I should have been a pair of ragged claws." But the speaker of "Preludes" sees it as wiping out individuality. "The morning comes to consciousness" means there is no distinction among all the people who come to minimal consciousness because it is morning:

> One thinks of all the hands

> That are raising dingy shades
> In a thousand furnished rooms.

In "Preludes" IV, the soul of the clerk returning from work at evening is trampled like the street "by insistent feet." His soul is also "stretched tight across the skies," suggesting perhaps his taut nerves.

> And short square fingers stuffing pipes,
> And evening newspapers, and eyes
> Assured of certain certainties,
> The conscience of a blackened street
> Impatient to assume the world.

The certainties of such people, certainties derived from the mass media and from urban sensations, are as determined and insensitive as the street blackened by trampling. Their certainties are almost as automatic as the grasping reflex of the crab in "Rhapsody."

In "Rhapsody," the speaker on his way home late at night recognizes the number on his door. "'Memory!'" says the street lamp sardonically, contrasting the mechanical memory of one's address with Wordsworthian memory. The indoor lamp "'spreads a ring on the stair,'" giving another kind of light from the moon's.

> "Mount.
> The bed is open; the tooth-brush hangs on the wall,
> Put your shoes at the door, sleep, prepare for life."

> The last twist of the knife.

If the moonlight has yielded such mechanical sensations and memories, what can be expected of ordinary life? The speaker's thoughts are given to him by the street lamps—a sign that perceiver and perceived are not distinguished.

The view of the self in these two poems was either influenced by Bradley, or else, what is more likely, Bradley confirmed for Eliot a view of the self he had already arrived at on his own.[11] F.H. Bradley, the turn-of-the-century English philosopher, taught that the self can be known only through experience; for the self cannot be distinguished from its psychical contents, its sensations and memories of sensations. For the same reason, the self is in experience hardly distinguishable from the not-self—each fills and determines the other. "We have no right, except in the most provisional way," says Eliot in explaining Bradley, "to speak of *my* experience, since the I is a construction out of experience, an abstraction from it."[12] Bradley speaks, therefore, not of subjective perceivers but of subjective-objective centers of experience—"finite centres." There are as many universes as there are finite centres; for as Bradley puts it: "My external sensations are no less private to myself than are my thoughts or my feelings. In either case my experience falls within my own circle, a circle closed on the outside; and, with all its elements alike, every sphere is opaque to the others which surround it.... In brief, regarded as an existence which appears in a soul, the whole world for each is peculiar and private to that soul." Eliot quotes this passage in a note to lines v, 411–13 of *The Waste Land*—lines in which the self as so described is the thing to be overcome. Through an analogy to the prison in which Dante's Count Ugolino was locked up to starve to death, Eliot, in meditating on the Sanskrit precept *Dayadhvam* (sympathize), is saying we must break out of the Bradleyan prisonhouse of self.

In "Preludes" and "Rhapsody," the Bradleyan view of self as opaque and discontinuous ("The usual self of one period is not the usual self of another")[13] is presented as true but awful. In both poems, the word *I* is severely repressed. But we can tell from the perceived details that the *speakers*—as distinguished from the characters they perceive—have in reserve an unacknowledged ideal by which they judge the mechanical life they portray. In "Preludes," the speaker finally uses *I* to express through the trampled souls on trampled streets an accumulating sense of violation, and to suggest that even these mechanical registers of sensation may obscurely feel some core of self that has been violated.

> I am moved by fancies that are curled
> Around these images, and cling:
> The notion of some infinitely gentle
> Infinitely suffering thing.

But no, this is only fancy; the universe is as sordid and meaningless as the urban scene:

> Wipe your hand across your mouth, and laugh;
> The worlds revolve like ancient women
> Gathering fuel in vacant lots.

Yet the fancy of some other possibility remains with us here and in "Rhapsody."

Having dissolved the distinction between subject and object, Bradley himself acknowledges a "limit of this interchange of content between the not-self and the self." He admits that we do nevertheless entertain obscure "sensations of an essential selfhood," which derive from "our ability to feel a discrepancy between our felt self and any object before it. This ... gives us the idea of an unreduced residue."[14] It is out of this unreduced residue, sensed in spite of the problematical nature of the self, that modern literature generates the mysteries of identity. And it is this unreduced residue—sensed as a mere perceptual bias in "Preludes" and "Rhapsody," and in the blank young man in "Portrait" who responds to the street piano and the smell of hyacinths—that develops into a positive force in *The Waste Land*.

The structure of "Preludes" anticipates that of *The Waste Land*. Both present separate vignettes of city life; yet the vignettes are unified by the central consciousness which must be understood as perceiving or imagining them all. The speaker of "Preludes," having thought of all the morning hands "raising dingy shades/ In a thousand furnished rooms," imagines himself in the furnished room where the streetwalker wakes up alone. In the same way, the protagonist of *The Waste Land* imagines himself at evening in the furnished room where the typist receives the clerk; and he does this after envisioning the city's taut nerves at the end of a working day:

> At the violet hour, when the eyes and back
> Turn upward from the desk, when the human engine waits
> Like a taxi throbbing waiting.

Not rest but stimulation is wanted (in the original draft, the next line was: "To spring to pleasure through the horn or ivory gate"); hence the intercourse that turns out as mechanical as the throbbing. This typist and clerk, too, have had their souls trampled by the "insistent feet" returning from work.

"Preludes" gives us a world where people live alone in furnished rooms; the speaker of "Rhapsody" returns to such a room. *The Waste Land* gives us a world in which people do not communicate. Dialogues are one-sided; the answer, when there is an answer, is thought rather than spoken and does not answer the question:

> "Speak to me. Why do you never speak. Speak.
> "What are you thinking of?" ...
> I think we are in rats' alley
> Where the dead men lost their bones.

But this isolation is counteracted by the ability of the speaker in "Preludes" and the protagonist in *The Waste Land* to project into the other characters. Hence the speaker's fancy in "Preludes" is of a compassionate humanity they all share, and his view remains general when he reverses himself to see that our general fate, instead, is as loveless as the force that moves the stars. The final lines may invoke an ironical comparison with Dante's final vision in *Paradiso* of "Love that moves the sun and the other stars." And, indeed, the minimal "notion of some infinitely gentle/ Infinitely suffering thing" is just the unreduced residue of feeling out of which Christian mythology takes shape.

In *The Waste Land*, the speaker's projection into the typist's room takes shape in the figure of Tiresias. Bound up with the original draft of *The Waste Land* are some poems that demonstrate the projective sensibility that was to produce Tiresias. In "The death of Saint Narcissus," the speaker knows he has been a tree, a fish, "a young girl/ Caught in the woods by a drunken old man"; now he is happy to experience even martyrdom. "Song. [For the Opherion]" speaks of "Bleeding between two lives"; and some untitled lines help us understand how the protagonist of *The Waste Land* can be both Quester and Fisher King:

> I am the Resurrection and the Life
> I am the things that stay, and those that flow.
> I am the husband and the wife
> And the victim and the sacrificial knife.

The protagonist's projective imagination, which sees or creates the connections among the characters, sees in them a memory of and yearning for a communal identity, and that communal identity is expressed through the mythical figures in the poem, most notably the figures of the Tarot cards. In a 1916 paper, "Leibniz' Monads and Bradley's Finite Centres," Eliot threw light on the method of establishing identities he was to use in *The Waste Land*: "Nothing is real, except experience present in finite centres. The world, for Bradley, is simply the *intending* of a world by several souls or centres.... For Bradley, I take it, an object is a common intention of several souls, cut out (as in a sense are the souls themselves) from immediate experience. The genesis of the common world can only be described by admitted fictions."[15]

Thus the mythical figures and patterns—the Grail Quest, the vegetation myths leading to the Christian myth—are the admitted fictions rising out of the characters' memories and desires, their unreduced residue of feeling. The vision encountered and lost of the hyacinth girl leads to a desire for recovery expressed through the fiction of the Quest. The longing everyone has for water recalls the seasonal alternation of drought and rain; while winter and spring are recalled by the longing for death that leads in the end to the longing for rebirth. The whole connection of human emotions with the cycle of the seasons is expressed through the fictions of the vegetation myths.

The sense of violation we detected in "Preludes" permeates the first three parts of *The Waste Land*. The theme is established through the fiction, represented in the rich Belladonna's painting, of Philomela's rape; and that fiction applies to all the women in the poem, including such recollected victims as Dante's La Pia and Ophelia (III, 293–94, 306). The Christian imagery of Part V makes explicit our accumulating sense that all the violations come together in the figure of Jesus, the arch-victim.

The movement from the fire of Part III to the relief, in Part IV, through water prepares the sensuous texture out of which, in Part V, the figures of Jesus and other redeemers take shape. They take shape because the senses require them to take shape, the senses as objective correlatives to the protagonist's emotions:

> Ganga was sunken, and the limp leaves
> Waited for rain, while the black clouds
> Gathered far distant, over Himavant.
> The jungle crouched, humped in silence.
> Then spoke the thunder.

Earlier, a similar rendition of thirst gives rise to the figure of Jesus:

> If there were the sound of water only
> Not the cicada
> And dry grass singing
> But sound of water over a rock
> Where the hermit-thrush sings in the pine trees
> Drip drop drip drop drop drop drop
> But there is no water.

The longing for water, for even the sound of water, together with the hope offered by the lovely water-dripping song of the hermit-thrush, leads to "Who is the third?" The third, as we have seen, is the unrecognized apparition born of the Antarctic explorers' despair, and the unrecognized apparition of Jesus born of the disciples' grief over the Crucifixion. In both cases the apparition was delivering. *The Waste Land's* positive force derives from the characters' ability to generate, from an unreduced residue of feeling, an archetypal identity which delivers them from the closed circle of the Bradleyan self and the immediate historical moment.

NOTES

1. Conrad Aiken, "An Anatomy of Melancholy," *New Republic*, 7 February 1923; I.A. Richards, *Science and Poetry*, *Principles of Literary Criticism* (London, 1926); F.R. Leavis, *New Bearings in English Poetry* (London, 1932); F.O. Matthiessen, *The Achievement of T.S. Eliot* (New York, 1935); Cleanth Brooks, *Modern Poetry and the Tradition* (Chapel Hill, 1939); George Williamson, *A Reader's Guide to T.S. Eliot* (New York, 1953); Hugh Kenner, *The Invisible Poet: T.S. Eliot* (New York, 1959).

2. In an autograph letter to L.A.G. Strong, 3 July 1923, quoted in *An Exhibition of Manuscripts and First Editions of T.S. Eliot* (Austin, 1961), p. 10.

3. *The Letters of Ezra Pound 1907–1941*, ed. D.D. Paige (New York, 1950), [? January] 1922, p. 171.

4. *The Waste Land: A Facsimile and Transcript of the Original Drafts Including the Annotations of Ezra Pound*, edited with an Introduction by Valerie Eliot (New York, 1971). The draft is part manuscript, part typescript.

5. *Knowledge and Experience in the Philosophy of F.H. Bradley* (London, 1964).

6. Eliot will be quoted from *Collected Poems 1909–1962* (London, 1963).

7. See *Facsimile*, Introduction, pp. xx–xxi.

8. Eliot knew Colin Still's interpretation of *The Tempest* as a Mystery ritual of initiation (*Shakespeare's Mystery Play*, London, 1921).

9. *Facsimile*, p. 47.

10. *From Ritual to Romance* (Cambridge, 1920).

11. We do not know when Eliot first read Bradley, but he did not begin to study him until he returned from Paris to Harvard in autumn 1911 to work for a doctorate in philosophy.

12. *Knowledge and Experience*, p. 19.

13. *Appearance and Reality*, 2nd ed. (London, 1902), pp. 346, 79.

14. *Appearance and Reality*, pp. 92–93.

15. Reprinted as Appendix in *Knowledge and Experience* pp. 203–04.

RICHARD POIRIER

Soundings for Home

Frost's poetry of "home" is a dramatization of the human costs and human benefits of decorum. As a reader becomes more intimate with the poems, however, it is hard to resist what seem like solicitations to think of social or psychological or domestic decorums as somehow synonymous with poetic ones. How much "extravagance" is possible within decorum; how much can be mediated by it; what extremities are induced by the constraints or failures of mediation; and what, in case of failure, are the prospects beyond decorum or mediation except nothingness or madness? These are issues central to English poetry, especially since 1800, and to the great Americans, Whitman and Stevens. One of the reasons Frost has not been taken as seriously as Stevens is in part explained by the fact that though he can be found working within some of the same dialectical oppositions, he chose resolutely, even defiantly, to work also within the circumstantially or topically familiar, as if from a list of the hundred most famous poetic and novelistic situations. So insistently ordinary, so particularized is the domestic drama of his work that it appears to be written *against* that kind of poetry which is an interpretation of itself and of its potentialities. Of some importance, too, when it comes to the understandably Anglophilic bias of literary critics, is the fact that Frost chose a landscape—for the early poems it is the intervales of the White Mountains and the countryside around Derry in southern New Hampshire;

From *Robert Frost: The Work of Knowing.* © 1977 by Oxford University Press, Inc.

for the later ones, the Taconic Mountains around Shaftesbury and the Green Mountains around Ripton in central Vermont—which does not have anything storied about it. Even Emerson complained in his "Ode Inscribed to W.H. Channing" (and Frost repeats the complaint in his poem "New Hampshire") that "The God who made New Hampshire / Taunted the lofty land with little men." It was a landscape without poetic or sublime associations and Frost got credit for being able even to report on a region and a people so uninspiring.

Frost was treated mostly as the brilliant poet of the average human lot, and that attitude continues (despite earlier recognitions from Robert Graves and Edwin Muir, from Allen Tate, Robert Penn Warren, and especially Jarrell, and also from a more recent critic like James Cox) to stand in the way of efforts to give him credit for being a great poet precisely because it was within that human lot that he found the glories and plights of poetry itself.

It is difficult even now to get accustomed to this combination, no matter how many precedents are brought to bear from Wordsworth or Coleridge. Whenever there is a poem by one of these three involving "home" and "extra-vagance," there is provision for a place where the poet or central figure belongs, a kind of home base, and for something beyond, on which the figure gazes while he is out walking or while he is sitting on a hillside. Both the viewer and the view are made to seem at least latently mythological either by being put in a reciprocally enhancing relationship to one another or by suggesting the degree to which human consciousness prevents rather than assists such a relationship.

And yet it is obvious that Wordsworth and Coleridge have proved far more accommodating than has Frost to critics who like their poems to be about poetry. The reason, I think, is that while it is possible, as we have already seen, to infer from Frost's poems an interest in the drama of poetic "making," he is some of the time even tiresomely determined not to surrender the human actuality of his poems to a rhetoric by which action is transformed immediately into ritual, as in the account of the boy stealing the boat in *The Prelude*. Where such enlargement of rhetoric occurs in Frost, it redounds almost invariably to the disadvantage of the speaker; he must face the opposition both of nature and of the decorum, however pliant, which Frost establishes between himself and the reader. There are "over-reachers" in Frost, like Meserve in "Snow," but Meserve is never allowed to "*sound*" like one, and the "extra-vagance" of his conduct is accepted by his neighbors with an admiration that is both begrudging and impatient, until they can get him safely back home. Frost sets up obstacles to his own capacities for transcendence, and I can think of no poem in which he allows himself (without all kinds of subtle vernacular modulations and deflations) the sustained rhetorical eloquence he admired in a poem like Shirley's "The Glories of Our Blood and State." Having met the challenge that no one can turn certain kinds of New England and especially household experience into metaphor, he then, with an exquisite pride, wants to show that he does not choose ostentatiously to extend his metaphor into a fashionable literariness. A great poem like "Home Burial" thus has to win its way, with a lean and sinewy and finally irresistible necessity, to a reading that tells us not only about lives but about Frost's own life in the writing of poetry and about his rescue of a life for poetry out of his own desperate need for circumscriptions.

He is a poet who finds his freedom of movement out of a sense of restraint: the movement to one extreme is provoked by the imminence of the other. "The Wood-Pile" is like a sequel to "Home Burial," with the man in this instance wandering from a "home" that seems little more than an abstraction to him and to us. More a meditation than a dramatic narrative, it offers the soliloquy of a lone figure walking in a winter landscape. It is a desolate scene possessed of the loneliness of "Desert Places." Attention is focused on the activity of consciousness in this isolated wanderer, and nothing characterizes him as a social being or as having any relationships to another person. While the poem has resemblances, again, to Wordsworth's "Tintern Abbey," or Coleridge's "Dejection: An Ode," it is more random in its structuring and has none of the demarcations of the descriptive-reflective mode. A better way to describe the poem is suggested in a talk by A.R. Ammons, "A Poem as a Walk." "A walk involves the whole person; it is not reproducible; its shape occurs, unfolds; it has a motion characteristic of the walker" (*Epoch*, Fall, 1968, p. 118).

The man in the poem is not, like Stevens' Crispin, "a man come out of luminous traversing," but more like the "listener" in Stevens' "The Snow Man." In each poem is a recognition of a wintry barrenness made more so in Frost by a reductive process by which possibilities of metaphor—of finding some reassuring resemblances—are gradually disposed of. At the end, the speaker in Frost's poem is as "cool" as is the listener in Stevens, and also as peculiarly unanguished by the situation in which he finds himself. It is as if the wintry prospect, the arrival at something like Stevens' First Idea, a cold clarity without redeeming deceptions, has in itself been an achievement of the imagination. It is something won against all such conventional blandishments as the "misery" of what Harold Bloom calls the "Shelleyan wind" in "The Snow Man" or the flirtatious bird in "The Wood-Pile."

The persistent difference between Frost and Stevens applies here, too, however. It resides in the kind of context the reader is asked to supply for each of the poems. Thus, despite the absence of characterizing detail, the speaker in "The Wood-Pile" shapes, from his very opening words, a human presence for us in his sentence sounds, his voice; he makes us imagine him as someone in a human plight "far from home." By comparison, the "voice" in "The Snow Man" belongs not to a person but to a quality of rumination, and Bloom is succinctly generalizing about the poem—he calls it Stevens' "most crucial poem"—when he remarks of its author that "the text he produces is condemned to offer itself for interpretation as being already an interpretation of other interpretations, rather than as what it asserts itself to be, an interpretation of life" (*Poetry and Repression*, p. 270).

"The Wood-Pile" is about being impoverished, being on the dump—to recall two related states of consciousness in Stevens—with no clues by which to locate yourself in space. All you can assuredly know about "here" is that you are far from "home":

> Out walking in the frozen swamp one gray day,
> I paused and said, "I will turn back from here.
> No, I will go on farther—and we shall see."
> The hard snow held me, save where now and then
> One foot went through. The view was all in lines
> Straight up and down of tall slim trees
> Too much alike to mark or name a place by
> So as to say for certain I was here
> Or somewhere else: I was just far from home.

If this is a *situation* that resembles winter visions of Stevens, the *sound* resists any effort to bring visionary possibilities into being. The voice of this man ("So as to say for certain I was here / Or somewhere else") cannot be expected to test the poetic potentialities of what is seen and heard and can even less be expected to cheer itself up by indulging in the hyperbolic or the sublime vocabularies. There is an informality even in the initial placements—"out walking ... one gray day"—of the spondaic effect of "gray day," as if it were a scheduled occurrence (like "pay day") and of the possible metaphoric weight in what he says, as in the allusion (but not really) to the lack of adequate support he can expect in this landscape ("The hard snow held me, save where now and then / One foot went through"). Such anxious and innocuous precision about the relative hardness of the snow or the size and contour of the trees is humanly and characterologically right. It expresses the kind of paranoia that goes with any feeling of being lost and of losing thereby a confident sense of self. Paranoia, displaced onto a small bird chancing by, becomes the motive for metaphor: the bird is endowed with the characteristics being displayed by the man observing him:

> A small bird flew before me. He was careful
> To put a tree between us when he lighted,
> And say no word to tell me who he was
> Who was so foolish as to think what *he* thought,
> He thought that I was after him for a feather—
> The white one in his tail; like one who takes
> Everything said as personal to himself.
> One flight out sideways would have undeceived him.
> And then there was a pile of wood for which
> I forgot him and let his little fear
> Carry him off the way I might have gone,
> Without so much as wishing him good-night.

There is a combination here of yearning, competitiveness, and resentment that threatens to become ludicrous, a parody of the romantic search for associations and resemblances. And the parodistic possibility is increased by the syntax of the lines about the bird's tailfeathers. They could mean that the bird was foolish to think that the man had this particular design upon him. But the lines could also be the speaker's rendition or imitation of what he thought the bird was thinking, i.e., "Who does that man think he is to think that he can get hold of my tailfeathers?" In any event, there is more "thinking" proposed than could possibly or profitably be going on. That the paranoia and self-regard confusingly attributed to the bird are really a characterization of the man who is observing the bird is further suggested by the accusation that the bird is "like one who takes / Everything said as personal to himself"—a jocular simile, given the fact that there is only "one" person around to whom the comparison might apply. If all this is to some degree comic, it is feverishly so, the product of intense loneliness and displacement. From its opening moment the poem becomes a human drama of dispossession, of failed possessiveness, and of the need to structure realities which are not "here," to replace, in the words of Stevens, "nothing that is not there" with "the nothing that is."

The only probable evidence of structure that he does find, already put together, is the "wood-pile," a forgotten remnant of earlier efforts to make a "home" by people who, when they did it, were also away from home. The pile of wood, which lets the speaker promptly forget the bird, once more excites his anxious precisions. He still needs to find some human resemblances, evidences in zones and demarcations for the human capacity to make a claim on an alien landscape. What he discovers is sparse indeed, his reassurance equally so, as we can note in his rather pathetic exactitudes:

> It was a cord of maple, cut and split
> And piled—and measured, four by four by eight.
> And not another like it could I see.
> No runner tracks in this year's snow looped near it.
> And it was older sure than this year's cutting,
> Or even last year's or the year's before.
> The wood was gray and the bark warping off it
> And the pile somewhat sunken. Clematis
> Had wound strings round and round it like a bundle.
> What held it, though, on one side was a tree
> Still growing, and on one a stake and prop,
> These latter about to fall. I thought that only
> Someone who lived in turning to fresh tasks
> Could so forget his handiwork on which
> He spent himself, the labor of his ax,
> And leave it there far from a useful fireplace
> To warm the frozen swamp as best it could
> With the slow smokeless burning of decay.

The poem here could be read as a commentary on the earlier "The Tuft of Flowers" where, instead of a bird, a butterfly acts as a kind of pointer who "led my eye to look / At a tall tuft of flowers beside a brook" and where these flowers, in turn, direct his attention to signs of work having been done by another man with "A spirit kindred to my own; / So that henceforth I worked no more alone." "The Wood-Pile" is obviously a much starker poem. The "tuft of flowers" was left as a kind of signature, a greeting and communication; the pile of wood was simply forgotten by the man who cut and carefully stacked it, as he went on to the distractions of other things. The wood-pile cannot therefore prompt the gregarious aphorisms which bring "The Tuft of Flowers" to a close: " 'Men work together,' I told him from the heart, / 'Whether they work together or apart.' " Remnants of a human presence in the swamp only remind the walker that he is completely alone in a place that has been deserted. And his aloneness is the more complete because there are no alternatives outside the present circumstances which give him any comfort. Even when he thinks of a fireplace it is not with images of conviviality but only with the observation that it would be "useful."

The wood burns of itself, with a warmth that cannot be felt and without giving any evidence whatever that it belongs in the world of men and women. "With the slow smokeless burning of decay" is a line whose sound carries an extraordinary authority and dignity because it has emerged out of the more sauntering vernacular movements at the beginning of the poem. It induces a kind of awe because it is the acknowledgment of nature as a realm wholly independent of human need or even human perception, and it belongs not only in what it says but in its very cadence with Wordsworth's evocation at the end of his sonnet "Mutability" of "the unimaginable touch of Time."

If the speaker "resembles" anything at the end of the poem, it is the wood-pile itself, something without even a semblance of consciousness; it is wholly self-consuming. As in "Desert Places," another poem about a lonely man walking in a landscape of snow, the man in "The Wood-Pile" could say that "The loneliness includes me unawares." This line is a little poem in itself. It has a syntactical ambiguity more common in Stevens than in Frost. It can mean both that the loneliness includes him but is unaware of doing so, and that the loneliness includes him and *he* is not aware of its doing so by virtue of his near obliteration. In either case he is not so much included as wiped out; he is included as if he were inseparable from, indistinguishable from, the thing that includes him. He is on the point of being obliterated by the landscape, rather than allowed to exist even as an observer of it, much less a mediating or transcending presence.

Despite Frost's devotion to Emerson, it was impossible for him ever to feel that to become "nothing" on a "bare common" is also to become, as in the opening paragraphs of *Nature*, a "part or parcel of God." For Frost's lonely walkers, far from "home," nothing can come from such nothing, and they therefore must try to speak again and in such a way as to make known an ordinary human presence. Frost in this mood is bleaker than Stevens. He resists the transcendentalist willingness to disentangle the self from the ties of "home" and from any responsibility to domesticate whatever might be encountered while one is "extra-vagant." Stevens, but not Frost, could say with Emerson that on that "bare common," faced with evidences of a primal and impoverished reality of "snow puddles at twilight under a clouded sky," it is possible by the power of heightened imagination so to transform reality that

the name of the nearest friend sounds then foreign and accidental: to be brothers, to be acquaintances, master or servant, is then a trifle and a disturbance. I am the lover of uncontained and immortal beauty. In the wilderness, I find something more dear and connate than in streets or villages. In the tranquil landscape, and especially in the distant line of the horizon, man beholds somewhat as beautiful as his own nature.

Frost's whole theory of "sentence sounds" is implicitly a way of taking an exception to transcendental vision and to the Sublime as an alternative to the discovery of barrenness: "I cultivate ... the hearing imagination rather than the seeing imagination though I should not want to be without the latter" (Thompson, *Letters*, p. 130). Barrenness, poverty, the mind of winter are posited as conditions of life and of poverty by both Frost and Stevens. But while in Stevens these exist in a tradition that passed from Emerson through Santayana, with a dialectic weighted toward sublimity and supreme fiction, in Frost, following a tradition that passed from Emerson through William James, these same conditions are held within a quite different dialectical tension. "Home" exerts such a simultaneous restraint on and incentive to "extra-vagance" that anyone who feels it must become pugnacious in the expressed need for ventilation, for some degree of imaginative license. Hence the sharply more individuated and personalized tone of Frost's poems. In that respect, "The Wood-Pile" is perhaps more quiescent than "Desert Places," in that it does not, or cannot, go on to some final combative assertion of a confronted self, the sort of thing we hear in

> They cannot scare me with their empty spaces
> Between stars—on stars where no human race is.
> I have it in me so much nearer home
> To scare myself with my own desert places.

The self-assertion here is implicit in the slangy schoolyard tone of "They cannot scare me" as it applies itself to something akin to Eliot's "vacant interstellar spaces." It is typical of Frost that he would bring, without any signaling, a fashionable-sounding phraseology of self-diminishment into combination with that kind of vernacular voice which draws its strength from a sense of rootedness, no matter how unfertile the soil. "Home" is the place where one might hear a phrase like "they cannot scare me"; the anxious tension that goes into that sound is what induced Frost to change the second line of this passage from its original form in the first printing (*The American Mercury*, April, 1934), where it read "Between stars—on stars void of human races." Frost settled on a sound altogether more vernacular and idiomatic and which got rid of the literarily portentous word "void."

Voice is the most important, distinguishing, and conspicuously insistent feature of Frost's poetry and of his writing about poetry. There is scarcely a single poem which does not ask the reader to imagine a human character equivalent to the movement of voice, and there is no other poet in English of whom this is so emphatically the case. Behind the theory of "voice" and "sentence sounds" that he presented wholly as a literary choice, behind his related insistence that poetry was as good as it was "dramatic," there is a psychological and moral imperative. It can be most simply described as a revulsion against the idea of human transparency. Under any and all circumstances he would resist becoming a "transparent eyeball." It would mean getting lost. This was never an agreeable prospect for him, despite little hints to the contrary in "Directive," and there are therefore no poems by him of visionary afflatus. There are, however, close to terrifying poems about wandering off, losing the self, or belonging nowhere. That is the plight of the men in the poems we have been considering and of the man in "Acquainted with the Night" who has "out-walked the furthest city light."

> I have stood still and stopped the sound of feet
> When far away an interrupted cry
> Came over houses from another street,
>
> But not to call me back or say good-by....

The deprived figure in "Desert Places" is faced with another threat of the same kind: of disappearing without any record of his having been there or any protest at his going. He is confronted with "a blanker whiteness of benighted snow / With no expression, nothing to express." We hear their voices in a kind of wilderness. The situation in which these Frosty figures find themselves does have an equivalence in Stevens where the observer in "The Snow Man" "listens in the snow, / And, nothing himself, beholds / Nothing that is not there and the nothing that is." But the very suppleness of syntactical maneuverings in these lines, and in much of Stevens' poetry, with its intricate patterns of repetition and echoing, is meant to dissuade any reader from finding evidences in the voice of an imaginable speaker. Both poets propose a similar plight, but in one it is of life and in the other of the poetic imagination.

Stevens and Frost part company at the point where Stevens exercises his belief, with Santayana, that the power of the imagination can create realities in a poem that can exist in defiance of the evoked realities of a "fact." Truth was not required, as it was for Frost and the William James of *Pragmatism*, to "grow up inside of" finite experiences; rather, it was something that imagination could *create* as an alternative form of experience. Stevens himself very beautifully argues the case, using metaphors of "home" and "extra-vagance," in Part One of "Three Academic Pieces":

> ... the intensification of reality by resemblance increases realization and this increased realization is pleasurable. It is as if a man who lived indoors should go outdoors on a day of sympathetic weather. His realization of the weather would exceed that of a man who lives outdoors. It might, in fact, be intense enough to convert the real world about him into an imagined world. In short, a sense of reality keen enough to be in excess of the normal sense of reality creates a reality of its own. Here what matters is that the intensification of the sense of reality creates a resemblance: that reality of its own is a reality. This may be going round a circle, first clockwise, then anti-clockwise. If the savor of life is the savor of reality, the fact will establish itself whichever way one approaches it.

True "realization" for Frost occurs *after* the man who went outdoors comes back in. "I opened the door so my last look / Should be taken outside a house and book." Thus Frost begins a poem called "One More Brevity," in his last volume. But the "look," while a perfectly "extravagant" one, in that it is beyond both "home" and literature, is really a way of assuring himself that the stars are in place so that he may sleep more securely: "I said I would see how Sirius kept / His watchdog eye on what remains/ To be gone into if not explained." "Intensifications" while "out of doors" are not in themselves a true form of "realization," so far as Frost is concerned, since the very nature of metaphor involves for him a constant pressure, *at some point*, against intensifications and the excesses that go with them. Quite charmingly, while the man is looking up at the star Sirius a dog slips by "to be my problem guest: / Not a heavenly dog made manifest, / But an earthly dog of the carriage breed." This is a fine example of what Frost means when he says "I would be willing to throw away everything else but that: enthusiasm tamed by metaphor" ("Education by Poetry").

For Stevens, on the other hand, metaphor, or "resemblances," *creates* the conditions for enthusiasm:

> ... it is not too extravagant to think of resemblances and of the repetition of resemblances as a source of the ideal. In short, metaphor has its aspect of the ideal. This aspect of it cannot be

dismissed merely because we think that we have long since outlived the ideal. The truth is that we are constantly outliving it and yet the ideal itself remains alive with an enormous life (Part One, "Three Academic Pieces").

In Frost, the ideal aspect of metaphor exists only that it may be tested. Metaphor is an education by which the reader learns to be "at ease with figurative values," at ease not to luxuriate but the better to know "how far [he] may expect to ride" a metaphor "and when it may break down with [him]" ("Education by Poetry"). That is how one becomes "safe in history" or "in" science. Being "safe in" anything is clearly not a condition proposed by Stevens' "Notes Toward a Supreme Fiction." Stevens therefore can write a kind of ecstatically imagined poetry seldom found in Frost:

> Close the cantina. Hood the chandelier.
> The moonlight is not yellow but a white
> That silences the ever-faithful town.
> How pale and how possessed a night it is,
> How full of exhalations of the sea ...
> All this is older than its oldest hymn,
> Has no more meaning than tomorrow's bread.
> But let the poet on his balcony
> Speak and the sleepers in their sleep shall move,
> Waken, and watch the moonlight on their floors.
> This may be benediction, sepulcher,
> And epitaph. It may, however, be
> An incantation that the moon defines
> By mere example opulently clear.
> And the old casino likewise may define
> An infinite incantation of our selves
> In the grand decadence of the perished swans.
>   (From "Academic Discourse at Havana")

Stevens' is a poetry of possible impossibility, a poetry of vacation, which is at least as valuable as any "momentary stay against confusion," and bound to be more rapturous.

When Stevens and Frost met, not for the first time, in February 1940 in Key West, Stevens remarked, "Your trouble, Robert, is that you write poems about—*things*." To which Frost replied, "Your trouble, Wallace, is that you write poems about—bric a brac" (Thompson, II, 666). In an earlier meeting, in Florida during the spring of 1935, Stevens had apparently complained that Frost simply wrote too much. " 'You have written on subjects that were assigned,' is what he meant," Frost remarked in March 1935 in a talk at the University of Miami (Florida) in apparent allusion to Stevens. Frost's answer, if he gave one, can be guessed from what he says a year later, 12 March 1936, in a letter to L.W. Payne, Jr.:

> Oh I mustnt forget I wanted to correct you in a matter. Somewhere I found you saying lately that my formula of twenty-five years ago—Common in experience and uncommon in writing—meant that the subject should be common in experience but that it should be written up in an uncommon style. I believe that may be Munson's mistake. [Frost is referring to a book by Gorham B. Munson: *Robert Frost: A Study in Sensibility and Good Sense* (New York, 1927).] You're not to blame for it. The subject should be common in experience and uncommon in books is a better way to put it. It should have happened to everyone but it should have occurred to no one before as material. That's quite different. I was silent as to the need of giving old themes a new setting of words. I am silent still (Thompson, *Letters*, pp. 426–27).

What is "common in experience"? Obviously it could be said that one common experience is "impoverishment," as in a run-down house, and that another is the attempt at solace, as in painting the house. And it could also be said that these "experiences" can be found as frequently in Stevens as in Frost. But the difference is that in Stevens they are not "common"; it can be said without disparagement that they are instead literary and theoretical; they are states of poetic rather than of social consciousness; they call for actions of mind rather than actions of bodies. The leaves which fall in Frost's "The Leaf-Treader" are not the Shelleyan leaves of Stevens' "Domination of Black," and the response to them, as a threat of death, is in Frost not a swirling rhetoric of cosmic incantatory fear but rather a pep talk to the speaker's knee: "But it was no reason I had to go because they had to go. / Now up, my knee, to keep on top of another year of snow." Similarly, the "dirty house" in Stevens' "A Postcard from the Volcano" gets at the end "smeared with the gold of the opulent sun," while the "old old house" in Frost's "The Investment" is "renewed with paint" because the man and wife want to "get some color and music out of life."

So "common" is the experience in Frost that the phrasing of that last line is purposefully clichéd. Or rather it is not so much clichéd as an allusion to cliché. The reader is asked to indulge in a cliché, and to do so without irony, without even the patronizations of compassion. After all, that paint cost money; it truly means something in the life of a couple who share a community of deprivation and respond to it with practical imagination. A reader and writer who conspire in a sympathetic understanding of domestic and social clichés are in a different relationship to one another than are a reader and writer who conspire in the understanding of literary allusions or the pressure of one literary text or tradition on another. Frost asks us to be *both* kinds of readers; and his unique difficulty is in the demand that we be common and literary all at once. Which is a way of suggesting, again, the great difference sometimes between Frost, whose extensive literary allusiveness is always less apparent than are his allusions to clichés, and any of the other great figures of the first half of this century.

West-Running Brook, where "The Investment" appears, has other poems of deprivation, some well known, like "Bereft" and "Acquainted with the Night," but also some little known, like "The Cocoon":

> As far as I can see, this autumn haze
> That spreading in the evening air both ways
> Makes the new moon look anything but new
> And pours the elm tree meadow full of blue,
> Is all the smoke from one poor house alone,
> With but one chimney it can call its own;
> So close it will not light an early light,
> Keeping its life so close and out of sight
> No one for hours has set a foot outdoors
> So much as to take care of evening chores.
> The inmates may be lonely womenfolk.
> I want to tell them that with all this smoke
> They prudently are spinning their cocoon
> And anchoring it to an earth and moon
> From which no winter gale can hope to blow it—
> Spinning their own cocoon did they but know it.

Once again, "a poor house alone," with scarcely a sign of habitation or embellishment; once again, an observer with some admitted limitation of view ("As far as I can see"); once again, a question about the nature of a "home" when there are almost no signs of life around it. The observer is much like the man in "The Census-Taker" who wonders "what to do that could be done— / About the house—about the people not there." "The

Cocoon" is a poem of seeing more than of walking, and the extravagance consists in the effort to sustain the metaphor of a "cocoon" when there is so little to support it. The observer is offered some chimney smoke, to be sure—more, at least, than "the smokeless burning of decay" in "The Wood-Pile"—and this is apparently enough to warrant an "investment" of imagination, a kind of poetic imitation of the action of the couple who renew the paint on their old, old home. Nonetheless, the speaker here is bothered—he has been looking at the house "for hours"—by the disparity between his rather modest metaphor, on the one hand, his bit of extravagance about the curling smoke, and, on the other, the lonely obliviousness of the people—if, indeed, there are any inside the house—to the significance of their fire smoke. Clearly, there is nothing extravagant about them; the house keeps whatever life it has "close and out of sight." He "wants to tell them" they are spinning a cocoon, and that in so doing they are making a link between heaven and earth. But this is something that they do not and cannot "know."

There is a desire, not urgent but nonetheless humanly and poetically challenging, to see what can be "made" of the "poor" house here, the old house in "The Investment," and even the house that has been left behind in "The Wood-Pile," with its merely "useful fireplace." The places and persons in these poems are not so much drab as stripped and bare, and the details given about them dispel rather than suggest any possibility of character or of eccentricity. It is a barrenness that is exemplary or even mythological in tendency, establishing a testing ground for observers who want to make something up about it—not a supreme fiction, perhaps no more than "some color and music" or an encouraging metaphor.

These poems are thus somewhat different from the dramatizations already looked into of marital struggles or of ambulatory itineraries away from home and back again. They are not the kind most commonly associated with Frost and are seldom anthologized or discussed. As a result they have not as yet established a context for themselves by which the familiar Frostean disengagement from any sort of motionlessness or stasis can be seen not only as a moral but as a literary act. In these particular instances, the literary element, the degree to which the poems become a species of literary criticism, is especially strong because the speaker in something like "The Cocoon," even more evidently than in "The Wood-Pile," is a poet as well as a chance observer. But he is a poet about whom Frost, as an overarching presence, exercises some of his most subtle and most gentle discriminations.

Two other poems in this group, "On the Heart's Beginning to Cloud the Mind" and "The Figure in the Doorway," are about houses looked at with some sort of ulterior, "creative" intention by a poet-observer from a passing train. The poems are placed next to one another in *A Further Range*, which also includes "Desert Places," "Design," and "Provide, Provide." All these are meditations on bleakness, a subject of increasing frequency in Frost's work beginning with his fourth volume, *New Hampshire*. They are different from earlier poems about the failures of "home" to nourish the imagination in that the narrator is disengaged and relatively dispassionate. The houses are discovered by accident, and it is implied that the viewer is somebody who wanders less in a search for signs and embodiments than to amuse himself with the possibility of their existence.

The title "On the Heart's Beginning to Cloud the Mind" admits to something implicit in the other poems in this group: that because the observer has no active part in whatever is going on inside the house, he makes things up which are not only fictitious (that, of course, is his right) but also wrong-headed and banal. The opening of the poem—"Something I saw or thought I saw / In the desert at midnight in Utah"—is a possible allusion to Virgil's *Aut videt aut videsse putat*, as Reuben Brower observes, or, as likely, to *Paradise Lost*, where at the end of Book I, "some belated peasant sees / Or dreams he sees" some fairy elves. But the comic rhyme "I saw / Utah" makes the allusion parodistic. We can be reminded also of "For Once, Then, Something," which is also a poem about trying to have a vision, trying to see "something" which is probably only that—"some thing" and not a metaphor for any thing. Here, the landscape is a barren desert observed from the lower berth of a fast train. The man sees "A flickering human pathetic light / That was maintained against the night, / It seemed to me, by the people there, / With a God-forsaken brute despair." It is this mere supposition ("it seemed to me") which makes him think that his heart is "beginning to cloud" his mind. The alternative possibility—that the light is a burning tree kept flaming by various people at their pleasure—is, he has to admit, only "a tale of a better kind." But his fictionalizing is at least adequate to a further conjuration: he invents a domestic scene wherein a woman in the darkened room of this hypothetical house shares with him a view of the desert scene. She, however, is without fear or suspicion. He guesses that she knows, as he does not, what the lights "really" mean, and as the poem nears its end he manages to "typify" the woman and her husband in a nascently mythological way:

> Life is not so sinister-grave.
> Matter of fact has made them brave.
> He is husband, she is wife.

> She fears not him, they fear not life.
> They know where another light has been,
> And more than one, to theirs akin,
> But earlier out for bed tonight,
> So lost on me in my surface flight.

"Surface flight" necessarily describes more than the train's movement. It reminds us of the unabashed superficiality of the man's vision. The concluding lines are justly critical of the poetic vision or realization that precedes them: the engine smoke abets the sentimentality of his "clouded mind." The claim that he sees "far into" anything suggests distance rather than powers of penetration:

> This I saw when waking late,
> Going by at a railroad rate,
> Looking through wreaths of engine smoke
> Far into the lives of other folk.

The poem is a critical inquiry into itself and its own procedures. It dramatizes the action of a mind attempting to make metaphorical enhancements, but its language suggests that the action is too casually a violation of privacies. The kind of mythologizing in which this man engages is often a "flight" over the surface of reality rather than into it. Lawrence's delighted remark about Whitman comes to mind: "ALLNESS! shrieks Walt at a crossroads, going whizz over an unwary Red Cap Indian."

As if spoken from the same train window, "The Figure in the Doorway" reads like an effort to correct such poetic "flights" from wobbling off course. Frost's train-window poems are different from Rossetti's—as in the series "A Trip to Paris and Belgium"—in that they raise not merely phenomenological problems but questions of misreading, of necessary failures of perception:

> The grade surmounted, we were riding high
> Through level mountains nothing to the eye
> But scrub oak, scrub oak and the lack of earth
> That kept the oaks from getting any girth.
> But as through the monotony we ran,
> We came to where there was a living man.
> His great gaunt figure filled his cabin door,
> And had he fallen inward on the floor,

He must have measured to the further wall.
But we who passed were not to see him fall.
The miles and miles he lived from anywhere
Were evidently something he could bear.
He stood unshaken, and if grim and gaunt,
It was not necessarily from want.
He had the oaks for heating and for light.
He had a hen, he had a pig in sight.
He had a well, he had the rain to catch.
He had a ten-by-twenty garden patch.
Nor did he lack for common entertainment.
That I assume was what our passing train meant.
He could look at us in our diner eating,
And if so moved uncurl a hand in greeting.

The vision of the "great gaunt figure" filling the cabin door prompts little more than superficial reportage. Four lines in a row begin with the repeated "he had"; the man's possessions are then as dutifully listed. It reads as if the speaker were determined not to make anything out of what he sees. Beyond these measurements, all we learn about the man is the merest guesswork. In an Empsonian sense, the poem has a pastoral inclination: it is "assumed" that the passing train is "common entertainment" for the "grim" figure in the cabin door and that he must sometimes be moved (even though he is not on this one occasion, when the speaker has opportunity to see him) to "uncurl a hand in greeting." As in "On the Heart's Beginning to Cloud the Mind," there is scarcely any scene at all here; there is no material for poetry except what might be guessed *if* the spectator were in a position to watch long enough. This, then, for all its self-discipline, also becomes a "surface flight," and the best he can do with the image of the giant man in the doorway is to make a "tall tale," in a grotesque sense of the term, about what might happen at some future time: "And had he fallen inward on the floor, / He must have measured to the further wall. / But we who passed were not to see him fall." Frost's evident intentions in the poem are pleasantly confirmed in a speech given at Bread Loaf on July 2, 1956, where he said of "The Figure in the Doorway" that "it might not be true of him at all, but there is such a thing. I might have been all wrong about him. He might have been a candidate for the Democratic party" (Cook, p. 110).

These poems are evidence of Frost's congenital circumspection about "extra-vagance"—about making things up while "in flight," about inventing other people's lives without getting intimately involved with them, about the problematics of mere accidental relationships, mere glimpses of a "field looked into going past" ("Desert Places") or glimpses of a desert or a house from a fast train, or something so grandly and therefore remotely conceived as is "the universe" by the young man who cries out at the beginning of "The Most of It":

> He thought he kept the universe alone;
> For all the voice in answer he could wake
> Was but the mocking echo of his own
> From some tree-hidden cliff across the lake.
> Some morning from the boulder-broken beach   5
> He would cry out on life, that what it wants
> Is not its own love back in copy speech,
> But counter-love, original response.
> And nothing ever came of what he cried
> Unless it was the embodiment that crashed   10
> In the cliff's talus on the other side,
> And then in the far-distant water splashed,
> But after a time allowed for it to swim,
> Instead of proving human when it neared
> And someone else additional to him,   15
> As a great buck it powerfully appeared,
> Pushing the crumpled water up ahead,
> And landed pouring like a waterfall,
> And stumbled through the rocks with horny tread,
> And forced the underbrush—and that was all.   20

This is the most powerful of what might be called his spectatorial poems, those in which a wandering figure tries to locate a "home" by the exercise of vision, the making of metaphor, or the making of sound to which an answering call is expected. Along with the poems being discussed in this section (and "Neither Out Far nor In Deep") "The Most of It" is a poem in which "life" is being asked to do some or all of a "poet's" work. The request is illegitimate, and it is made not by Frost but by the speakers or spectators— or would-be poets—in his poems. If their calls on "life" have a pathos of innocence, they also elicit that Frostean exasperation which is aroused by anyone who acts politically, or poetically, as if the world owes him a living, or as if it is easy to be "at home in the metaphors" one contrives about the world.

Metaphors, like other marriages, are not made in heaven. About this, Frost and Stevens would agree. Metaphors are made by poets, either by those who write poems or by the kind of Emersonian poet who is potentially in any one of us. Significantly, the poem following "The Most of It" is "Never Again Would Birds' Song Be the Same." There, the world itself has already been made our "home," partly by the fact that the "birds" "from having heard the daylong voice of Eve / Had added to their own an oversound." It is a sound that still "persists" in the wilderness which is of our present moment. But her "sound," her "voice," was not, we have to remember, directed to birds at all in any naive expectation that they would answer her in kind or in any other way. The birds simply heard her voice as it was "carried aloft" from the intercourse between Adam and Eve, the "call or laughter" of their daily life together before the Fall. To the extent, then, that the sound of birds has been crossed with and become an echo of human sound, it is not to be confused with the kind of sound the man in the opening lines of "The Most of It" requests as an answering call from the wilderness around him. Keeping the universe alone, he is an Adam without an Eve. To paraphrase a passage from Frost's "The Constant Symbol" which we have already looked at, it might be said that he wants to "keep" the universe without spending very much on it. He has not learned the essential lesson that "strongly spent is synonymous with kept." Or, to make another comparison, he "keeps" the world the way the old man keeps house in "An Old Man's Winter Night," forever making sounds, even to "beating on a box," in order to lay some claim to the world around him: "One aged man— one man—can't keep a house / A farm, a countryside, or if he can / It's thus he does it of a winter's night."

The supposed model for this isolate and solitary man, this man who has not entered into or engaged upon any kind of "marriage," was, according to Thompson, a young poet named Wade Van Dore whom Frost met first in Littleton, New Hampshire, in 1922 and later at the University of Michigan in 1925. Frost helped Van Dore with the publication of his first volume of poetry, *Far Lake*, in 1930, which included one poem, "Man Alone," and excluded another, "The Echo," whose superficial resemblances to "The Most of It" encourage Thompson to claim that Frost's poem, especially under its original title "Making the Most of It," was meant as an "ironic reply" to Van Dore's work (Thompson, II, 361). And indeed some passages from Van Dore might easily have provoked Frost, like the following from "The Echo":

> Made mellow by a wall of trees
> My call came swiftly back to me.
> My word the forest would not take
> Came bounding back across the lake.

Through outer trees to shade grown black
I peered and saw, like strips of snow
That form in rocks the ages crack
The trunks of birches, half aglow.
Again I called, and now I stirred
A fearful bird to swiftly fly.
Far off I heard his angry scream,
But not a gladdened human cry.
It seemed I could not overthrow
The brooding barrier of the trees.
My voice grew swift, my call more keen,
But always backward came the word
Of it to me, that seemed to sigh
For him I sought, for all reply.

Or this passage from "Man Alone":

If he should loudly call, then stand and wait
Until the sound had traveled far and made
A voice reply, he'd know the forest held
No mate for him. An echo would reply,
Giving him back his lonely call and word.
A deer might start....

The similarities of circumstance and phrasing between these poems
and Frost's "The Most of It" are extensive enough not to need comment, and
it seems probable that Van Dore's poems were an incentive for Frost's. But
to treat "The Most of It" as an ironic "reply" to Van Dore is to miss the
altogether more important fact that Frost's poem is too powerful for such
irony. Van Dore provided no more than a nudge, if that, pushing Frost in the
direction of a poem already waiting in him to be written, a great poem that
is a culmination of the motifs and themes we have been looking into. In some
sense, too, it brings into sharper focus many of his poems about echoing and
shows the degree to which his poetry absorbs and continually comments
upon the echoing streams, hills, and rocks of pastoral poetry, the "Sweet
Echo, sweetest nymph that lives unseen" of Milton's "Comus," and especially
the echoes that greet Wordsworth's Boy of Winander. The poem exists
within a large poetic context of "echoing" that has been best located in
English poetry by John Hollander and Angus Fletcher. In that sense,
Wordsworth's "There Was a Boy" must be thought to have had a stronger

claim on Frost than a quite minor poem by Van Dore which itself, directly or indirectly, derives from passages like the following, taken from the 1805 version of *The Prelude*, Book V:

> There was a Boy, ye knew him well, ye Cliffs
> And Islands of Winander! many a time,
> At evening, when the stars had just begun
> To move along the edges of the hills,
> Rising or setting, would he stand alone,
> Beneath the trees, or by the glimmering lake;
> And there, with fingers interwoven, both hands
> Pressed closely palm to palm and to his mouth
> Uplifted, he, as through an instrument,
> Blew mimic hootings to the silent owls
> That they might answer him. And they would shout
> Across the watery vale, and shout again
> Responsive to his call, with quivering peals,
> And long halloos, and screams, and echoes loud
> Redoubled and redoubled; concourse wild
> Of mirth and jocund din! And, when it chanced
> That pauses of deep silence mocked his skill,
> Then, sometimes, in that silence, while he hung
> Listening, a gentle shock of mild surprise
> Has carried far into his heart the voice
> Of mountain torrents; or the visible scene
> Would enter unawares into his mind
> With all its solemn imagery, its rocks
> Its woods, and that uncertain heaven, received
> Into the bosom of the steady lake.
>
> This Boy was taken from his Mates and died
> In childhood, ere he was ten years old.
> Fair are the woods, and beauteous is the spot,
> The Vale where he was born: the Church-yard hangs
> Upon a slope above the Village School,
> And there, along that bank, when I have passed
> At evening, I believe, that oftentimes
> A full half-hour together I have stood
> Mute—looking at the grave in which he lies.

Wordsworth's poem is closer to Frost's than its "echoes loud /
Redoubled and redoubled" might superficially suggest. Nature responds, but
only with what is initially rejected as inadequate in "The Most of It" and with
what becomes inadequate in Wordsworth—with "copy speech." The Boy has
to blow "*mimic* hootings," an echo of the echo he seeks, before he hears
anything at all, and even this eventually gives way to a "deep silence" that
"mocks his skill." During these "pauses" the images "carried far into his
heart" may be less awesome but are no less mysterious than "it" or "the
buck." The poem ends with a "muteness" confirmed by the Boy's death and
by the reflective man who stands as a "mute observer" beside his grave. We
are left with a mere chronicler of echoes no longer to be heard; the man can
himself call no voices out of silence, even his own. Under circumstances so
imposingly mythological (the Boy is dead before the poem but lives in the
memory of the man and of the cliffs and islands), "deep silence" is not meant
to be *less* than echoing sound, and possibly it is more. So, too, with the
"response" in "The Most of It": to be told that "that was all" does not,
needless to say, mean that "all" is nothing.

The difference between the Wordsworth and the Frost poems is that
in Frost the spectator can draw no sustenance from memories of anyone like
"The Boy of Winander," and must face the likelihood that his human
presence is altogether an irrelevance. But that does not mean that the "it" at
the end should be written off, as it generally is, as a mere terrifying negation
of meaning. It is an awe-inspiring and wonderful representation of what we
do not know and cannot name—what poets cannot name any more. The final
words of the poem, "and that was all," are addressed not to the inadequacy
of the buck to live up to the spectator's sentimental expectations but to the
incapacity of the spectator, and of us, to find any way to account for the buck,
its power and fantastic indifference. If one wants to talk about irony in the
poem, then the irony is directed not toward the romantic attitude but toward
a naive version of it, one that takes no account of what Wordsworth himself
saw as the merely contingent boundaries of the self in the face of
undefinable, inarticulable influences.

Of the opening, Frost remarked in "On Extravagance," "It begins with
this kind of person: 'he thought he kept the universe alone;' ... just that one
line could be the whole poem, you know." I think Frost wanted to suggest
that very likely nothing would be "realizable" from the person from whom
the rest of the poem issued, a person who cannot "*make* the most of it." A
benighted version of Wordsworth's boy who lets whatever occurs be "carried
far into his heart" or "enter unawares into his mind," this man apparently
will not let himself be satisfied with anything that comes back to him, echo,

silence, or embodiment. But he stands there bathed in a mythological heroism nevertheless. What does happen at the end, in fact or in his mind, is far too awesome and magnificent to have been conceived merely as an ironic commentary on a pathetic but hardly disreputable desire to find "counter-love, original response" in nature. Though the spectator does not get what he apparently wants, he does get, and the reader with him, a vision of some fabulousness beyond domestication.

"The Most of It" is a kind of poem which creates adherents rather than readers. Any "analysis" is resented as reductive, and of course it is. The poem suspends itself brilliantly in such a large but wavering mythological context that its grandeur depends upon our not being able very precisely to answer those questions which, again, Frost himself persistently wanted to put to a poem: "By whom, where and when is the question" (Preface to *A Way Out*). As for "whom," the wholly elusive "he" is never characterized even by a speaking voice, and yet "he" is placed over against an immense "where," the "universe" and later the "boulder-broken beach" that looks toward a cliff hidden by trees. As for "when" his calling could have taken place, line 5 hints at a specific time ("Some morning"), but lines 9 and 10 ("and nothing ever came of what he cried / Unless it was the embodiment ...") suggest that he "called out" whenever he felt like it. To specify a specific dramatic situation here or in other crucial poems by Frost, like "Spring Pools" or "Hyla Brook" or "The Silken Tent," is to expose to ridicule both the situation and the person speaking. By its impressive generality of reference, to "the universe," to "life," to "counter-love," the poem implicitly requests us *not* to localize. Indeed, grammatically at least, the evidence is that "life" itself wants an answer as much as does the man: "He would cry out on life that what it wants / Is not its own love back in copy speech, / But counter-love, original response." Those phrases are peculiar; their rather technical angularity makes it sound as if a prescription were being called for. And "original response" is close to oxymoronic since to call for a sound that has an unprecedented origin is to deny its capacity to be "re-sponsive," a word which in the Latin sense means to pledge back something that has once been received. It is as if "life" itself were making the demand on the world through the demand of this single man in it, and as if life's demands were inherently wonderful as well as impossible.

In the best and simplest sense the poem is exciting for the largeness of its embrace, and because the man is beautifully anxious that "life" be allowed to exalt and enrapture itself. So that even without knowing classical literary analogues in echo literature, and all that is implied therein about man and his relation to the universe, any reader feels the presence and pressure here of a great human tradition and a great human predicament. In the expansive gestures of inclusiveness made at the outset, in the efforts to bring a universe into the focus of the self and its immediate environments, the poem is about the attempt to "make" a home by demanding a "return," a coming back of sound enriched and transformed by its movements out into the universe. If the man or "life" asks too much, then the response which they do get by the end of the poem is at least to that degree more powerfully informative about the nature of things than if they had asked for too little. If the aspiration is always to bring "home" what would otherwise be unseen, an element left to chaos, then at least the effort should show not only what can but also what cannot be given house room. Apparently that includes this horny-hoofed creature, if indeed it even exists, who "lands" only to "stumble" and "force" its way back into the obscurity from which it came. "The most exciting movement in nature," Frost says in "The Poetry of Amy Lowell," "is not progress, advance, but expansion and contraction, the opening and shutting of the eye, the hand, the heart, the mind. We throw our arms wide with a gesture of religion to the universe; we close them around a person."

The image of this man throwing his arms "wide," as it were, "with a gesture of religion to the universe," dominates the poem only to line 10; after that, the poem more or less ignores him, and devotes itself to the great buck. It is said to be an "embodiment" but of what? It is possible to read lines 9 and 10, "and nothing ever came of what he cried / Unless it was the embodiment that crashed" so that "it" refers to "nothing." The embodiment in that case becomes his hallucination of—to quote again the ever-useful phrase from Stevens—the "nothing that is not there and the nothing that is." Even if the embodiment does physically exist, its appearance is wholly fortuitous; it is no necessary "response" at all. Frost's use of the word "unless" is characteristic, as already seen in "A Cliff Dwelling" where "no habitation meets the eye / Unless in the horizon rim ..." And it functions, as do his frequent uses of "as if" or "something," when talking about presences, to induce in his meditative poems some of the speculative excitement that belongs also to his narratives of haunts or ghosts, like "The Witch of Coös." Symbols are thus poised ready to come into being, but only into the most uncertain kind of significance. The end of the poem, "and that was all," suggests that something happened for which we have no better language. Doubtless Thoreau would have been satisfied, if we are to believe a passage from *Walden*, another example of how various are the writings, including Cowper's "The Castaway," which Frost might have had in mind as he wrote this poem:

When, as was commonly the case, I had none to commune with,
I used to raise the echoes by striking with a paddle on the side of
my boat, filling the surrounding woods with circling and dilating
sound, stirring them up as the keeper of the menagerie his wild
beasts, until I elicited a growl from every wooded vale and hillside
("The Ponds").

But Thoreau, famously, was not looking for someone else additional to
him; far from being worried that he "kept the universe alone" he seemed
quite happy to be "the keeper of a menagerie" of wild beasts. The man in the
poem is not so lucky—or so superficial. He wants more, the "most," but his
gesture to the universe does not close even around a person. Rather, we are
left with the possibility that the gesture remains open, unless it closes, self-
protectively, before an image of vastation or of animal necessity which
admits, as the repeated use of the word "and" in the last three lines suggests,
of no subordination or modification or taming. This "embodiment" could be
in no one's menagerie.

One further way of allowing the poem its proper resonance is to read
it as part of the sequence of three poems in which Frost placed it in *A Witness
Tree*. It appears first, followed by "Never Again Would Birds' Song Be the
Same" and then by "The Subverted Flower." All three suggest, as indeed do
Frost's earliest love poems in *A Boy's Will*, that consciousness is determined
in part by the way one "reads" the response of nature to human sound. By
placing "Never Again Would Birds' Song be the Same" between "The Most
of It" and "The Subverted Flower," Frost once again reveals his deep
commitment to married love as a precondition for discovering human
"embodiments" in nature, for discovering Adam and Eve, whose intercourse
included the "call or laughter" that was "carried aloft" where ever since it has
been "crossed" with the song of birds:

> He would declare and could himself believe
> That the birds there in all the garden round
> From having heard the daylong voice of Eve
> Had added to their own an oversound,
> Her tone of meaning but without the words.   5
> Admittedly an eloquence so soft
> Could only have had an influence on birds
> When call or laughter carried it aloft.
> Be that as may be, she was in their song.
> Moreover her voice upon their voices crossed   10

> Had now persisted in the woods so long
> That probably it never would be lost.
> Never again would birds' song be the same.
> And to do that to birds was why she came.

Nothing in Frost more beautifully exemplifies the degree to which "tone of meaning" or sounds of voice create resemblances between birds and Eve, between our first parents and us, between the unfallen and the fallen world. On such resemblances as these Frost would have us imagine a habitable world and a human history. This is a poem which establishes differentiations only that it may then blur them. The delicate hint of a possible but very light sarcasm in the first line blends into but is not wholly dissipated by a concessive "admittedly" in the sixth line. This is one man allowing for another's pride of love but unable to resist the suggestion that perhaps his friend is a bit overindulgent. And the other concessive phrasings, "Be that as may be" and "Moreover," are equally delicate in their effectiveness. For one thing, they tend to take the sting out of the possibly ironic statement that the eloquence of Eve "could only have had an influence on birds"; for another, they lighten the force of "persisted"; and they allow for an almost unnoticeable transition by which the reader is moved from the "garden round" of the second line to "the woods" in line 11.

The tone of the poem is of a speaker who is now here with us and of our time and destiny, while it is at the same time full of a nice camaraderie with our first parents. It is loving and responsible all at once, accepting the parentage of Adam and Eve and the necessary consequences of the Fall, along with the acknowledgment of the possibly good fortunes that also attended it. Eve did come—from Adam and with Adam—in order that the song of birds should, by being changed, *mean* more than it otherwise would have. The force of the word "aloft" is ever so discreetly crucial here. Her eloquence had power not indiscriminately but only when it was carried to a "loftiness" that belongs to great love and great poetry, neither of which need be separated from the delights of "call or laughter." The "voice upon their voices crossed" became part of Emerson's fossil poetry, awaiting discovery by future readers, and lovers. The ability to hear the "daylong" voice of Eve in bird song teaches us that our own voices, like the voice in this poem, still carry something of our first parents and their difficult history. Mythological identification in this poem consists of voices finding a way to acknowledge and also to transcend historical differences and historical catastrophes. The birds' oversound in relation to words resembles the "sentence sounds" described in the letter, already quoted, which Frost wrote in February 1914 to John Bartlett: "A sentence is a sound in itself on which other sounds called words may be strung." And a bit later he insists that "the ear is the only true writer and the only true reader ... remember that the sentence sound often says more than the words" (Thompson, *Letters*, pp. 111, 113).

"Never Again Would Birds' Song Be the Same" is quite properly located between two poems in which human sound fails in an attempted transaction with nature. It is as if the young man and the woman of "The Subverted Flower," the last of the three poems, were in a post-lapsarian world where flowers and sex have the power to transform them into beasts, while the man alone in "The Most of It" is in the world without an Eve of any kind, and where the only form of animal life which can be heard, seen, or imagined in response to a cry of loneliness is so alien as to be called "it." In both poems the world is devoid of love, and consequently, as Frost would have it, of the power to realize a human extension, "someone else additional to him," a metaphor, like Adam and Eve, that would augment the human animal and allow it to make a human "home." These three great poems are profoundly about finding a "home" in the largest sense—by propagating the self through love, through the metaphorical discovery of self in another. "You must have read the famous valentine / Pericles sent Aspasia in absentia," Frost writes at the end of the late poem (1951) "How Hard It Is to Keep from Being King When It's in You and in the Situation." And he then gives his version of the valentine:

> For God himself the height of feeling free
> Must have been His success in simile
> When at sight of you He thought of me.

Simile or metaphor is the act of love, the act of writing poetry, and also evidence in each of these of how something as frighteningly big and potentially chaotic as the "universe" can be "kept" to a human measure. In the disproportion between these two words, "universe" and "kept," is both the pathos of "The Most of It" and a clue to Frost's sense that his own personal and poetic salvation lay in facing up to the full cost, in poetry and in daily living, of the metaphors he makes. "Earth's the right place for love," we are told in "Birches," and while there are times when the speaker of that poem would "like to get away from earth awhile," his aspiration for escape to something "larger" is safely controlled by the recognition that birch trees will only bear so much climbing before returning you, under the pressure of human weight, back home.

WORKS CITED

Following is a list of works frequently referred to in the text by short title only:

The Poetry of Robert Frost, edited by Edward Connery Lathem. New York: Holt, Rinehart and Winston, 1969.

Selected Prose of Robert Frost, edited by Hyde Cox and Edward Connery Lathem. New York: Collier, 1966.

Robert Frost: Poetry and Prose, edited by Edward Connery Lathem and Lawrance Thompson. New York: Holt, Rinehart and Winston, 1972.

Selected Letters of Robert Frost, edited by Lawrance Thompson. New York: Holt, Rinehart and Winston, 1964.

The Letters of Robert Frost to Louis Untermeyer, edited by Louis Untermeyer. New York: Holt, Rinehart and Winston, 1963.

Interviews with Robert Frost, edited by Edward Connery Lathem. New York: Holt, Rinehart and Winston, 1966.

Writers at Work: The Paris Review Interviews, Second Series, edited by George Plimpton. New York: Viking, 1963.

Cook, Reginald L. *Robert Frost: A Living Voice*. Amherst: University of Massachusetts Press, 1974. (Includes transcripts of twelve talks given by Frost in the last decade of his life.)

Thompson, Lawrance. *Robert Frost: The Early Years, 1874–1915*. New York: Holt, Rinehart and Winston, 1966.

———. *Robert Frost: The Years of Triumph, 1915–1938*. New York: Holt, Rinehart and Winston, 1970.

Thompson, Lawrance, and Winnick, R.H. *Robert Frost: The Later Years, 1938–1963*. New York: Holt, Rinehart and Winston, 1976.

JAMES E. MILLER, JR.

How Shall I Be Mirror to This Modernity?: William Carlos Williams's "Paterson"

Williams is part of the great breath of our literature. *Paterson* is our
Leaves of Grass.
—*Robert Lowell, "William Carlos Williams"*

1

In the poem that stands first in his *Collected Earlier Poems*, in Whitmanesque
lines that Williams first published in 1914, he says:

> But one day, crossing the ferry
> With the great towers of Manhattan before me,
> Out at the prow with the sea wind blowing,
> I had been wearying many questions
> Which she had put on to try me:
> How shall I be a mirror to this modernity?
>
> $(CEP,$ p. 3)[1]

The "she" of these lines, "old, painted— / With bright lips," looks startlingly
like a descendant of Whitman's muse which he discovered "install'd amid the
kitchen ware!" The ferry on which Williams rides in these lines may not be
Whitman's Brooklyn ferry, but it conjures up some of the same kinds of
poetic vision.

From *The American Quest for a Supreme Fiction: Whitman's Legacy in the Personal Epic.* © 1979 by
The University of Chicago.

The road from the 1914 "Wanderer" to the first Book of *Paterson* in 1946 is a long and open one, and it is not easy to assess the extent to which Whitman was a camerado in arms. In his *Autobiography* (1951), Williams freely confessed the unhealthy influence of Keats on his early poetry, an influence that he was able to lay to rest rather quickly under the scathing criticism of his friend Ezra Pound. But at the same time that he acknowledged the obsessions with Keats, Williams said: "For my notebooks, however (which I don't think anyone ever saw), I reserved my Whitmanesque 'thought,' a sort of purgation and confessional, to clear my head and my heart from turgid obsessions" (*A*, p. 53). Of his first book of poetry, Williams wrote: "The poems were bad Keats, nothing else—oh well, bad Whitman too. But I sure loved them" (*A*, p. 107).

Although Keats seemed to drop out of Williams's vocabulary rather early without much problem, Whitman remained in it over the years, as a focus of discussion or a point of reference. As early as 1917 Williams attempted to disentangle Whitman's significance for poetry and for him: "Whitman created the art [of poetry] in America.... There is no art of poetry save by grace of other poetry. So Dante to me can only be another way of saying Whitman. Yet without a Whitman there can be for me no Dante." Whitman was the "rock," the "first primitive," and modern poets could not "advance" until they had "grasped Whitman and then built upon him." But straight imitation was wrong: "The only way to be like Whitman is to write *unlike* Whitman. Do I expect to be a companion to Whitman by mimicking his manners?"[2] The line that Williams established in this little essay was one that he elaborated repeatedly in a variety of places. At times he was more, at times less, critical of Whitman—in a way carrying on a love-hate relationship not unlike that of Pound in his "Pact," and seeing himself (as did the early Pound) as one of Whitman's "encrustations" to come in "ages and ages." One of the most interesting of Williams's comments on Whitman came in that strange, early book, *Spring and All* (1923), filled with some of Williams's finest early poems together with seemingly random comments on the art and nature of poetry: "Whitman's proposals are of the same piece with the modern trend toward imaginative understanding of life. The largeness which he interprets as his identity with the least and the greatest about him, his 'democracy' represents the vigor of his imaginative life" (*I*, pp. 112–13).

This aspect of Whitman was perhaps the most enduring in its impact on Williams, in both his poetry and fiction. But it was Whitman's technical innovation that inspired Williams's most extensive and complicated commentary. In "Against the Weather: A Study of the Artist" (1939), Williams identified Whitman as "a key man to whom I keep returning ...

tremendously important in the history of modern poetry" (*SE*, p. 218). Whitman's importance is dramatically identifiable: "He broke through the deadness of copied forms which keep shouting above everything that wants to get said today drowning out one man with the accumulated weight of a thousand voices in the past—re-establishing the tyrannies of the past, the very tyrannies that we are seeking to diminish. The structure of the old is active, it says no! to everything in propaganda and poetry that wants to say yes. Whitman broke through that. That was basic and good" (*SE*, p. 218). But Whitman's innovation, however remarkable, was beyond his own full understanding: "Whitman was never able fully to realize the significance of his structural innovations. As a result he fell back to the overstuffed catalogues of his later poems and a sort of looseness that was not freedom but lack of measure. Selection, structural selection was lacking" (*SE*, p. 212). In brief, Whitman "broke the new wood"; now is the "time for carving" (as Pound had written in "A Pact").

By the 1950s, Williams's view of Whitman as the great innovator who somehow fell short of his own discoveries became a recurring theme, with variations. In 1954: "Whitman was right in breaking our bounds but, having no valid restraints to hold him went wild.... Whitman, great as he was in his instinctive drive, was also the cause of our going astray. I among the rest have much to answer for. No verse can be free, it must be governed by some measure, but not by the old measure. There Whitman was right but there, at the same time, his leadership failed him. The time was not ready for it. We have to return to some measure but a measure consonant with our time and not a mode so rotten that it stinks" (*SE*, p. 339). In 1955 (in "An Essay on *Leaves of Grass*"): "Whitman's so-called 'free verse' was an assault on the very citadel of the poem itself: it constituted a direct challenge to all living poets to show cause why they should not do likewise. It is a challenge that still holds good after a century of vigorous life during which it has been practically continuously under fire but never defeated." Yes, but: "He had seen a great light but forgot almost at once after the first revelation everything but his 'message,' the idea which originally set him in motion, the idea on which he had been nurtured, the idea of democracy—and took his eye off the words themselves which should have held him."[3] By the time Williams wrote these comments, he himself was in process of exploiting the new "variable foot" and "triadic line" which he had hit upon in the writing of Book II of *Paterson* (1948).

Later, Williams's view of Whitman became somewhat more expansive. In an important little essay entitled "The American Idiom" (1961), he wrote: "The American idiom is the language we speak in the United States. It is characterized by certain differences from the language used among cultured Englishmen, being completely free from all influences which can be summed up as having to do with 'the Establishment.' This, pared to essentials, is the language which governed Walt Whitman in his choice of words. It constituted a revolution in the language." Williams asserted that the revolution is continuing, and the modern reply to the "fixed foot of the ancient line" is "the variable foot which we are beginning to discover after Whitman's advent.... Whitman lived in the nineteenth century but he, it must be acknowledged, proceeded instinctively by rule of thumb and a tough head, correctly, in the construction of his verses. He knew nothing of the importance of what he had stumbled on, unconscious of the concept of the variable foot."[4]

It is clear from these scattered comments on Whitman that Williams felt affinities and at the same time felt the necessity of declaring his independence; after all, in his drive to discover the new, Williams could not give over his allegiance totally to any poet of the past—not even Whitman. But there is one more significant comment on Whitman to be noted. In all of *Paterson*, Whitman's name is not to be found (except in one of the Allen Ginsberg letters—"I do have a whitmanic mania & nostalgia for cities and detail & panorama and isolation in jungle and pole, like the images you pick up") (*P*, p. 213). But Williams goes out of his way to inject Whitman's name in a brief commentary on *Paterson* at the end of his *Autobiography*. Williams published what he assumed to be then the final book, Book IV, of *Paterson* that same year (1951): the poem fulfilled his plans as publicly announced and he saw it as finished. His brief comments in his *Autobiography*, in the final chapter entitled "The Poem Paterson," are mostly of a general nature, but one of the few paragraphs turns almost interpretive: "In the end the man rises from the sea where the river appears to have lost its identity and accompanied by his faithful bitch, obviously a Chesapeake Bay retriever, turns inland toward Camden where Walt Whitman, much traduced, lived the latter years of his life and died. He always said that the poems, which had broken the dominance of the iambic pentameter in English prosody, had only begun his theme. I agree. It is up to us, in the new dialect, to continue it by a new contruction upon the syllables" (*A*, p. 392). This is a remarkable comment, hardly to be derived from the poetic text itself, but clearly earnest and almost defiant (earlier in the passage Williams addresses his critics); at this critical final (final as of 1951) moment in his poem, Williams's imagination evokes Whitman—as Pound had done in Canto 82, as Crane had done in Part IV of *The Bridge*.

2

But before attempting to fathom Williams's meaning here ("It is up to us ... to continue" the theme which Whitman "had only begun"), we must trace in outline the emergence of Williams's *Paterson*. For this, two other poets are of considerable importance. If Whitman was a poet with whom Williams connected and of whom he felt himself a continuation, the expatriates T.S. Eliot and Ezra Pound (the latter a lifelong friend) constituted poets against whom he felt himself in reaction. There is no need here to trace out the relations in detail—these have been illuminatingly explored in Louis Simpson's *Three on the Tower*[5]—but Williams's strong feelings against some aspects of their poetry shaped his own ideas of *Paterson*. Williams came to view *The Waste Land* as "the great catastrophe to our letters" (*A*, p. 146), and he wrote with passionate intensity of his memory of the poem's publication:

> Then out of the blue *The Dial* brought out *The Waste Land* and all our hilarity ended. It wiped out our world as if an atom bomb had been dropped upon it and our brave sallies into the unknown were turned to dust.
>
> To me especially it struck like a sardonic bullet. I felt at once that it had set me back twenty years, and I'm sure it did. Critically Eliot returned us to the classroom just at the moment when I felt that we were on the point of an escape to matters much closer to the essence of a new art form itself—rooted in the locality which should give it fruit. I knew at once that in certain ways I was most defeated.
>
> Eliot had turned his back on the possibility of reviving my world. And being an accomplished craftsman, better skilled in some ways that I could ever hope to be, I had to watch him carry my world off with him, the fool, to the enemy. (*A*, p. 174)

Although Williams's relationship with Pound was much more complex (as, for example, note Williams's appreciative review of *A Draft of XXX Cantos* [1931]), his reservations about Pound's epic were deep. He wrote in 1939:

> The truth is that news offers the precise incentive to epic poetry, the poetry of events; and now is precisely the time for it since never by any chance is the character of a single fact ever truthfully represented today. If ever we are to have any understanding of

what is going on about us we shall need some other means for discovering it.

The epic poem would be our "newspaper," Pound's cantos are the algebraic equivalent but too perversely individual to achieve the universal understanding required. The epic if you please is what we're after, but not the lyric-epic sing-song. It must be a concise sharpshooting epic style. Machine gun style. Facts, facts, facts, tearing into us to blast away our stinking flesh of news. Bullets.[6]

When Williams wrote in the italicized epigraph to *Paterson*—"a reply to Greek and Latin with the bare hands"—he was pitting his epic against the long poems of Eliot and Pound; and throughout *Paterson* Williams continued his response to them (as at the end when Paterson rises from the sea they followed to Europe and turns back to the land, Camden, and Whitman).

Although the first book of *Paterson* appeared in 1946, when Williams was sixty-three, and other books appeared in 1948, 1949, 1951, and 1958 (when he was seventy-five; notes for Book VI were found at his death in 1963), some of the lines were written as early as 1914, in the poem "The Wanderer," when he was only thirty-one. From 1914 to 1958 is forty-four years—a long time to live with a poem. And that thirty-two-year lag (a minimal period, since we don't have a complete record of Williams's mind) from embryonic idea to first execution surely constitutes the kind of "long foreground" which Emerson detected behind *Leaves of Grass* on its appearance in 1855. The 1939 comment quoted above (on the nature of the "epic poem") appears to have been made by a man who had long since determined not only what constituted an epic but also that he was going to write one. The first line from a strange prose piece entitled "Notes in Diary Form" and dated 1927 flashes out to arrest attention: "I will make a big, serious portrait of my time" (*SE*, p. 62). In 1927 Williams also published a poem entitled "Paterson," in which for the first time he introduces a Mr. Paterson who has some of the aspects of a city ("Inside the bus one sees / his thoughts sitting and standing" [*CEP*, p. 233]), and in which he reiterates: "Say it, no ideas but in things" (*CEP*, p. 233). Both lines and ideas from this poem ended up in the later epic: by 1927 the embryo had developed recognizable features, but still had to wait out a long gestation.

In 1937 appeared "Paterson: Episode 17," the very title suggesting a long poem well along in progress, if not in fact at least in conception. If this conception was to change considerably over the next nine years before the publication of Book I, there would still be room in Book III (1949) for many lines and the main themes of "Paterson: Episode 17": "Beautiful Thing," detected in the form of a maid beating a rug, a comely girl with a mixed sexual history who, in spite of violence and violation, retains a kind of innocence and purity, her rhythmic action containing the beat of poetry itself:

> The stroke begins again—
>   regularly
> automatic
>   contrapuntal to
> the flogging
> like the beat of famous lines
> in the few excellent poems
>   woven to make you
>   gracious
> and on frequent occasions
>   foul drunk
>   Beautiful Thing
> pulse of release
>   to the attentive
> and obedient mind.
>   (*CEP*, pp, 441–42)

Inasmuch as *Paterson* is a poem portraying a quest for beauty, and specifically Beautiful Thing, and particularly since in the long poem the poet finds Beautiful Thing in essentially the same embodiment as he did in this 1937 poem, we might assume that by this year Williams had brought into focus an important part of his epic's scope and meaning. As fragments of "Paterson: Episode 17" appear in Book III of *Paterson* (contrapuntally with the burning of the library), the phrase Beautiful Thing takes on resonance and almost visionary meaning—a meaning worthy of exploration in its proper place in the poem.

Of Williams's many works that might be cited as important milestones on the road to *Paterson*, two prose volumes must be singled out for mention. The first of these is *In the American Grain* (1925), an extraordinary exploration of the American past through the accounts and histories of America's discoverers, explorers, founders, adventurers, warriors, leaders, and writers. The cumulative picture is not a pretty one, and is filled with cruelty and violence, as Williams permits many of the personages to condemn themselves through their own incredible narratives—as, for

example, Cotton Mather does in his accounts of the witches of Salem in
chapters from *Wonders of the Invisible World.* Williams reveals something of
his purpose in the book when he records his reply to a question (in Paris) as
to why Americans don't speak more often of the things he has just recounted
(much like the things of this book): "Because the fools do not believe that
they have sprung from anything: bone, thought and action. They will not see
that what they are is growing on these roots. They will not look. They float
without question. Their history is to them an enigma" (*IAG,* p. 113). If this
unromantic examination of the American past brought Williams closer to his
epic vision, his volume of short stories published in 1938, *Life along the
Passaic River,* brought him still closer. In the former book Williams located
himself as an American in time (in relation to the past); in the latter he found
himself in place (in relation to locality and the local). The stories of *Life along
the Passaic River* are sketches of ordinary, mostly humble people with whom
Williams has shared some experience in his role as family doctor delivering
babies and caring for children. Williams not only finds his material in the
locality where he lives and works, but he also finds his values there—material
and values that were to figure prominently in the epic then shaping.

3

Williams's "long foreground" gave him time to work out, change, and
work out again many plans for *Paterson,* but his conception of a Mr. Paterson
seems to have endured from his first appearance in the 1927 poem. Paterson
is a shifting identity: the city, but also a man, everyman, modern man, a poet,
a doctor, and, of course, William Carlos Williams himself. If there is
ambiguity as to the "I" or speaker in the poem, it is no doubt intentional and
is in the tradition of ambiguity that Whitman established in *Leaves of Grass,*
where the "I" may be any one of a number of identities, not unlike many of
those *Paterson* assumes. Although the identity of Paterson may sometimes be
confusing when we first enter the poem, as we move into the later books the
speaker of the poem becomes more and more clearly identifiable as William
Carlos Williams. Like *Leaves of Grass, Paterson* contains a great deal of
autobiography, all put in the service of the poetry.

Like other epics we are examining, the basic structure of *Paterson* is the
structure of the journey or voyage, the inner or spiritual quest in search of—
what? Knowledge? Awareness? Beauty? Language? All these, and perhaps
more. The opening lines of the poem's "Preface" state bluntly: "Rigor of
beauty is the quest. But how will you find beauty / when it is locked in the
mind past all remonstrance?" (*P,* p. 3). At one time, Williams had added to

these lines: "It is not in the things nearest us unless transported there by our employment. Make it free, then, by the art you have, to enter these starved and broken pieces."[7] The beauty is there, in the local, but only art can *make it free*. These are words to remember as we pursue (with Williams) Beautiful Thing in Book III of *Paterson*.

But if Paterson the man is an Odysseus figure (and the metaphor is used on occasion, as at the end of Book IV), he is an Odysseus who travels at home, his highest adventure a Sunday walk in the park, a dunking in the ocean near the shore. *Paterson* is rigorously local, and only by so being could it become American or universal: "The first idea centering upon the poem, *Paterson*, came alive early: to find an image large enough to embody the whole knowable world about me. The longer I lived in my place, among the details of my life, I realized that these isolated observations and experiences needed pulling together to gain 'profundity'" (*A*, p. 391). But the "whole knowable world" could not be embodied in a poem about the universe, the globe, the country, but only about a specific locale: "That is the poet's business. Not to talk in vague categories but to write particularly, as a physician works, upon a patient, upon the thing before him, in the particular to discover the universal. John Dewey had said (I discovered it quite by chance), 'The local is the only universal, upon that all art builds.' " (*A*, p. 391). *Paterson*, then, conceived in these terms and with these purposes, provides far larger boundaries for the imagination than the geographic. We do not want to use the term "symbolic" because it was a term that Williams avoided, condemned as a grasping after that universal without the local. But neither do we want to mistake *Paterson* as providing locale for the purpose of mere local color. Williams put it: "If it rose to flutter into life awhile—it would be as itself, locally, and so like every other place in the world. For it is in that, that it be particular to its own idiom, that it lives" (*A*, p. 392).

The basic form, the quest. Then what? After only a few pages into the poem, the poetry is interrupted by fragments of prose—letters, historical accounts, statistics, advertisements, recorded interviews, and so on—some of them quite long, interrupting the poetic flow for several pages, or standing at important junctures, as, for example, the eight-page letter at the end of Book II. What kind of "poetry" can this be? In response to Wallace Stevens's suggestion that the prose passages were "anti-poetic," Williams wrote:

All the prose, including the tail which would have liked to have wagged the dog, has primarily the purpose of giving a metrical meaning to or of emphasizing a metrical continuity between all word use. It is *not* an anti-poetic device, the repeating of which piece of miscalculation makes me want to puke. It is that prose and verse are both *writing*, both a matter of the words and an interrelation between words for the purpose of exposition, or other better defined purpose of *the art*. Please do not stress other "meanings." I want to say that prose and verse are to me the same thing, that verse (as in Chaucer's tales) belongs *with* prose, as the poet belongs with "Mine host," who says in so many words to Chaucer, "Namoor, all that rhyming is not worth a toord." Poetry does not *have* to be kept away from prose as Mr. Eliot might insist, it goes *along with* prose and, companionably, by itself, without aid or excuse or need for separation or bolstering, shows itself by *itself* for what it is. *It belongs* there, in the gutter. Not anywhere else or wherever it is, it is the same: the poem. (*SL*, p. 263)

In the gutter?

Williams's explanation verges on the irrational—a term that he himself evoked in another attempt on his part to explain the prose insertions in *Paterson*:

... one fault in modern compositions ... is that the irrational has no place. Yet in life (you show it by your tolerance of things which you feel no loss at not understanding) there is much that men exclude because they do not understand. The truly great heart *includes* what it does not at once grasp, just as the great artist includes things which go beyond him.... The irrational enters the poem in those letters, included in the text, which do not seem to refer to anything in the "story" yet do belong somehow to the poem—how, it is not easy to say. (*SL*, p. 309)

Here Williams seems to be as puzzled about the prose in *Paterson* as some of his readers, who might take Williams's reaction as an invitation to discover their own rationale for the presence of the prose in the poem. In the first place, the prose is a way of extending the poem beyond its poetic boundaries—in the direction of the comprehensive. Elements are injected— an Indian massacre, letters of a quasi-neurotic poetess, a handbill on social credit—that extend the reach of the poem suddenly, forcefully, and with an immediacy that would be hard to achieve in a rational introduction of the subject into the verse. The prose pieces are all intensely "local" artifacts whose grounding in feeling and passion, time and place, is indisputable.

They provide, then, through their supreme particularity, much of the poem's reach for universality. In this way they resemble the long catalogs in *Leaves of Grass*—those lists of items, persons, scenes, activities, thoughts, all of which, by near-exhaustion of possibilities, convey the sense of totality: all of life is included here, Whitman and Williams seem to say, and belongs here and cannot be excluded, the poetic and the anti-poetic, the rational and the irrational, the important and the trivial, the poetry and the prose of life.

Allied perhaps to this purpose of comprehensiveness is the attempt to keep the poem close to reality—the real reality of life as daily experienced by all of us. We have read such accounts, we have heard of such massacres, we have talked of such sensational behavior, we have feared such violence, and we have received or written such letters. We recognize the painful reality of the exposures, and we perhaps squirm a bit in discomfort. Williams must have thought: the poem in its poetry, at such length, is likely to wander away from reality too easily (language is tricky, deceptive); the way to keep it near things as they are is to have these periodic injections of prose, real prose, taken out of my life as I live it in this place, from these people I know, from these books I read, from these handbills I receive, from these statistics I ponder. Some such reasoning, conscious or unconscious, we might imagine on Williams's part. And he might have thought, too, that since his theme is importantly about language, the varieties of language introduced by the prose would reinforce his theme in subtle ways. There is a wide range of usage, tone, level in the language of the prose—nearly always jarring, striking, or puzzling. There is language that is groping, language that is inarticulate, salty language, stilted language, passionless and impassioned language, language that cries and language that laughs—and it is all language that brings to the reader the shock of recognition, of reality. Has the poem drifted too far in its measured language? Then tear out a page from daily life and stick it in to bring it back close to earth; the language will signal its reality. And since the poet works intuitively, to his own rhythmic sense of pacing—the prose appearing rhythmically spaced—there will be reverberations, resonance, ironic echoes and reechoes. The theme is art or poetry? Then the letters will be from artists and poets; the reader may test the poem's reality directly in its interwoven stream of quotidian reality in subjects and themes openly or subterraneously related.

Such must have been some of the unformulated theory that lay behind the prose passages. They are compatible—meld—with what is perhaps the poem's geographic centerpiece, the falls: "Paterson lies in the valley under the Passaic Falls." (Williams remarked of his choice of the city Paterson in 1951, "It has ... a central feature, the Passaic Falls which as I began to think about it became more and more the lucky burden of what I wanted to say,")[8] The ears of the man-city are the rocks that lie under the falls. Williams wrote in his *Autobiography:* "The Falls let out a roar as it crashed upon the rocks at its base. In the imagination this roar is a speech or a voice, a speech in particular: it is the poem itself that is the answer" (*A*, p. 392). The first full description of the falls comes after a prose insert (fragment of a letter from a frustrated woman poet):

> Jostled as are the waters approaching
> the brink, his thoughts
> interlace, repel and cut under,
> rise rock-thwarted and turn aside
> but forever strain forward—or strike
> an eddy and whirl, marked by a
> leaf or curdy spume, seeming
> to forget
>
> (*P*, p. 7)

Here Paterson's thoughts and, implicitly, the letter's pleading, are mixed in the waters that move to the edge to—

> fall, fall in air! as if
> floating, relieved of their weight,
> split apart, ribbons; dazed, drunk
> with the catastrophe of the descent
> floating unsupported
> to hit the rocks: to a thunder,
> as if lightning had struck
>
> (*P*, p. 8)

"Catastrophe of the descent": here is the lost history of Paterson that has cried out in descent only to "hit the rocks," the deaf ears of mankind. "The language, the language / fails them / They do not know the words / or have not / the courage to use them" (*P*, p. 11). Only in the local may be found the universal: the lost history of Paterson, the lost history of America, the lost history of mankind has poured with thunder over those falls, falling on stone ears. The poet sets himself the task of "combing out" the language of the falls—and that includes watching, listening, observing language from its every direction as it pours down on the poet. What is the significance of "insignificant" lives; what is the meaning of the "meaningless" flow of events in the voiceless currents of ceaseless experience? Book I concludes: "Earth, the chatterer, father of all / speech." The poet struggles to unstop his stone ear.

4

Readers of *Paterson* quickly realize that they are not reading a traditional narrative, but they soon begin to catch glimpses of a fugitive narrative. Paterson's journey through the local does, finally, reach some kind of awareness. And the arrangements of the books of *Paterson* represent to some extent stages on that journey to awareness. The form is open-ended inasmuch as such journeys are never concluded until the death of the poet; thus *Paterson* has its concluding fragments, just as *The Cantos* has its and *Leaves of Grass* the Annexes. But the open-endedness does not preclude conclusion. In a sense, each book of *Paterson* is a conclusion, and the first four books especially lead to a conclusion, but Book V carries the reader further along to another stage in the poet-Paterson's insight or vision, combing further the language of the falls.

There are abundant suggestions of an elemental organization of *Paterson*, especially in the various descriptions that Williams drew up for the poem. One of the earliest available of these is the poem, "Paterson: The Falls," which appeared in the 1944 volume, *The Wedge:*

> What common language to unravel?
> The Falls, combed into straight lines
> from the rafter of a rock's
> lip. Strike in! the middle of
> some trenchant phrase, some
> well packed clause. Then ...
> This is my plan. 4 sections:
> (*CLP,* p. 10)

The poem's remaining eight stanzas give an outline of the poem as Williams planned it. "First, / the archaic persons of the drama." Here will be "an eternity of bird and bush," and "an unraveling: / the confused streams aligned, side / by side, speaking!" Next, "The wild / voice of the shirt-sleeved / Evangelist rivaling," his voice "echoing / among the bass and pickerel." And then, "Third, the old town: Alexander Hamilton / working up from St. Croix," but "stopped cold / by that unmoving roar." And finally,

Fourth,
the modern town, a
disembodied roar! the cataract and
its clamor broken apart—and from
all learning, the empty
ear struck from within, roaring.

                                    (*CLP*, p. 11)

This early conception of the poem is clearly comprehensive at the same time
that it omits much vital to the finished poem. And if the plan for Part Four—
"the empty / ear struck from within, roaring"—was for some climactic
interior vision, the plan was not apparently fulfilled, until, perhaps, Part Five
with its vision of death as "a hole," through which the "imagination / escapes
intact" (*P*, p. 212).

    When Book I appeared in 1946, Williams wrote: "Part One introduces
the elemental character of the place. The Second Part comprises the modern
replicas. Three will seek a language to make them vocal, and Four, the river
below the falls, will be reminiscent of episodes—all that any one man may
achieve in a lifetime" (*P*, p. 1). The epigraph to *Paterson* suggests seasonal
analogies: "*spring, summer, fall and the sea*" (*P*, p. 2). Writing on the
publication of Book III, Williams said: "From the beginning I decided there
would be four books following the course of the river whose life seemed
more and more to resemble my own life as I more and more thought of it:
the river above the Falls, the catastrophe of the Falls itself, the river below
the Falls, and the entrance at the end into the great sea." Williams then
defined the poem's structure in terms of a quest: "The brunt of the four
books is a search for the redeeming language by which a man's premature
death ... might have been prevented. Book IV shows the perverse confusions
that come of a failure to untangle the language and make it our own as both
man and woman are carried helplessly toward the sea (of blood) which, by
their failure of speech, awaits them. The poet alone in this world holds the
key to their final rescue."[9]

    In 1951, Williams reviewed his plans for *Paterson*, and confessed:

    There were a hundred modifications of this general plan as,
    following the theme rather than the river itself, I allowed myself
    to be drawn on. The noise of the Falls seemed to me to be a
    language which we were and are seeking, and my search, as I
    looked about, became the struggle to interpret and use this
    language. This is the substance of the poem. But the poem is also

the search of the poet after his language, his own language which I, quite apart from the material theme, had to use to write at all. I had to write in a certain way to gain a verisimilitude with the object I had in mind.

Williams's own intuitive way of working is suggested by his statement: "So the objective became complex. It fascinated me, it instructed me besides." The concluding book then became a challenge:

And I had to think hard as to how I was going to end the poem. It wouldn't do to have a grand and soul-satisfying conclusion, because I didn't see any in my subject. Nor was I going to be confused or depressed or evangelical about it. It didn't belong to my subject. It would have been easy to make a great smash up with a "beautiful" sunset at sea, or a flight of pigeons, love's end and the welter of man's fate. Instead, after the little girl gets herself mixed up at last in the pathetic sophisticate of the great city, no less defeated and understandable, even lovable, than she is herself, we come to the sea at last. Odysseus swims in as a man must always do, he doesn't drown, he is too able, but, accompanied by his dog, strikes inland again (toward Camden) to begin again.[10]

Book V of *Paterson* never figured in the early planning of the poem, but it was not long after the publication of Book IV in 1951 that Williams began musing on the possibility of Book V. In 1953 he remarked to John Thirlwall: "At first I didn't have any plans. It ends with the river mingling with the ocean. You come to the ocean and that's the end of all life; that's the end of the river and the end of everything that concerns the river. But the fifth book, well, you might logically say there shouldn't be an end. But, as you recollect, as you look back to find a meaning, nobody knows anything about death and whether it is an end. It possibly isn't an end. It's a possibility that there's something more to be said." In this same conversation, Williams remarked of the earlier books: "It's a man in his own life going through, not revealing very much of his own life, but telling of the region which he's inhabited for a certain number of years and what it meant to him so far as it can be told. Many things are to be inferred."[11]

Whatever Williams's plans, and whatever his remembrance of *Paterson*, the achieved poem escapes the outlines. As someone has said of linguistics— all grammars leak. All the structures of any complex poem, even those of the maker, leak: there are elements, depths, dimensions that escape the net. *Paterson* may be viewed as a sequence of stages on the way (an endless way) to knowing. The dominant elements of each of the books then come to focus in patterns and relationships that begin to make a whole:

Book I, "The Delineaments of the Giants": blockage and divorce as Paterson's historical inheritance. The two most vivid examples, Sam Patch (Noah Faitoute Paterson) who jumps to his death (in 1829) in the Genesee River falls, his body later found in a cake of ice; and Mrs. Sarah Cumming, recently married to the Reverend Hopper Cumming, who fell without a word, probably deliberately, over the Passaic Falls in 1812. Appearing contrapuntally with these two vivid and recurring images of language failure is the image of an old *National Geographic* picture of the nine women of an African chief, a picture that speaks of something enigmatic in spite of its silence.

Book II, "Sunday in the Park": the book of place—here; the shoddy and the sordid; deformity and drunkenness. The Sunday walk in the park above the falls presents a sequence of vignettes that might at first glance constitute a wasteland of modern urban industrial life; Hamilton's "great beast," the common people, in meaningless and purposeless Sunday relaxation and torpor. There are two contrapuntal threads of action that vividly mark the walk: a pair of lovers caught sleepily in their desire, frustrated, dozing; and an itinerant minister who has given over all his riches in order to preach salvation. The dominant prose injection of this book is the sequence of letters from the anxiety-ridden female poet, and the book ends in a long denunciation of Paterson by the poetess.

Book III, "The Library": the book of time—now; the library's stench, purified by storm, fire, flood. As Book II was a walk in the park, Book III is a walk in the past, through books. "The library is desolation, it has a smell of its own / of stagnation and death" (*P*, p. 100). The contrapuntal theme is the search for Beautiful Thing, found in a Negress beating a rug—far from the environment or concerns of the books of a library. The prose passages inject considerable violence, particularly historical accounts of the killing of Indians (juxtaposed to Beautiful Thing).

Book IV, "The Run to the Sea": "perverse confusions"; the Lesbian poetess and Paterson vie for Phyllis in an ironic modern Idyl. Images of blockage and divorce dominate—the atom bomb, Billy Sunday, usury, violence (especially in the prose accounts of murder); but there are contrapuntal themes, particularly in the account of Madame Curie's discovery of radium and in Paterson's vigorous return from the "sea of blood" ("the sea is not our home") at the end and striding off inland with refreshed spirit for a new beginning.

Book V: bridging the way from life to death; the Unicorn tapestries and the immortal vision of art. Out of the tapestries at the Cloisters museum in New York City, Paterson weaves a final poem of discovery beyond the Paterson of Book IV: he discovers a "hole" through the bottom of death—the imagination of art. But this book of death is filled with a lively life: the life of love triumphant over blockage and divorce. Love walks the bridge of imagination (and art) to and *through* death. The poet advises himself (and his reader), "keep your pecker up." The book ends with the "measured dance," a dance of life made up (like the serpent with its tale in its mouth) of both the joyous and the painful, of love and death; "dance to a measure / Satyrically, the tragic foot."

In this summary view of *Paterson*, much has leaked away that is vital to the poem. But the overview might serve as the basis for a longitudinal approach which will constitute a kind of combing out of the major languages of the poems as they thread and entangle their way through all the books of *Paterson*. Williams repeatedly asserted that his poem constituted a search for a redeeming language. The question remains, Did he find it? The answer to this question involves us in passages of the poem passed over in the above summary view. Of the poem's many languages, there is first and foremost the Language of Chaos: there is the unmistakably less robust Language of Beauty; and there is the more fragile Language of Redemption. As we comb out these languages we shall simplify, but they will immediately re-entangle themselves in the poem where they shall remain inviolate.

5

The loudest language of *Paterson* is the language of chaos, of criticism, the language which the poet finds as the reality of Paterson, the reality of America. Indeed, a first reading of the poem might well leave the impression that it is the only language because it is so dominant. The voiceless drownings of Sam Patch (who used the symbolic name of Noah Faitoute Paterson, thus enabling the poet to identify with him) and Mrs. Cumming offer a paradigm for a languageless, perishing America, suffering from "blockage" (it's there but it's dammed up, blocked) and from "divorce," a failure of connecting humanly because of a failure of language. But the Patch-Cumming episodes are only the most vivid of a large cluster of related images of failure:

The language, the language
    fails them

They do not know the words
    or have not
the courage to use them   .
    —girls from
families that have decayed and
taken to the hills. no words.
They may look at the torrent in
    their minds
and it is foreign to them.   .
They turn their backs
and grow faint—but recover!
    Life is sweet
they say: the language!
    —the language
is divorced from their minds,
the language . . the language!
               (*P,* pp. 11–12)

It is not, of course, that there is no language at all: worse, there is abundant language (or sound) that misleads and betrays:

A false language. A true. A false language pouring—a
language (misunderstood) pouring (misinterpreted) without
dignity, without minister, crashing upon a stone ear.
(*P,* p. 15)

By divorce Williams does not of course have reference simply to matrimony: his notion of divorce goes much deeper, with profounder consequences:

    a bud forever green,
tight-curled, upon the pavement, perfect
in juice and substance but divorced, divorced
from its fellows, fallen low—
    Divorce is
the sign of knowledge in our time,
divorce! divorce!
    with the roar of the river
forever in our ears (arrears)
inducing sleep and silence, the roar

of eternal sleep ... challenging
our waking—

(*P,* p. 18)

This divorce is a severance from the fruition of life itself. In divorce "from its fellows," the bud remains "forever green." Thus Williams suggests a profound immaturity characteristic of America, with the energy and potential present but unrealized. And the divorce is clearly related to the "roar" which communicates nothing but its uncombed sound, rendering genuine human connection difficult if not impossible. Life roars by and leaves nothing in its wake but a trailing silence, "the roar / of eternal sleep," death, the final and lasting divorce.

In Book II of *Paterson*, the poet-protagonist's Sunday walk through the park brings into focus some of the causes of blockage and divorce. There is, first of all, the people—Alexander Hamilton's "great beast"—coarsened by a life of hard work:

... the ugly legs of the young girls,
pistons too powerful for delicacy!
the men's arms, red, used to heat and cold,
to toss quartered beeves and   .

(*P,* p. 44)

Their Sunday relaxation suggests the nature of the other days of their lives—days in the factories and businesses of Paterson earning the money for survival. In what is potentially an Eliotic *Waste Land* scene, the "great beast" of the people ignoring the traditional meaning of Sunday and wasting their time in meaningless activities, drinking beer, playing ball, quarreling and napping, we encounter a vision closer to Whitman's than to Eliot's: there is sympathy and understanding and searching as Paterson walks through the park. "Cash is mulct of them that others may live / secure / . . and knowledge restricted" (*P,* p. 72). A significant part of the poet's vision comes in a prose passage: "Even during the Revolution Hamilton had been impressed by the site of the Great Falls of the Passaic. His fertile imagination envisioned a great manufacturing center, a great Federal City, to supply the needs of the country. Here was water-power to turn the mill wheels and the navigable river to carry manufactured goods to the market centers: a national manufactury" (*P,* p. 69). Williams had been attracted to Paterson and its Passaic Falls precisely because of Hamilton's historical involvement, his vision of great material wealth, prototype of the American dream. Somewhere, back in the past, in the visionary planning of such as Hamilton, lies the cause of the wastes on display on Sunday in the park.

There is one man in the park who speaks a torrent of words: Klaus, the "Protestant! protesting—as / though the world were his own." In telling his story to the Sunday park strollers, he reveals himself the victim of the American dream—victim in the sense that he came to America, made the riches he dreamed of, and discovered in a visitation from "our blessed Lord" that he was not happy. He followed the injunction to give away all his money and found finally in his evangelism the way to happiness: "There is no / end to the treasures of our Blessed Lord who / died on the Cross for us that we may be saved" (P, p. 73). We no sooner read the "Amen" to Klaus's familiar revival sermon than we find ourselves in a prose passage describing the Federal Reserve System in the U.S., a private enterprise that creates money and lends it at high interest, forcing the people to "pay interest to the banks in the form of high taxes" (P, p. 73). Usury, a familiar theme from Ezra Pound's *Cantos* here divulged as lying obscurely behind the ugliness of Sunday in the park: "The Federal Reserve Banks constitute a Legalized National Usury System." (P, p. 74). Klaus's torrent of words misses the economic reality. The people comprehend neither him nor the system his mythology distorts and veils. The roar goes on, unattended, uncombed.

The Library, in Book III, turns out to be the repository not of the wisdom of the past, but of the cumulative horrors of history. Accumulated newspapers reveal that the past is simply more of the present:

> Old newspaper files,
> to find—a child burned in a field,
> no language. Tried, aflame, to crawl under
> a fence to go home. So be it. Two others,
> boy and girl, clasped in each others' arms
> (clasped also by the water) So be it. Drowned
> wordless in the canal. So be it.
>
> (P, pp. 97–98)

From newspapers Paterson turns to the books: "A library—of books! decrying all books / that enfeeble the mind's intent" (P, p. 102). It is soon clear that the books do not contain the revelation for which the poet seeks:

The place sweats of staleness and of rot
a back-house stench   .   a
library stench

(P, p. 103)

Paterson realizes that the books "cannot penetrate and cannot waken, to be again / active but remain—books / that is, men in hell, / their reign over the living ended" (P, p. 115). In the midst of this awareness, one of the most violent of the prose inserts relates the story of the torture and murder of innocent Indians by American colonists, witnessed by "leaders" who "stood laughing heartily at the fun" (P, p. 102). The reader muses: where are the books in this library that reveal the reality of this American pioneer past? By the time the tornado strikes, followed by the fire and the flood, the reader yearns with Paterson for the cleansing of the past to make way for a new beginning.

Book III concludes with some of the most Whitmanian lines of *Paterson*. Unlike Eliot and Pound, very much like Emerson and Whitman, Paterson learns from the Library experience—

The past above, the future below
And the present pouring down: the roar,
the roar of the present, a speech—
is, of necessity, my sole concern   .

(P, p. 144)

Whitman put it this way in his 1855 Preface: "The direct trial of him who would be the greatest poet is today. If he does not flood himself with the immediate age as with vast oceanic tides ... and if he be not himself the age transfigured ... let him ... wait his development."[12] Paterson seems determined to be the Whitmanian poet:

I cannot stay here
to spend my life looking into the past;

the future's no answer. I must
find my meaning and lay it, white,
beside the sliding water: myself—
comb out the language—or succumb

—whatever the complexion. Let

me out! (Well, go!) this rhetoric
is real!
(*P*, p. 145)

Whitman always declared that his rhetoric was of the flesh: "Camerado, this is no book, / Who touches this touches a man."[13]

Book IV, which was once thought to complete *Paterson*, pleased almost nobody, and even Williams felt moved to add another book. No doubt a major reason for the critical displeasure with the book is the dominance of the language of chaos, with vignettes and images of perversion, sexual frustration, violence and death. Readers have not known how to interpret the opening section, portraying a Lesbian poetess vying with Dr. Paterson for the sexual favors of a beautiful nurse. Critics have tended to be more condemnatory morally than Williams himself, who commented: "The little girl gets herself mixed up at last in the pathetic sophisticate of the great city, no less defeated and understandable, even lovable, than she is herself."[14] Clearly Williams did not intend the episode in an Eliotic sense—sexual perversion as emblematic of moral and spiritual perversion. His sympathies for all the frustrated participants come through the long sketch, and his admiration for the girl shines brightly in the poetry. What has not been much noticed about the narrative is its mixture of languages. The poetess in the "Idyl" is a creature out of the library of Book III, her version of reality framed by poetic visions from the past, classical or modern; she forces her life into the unreal form of a pastoral, and she writes Phyllis a poem with lines that even she recognizes from Yeats. Paterson, too, sees his experience with Phyllis framed in an Eliotic vision: "Oh Paterson! Oh married man! / He is the city of cheap hotels and private entrances" (*P*, p. 154). As he departs from a rendezvous, he remembers that there is something he wanted to say—"but I've forgotten / what it was . something I wanted / to tell you. Completely gone! Completely" (*P*, p. 154). The only entirely genuine language in this frustrated triangle is the language of the down-to-earth letters that Phyllis writes to her alcoholic father, reeking with a refreshing reality that points up the phoniness of the rest: "Look, Big Shot, I refuse to come home until you promise to cut out the booze" (*P*, p. 150).

Book IV presents other images of chaos, images of the atomic bomb, of "the cancer, usury," and of violence. Perhaps the most impressive of these are the prose accounts (in Part Three) of several murders, one the story of a young man killing his own infant daughter when "her crying annoyed him," and another the story (1850) of one John Johnson, a sometime hired hand (an inverse of Robert Frost's), who killed his former employer and wife, and then "was hung in full view of thousands who had gathered on Garrett Mountain and adjacent house tops to witness the spectacle" (*P*, p. 203). What gives this passage authority is its position within five short lines of the conclusion of Book IV (and one time the end of the poem). It is, indeed, the final image of the book, and is almost like a slap in the face for readers who have smiled affirmatively as they have just witnessed Paterson wade out of the "sea of blood" and strike inland for what seems to be a new beginning. The closing lines: "This is the blast / the eternal close / the spiral / the final somersault / the end." Thus readers are not permitted a sentimental conclusion; they are reminded of the reality of violence as it exists not only in Johnson but also in the crowds come to witness, among whom the reader might even, if he looks hard enough, discover himself.

In Book V of *Paterson*, the images of chaos decrease considerably, and they are integrated almost inseparably with images of renewal—the unicorn suffers death, but transcends death. In Part Two, Paterson exclaims:

> I saw love
> > mounted naked on a horse
> > > on a swan
> > the tail of a fish
> > > the bloodthirsty conger eel
> > > > and laughed
> > recalling the Jew
> > > in the pit
> > > > among his fellows
> > when the indifferent chap
> > > with the machine gun
> > > > was spraying the heap
> > he had not yet been hit
> > > but smiled
> > comforting his companions
> > > comforting
> > > > his companions.
> > > > > (*P*, p. 223)

Paterson does not evade evil and horror, but seems now to see it in a totality that balances: there is the man who shoots, but there is also the man who comforts—a Whitmanian figure bringing succor to the suffering (as in "Song of Myself"). The serpent with its tail in its mouth; evil begetting good, good begetting evil, evil begetting good: "the river has returned to its beginnings" (*P*, p. 233). Paterson goes on—

   Dreams possess me
    and the dance
     of my thoughts
   involving animals
    the blameless beasts
       (*P*, p. 224)

Whitman said: "I think I could turn and live with animals, they are so placid and self-contain'd, / I stand and look at them long and long."[15] Paterson's dance, the dance of his thoughts and the dance that ends the poem, is a dance of acceptance that embraces (as "all we know") both the joyous and the tragic.

6

  Paterson's Preface opens, "Rigor of beauty is the quest. But how will you find beauty when it is locked in the mind past all remonstrance" (*P*, p. 3). At one time, Williams had added: "It is not in the things nearest us unless transposed there by our employment."[16] Language must be used in explorations for beauty, and much of *Paterson* is given over to its discovery and delineation, its tenuous embodiment in an elusive language. Paterson does indeed find beauty in "the things nearest us," but it is only by employment of his art that it is "transposed there."
  The first extended probing for beauty comes in Book I, with minute examination in memory of an old photograph from the *National Geographic:*

   I remember
 a *Geographic* picture, the 9 women
 of some African chief semi-naked
 astraddle a log, an official log to
 be presumed, head left:
      (*P*, p. 13)

Paterson's eye of memory moves from the youngest, most recent wife along the line to the "last, the first wife, / present! supporting all the rest growing up from her." Her breasts sag "from hard use," but on her face there is a "vague smile, / unattached, floating like a pigeon / after a long flight to his cote." After presenting the examples of Sam Patch and Mrs. Cumming (blockage and divorce), Paterson's mind returns to this enigmatic woman:

Which is to say, though it be poorly
said, there is a first wife
and a first beauty, complex, ovate—
the woody sepals standing back under
the stress to hold it there, innate

a flower within a flower whose history
(within the mind) crouching
among the ferny rocks, laughs at the names
by which they think to trap it. Escapes!
Never by running but by lying still—

(P, p. 22)

Beauty locked—or lurking—in the mind? An unlikely place, this—an old
African woman with sagging breasts—to begin the search for beauty. But for the
African chieftain, the beauty of his first wife crouches there among the "ferny
rocks" of *his* mind, and is obscurely translated through the eight successors.
Paterson will seek—and find—beauty in the most unlikely of places.

In "Sunday in the Park" (Book II), Paterson spots two lovers in a
"grassy den," the woman "lies sweating" at the side of a dozing man—

> She stirs, distraught,
against him—wounded (drunk), moves
against him (a lump) desiring,
against him, bored

flagrantly bored and sleeping, a
beer bottle still grasped spear-like
in his hand   .

(P, p. 59)

Small boys peer down on the frustrated lovers. The woman moves nearer the
man, "her lean belly to the man's backside," but he does not waken:

> —to which he adds his useless voice:
until there moves in his sleep
a music that is whole, unequivocal (in
his sleep, sweating in his sleep—laboring
against sleep, agasp!)
>   —and does not waken.

Sees, alive (asleep)
          —the fall's roar entering
his sleep (to be fulfilled)
                              reborn
in his sleep—scattered over the mountain
severally
          —by which he woos her, severally.
                                        (*P,* p. 60)

Later in the day, Paterson passes by once again and notices that "the drunken lovers slept, now, both of them" (*P,* p. 62).

Later, after listening to the evangelist Klaus, Paterson ponders and puzzles over beauty—"These women are not / beautiful and reflect / no beauty but gross . . / Unless it is beauty / to be, anywhere, / so flagrant in desire" (*P,* p. 71). *Unless, unless.* Before presenting the frustrated Sunday park lovers, Paterson remembered a scene from an Eisenstein film in which an old peasant is drinking with abandon in a kind of sexual celebration: "the female of it facing the male, the satyr— / (Priapus!)" (*P,* p. 58). The priapus principle of life has been frustrated in the lovers in the park—but affirmed by the poet. These lovers are not re-creations of Eliot's typist and "young man carbuncular," but rather, perhaps, answers to them. Their desire is healthy and life-affirming, not sordid and meaningless. It is the beauty that the poet seeks, and he works to "transpose" it there without falsifying or sentimentalizing or satirizing. Many readers have been misled by this passage, seeing it in the context of Eliot's *Waste Land* view of sex. But Williams has made it clear, both in the poem and out of it, that he is on the side of the frustrated lovers. He remarked in 1954: "I was always concerned with the plight of the young in the industrial age who are affected by love. It's a classic theme because a tragic theme—because love is much thought about and written about. It's tragedy when it is realized by an artist and comes out in a form like this. I love the impassioned simplicity of young lovers. When it's thwarted, and they don't know it's thwarted, then the vulgarity is lifted to distinction by being treated with the very greatest art which I can conceive." Williams saw the "love" scene as vital to the poem: "It's easy to miss, but the whole theme of *Paterson* is brought out in this passage, the contrast between the mythic beauty of the Falls and Mountain and the industrial hideousness.... so in this scene love has triumphed."[17] Beauty locked in the mind—released.

In Book III, "The Library," the quest for beauty surges to the fore, flashing in Paterson's (and the reader's) mind in the strangely vague refrain,

"Beautiful Thing." But the vagueness perhaps suits the poet's purposes in appearing rather common (and undistinguished) language but suggesting reverberations that go beyond any specific attachment. The refrain has a long history in the conception of *Paterson*. It appeared first at the end of the Columbus chapter, "The Discovery of the Indies," in *In the American Grain* (1925): Columbus has sent his men off for water in the new land of his discovery, and during the two hours he contemplates this new world: "During that time I walked among the trees which was the most beautiful thing which I had ever seen" (*IAG*, p. 26). Williams inserted this passage in *Paterson* IV, ii (*P*, p. 178) (changing only the last word to *known*), himself calling attention to the historic and national dimension of the refrain: Beautiful Thing was there for the simple viewing, not locked away in the mind, not hidden deep within the sordid surfaces—in the beginning of the American experience. What had become of it (or what we had done to it) in the centuries since was a different matter.

As we have already observed, Beautiful Thing figured centrally in Williams's 1937 poem, "Paterson: Episode 17," and many of the passages of this poem turn up in Book III of Paterson. The idea and the phrase embodying it, then, seem to have been an important part of the poem's beginning. Throughout Book III, Beautiful Thing seems to be set over against the library, offering a meaning and vitality that the books of the dead past cannot match. The Beautiful Thing of the original poem is a beautiful Negro servant girl, loved and violated by many, caught in the lively moment of beating a rug. But in *Paterson* she seems raised to mythic level—"tall / as you already were— / till your head / through fruitful exaggeration / was reaching the sky and the / prickles of its ecstasy / Beautiful Thing!" (*P*, pp. 126–27). In this role, she reaches back in the poem to Book I to connect with the old (first) wife of the African chieftain of the *National Geographic* picture and to Book II to connect with the girl filled with frustrated desire in the park; and she reaches forward in the poem to connect with Phyllis of the Idyl and with Madame Curie (Book IV) and with the "whore and virgin" of Book V: the mystery of woman, the mystery of sex, the mystery of love, the mystery of creativity—themes of Whitman throughout *Leaves of Grass*, but especially in the sex poems of "Children of Adam."

For a time in Book III, Paterson seems to hold the "answer" in his mind:

What end but love, that stares death in the eye?
A city, a marriage—that stares death
in the eye

the riddle of a man and a woman
For what is there but love, that stares death
in the eye, love, begetting marriage
not infamy, not death
(*P,* p. 106)

The line turns almost Whitmanian in the midst of this new awareness:

Sing me a song to make death tolerable, a song
of a man and woman: the riddle of a man
and a woman.
        What language could allay our thirsts,
what winds lift us, what floods bear us past defeats
but song but deathless song   ?
                                                         (*P,* p. 107)

Language, love, death: beauty is the key, beauty locked in the mind released,
beauty "transposed" to the simple scene of Beautiful Thing in all her vitality
and appeal:

        Beautiful thing, your
vulgarity of beauty surpasses all their
perfections!
        Vulgarity surpasses all perfections
—it leaps from a varnish pot and we see
it pass—in flames!
                                                         (*P,* pp. 119–20)

The books cannot substitute for the reality, however "vulgar":

        But you are the dream
of dead men
                Beautiful Thing!
Let them explain you and you will be
the heart of the explanation. Nameless,
you will appear
                Beautiful Thing
the flame's lover—
                                                         (*P,* pp. 122–23)

It was the Emersonian-Whitmanian transcendental tradition to reject books (and the past) when experience itself offered directly what the books could offer only indirectly. Williams clearly places himself in this tradition.

Beautiful Thing appears (as we noted above) in numerous incarnations in *Paterson*, but perhaps receives her apotheosis in Book V in the fused vision of the virgin and the whore. "The moral / proclaimed by the whorehouse / could not be better proclaimed / by the virgin, a price on her head, / her maidenhead!" (*P*, p. 208). Again: "The whore and the virgin, an identity: / —through its disguises" (*P*, p. 210). And again: "the virgin and the whore, which / most endures? the world / of the imagination most endures" (*P*, p. 213). The Unicorn legend woven into the tapestries of the Cloisters invites this fusion of identities, as it brought together both religious and secular meanings, the Unicorn itself representing Christ, but also, with his phallic horn, the lover-bridegroom. Thus the poet allies himself to a long tradition in seeing the two designations—virgin and whore—based on a single identification of sexuality, evocative of fundamentally identical creative sexual energy: "every married man carries in his head / the beloved and sacred image / of a virgin / whom he has whored" (*P*, p. 234). And he can assert paradoxically: "no woman is virtuous / who does not give herself to her lover / —forthwith" (*P*, p. 229).

In Part Two of Book V of *Paterson* there appears what seems to be an independent poem, beginning:

> There is a woman in our town
> walks rapidly, flat bellied
> in worn slacks upon the street
> where I saw her.
> > neither short
> nor tall, nor old nor young
> her
> > face would attract no
> adolescent.
> > > (*P*, p. 219)

This woman could be Beautiful Thing in another guise. Her appearance is not extraordinary, but her effect on the poet is: "She stopped / me in my tracks—until I saw / her / disappear in the crowd." And he exclaims, "if ever I see you again / as I have sought you / daily without success / I'll speak to you, alas / too late!" The poem might be read as an updated version of a Whitman "Children of Adam" poem ("A Woman Waits for Me," perhaps),

and the poet adds at the end: "have you read anything that I have written? /
It is all for you" (*P*, pp. 255–56).

Beautiful Thing, sexual-creative energy, the phallic-priapus principle,
love against death: these themes intermingle and become vital in *Paterson*,
culminating in Book V: "The Unicorn roams the forest of all true lovers's
minds. They hunt it down. Bow wow! sing hey the green holly!" (*P*, p. 234).
The poet admonishes himself: "Paterson, / keep your pecker up / whatever
the detail!" (*P*, p. 235). Sexuality and creativity, like the virgin and whore,
fuse, and the energy of the "pecker" is as important to creating poetry as for
making love. For "to measure is all we know, / a choice among the measures
/ . . / the measured dance." And this "measure" is made up of the eternal satyr
in man as well as the eternally tragic—"to dance to a measure /
contrapuntally, / Satyrically, the tragic foot" (*P*, p. 239).

7

Paterson's search for a redeeming language turns up a language of
redemption, but it is a delicate thread winding its way through the poem. In
the first book the emphasis is on descent, as Paterson himself identifies with
Sam Patch in his leap into Passaic Falls, ending up in a cake of ice. Paterson
hovers near the edge—

> The thought returns: Why have I not
> but for imagined beauty where there is none
> or none available, long since
> put myself deliberately in the way of death?
>
> (*P*, p. 20)

The imagination as man's redeemer? Possibly, as we shall see in Book V. But
meanwhile, the nul and the descent must be faced. Part Three of Book II
opens with the admonition: "Look for the nul / defeats it all." This "nul" is
"the N of all / equations," "the blank / that holds them up." It is "that nul /
that's past all seeing / the death of all that's past / all being" (*P*, p. 77). This
blankness and nullity appear to be very close to that palsied whiteness that
Melville's Ishmael (in *Moby-Dick*) saw in the heart of all matter, the whiteness
that "shadows forth the heartless voids and immensities of the universe, and
thus stabs us from behind with the thought of annihilation."[18]

Then Paterson suddenly breaks off from contemplation of the nul:
"But Spring shall come and flowers will bloom / and man must chatter of
his doom." This is self-admonition, a turning away from abstract ideas of

nullity and blankness to the apprehendable realities of spring and flowers ("no ideas but in things"). There follows the justifiably famous passage in which Williams discovered his beloved triadic line—as well as affirmation in nullity:

> The descent beckons
>> as the ascent beckoned
>>> Memory is a kind
> of accomplishment
>> a sort of renewal
>>> even
> an initiation, since the spaces it opens are new
> places
>> inhabited by hordes
>>> heretofore unrealized,
> of new kinds—
>> since their movements
>>> are towards new objectives
> (even though formerly they were abandoned)
> No defeat is made up entirely of defeat—since
> the world it opens is always a place
>> formerly
>>> unsuspected. A
> world lost,
>> a world unsuspected
>>> beckons to new places
> and no whiteness (lost) is so white as the memory
> of whiteness   .

$$(P, \text{pp. } 77\text{–}78)$$

The vision here may be reminiscent of Ezra Pound's descent described in the "Pisan Cantos," resulting in the unanticipated new awareness on Pound's part—"What thou lov'st well remains,"[19] a reservoir of the memory that is "a kind of accomplishment," "a sort of renewal." Like Pound, Paterson finds in descent a reversal—

> The descent
>> made up of despairs
>>> and without accomplishment
> realizes a new awakening   :

which is a reversal
of despair.

(*P*, p. 78)

The nul, the blank, the descent, confronted in their reality, open up new spaces for the imagination.

In contrast with Eliot's wasteland negativism, Williams's vision might be called creative despair—that which brings reversal not by sentimental avoidance but by inhabiting the new spaces revealed. It is very much like the reversal that comes in Whitman's "Song of Myself," where the poet has come (in section 33) to identify with all the miserable of the world—"Hell and despair are upon me," "Agonies are one of my changes of garments." But as he reaches the nadir of his despair ("I project my hat, sit shame-faced, and beg"), he also reaches one of those open spaces, and he experiences reversal of despair in a new awareness. He cries out "Enough! enough! enough!" as he remembers the "overstaid fraction," discovering new spiritual or imaginative energy which he can share through his poetry.[20]

This theme of renewal through despair is echoed throughout *Paterson*, as, for example, in Book III, in the midst of the burning of the library—

An old bottle, mauled by the fire
gets a new glaze, the glass warped
to a new distinction, reclaiming the
undefined. A hot stone, reached
by the tide, crackled over by fine
lines, the glaze unspoiled
Annihilation ameliorated:

(*P*, p. 118)

In the renewal of the bottle (found in its "new space") there is vital reversal—

the flame that wrapped the glass
deflowered, reflowered there by
the flame: a second flame, surpassing
heat

(*P*, 118)

Deflowered: reflowered. Despair, reversal of despair. Descent: renewal. Paterson contemplates the example of the reflowered bottle:

Hell's fire. Fire Sit your horny ass
down. What's your game? Beat you
at your own game, Fire. Outlast you:
Poet Beats Fire at Its Own Game! The bottle!
the bottle! the bottle! the bottle! I
give you the bottle! What's burning
now, Fire?

                              (*P*, p. 118)

It is the poet's language of redemption that has beaten the fire at its own
game, turning destruction into creation, resurrecting (and preserving) the
bottle in its new incarnation.

In Book IV, Madame Curie's discovery of radium constitutes a similar
reversal—

A dissonance
in the valence of Uranium
led to the discovery
Dissonance
(if you are interested)
leads to discovery

                              (*P*, p. 176)

At a critical moment in the Curie investigations, there appeared the nul, the
blankness—but

a stain at the bottom of the retort
without weight, a failure, a
nothing. And then, returning in the
night, to find it
                    LUMINOUS
                              (*P*, p. 178)

The luminosity derives from the assumed nothing—the blank space that
gave room for the new awakening.

The pattern of descent and renewal is the pattern of the central
action of the poem. Paterson takes on the identity of Sam Patch fallen to his
doom and encased in a cake of ice in the opening of the poem. If the doom
is final, Patch-Paterson should disappear in the sea at the end of the descent

of the falls as the river runs to the sea—the "sea of blood"—in the conclusion
of Book IV:

> the nostalgic sea
> sopped with our cries
> Thalassa! Thalassa!
> calling us home   .
> I say to you, Put wax rather in your
> ears against the hungry sea
> it is not our home!
> (*P,* p. 201)

With the recurring cry, "the sea is not our home," Paterson wades out of the
"blood dark sea" at the end of Book IV and has a refreshing nap on the beach.
All the imagery in the closing lines describing Paterson's action is the
imagery of life—the dog who accompanies him, the girls he notices playing
on the beach, the beach plums he samples (spitting out the seed, emblem of
renewal), his striking out energetically inland.

The language of redemption moves to the central position in Book V of
Paterson, inherent in the very nature and narrative of the Unicorn tapestries.
The story is a story of death and resurrection. The most magnificent of all the
tapestries is the last, in which the Unicorn appears alone, chained to a tree,
surrounded by a wooden fence in an incredibly beautiful field of multicolored
flowers. Here the Unicorn may be the risen Christ in Paradise, or he may be
the lover finally secured by his lady-love, a fusion of sexual-religious
symbolism that goes to the heart of Williams's purposes:

> in a field crowded with small flowers
> .   .   its neck
> circled by a crown!
> from a regal tapestry of stars!
> lying wounded on his belly
> legs folded under him
> the bearded head held
> regally aloft   .
> (*P,* p. 211)

The risen (erect?) unicorn "has no match / or mate," just as "the artist / has
no peer": "Death / has no peer." The Unicorn has been killed, yet lives—

> We shall not get to the bottom:
> death is a hole
> in which we are all buried
> Gentile and Jew.
> The flower dies down
> and rots away   .
> But there is a hole
> in the bottom of the bag.
> It is the imagination
> which cannot be fathomed.
> It is through this hole
> we escape   .   .
> So through art alone, male and female, a field of
> flowers, tapestry, spring flowers unequaled
> in loveliness.
>   (*P*, pp. 211–12)

The descent of death is the final descent: but there are new spaces even here, and a reversal of despair: the imagination finds the hole at the bottom of death through which to escape—as the resurrected Unicorn has escaped in the tapestry.

> Through this hole
> at the bottom of the cavern
> of death, the imagination
> escapes intact.

> he bears a collar round his neck
> hid in the bristling hair.
>   (*P*, p. 212)

Immediately following this defiant assertion appears a letter from the young, then unknown poet Allen Ginsberg, setting out to dedicate his life to the poetic imagination. The letter thanks Williams for writing his introduction (to *Howl!*), and proclaims his "whitmanic mania": "In any case Beauty is where I hang my hat. And reality. And America" (*P*, p. 213). Williams-Paterson's Unicorn, perhaps? Redemption, resurrection, through the imagination, of Whitman's "ages' and ages' encrustations." But of course, Williams's Unicorn of the seventh tapestry is the poem *Paterson* itself. It has handsomely escaped through the hole at the bottom of death. And many readers would conclude with Robert Lowell's judgment, in proclaiming Williams as "part of the great breath of our literature, that *"Paterson* is our *Leaves of Grass."*[21]

> *A final word:*
> *from*
> "An Elegy for W.C.W., the lovely man"
> *John Berryman*
>
> Henry in Ireland to Bill underground:
> Rest well, who worked so hard, who made a good sound
> constantly, for so many years:
> your high-jinks delighted the continents & our ears:
> you had so many girls your life was a triumph
> and you loved your one wife.
>
> At dawn you rose & wrote—the books poured forth—   .
> you delivered infinite babies, in one great birth—
> and your generosity
> to juniors made you deeply loved, deeply:
> if envy was a Henry trademark, he would envy you,
> especially the being through.[22]

NOTES

1. Williams quotations are cited in the text, using the following abbreviations:
A: Autobiography (New York: Random House, 1951; rpt. New Directions, 1967)
CEP: The Collected Early Poems (New York: New Directions, 1951)
CLP: The Collected Later Poems (New York: New Directions, 1963)
I: Imaginations (containing *Kora in Hell, Spring and All, The Great American Novel, The Descent of Winter, A Novelette and Other Prose*) (New York: New Directions, 1970)
IAG: In the American Grain (New York: New Directions, 1956)
P: Paterson (New York: New Directions, 1963)
SE: Selected Essays (New York: New Directions, 1969)
SL: Selected Letters, ed. John C. Thirlwall (New York: McDowell, Oblensky, 1957)
2. William Carlos Williams, "America, Whitman, and the Art of Poetry," *Poetry Journal* 8 (Nov. 1917): 27, 31.
3. William Carlos Williams, "An Essay on *Leaves of Grass," Leaves of Grass One Hundred Years After,* ed. Milton Hindus (Stanford: Stanford University Press, 1955), p. 22.
4. William Carlos Williams, "The American Idiom," *New Directions* 17 (New York: New Directions, 1961), pp. 250–51.
5. Louis Simpson, *Three on the Tower: The Lives and Works of Ezra Pound, T.S. Eliot,*

and William Carlos Williams (New York: William Morrow & Co., 1975). This work is most valuable in interweaving and relating the lives and works of the three poets.

6. Quoted in Mike Weaver, *William Carlos Williams: The American Background* (Cambridge: Cambridge University Press, 1971), p. 120.

7. Ibid., p. 201.

8. Quoted in John C. Thirlwall, "William Carlos Williams' *Paterson,*" *New Directions* 17, p. 263.

9. Ibid., p. 254.

10. Ibid., pp. 263–64.

11. Ibid., p. 281.

12. Walt Whitman, *Complete Poetry and Selected Prose* (Boston: Houghton Mifflin Co., 1959), pp. 424–25. Hereafter cited as *CPSP.*

13. Ibid., p. 349.

14. Quoted in Thirlwall, "William Carlos Williams' *Paterson,*" p. 264.

15. Whitman, *CPSP,* p. 47.

16. Quoted in Joel Conarroe, *William Carlos Williams' Paterson* (Philadelphia: University of Pennsylvania Press, 1970), p. 55.

17. Quoted in John C. Thirlwall, "William Carlos Williams' *Paterson,*" pp. 276–77.

18. Herman Melville, *Moby-Dick,* ed. Harrison Hayford and Hershel Parker (New York: W.W. Norton & Co., 1967), p. 169.

19. Ezra Pound, *The Cantos* (New York: New Directions, 1972), pp. 520–21.

20. Whitman, *CPSP,* pp. 52, 56.

21. Robert Lowell, "William Carlos Williams," *William Carlos Williams: A Collection of Critical Essays,* ed. J. Hillis Miller (Englewood Cliffs, N.J.: Prentice-Hall, 1966), p. 158.

22. John Berryman, *The Dream Songs* (New York: Farrar, Straus & Giroux, 1969), p. 346.

ELEANOR COOK

Late Poems:
Places, Common and Other

One turns with something like ferocity toward a land that one
loves, to which one is really and essentially native, to demand that
it surrender, reveal, that in itself which one loves. This is a vital
affair, not an affair of the heart (as it may be in one's first poems),
but an affair of the whole being (as in one's last poems), a
fundamental affair of life, or, rather, an affair of fundamental life;
so that one's cry of O Jerusalem becomes little by little a cry to
something a little nearer and nearer until at last one cries out to
a living name, a living place, a living thing, and in crying out
confesses openly all the bitter secretions of experience. (*OP* 260,
1948)

I have moved from the end of *Transport to Summer* to *An Ordinary Evening in
New Haven*, the major long poem of Stevens' next volume. That poem, and
the volume's title poem, *Auroras of Autumn* explore ways of saying farewell.
At the same time, Stevens increasingly writes short poems of peculiar force
and intensity that do not give the effect of meditating on farewells, except by
indirection. Randall Jarrell describes them as the work of a man "at once very
old and beyond the dominion of age; such men seem to have entered into (or
are able to create for us) a new existence, a world in which everything is

From *Poetry, Word-Play, and Word-War in Wallace Stevens*. © 1988 by Princeton University Press.

enlarged and yet no more than itself, transfigured and yet beyond the need of transfiguration."[1]

It is hard to find a language in which to speak well of these extraordinary late lyrics. We speak again and again of a sense of doubleness in them, of the strange and right combining of the everyday and the visionary. The everyday and the visionary come together yet are held apart, before us; or, to change the metaphor, we cross easily back and forth from one area to the other. Things familiar and ordinary live in tension with their own unfamiliarity and extraordinariness. There is no sense of blocking, and this is one difference from the early poems. It is not at all that outside place and the order of words are made to sound stable. It is that the word "stable" and the inside-outside metaphor seem insufficient, even wrong. In *Things of August*, for example, are we inside or outside the egg?

> Spread sail, we say, spread white, spread way.
> The shell is a shore....
> Spread outward. Crack the round dome. Break through....

Outside if we are cracking a breakfast egg, and inside if we are cracking the old egg of the world. The egg turns inside out and outside in (and we all began in or as an egg), like words themselves: "It is a world of words to the end of it" (which we usually misread through insufficient attention to the word "it"). In the opening poems, the figures seemed to belong properly to neither mimetic nor legendary nor allegorical worlds. The figures in these late poems seem to belong properly to different worlds at the same time. Stevens admits what he can of older tropes, legends, beliefs, ideas, and even some old ghosts. He has tried them as by fire, and he knows to the last syllable what he can allow into his poetic world.

Thematically, these are poems of last things, of memories, of repetitions, of attentuations, yet also of a fierce will to live and a love of this earth. They are poems of being at home yet also of seeking home. (It is little wonder that the Ulysses figure reappears in force.) Generically, we may usefully think of some as tombeau or epitaph poems, as Charles Berger suggests,[2] or as testamentary poems. There is a high proportion of fluency poems, this subgenre being appropriate for a man musing on the river of time.

Much of Stevens' familiar word-play is here, with his tactics often foregrounded. From the beginning, Stevens' lines could do what they described. From the beginning, Stevens could find language for his methods of doing and describing. These late poems are different in the simplicity and obviousness of Stevens' language for his methods. Here Stevens achieves the seemingly impossible, as he did also in *An Ordinary Evening in New Haven*: to look through and at language at the same time. He opens his 1950 volume, *The Rock*, with a poem ending on the line, "The river motion, the drowsy motion of the river R." The wordplay is presented to the reader as if in a Shakespearean epilogue. Reader, the poem says, we all know of that old trope and allegory, the river of time, the river of being, the capital-R River of Are. Once more, here it is, repeated yet new, simple and evident, like this cadence. It is as if the river began to say its own proper name, then fell asleep like an old man, for this is a poem titled *An Old Man Asleep*. Stevens is writing of an old man's river, and Old Man River too—not the Mississippi but the typic River.

I have isolated this one line, though my reading depends on the rest of this short poem, and it is instructive to consider how:

> The two worlds are asleep, are sleeping, now.
> A dumb sense possesses them in a kind of solemnity.
>
> The self and the earth—your thoughts, your feelings,
> Your beliefs and disbeliefs, your whole peculiar plot;
>
> The redness of your reddish chestnut trees,
> The river motion, the drowsy motion of the river R.

We hear behind this poem Stevens' earlier fluency poems and somnambulist poems: *Hibiscus on the Sleeping Shore*, *Frogs Eat Butterflies*, and especially the powerful poem, *Somnambulisma*.[3] What keeps this late lyric from sliding back into a pleasing exercise like the first two poems? Two things, I think, that are largely present in the late lyrics: a sense of dialectic, and the universal human subject of the way things look and feel when one is old. Stevens' dialectic in the late poems may be muted but it is clearly present. His subject matter is strongly human, and his "I" or "he" emerges as acting, willing, desiring. Word-play can afford to be as obvious as "the river R" when it plays against a tough dialectic and on a human subject. The danger for a lesser poet would be portentousness, but Stevens' touch is sure.

Stevens' familiar play with grammar goes on, for example with prepositions, a play I have noted from the start. *The Woman in Sunshine* turns on an unexpected use of "in"; the effect is obvious. In *The Plain Sense of Things*, the play with "in" is unobtrusive. The last stanza of Stevens' ten-part elegy, *Auroras of Autumn*, sounds baroque in its prepositions; it has more play of prepositions than any three lines I know. They challenge and establish different senses of place:

> As if he lived all lives, that he might know,
>
> In hall harridan, not hushful paradise,
> To a haggling of wind and weather, by these lights
> Like a blaze of summer straw, in winter's nick.

One grammatical-rhetorical punning is especially fine, a pun on apostrophe, to which I shall return. As for play with figures, I hear less of this, though it includes one example that is especially remarkable because Stevens admits anagogic metaphor. This is *Of Mere Being*, to which I shall also return.

The etymological play continues, and we need it in order to read well such a poem as *This Solitude of Cataracts*. In *The River of Rivers in Connecticut*, "there is no ferryman. / He could not bend against its propelling force." The ferryman would be Charon if he were there, just as the preceding "shadow" would be a shade of the dead if it were present. "Bend against" is so nearly, and yet not quite, the literal, etymological meaning of "reflect" ("bend again"). Stevens is punning richly and beautifully and fiercely, punning his life-force against all the pull of the dead.

Tropes continue to be literalized, dead metaphors revived, idioms punned upon. "Fixed one for good" (*CP* 529) can be deadly (good = forever) or excellent (good = the cause of goodness). In *July Mountain* (*OP* 114–15),

> We live in a constellation
> Of patches and of pitches ...
> In an always incipient cosmos,
> The way, when we climb a mountain,
> Vermont throws itself together.

"Ver" and "mont" do combine to make the green mountain, Vermont. And Greek *symballein*, whence our "symbol," means "throw together." When we climb a mountain, then, word and state and the etymological "mountain" of Vermont self-symbolize. It is not that they "are symbolized." This is not Coleridgean symbolism, but a composing like "piece the world together, boys" or "patches the moon together."

One late poem that is close to a riddle poem literalizes a common trope. This is *The Desire To Make Love in a Pagoda* (*OP* 91).

Among the second selves, sailor, observe
The rioter that appears when things are changed,

Asserting itself in an element that is free,
In the alien freedom that such selves degustate:

In the first inch of night, the stellar summering
At three-quarters gone, the morning's prescience,

As if, alone on a mountain, it saw far-off
An innocence approaching toward its peak.

Stevens' title plays with the preposition "in," for this is both, the desire felt by a human to make love in a pagoda, and the desire felt by a pagoda to make love. Stevens also plays with the different senses of "peak," for the act of making love has a peak both physiologically and emotionally. (And pagodas are "strange buildings that come to a point at the end," as Ruskin says.) We recall the old trope of the body as a temple of the Lord, and remember that for most of Stevens' readers, a pagoda is a foreign or "alien" temple. If we read the noun clause in the second line as describing itself, we note also that a "rioter," "when things are changed," is anagrammatically a near-complete erotic, an appropriate enough change in a poem about a desire to make love. The poem is a gently witty, erotic, multilayered verse on overlapping subjects: on desires of the body and of feelings; on primal desires for morning, which a temple might desire, as in love; on the desire to make riots, or anagrams, of letters, and to trope. The poem is close to a riddle poem. (Query: Is the body a temple? A temple of the Lord? Answer: Sometimes it is a pagoda.)

After I argued this case in 1983, two people mentioned the existence of an actual pagoda that Stevens knew, the one overlooking Reading.[4] On reflection, this made perfect sense. Once more, Stevens' word-play is connected with an actual place, even as he sums up over a history of troping, and brings it and an actual place alive for us. We read freshly Shakespeare's "heaven-kissing hill" or Wordsworth's more neutral verb: "these steep and lofty hills ... connect / The landscape with the quiet of the sky" *Tintern Abbey.)* Other writers can use tropes that are rude and funny. We look more closely at the way tall buildings or trees or hills "meet" the sky, and see them more fully in the act of considering our words.

The crowded style and self-lacerating wit of *The Comedian as the Letter C* have gone. There is little irony left, and it tends to be simple and clear, as in "St. Armorer's was once an immense success, / It rose loftily and stood massively" (*CP* 529). The tone makes us supply quotation marks: "St. Armorer's was once an 'immense success,' " etc. The attack here will offend no one. In fact, it is Stevens' retrievals from Christianity rather than his attacks that sometimes cause offense. Such retrievals as "God and the imagination are one" or the end of *St. Armorer's Church from the Outside* are variously read. The orthodox are sometimes angered, while those more accommodating sometimes assimilate Stevens a shade too easily into the Christian fold.[5] (He did say, after all, that his aim was to make the Archbishop of Canterbury jump off the end of the dock.) Geoffrey Hill's phrase is both generous and rightly placed: "magnificent agnostic faith."[6]

Stevens' echoing in the late lyrics is very quiet for the most part. We are unlikely to hear it unless we have attended to the earlier, louder, combative echoes. It is as if he were smiling to himself at the old battles, remembering them clearly but softly, now past combat. When he does send echoes to war, he signals his procedure very clearly. Thus in *In the Element of Antagonisms*: "Birds twitter pandemoniums around / The idea of the chevalier of chevaliers" (*CP* 426). Keats and Milton and Hopkins are once more recalled, though not as in the quiet closing of *Sunday Morning* but "in the element of antagonisms." Stevens uses a different verb from *To Autumn* ("twitter," not "whistle") and a discordant noise from *Paradise Lost* (though without a capital) in order to attack a "chevalier of chevaliers" ("O my chevalier," said Hopkins of a bird). Or rather, to attack such an "idea." Medieval bird debate could hardly do better.

I hear little of Stevens' extraordinary metaleptic or leaping-over echoes, as for example the leap of the mockingbirds over Keats. I hear little of his extraordinary hearing-through echoes, as for example we gradually hear Milton's serene angelic gaze through Wordsworth. In *This Solitude of Cataracts*, the echoing takes disagreement for granted, and goes back from Wordsworth to end with Milton and the unusual wish to possess a Miltonic or biblical sense of the world. Other old echoes are reechoed: Theseus on the lover, the lunatic, and the poet: "The lover, the believer and the poet. / Their words are chosen out of their desire ... The lover writes, the believer hears, / The poet mumbles" (*CP* 441–43). Or the Exodus journey: "These locusts by day, these crickets by night" (*CP* 489). And Stevens reechoes his own work, time and again. "Oto-otu-bre" from *Metamorphosis* comes back: "Otu-bre's lion-roses have turned to paper / And the shadows of trees / Are liked wrecked umbrellas" (*CP* 506).

Among other old subjects, we might note the late form of Florida as Madame la Fleurie, a wicked fairy-tale earth mother whose reality awaits us all. Venus has mostly vanished, though there is "a mother with vague severed arms" (*CP* 438). As a force, she has become Penelope, the longed-for and longing woman of this earth. As with old subjects and arguments, so with old topoi. The leaves, birdsong, light, evening, flowers, fire, ghosts, dwelling places: Stevens sums up over these familiar topoi. Some old figues reappear though not others: the ghosts, the angel, the reader, but not the scholar or rabbi or mentor. Of his old selves, the Spaniard remains (I shall come to him), and a new name comes forward, retrieved from the early letters, Ariel. Not Prospero, commanding then leaving a world, but Ariel, also leaving a world, about to be released into his own element, air: "Ariel was glad he had written his poems." Stevens' memory is going back forty-four years. "I like to write most when the young Ariel sits, as you know how, at the head of my pen and whispers to me—many things; for I like his fancies, and his occasional music.... Now, Ariel, rescue me.... Ariel was wrong, I see" (*L* 123, 124, June 17 and 19,1909; *CP* 532).

I mentioned the reappearance of Ulysses in these late poems, reappearance because Ulysses like Virgil was there at the start. Crispin's journey is an "Odyssey"; du Bellay's sonnet on Ulysses is mentioned more than once. Among the gods, Vulcan is closest to Stevens. Among legendary mortals, Ulysses is his alter ego, just as *pius* Aeneas is Eliot's. Many-sided Odysseus, wily, resourceful, gifted with words and so loved by Athena, is nonetheless simple in feeling and desire. I think Stevens liked him especially because he journeyed to earthly paradises, cohabited with goddesses, was promised immortality if he would stay, and always refused. "The nymph Calypso ... yearning that he should be her husband ... tended him, and said that she would make him immortal and ageless all his days; yet she could never persuade the heart in his breast" (*Odyssey* xxiii.333–36, repeating vii.256–57, Loeb). Penelope and Ithaca, that poor land and that rich woman, make a home for Ulysses that no heaven can provide. It is that sense of home, which is also du Bellay's sense, that makes Ulysses a potent figure in Stevens' late poetry. Du Bellay also reppears in the late work (*OP* 198, 1951).

Stevens' old genius for borrowing and inventing proper names continues. Throughout his work, there are a surprising number of actual names, surprising because our memory may tell us that there are not many. Actual names sometimes act as a metonymy for a system of belief or ideas, or for the spirit of an age, or for a tradition of thought: "In the John-begat-Jacob of what we know ... In the generations of thought" (*OP* 103). Thus also in *Description without Place*, with Calvin or Queen Anne of England or Lenin: "Things are as they seemed to Calvin...." Stevens occasionally uses the names of friends and acquaintances, as well as family names like John Zeller.

Châtillon is, I think, a family name, or at least a desired family name, for Stevens liked the thought that this Protestant reformer was among his ancestors.[7] Some random names give a flavor in themselves; their function is generic (Bonnie and Josie, Mrs. Dooley, Swenson, Solange).[8] Stevens can play with the authority of names and titles, as we know from his Canon and Professor and Herr Doktor. As for the name of greatest authority, the name of God, Stevens sometimes treats it with humor, genial and other ("the Got whome we serve," "Herr Gott"). God's name for himself, "I am that I am," echoes through *Notes toward a Supreme Fiction*, together with some of our human echoes of "I am" (those of Coleridge and Descartes). In the late poetry, he returns to it in *The Sail of Ulysses (OP* 99): "As I know, I am and have / The right to be." (He is punning on "as," revising Descartes's "ergo," and using enjambment to play on the verb "have.") He was always as interested in American place names as Milton was in English or Latin ones.[9] And he always enjoyed inventing place names, including typic place names like Indyterranean, on the model of Mediterranean. He invents allegorical and onomatopoeic rivers in the late poetry, with no loss of the sense of actual flowing water: the z sounds of a river in Brazil, "the river R."

It is Stevens' invented personal names that especially surprise and delight us as we look back over his poetry: Chief Iffucan, Bawda, Nanzia Nunzio, Mr. Blank, Madame la Fleurie, Mac Mort, Mr. Homburg, Hoon, Flora Lowzen, General du Puy, Mrs. Alfred Uruguay, Berserk, Augusta Moon and Alpha and Omega. Lulu Gay and Lulu Morose are wonderfully funny, though their poems are strained (*OP* 26–27). Stevens invented them after he received from Harriet Monroe a book called *Lillygay: An Anthology of Anonymous Poems* (*L* 221, March 14, 1921). Lulu Gay is l'Allegro, 1921 style, female version, with a refrain of ululate, sung by eunuchs. Lulu Morose is Il Penseroso, 1921 style, female version. Stevens' "diva-dame" (*CP* 353) is presumably a late form of the sybil—Dryden's "mad divining dame" (*Aeneid* VI.54) in operatic mood. Phoebus Apothicaire (*CP* 105) should be Phoebus Apollo—or Apollinaire, but what the connection is with Guillaume, I must leave to others.

Stevens is especially inventive in names for his (and our) various public and private selves, as well as his poetic selves. His early poetic selves are like Chaplin characters: the bumbler, the modest poet, the clown. They come out of Shakespeare or Dickens or old comedy, and they come with c-sounds, on which Stevens commented, and with p-sounds, on which he did not: Peter Quince, Pecksniff, Crispin. Later, Stevens invents names, still with c- and p-sounds: a clerical figure for an aspiring self, Canon Aspirin; a professor for an earnest self, Professor Eucalyptus. Stevens figures as Pierrot in letters to his future wife,[10] and also as Ariel, a figure who enters his poetry only late in life. Comic in sound (said Stevens), bumbling and so part of a modesty topos, these early masks are mostly drawn from other worlds. Milton Bates has provided a fine account of them.[11] Their function is not simple, as witness our disputes over Peter Quince's role in his poem. Sometimes they approach a dramatic character, for example, Crispin. Sometimes they seem something like dramatic masks, or characters who speak the prologue or epilogue, presenters under whose aegis a poem goes forward. Michael Hamburger's term, a "mask of style," fits them well.[12] They are at once part of the action yet detached from it, mediators of a kind between audience and poem. Sometimes they seem defensive. Stevens remarked on the different characters present within all of us, and imagined a trunkful of costumes in our mental makeup: "There is a perfect rout of characters in every man—and every man is like an actor's trunk, full of strange creatures, new & old. But an actor and his trunk are two different things" (SP 166). Stevens does not write dramatic monologues proper, but his word-play with names, and with the word "mask," make his interest in dramatic functions clear. Our discussions of the changing dramatic monologue, of dramatis personae, and of theories of the mask should look again at Stevens' names.

One series of characters has not been remarked on, and that is the Spanish series of figures that appear all through Stevens' work. They run from Don Joost in 1921 to the demanding hidalgo in 1949 (CP 483), a tutelary spirit and poetic conscience in one. "Don Joost is a jovial Don Quixote," said Stevens (L 464), a remark that makes no sense of his unjovial poem, From the Misery of Don Joost. (It follows The Comedian as the Letter C, also a very uncomfortable mixture of joviality and misery.) Sometimes the Spaniard plays a guitar, as Stevens himself did literally and also poetically. He may be Don John (CP 49) or Don Juan (OP 64) or simply Don Don (CP 104). Stevens does not especially like him in these last manifestations, nor as the "moralist hidalgo" (CP 186). It is in the mature verse that the hidalgo comes into his own: "The knowledge of Spain and of the hidalgo's hat— / A seeming of the Spaniard, a style of life, / The invention of a nation in a phrase (CP 345) ... This was / Who watched him, always, for unfaithful thought. / This sat beside his bed, with its guitar ... Nothing about him ever stayed the same, / Except this hidalgo and his eye and tune" (CP 483). The Spaniard is a singer and a lover and a fighter. In one desperately bitter, uncollected poem, he considers mock-fighting like mon oncle's, and gives it up (The Woman Who Blamed Life on a Spaniard [OP 34]).

Once we hear this Spanish figure through Stevens' work, we begin to discover other appearances. The "Spaniard of the rose" (CP 316) is still

unidentified but he is related, and somehow through the Order of the
Knights of the Rose. The Pastor Caballero (another c-plus-p name) follows
the Pastoral Nun to end the short poems of *Transport to Summer*. Christian
"pastoral" is not quite the same as a pastor that goes with a caballero (a
knight), whose poem opens thus:

> The importance of a hat to a form becomes
> More definite. The sweeping brim of the hat
> Makes of the form Most Merciful Capitan,
>
> If the observer says so: grandiloquent
> Locution of a hand in a rhapsody.
> Its line moves quickly with the genius
>
> Of its improvisation until, at length,
> It enfolds the head in a vital ambiance,
> A vital, linear ambiance. The flare
>
> In the sweeping brim becomes the origin
> Of a human evocation, so disclosed
> That, nameless, it creates an affectionate name,
>
> Derived from adjectives of deepest mine.

"Mine" indeed, we murmur, thinking of Stevens' affection for his Spanish
self. This poem sweeps (not strides) in enjambment, and makes "a human
evocation." (It reminds, it calls forth.) The pastor is nameless, and which
word of "pastor caballero" is adjective, I do not know, yet the lines also create
"an affectionate name." We speak of donning this or that hat, when we take
on certain jobs or roles. This is a Spanish hat, become a role through idiom
and through analogy.

   The Spaniard is a compound figure whose clearest ancestor is Don
Quixote. His immediate relatives are Stevens' mentor at Harvard, George
Santayana, and his contemporary, Picasso. Santayana is obvious but Picasso
may not be, especially if we recall Stevens' phrase about the "dilapidations of
Picasso." A notebook entry makes Picasso's presence—or at least, the
presence of his Spanishness—in Stevens' imagination clearer: "In a review of
Middle Spain by George Santayana, in *The New Statesman* June 26, 1948,
Raymond Mortimer joined him with Picasso as the two living Spaniards
most conspicuous for genius and said . . they have both chosen to be

expatriates yet retain under their cosmopolitanism a deep Spanishness—the sense 'that in the service of love and imagination nothing can be too lavish, too sublime or too festive; yet that all this passion is a caprice, a farce, a contortion, a comedy of illusions.'"[13] The passage is especially interesting because of the combination, sometimes strange to an Anglo-Saxon mode of behavior, of entire devotion and seriousness with complete comic grace. It is serious play, Spanish style, and Stevens, from the beginning, liked to take on what Cervantes calls "the syle of a Don."

The Spaniard's last appearance is in 1954 in *Farewell without a Guitar* (*OP* 98):

> Spring's bright paradise has come to this.
> Now the thousand-leaved green falls to the ground.
> Farewell, my days.

This short poem, of great poignancy, speaks quietly back over Stevens' whole life.

Some of Stevens' late poems become clearer from a knowledge of his earlier work, for example, *Study of Images II*:

> The frequency of images of the moon
> Is more or less. The pearly women that drop
> From heaven and float in air, like animals
>
> Of ether, exceed the excelling witches, whence
> They came. But, brown, the ice-bear sleeping in ice-month
> In his cave, remains dismissed without a dream,
>
> As if the centre of images had its
> Congenial mannequins, alert to please,
> Beings of other beings manifold—
>
> The shadowless moon wholly composed of shade,
> Women with other lives in their live hair,
> Rose—women as half-fishes of salt shine,
>
> As if, as if, as if the disparate halves
> Of things were waiting in a betrothal known
> To none, awaiting espousal to the sound

> Of right joining, a music of ideas, the burning
> And breeding and bearing birth of harmony,
> The final relation, the marriage of the rest.

We may start with the title, taking it as a directive, and follow the old-fashioned method of image study. Moon images as a series of "pearly women" are not hard to read, though we may quarrel about their "witchy origins." The moon as brown bear in a cave is an image that "remains dismissed," as Stevens says. When we recall his own "brown moon" that opens *Transport to Summer*, the two antithetical moon types come clear. Stevens is inventing a land of images, like the *pays de la métaphore*, a place inhabited by images who are "congenial mannequins, alert to please"—model models, so to speak. He devises moon images drawn from the sea, for half- or quarter-moons may be reflected as shiny mermaids, "women as half-fashion of salt shine." (The acoustic effects are very fine here.) And he reads a fable from the light and dark halves of the moon, in which the two halves yearn for each other, are betrothed, and await marriage, consummation, and the birth of harmony. *The Motive for Metaphor* helps us read this fable, as does Harmony, daughter of contraries, of Venus and Mars, allegorically Love and Strife, and one presiding genius of Stevens' volume *Harmonium*. Many of Stevens' late poems are like this; they play back over his own work, echoing it, reshaping it, enlightening it. Here, for example, we might ask if *The Motive for Metaphor* is also a fable of moon and sun. (We recall that its land of the moon is half- and quarter- and mutable. Its land of the sun is full, and fixes, as with the classical sun, "He Who Smites from Afar.") Stevens' vision of union and harmony here is a metaphor, resting grammatically on a repeated "as if." Yet his tercet of appositive phrases sounds like positive affirmation. The poem is a remarkable summing-up.

　　This Solitude of Cataracts (*CP* 424) is a fluency poem of sorts, and a rich one. It is a poem of desire, not so much the desire to stop time as the desire to make it keep on flowing in the same way. The tension is between familiar change and unfamiliar change. Stevens opens with a variation on Heraclitus: "He never felt twice the same about the flecked river, / Which kept flowing and never the same way twice, flowing...." The poem is full of doublenesses that are near but not complete, whether syntactical or mimetic. The reflections in the water are like the reflections of thought, "thought-like Monadnocks" (with a ghost of Leibniz rendering that Indian name and actual mountain "thought-like"). Yet they are not the same, not even a mirror image, for on the surface, "wild ducks fluttered, / Ruffling its common reflections." (Auden also uses the word "ruffled" in a poem of doubleness and reflection to imply that we only see on or into water when it is still: "Fish in the unruffled lake.") Common reflections in both senses of the word are ruffled when their surface is fluttered. The poem also "flows through many places, as if it stood still in one" (representations of actual places like Mount Monadnock and also the topoi of poetry). As in many late poems, Stevens moves from wit to intense desire:

> He wanted to feel the same way over and over.
>
> He wanted the river to go on flowing the same way,
> To keep on flowing.

"Feel," rhyming with both "real" and "not real" in the preceding line, alters the tone of the opening line. Something is suppressed here, like a lament—or in Stevens' unexpected metaphor, like an apostrophe: "There seemed to be an apostrophe that was not spoken." What is this apostrophe? Like the one forbidden on the funicular, as we travel up a nonvisionary mountain? Like the spouting "volcano Apostrophe"? We may hear a suppressed "O" flowing through the poem, as if Stevens thought something like "O wild West Wind," but would not speak it. His negative, "not spoken," plays on a paradox of absence and presence. This line is especially fine because of the pun on apostrophe, a pun that current theories of apostrophe have not thought of. An apostrophe is also a mark of elision. In this sense, apostrophe is *defined* as something "not spoken," so that "there seemed to be" an elision, a contraction, something omitted but understood. This is a secondary meaning that limits the sense of loss or suppression in something "not spoken." It is as if Stevens said: I could write an apostrophe but will only evoke the thought of one, eliding it like apostrophe in another sense; that little mark stands for, or evokes, the "O," etc., of appropriate apostrophe. As it happens, there are no apostrophes of either kind in the poem; the grammatical and rhetorical pun is "not spoken."

Thematically, this is a poem of solitude, recalling other solitudes in Stevens' poetry. It closes on a most unusual desire for him, a desire to feel oneness, unity, paradisal vision—or to feel what it would be like to feel that way. It remains only a passing desire. Stevens' poem begins with paradox, and goes on to meditation on the fact that some things, though changed, look and feel so nearly the same. This is as true of nature as of the self, and the two may be connected. Wordsworth is our most familiar writer on this theme. "Though changed," he comes again for restoration to the river Wye. The question of its change is not raised, and its restorative power seems constant. Doubleness that is not quite the same is felt differently by a twenty-eight-year-old looking back five years and a sixty-nine-year-old.

Stevens' word "cataracts" is surprising if read descriptively, for there is no reference to cataracts in the body of the poem. (This quiet riddling device is one he likes, as we know from *Invective against Swans* and *Ghosts as Cocoons*.) Allegorically, the word implies a turbulence of feeling that is not spoken. Allusively, the word recalls some of Wordsworth's most memorable lines: "I cannot paint / What then I was. The sounding cataract / Haunted me like a passion." Stevens works against Wordsworth's sense of how memory may refresh us and become "the bliss of solitude." His title responds to Wordsworth *sotto voce* when we emphasize its first word: *This Solitude of Cataracts*. His desire is not just for what he has had, but for what he never had—that biblical and Miltonic sense of being at the center:

> He wanted the river to go on flowing the same way,
> To keep on flowing. He wanted to walk beside it,
>
> Under the buttonwoods, beneath a moon nailed fast....
>
> Just to know how it would feel, released from destruction,
> To be a bronze man breathing under archaic lapis,
>
> Without the oscillations of planetary pass-pass,
> Breathing his bronzen breath at the azury centre of time.

This is desire for an earthly paradise, American version, as the "buttonwood" tells us. (The tree is the *Platanis occidentalis*, the American plane-tree, another species of the genus under which Eve first saw Adam, a tree of felicitous associations.) The diction, beautifully ordinary and clear, comes with the resonance of associative sound. The moon of mutability is stopped here, nailed as if on some stage set. If Stevens could "be a bronze man breathing under archaic lapis," he would be under the archaic lapis of the biblical heavens, like Milton's steps "on Heavens azure" (*PL*1.297). Stevens' word "archaic" is pointing us toward archaic usage. "Breathing his bronzen breath at the azury centre of time" links "azury" and "archaic lapis" in an implied lapis lazuli, which is the Arabian origin of the word "azure." The two words are quite separate in modern usage, but once were nearly the same like so many other near-doubles in this poem.

The "planetary pass-pass," punning finely on French *passe-passe* or sleight of hand, suggests the illusion in our reading of the passing planets.

They do seem to return to the same orbits as they pass and then pass again, with "pass-pass" accelerating the pace. Yet they do not: that seeming sameness by which "pass" reduplicates "pass" is itself a passe-passe or illusion, with the eye deceived by a motion. The second word "pass" is not the same as the first, because it comes after itself and so sets up an echoing compound. The planets, once assumed to be beyond change, follow the same pattern of near-sameness, for their orbits vary slightly each time.

With these senses of "pass-pass" and "azure" in mind, we return to the word "cataracts" and consider it diachronically or in its "pass-pass" aspect. Like "azure," "cataracts" has an archaic meaning (OED 1). It once meant the floodgates of heaven, which in the old cosmography were thought to keep back the rains. When they go, the deluge comes. (*Cataractae*, says the Vulgate.) Either as something dashing down or something holding back complete inundation, the word is a powerful figure for an aging human being. The ghost of an old cosmography hovers in "cataracts" and "lapis" and "azury." But in the end, Stevens' desire to be part of an old scheme is unreal for him.

Stevens returns to his earlier vexed subject of birdsong. *Song of Fixed Accord* evokes the maddeningly insistent cooing of mourning doves on spring mornings. Poets see various suns at five and six and seven of a spring morning, but this dove accepts them, "Like a fixed heaven, / Not subject to change." "Fixed accord" of the title implies a song about fixed accord or a song made by fixed accord. The various sound patterns wonderfully imitate the dove, and one repetition imitates it visually: "hail-bow, hail-bow, / To this morrow" and we see the bobbing head of the dove. One small sound, "a little wet of wing," evokes an early line from *Le Monocle*, "Among the choirs of wind and wet and wing," a farewell to torrents of erotic song. "Softly she piped" also allows back into Stevens' work the much-abused trope of pipes.

Yet the poem comes with a caveat, gentle and insistent like the song of a mourning dove. This is *her* song of fixed accord; we are free to hear something more. There is a fine unobtrusive movement from simile to metaphor over the ellipsis. The dove speaks "like the sooth lord of sorrow" in line 2, and "the lord of love and of sooth sorrow" arrives at the end. This is day's "invisible beginner" as against the visible beginner, the sun. "The lord of love and of sooth sorrow, / Lay on the roof / And made much within her." She appears to have summoned her lord, muse, and male all at once. Stevens' play with archaic and religious diction makes this an earthly version of the bird of the Holy Ghost. Milton's inspiring Holy Spirit has, dovelike, satst brooding, not on the vast abyss and made it pregnant, but on one female dove and made her pregnant, whether with song or more, Stevens keeps unclear. The play with the dove is like Joyce but the effects are Stevens' own, and finely controlled as they must be.

"Part of the res itself and not about it," Stevens said in *An Ordinary Evening in New Haven*, in the canto beginning "The poem is the cry of its occasion." In *Not Ideas about the Thing but the Thing Itself*, the cry is "a bird's cry." Not birdsong but a call. (The call and the song of birds differ for many species.) This is an Alpha cry, so to speak, as Stevens catches the strange predawn effect of the first bird-sound. And the first strange predawn effect of March, a very early beginning to birdsong at dawn. It will become loud enough to interrupt sleep by May, and a little louder on this March morning as other birds join in. Hence:

> That scrawny cry—it was
> A chorister whose c preceded the choir.
> It was part of the colossal sun,
>
> Surrounded by its choral rings,
> Still far away. It was like
> A new knowledge of reality.

The tentative, then surer, placing of that bird-cry imitates the mind and ear coming to consciousness, at first hearing as in a dream, then realizing actual sound, outside. The sound of the predawn that Stevens loves comes as a kind of gift. He plays easily with old arguments of inside and outside, with a sense of place, with puns and echoes, as he closes his poem and his volume on these stanzas. He repeats "scrawny cry" three times, a repetition and mimesis enriched by memory. For "scrawny" is our modern form of the word "scrannel," Milton's word in "Grate on their scrannel pipes of wretched straw." Stevens here writes of neither nightingale nor grackle nor any named bird. This March sound recalls his autumn refrain of "skreak and skritter" and "grackles" and "grates"—recalls and rewrites it, turning thin, false-piped scr-sounds into thin, earliest sounds like "scrawny." The old play with the letter c is here too, placed before the reader with simple charm. The bird-cry lines are full of c-sounds; the old wintry and sleepy worlds sound out "sh" ("panache," "papier-mâché"); c-sounds intrude slowly into non-c "knowledge" in stanza ii and make a firm non-c simile at the end. Here is a "nota," c, that pre-cedes the sound of the choir, and, as a letter, is "part of the colossal sun." Like some precentor with a tuning fork, the bird sounds out his note. Stevens moves among different senses in his old c-see pun, which makes "choral rings" seen as well as heard.

The series "chorister," "choir," "choral," is a little insistent, again because of memory, I think. At least two memories are at work here, one of song and eros, and one of song and the divine. One memory is Shakespeare's Sonnet 73 and its "bare ruin'd choirs where late the sweet birds sang," repudiated in *Le Monocle de Mon Oncle* and attenuated in the bough of *An Ordinary Evening in New Haven*. Choirs have ceased vexing Stevens, and a scrawny cry can be much. He centers things on the sun, not on the light of God, like Dante's choral rings at the end of the *Paradiso*. He makes choral rings, not perfect rounds. "Item: The wind is never rounding O," he wrote in 1942 (*CP* 263). Item, we add: the choir is never rounding O but only C.[14] Coleridge's great "choral echo" at the end of the *Biographia Literaria* echoes the great "I am." Stevens' bird-cry is "part of" something, where "part of" implies no transcendence, no sacramental symbolism, no associative analogy. Recalling complex rhetorical and dialectical matters for some readers, the poem remains simple and moving, scrupulously placed, a hymn.

Of Mere Being (*Palm* 398) allows what Stevens has not allowed before, anagogic metaphor, which we may hear in his explicit and implicit wordplay:

> The palm at the end of the mind,
> Beyond the last thought, rises
> In the bronze decor,
>
> A gold-feathered bird
> Sings in the palm, without human meaning,
> Without human feeling, a foreign song.
>
> You know then that it is not the reason
> That makes us happy or unhappy.
> The bird sings. Its feathers shine.
>
> The palm stands on the edge of space.
> The wind moves slowly in the branches.
> The bird's fire-fangled feathers dangle down.

This slowly moving play of exaltation begins with the title and its obvious double sense of "mere." This is mere (bare, only) being and also mere (utter, very) being. On the edge of things, including life, this is how being may be. The implicit pun is on the word "phoenix," which is what this fiery bird is. The Greek word for this fabulous sacred bird is also used for a date-palm. The bird "sings in the palm" and through a pun *is* the palm. So also the poem is contained in its words or its leaves, and vice versa; it also *is* its words or leaves. So also space is contained in the mind, and vice versa; it also *is* the mind.

This use of "is" sounds like the merest play of the verb "to be" or of "being." Yet such a visionary sense "at the end of the mind" is also of utter and very being. These are no longer the "intricate evasions of as"; here "as and is are one" (*CP* 476, 486). This is being as in the A *is* B of anagogic metaphor. And we recall Stevens' old play with "B," "be," "to be"—of mere being, so to speak. Anagogic metaphor is paradisal: this is as close to paradisal language as Stevens will allow himself. He echoes the bird of the earthly paradise from the lemon-tree land of *An Ordinary Evening* in "dangle down," also rhymed on. He evokes the sun once more, for the phoenix lives in the City of the Sun (Ovid, *Met.* XV.391–407). He uses no language of upwardness and no language of home. The poem is of mortality yet with a sense of immortality, though not personal immortality. It is a kind of will and testament of song. Thus, I think, the touching on Yeats; this is a Byzantium poem of sorts, a land of gold and kinds of transmutation. The "last thought" is the last thought possible before we move beyond reason, whether toward imagination or toward death.

I began by looking for the point at which Stevens' poems break with our expectations. More and more, his poetry ceases to have one or two or three such points. They multiply, and the language "flitters," to use a word from *Notes*. If the late poetry displaces the reader at all, it is in a very different way from the early work. And it also attaches, for it makes this too loved earth lovelier still. These are poems of a man who loves this earth and does not want to leave it. Nothing of this passion sounds in the early poems for all their wit and pleasure. And paradoxically, for all their sensuousness. The early poems may have been poems of Stevens' heart. The late poems, some of deprivation, are often poems of Stevens' whole being.

NOTES

1. Jarrell, *The Third Book of Criticism* (New York: Farrar, Straus, & Giroux, 1979), p. 60.

2. Berger, *Forms of Farewell: The Late Poems of Wallace Stevens* (Madison: University of Wisconsin Press, 1985), pp. 143–45.

3. See Helen Vendler's fine commentary in her *Wallace Stevens: Words Chosen Out of Desire* (Knoxville: University of Tennesse Press, 1984), pp. 69–72.

4. See my "Riddles, Charms, and Fictions in Wallace Stevens," *Centre and Labyrinth: Essays in Honour of Northrop Frye* ed. Eleanor Cook et al. (Toronto: University of Toronto Press, 1983), p. 228. See also Joan Richardson, *Wallace Stevens: A Biography* (New York:

Beech Tree Books, 1986), vol. 1, p. 349. "Look for me in Sacred Pagodas," Stevens wrote when young (ibid., p. 340).

5. I find both Adelaide Kirby Morris and Milton Bates a shade accommodating in their assimilation of Stevens.

6. Geoffrey Hill, *The Lords of Limit: Essays on Literature and Ideas* (New York: Oxford University Press, 1984), pp. 16–17.

7. Stevens speaks of his ancestor, Gaspard de Châtillon, grandson of Coligny, "one of the great Protestant figures of his time," in a letter to Paule Vidal, May 21, 1945 (WAS 2887, Huntington Library, quoted by permission of Holly Stevens and the Huntington Library).

8. Cf. Alastair Fowler, *Kinds of Literature: An Introduction to the Theory of Genres and Modes* (Cambridge, Mass.: Harvard University Press, 1982), "Generic Names," pp. 75–87.

9. Cf. T.S. Eliot: "It remained for Marlowe to discover, and Milton to perfect, the musical possibilities of classical names almost to a point of incantation" (*Selected Essays*, 3d ed. [London: Faber & Faber, 1951], p. 103). Or cf. Ezra Pound: "I have read a reasonable amount of bad American magazine verse, pseudo-Masefieldian false pastoral and so on. Not one of the writers had the sense, which Mr Ford shows here, in calling up the reality of the Middle West by the very simple device of names" (*Egoist* 2:1 [January 1,1915], 12).

10. Jacques Derrida offers a "library of Pierrots" in "The Double Session," *Dissemination*, trans. Barbara Johnson (Chicago and London: University of Chicago Press, 1972, 1981), p. 205n 23. The question of "specular doubling" is of interest for Stevens.

11. *Wallace Stevens: A Mythology of Self* (Berkeley and London: University of California Press, 1985), pp. 55–60 and *passim*.

12. Hamburger, *The Truth of Poetry: Tensions in Modern Poetry from Baudelaire to the 1960s* (London and New York: Methuen, 1969, 1982), p. 110. David Walker distinguishes between poems written in the traditions of the dramatic monologue and dramatic lyric and those written as "transparent lyrics," which replace "the lyric speaker with the reader as the center of dramatic attention" (*The Transparent Lyric: Reading and Meaning in the Poetry of Stevens and Williams* [Princeton: Princeton University Press, 1984], p. xii).

13. Commonplace Book, II, 12, WAS 70–73, Huntington Library, quoted by permission of Holly Stevens and the Huntington Library.

14. I am indebted for this point to Carolyn Masel.

EDWARD HIRSCH

Helmet of Fire:
American Poetry in the 1920s

All my beautiful safe world blew up....
> —F. Scott Fitzgerald, *Tender Is the Night*

The age demanded an image
Of its accelerated grimace....
> —Ezra Pound, "Hugh Selwyn Mauberley"

The decade of the twenties rightfully begins in November 1918, at the end of fifty-two slaughterous months that changed the world forever. It is difficult to underestimate the impact of World War I on a generation that had been trained and prepared for one kind of world—one that in retrospect seems almost prelapsarian—and then discovered that it existed in another kind of world altogether. By the time the war began in 1914, the Modernist revolution was well underway, but the sordid experience and reality of modern warfare propelled that revolution forward in an unprecedented and violent way. Poets who wrote in the aftermath of the war could never again forget its particular horrors, how the so-called civilized world put on a modern helmet of fire. In this sense, as Francis Hope has stated, "All poetry written since 1918 is war poetry."[1] In particular, the poets who wrote between 1918 and 1929 (the year of the stock market crash and the beginning of the Great Depression that so radically altered American life)

From *A Profile of Twentieth-Century American Poetry*. © 1991 by the Board of Trustees, Southern Illinois University.

inherited a fallen world, a world changed by the experience and knowledge of trench warfare, the blood-drenched reality of murderous carnage, what Ezra Pound's seminal postwar poem, "Hugh Selwyn Mauberley" (1920), calls "wastage as never before" and

> disillusions as never told in the old days,
> hysterias, trench confessions,
> laughter out of dead bellies.[2]

Pound's poem inaugurates the decade and sums up the Modernist poets' sense of a "botched civilization," their communal belief in the dramatic failure of modern life. In a crucial way the war years delivered the final death-blows to the nineteenth century.

Experience seemed more chaotic and disjunctive for most writers; consciousness, language, and writing itself seemed more problematic than in previous times.[3] These changes help to account for the grave crisis in poetry in the late teens and early twenties, the final overhaul of the genteel and fin de siècle tradition in American letters, the complex and sometimes adversarial relationship between writers and readers as well as for the notorious difficulty of much modern poetry which was fueled by, and indeed assaulted its audience with, images of fragmentation, discontinuity, and collapse, what in "Mauberley" is called "consciousness disjunct." In 1921, T.S. Eliot, who was deep in the throes of *The Waste Land* at the time, put the case for the fragmented and "difficult" text succinctly in what turned out to be one of the key critical essays of the decade, "The Metaphysical Poets": "We can only say that it appears likely that poets in our civilization, as it exists at present, must be difficult. Our civilization comprehends great variety and complexity, and this variety and complexity, playing upon a refined sensibility, must produce various and complex results. The poet must become more and more comprehensive, more allusive, more indirect, in order to force, to dislocate if necessary, language into his meaning."[4]

There was an explosive sense of tension and energy at the end of the war. The war years created a bottled-up and nearly hysterical intensity that for most writers soon yielded to a mood of postwar disillusionment and despair, a feeling of large moral and cultural decay. That pessimism was perhaps most total and vehement in the work of Robinson Jeffers, who, in the six books he published in the twenties, universalized it into a critique of all human behavior, civilization itself. In a more representative way, *The Waste Land* (1922)—with its sense of the unreal city and the walking dead, hysterical voices and fragmented experiences—was unquestionably the central summary text of generational despair over the decline of the West. In Archibald MacLeish's words, "*The Waste Land* provided the vocabulary of our understanding."[5] Eliot himself repeatedly insisted that he never intended the poem to express what I.A. Richards called "the disillusionment of a generation," but nonetheless that was how it was understood by a large number of young writers. Almost immediately it became the central canonical text of the decade and, indeed, of Modernism itself, the single postwar poem to which all other poets responded in one way or another. Whereas most young American writers found in the poem a symbol answerable to their own pessimistic sense and even diagnosis of contemporary life, others like William Carlos Williams and Hart Crane disliked the negativism of the poem and felt betrayed by it. They believed it moved American poetry powerfully in the wrong direction, that the death of the old order could be a prelude to the birth of a new one, the beginning of what Crane in "The Wine Menagerie" calls "new thresholds, new anatomies!" But whatever their response to Eliot's radical poetic methodology, his strategy of juxtaposition and collage, his gloomy prognosis and nearly pathological anatomizing of the death of modern civilization, and whatever their political slant or persuasion, for all but the most naïve of writers the war and its aftermath problematized and finally punctured forever the American myth of progress and improvement. What Van Wyck Brooks called "the confident years" (1885–1915) were over.

The twenties was the decade when, as Frederick Hoffman pointed out, "All forms of rebellion, protest, satire and experiment ... were admitted."[6] It was also an era when the most puritanical and the most expansive and liberated aspects of American culture came into dramatic conflict and confrontation. The repressive aspects of American culture can be symbolized by the Prohibition amendment (which took effect on 1 January 1920 and wasn't repealed until 1933) and the Red Scare (the intolerant, paranoid form of patriotism which peaked with the arrest of Sacco and Vanzetti in one of the most celebrated legal cases of the decade). Beginning with the general strike in Seattle, the country was also torn apart by some three thousand labor strikes which were broken one after the other, leaving a heritage of failure for organized labor in the twenties. So, too, there was a tremendous black migration to Northern cities after the war, a strong reaction of repressive violence by many whites and, consequently, for a complex of reasons, there were race riots in some twenty-five cities during the "red summer" of 1919. At the same time the great northern migration also helped to lay the foundations for the creative ferment which would become the Harlem Renaissance.[7]

After the war a deep change took place in black consciousness around the country. The writers of the Harlem Renaissance were inflamed with a fresh faith in blackness and a fervent racial pride, the symbol and gospel of the New Negro. Harlem emerged as the new cultural center of black life. The lyric outpouring and achievement of the bright firmament of Claude McCay, Countee Cullen, Jean Toomer, and Langston Hughes essentially grew out of the radical evolution and change in American black life between the war years and the Depression. In the twenties the writers of the Harlem Renaissance self-consciously forged a distinct black aesthetic—reinventing and rediscovering traditional folk forms and, simultaneously, inventing a new formal expression of black life. As Langston Hughes asserted in 1926, "We younger Negro artists who create now intend to express our individual dark-skinned selves without fear or shame."[8] The collective work of the Harlem Renaissance poets forever redefined black life in literature. It marked a major watershed in black and, consequently, in American literary history.[9]

The more expansive and liberated aspects of American culture in the twenties can be symbolized not only by a changing black consciousness, but also by political developments such as the national woman's suffrage movement (women at last received the right to vote in 1920) and, in social terms, what came to be called the Jazz Age, an era of flappers and flaming youth, changing sexual mores and moral standards, a new bohemianism. Edna St. Vincent Millay and E.E. Cummings were the poets who seemed to express this bohemian aspect of the era most effectively and representatively in their work. Despite their different poetic modes and sensibilities, both Millay and Cummings were romantic individualists who had gravitated to Greenwich Village as the unquestioned center of bohemia. (So, too, Gertrude Stein and the young men she called "the lost generation" helped establish Paris as the center of romantic expatriatism in the twenties.) Millay and Cummings were writing in revolt against social and sexual puritanism, an outdated moral code. "Let's live suddenly without thinking," Cummings asserted in one poem. As Millay wrote in what was perhaps the most widely quoted quatrain of the decade:

> My candle burns at both ends;
>   It will not last the night;
> But ah, my foes, and oh, my friends—
>   It gives a lovely light.[10]

Millay and Cummings were poets of extravagant feeling writing on behalf of a changing system of manners. Their work reflected a new ethic. Thus, for the younger generation the Jazz Age—which was also an Age of Dismay—was a liberating time. F. Scott Fitzgerald referred to it as "the greatest, gaudiest spree in history."[11]

It was also during the twenties that the reigning ethic of middle-class America became a kind of rampant consumerism. Wilsonian idealism died, and under the leadership of Harding and Coolidge the route to normalcy became the road to a new commercialism and economic prosperity accompanied by an acquisitive spirit of materialism. Most writers reacted violently against America's materialistic ethics and, in alienated distrust, American poetry turned increasingly inward and away from social action.

At the beginning of the decade, it was still possible for critics to argue that modern American poetry scarcely existed. In "The Literary Life," his contribution to *Civilization in the United States*, Van Wyck Brooks surveyed the history of American literature as a "very weak and sickly plant" that couldn't be expected to flourish in the decaying soil of American civilization. Critics everywhere were willing to echo Brooks's opinion that, in comparison to contemporary European literature, American literature "is indeed one long list of spiritual casualties. For it is not that the talent is wanting, but that somehow that talent fails to fulfill itself."[12] Ten years later that opinion was scarcely possible. The twenties witnessed what R.P. Blackmur called an extraordinary "explosion of talent" that did, in fact, fulfill itself. A renaissance took place which established American poetry once and for all, at home and abroad, at the center of twentieth-century poetry. By the end of the decade American poetry had been recast and re-created as High Modernism. One result was a literary canon practically unsurpassed in American poetry.

T.S. Eliot and Ezra Pound together created an American version of continental Modernism. Their work of the late teens and early twenties has a closer affinity to Wyndham Lewis's Vorticist paintings and James Joyce's *Ulysses* than it does to the New World imperatives and ingenuities of William Carlos Williams and Marianne Moore, Hart Crane and Wallace Stevens. By 1920 the two expatriate American poets who had done so much to extricate twentieth-century poetry from the vagaries of late-Victorian verse were intent on reestablishing the connection between a fragmentary and chaotic present and a harmonious European past. In his seminal essay, "Tradition and the Individual Talent" (1919), Eliot argues that the contemporary poet needs to write with a strong historical sense "not only of the pastness of the past, but of its presence," with the feeling "that the whole of the literature of Europe from Homer and within it the whole of the literature of his own country has a simultaneous existence and composes a simultaneous order."

Eliot's idea of historical continuity and coherence, his idealized version of the comprehensive "mind of Europe," placed American poetry firmly in a European context and tradition. (In 1933, Pound concurred that "Eliot and I are in agreement or 'belong to the same school of critics,' in so far as we both believe that existing works form a complete order which is changed by the introduction of the 'really new' work.")[13] As a corollary to his emphasis on the interrelationship between the individual poet and the preceding tradition, the avant-garde artist and the deep (as opposed to the recent) past, Eliot also argued for the depersonalization of poetry in his well-known formulation, "The progress of the artist is a continual self-sacrifice, a continual extinction of personality." The essays in Eliot's first critical book, *The Sacred Wood* (1920), emphasize traditionalism, impersonality, and a transcendental European authority. They ask the critic to focus on the poem itself rather than on the personality or emotions of the poet; they call for "analysis and comparison" in considering the poem as an object. Although Eliot himself never practiced the method of close analysis and systematic criticism that would derive from the work of I.A. Richards (*Practical Criticism*, 1926) and William Empson (*Seven Types of Ambiguity*, 1928), his focus on the work of art as an ontological object is the inaugural step in a critical method that would become formulated as New Criticism during the thirties.[14]

In the July 1932 issue of the *Criterion*, Pound looked back to the moment when he and Eliot decided that free verse had to be replaced by regular forms:

> That is to say, at a particular date in a particular room, two authors, neither engaged in picking the other's pocket, decided that the dilution of *vers libre*, Amygism, Lee Masterism, general floppiness had gone too far and that some counter-current needed to be set going ... Remedy prescribed "Émaux et Camées" (or the Bay State Hymn Book). Rhyme and regular strophes.
>
>   Results: Poems in Mr. Eliots *second* volume not contained in his first (*Prufrock*, Egoist, 1917), also "H.S. Mauberley"[15]

There are twelve new poems in Eliot's second volume, *Poems* (1920). Eliot wrote four of the poems in French under the influence of Corbière to get himself unlocked from a stagnant period, seven in quatrains derived from Gautier (though the ironic diction harks back to Laforgue and the violent wit is reminscent of Donne). The quatrains are allusive, chilly, condensed, witty. Their rigid structure emphasizes coherence and control, an idea of imposed order. George Williamson calls the quatrains "a temporary discipline rather than a lasting form," and, tellingly, the book's most important single poem,

"Gerontion," is a free-verse dramatic monologue which stands in the line of "Prufrock" and as a prelude to *The Waste Land*.[16]

Ezra Pound called "Hugh Selwyn Mauberley: Life and Contacts" both "a farewell to London" and "a study in form, an attempt to condense the Jamesian novel."[17] It is the poem that marks the end of Pound's London days as well as the close of his early work. Thereafter he would become the poet of his evolving Modernist epic, *The Cantos*. One of the central themes of "Mauberley" is the overriding tyranny of modern life, the relentless pressure it exerts upon the individual. Mauberley's limited Paterian aesthetic can't satisfy the demands of the age, and the poem ends with his isolation and death. Thus the poem becomes an elegy not only for the character of Mauberley but also for the heritage of aestheticism. By 1920 Pound had already published a version of the first three cantos and had begun to work toward *A Draft of XVI Cantos* (1925). One of the ways he turned away from aestheticism was by embarking on an epic poem that would tell "the tale of the tribe." In formal terms, the chiseled quatrains of "Mauberley" derive from Pound's reading of Gautier as well as of Bion's *Adonis*, though the material is grafted together and presented through a series of abrupt cuts and shifts that give the feeling of a Modernist collage. Many of its formal devices—especially the way it radically changes ground, shifting perspective, juxtaposing fragments and languages, mixing classical allusions and contemporary events—also anticipate the method of *The Waste Land*.

The most important poem of our century (and also the most explicated one) began, in T.S. Eliot's own words, as "the relief of a personal ... grouse against life."[18] Eliot had been collecting fragments and planning a long poem for years, but he finally managed to draft most of the poem which would eventually become *The Waste Land* in 1921 in a sanitorium at Lausanne where he was taking a rest cure. On one level, the poem recapitulates his tormented personal life over the previous ten years—his full-scale depression, his disastrous marriage to a woman both sickly and high-strung ("My nerves are bad tonight. Yes, bad. Stay with me," her stand-in says in the final poem), his sense of being enslaved to a job at Lloyds Bank, his own fear of psychosis, hypersensitivity to noise, indecisiveness, and suffering from "nerves." The poem arises out of what he once called "some rude unknown *psychic materials*."[19] In a psychoanalytic sense, the poem— which one of his friends called "Tom's Autobiography"—represents the psychic disintegration and reconstitution of a self.[20] The writing itself became "these fragments I have shored against my ruin," a psychic as well as a religious journey from sin to revelation. At the same time, as Eliot acknowledged many years later in a piece about Virgil, "A poet may believe that he is expressing only his private experiences ... yet for his readers what he has written may come to be the expression both of their own secret feelings and of the exultation or despair of a generation."[21] Eliot's own inner nightmare correlated to what others perceived as an outer social nightmare, and thus his spiritual autobiography simultaneously became an account of a collapsing postwar society.

The Waste Land is an open structure of fragments, a poem without a fixed center. It has no single interpretation or truth, no one narrator or narrative thread to hold it together. It disseminates the self. It contains scenes and vignettes from a wide variety of times and places: agitated scraps of conversations, parodies, intertextual allusions, unattributed and often broken quotations, a medley of radically shifting languages, a disturbing cacophony of voices. The result is a poem with the feeling of a nightmare. As the facsimile edition of The Waste Land now makes clear, the manuscript which Eliot originally brought to Pound was much more sprawling and chaotic than the final poem. Pound ruthlessly cut the poem from about a thousand lines to its final four hundred and thirty-three lines, deleted eight major sections, made dozens of minor changes, recommended against the title ("He Do the Police in Different Voices"), against using an epigraph from Conrad ("the horror! the horror!"), and against using "Gerontion" as a prelude to the poem. The author of "Mauberley" was more comfortable with the poetics of fragmentation and collage, and his severe cuts foregrounded the poem's wrenching dislocations and juxtapositions. The result is a poem which is rhetorically discontinuous.

Eliot's method of dislocating language suits the basic despairing tone and vision of the poem—the theme of a ruined postwar world. The backdrop of the poem is the "unreal city" of London and, beyond that, the larger collapse of two thousand years of European history. The people who inhabit the waste land are the walking dead. The philosophic principle animating the poem is solipsism, F.H. Bradley's idea that, as Eliot says in a note to the poem, "the whole world for each is peculiar and private to that soul." Thus there is no genuine sharing of worlds—the experience of each person is "a circle closed on the outside." The medley of voices that inhabit The Waste Land never connect. The idea of a contemporary world without meaning or connection is also highlighted in Eliot's next major poem, a kind of epilogue to The Waste Land, "The Hollow Men" (1925).

The Waste Land first appeared, without notes, in the Criterion in 1922. (Eliot became the editor of the journal in 1923 and stayed on until the late thirties.) The title of the poem and what to many critics has seemed to be its controlling myth (the Grail legend) were late additions and impositions on the poem. In his essay on Joyce's *Ulysses*, "Ulysses, Order, and Myth," Eliot defined the mythical method as "a way of controlling, of ordering, of giving a shape and a significance to the immense panorama of futility and anarchy which is contemporary history."[22] Eliot saw his own experience as well as contemporary history as a vast chaos and anarchy. He projected his personal life onto history and sought a way to shape and order that chaos. Thus his conservative turn. By the end of the decade he had declared himself a classicist in literature, a royalist in politics, and an Anglo-Catholic in religion.[23]

The Modernism of the twenties took regional form in the work of three Southern poets—John Crowe Ransom, Allen Tate, and the young Robert Penn Warren, all of whom were associated with the Nashville Fugitives and helped to publish the literary magazine the *Fugitive* from 1922 to 1925. Of the sixteen poets in the Fugitive group, Ransom was the one significant writer who reached his full (and nearly complete) poetic development in the twenties.[24] Tate, the recognized champion of experimental Modernism in the group, developed many of his key ideas during the decade and published his first book, *Mr. Pope and Other Poems*, in 1928. During the decade, Warren established his basic poetic dualism, his tragic vision of the fall of man, his interest in irony as a reigning, inclusive poetic mode, and perhaps even his redemptive vision of language; but his major poetic work rightly belongs to later decades in American poetry.

In formal terms, the Fugitive poets began at the same place that Eliot and Pound had come to by the early twenties—with the sense that the free-verse revolution needed a countercurrent. Consequently, they worked within traditional forms. In their commitment to the historical past, their antiindustrialism, their hatred of abstraction, their diagnosis of what Tate called the "deep illness of the mind," dissociation of sensibility, their belief in what Ransom defined as the "antipathy between art and science," and their prevailing sense of the tragedy of modern man, the Fugitives also developed a brand of what might be called Traditionalist Modernism which was related to the cultural critiques leveled at modern civilization by Eliot and Pound.[25] At the same time their work grew directly out of their own native region. One might say that the American current of European Modernism took a strong, unexpected turn in the modern South.

The first issue of the *Fugitive* proclaimed that the phenomenon sometimes "known rather euphemistically as Southern Literature has expired" and that "*The Fugitive* flees from nothing faster than the high-caste Brahmins of the Old South."[26] The Fugitive poets began in rebellion against apologetic, official Southern literature, the "moonlight and magnolia" school of post–Civil War Southern poetry. Initially, they showed little interest in regional self-consciousness and self-definition. Their most common and persistent theme was the alienation of the artist from society, especially Southern society. But the South suffered a powerful economic and social shock after the end of the war as an essentially closed and static society increasingly opened up to industrialism and mass culture. As the twenties progressed, modern industrialism encroached further and further into traditional Southern culture. After the national attention and criticism directed at the South during the Scopes trial, the Fugitives began to rethink their ideas of the old South and how it might resist the spirit of technology and science as well as the onslaught of American materialism. They were already classicists in literature, traditionalists in religion—they also became regionalists. By the end of the decade they had turned into Agrarians, a movement which culminated in the manifesto *I'll Take My Stand* (1930). In that book, twelve Southern writers defended an agrarian economy and looked back nostalgically to a preindustrial, racially segregated, Christian South. In so doing they turned away from the progressivism of contemporary America and toward the conservatism of older European traditions.

John Crowe Ransom's first book, *Poems about God* (1919), consisted of poems which Randall Jarrell once described as "old-fashioned amateurishly direct jobs that remind you of the Longfellow-Whittier-Lowell section of your sixth-grade reader."[27] Ransom himself came to consider them apprentice work, and none survived into his later *Selected Poems.* They do indicate, however, the beginning of Ransom's furious war against abstractionism, his desire to knit up what he perceived to be the modern dissociation of reason from sensibility. Ransom's development as a poet was so rapid that in a few years he had discovered and mastered his mature style—with its formal elegance and technical skillfulness, its complex mix of dictions and tones, its wry wit and understatement, its cool surface and subtle use of irony—and written about a dozen or so nearly flawless lyrics. His two books *Chills and Fever* (1924) and *Two Gentlemen in Bonds* (1927) contain nearly all of the poems he wished to preserve. They represent his primary achievement in poetry. By the end of the decade Ransom had mainly stopped writing poetry and turned his attention to philosophical literary and social criticism.

The principal theme that runs through all of Ransom's work is our curious and tragic human doubleness, our divided natures and sensibilities. He once told Robert Penn Warren that he thought of man as an "oscillating mechanism," and for him Eliot's notion of the fragmented modern psyche was a psychological rather than a historical truth.[28] Ransom's poems chart a war of inner human tensions and oppositions—the split between body and soul, desire and need, illusion and reality, emotion and rational intellect. His most characteristic poems enact a theme of thwarted love or else dramatize and investigate the relentless inevitability of death and how we respond to it. The tragedy of Ransom's characters is their inability to accept their own duality, oscillating between extremes, paralyzed and tortured—as the equilibrists are—by opposing forces in their own natures. The only reconciliation they can find is in their own death. Despite his playfulness and wit, a Hardyesque fatalism runs through all of Ransom's poems.

Ransom's typical poetic strategy is to take a passionate subject and hold it up at a certain distance, creating a feeling of balance and tension, emotions held in check, fever and chills. He created a detached surface and linguistic tension by mixing a raw, colloquial, and informal speech with an archaic and elegant diction. And his central poetic mode was irony. He believed that irony was the most inclusive response to human duality and in 1924 praised it in *the Fugitive* as "the rarest of the states of mind, because it is the most inclusive; the whole mind has been active in arriving at it, both creation and criticism, both poetry and science."[29] Thus out of his own poetic practice and experience, his idea of the proper response to man's perception of his difference from nature, Ransom began to define the term that would be the foundation stone for New Criticism.

In the early twenties Allen Tate carried on what he called "an impertinent campaign on Eliot's behalf in the South." Tate's first book, *Mr. Pope and Other Poems*, combines a traditional formality with a Modernist subject matter and was heavily influenced by Eliot's *Poems*. His style is chiseled, concentrated, difficult. Tate arranged the poems under three categories, "Space," "Time," and "History," but they all deal with the same essential theme—the suffering of the modern citizen who must live in a world of bewildering complexity (with understanding divorced from reason) and under the dispensation of a scientific and technological age.

Tate's most important single poem, "Ode to the Confederate Dead," is a kind of Southern analogue to *The Waste Land*. As opposed to Ransom, who thought *The Waste Land* "seemed to bring to a head all the specifically modern errors," Tate defended the way Eliot's poem embraced "the entire range of consciousness" and impersonally dramatized the tragic situation of those who live in modern times.[30] Tate's "Ode" treats that situation in specifically Southern terms. The poem presents the symbolic dilemma of a man who has stopped at the gate of a Confederate graveyard. He is trapped in time, isolated, alone, self-conscious, caught between a heroic Civil War past, which is irrecoverable, and the chaotic, degenerate present. In his essay

"Narcissus as Narcissus," Tate argues that "the poem is 'about' solipsism, a philosophical doctrine which says that we create the world in the act of perceiving it, or about Narcissism, or any other *ism* that denotes the failure of the human personality to function objectively in nature and society."[31] As the poem develops, it becomes a drama of "the cut-offness of the modern 'intellectual man' from the world." The situation of the speaker is symptomatic of the crisis of his region—the crisis of the Old and the New South after World War I. In its diagnosis of that historical situation, the "Ode" is an Agrarian poem. It universalizes from the situation of the South in the middle and late twenties to the larger condition of the modern world.

In the twenties William Carlos Williams and Marianne Moore helped to continue to create and define a Modernist poetry of the New World, a local, homemade American poetic. Their "experiments in composition" are akin to the typographical innovations of E.E. Cummings and the verbal portraits of Gertrude Stein as well as to the more minor free-verse experiments of Mina Loy, Alfred Kreymborg, and Walter Arensberg. Their urgent struggle to create an indigenous American poetry parallels the innovative prose experiments of the expatriates Hemingway and Fitzgerald in the twenties. They had an even stronger and more direct connection to the visual artists who clustered around the photographer Alfred Stieglitz's gallery, "291" (Marianne Moore called it "an American Acropolis"), especially John Marin, Marsden Hartley, Arthur Dove, Charles Demuth, and Charles Sheeler. Along with the cultural journalists Waldo Frank (*Our America*, 1919) and Paul Rosenfeld (*Port of New York*, 1924), these artists emphasized immediate visual experience and the need for establishing American values in art. Out of this milieu, surrounded by the call for the emancipation of American art and literature, Moore and Williams created a body of early work (*Observations* and *Spring and All* are its masterpieces) that stands as a direct alternative to Continental American Modernism.

Williams's response to *The Waste Land* is the most extreme example of the way two strains of American poetry diverged in the twenties. Williams wanted a poetry that was forward-looking and experimental, self-consciously rooted in American soil. Years later he recalled how he felt when *The Waste Land* first appeared:

> It wiped out our world as if an atom bomb had been dropped upon it and our brave sallies into the unknown were turned to dust.
> To me especially it struck like a sardonic bullet. I felt at once that it had set me back twenty years, and I'm sure it did. Critically

Eliot returned us to the classroom just at the moment when I felt that we were on the point of an escape to matters much closer to the essence of a new art form itself—rooted in the locality which should give it fruit.[32]

The poetry which Williams wrote and sponsored in the twenties was directly posed against Eliot's version of Modernism.

Williams and Moore are poets of immanence, anti-Symbolists. For them meaning inheres primarily in the external world, and their poems accord to objects a life of their own. They featured and appraised objects (also animals and other people) in and of themselves, not for what they represented. Williams said of Moore, "To Miss Moore an apple remains an apple whether it be in Eden or the fruit bowl where it curls."[33] There is no depth of transcendence in their world, no secret, symbolic nature in things, no hidden correspondences to another world. So, too, for them words were fundamentally things in themselves, solid objects that match the particular things they name. Williams writes in *Spring and All*, "Of course it must be understood that writing deals with words and words only and that all discussions of it deal with single words and their associations in groups." At the same time words are themselves marked by "the shapes of men's lives in places."[34] Words are objects interacting in their own right which simultaneously name and parallel the local, external world. This dual sense of language is the beginning of an Objectivist aesthetic.

To render the external world accurately also meant to break radically with traditional ways of presenting and describing that world as well as with traditional or received forms of poetry. The goal was not loveliness but reality itself. This is the basic premise behind Williams's claim that "destruction and creation / are simultaneous."[35] "Poetry," Moore's most celebrated early poem, begins with the assertion

> I, too, dislike it: there are things that are important
>   beyond all this fiddle.
> Reading it, however, with a perfect contempt for it, one
>   discovers in
> it after all, a place for the genuine.[36]

Moore and Williams are revolutionary poets in the way they destroy preexisting forms in order to create new ones.

Williams published three books of poems in the twenties: *Kora in Hell: Improvisations* (1920), *Sour Grapes* (1921), and *Spring and All* (1923). All are

what Webster Schott terms "crisis books."[37] Written in white heat, their
style is fervent, headlong, embattled, often obscure and contradictory,
sometimes radiantly clear and luminous. They are also the key books of
Williams's early career, for they contain the basic premises of his mature
thought. They show him trying to create a platform for his evolving aesthetic
in prose even as he embodied that aesthetic in some of his most memorable
short poems.

Kora in Hell is a book of experimental prose poems, a culling of journal
meditations which Williams jotted down as a kind of automatic writing every
night for a year. Later he added comments and explanatory notes, many of
them equally dense and obscure. The title refers to the legend of Spring
captured and taken to Hades. As Williams recalled years later, "I thought of
myself as Springtime and I felt I was on my way to Hell."[38] Inspired by
Rimbaud's Illuminations, Kora in Hell is one of Williams's most puzzling,
disjunctive, and surreal texts, a broken composition that continually defies
rational logic and coherence. Kora in Hell is a text divided against itself,
energetically trying to find an equilibrium, holding together two conflicting
forces and impulses. On the one hand, the improvisations are impromptu
and open-ended, asserting the freedom and primacy of the imagination.
They are fueled by what J. Hillis Miller calls an "anarchistic rage to demolish
everything, all logical or rational forms, all the continuities of history."[39] The
destruction of received models and forms is necessary in order to clear a
space for spontaneous thought to arise. On the other hand, Williams's
aesthetic asserts the primacy of treating objects in the world directly. Thus
his thought oscillates between process and the thing itself. Williams's poetic
struggle involved finding an equilibrium between these opposing energies
and polarities. "Between two contending forces there may at all times arrive
that moment when the stress is equal on both sides so that with a great
pushing a great stability results giving a picture of perfect rest."[40]

Spring and All (1923)—first published by Robert McAlmon's Contact
Publishing Company—is an experimental weaving together of poems and
prose manifestoes about poetry. It is, as Williams said, "a travesty on the
idea" of typographical form.[41] Chapter headings are printed upside down,
chapters are numbered in the wrong order. The poems are untitled. The
prose combines violent indictments of contemporary civilization and
impassioned pleas on behalf of the imagination. As Kora in Hell is a descent
into winter and hell, so Spring and All is a difficult ascent into the radiance of
spring and the temporal world. The underlying subject of the book is the
hard necessity of creating "new forms, new names for experience." In this

cause, the prose rails against the false values of a rootless, materialistic society and calls for the annhilation of old values and forms. Against this materialistic malaise Williams poses the compensating imagination: "To refine, to clarify, to intensify that eternal moment in which we alone live there is but a single force—the imagination."[42] There are poems of great visual accuracy and precision, lyrics in which familiar objects are clarified and presented in a fresh context, such as the red wheelbarrow upon which "so much depends" and the flowerpot "gay with rough moss" (11). The primary subject of the poems in *Spring and All* is the difficult struggle to be reborn. The introductory poem sounds the call for a new world, describes the way the plants, still dazed and "lifeless in appearance,"

> ... enter the new world naked,
> cold, uncertain of all
> save that they enter....[43]

Later they "grip down and begin to awaken." In these poems consciousness and the world permeate each other. Subject and object are fused, and oppositions disappear between the inner world of the self and the outer world of things. This is Williams's central post-Romantic breakthrough. All of his work in the next decades would build on the basic premises and fundamental achievement of *Spring and All*.[44]

Marianne Moore's first pamphlet of twenty-four poems, *Poems* (London: Egoist Press, 1921) was published without her knowledge at the instigation of her friends Bryer and H.D. Her first American book, *Observations* (1924), contained all but three of the poems in the original pamphlet and added some thirty-two others. For Moore, poems *were* observations. Her poems have an acute visual sense, motivated as if by a painter's eye and a biologist's curious scrutiny. To borrow one of her phrases, her observations have a "relentless accuracy." She is a precisionist meticulously rendering visual phenomena, and her policy of exact comparison and the perfect word serves the facticity of the world. Her poems consist of scrupulous, and many separate, acts of attention to small and otherwise unnoticed animals and things. It is, as Hugh Kenner says, "the poetic of the solitary observer" confronted by a mute world that "seems to want *describing*."[45] Moore writes as if seeing things for the first time, defamiliarizing the natural world. Her descriptions of things-as-they-are stands as a corrective to the overhumanizing impulse to turn the world into a mirror for human beings. The testimony of the eye constitutes the basic premise of her ethics. In her early work both her morals (and all of her work has a moral inflection) and her ideas about things grow out of the primary ground of her Objectivist aesthetic.

Moore's poems are so clear and "objective," her individual words so concrete and singular, her descriptions so vivid and precise, that it is as if her language had been cleaned and held up to the light at a slight distance. Williams said of her language:

> With Miss Moore a word is a word most when it is separated out by science, treated with acid to remove the smudges, washed, dried, and placed right side up on a clean surface. Now one may say that this is a word. Now it may be used, and how?
>
> It may be used not to smear it again with thinking (the attachments of thought) but in such a way that it will remain scrupulously itself, clean perfect, unnicked beside other words in parade. There must be edges.[46]

Moore's elaborate syllabic patterns foreground the visual aspect of her work. The stanza, as opposed to the line, is her operative unit, and her characteristic poems are an arrangement of stanzas, each a formal replica of the previous one. "The Past Is the Present" concludes: "Ecstasy affords / the occasion and expediency determines the form."[47] Moore's expedient forms rely on the cadences of prose as well as the music of colloquial speech. They shun traditional effects, seem hammered out on a typewriter. The formal arrangement of her work gives the impression not so much of a thing *said* as of a thing *made*. Implicitly the poems stand as a corrective to the formless and shoddy in life and art.

Moore is particularly American in her belief in "accessibility to experience" ("New York") and her faith in locale, her aesthetic of the independent observer looking intently at the brute forces of nature. *Observations* also looks acutely and knowledgeably at "this grassless, linksless, languageless country in which letters are written / not in Spanish, not in Greek, not in Latin, not in shorthand, / but in plain American which cats and dogs can read!" ("England").[48]

Like Williams and Moore, E.E. Cummings was a poet of contact and immediacy, the present moment. A lesser poet than either—in an ultimate sense he altered no language but his own—he was nonetheless allied with them in. a commitment to the new and experimental. In a way he combined the romantic bohemian sensibility of Millay with the restless formal experimentation of Williams. On the surface his style was aggressively and typographically innovative. Cummings was extreme in the way he fractured spelling and syntax and played with capitalization, lineation, and stanzaic divisions, creating his own eccentric mode of punctuation and spacing, sometimes breaking up the integrity of individual words themselves. He was a determined individualist who signed his name in the lower case and defined the self with a small *i*. A feeling of adolescent rebelliousness still clings to a large number of his typographical experiments, and often the language seems wrenched into new shapes rather than truly renovated. More profoundly, his aesthetic favored spontaneity, motion, speed, process over product. As he wrote in the foreword to *Is 5*, "If a poet is anybody, he is somebody to whom things made matter very little—somebody who is obsessed by Making."[49] His favorite modern poet was Pound—he was especially influenced by the satirical aspect of "Mauberley"—and indeed his poems often move with a Poundian sense of juxtaposition and collage. At the same time, the subject matter of many of Cummings's poems is the time-honored, circumscribed, and conventional subject matter of much traditional lyric poetry: love, death, and the changing of the seasons.

Cummings's first book, *The Enormous Room* (1922), a striking prose memoir of his experiences as a prisoner in France during the war, established him as one of the representative voices of freedom for the new postwar generation. So did his first four books of poems—the work which defined his lifelong preoccupations as well as his basic stylistic method—all of which were published in the twenties: *Tulips and Chimneys* (1923), *XLI* and *&* (both in 1925), and *Is 5* (1926). The book *&*, more than any other, established him as a poet of erotic love just as his next book, *Is 5*, established him as a satirist who staunchly condemned America's moral corruption.

The central oppositions of *Tulips and Chimneys* defined the basic terms that would animate much of Cummings's work to come: the country against the city, the spontaneous against the planned, the organic against the lifeless, the natural against the artificial, the individual against the crowd, the beautiful against the ugly, the emotions against the rational intellect. His oppositions were forceful, elementary, reductive. Always he spoke up for the spontaneity of feeling—the new, the irreverent, the unselfconscious—and sang in celebration of love and the individual self. There may be what R.P. Blackmur called "a sentimental denial of the intelligence" in his work, but he also had an imagination which John Dos Passos called "essentially extemporaneous."[50] His best work gave a sense of freedom and buoyancy to the struggle to create an innovative, indigenous, process-oriented American poetry in the twenties.

A few years before *The Waste Land* appeared, Robert Frost wrote to Hamlin Garland, "I wonder if you think as I do it is time for consolidating our resources a little against outside influences on our literature and particularly against those among us who would like nothing better than to help us lose our identity."[51] Frost's two books in the twenties—*New Hampshire* (1923) and *West-Running Brook* (1928)—are a consolidating of resources, a strong affirmation of his local identity. For several years after he returned to New Hampshire in 1915, Frost made a renewed effort to insert himself into the tradition of New England regional literature. His most immediate precursor in that tradition was E.A. Robinson, who in the twenties was primarily engaged in a series of long, ultimately unsuccessful narrative poems. *New Hampshire* is one of Frost's most self-consciously regional books. It announces his commitment to the local, to "the need of being versed in country things," to a state which has "one of everything as in a showcase" ("New Hampshire"). The debilitating aspect of the regional tradition can be seen in the way Frost assumed the pose and role of the homiletic Yankee sage, acting not as an observer and analyst, as he had done in the great narrative poems of *North of Boston*, but as a patriotic spokesman for the region.

Against these editorializing tendencies one may pose such dark, playful, and compelling lyrics of the twenties as "Fire and Ice," "Dust of Snow," "Nothing Gold Can Stay," "To E.T.," "Stopping by Woods on a Snowy Evening," "To Earthward," and "Not to Keep" (from *New Hampshire*) and "Spring Pools," "The Freedom of the Moon," and "Acquainted with the Night" (from *West-Running Brook*), as well as the major dramatic dialogues "The Witch of Coos" and "West-Running Brook." These poems enact genuine dilemmas and contraries, confrontations with nothingness, playful differences in perspective, dark tensions, conflicts, and interactions between the inner self and the outer world. They seem spoken by a person in a scene or setting, and they register the colloquial nuances of a speaking voice played off against the rhythms of a traditional metric. As Frost said in the preface to his one-act play, *A Way Out* (1929), "Everything written is as good as it is dramatic."[52]

One of the central subjects of Frost's lyrics in the twenties is the longing for absorption or escape from the self against the desire to maintain the boundaries and integrity of that self. The full burden of loneliness is expressed in "Acquainted with the Night," in which the speaker, who walks away from home and town and is not called back by any one, is surrounded by an isolating darkness. Frost's acquaintance with the desolations of night and the gloom of consciousness closely parallels Stevens's understanding of the "mind of winter," the termless terms of nature, in "The Snow Man." The desire to escape consciousness and find peace in oblivion is at the center of

Frost's well-known lyric "Stopping by Woods on a Snowy Evening," in which the speaker turns away from the lure of the woods' annihilating beauty and back to the world of human bonds and contracts. This is Frost's characteristic move, the mind pressing back against the desolations of reality. The self is most exposed and present in Frost's middle work when he is testing its limits (as in "To Earthward") or playing with its various perceptions (as in "The Freedom of the Moon"). Ultimately, he refuses to give the mind up to its own transcendental urges.[53]

In addition to the international Modernism of Pound and Eliot and the indigenous Modernism of Moore and Williams, the romanticism of Wallace Stevens, Hart Crane, and, to a much lesser degree, Archibald MacLeish stands as a third powerful tradition to emerge in American poetry in the twenties. In radically different ways, Stevens and Crane reconciled the demands of being both Modernist and Romantic poets. In the process they re-created an American visionary poetic, and their work directly relates to and extends the Anglo-American Romantic tradition—the work of Blake, Wordworth, Keats, and Shelley in England, and Emerson, Whitman, Melville, and Dickinson in America. Stevens's claim that "the whole effort of the imagination is toward the production of the romantic" and even that "the imagination is the romantic" is one of the motivating premises of their explicitly Modernist poetic.[54] Stevens and Crane questioned and refigured the problem and validity of belief in a faithless age. They are post-Symbolist poets of great verbal energy and extravagance, an exultant language and lavish music, who sought "a new order of consciousness" (Crane) and "a new knowledge of reality" (Stevens). Theirs is the psychology of American Adamic poets in a relativist time, alone before the brute forces of nature, trusting their own inner experiences, accepting the burden of examining their own individual states of consciousness and reporting on the evidence. Their poems attempt to move beyond the isolating negations of *The Waste Land*, to pass beyond the poetics of irony and alienation and, through the saving compensatory powers of the imagination, to reconcile self and world, imagination and reality. In his last major poem, "The Broken Tower," Crane writes: "And so it was I entered the broken world / To trace the visionary company of love."[55] These lines encapsulate the central redemptive struggle of the late-Romantic poet in a Modernist era.

Stevens entered the broken world with the fundamental premise of Modernism—that God and the gods are dead. The poems in *Harmonium* (1923, 1931) begin with the idea of the death of the gods and meditate on the unsponsored world we live in without them. A relentless skepticism became the basis for Stevens's radical humanism, his belief that the modern poet must rediscover the earth. In the essay "Imagination as Value" he wrote, "The great poems of heaven and hell have been written and the great poem of the earth remains to be written."[56] Stevens's own goal was to write that earthly poem. He came to believe in the imagination, the gaiety of language he defined as poetry, as the consoling force in a world bereft of certainty: "After one has abandoned a belief in god, poetry is that essence which takes its place as life's redemption."[57] The refusal to accept the consolations of orthodox Christianity or of any revealed religion is the subject of Stevens's first major poem of earth, "Sunday Morning." It was through his aestheticism and sensibility, the mind turning to the world of sensations and the splendors of its own productions rather than to the certainties of false belief, that Stevens traced the visionary company.

In *Harmonium* Stevens expresses a strong determination to be true to one's own inner experiences and sensations. Many of his poems record a world of exquisitely changing surfaces and appearances, things moving rapidly in the external flux of experience. Such lyrics as "Thirteen Ways of Looking at a Blackbird," "Six Significant Landscapes," "Metaphors of a Magnifico," and "Sea Surface Full of Clouds" are a collection of sensations, naturalistic notes of the eye recording natural phenomena. At the same time they track the interrelationship between mind and landscape, the solitary consciousness reacting to an external and wholly separate world which cannot be known apart from our awareness of it. Poems of appearance are also poems of perception. The self, too, is an unstable, fluctuating element in a world of flux. "The Comedian as the Letter C" asks, "Can one man think one thing and think it long? / Can one man be one thing and be it long?"[58] The implicit answer: no. Stevens's skeptical intelligence refused to rest in any single certainty or explanation of the world.

For Stevens, the imagination acts as a way to order a constantly changing and chaotic world. It takes the place of empty heaven. In the parable "Anecdote of the Jar," the speaker places a jar in Tennessee and the jar organizes the "slovenly wilderness": "The wilderness rose up to it, / And sprawled around, no longer wild."[59] Thus the human artifact, emblem of the imagination, structures everything around it. The mind transforms the place, creating order out of wilderness. At the same time the mind doesn't create a single unchanging or "true" world, but only versions of that world. Every new jar, every new combination of words also creates a new window, a fresh revelation about reality itself. This helps to account for the range of tones in *Harmonium*—from the verbal gaudiness of "Bantams in Pine Woods" and "The Emperor of Ice Cream" to the solemn musings of "The Snow Man" and "Sunday Morning." In a way all of Stevens's poems about the relationship between imagination and reality are also justifications of poetry. *Harmonium* was the first major testament in his lifelong romantic struggle to "live in the world but outside of existing conceptions of it."[60]

The sole collection of lyrics that Hart Crane published in his lifetime, *White Buildings* (1926) is a thickly textured and radiant record of his quest to transcend the spirit of negation and become a poet of joy, a seer testifying to the reality of the absolute. As he suggested in "General Aims and Theories," Crane emulated his precursors Rimbaud and Blake and tried to see *through* and not *with* the eye, to use the real world as a springboard for what Blake called "innocence" and he called "absolute beauty," seeking a higher consciousness and transcendental realm, "moments of eternity."[61] His poems often descend into a depth of horror or squalor out of which a grail of light suddenly radiates:

> Look steadily—how the wind feasts and spins
> The brain's disk shivered against lust. Then watch
> While darkness, like an ape's face, falls away,
> And gradually white buildings answer day.[62]

One of the principal dramas in all of Crane's work is the attempt to reconcile the rival claims of the actual and the ideal, the sensuous and spiritual worlds.

There are twenty-eight poems in *White Buildings*, all but two of them written between 1920 and 1925 when Crane forged his central aesthetic. Early poems such as "In Shadow," "Pastorale," and "My Grandmother's Love Letters" have a quasi-Imagist impressionism and a lyrical fragility. Crane was seeking a more charged language and more contemporary feeling in his poems, and by 1919 had turned toward Pound and Eliot for his poetic values and, through them, to the work of Laforgue and the Elizabethans. He confessed he read "Prufrock" and "Preludes" continually, and one sees Eliot's verbal hardness and ironic literary allusions in the quatrains of such early poems as "Praise for an Urn" and "Black Tambourine." He translated Laforgue's "Locutions des Pierrots," and in his most Laforgian poem, "Chaplinesque"—inspired by Chaplin's *The Kid*—he adapted the French poet's complex tone and wit in order to parallel the situation of the modern poet with that of the lonely, abused tramp of the movie. Crane was most lastingly influenced by "the vocabulary and blank verse of the Elizabethans" (in one of his letters he refers to his "Elizabethan fanaticism"), and his work often relies on a high rhetoric derived from reading Marlowe, Webster, and Donne.[63]

Crane's poems are "drunk with words." He was more interested in associational meanings than in ordinary logic and characteristically took unusual and highly connotative words and combined them in unexpected and musical ways. Reproved by the editor of *Poetry* for the difficult obscurity of his work, especially "At Melville's Tomb," he responded that his goal was to find "a logic of metaphor" beyond the boundaries of "so-called pure logic."[64] The principle of organizing a poem through the "emotional dynamics" of suddenly forced conjunctions correlates to the visionary subject and goal of the poems. Crane's verbal excess, his metaphorical and extralogical way of organizing a poem and, ultimately, his idealism, were attacked by such antiromantic critics as R.P. Blackmur, Yvor Winters, and his friend Allen Tate, although their pioneering essays helped to uncover the motivating romantic principles of Crane's poetic.[65]

Crane admired and imitated the way that Eliot's poems encompassed contemporary life, but after the publication of The *Waste Land* he began to think of his work as a positive alternative and direct counterstatement to Eliot. In a letter to Allen Tate, he declared: "In his own realm Eliot presents us with an absolute *impasse*, yet oddly enough, he can be utilized to lead us to, intelligently point to, other positions and 'pastures new.' Having absorbed him enough we can trust ourselves as never before, in the air or on the sea. I, for instance, would like to leave a few of his 'negations' behind me, risk the realm of the obvious more, in quest of new sensations, *humeurs*."[66] Six months later he emphasized his own "more positive, or (if [I] must put it so in a skeptical age) ecstatic goal ... I feel that Eliot ignores certain spiritual events and possibilities as real and powerful now as, say, in the time of Blake.... After his perfection of death—nothing is possible in motion but a resurrection of some kind."[67]

"For the Marriage of Faustus and Helen" is the first fruit of Crane's attempt to break away from the poetry of negation. It is his first long poem, a direct precursor to *The Bridge* in its countering of pessimism and in its expression of a renewed hope in the American city. The poem employs Crane's own version of the mythical method, fusing the present with the past, paralleling contemporary life and ancient culture through the symbolism of Faustus (imaginative man) and Helen (ideal beauty). In a way Crane uses a reduced version of Eliot's method in order to "answer" *The Waste Land*, insisting—in a Blakean formulation—that we "Greet naively—yet intrepidly / New soothings, new amazements."[68] "Faustus and Helen" is the first poem in which Crane tries to absorb the influences of the modern era—jazz, electric light displays, advertising—and become a visionary poet of the Machine Age. As he wrote to Tate, "Let us invent an idiom for the proper transposition of jazz into words! Something clean, sparkling, elusive."[69] This transposition became his method of trying to move "beyond despair," showing "one inconspicuous, glowing orb of praise."

Crane's lyrical masterpiece "Voyages" is a coherent sequence or "suite" of six sea poems that he wrote between 1921 and 1925. His most personal poem, it traces a homosexual love affair with a young sailor, commonly designated as E.O., through the arc of elation, excitement, separation, betrayal, and loss. The final poem ends with the poet's solitary vision of ideal beauty. Crane's attempt to reconcile the erotic and the spiritual in love, indeed to comprehend the psychology of romantic love, is played out against the constant backdrop of the sea, which appears in the sequence as dangerous and threatening as well as "a great wink of eternity" and, finally, a source of visionary solace. Crane borrowed some of the sea imagery from the unpublished poems of Samuel Greenberg, who died in 1916 at the age of twenty-three; more profoundly, his poem is saturated with the arresting vocabulary and imagery of Melville's *Moby-Dick*. In "Voyages" Crane uses the sea to mirror and record the experience of love and its loss. His great subject is the precariousness of ecstasy in a phenomenal world and the necessary, doomed quest for spiritual wholeness. In the final lyric, the vision of Belle Isle and poetry itself become the compensation for the death of love: "It is the unbetrayable reply / Whose accent no farewell can know."[70]

The Bridge is a loosely joined sequence of fifteen poems that Crane wrote between 1923 and 1929. His original idea was to present the "Myth of America," a "mystical synthesis" of the American past, present, and future. His ambition was to become "a suitable Pindar for the dawn of the machine age," and he intended his poem as an "epic of modern consciousness," a full-scale reply to *The Waste Land* and a simultaneous embrace of contemporary life. Whitman acts as the presiding spirit of the poem, and Crane asserts a spiritual alliance with Whitman's large, transcendental vision of America. In the many years of writing his lyrical epic, however, he often suffered a wavering confidence about the spiritual worthiness of American life in an industrial and scientific era: "If only America were half as worthy today to be spoken of as Whitman spoke of it fifty years ago there might be something for me to say—not that Whitman received or required any tangible proof of his intimations, but that time has shown how increasingly lonely and ineffectual his confidence stands."[71] One of the underlying dramas of *The Bridge* is Crane's struggle to maintain his initial optimistic faith in the spiritual possibilities of America in the twenties. Along with such writers as Waldo Frank and Lewis Mumford, he sought to repudiate American materialism by finding a higher idealism in American culture. At the same time he read the development of American experience as analogous to the growth of spiritual consciousness.

The crucial fact and symbol of Crane's poem is Brooklyn Bridge itself. To Crane the bridge not only connected Brooklyn to Manhattan, but also linked the past to the present, earth to heaven. It was a product of modern technology and science as well as a work of labor and art, a symbol of America's "constructive future" and "unique identity." Beyond its commercial and practical purposes, Crane also read it as a "harp and altar," a magnificent span between time and eternity, "terrific threshold of the prophet's pledge" ("Proem"), a sign of America's religious need to transcend the realm of ordinary experience in quest of ideal purity and permanence. Crane's different protagonists—Columbus in "Ave Maria," the poet/pilgrim in various guises and moods, whether contemplating Pocahontas and his own childhood (section 1), giving an account of American history (section 4), or riding and thinking about the subway as a modern hell (section 7)—are all versions of the American wanderer or prodigal in a restive search for America's lost patrimony.[72] The urgency and importance of this quest signal Crane's full visionary ambition. His most important poem stands as a record not so much of man's spiritual fulfillment as of his enormous spiritual desire and aspiration.

There were some compelling female lyricists in the twenties, all of them—in one way or another—Romantic poets. Elinor Wylie, Sara Teasdale, Edna St. Vincent Millay, Leonie Adams, and Louise Bogan (in her first two books) created a substantial body of lyric poetry that is essentially romantic in its procedures, its rhetoric, and its attitudes.[73] Their poems— many of them comparable to Elizabethan songs—assert the authority of the female self through musical lyrics of intense personal feeling. Their work belongs to the formal tradition of Anglo-American poetry and stands apart from the stylistic revolution in American poetry in the twentieth century. It also belongs to an alternative tradition of women's poetry.

Modernism precipitated two distinct styles of women's poetry that had divided clearly by the twenties.[74] One style was the innovative Modernism of such poets as Marianne Moore, Gertrude Stein, Amy Lowell, Mina Loy, and H.D. These poets were experimental in their methodologies. The female lyric poets, on the other hand, projected themselves more personally through a received poetic style and form. Their pared-down language and the direct way in which they treated their subjects were Modernist, but their work repudiated free verse and generally observed the conventions of the traditional nineteenth-century short poem. Their well-crafted lyrics have the colorings of Romantic poetry.

Wylie, Teasdale, Bogan, Adams, and, to a lesser extent, Millay were skilled metricists who embraced a poetics of closure and often wrote lyrics, ballads, odes, and sonnets. Their work is carefully wrought and has the formalist quality, as Moore said of Bogan, of "compactness compacted."[75] Each owes a large debt to the Metaphysical poets who were in ascendance in the early twenties, and each in her own way adapts a poetry of paradox and wit to a Romantic sensibility. Ultimately, they are poets of the expressive self, of a radical subjectivity committed to emotion. In Bogan's words, emotion is "the kernel which builds outward form from inward intensity."[76] Their neo-Romanticism was also a revolt against Victorian sentimentality, against false emotions and posturing, and against decorative ornamentation. There is a tension and conflict in their work between exuberant desire and romantic aspiration and the requirements of limited form, the demands of hardness, clarity, precision. Millay was the most florid and expansive of the poets, Bogan the most clipped and austere, but each expressed a deep longing for escape in strictly determined forms. Love is the circumscribed subject in most of their poetry—partially because the love poem was a form of discourse that included women in a way that the poetry of history did not include them. In these lyrics women are not idealized objects or muses, but motivating subjects: self-assertive, joyous, sometimes arrogant, singing of extreme emotional deprivation or thwarted passion, insisting, too, on physical passion and sensuality, the profound conflict between mind and body.

The traditional female lyricists of the twenties inherited a heritage of the divided self. Their poems enact a series of conflicts and unresolved contraries: passion against restraint, easy flow against containment, the outward suppression of the female personality in a male-dominated society against the inner desire for self-assertion and authorship. Often the need for self-expression and the desire for freedom from restrictive social roles is coded in terms of a timeless quest for spiritual loveliness and beauty. Inspired by Shelley and Christina Rosetti as well as by Donne and Jonson, their lyrics—especially the lyrics of Wylie and Teasdale—suggest a succession of strategies for fending off a hostile outside world and maintaining the fragile integrity of the individual self. Their Platonism and ecstatic love of beauty, their concern with ultimate themes, expresses a veiled personal and social need for autonomy. So, too, their poetry is visionary in its determined quest for an absolute truth to replace a lost god.

In their work in the twenties, Elinor Wylie, Sara Teasdale, and Louise Bogan, as well as Hart Crane and Wallace Stevens, showed themselves to be redemptive poets writing at perhaps an unredeemable time in American history. One of the romantic splendors of their poetry is its persistent spiritual aspiration in a world resistant and even hostile to that aspiration. And yet, as Wallace Stevens wrote, "After the final no there comes a yes / And on that yes the future world depends."[77]

NOTES

1. Quoted in Paul Fussell, *The Great War and Modern Memory* (New York: Oxford University Press, 1975) 325.

3. Peter Faulkner, *Modernism* (London: Methuen, 1977), 14–15.

4. *Selected Prose of T.S. Eliot*, ed. Frank Kermode (New York: Harcourt and Farrar, 1975), 65.

5. Quoted in Gorham Munson, *The Awakening Twenties* (Baton Rouge: Louisiana State University Press, 1985), 291.

6. Frederick Hoffman, *The Twenties: American Writing in the Postwar Decade* (New York: Free Press, 1962), 441.

7. Geoffrey Perrett, *America in the Twenties* (New York: Simon and Schuster, 1982), 15–143.

8. Hughes, "The Negro Artist and the Racial Mountain," in *The Black Aesthetic*, ed. Addison Gayle, Jr. (Garden City, N.Y.: Doubleday, 1972), 172.

9. For a fuller discussion of the black movement, see Timothy Seibles, "A Quilt in Shades of Black: The Black Aesthetic in Twentieth-Century African-American Poetry," 158–90.

10. Cummings, *Poems 1923–1954* (New York: Harcourt, 1968), 121; Millay, *Collected Poems* (New York: Harper, 1956), 127.

11. Quoted in Malcolm Cowley, "Fitzgerald: The Romance of Money" (1956), in *F. Scott Fitzgerald: Modern Critical Views*, ed. Harold Bloom (New York: Chelsea, 1985), 53.

12. *Civilization in the United States*, ed. Harold Stearns (1922; rpt. Carbondale: Southern Illinois University Press, 1964), 181.

13. Pound, "Praefatio aut Tumulus Cimicius," *Active Anthology* (London: Faber and Faber, 1933), 9.

14. Bernard Bergonzi, *T.S. Eliot* (New York: Macmillan, 1972), 60.

15. Pound, "Harold Monro," *Criterion* 11, no. 45 (July 1932): 590.

16. Williamson, *A Reader's Guide to T.S. Eliot* (New York: Noonday, 1953), 89.

17. Pound, *Personae*, 185, and *The Letters of Ezra Pound, 1907–1941*, ed. D.D. Paige, (New York: Harcourt, 1950), 180.

18. Eliot, *The Waste Land: A Facsimile and Transcript of the Original Drafts Including the Annotations of Ezra Pound*, ed. Valerie Eliot (New York: Harcourt, 1971), 1.

19. Eliot, *On Poetry and Poets* (New York: Farrar, Straus and Giroux, 1957), 111.

20. Mary Hutchinson interpreted the poem as "Tom's Autobiography—A Melancholy One," according to *The Diary of Virginia Woolf*, ed. Anne Olivier Bell (New York: Harcourt, 1978), 2:178. For a psychoanalytic reading of the poem, see Harry Trossman, "T.S. Eliot and *The Waste Land*: Psychopathological Antecendents and Transformations," *Archives of General Psychiatry* 30 (May 1974): 709–17, and Ronald Bush, *T.S. Eliot: A Study in Character and Style*, (New York: Oxford University Press, 1983), 68–69.

21. Eliot, "Virgil and the Christian World," in *On Poetry and Poets*, 137.

22. Eliot, *Selected Prose*, 177.

23. Eliot, *For Lancelot Andrewes: Essays on Style and Order* (Garden City, N.Y.: Doubleday, 1929), vii.

24. They are John Crowe Ransom, Allen Tate, Robert Penn Warren, Donald Davidson, Merrill Moore, Laura Riding, Walter Clyde Curry, Jesse Wills, Alec B. Stevenson, Sidney Hirsch, Stanley Johnson, William Yandell Elliott, William Frierson, Ridley Wills, James Frank, and Alfred Starr.

25. Tate, *Reason in Madness* (New York: Putnam's, 1941), ix; John Crowe Ranson, "Classical and Romantic," *Saturday Review of Literature* 6 (14 Sept. 1929): 125–27. See also Monroe Spears, *Dionysius and the City* (New York: Oxford University Press, 1970), 153–54.

26. Quoted in Louise Cowan, *The Fugitive Group: A Literary History* (Baton Rouge: Louisiana State University Press, 1959), 48.

27. Jarrell, "John Ransom's Poetry," *Sewanee Review* 56 (Summer 1948): 389.

28. Spears, *Dionysius and the City*, 154.

29. Quoted in *The Fugitive Poets*, ed. William Pratt (New York: Dutton, 1965), 27.

30. John M. Bradbury. *The Fugitives: A Critical Account* (Chapel Hill: University of North Carolina Press, 1958), 21–24.

31. Tate, *Reason in Madness*, 136.

32. Williams, *The Autobiography of William Carlos Williams* (New York: Random 1951) 174

34. Ibid., 145, 357.

35. Ibid., 127.

37. Williams, *Imaginations*, xii.

38. Williams, *I Wanted to Write a Poem*, ed. Edith Heal (Boston: Beacon, 1958), 29.

39. Miller, *Poets of Reality* (New York: Atheneum, 1969), 338.

40. Williams, *Imaginations*, 32–33.

41. Williams, *I Wanted to Write a Poem*, 36.

42. Williams, *Imaginations*, 89.

43. Ibid., 95.

44. Miller, *Poets of Reality*, 287.

45. Kenner, *A Homemade World* (New York: Knopf, 1975), 92.

46. Williams, *Imaginations*, 316.

47. Moore, *Complete Poems*, 88.

48. Ibid., 46.

49. Cummings, *Poems 1923–1954*, 163.

50. Blackmur, "Notes on E.E. Cummings's Language" (1931), in *Critical Essays on E.E. Cummings*, ed. Gary Rotella (Boston: G.K. Hall, 1984), 107; John Dos Passos, *The Best Times* (New York: New American Library, 1966), 83.

51. Frost, *Selected Letters of Robert Frost*, ed. Lawrence Thompson (New York: Holt, 1964), 265–66.

52. Frost, *Selected Prose of Robert Frost*, ed. Hyde Cox and E.C. Lathem (New York: Collier, 1968), 13.

53. Frank Lentricchia, *Robert Frost: Modern Poetics and the Landscape of the Self* (Durham, N.C.: Duke University Press, 1975), 101–19; and Richard Poirier, *Robert Frost: The Work of Knowing* (New York: Oxford University Press, 1977), 173–225.

54. Stevens, *Opus Posthumous*, ed. Samuel French Morse (New York: Random, Vintage, 1982), 163.

56. Stevens, *The Necessary Angel* (London: Faber and Faber, 1951), 142.

57. Stevens, *Opus Posthumous*, 158.

58. Stevens, *The Palm at the End of the Mind*, ed. Holly Stevens (New York: Random, Vintage, 1971), 71.

59. Ibid., 46.

60. Ibid., 164.

61. Crane, *Complete Poems*, 220–21.

62. Ibid., 25.

63. Crane, *The Letters of Hart Crane 1916–1932*, ed. Brom Weber (Berkeley: University of California Press, 1965), 71.

64. Crane, *Complete Poems*, 234–40.

65. Blackmur, "New Thresholds, New Anatomies," in *Form and Value in Modern Poetry* (Garden City, N.Y.: Doubleday, 1957), 269–86; Allen Tate, "Hart Crane" and "Crane: The Poet as Hero," in *Collected Essays* (Denver: Allan Swallow, 1959), 225–37, 528–32; Yvor Winters, "The Significance of *The Bridge* by Hart Crane, or What Are We to Think of Professor X?" in *In Defense of Reason* (Denver: Denver University Press, 1943), 575–603.

66. Crane, *Letters*, 90.

67. Ibid., 114–15.

68. Crane, *Complete Poems*, 30.

69. Crane, *Letters*, 89.

70. Crane, *Complete Poems*, 41.

71. Crane, *Letters*, 274, 305, 124, 129, 308.

72. R.W.B. Lewis, *The Poetry of Hart Crane* (Princeton: Princeton University Press, 1967), 219–45.

73. Elinor Wylie: *Nets to Catch the Wind* (1921), *Black Armour* (1923), *Trivial Breath* (1928), *Angels and Earthly Creatures* (1929). Sara Teasdale: *Flame and Shadow* (1920), *Dance of the Moon* (1926). Edna St. Vincent Millay: *A Few Figs from Thistles* (1920), *Second April* (1921), *The Harp-Weaver* (1923), *The Buck in the Snow* (1928). Leonie Adams: *Those Not Elect* (1925), *High Falcon* (1929). Louise Bogan: *Body of This Death* (1923), *Dark Summer* (1929).

74. Alicia Suskin Ostriker, *Stealing the Language: The Emergence of Women's Poetry in America* (Boston: Beacon, 1981) 44.

75. Marianne Moore, *Predilections* (New York: Viking, 1955), 130.

76. Quoted in Moore, *Predilections*, 130.

77. Stevens, *The Palm at the End of the Mind*, 190.

LANGDON HAMMER

Dice of Drowned Men's Bones

If after all these fearful fainting trances, the verdict be, the golden haven
was not gained;—yet in bold quest thereof, better to sink in boundless
deeps than float on vulgar shoals; and give me, ye gods, an utter wreck,
if wreck i do.

—Herman Melville, *Mardi*[1]

By the fall of 1925, the manuscript of *White Buildings* had circulated for
more than a year without securing a publisher.[2] Nor, in this period, had
Crane had much success placing his poems with magazines. Tate took
"Legend" and "Lachrymae Christi" for the *Fugitive*, but Marianne Moore
rejected "Passage" for the *Dial*, and Eliot rejected the same poem for the
Criterion. When Eliot rejected "The Wine Menagerie" as well, Crane again
tried Moore. This time Moore accepted Crane's poem, but with certain
changes, which she took it upon herself to make; and these changes, it turned
out, entailed the reduction of Crane's eleven pentameter quatrains to three
much abridged, strangely Moore-like strophes, enigmatically retitled
"Again."[3] Crane, it seems, would either have to see his work rejected by Eliot
and Moore, or submit to their correction.

When he drafted "At Melville's Tomb" in late October 1925, Crane
turned away from the modernist community represented by Eliot and
Moore, as the speaker of this poem turns his back on the shore. At the same

From *Hart Crane & Allen Tate: Janus-Faced Modernism.* © 1993 by Princeton University Press.

time, Crane turned toward the sea, toward the past, and toward Melville, the history of whose reception gave Crane a means to dramatize and interpret the vicissitudes of his own. Melville was an off-shore ally. His imaginative world gave literary sanction to Crane's erotic life, in particular to Crane's pursuit of sailors. In another sense, Crane's sexual voyages in Lower Manhattan or on the Brooklyn waterfront acted out literary motifs and ambitions, such as he found in Melville. "Under thy shadow by the piers I waited," Crane says to Brooklyn Bridge; it is a scene of desiring that is neither merely sexual nor wholly literary (Crane, *Poems*, 44). Melville gave Crane ways to link the homosexual company he found by the piers and "the visionary company of love" he projected in his poems (Crane, *Poems*, 160). But Crane did not find in Melville healing and unity of the kind represented in "Episode of Hands." The Melville Crane addressed stood for boundless and despised desires.

"At Melville's Tomb" proposes a literary history in which Crane would have a place; in the act of reading Melville, the poem projects a reader for Crane. An intimate bond with the reader was essential to the kind of "obscure" poem Crane wrote. The difficulty of Crane's work calls forth— and is premised upon—an ideal reader; it is an appeal for aid and connection, as Crane explained during 1926 in a series of important and related documents, letters to Gorham Munson and to Harriet Monroe and the essay (or really the notes) called "General Aims and Theories." In this chapter, I plan to meditate on "At Melville's Tomb" and the prose texts that grew out of it in order to extract the basic terms of Crane's poetics and set them against those of Tate and Eliot. In conclusion, I will turn briefly to "Repose of Rivers." Written just after Crane left Patterson in April 1926, "Repose of Rivers" draws this stage of Crane's writing life to a close. It also looks ahead to *The Bridge*.

Who exactly was Melville in 1925? Whom did Crane invoke by that name? He was and was not the author who occupies a central position in the temple of the American Renaissance. That author was available to Crane in D.H. Lawrence's *Studies in Classic American Literature* (1923) or in writing influenced by Van Wyck Brooks's reevaluation of American romanticism, including Frank's *Our America* (1919) and Lewis Mumford's *The Golden Day* (1926). Crane, who sent his first draft of the poem to Frank, understood "At Melville's Tomb" as a contribution to this ongoing cultural labor, this search for "a usable past." But Melville was not an important figure in Brooks's canon, and less important still in "the genteel tradition" Brooks's canon was intended to displace. When Melville was revived in the early 1920s, it was later than Whitman, say, or Twain,[4] and under different circumstances: he had never been entirely alive. Melville was a minor author of sea tales whose appeal was closely associated with his own life as vagabond, *isolato*, and adventurer. Melville's later fiction, where it was known, was considered the imaginative failure of an embittered man; and *Moby-Dick*, if it was admired, was chiefly admired abroad.[5] In 1925, then, Melville carried with him the aura of an American *maudit*—an obscure author with a criminal appeal not unlike that which attracted Crane to Joyce. Crane, known to dress himself as "an Indian" or "a cannibal" at parties, saw a brother in Melville, "who lived among the cannibals"; like Crane, Melville was a sailor and a symbolist—or, as the subtitle of Raymond Weaver's biography of Melville identifies him, a *Mariner and Mystic*.[6]

The epigraph with which this chapter begins comes from Melville's *Mardi* in a passage Weaver quotes to describe Melville's early ambition. Crane read Weaver's biography of Melville, which was published in 1921; he read *Moby-Dick* four times, read *White-Jacket*, *Typee*, *Omoo*, *Mardi*, and *Israel Potter*, read *Piazza Tales*, and read Melville's poems.[7] The life-narrative Crane found in these books is summarized by Weaver as an ongoing conflict between the claims of desire and "reality":

> Throughout Melville's long life his warring and untamed desires were in violent conflict with his physical and spiritual environment. His whole history is the record of an attempt to escape from an inexorable and intolerable world of reality: a quenchless and essentially tragic Odyssey away from home, out in search of "the unpeopled world behind the sun." In the blood and bone of his youth he sailed away in brave quest of such a harbour, to face inevitable defeat. For this rebuff he sought both solace and revenge in literature. But by literature he also sought his livelihood.... Held closer to reality by financial worry and the hostages of wife and children, the conflict within him was heightened. By a vicious circle, with brooding disappointment came ill health. (Weaver, *Melville*, 19)

As Weaver's rhetoric rises to the level of Melville's in *Mardi*, he depicts Melville's literary project as "solace and revenge" for the failure of his youthful "Odyssey away from home," his longed-for deliverance from "the vulgar shoals" of "an inexorable and intolerable world of reality." Melville's youthful urge to escape the confines of bourgeois civility and "home" (later, the wife and children he holds hostage) is renewed in Melville's will to transcend "fireside literature," and produce a kind of writing that would mean more than his livelihood. Both of these quests, being dedicated to absolute satisfactions, necessarily encounter defeat, imagined as shipwreck, or as a writer's production of an unread (perhaps an unreadable) text. Weaver's Melville remains true to the "untamed desires" of his youth, but at the cost of becoming "the Devil's Advocate," a novelist created in the image of the Satanic Poet willing to commit himself to hell rather than repent. It is a version of the story Tate tells about Keats and Crane, but unlike Tate, Weaver does not endorse moral "realism"; Melville is for Weaver a tragic figure because he keeps faith with his desires, not because he gives them up.

This is the moral, and history of Crane's Melville too. But to refuse to repent, to abandon the consolations of "home," is not, in Crane's poem, to cut oneself off from all bonds; it is to enter into a different kind of community, a league of "drowned men," from which it is possible to draw hope. In the first stanza of Crane's poem, the persistence of this community across time, even in "defeat," is figured in the repeated action of the waves as they rise and fall, breaking on the shore.

> Often beneath the wave, wide from this ledge
> The dice of drowned men's bones he saw bequeath
> An embassy. Their numbers as he watched,
> Beat on the dusty shore and were obscured.
> (Crane, *Poems*, 33)

The trochaic substitutions in the first and fourth feet of line 1 introduce a tension between iambic and trochaic schemes, the metrical norm and its reversal, which, as we will see, is encoded on another level in Crane's images of rising and falling, lifting and sinking. In this first instance the metrical alternation, a movement of arrest and renewal, is coordinated with the action of the waves. The trochaic word "Often" locates this action in time while the phrase "wide from this ledge" locates it in space. That initial phrase invokes a recurring possibility of vision—at once enduring *and* discontinuous—of the kind invoked in the first line of *The Bridge*: "How many dawns, chill from his rippling rest" (Crane, *Poems*, 43). In fact, the beginning of *The Bridge* specifically reworks the beginning of Crane's draft, "How many times the jewelled dice spoke."[8] In both cases, Crane begins a poem in such a way as to place his own action within a *series* of beginnings. The effect, here, is to emphasize the continuity between Crane's and Melville's perspectives even as it emphasizes the discontinuity, or seriality, of this perspective as such. In the preface to *White Buildings*, Tate faults Crane's "masters"—Whitman, Melville, and Poe—for establishing only a discontinuous tradition of false starts, repeated beginnings; in "At Melville's Tomb," Crane claims that discontinuity as a sign of generative power and a principle of historical connection.

The vision Melville and Crane share—"wide from this ledge"— introduces an expanded field of possibility. "Wide" is a peculiarly Cranean modifier, a *positional* term, implying breadth, lateral movement, and scope. It points to both separation and extension, and it turns up repeatedly in Crane's poems about the sea, which are also poems about Crane's relation to nineteenth-century American male authors like Melville and Whitman. "Wide" (sometimes "widening" or "wider") occurs four times in "Voyages," once in "The Harbor Dawn" and in "Ave Maria," and twice more in both "The River" and "Cape Hatteras." In "Voyages I," the word describes the danger of engulfment by "caresses / Too lichen-faithful from too wide a breast" (Crane, *Poems*, 34); and in "Voyages II," this threat is matched and overcome by "The seal's wide spindrift gaze toward paradise" (Crane, *Poems*, 35).

Here, in the first line of "At Melville's Tomb," "wide" describes the poet's latitude of vision across the extrasocial space of the sea, a place without limits, of "rimless floods, unfettered leewardings" ("Voyages II" [Crane, *Poems*, 35]), an imaginative domain very different from the strictly circumscribed and highly structured space of Tate's cemetery.[9] The sea's boundaries, defined by the tides, are continually in flux; as Crane imagines it, the sea is destructive—or not so much destructive as destructuring, a medium of transformation, process, and change. For these reasons, as Lee Edelman has argued, the sea in Crane's poems can be discussed in Lacanian terms as a "maternal" space unmediated by—and unconstrained by—the symbolic coordinates of the Father (Edelman, *Transmemberment of Song*, 135–37). In the fragment "The Sea Raised Up," from the winter of 1927, the sea is the site of a regressive, incestual fantasy of union, collapsing male poet and mother in the compound identity "—me—her":

> The sea raised up a campanile ... The wind I heard
> Of brine partaking, whirling into shower
> Of column that breakers sheared in shower.
> Back into bosom, —me—her, into natal power ...
> (Crane, *Poems*, 213)

The "natal power" spoken of here is a mother tongue; it suggests that the anachronistic language of Crane's high style is not (in contrast to the "grand manner" Tate coveted) a language of the fathers. Rather, it is a transgressive discourse cut loose from—"wide from"—the proprieties of conventional reference, and therefore "shocking to the scholar and the historians of logic."

Crane's decision to locate Melville's tomb at sea—as if the author had been lost at sea—has not sufficiently surprised his critics. To deny Melville his actual resting place on land is to rededicate his spirit to the youthful quest Weaver describes; to deny, in effect, that Melville ever had or could come home. For Crane's *cimetière marin* is imagined in such a way as to refuse, as Tate's cemetery does not, the possibility of representing and enclosing the heroic dead. Tate's headstones ("Row after row," "Rank upon rank") depict a static temporality Eliot conceived of as an ideal order of monuments. They are first of all *containers*—like Mr. Pope's well-wrought urn; they *stand for* bodies; and they describe a poetics, exemplified by "Ode to the Confederate Dead," wherein the poet cannot be present, cannot act, except as the disembodied intelligence that contemplates the scene from this side of the gate. The charge brought by Davidson against this poetics—that it assigns the poet to a point of view which, in its absolute removal from the site, is structurally analogous to that of the dead—was freely, although unhappily, admitted by Tate. The charge brought by Tate against Crane's poetics is exactly complementary: that the poet in Crane's poems cannot be assigned a point of view outside of them, and thus is not in a position to control and interpret his materials, only to be absorbed by them. Crane's "pantheism," Tate explained, "is necessarily a philosophy of sensation without a point of view" (Tate, *Essays of Four Decades*, 319). Despite the moral that clings to it, Tate's remark touches Crane's deepest ambition; for the poet in Crane's poems seeks to fully participate in the visionary events he describes.

This ambition places the reader of Crane's poems—unnervingly, disorientingly—in a position conventionally assigned to the poet. R.W.B. Lewis defines this effect when he quotes and comments on the aims Crane stated in defense of "At Melville's Tomb": "'Fresh concepts, more inclusive evaluations ... added consciousness and increased perceptions.' There is the vital essence of Crane's theory, and an abstract of his practice.... Aiming at those things, Crane's poems are persistently *about* them, and about aiming at them; when, with our active cooperation, they succeed, they increase our consciousness of what is involved in the effort to increase our consciousness" (Lewis, *Poetry of Crane*, 206). In Lewis's account of Crane's practice, Crane's reader is placed in the position of the speaker on shore in "At Melville's Tomb," a position in which the reader is charged with receiving and thus completing the message or "embassy" that the drowned men's bones "bequeath." If Lewis's logic looks circular, or his language convoluted, it is because Crane's contract with the reader is imagined as a circuit, as a circulation of energy and meaning, which is figured, in subsequent stanzas, in Crane's vortical images of "shells," "calyx," and "coil." These are images of the structure of the poem itself, because the poem's circular forms, its inward "corridors of shells," represent in spatial terms the vision Crane and Melville—and Crane's reader—share across time. That vision is discontinuous, despite its endurance across time, because it is continually passing—and continually renewed—with every reading of the poem. Meaning is repeatedly promised and deferred in Crane's poems; it is virtual, preludial, prospective—intended to increase "our consciousness of what is involved in the effort to increase our consciousness"; and it is carried to shore, like "the dice of drowned men's bones," only in the moment before it is "obscured."

Lewis describes Crane's aims ("Fresh concepts, more inclusive evaluations") by quoting from Crane's own statement of them in "A Letter to Harriet Monroe," a reply to the editor of *Poetry*, which appeared in the magazine with "At Melville's Tomb" in October 1926. The obscurity of Crane's meanings, apparently, had made the poem all but unpublishable; it circulated for almost a year before Monroe, somewhat grudgingly, accommodated it along with Crane's explanation. That explanation is, as he knew it would be, Crane's most widely known performance as a critic and theorist, and it bears the strain of Crane's obligation to prove his sophistication, intelligence, and good faith to several audiences at once. Privately, Crane ridiculed Monroe; "Aunt Harriet" was a recurrent figure of fun in communications with Tate. Crane's antipathy toward Monroe, as well as Moore, whom he called names like "the Rt. Rev. Miss Mountjoy" (Crane, *Letters*, 218), leagued him with other modernist men. In his letter to Monroe, Crane took the side of his male colleagues by defending modernist "difficulty" against genteel standards, which are seen here as, at least implicitly, female ones. But one function of Crane's obscurity, as of his misogyny, was to disguise his sexual desires, and this motive divided him from Tate and Monroe both. Defending obscurity, Crane was defending his right to a language in which the unspeakable could be spoken.

Crane's metaphor "the dice of drowned men's bones" vexed Monroe particularly. Crane's gloss remains cogent:

Dice bequeath an embassy, in the first place, by being ground (in this connection only, of course) in little cubes from the bones of drowned men by the action of the sea, and are finally thrown up on the sand, having "numbers" but no identification. These being the bones of dead men who never completed their voyage, it seems legitimate to refer to them as the only surviving evidence

of certain messages undelivered, mute evidence of certain things,
experiences that the dead mariners might have had to deliver.
Dice as a symbol of chance and circumstance is also implied.
(Crane, *Complete Poems and Selected Prose*, 238)

"Dead letters! does it not sound like dead men?" (Melville, *Writings of
Herman Melville*, Vol. 9, *Piazza Tales*, 45). It is hard not to hear Crane's gloss
as an affirmative reply to the pained exclamation of the narrator of Melville's
"Bartleby." We can see the "dice of drowned men's bones" as a figure for "the
homosexual text," in Yingling's terms, insofar as the "obscurity" imposed on
and by homosexual desire presents a fable for the textualization of the self.
On the one hand, Crane's mariners cannot deliver their messages—they are
converted to "numbers," perhaps as Wilde is when he becomes "C 33"; on
the other hand, their experience is precisely and narrowly textual—in code,
accessible only through reading. The writing they do here—their
transmissions of self as text—is identified with dying, and specifically with
death by water. The metaphor follows the consequences of wagering the self
in literary exploit to the marking not of paper, but of bone—as if the attempt
to put oneself into words could only issue in the fragmentation,
formalization, and inscription of the body. Rather than expression, then,
what is recovered is the impression of the transforming medium itself—"the
action of the sea"—which is equated with the pure form manifest in poetic
"numbers." The mariners of "At Melville's Tomb" are absorbed into and
changed by a textual process Crane associates with the determinate structure
of metrical order and the nonhuman violence of the waves.

The contrast between Crane's account of this process and the
drowning of Eliot's Phlebas, or the erosion of Tate's headstones in the ode, is
worth contemplating. In Eliot, the death of the handsome sailor removes
him from quest-romance and places him in an archetypal framework from
which his failure could be foreseen. In Tate, the headstones that "yield their
names to the element" figure an effacement of personal identity consistent
with the submission to an ethical order outside the self. In both cases, we
encounter representations of the sacrifice of self that is necessary for the
integration of parts into a whole; whether this whole is imagined as "the
harmony of archetypal spheres," or the harmony of the so-called traditional
society, it is located in a remote and idealized past. In *The Waste Land*, the
passage from the present to the past is represented by the regressive vortex
of the whirlpool, a circular movement that reverses the drowned mariner's
direction, returning Phlebas "through the stages of his age and youth" to a
point at which individuality dissolves into the scholar's archetype.

Eliot's vortex returns in "At Melville's Tomb," but Crane's interest is in the centrifugal force of the whirlpool, its power to cast up and disseminate traces of the voyage it consumes:

And wrecks passed without sound of bells,
The calyx of death's bounty giving back
A scattered chapter, livid hieroglyph,
The portent wound in corridors of shells.
                                        (Crane, *Poems*, 33)

The vortex or whirlpool (in other poems, the waterspout and the hurricane) symbolizes the rhetorical operations of expanding and compacting, widening and winding, that structure Crane's condensed and overtaxed poetry. John Irwin explains: "In Crane's verse the metaphoric relationship 'A is B' takes by ellipsis the form of a complex word or phrase 'AB,' and this complex word or phrase becomes in turn part of the metaphoric relationship 'C is AB,' and so on, with mounting complexity."[10] The will to activate and include all "the so-called illogical impingements of the connotations of words on the consciousness" (Crane, *Complete Poems and Selected Prose*, 234) results in the excess and eliding of references for which Crane's work remains notorious. "This crowding of the frame," Grossman writes, "came to constitute a trope peculiar to him—not the modernist 'ambiguity,' which hierarchizes, or ironically totalizes a plurality of meanings—but a singularly naive rhetoric of shadowed wholeness (the impossible simultaneity of all the implications of desire) that struggles merely to include all meanings in the one space of appearance" (Grossman, "Crane's Intense Poetics," 230). What emerges from that struggle, the failure of which Crane images as a shipwreck and descent into the whirlpool, is not "shadowed wholeness" but the isolated fragments of this whole, "A scattered chapter, livid hieroglyph, / The portent wound in corridors of shells." This cycle of absorption and redistribution represents a narrative of poetic composition in which the whole, as it is engrossed in the part ("the one space of appearance"), which cannot possibly sustain it, is both torn apart *and* disseminated. The "wholeness" Crane envisions is "shadowed," or "obscured," precisely in the sense of "foreshadowed"—still waiting to be constituted and received; its destruction (simultaneous with its arrival on shore) is also the condition of its postponement, its transmission as a "portent." Unlike the "unity of sensibility" Eliot and Tate looked for in the past, Crane's deferred harmony refers to the future.

The distinction can be clarified by examining the difference between

Tate's sense of poetic structure as container and Crane's sense of poetic structure as "portent"—as a sign both necessary and inadequate to the expression of its referent. For example, Harvey Gross has shown the extent to which the intelligibility of Crane's poems *depends upon* verse form—and particularly meter—to mitigate "uncertain, almost haphazard syntactical progression."[11] Gross's insight is borne out by the poem at hand to the extent that the multiple figures in the second stanza's substitutive chain (wrecks—calyx—chapter—hieroglyph—portent) are organized *as* a chain and not as a random series less by logic or grammatical relation than by the catena of pentameter. This is frequently the state of affairs in Crane's poems, where meter takes over the work of grammar in the construction of an elaborate apostrophe or an extended series of appositive phrases. Yet even metrical order, however necessary to intelligibility, remained for Crane a compromise of his intentions. "Poetic structure, whether the phantom modernism of *The Bridge* or the nineteenth-century French formality of 'The Broken Tower,' was unaccommodated to [Crane's] meaning because no structure, the function of which is to bear meaning into the world of appearance, is free from the finitizations that are the sufficient condition of appearing at all" (Grossman, "Crane's Intense Poetics," 239).

In "The Broken Tower," Crane represents the costs of this compromise, of the "finitizations" attendant on poetic structure, as an engraving of "Membrane through marrow," which recalls the inscription of "numbers" on "the dice of drowned men's bones." The "scattered chapter" that these bones constitute returns, in the same stanza of "The Broken Tower," as "my long-scattered score / Of broken intervals" (Crane, *Poems*, 160). This is, in Crane's "final" poem, a retrospective reflection on the shape of Crane's career, an embittered comment on the intermittency of writing. But it also describes the disseminative violence that Crane's poems, from the beginning, participate in and celebrate. For Crane, the entrance into poetry is imagined as a breaking or scattering of the whole of his desire, ambition, identity; it is a passage into structure that is, paradoxically, destructuring. Verse form, understood here both as abstract pattern and concrete instance, fragments Crane's utterance at the same time that it shapes and upholds it.[12] This is fundamentally the paradox of a discourse—a homosexual discourse for Crane—in which to speak is to be silenced. The point of the poet's appearance is also that of his disappearance, and the message of the drowned is communicated in the moment it is obscured.

"The dice of drowned men's bones" might be regarded, then, as emblems of Crane's own quatrains, which are forms fashioned in the tension between structure and flux, necessity and "chance," and which present the reader with "a livid hieroglyph." They are the decipherable but complexly encoded, complexly burdened parts of an inaccessible self, the fragments of a mutilated—because unrepresentable—whole. The question is: How did Crane find hope in this sea change? How does the fragmentation of word and self in "At Melville's Tomb" differ from the "song of minor, broken strain" in "C 33"? How could the mutilation of the body possibly anticipate its restoration?

In *American Hieroglyphics*, John Irwin suggests one answer to these questions when he calls attention to the way in which the drowning of Bulkington, in "The Lee Shore" chapter of *Moby-Dick*, functions synecdochically to describe the work of synecdoche in Melville's novel as a whole. Bulkington, a handsome sailor in a line running beyond Billy Budd to Phlebas and Crane's Melville, gives one "glimpses ... of that mortally intolerable truth" that the natural elements of the air and sea always drive any "deep, earnest thinking" back upon "the treacherous, slavish shore." Melville's Ishmael continues: "But as in landlessness alone resides the highest truth, shoreless, indefinite as God—so, better is it to perish in that howling infinite, than be ingloriously dashed upon the lee, even if that were safety! ... O Bulkington! Bear thee grimly, demigod! Up from the spray of thy ocean-perishing—straight up, leaps thy apotheosis!" (Melville, *Writings of Melville*, Vol. 6, *Moby-Dick*, 107). The "six-inch chapter" of "The Lee Shore," Ishmael tells us, is itself "the stoneless grave of Bulkington." Irwin, who interprets this epitaph as a prefiguration of the wreck of the *Pequod*, writes: "What leaps up from the spray of his ocean perishing is the phallic coffin/life preserver/book—the part-whole relation of the phallic six-inch chapter to the body of the text prefiguring the symbolic relationship of the book to the self."[13] The relation of the chapter to the whole of the book, like that of Crane's own "scattered chapter" to "any complete record of the recent ship and her crew" (Crane, *Complete Poems and Selected Letters*, 239), is a relation of survival *through* dismemberment, of the whole persisting in its parts. By the end of the novel, Bulkington is returned whole, even as the *Pequod* itself is lost, when Ishmael rises from—is cast up by—the vortex of its grave, buoyed by "the phallic coffin/life preserver/book." Ishmael, at the same time, survives the unsurvivable voyage not by renouncing but by reaffirming the moral imperative of the quest, allowing us to identify character and narrator in a way we could not in the case of modernist narratives like *The Waste Land* or *A Portrait of the Artist as a Young Man*.

The structure of Melville's novel presents a narrative unfolding of Crane's desired union of author and hero, self and text. As Irwin indicates in his comments on "The Lee Shore," the English word "chapter" derives, like "capital," the architectural term for the crown of a column, from the Latin *caput* for "head." It is possible, with this etymology in mind, to read Crane's "scattered chapter" as a simple restatement of the initial figure of "the dice of drowned men's bones," and to see both phrases as early versions of the architectural collapse announced in the title of "The Broken Tower." In each of these phrases, the dismembering of the body, conceived of as structure, instrument, or vehicle, is identified with the dismembering of texts, because word and flesh are fractured under the pressure of Crane's effort to lift and connect them, to turn each one into the other. It is not at all an admission of failure, therefore, when a petulant Crane tells Monroe that she should expect "about as much definite knowledge" to be had from a "scattered chapter" and "livid hieroglyph" "as anyone might gain from the roar of his own veins, which is easily heard (haven't you ever done it?) by holding a shell close to one's ear" (Crane, *Complete Poems and Selected Prose*, 239). For Crane is willing to sacrifice claims to a conventional mimesis (claims that he is at pains to defend elsewhere in this letter) in order to interpret the sound of the sea, remembered in the form of the shell ("The portent wound in corridors of shell"), as the present sound (and not the echo) of "the roar in his own veins."[14] The poem does not simply record the passions of the body; it *consists in* those passions, and magically transmits them.

This turn of mind anticipates Crane's identification of Shakespeare with a Prospero absorbed into the fury of his own creating: the author that Crane apostrophizes in "To Shakespeare" is "pilot,—tempest, too!" (Crane, *Poems*, 131). In a letter to Munson written in March 1926, and more or less contemporary with "General Aims and Theories" (which was based upon, if it did not in fact constitute, the notes that Crane sent Eugene O'Neill for his undelivered preface to *White Buildings*),[15] Crane described his poems as "incarnate *evidence*" of a kind of knowledge that can be experienced but not properly named, since one enters—as writer or reader—so fully into that experience: "Poetry, in so far as the metaphysics of any absolute knowledge extends, is simply the concrete *evidence* of the *experience* of a recognition (*knowledge* if you like). It can give you a *ratio* of fact and experience, and in this sense it is both perception and thing perceived" (Crane, *Letters*, 237). Despite Crane's confidence about poetry's unmediated access to experience, there is nothing very simple about this definition. Indeed, as Edelman has shown in a fine deconstruction of the passage, the "concrete *evidence*" Crane writes of, because it refers us to a prior "*experience* of recognition," "must be founded not on the presence, but on the absence of the experience to which it refers; it presents itself, that is, as a mediated version of an originally unmediated vision" (Edelmen, *Transmemberment of Song*, 33–34). This is not an indication of the inadequacy of Crane's exposition so much as an accurate description of the contradictory character of its claims. It is consistent, that is, with the impossible condition of a poetry that seeks to become both sign and signified, "both perception and thing perceived," a poetry projected by a poet who imagines himself as "pilot,—tempest, too!"

Grossman, who claims that Crane's poetry, in the absence of "new structures" of its own to deploy, "tends to hallucinate or thematize" such structures (Grossman, "Crane's Intense Poetics," 224), and Edelman, who shows how "the structural principles that generate Crane's figures also generate recurrent narrative and thematic concerns" (Edelman, *Transmemberment of Song*, 14),[16] both point to Crane's lack of a language—apart from the figural and formal operations of the poetry itself—that would be capable of explaining and legitimating those operations. Crane has this problem in mind when, in a letter to Otto Kahn, he says it is "next to impossible to describe [*The Bridge*] without resorting to the actual metaphors of the poem" (Crane, *Letters*, 241). This is the case both because Crane's poems leave vacant the position of the poet-critic established in modernist convention and because Crane's poems specifically seek a language *prior* to criticism, a language Crane connected (misleadingly or not) with "experience." Crane's stylistic anachronism is a sign of this primary language. I compared it earlier to a "mother" tongue; Crane usually called it "a logic of metaphor." This logic, Crane argued, "antedates our so-called pure logic, and ... is the genetic basis of all speech" (Crane, *Complete Poems and Selected Prose*, 221); yet it does not refer, strictly speaking, to the past. Crane preferred to describe it, as he does in "General Aims and Theories," as a language of "*causes* (metaphysical)" and "spiritual consequences" (Crane, *Complete Poems and Selected Prose*, 220). It is a nonnarrative language condensing beginnings and ends, "causes" and "consequences," signs and signifieds, in a medium that exists outside history in the timeless present that Crane invokes at the beginning of "At Melville's Tomb" and of *The Bridge*.

In this sense, the archaic language Crane seeks is also radically "new." "It is as though," Crane speculates in "General Aims and Theories," "a poem gave the reader as he left it a single, new *word*, never before spoken and impossible to actually enunciate, but self-evident as an active principle in the reader's consciousness henceforward" (Crane, *Complete Poems and Selected Letters*, 221). Never before spoken, that is, *because* it is "impossible to actually enunciate"; it can only be transmitted as an *event*, as a transaction between the poem and a reader who retains this new word as fragment or token, as the kind of "self-evident" and untranslatable sign that Crane describes simply as "mute evidence of certain things, experiences that the dead mariners might have had to deliver." The mystical "new *word*" is a secular synecdoche of a sacred Word, colored by Crane's experience with the subliminal codes of both advertising and gay culture. But what that word means is hard to say. Crane's own critical language typically falls mute when called upon to specify the content of his poems' prophecy (merely "certain messages," "certain things," "certain spiritual events and possibilities"). Munson, Winters, Tate, and Blackmur, echoing Arnold's evaluation of the Romantic Poets, judged that reticence harshly; they claimed Crane did not know enough. But what they called a lack of knowledge was Crane's commitment, in his life, to the role of the autodidact, and his decision, in his work, *not* to arrive at "definite knowledge," not to submit to the various forms of doctrine that were required by his critics.[17]

In "General Aims and Theories," Crane speaks of his search for "a morality essentialized from experience directly, and not from previous precepts or preconceptions" (Crane, *Complete Poems and Selected Prose*, 221). Crane's statement is the basis for an ethics, linked to his defense of Joyce's *Portrait*, and a poetics, linked to his defense of "At Melville's Tomb." "If the poet is to be held completely to the already evolved and exploited sequences of imagery and logic," Crane wrote to Monroe, "—what field of added consciousness and increased perceptions (the actual province of poetry, if not lullabies) can be expected when one has to relatively return to the alphabet every breath or so?" (Crane, *Complete Poems and Selected Prose*, 237). The point of novelty, of Crane's "new *word*," is to liberate the poet's language from "precepts or preconceptions," the received order of "the alphabet." The "new *word*" is new, therefore, because it is obscure, and it is obscure because it breaks with "already evolved and exploited" systems of reference, which Crane sees as sequential ("already evolved") systems. "Obscurity," Barbara Johnson has written, "... is not encountered on the way to intelligibility, like an obstacle, but rather lies beyond it.... Obscurity is an excess, not a deficiency, of meaning."[18] Johnson's comments refer to Mallarmé's *Mystère dans les lettres*, but they are also a statement of the issues at stake in Crane's letter to Monroe, an essay in which Crane defends himself from the charge of obscurity by asserting his right to language that exceeds and transgresses (goes "beyond") normative expectations, which are experienced by Crane as proscriptions. To write a "new word," which is also to write a forbidden word, is to violate the sequential order Crane ascribes to both "history" and "logic."

To deny the poet this transgressive authority, Crane told Monroe, is not simply to circumscribe present possibilities; it is "to limit the scope of the medium so considerably as to outlaw some of the richest genius of the past"

(Crane, *Complete Poems and Selected Prose*, 235). In "At Melville's Tomb," Crane seeks to recover an outlaw and genius of the past, a venture in which he is motivated by his sense of himself as a poet whose faith in the authority of personal "genius" had been cast into disrepute, if not outlawed, by "the rational order of criticism." Behind this project is Crane's ongoing struggle to find sanction for a criminalized homoeroticism that he fetishistically identified with the sailor—a marginalized man, like the hoboes of "The River," who is not at home in the productive economies of home and workplace, but who remains dedicated, in exile, to the sexual community of other "drowned" men.

The codes and conditions of male homosexual fellowship inform Crane's projection of a relation between reader and poet that is not properly sexual, perhaps, but peculiarly, even transgressively intimate, secretive, and physical. Recall the way Crane's "new *word*" is transmitted: it remains unspeakable ("impossible to actually enunciate") even while it continues to operate, like a password, "as an active principle in the reader's consciousness henceforward." In "A Letter to Harriet Monroe," Crane expands on this notion with a question: "In the minds of people who have sensitively read, seen, and experienced a great deal, isn't there a terminology something like short-hand as compared to usual description and dialectics, which the artist ought to be right in trusting as a reasonable connective agent toward fresh concepts, more inclusive evaluations?" (Crane, *Complete Poems and Selected Prose*, 237–38). What Crane describes as a "short-hand" code, or "connective agent," is the rhetorical strategy he elsewhere calls "inferential mention." The special persons sensitized to such inferences form a kind of league, and they seek each other. The examples of this rhetorical strategy Crane gives come from Blake and Eliot. In effect, Crane makes Blake a modernist, and claims a place in modernism for Crane's Blakean stance; he is also trying to show how Blakean Eliot is, or could be. Implicitly, Crane is trying to validate his own early readings of both Blake and Eliot.

Crane explains Eliot's simile in "Rhapsody on a Windy Night," "Every street lamp that I pass / Beats like a fatalistic drum," in this way: "There are plenty of people who have never accumulated a sufficient series of reflections (and these of a rather special nature) to perceive the relation between a *drum* and a *street lamp*—*via* the *unmentioned* throbbing of the heart and nerves in a distraught man which *tacitly* creates the reason and 'logic' of the Eliot metaphor" (Crane, *Complete Poems and Selected Prose*, 237). Whatever value this has for reading Eliot, it has a great deal of value for reading Crane. Metaphor works in Crane's account as a relation between two terms the logic of whose connection is to be inferred or implied by those who are in a position to infer it on the basis of their own experience; and what is implied, in this case, is most significant: it is the throbbing of the heart and nerves of a distraught man—a highly private ("subjective") sensation, a tremor located in the male poet's body as he walks the Nighttown streets. To read Eliot's line rightly, one must have "read, seen, and experienced" enough to recognize in one's own body the unmentioned but urgent and inferred sensations in the poet's.

Unmentioned and unmentionable: the tawdry streets and urban night of Eliot's "Rhapsody" are both a homosexual and a modernist topos for Crane. Linking that scene with the scene of reading as such, Crane imagines the act of reading a modern poem—when it is successful, when the reader and poet really "spark" (a slang word Crane used)—as a tryst. Reading is like cruising; it calls for shared recognitions; it communicates pleasure and pain. Even the arbitrariness of the union between a modern poet and a reader, the necessary impersonality of their bond, becomes the ground of a profoundly personal relation, a communication that exceeds the demands and conventions of civil reference. When a poem is truly and fully read, poet and reader encounter each other as equal and kindred, "twin shadowed halves"; they recognize an essential relation beyond their random connection, assuaging the loneliness each of them feels in his body. For Crane, the intelligibility of Eliot's "obscure" poems, as of his own, ultimately presumes a transaction or pact like the unspoken, physical connection (the meeting of smiles and eyes) that concludes "Episode of Hands."

The bond between speaker and addressee in "At Melville's Tomb" dramatizes another version of this mutuality. Earlier I talked about the problem of perspective in Crane's poem as if only time separated Melville and this speaker, who are otherwise bound by a shared vision. The problem is more complicated. The opening lines of the poem do not make it clear whether Melville "watched" the waves from "this ledge" or from a position somehow "beneath the wave" itself. This ambiguity is coordinated with that of the poet's own perspective. Although he speaks "from this ledge," he is clearly identified with the drowned mariners, and speaks "for" them, from their point of view. For Crane's poet is charged with receiving and reading the messages of the drowned; yet his own message does not represent a decoding, so much as a repetition, of theirs; and this repetition in turn places the reader in the position of receiver, the poet onshore. If, in Tate's poems, the poet takes up the position of the reader or critic, the reader in "At Melville's Tomb" is invited to take up the position of the poet. But the completed communication or communion (implicitly, a kind of rescue) that the message's transmission would mean is repeatedly deferred through repetition of the event; and the reciprocity that author and reader demand and project results in the oscillation between their two positions, which is figured as the bond between those on shore looking out to sea and those still at sea appealing to the shore.

In the first quatrain, this oscillation is implicated in the recurrent rising and falling of waves; in the third quatrain, in the lifted gaze of the mariners as they sink to their deaths:

> Then in the circuit calm of one vast coil,
> Its lashings charmed and malice reconciled,
> Frosted eyes there were that lifted altars;
> And silent answers crept across the stars.
>
> (Crane, *Poems*, 33)

The vortex imaged in the second quatrain as "The calyx of death's bounty" is triumphant here in its expansion to the point of "one vast coil," the point of "calm" arrived at beyond the violent competition ("lashings") of regressive and progressive currents. This "circuit calm" designates, if not a moment of rescue, then one of suspension, of reconciliation, which is induced under the sway of a specifically aesthetic "charm." The communication between these starlike "Frosted eyes" and the gazing stars above them is perhaps an instance of the "new *word*" Crane speaks of; it is certainly a "silent" communication, "impossible to actually enunciate," which extends the figuration of the author's appeal to the reader to the vertical axis Crane invokes when he wrote to Munson about "a resurrection of some kind." Here, it is not a matter of exchanging a message between sea and shore, but between earth and heaven.

Syntactically, the inversion in the third line of the third quatrain—that is, the placement of "Frosted eyes" *before* "there were"—suggests a similar kind of exchange in the construction of the line itself. Compare the published with the draft version of lines 8 and 9:

> Frosted eyes there were that lifted altars;
> And silent answers crept across the stars.
>
> Some frosted altar there was kept by eyes
> Unanswering back across the tangent beams.

One effect of the revision is to eliminate the enjambment and stabilize both lines as individual units. (The only enjambments in the published text come in the first and fourth quatrains, deferring the objects of the verbs "bequeath" and "contrive.") The other effects produced by the exchange of "altars" and "eyes" *across* line 8 are more subtle. Even the process by which Crane came to a final version of this line enacts the sort of substitution, the reciprocity and reversibility, that the line itself evokes: one feels that, in whatever order Crane deploys them, there will be "eyes" and "altars" here so long as subject and object continue to reciprocally sustain each other across the line—which, as Crane's placement, in both cases, of "eyes" and "altars" at each end suggests, is itself "a tangent beam."

The revision shifts Crane's sentence from the passive to the active voice, as it introduces the key verb "lift," and so gives definite expression to Crane's faith that (as he said to Monroe) "a man, not knowing perhaps a definite god yet being endowed with a reverence for deity—such a man naturally postulates a deity somehow, and the altar of that deity simply by the very *action* of the eyes *lifted* in searching" (Crane, *Complete Poems and Selected Prose*, 239). In Crane's gloss, it is "the eyes," not "altars," that are "lifted." The grammatical shift that comes with Crane's rendering of the line into prose again enacts the reciprocity we are concerned with, which, in Crane's account of his "faith," is understood as the power of the human subject to construct, of its own action, the object of its desire. This is a "mystic" claim, validating stylistic, spiritual, and sexual goals disallowed in the theory and practice of Crane's peers. The phrase "definite god" specifically recalls Crane's refusal of the demand—central to Tate's literary criticism—for "definite knowledge"; and "the eyes *lifted* in searching"—rejecting Eliot's skepticism as well as his later orthodoxy—approve the autodidact's decision to proceed without "precepts or preconceptions." Whether the stars give "silent answers" to these searchers or are "Unanswering," is a question that the poem does less to resolve than to retain in suspension.

This state of suspension is momentarily audible in the metrical structure of Crane's line. I mentioned, early on, the tension between iambic and trochaic impulses in the first line. In the revision of line 8, Crane not only moves from a passive to an active construction, but from an iambic to a trochaic pattern. The draft version, "Some frosted altar there was kept by eyes," is consistent with the iambic scheme of the whole, whereas the published text, "Frosted eyes there were that lifted altars," introduces a line of trochaic pentameter. In this strongly iambic context, the alternation represents a halt, a moment of resistance or reversal, before the meter of line 9, "And silent answers crept across the stars," returns the poem to its normative cadence (and emphasizes, by contrast, the dominance of that cadence). The metrical alternation is itself a structure of inversion, then, which interrupts, if it does not really suspend, the progress of the poem at that moment when the mariners, fixing their eyes on the stars, can still resist the fact of drowning.

Crane's poems create enclosed spaces *that offer no shelter* because the structural features of their enclosure (the specular identity of eyes and stars, the chiasmatic exchange of sea and shore, the simultaneity of past and present visions) are figures for an endless and impossible circulation. This circulation is sometimes represented in Crane's poems as the poet's power to speak to readers from beyond the grave. In the fragment beginning, "So dream thy sails, O phantom bark," whose pentameter quatrains make it an uncanny companion piece to "At Melville's Tomb," Crane imagines a power of posthumous speech such that "I thy drowned men may speak again" (Crane, *Poems*, 214)—a phrase that, again according to an Elizabethan formula, equivocates as to whether "drowned men" is an appositive subject or an object (i.e., the poet may be speaking *as* or on *behalf* of "thy drowned men"). The position of the posthumous speaker in this and other Crane poems is not like that of Whitman's poet in "Crossing Brooklyn Ferry," whose life in time is perpetuated by the poem's enduring power to address a future audience, but like that of Dickinson's poet in "I heard a Fly buzz— when I died—," whose speech comes to us from a station outside of time, a place that Crane and Dickinson both call "Eternity."[19] Unlike Whitman's democratic address to the crowd, the mode of address Crane shares with Dickinson is strangely private or elite, intimating, as Crane puts it in his sonnet "To Emily Dickinson," "Some reconcilement of remotest mind" (Crane, *Poems*, 128).

This remote "reconcilement" is the kind of agreement between poet and reader that Crane looks for in "At Melville's Tomb," in which Crane imagines reading as the recovery of a message the drowned "bequeath." In "Voyages II," we encounter another bequest, only this time the speaker of Crane's poem is not the inheritor but that which is inherited:

Bind us in time, O Seasons clear, and awe.
O minstrel galleons of Carib fire,
Bequeath us to no earthly shore until
Is answered in the vortex of our grave
The seal's wide spindrift gaze toward paradise.
(Crane, *Poems*, 35)

To be bound "in time" is to be bound by a vortex consuming and renewing the self as it casts up, out of time, as bequest, "The seal's wide spindrift gaze toward paradise." Both "spindrift" and the odd word—"findrinny"—that it replaced in Crane's revision are "new" words from Melville's *Moby-Dick* (Unterecker, *Voyager*, 389); and the sentence they complete is a reimagining of the conclusion of that book, placing the speaker in the position at once of Tashtego, the last sailor to be drowned, and of Ishmael, who survives to tell the story. This is an impossible position in which the poet imagines speaking both from death and beyond it—as if, by passing through this form of "negation," he might affirm his original, "more positive" goal—and it calls to mind Crane's contradictory plan to undo the direction modernism had taken in Eliot's work. Perhaps the unusual, winding syntax in the subordinate clause, in which the verb ("Is answered") supplants and defers the subject ("The seal's wide spindrift gaze"), exemplifies the reversal Crane sought; certainly it is a reordering of grammatical sequence, a substitution of beginning for end ("cause" for "consequence"), which evokes, in this case, the substitution of life for death. The poem closes, then, with an image not of the shut "grave," but of the open "gaze," as a visionary action of lifting—or postulation—issues from the whirlpool of *The Waste Land*. The "answers" Crane submits here, as in "At Melville's Tomb," are "silent" ones; and the paradise his seal seeks remains a remote destination. But the structure of Crane's syntax is such that the answer (of the grave) precedes the question (of the gaze) with the effect of affirming, in and through death, the survival of the latter.

The end of "Voyages II" is a striking and deliberate contrast to the end of "Procession" and other Tate poems that define closure as "death, and death, and death!" In the final quatrain of "At Melville's Tomb," Crane offers another kind of resurrection. The initial conceit of Crane's poem—that Melville is buried at sea—is surprising, but it merely prepares for the more daring claim that Melville is to be found neither at sea nor on land but in the "azure steeps" shadowed by the rolling sea.

> Compass, quadrant and sextant contrive
> No farther tides ... High in the azure steeps
> Monody shall not wake the mariner.
> This fabulous shadow only the sea keeps.
>
> (Crane, *Poems*, 33)

Remember Crane's intention to appropriate "the gifts of the past" (among them, Eliot's "erudition and technique") as "instruments" with which to catch and fix "the voice of the present." This Daedalian definition of language as *techne* should be contrasted with "the voice of the present" in the resonant sentence that ends "General Aims and Theories": "Language has built towers and bridges, but itself is inevitably as fluid as always" (Crane, *Complete Poems and Selected Prose*, 223). As structure or *techne*, language operates in time; as "itself," language operates in the eternity of the continuous present ("is ... always"), imagined as the fluid and destructured space of the open sea. Here, in the final quatrain of "At Melville's Tomb," Crane arrives at the point at which instruments ("Compass, quadrant and sextant") no longer function but cede control to the medium ("farther tides") as it exists by and for itself—the vanishing point of infinity that Crane designates simply and characteristically by an ellipsis.

In this final quatrain, for the first time in the poem, Crane shifts from the past into the present tense—a change that is coordinated with Crane's elevation of Melville from the place he seems to occupy "beneath the wave" to somewhere "High in the azure steeps." As John Hollander observes, "steeps" takes the place of the rhyming antonym a reader expects: "deep" (Hollander, *Figure of Echo*, 141), in a final instance of the kind of specular reversal we have been studying in the poem. The use of the word here resonates with Crane's image for the "high" interior of the sea at the epiphanic center of "Voyages":

> where death, if shed,
> Presumes no carnage, but this single change,—
> Upon the steep floor flung from dawn to dawn
> The silken skilled transmemberment of song;
> Permit me voyage, love, into your hands ...
> (Crane, *Poems*, 36)

The point where the "floor" of the sea is made "steep" by, or is "flung" by, the embrace of the lovers "from dawn to dawn," establishes the enclosed circuit of a single day in which two bodies, as they submit to "this single change," can know "transmemberment" by and in "song." Crane's phrase "azure steeps" reconstitutes this interior space in the air, and identifies the voyager-lover of "Voyages III" with the voyager-author Melville (transmembered, once he is finally and fully "steeped" in the medium of his quest). If, in the third quatrain of "At Melville's Tomb," the searching eyes of the mariners found only the "silent" response of the stars, in the final quatrain of the poem Crane's poet is given a vision of human connection through song, which, although it "will not wake the mariner," still reconciles height and depth, present and past.

Crane's term "monody" places this poet and his poem in the line of several songs and singers of the past, invoking as it does the subtitles of

Milton's "Lycidas" and Matthew Arnold's "Thyrsis" (Arnold's elegy for
Arthur Hugh Clough) as well as Melville's own title "Monody"—the brief,
late elegy for Hawthorne collected in *Timoleon* (Hollander, *Figure of Echo*,
92). In the cases of Arnold and Melville, the allusion to Milton's elegy draws
some of its force from the special power of a friendship mourned, allowing
the generic marker—monody—to indicate a state of private isolation and
bereavement: only one is left to sing. The same marker in Crane resists the
separation of the living and the dead—as Crane's draft version, employing
the first-person plural, suggests:

> Our monody shall not wake the mariner
> Whose fabulous shadow only the sea keeps.

"Monody," in this sense, reverberates with those "beating leagues of
monotone" that a shell is said to "secrete" in "Voyages VI" (Crane, *Poems*,
39); it is a song of unity and of union that is achieved by every singer steeped
in the sea; and it presumes no disjunction but that "single change" that Crane
calls "transmemberment."

As a figure for historical relation, the neologism "transmemberment"
eschews the lesser reconcilements of memory to affirm the transfiguration of
the past in the present. As a rhetorical strategy, the term indicates the mode
of transumptive allusion that Hollander, Edelman, Irwin, and Bloom have
studied in Crane's work.[20] For Crane, the goal of such a strategy is to admit
no distance—or rather: no distance that cannot be spanned—between his
own song and, in this instance, Melville's, which, under the auspices of the
reciprocity we have been discussing, is itself shown, retrospectively, to be an
elegy and interpretation of *Crane's* song. By the most curious kind of reversal,
Melville emerges here, in Grossman's suggestive phrase, as "a hermeneutic
friend" (Grossman, "Crane's Intense Poetics," 227), a version of the ideal
reader who is able to receive the message Crane bequeaths. He does so,
again, in the space of "eternity," identified here with "the azure steeps," the
earthly shadow or type of which only the sea "keeps." In choosing to break
his syntax at the penultimate line, excise the possessive "Whose" and admit
the demonstrative "This," Crane again chooses to suspend reference. "*This*
fabulous shadow" might designate either Melville's shade or Crane's—or, for
that matter, the poem itself, which is given over to the sea in a form of ritual
burial recalling the ceremonial scattering that concludes Shelley's "Ode to
the West Wind" or Crane's own "Praise for an Urn." "At Melville's Tomb"
is commended to the sea as the shadow of the fable that connects Crane and
Melville, and that together they transmit.

"At Melville's Tomb" was probably completed before Crane came to live with Tate and Gordon in December 1925. Blaming Gordon for the dispute that made him leave four months later, Crane told Underwood, in a postcard from Cuba, that she and Tate were jealous over the money Kahn had given him to work on *The Bridge;* they had gossiped about him with other friends, he said, and betrayed his "faith" in them, causing Crane in turn to lose "faith" in the "material" of *The Bridge.* "It's all been very tiresome—," Crane complained, "and I'd rather lose such elite for the old society of vagabonds and sailors—who don't enjoy chitchat" (Crane, *Letters,* 264). With the sailor, in contrast to that "elite," "no faith or such is properly *expected* and how jolly and cordial and warm the tonsiling *is* sometimes, after all" (Crane, *Letters,* 264). Crane would return several times to Mrs. Turner's house in Patterson—Tate and Gordon left in the summer of 1926—and he returned to Brooklyn as well. But Crane remained in no place long—and for the most part he remained unemployed—during the final five years of his life (a period Crane spent in Cuba, New York, Connecticut, Ohio, California, England, France, and Mexico in rented rooms, in the homes of friends and family, on trains, and aboard ships).

The state of exposure and mobility that Crane chose when he left for Cuba in 1926 is the subject of "Repose of Rivers."[21] The poem's alliterative title introduces antithetical terms, linking stasis and motion, the singular and the plural, in anticipation of the oxymoronic figures that dominate the poem. There is in "Repose," I think, a connotation of putting things *back* into place—as if Crane's use of the word were modeled on "return." But what is returned to here—the great mouth of the river, where the river meets the sea and is absorbed by it—is not an origin but an end. The poem is an account of a career, identifying the course of the poet with that of a river, through the ancient association of eloquence with fluency, and the progress it traces is a story of immersion in the liquid Crane called "language itself," an itinerary— at once homosexual and visionary—that concludes at the point of the speaker's engulfment.

Because the power of poetic utterance depends, in the mythology of this poem, on its unimpeded flow, the seaward course of the river-poet requires him to resist or escape from a series of traps. These are the burden of the second and third strophes:

> Flags, weeds. And remembrance of steep alcoves
> Where cypresses shared the noon's
> Tyranny; they drew me into hades almost.
> And mammoth turtles climbing sulphur dreams

Yielded, while sun-silt rippled them
Asunder ...

How much I would have bartered! the black gorge
And all the singular nestings in the hills
Where beavers learn stitch and tooth.
The pond I entered once and quickly fled—
I remember now its singing willow rim.

                                    (Crane, *Poems*, 16)

These are all sites of seduction—versions, perhaps, of possible "homes"—
which threaten to draw the poet down and "into" their enigmatic enclosures.
The human experience in this narrative is highly fraught, and hard to
decode, but Harold Bloom provides a good starting place: "Embowered by
steep alcoves of cypresses, intensifying the dominant noon sun, Crane nearly
yields to the sexual phantasmagoria of 'flags, weeds,' and the sound play
alcoves / almost intensifies the narrowness of the escape from a primary
sexuality, presumably an incestuous heterosexuality." In Bloom's account,
what Crane "would have bartered, indeed did barter, was nature for poetry,"
in such a way as to relate "the inevitability of sexual orientation to the
assumption of his poethood" (Bloom, "Introduction," *Crane: Critical Views*,
4–5). This is useful, because it defines the relation between Crane's poetry
and his sexuality by the opposition to "nature" that they share, linking
Crane's rejection of his place as son in the Oedipal succession to his
"unnatural," visionary poetics, a way of writing that was always a refusal to
reproduce the world as he found it.

    For this reason, homosexuality is difficult to find on the level of plot.
As Yingling explains, building on the readings of Bloom and Robert K.
Martin, "Repose of Rivers" does not "depict an actual relationship between
two men; it focuses instead on the problem of homosexual self-authorization
as an issue of internal resolution where one comes to maturity through a
rejection of Oedipal models of development and an adoption of homosexual
ones" (Yingling, *Crane and the Homosexual Text*, 139). With this genetic
model in mind, Yingling reads the "mammoth turtles" of the second strophe
as emblems of "Oedipal masculinity," enacting sexuality as a drama of
"division and competition" under the "tyranny" of the midday sun, "a trope
for the overpowering but false authority of patriarchal reality" (Yingling,
Crane and the Homosexual Text, 141). This is compatible with Bloom's
reading, in which the scene calls up the lure and threat of "a primary
sexuality, presumably an incestuous heterosexuality." But one could also view

Crane's "steep alcoves" as a kind of closet in which homosexual desire has been confined under a Circean spell. As Bloom remarks, these turtles seem to recall Melville's "The Encantadas," a tale concerning the "emphatic uninhabitableness" of the Galapagos Islands and, among their unlikely inhabitants, the gigantic tortoises. These, it is reported, sailors held to be "wicked sea-officers" transformed after death ("in some cases, before death") and about whom there was "something strangely self-condemned" (Melville, *Writings of Melville*, Vol. 9, *Piazza Tales*, 128–29).[22] The giant creatures in Crane's poem, seen in this light, belong among his other representations of homosexual banishment, imprisonment, and metamorphosis, from "C 33" to a cryptic late lyric like "The Mermen" (Crane, *Poems*, 113).[23]

But Crane's anthropomorphic beasts resist the impulse to decode them in human terms, even psychoanalytic ones, because "Repose of Rivers" is not an autobiography, but a refusal of autobiography. The poem is about breaking bounds. Its action is indeed one of "homosexual self-authorization," but it identifies Crane's particular homosexual poetics with boundlessness—or with the pursuit of boundlessness, a pursuit that overrides the representational means by which identities are conventionally fixed and counted, including that of the homosexual. "Repose of Rivers" converts the "negation" under which homosexuality takes its place in culture—its unrepresentability—into the motive for a poetry that eschews representational aims. What Crane's poet reclaims from his river-voyage, therefore, is a remembrance of thresholds behind which the object of desire—and reference—is withdrawn, as "the pond" is supplanted by the poet's memory of "its singing willow rim."

Memory supplants event in this poem ("remembrance of steep alcoves," not the alcoves themselves), but the memory is not of the past, as in Tate's or Eliot's nostalgic modernism; it is a memory *of the future* in which, Crane says in the fourth strophe, "all things nurse":

> And finally, in that memory all things nurse;
> After the city that I finally passed
> With scalding unguents spread and smoking darts
> The monsoon cut across the delta
> At gulf gates ... There, beyond the dykes
>
> I heard wind flaking sapphire, like this summer,
> And willows could not hold more steady sound.

The sexual arts and violence of the city ("scalding unguents," "smoking darts") are a prelude to the poet's entrance into the gulf, the poem's ultimate space of enclosure beyond all enclosures, out "beyond the dykes," where a "monsoon" cuts across the delta. The cutting action of the hurricane, like the wind that "flakes" the "sapphire" sky ("breaking up," Bloom writes, "and yet also distributing the Shelleyan azure of vision" [Bloom, "Introduction," *Crane: Critical Views*, 5]), recalls the mowing of the wind in the first strophe:

> The willows carried a slow sound,
> A sarabande the wind mowed on the mead.
> I could never remember
> That seething, steady leveling of the marshes
> Till age had brought me to the sea.
>
> (Crane, *Poems*, 16)

The actions of mowing, leveling, cutting, and flaking described at the beginning and end of the poem emphasize that the recovery of origin that "Repose of Rivers" projects is an apocalyptic event, connecting origin and end in a vision of unity that is acquired at the cost of a radical reduction of life, imaged in the grasses Crane has drawn as much from Proverbs as from Whitman. Still the actual articulation of that unity, like the ineffable present moment of composition Crane alludes to as "this summer," remains outside and beyond the limiting structures of the poem, past "gulf gates." Beginning with the images it ends with, therefore, and ending with those it begins with, "Repose of Rivers" turns on itself in a circulation of figure and energy, a "circumlocution" that refers us again to Crane's hurricane and vortex, as well as to the controlling figure of *The Bridge*. What emerges from this perpetual motion is, curiously enough, repose, or "steady" sound, a song that is figured as a "sarabande," or dance, both sexual and elemental, and that is also represented as the "singing" of the pond's willow rim. Beyond that threshold is the "absolute music" of "Atlantis."

NOTES

1. Melville, *The Writings of Herman Melville*, Vol. 3, *Mardi, and a Voyage Thither*, ed. Harrison Hayford, Alma A. MacDougall, and G. Thomas Tanselle (Evanston and Chicago, 1970), 81.
2. The history of the publication of *White Buildings* is told from the perspective of Crane's publisher by Walker Gilmer, *Horace Liveright: Publisher of the Twenties* (New York, 1970), 129–33. Unterecker mentions, along with the story of Crane's difficulty getting *White Buildings* published, an interesting mix-up: "An article by Allen Tate on the 'Voyages' set that was intended to accompany the poems in *The Guardian*, a Philadelphia magazine, never appeared, although a disastrous advance announcement did," reading

"'Voyages,' four remarkable poems by Allen Tate will appear in the next issue.'" The magazine folded before the error could be corrected. See Unterecker, *Voyager*, 407.

3. *Dial* 80, no. 5 (May 1926): 370.

4. Consider a transitional text such as John Macy's *The Spirit of American Literature* (Garden City, N.Y., 1913). Macy's history includes chapters on figures from the nineteenth-century canon (Whittier, Longfellow, Irving) and from the twentieth-century canon (Whitman, Twain, James), but mentions Melville only once (beside Stowe and Norris).

5. See Merton M. Sealts, Jr., *Pursuing Melville 1940–1980* (Madison, Wis., 1982), especially 232–49. Carl Van Doren's comments on Melville in *The Cambridge History of American Literature* isolate a point at which Melville's reputation as a romancer classed with Cooper begins to give way to his reputation as a novelist classed with Hawthorne.

6. Melville calls himself a man "who lived among the cannibals," describing his fears for his reputation, in a letter to Hawthorne, which is quoted by Raymond Weaver, *Herman Melville: Mariner and Mystic* (New York, 1921), 21. On Crane's "cannibal" costume, see Unterecker, *Voyager*, 404, and Tate's comments mentioned above in Chapter Two.

7. On Crane's response to Melville, see R.W.B. Lewis, *The Poetry of Crane: A Critical Study* (Princeton, 1967), 202–3 and passim, and Joseph Warren Beach, "Hart Crane and Moby-Dick," in Trachtenberg, ed., *Hart Crane: A Collection of Critical Essays*, (Englewood Cliffs, N.J., 1982), 65–79.

8. A copy of the draft Crane sent to Frank, October 26, 1925 (Beinecke Library, Yale University).

9. R.W.B. Lewis and John Hollander both note that Crane's phrase elides the first part of the familiar phrase, "far and wide." See Lewis, *The Poetry of Hart Crane*, 204, and Hollander, *The Figure of Echo*, 92. This characteristic gesture brings out the spatial continuity implied in "wide" and suppresses the temporal discontinuity in "far"; it is part of Crane's effort to disregard his irreversable distance in time from Melville by reimagining it as a traversable distance in space.

10. John T. Irwin, "Naming Names: Hart Crane's 'Logic of Metaphor,'" *Southern Review* 11, no. 2 (1975): 286.

11. Harvey Gross, "Hart Crane and Wallace Stevens," in Bloom, ed., *Hart Crane: Modern Critical Views*, 49. Gross's comments, which concern the pentameter in "To Brooklyn Bridge," come from his study *Sound and Form in Modern Poetry: A Study of Prosody from Thomas Hardy to Robert Lowell* (Ann Arbor, Mich., 1964). Gross continues: "Perhaps, by definition, the apostrophe requires no explicit grammar.... But without the binding meter, the omission of verbs and uncertain use of reference would be destructively apparent." Herbert Liebowitz makes a related point with reference to Crane's image of the vortex: "The centrifugal force of Crane's emotions needed to be counteracted by the centripetal force of established verse structures." See Liebowitz, *Hart Crane: An Introduction to the Poetry* (New York, 1968), 164.

12. Sharon Cameron provides this phenomenology of Crane's composition in "The Broken Tower": "In the dawn rung in by the bells during which 'The stars are caught and hived in the sun's ray,' the swarming of fragmentary radiance to a honey-colored whole literalizes on another, natural level the gathering of plenitude to one entity.... In fact it is the gathering of the stars to the mass of the sun that overflows the bounds of conceptual fullness and compels the 'breaking' in the next stanza. The release from permanent form, the spilling of plenty back into the world, leads to the dissolution of

wholeness, to 'broken intervals.'" Cameron, *Lyric Time: Dickinson and the Limits of Genre* (Baltimore, 1979), 231.

13. John T. Irwin, *American Hieroglyphics: The Symbol of the Egyptian Hieroglyphics in the American Renaissance* (New Haven, 1980), 349.

14. John Hollander charts the literary history of the music of the shell in *Images of Voice: Music and Sound in Romantic Poetry*, Churchill College Overseas Fellowship Lectures No. 5 (Cambridge, 1970). Hollander distinguishes two myths about the meaning of the sound "inside" shells: one, that it is the sound of the sea; two, that it is "the roar of one's own veins." "If the first myth is ... Romantic, the substituted one is just as certainly Symbolist, in, among other things, re-authenticating the imagined exterior sea-sound in the inner perception of an equivalent blood-tide: a Mallarmean shell, and a metaphoric presence not wholly absent from Hart Crane's image of a shell that 'secretes / Its beating leagues of monotone.'" Hollander, *Images of Voice*, 17.

15. In a postscript to his letter to Munson, composed March 17, 1926, Crane describes with approval the treatment of "the logic of metaphor" and "the dynamics of inferential mention" in the notes he had prepared for O'Neill and passed along to Munson (Crane, *Letters*, 237). "General Aims and Theories," this letter to Munson, and "A Letter to Harriet Monroe" are so closely related as to read like versions of one document.

16. This is the generative insight of Edelman's own study, which proceeds as an anatomy of three figural strategies in Crane's work—anacoluthon, chiasmus, catachresis— identified not only with three thematized actions—breaking, bending, bridging—but with the three phases of Crane's career represented by (again in series) "For the Marriage of Faustus and Helen," "Voyages," and *The Bridge*.

17. Crane's most important statement of that refusal, which links a defense of his homosexuality and a defense of his tastes and practices as a poet, is the letter he wrote to Winters on May 29, 1927, beginning, "You need a good drubbing for all your recent easy talk about 'the complete man,' the poet and his ethical place in society, etc." For a text of the letter and a commentary on the relationship between the two men, see Thomas Parkinson, *Hart Crane and Yvor Winters: Their Literary Correspondence* (Berkeley, 1978), especially 84–93.

18. Barbara Johnson, *The Critical Difference* (Baltimore, 1980), 68.

19. Sharon Cameron describes this strategy in a way useful for thinking about Crane: "Dickinson's lyrics are in fact conceived within a tradition of utterance that imagines redemption itself to rest upon a speaker's ability to fight free of the grip of this world, and to embrace instead that unthinkable space whose time exacts no separations" (Cameron, *Lyric Time*, 259). Mutlu Konuk Blasing persuasively links Crane and Dickinson in her rhetorical study of American poetry. She uses Crane's image of the vortex to explain: "Technically, Crane adopts Dickinson's subversive strategies, pitting the centripetal force of formal and literal limitation against the centrifugal force of semantic expansion. The meaning of such poetry lies precisely in its articulating and disarticulating rhetoric and syntax, which precludes certainties and unequivocal readings." Blasing, *American Poetry: The Rhetoric of Its Forms* (New Haven, 1987), 189.

20. Edelman, *Transmemberment of Song*, especially 210–15; Bloom, "Introduction," in Bloom, ed., *Hart Crane: Modern Critical Views;* and Irwin, "Figurations of the Writer's Death." For a systematic definition and history of the trope, see Hollander, *The Figure of Echo*, 133–49.

21. Edward Brunner presents a strong argument for locating the poem's composition

between April 24 and May 1, 1926, as opposed to June 1926, during the weeks of intense depression before Crane renewed his work on *The Bridge*, as has usually been the case (Lewis, *The Poetry of Hart Crane*, 211–15). "Instead of being a product of his early weeks of creative stasis on the Isle of Pines, the poem is a product of his joyful days in New York, after his mother had given permission to visit the family cottage in the Caribbean (a permission asked for previously but always denied); the poem looks ahead with optimism to a period of renewed vigor" (Brunner, "Appendix A: A New Background for 'Repose of Rivers,'" in Brunner, *Splendid Failure*, 246–49).

22. When he arrived in Cuba, Crane wrote to Slater Brown and Susan Jenkins back in Patterson: "To me, the mountains, strange greens, native thatched huts, perfume, etc. brought me straight to Melville.... Oleanders and mimosas in full bloom now make the air almost too heavy with perfume, it's another world—and a little like Rimbaud" (Crane, *Letters*, 252).

23. Crane sent this odd poem, with a dedication, to Underwood on November 22, 1928 (Beinecke Library, Yale University). Underwood (to whom Crane only seldom sent his work) might have read himself as one of the underwater men Crane writes about here.

KATHERINE KEARNS

Lyricism:
At the Back of the North Wind

I'm not here to make exorbitant claims for poetry, lest they seem
personal, but one thing must be said about poetry—it's the ultimate. The
nearest thing to it is penultimate, even religion. Poetry is the thoughts
of the heart.... It's a thought-felt thing. Poetry is the thing that laughs
and cries about everything as it's going on—and makes you take it.

—Robert Frost, in Thompson, *Robert Frost:*
The Later Years 238

A poet is a person who thinks there is something special about a poet and
about his loving one unattainable woman. You'll usually find he takes the
physical out on whores. I am defining a romantic poet—and there is no
other kind. An unromantic poet is a self-contradiction like the
democratic aristocrat that reads the Atlantic Monthly. Ink, mink, pepper,
stink, I, am, out! I am not a poet. What am I then? Not a farmer—never
was—never said I was.

—Robert Frost, in Thompson, *Robert Frost:*
The Years of Triumph 381

In Frost's poetry the birds never seem to fly very high, and when they do take
flight they risk being overtaken by darkness. For them, the trees become
both havens and traps, to be flown to for cover at twilight and, more

From *Robert Frost and a Poetics of Appetite.* © 1994 Cambridge University Press.

311

treacherously, to be flown against after sundown. Ousted from their safe
perches in "The Thatch," the birds "must brood where they [fall] in mulch
and mire, / Trusting feathers and inward fire / Till daylight [makes] it safe for
a flyer." Trapped by a spring snow in "Our Singing Strength," they sit
huddled and vulnerable on the muddy road where the speaker drives them
"underfoot in bits of flight." In "A Line-Storm Song," caught in "the wood-
world's torn despair," their songs are "crushed like some / Wild, easily
shattered rose." The cautious, small bird of "The Woodpile" is silent and
fearful; he will "say no word to tell … who he [is]," and his "little fear" makes
his evasive movements erratic and small. These birds that do not fly, that
secret themselves in the evening forest in "Come In" to call the speaker to
"come in / To the dark and lament," seem defeated or resigned, tethered to
the ground. In "Acceptance" the mated birds are forlorn creatures separated
by night; the female closes a "faded eye" and the lost male is a "waif." In
"The Exposed Nest" baby birds lay revealed and vulnerable, their nest torn
by the plow blade; the speaker imagines that they will die before they fledge,
abandoned by parents too fearful to return to them. Like the infant son in
"Home Burial," these nestlings will return to the ground, which is plowed
and open to receive them. No blithe spirits, Frost's birds never rain pure
melody down from the sky.

    These seemingly negligible birds, symbols of the lyric voice, have
intuited the Oven Bird's lesson and are the signs by which one is meant to
divine Frost's acceptance of the linguistic implications of the fall from
innocence. The Oven Bird, who watching "That other fall we name the fall"
come to cover the world with dust, "Knows in singing not to sing." Instead,
"The question that he frames in all but words / Is what to make of a
diminished thing." The fall, in necessitating both birth and death, imposes a
continuum of identity that compromises naming. The process toward death,
begun with birth, transmutes and gradually diminishes form, thus adding to
the equation—words are things before they become words and things again
when they do—an element of inevitable, perpetual senescence. The birds of
"A Winter Eden" say "which buds are leaf and which are bloom," but the
names are always premature or too late: gold goes to green, dawn to day,
everything rises and falls and is transformed. Thus the Oven Bird says,
"Midsummer is to spring as one to ten," because a season—this or any
other—may only be codified analogously. "Fall" takes on a series of
identities: petal fall, the fall season, the first and fortunate fall, each of which
bears, at the moment of articulation, the burden of a whole complex of
moral, aesthetic, and literary valuations. This bird is a "midsummer and a
midwood bird" that sees things at the moment of capitulation to the

imperatives of fall. Loud, he predicts the inevitable, and his "language" reflects the potential meaninglessness of a world in which one is forced to define a thing by what it departs from or approaches rather than what it "is." To anticipate and recognize in the full-blown flower only its inevitable decay is to miss the mark, but to ignore its ephemerality is an equal failure. The paradox of the Oven Bird's assertive voice completes the suggestion that only a new "language" can accommodate the diminishing of things, for he neither sings nor speaks: he "knows in singing not to sing" and he frames his question "in all but words." He neither sinks nor soars, and he lives in a solid, domed house that typifies his Yankee ingenuity, his forethought, his prudence. In a voice of virile moderation, loud but unhysterical, he sets out to articulate his surroundings.

But *at the same time*, and in a way that refuses to cancel out this message, Frost obliquely mocks his meager lyric birds and the compromised, oven-bird speakers throughout his poetry who are equally pinioned, held by their own voices from transcendence. He is ironically and ambivalently aware of the Palgravian definition of "lyric poetry." (Lentricchia sums it up: "No narrative allowed, no description of local reference, no didacticism, no personal, occasional, or religious material, no humor—the very antithesis of the 'poetical'—no dramatic textures of blank verse because the speaking voice is alien to song lyric," etc.)[1] And Frost is very much dedicated to deconstructing this mode with his own lyricism: he writes to Amy Lowell: "The great thing is that you and some of the rest of us have landed with both feet on all the little chipping poetry of a while ago. We have busted 'em up as with cavalry. We have, we have, we have."[2] Yet paradoxically, Frost holds on to lyric power by seeming to abnegate it: there is in this erotically declined game of loving (an abased and abasing) language an element of what can only be called sadomasochism. If poetry takes "a little rough handling once in a while," Frost is willing to "do it violence" in order to maintain his own poetic potency (*Letters* 182); yet he is both the abased—with his words— and the abaser—with his prosodically virile sound. Like ice shrieking across a red-hot griddle, his poetry does, indeed, ride on its own melting. One cannot, and Frost has ensured this absolutely with his unstable irony, make a validated choice between the fire and the ice, or between the language, so insistently mundane, and the potent oversound. Fire and ice are, after all, the inextricable complementarities of one apocalyptic vision: that endlessly regenerative cycle of desire and (self) hatred that necessarily brings the productive poet to scourge his own voice as he mocks both the poetic vocation and the state to which poetry—and if poetry then all language—has come. Frost anticipates modernism's lament and, it may be said, prefigures in his dualism its dubious palliative of self-referential irony. The lyric birds and the weary speakers tell us the genuine Frostian wisdom of achieving a commonsensical accommodation with the fallen world, while inciting at another, and ineffable, level a profound disquiet.

His virile prosody does not, then, merely supersede what Frost has to say about the necessary failure of lyricism when language fails to hold meaning. As if there were not this contradictory prosodic claim to an ironic distance from the problem that must plague lesser men, one must consider Frost's apparently genuine sense of his own lyric dilemma. Given his typical bifurcation between a gravity-bound voice and the ludicrous, gaseous immensities of speculative and traditionally "poetic" language, one must ask where the possibilities for lyricism lie. Where would an ascending bird fly *to* in the frangible dome that is Frost's vision of the arced sky; can it escape to sing hymns at heaven's gate like Shakespeare's lark or to rise like a cloud of fire or an unembodied joy into Heaven like Shelley's? The "dome" represents both form and necessary containment, so that the Oven Bird's arc of mud and sticks suggests its rounded view, while space is, and is a correlative for, formlessness. Thus "as a little bird / Before the mystery of glass" are these enclosed creatures under the sky. Earth may be a diminished place where everything is metamorphically inclined, but it is the only alternative to the void, where the only names are empty. Inside this dome the birds may not soar very high, but neither will they become distended, their songs "agape." To project a bird into the heavens is to imply that it is divinely inspired, that it may reach an ecstasy so close to celestial that it is posed at the gateway to God. But Frost's birds carry the weighty oversound of Eve's "daylong" fallen voice, "her voice upon their voices crossed," so that "Never again would birds' song be the same" as before God introduced woman into the garden.[3] Other lyric birds than Frost's may verify sensually a world outside of self, their songs evidence of some inhumanly orchestrated harmony or some divinely ordained artistry, but it is as if this function wanes inevitably in Frost's poetry with the suspicion that there is no truth outside of one's own capacity to make some (perhaps arbitrary) sound of sense and some sense of sound. The "Sunset Bird" sang "with an angelic gift" in a season long past, but in Frost's silent winter landscape the place where the bird once sang "sweet and swift" is empty, and silence prevails.

In fact, only when the flood is an external phenomenon rather than the internal surge of blood in the body documented in "The Flood" may the dove leave the ark and return with an olive branch as proof of another land that is not submerged. Birds are traditionally messengers carrying otherworldly news, harbingers whose very existence in a given time and place is a portent. As such, they become inviting embodiments for the Platonic soul, which may transcend visceral and appetitive apprehensions of reality to discover, and to sing, some alternative vision.[4] But even Frost's songbirds are bound to the standard metaphors from their literary pasts: in "The Valley's Singing Day," they sing "pearly-pearly," which the speaker translates into cliché: "(By which they mean the rain is pearls so early, / Before it changes to diamonds in the sun.)" (Like the songbirds, this speaker is a somewhat indifferent poet.) What the birds say here—or more to the point, what they are heard to say—represents an economic vision disguised as an aesthetic one, since pearls and diamonds maintain a precarious literary status only by virtue of their monetary worth. Like the birds, the metaphors are fallen, their "beauty" dependent on their post-Edenic market value and the hearer's recognition and admiration of them as a mark of exchange. Birds are a perfect paradox of connectedness and free flight, for they cannot remain on the wing forever, and where they touch down must exist sensually— whether it is heaven's gate, a golden bough, or an olive tree. To divest them of this capacity for translation, to tether them to low bushes, eaves, and roadbeds, to place worn-out lyric clichés in their weary beaks is to render them more human than otherwise.

Frost's birds, so often personified as defeated humans, are measured almost solely by their silence or by their voices, which are inevitably perceived as uttering some sad or aggrieved human message that seems to urge one to lamentation. It takes an enormous effort of will not to superimpose Eve's voice; as "The Need of Being Versed in Country Things" points out, the burned farmhouse and the abandoned barn are in reality only sorrowful to human eyes, but even to one who understands country things it is still almost impossible "Not to believe the phoebes wept." And Frost himself does not pretend to hear in this intimate country the unhumanized, nonpersonified sounds of nature: His birds are self-consciously literary creations, burdened with postlapsarian knowledge, correlatives for the saddened and diminished voices of people bereft of human love. Birds may not actually weep at human tragedy and despair, but to hear anything else in their voices is, for Frost's speakers, nearly impossible. The solemn speaker of "A Late Walk" who sees in his autumnal landscape all the signs of bereavement and death—the "headless aftermath of mowing," the bare trees—feels that "The whir of sober birds / Up from the tangle of withered weeds / Is sadder than any words." The "hill wife," who ultimately is herself subsumed into the natural world, knows that the birds she waits so eagerly to hear are preoccupied "But with each other and themselves," and she does not pretend to translate "whatever it is they sing" to each other. But even she, who might be expected to hear a wilder, more natural song, imposes upon them a sad domestic metaphor, believing them to "fill their breasts" selfishly only with thoughts for their mates, themselves, and "their built or driven nests." When Frost's birds sing, they are perceived to sing in a minor key— minor in its sense of lesser significance as much as in its musical sense; in "A Minor Bird," the speaker wants to banish the song whose tones must reflect (with myna-bird precision, if the title is any evidence) his own melancholy, self-blaming tune.

As personifications of the compromised poetic voice—the pinioned soul—these birds as often speak as sing, and they are used to call the speakers to account for their own mundane lives. They give them, as in "A Nature Note," "a piece of their bills." The double pun here suggests a thoroughly antiromantic vision: they are like the merchant from Porlock come to dun the dreaming Coleridge. The "note" is less musical than promissory (they sing "All out of time pell-mell!"), and the phrase "piece of their bills" suggests a cacophony of images and linguistic turns: the bill of a bird and the bill owed, the implied phrase "I'll give him a piece of my mind" connoting an angry speech but used synecdochally to suggest a language that comes from the mouth but not from the head. In other poems the birds are more quietly rational than the whippoorwills of "A Nature Note," but the message remains essentially unheroic: in "The Last Word of the Bluebird" the bluebird "sends word" through three parties that "The North wind last night / Almost made him cough his tailfeathers off."[5] The symbol of transcendence over despair has a bad cold, word of which is carried by a quiet but unmusical crow (who says, "Oh, / I was looking for you. / How do you do?") to the equally phlegmatic speaker who recounts the interchange. In "Our Singing Strength" the birds are reduced to "a talking twitter." More like cows than birds, they are herded on the road by the "Drover" / speaker, who, it may be assumed, has a song that is equally hemmed in and bound down (the birds can't leave the snowless roads for the snowfields, and they cannot fly upward into the "too much carven marble hall" of the trees). The speaker's voice manifests itself in matter-of-fact couplets; he drives the talking twitter down the page as he moves the birds down the road. By implication the combined mass of thrushes, bluebirds, blackbirds, sparrows, and robins might represent enough "singing strength" to bring spring out of winter if they could raise their voices above a nervous twitter. But when the spring snowfall melts, this potentially explosive chorus will immediately disperse—"Really a very few [come] to build and stay"—leaving the song unsung.

And just as Frost's lyric birds are burdened, weary creatures, so too do his speakers frequently and explicitly claim for themselves a noninspirational safety well out of the lyric-inducing wind. The standard romantic metaphor for inspiration, wind among Frost's speakers tends instead to be perceived as a force of disruption; internalized, it creates "inner weather" so turbulent as to threaten the careful poetic process. Inspirative possession is potentially dangerous, and for Frost's avowed purpose of bringing about wisdom through pleasure, it is more invasive than generative. That which is invasive or penetrative, that which transports a man outside his reason is, as we have seen, subversive of manliness; to be overwhelmed bespeaks a passivity as regards one's self that is defined as feminine and thus as highly suspect.[6] The manly course involves controlled choice and the imposition of a self-generated order that asserts Platonic shapeliness—as the speaker says in "Pertinax," "Let chaos storm! / Let cloud shapes swarm! / I wait for form." As "The Aim Was Song" (ironically?) points out, a little inspiration— translated here to mean, literally, an indrawn breath that penetrates no further than the lips and throat—may tame the "untaught" wind, which blows too loud and too hard: "He took a little in his mouth, / ... And then by measure blew it forth" to transform noise to song. The small taste of wind may be warmed and molded; one merely holds it "long enough for north / To be converted into south." By implication, the sounds the wind makes on its own are loud and wild; it thrums no aeolian harp, but shrieks indiscriminately across "any rough place where it caught." Too much of this wind, taken upon the body or into the lungs where inspirative singing begins, makes a bellows of the singer. This speaker seems to believe that it is better to sing a small song—the sound he produces, ambiguously described, may even be whistling—better to be a careful, self-controlled bird than one that is lofted by the wind to soar and sing uncontrolled.

"To the Thawing Wind" suggests explicitly that the wind-warmed natural world is subversive of the domesticated and tamed poetic vocation, causing a surrender of barriers that transforms the careful poet into a spring-fed rioter. In an image that suggests molten heat, the speaker imagines that the warm wind will "Bathe my window, make it flow / Melt it as the ice will go." As the window goes, so goes the house of words that makes a poem; the windowpane of ice that breaks in "After Apple-Picking" signals entrance into the half-world of dreams as barriers dissolve. The window that separates the sleeper in "The Hill Wife" from the wind-tossed "dark pine" with its tireless hands reduces the ominous tree to "seem as a little bird / Before the mystery of glass"; broken, the window would reverse the transformation of power to impotence—turning the lyric bird back into the ineffable tree—and the wind-animated tree is not seeking entrance to speak, but to "do." Once the panes in "To the Thawing Wind" are melted, the "Hermit's crucifix" that is left of the window will not suffice to keep the wind at bay. It will enter the monklike "narrow stall" and toss the tools of introspection, the books and pictures, about; it will "Scatter the poems on the floor; / Turn the poet out of door." A force of excess, the wind subverts vigilant moderation, inviting explicitly nonintellectual, nonmonkish pleasures.[7] By implication the Christian totem, the crucifix, has little power in this scenario of melting barriers.

In "Bereft," in the teeth of a powerful wind the figure on the porch is feminized, subject to violation and no longer in control of "the word." He sees the wind as an aggressor that might mistake his presence as a kind of availability: "What would it take my standing there for?" he wonders, as if his motives might be misapprehended in the same way that the girl / poet of "The Fear of Man," buffeted by wind and dust, might be misunderstood in what she/he means. He feels that the wind is there specifically because word has gotten out of his abandonment—"Word I was in the house alone / Somehow must have gotten abroad, / Word I was in my life alone, / Word I had no one left but God." This escaped "word" has been transformed to howling wind, much as Frost's escaped women are transformed elementally, and has become antithetical to order as it urges the world to the border of a storm. The wordless human figure, neither in nor out, neither man nor woman, is bereft of effective language as certainly as he is bereft of love: his "house" is sagging, indeed, as he is divested simultaneously of the woman and of the erotic power of the word. The wind's sound is a deep masculine roar, and the speaker hears "Something sinister in the tone." As if to provide a mocking symbol for the speaker's impotent rage at his abandonment, it has whipped the leaves up into a snakelike, hissing coil that strikes "blindly" at the speaker's knees and misses its mark: the snake that can only strike blindly and ineffectively is both phallically and verbally impotent, neither penetrative nor persuasive. The wind has churned the lake at the bottom of the hill into froth, as if to provide a symbol, too, for the absent female who has left the speaker "in [his] life alone."[8] The wind possesses, in short, the clear capacity to animate the speaker as well, for his feminized, passive state invites penetration, but with its words and not the speaker's own.

Frost's speakers, aware that submission to desire subverts their commonsensical version of how language is to work, thus seldom bare themselves willingly to feel the wind against their bodies, and so they tend to seem, like the urbane, ironic Drumlin woodchuck who is "instinctively thorough / About [its] crevice and burrow," the very embodiment of prudence. In keeping with the implication that to be ruled by outside forces signals a culpable appetitive uncontrol, the willingness to take on the wind may even signal a kind of licentiousness, suggested even in "To the Thawing Wind" by the uncloistered monk image. The Witch of Grafton is said by her husband to be out "kiting. / She thinks when the wind makes a night of it / She might as well herself." As one who "kites" she becomes a combination of things: she is one who soars on the wind; she is a bird of prey; she is by extension a person who preys on others; she is one who knows how the wind blows and who will, thus, "make a night of it," with the sexual license this term connotes. Borne by wind, she is at the mercy of her own rapacious desire. Similarly, but with less pejorative connotations, the wind in "A Line-Storm Song" is associated with rising desire that will flood the civilized land and crush its spokesmen, the lyric birds, with an orgasmic "ancient sea." Wind stirs ashes into sparks and drives sparks into conflagrations; both literally and figuratively, it is a force associated with cataclysm and purification.

Frost's speakers consistently place themselves in impotent opposition to elemental forces; they are there in the poems to choose their stated correlatives, to claim their own limitations of power—to confess. The speaker of "Bereft" locates himself clearly in the realm of nonpower; he and his sagging house are belittled by the roaring wind, which is a masculine correlative to his feminine powerlessness. The figure in "On Going Unnoticed" is the very emblem of abasement, and the "you" of which he speaks universalizes his impotence: grasping the "rugged pleat" of the great windswept tree, he is an abject figure, a child clinging to his mother's skirts, a slave prostrate at the feet of the master, a boy at the feet of a man. The figure of the speaker is metonymically contained in the phallic failure of the spotted and pallid coralroot whose "flowers hang meanly down," and the plucking out of this feeble root becomes, thus, a gesture encoded with the sadomasochism implicit in such willful abasement. The confessional impulses of these speakers reduce the potentially analogous relationships between man and nature to named metaphors that inevitably place the human figures in defensive, vulnerable positions: "I am like a woodchuck, or a coral root, or a fallen leaf, or a helpless, storm-tossed tree"; "I am like the frozen field of snow, frostbound to impotence"; "I am too absent-spirited to count." Even the urbane speaker of "For Once, Then, Something" qualifies his authority with his defensiveness about placing himself "wrong to the light," thus making his Apollonian pretensions at least potentially ironic and deprecating. It is no accident that in "Spring Pools," where hunger and the power to sate it are unqualified, the embodied human presence within the poem disappears: the trees "have in their pent-up buds / To darken nature" in a way that a speaking figure cannot, and in fact the distant voice remains cautionary, warning, "Let them think twice before they use their powers." Like the birds that symbolize Frost's stated version of his lyric voice, these figures do not claim to be lofted skyward, nor do they particularly wish to be—"May no fate willfully misunderstand me / ... and snatch me away," they pray.

"Misgiving" seems in this context a consciously parodic version of Shelley's "Ode to the West Wind," where the wintry West Wind drives the sickened and pestilential leaves before it along with the winged seeds that will give birth to spring. Shelley's speaker wants to be lifted by the wind, driven "Like withered leaves to quicken a new birth!" He begs to be taken and tossed by a wind so powerful that it can lift the clouds "Like the bright hair uplifted from the head / Of some fierce Maenad." But Frost's poem embodies an antithetical desire for rest and safety, a fear that when given the chance to be translated to some "knowledge beyond the bounds of life" he will prefer to rest like the sleepy leaves. The leaves first cry, "We will, go with you, O Wind!" having promised themselves ever since spring that they will "follow him." But they become oppressed by sleep, "And they end by bidding him stay with them." Unable to rise, they seek the shelter of walls, thickets, and hollows in which to rest, answering the wind "with an ever vaguer and vaguer stir." The speaker sees himself as like the autumn leaves, just as Shelley envisions himself as an autumnal forest, but Frost's vision is without the fire implicit in Shelley's hectic reds, yellows, and blacks that will scatter ashes and sparks of prophecy among humankind. His speaker's prayer is not to be lifted from the thorns of life, but is far more modest: "I only hope that when I am free ... It may not seem better to me to rest." He identifies himself with the leaves who choose an inglorious sleep and who ultimately seem more hibernatory than sacrificial.

For Frost, whose "The Bonfire" re-creates the romantic scenario of wind and fire in seriocomic, quasi-heroic terms, the generative effects of wind are compromised by its equal potential for subverting control. In "The Bonfire" the wind takes a flame that, in the breezeless, quiet afternoon, makes "a pinnacle to heaven" and spreads it in tongues across the ground. The mystical route from earth to heaven, the unmoving pillar of flame, is replaced with moving, all-consuming fire, and the speaker spends himself ecstatically in rubbing it out, thus saving civilization—the town—from wind-fed destruction. His battle with the fire that the wind awakens must be read at one level as an erotic one, and thus the victory may be seen as pyrrhic. Ecstatic release is accompanied in this case by acres of "coal-black," charred earth, yet he does, significantly, quell the wildfire before it reaches civilization. In actuality, Frost saved his home from the fire he had set, and in the poetic version the speaker saves the entire town;[9] in both cases the virile containment of the appetitive, tonguelike fire ensures domestic and civil order.

For the most part, Frost's equating of the wind with passion makes it a force productive of ambivalence and confusion. Without the wind, the fire of "The Bonfire" remains spiritually oriented, upright and heaven-directed like the central pole of "The Silken Tent," which may contain both soul and phallus simultaneously. In this manifestation love may be generative of a more immortal beauty, a Platonic communion of desire and spirit that produces, not human offspring, but "something lovelier and less mortal than human seed."[10] This state is, however, by nature tenuous, for a sudden wind can transform the spiritual flame into a "flaming sword." His speakers, who eschew the heroic stance, tend thus to find the low bushes and walls that make windbreaks and they mostly keep their windows closed. Outside, they find their correlatives in silently falling snow or in gray, windless landscapes; but "When the wind works against us in the dark / ... And whispers with a sort of stifled bark / The beast, / Come out! Come out!— / It takes no inward struggle not to go." "Lodged" presents the image of a bullying pair, the wind and the rain, lashing the piteous flowers into submission: "They so smote the garden bed / That the flowers actually knelt, / And lay lodged—though not dead." "I know how the flowers felt," the speaker says, again, as in "On Going Unnoticed," proclaiming metonymically his own humiliation envisioned in terms of enforced prostration and sadistic physical punishment.[11] In two poems where speakers are subjected to powerful winds—"The Thatch" and "Bereft"—they have been driven outside by domestic troubles, and as in "Storm Fear," they perceive the wind as actively aggressive, more dangerous than inspirational.[12] In an early poem, "Now Close the Windows," the speaker asks that the windows be shut to silence even the sounds of the wind, saying "So close the windows and not hear the wind, / But see all wind-stirred." He is able thus to create his own illusions, making this significant qualification: "No bird is singing now, and if there is, / Be it my Joss." The lyric birds who would sing in a winter gale are not birds he would want to hear, for the wind brings subversion of control and may awaken the passion that bruits down the sound of sense.

Even the trees that otherwise are filled with power and beauty, as the queenly maple in "Maple" or the sibylline trees of "On Going Unnoticed," lose their preeminence when the speaker of "Tree at My Window" associates them with himself. In "On Going Unnoticed" the trees sweep leafily by the dwarfed figure below, and they are "engaged [presumably in conversation] up there with the light and breeze" as equals. But in "Tree at My Window" the tree becomes insubstantial as it is made an external referent for the speaker: the tree outside his bedroom, made vague and diffuse as a cloud, does not toss down oracular leaves: "Not all your light tongues talking aloud / Could be profound," the speaker says. This tree, gossipy, familiar, is not engaged in a dialogue with the wind but is instead "taken and tossed" by it just as the speaker's dreams cause him to be "taken and swept / And all but lost." Both the man and the tree are in danger of being deprived of meaningful speech by too-powerful "weather," for just as the tree's leaves, its "light tongues," can only babble, so too can the man only dream, wordless, of chaos. The one a "fated" correlative for the other, they are both reduced to the status of victims: "The day she put our heads together, / Fate had her imagination about her, / Your head so much concerned with outer, / Mine with inner, weather."

And so what with all these symbolically pinioned birds and these self-deprecating, depressed speakers wary of inspirative power, it begins to seem that the sound of sense Frost aims for is exactly the down-home, conversational, and aphoristic "wisdom" of the Oven Bird. It seems that he really might have been shocked by Lionel Trilling's birthday compliment, that instead of desiring that Sophoclean capacity to terrify he might indeed rather wish to think that he lives "in the middle" at variance with no one and nothing.[13] Yet so laid out before us, this New Englander's version of the compromised lyric voice seems too patently symbolic and too straightforward in its message for one so ironically inclined as Frost. And in fact it may be said that Frost's modest and unaspiring birds and his wind-wary speakers and his battered flowers are decoys, the lyric sacrifices that "keep the overcurious out of the secret places" of his mind while freeing a metalyrical power that may not be fully articulated in any way the world knows how to speak (*Letters* 385).[14] As Poirier points out, Frost, all too wary of the "egotistical sublime," could not, nonetheless, completely give it up; the schizoid split between neoclassical reserve and visionary intensity that makes him so fond of mad Kit Smart is potential in his own devices of disguise and control.[15] If his lover's skeleton in "The Witch of Coös" is a veritable chandelier of consciously reticulated symbolisms constructed to aggrandize and undercut simultaneously love's body, his lyric symbols are another such wily, eccentric device.

Frost's birds beg to be taken at their word when they sing a commonsensical message of compromise—the Oven Bird is such a fruitful symbol as regards Frost's masculinist, deep-voiced rigor—and his dispirited speakers really do seem to argue against the sublime. But the full poetic song does not completely sanction their limited view. The birds demand in their consistency to be taken analogically, as rather obvious metaphors for the poet's commitment to the earth's being the right place for love, even if that means that love becomes a quarrelsome, mundane affair tainted by Eve's first betrayal. But Frost is contriving a way to sing that transcends words, goes beyond words to an aural source that is uncompromised and subverts rationality: he seeks "the abstract vitality of ... speech" that is "pure sound— pure form" (*Letters* 80). In this he is enacting a Frostian version of the Schopenhauerean premise that holds music forth as transcendent, a medium that moves one with a power beyond the rational, even as he repudiates the traditional poetic uses of music as a model by which harmonized vowels and consonants are brought to sing pretty songs (*Letters* 79).[16] In rediscovering and exploiting the "cave things," the sounds "living in the cave of the mouth" that "were before words were," he seeks to bring to poetry the true power of music, which may not be mimicked by language alone and which may not be sung by what Wallace Stevens calls, in "Thirteen Ways of Looking at a Blackbird," the "bawds of euphony" (*Letters* 191). The lyric bird may know in singing not to sing, but the poet with his virile oversound drums out the flagging lyric voice: he sets out "to make music out of what I may call the sound of sense" (*Letters* 79). The language of love, with its ambivalent impulses toward confession and aggrandizement and toward guilt and rapture, is dominated by a more powerful song.

Lyric poetry is exactly that locus which is most problematized for Frost, for at the same moment in poetic history when the lyric form is being indicted for its effeminacy and for its failure to accommodate the modern world, it is also having attributed to it the explicitly sexual energies seen as intrinsic to the revelatory mode.[17] By the time Frost gets to it, the lyric, classically associated only in part with love poetry, is caught in an inescapable tautology whereby it gradually removes itself from all that is not in some way correlative to sexual desire: love thus moves from a subset of lyric content to the standard by which lyric is measured. The underlying assumption that informs this tautology is based on a presupposition, articulated with detailed precision in Freud and long suspected as an implicit truth, at least literarily, before he so baldly laid it out: reality is sex.[18] One uncomfortable with this minimalist assertion might turn instead to Plato, who articulates a similar preoccupation with sex, which, codified and divested of its essential disorder, becomes the first necessary step toward Love, or the supreme Good, or the absolute Spirit; recognizing what he sees as love's preeminence, Plato makes the first of many philosophical attempts to integrate (sexual) love as an initiatory movement toward the divine.[19]

Or, in fact, one uncomfortable with this assertion might turn to Frost himself, who sees even his apprehension of Christ as infiltrated by an inescapable eroticism:

> You know Plato virtually says himself two thousand years before Freud that the love of the invisible, philosophy is a sublimation of τὰ ἐρότιΚα, sex love the mans love not only of fair girls but also of fair boys. The metaphor with him is always drawn from sex. Is it ever a single moment with Christ? Great play has been made with the ladies, not all of them sinless, he had around him.... It's reached a point with me where I've got to have it out with myself whether I can think of Christ but as another manifestation of Dionysus, wine in his beard and the love leer in his eye. Is he even a little Pagan? Isn't he pretty nearly all Puritan for better or worse? (*Letters* 313–14)

Even the most resolute effort of will, Frost seems to imply, cannot divest the metaphor-making process—"another manifestation of" *x*—of its eroticism. Whether or not this letter is meant, as Thompson asserts, to be one of Frost's many "provocations that bordered on insolence," its question appears to be quite genuine.

By this love—reality equation and by definition of lyric as a mode that expresses the genuine emotion of the speaker, any man who discovers his most fundamental lyric self will find desire and its concomitant states: empowerment and impotence, invigoration and enervation, the entire dialectic of appetite that mimics (or embodies) the inexhaustible tautologies of sadomasochism. The echoes one sends out come back virtually engorged with one's own virile power—this *is* the most of it, the most of what lyric poetry will inevitably reveal. A cry allegedly constructed, implies "The Most of It," to get "not its own love back in copy speech, / But counter-love, original response," the echo is embodied in the glorious beast that swims back toward the source: "As a great buck it powerfully appeared, / Pushing the crumpled water up ahead, / And landed pouring like a waterfall." Whether or not it is "true" that reality is sex, it is true that it has come for many to seem so and that Frost is not immune: his reality inevitably displays itself in sexual terms, with "love" at the center of it all—love as poetry, love as farming, love as love; poetry in the wild space, metaphor in the brothel, poetry and love like ice searing on the stove. To speak lyrically is to declare oneself sexually: the great buck "with horny tread" will have appeared, "forced the underbrush," and disappeared: such is the "copy speech" from Frost's lips. Yet to speak with candor of desire without the distancing devices of irony or other rhetorical strategies is a form of unmanning, a masochism that brings one, as in "The Fear of Man," to the desire for and fear of violation. On the other hand, to seem not to love, not to yield to the eroticism of a language that simultaneously unveils and regenerates this potent erotic source is also to invite impotence.

The (unreachable) ideal of lyric is to communicate feeling in its immediacy, but that failing, one must work to imply that there is a site of bliss, interdicted but imminent. That originally the form was indissociable from the lyre and the dance suggests its physical orientation and its proximity to a kind of possession. The lyric bird as it is romantically declined recapitulates in small these elements of musicality and dancing: "pant[ing] forth a flood of rapture so divine," Shelley's skylark springs from the earth, soars, floats, and runs, and it is its ability to articulate itself through unfettered movement as well as sound that both separates it from and joins it with the word-bound but participatory lyric poet. Ideally, then, the poem *is*, as Frost would have it, the same as love—an ecstatic song that, internalized in the movements of desire, approximates the dance in its power to alter stasis to ecstasy. Yet Frost chooses such birds as know not to fly too high or to sing too long, their "inspiration" lying in the "inspiration to desist" from singing before hostile ears might track them down ("On a Bird Singing in Its Sleep"). Described as "loveless" in "A Winter Eden," they deny their own lyric symbolism, and given in "Acceptance" a "faded eye," they abrogate their lyric vision for a diminished view. And yet in acknowledging that the speaking voice is its own source of impotence Frost empowers his own metalyrical sound.

There is, then, an inescapable discrepancy to be accounted for in this nearly absurdist reification of the lyric poet as oven bird: Frost's poetry itself is *not* mundane, despite frequent pretenses to the contrary. It is the speaking voice that tends to be mundane or preoccupied with life's daily insults. Those figures who embody themselves in the "I" that looks like Frost but, by virtue of Frost's ironic habits, can never quite *be* Frost show a consistent pattern of graceless attributes from self-aggrandizement to self-belittlement while the poetry prevails over their revealed weaknesses. Frost articulates this very disjunction in "A Minor Bird," which suggests the intimate connections and the asserted disparities among the singing bird, the speaking voice, and the poet. The poet denigrates the bird as "minor," and he displays the subject in predominately nine-syllable lines deployed in rhymed couplets. The poem, in fact, looks quite minor, its simplicity of form and its brevity proclaiming a kind of intended deflation of the lyric mode: this is not, despite its "Ode to a Nightingale" allusion, an ode, nor, the poet implies, does it deserve to be.

Ironically perceived, the poem could in fact be read as a veiled insult to another, unnamed poet making his poetic presence unendurable with its interminable, minor-keyed warble; there are, as "The Lesson for Today" makes clear, more than enough poets moaning about what is out of joint in the world to fit this bill (ll. 30–5).

But taken as serious, "A Minor Bird" has a remarkably resonant simplicity, as it suggests an intimate contiguity between speaker and bird, both of whom are masterfully represented in language reflective of the colorless nonspecifities of depression. "I have wished a bird would fly away," the speaker says, "And not sing by my house all day." In this opening one intuits the repetitive nature of his wish, and in the non-specificity of "a bird" one understands that *all* birds may sound to him the way this one does. The sad voice cannot muster the energy or will to extend himself to ten syllables; he cannot rouse himself from monosyllables (four two-syllable words out of sixty-six). The unexpected hand clapping of the second couplet—the only image of movement—is balanced by the admission that "it seemed as if I could bear no more." The third couplet is richly ambiguous, as the situation is perceived in terms of "fault" and "guilt," and the bird and speaker are conflated into correlatives of each other. At one level, the "fault"—the melancholy reaction awakened by the bird's song—is partly in the speaker, whose own hearing of the bird is, he feels, irrationally judgmental: one cannot blame a bird for singing its "little inborn tune" ("On a Bird Singing in Its Sleep"). At another level, this one reinforced by the punning title whereby the (mynah) bird mimics the speaker, it is the speaker interpreting the song who creates / causes the minor key: "a bird" or any bird would sound the same. Like one unable to imagine that the phoebes don't weep, he makes weeping where there may be none. In short, the speaker reveals himself as the minor bird, and the poet by his precisely appropriate form confirms him as the minor bird while confirming his own transcendent song. Plagued by what he senses to be his own serious limitation—there is "something wrong" with him for wanting to silence any song—he sings the very monotonal, abbreviated song that most aptly declares his own depressed state. By the logic of this poem, to silence the bird's song would be to silence himself.

As lyricists, Frost's speakers are such mynah birds as the self-revelatory figure of "A Minor Bird" who is made to perform the poet's service almost ventriloquistically. Because they talk they guarantee their own deconstruction: again, those sacrificial actors at their play.[20] This dynamic reiterates the essential mandate of the manly struggle for self-containment and self-control, for the man of moderation, the good Greek, is a man of *logos*, competent to command, to discuss, and to persuade.[21] He does not use the word to reveal his lyric (insecure, rhapsodic, depressed, narcissistic, impassioned) self. And so Frost's speakers are the (always compromised) lyricists, while Frost himself, forever potentially ironic and always in prosodic control, may seem the quintessential man of *logos*. In any event, with others deployed to say the parts of what he feels, he remains himself untouchable, seemingly possessed of immanent sense—the secret word— which can be neither refuted nor denied. Of course, the secret may in fact be nothing, Frost's cloaked nihilism which pervades this game of obfuscation and shares his balanced assessment that the unverifiable thing lying beneath the surface may be truth or a pebble of quartz, some thing or nothing. What he aspires to do is really quite extraordinary in its Socratic audacity, for he would both convince one of his capacity for the most intense emotions—be the lyricist—and convince one of his transcendence over those feelings to a state in which the absurdity of the human pretension to knowing is the one incandescent reality—be the consummate ironist.

And so, unlike the birds' apparent subscription to a fairly monotonal lament, the music of Frost's poetry is intricate, multileveled, and powerful. Poirier suggests this paradox in his assertion that Frost is "committed to the most subtle, insinuating, and diffident kind of self-perception"; even as the sound rises to assertiveness the message it speaks is of compromise, and thus it manages to deny possibilities for empowerment while "surreptitiously" keeping these possibilities alive.[22] It is always implied through his prosodic virility that he could obliterate the bird song and make his own "Line Storm Song" if he wished. "A Line-Storm Song" from *A Boy's Will* can be seen in the context of the bird metaphor as an early prediction of what he fantasizes might occur, poetically and sexually, when the moderate voice of reason is stilled; a world genuinely reflective of passion—a true lyric song if it were to be sung—is both sublime and terrible, productive of ecstasy and violence. The poem suggests in its punning title its self-consciously lyrical (and therefore potentially ironic) and generative nature; with each "line-storm" touching off another, the poem may be seen as an explosive "song" whose lines generate their own sequential energy. In "A Line-Storm Song," the birds are, quite literally, silenced; they "have less to say for themselves" than the long-silent elves, while the rain and wind supersede both human voices and the voices of the human-like birds. The speaker here calls for the wind to "bruit our singing down," and in the drowning of all sounds of sense, he feels in the east wind an ancient flood of desire. The use of the curiously ambiguous word "bruit" suggests the duality of the human/bird voice that articulates both passion and sense, for the term, also spelled *brute*, can mean "to noise abroad," "to rumor," or "to din." Singing that is "bruited down" is at once drowned out by the wind and noised abroad by it, as if the human love song has two levels, a commonsensical level that the wind batters down just as it has crushed the bird's voices, and a passionate oversound that resonates with the voices of the wind and the rain.

This world of passion is both lovely and violent: the birds' songs are "crushed like some / Wild, easily shattered rose" in order for the phallic "rain-fresh goldenrod" to prevail. (One must think, inevitably, of "The Subverted Flower" in the context of "A Line-Storm Song"; its female figure stands waist-high in goldenrod, while the woman of "A Line-Storm Song" is urged to wet her breast with "the rain-fresh goldenrod.") The speaker's fantasy of passion includes "rout" and apocalypse, with the return of a prehistoric sea that will retake dry land (which may be cultivated and civilized) in its flood. "A Line-Storm Song" reiterates the seemingly inextricable bond in Frost's poetry between sexuality and danger or violence—passion as line storms, as a bonfire, as a fireweed—and it suggests, too, the link Frost makes between nature and uncontrol. It also suggests that if Frost were to unleash his own lyric nature it would, he imagines, come in storm and whirlwind, in lines of storm, rather than disguised as a patient "minor" bird.

The bird metaphor in any of its manifestations must inevitably be self-conscious, as Frost well knows when he sets out to subvert its romantic status as an emblem of the free soul and the transcendent poetic spirit, but it cannot fully escape its association with transcendence. Birds can fly; humans cannot. Just as water is used to symbolize life because in a significant sense it *is* life, birds symbolize transcendence because they have wings. Meaning is thus not only inherited literarily but is inherent in form; the Oven Bird cannot eradicate the lark or the nightingale despite its own cast-iron weight, and, in fact, its preaching, premised upon their flightiness, brings them more inevitably to mind. One may reasonably extend this analogy to poetry; it may be disciplined at one level to carry the sound of (common) sense, but fundamentally it is closer to song than to prose. The compromised flight and the voice that knows in singing not to sing are thus Frost's conscious and somewhat ironic imposition of restraint on a form that he willfully encourages to sing its own prosodic harmonies and to create its own line storms. Like so many of Frost's images of precarious withholding—walls about to tumble, cold stars on the verge of wakening, still pools about to become revelatory—these birds carry in their hollow wing bones the potential to destroy their own enforced repose; their singing strength "though repressed and moody with the weather / [Is] nonetheless there ready to be freed /And sing the wild flowers up from root and seed." For Frost poetry resides not in free flight but in the beat of wings against the arc, words fluttering hard against structure. Like the dark pine that seems "as a little bird / Before the mystery of glass" in "The Hill Wife," poetry is force barely contained, leaving one to the fear and delight of "an oft-repeated dream / Of what the tree might do" if the glass were to break: bondage, and discipline, the barely concealed delight that comes from Frost's insight into the equivocal pleasures of containing and being contained. Frost, one might reasonably maintain, is himself like the "great tree" seeming to be a little bird, pushing against the barriers that he erects. These barriers are, it is implied, too strong for the traditional symbol of lyricism to shatter but necessary to contain the tremendous power of a less self-indulgent nature.

The bird metaphor carries a great deal of literary baggage, and thus the little birds cannot get very high off the ground. So too, Frost seems to be implying in his pinioning of the lyric birds, does poetry carry the excess baggage of its literary heritage: it must find a new song, a new metalanguage by which to regenerate itself. Frost may, in his domesticated, depressed birds, be making one of his most subtle and sophisticated puns about literary convention, in fact. In the autobiographical "The Bonfire," his bluebirds have the rug pulled out from under them—the "spent" breezes fail, leaving them "Short of the perch their languid flight was toward." But the poet's fire is first a pinnacle to heaven and then a wildfire. He starts the fire, he fuels it with an inspirative gust, and he rubs it out; the languid bluebird may be spent like the worn-out winter wind in April, but the poet emerges erect. The bluebird may be earthbound, but Frost "walk[s] ... light on air in heavy shoes," his "feet" bound in blank verse but his poetic spirit soaring. The bluebird is silent, freeing the poet to ignite a new kind of poetry. Frost's birds cannot measure up to his own poetic virility. They are talkers, but in a world such as the Oven Bird describes, where things and words that name them are metamorphic, language loses its penetrative function to fix or to pin down: what is immobilized in Frost's poetry is dead or hibernatory or momentarily frostbound. The overlay of unstable irony that echoes this suspicion of fixed "meaning" further keeps language from a "point" and suggests that its function lies elsewhere.

This is a condition of language that inevitably invites formalism to prevail over the epistemological circuities of unknowing, and, indeed, Frost's poetry has a formal rigor that resonates against unstable irony's resistance to closure and to the consummation of some mutual understanding with the reader. The closure this formal rigor affords is not rationally situated. He wants poetically to walk "light on air in heavy shoes," maintaining a lovingly disciplinarian relationship to the word rather than, like Keats, seeking to find the exact, lightly woven "sandals ... / To fit the naked foot of poesy": "her" word is necessarily not Frost's entire, manly message. Prosodically rigorous, Frost is committed to a nearly punitive relationship with language in which he sees himself as one who "like[s] to drag and break intonation ... across meter." What Keats sought to escape—the "chains" and "fetters" of rhyme and meter—Frost insists upon. Language itself may be diffusible into an endless "deferment of significance," but form—meter pounding against rhyme and line length, intonation pulsing against meter—has its own penetrative function.[23] It may even, as Lyotard has argued, subvert memory and thwart the backward gaze: "As meter takes precedence over accent in the production of sound ... time ceases to be a support for memory to become an immemorial beating that, in the absence of a notable separation between periods, prevents their being numbered, and consigns them to oblivion."[24] The subversion of memory is the subversion of rational thought, as it eradicates the premises upon which conclusions are built. Held in the poem's hermeneutic embrace, aroused to its rhythm, one may, in fact, feel temporarily the Nietzschean "strength to *forget* the past."[25] Frost consistently exploits the hypnotic potential of sound to countermand stated meaning, so that what one senses is something external to what the eye sees on the page. To "drag and break intonation ... across meter" is to postulate some truth beyond that which is signified by the word, as it takes language from a speaker's mouth and breaks it metrically to release something else.

Frost's own "lyric" voice (what we are made to feel are genuine, nonironic revelations as opposed to rhetorical postures) is never directly identifiable in the poetry through what is *spoken*, suggesting a cynicism about the power of language alone to communicate or to reveal the essential self. The birds, limited and ventriloquistic as they are, are merely components of Frost's metalyrical voice in which both emotion and control are displayed on equal terms. It being possible to describe only a border condition, not the state one is in but what one is moving toward or away from, any zero-order lyricism must reside extra-linguistically. The complex contradictions within the poetry, where the dialectic elements may be shifted into a near infinity of relationships—text versus subtext, stated meaning versus tone, allusion versus "theme," virile prosody versus claimed impotence, irony versus the straightforward, and all the permutations of these and other combinations— may be seen in this context as a form of oscillation that reproduces this state of disequilibrium. A tennis game that never ends, the back and forth between pairings nonetheless necessitates a net and boundary lines: containing this dynamically unstable condition necessitates a rigorous formalism if the energy is not to become dissolute. Spatial dissipation is a moral slippage as well, and formal control is imperative.

The reiterated image of the impotent bird becomes a limited version of the poet who must find a place from which to sing, for placement both mirrors and creates form. The Oven Bird's house is a concretized dome of mud; it re-creates the arc of heaven in small and sings from the middle ground that its "nest" suggests spatially. In "The Lockless Door" the speaker writes of himself as a timid bird who, at a knock on the door, "emptied [his] cage / To hide in the world / And alter with age."[26] Neither the domestic "cage" nor the natural hiding place can afford a perspective from which to impose form; caged or hibernatory, the madman or the tame bird or the woodchuck, one so encased does not create form but is formed by his space. "On a Bird Singing in Its Sleep" obliquely suggests in its version of evolutionary adaptation that the speaker endorses the safety of the unawakened, ventriloquistic voice that seems to come from where it isn't: "Partly because it sang ventriloquist / And had the inspiration to desist / Almost before the prick of hostile ears" the bird remained unharmed. The ventriloquistic function of the poet/bird—the mimicry of voices thrown onto wooden figures—ensures a very limited range and power; he sits on a low bush, hidden, and gives a short, muted whistle. But ventriloquism—thrown language—subverts form by disembodiment, and while Frost's "ventriloquism" vivifies a whole series of speakers, his full poetic voice makes it apparent that they remain just that: "speakers" who reproduce words but do not create or originate sound, meaning, or form.

Most frequently, Frost chooses to occupy poetically the borderlands between civilization and nature, a destabilized place where language is both created and destroyed but where, paradoxically, form may be perceived to emerge triumphant from the eternal decay and resurrection of particulars. His birds, another kind of border creature, are so humanized that they sit in nature taking as their view and as their theme human concerns. Frost, on the other hand, keeps an eye always on the outer boundaries, the place where cultivation yields to wildness. "My address is Amherst Mass, though really we are living in the abandoned town of Pelham so close to the woods that if the wood burn our house must go too," he writes to Amy Lowell (*Letters* 220). The successive qualifications of his literal place are telling—his address, what one would write down on a letter, is not really where he lives, just as in "New Hampshire" he is writing from Vermont. Where he is, actually, is in an abandoned town, which places it, as so many of his households are placed within the poetry, at a point of linguistic and actual transformation: when is a town no longer called a town and what does it then become?[27] For practical and perhaps for spiritual purposes he is part of the woods, for if they burn so too will the house and the "town" that abuts them. His poetic vision reiterates this ambiguous placement, and in examining as he does "the line where man leaves off and nature starts" ("New Hampshire"), Frost sets himself a more complex task than the birds' stated functions of qualifying, inspecting, defining, evaluating, and reminding: he looks directly at the place where transformation occurs, where words are coming unformed because meaning is always in flux. There are no formal gardens in the borderland he inhabits, no topiaries, no artificial, miniaturized grottos, and no Penshursts that embody the optimistic assumption that a man may order his physical and spiritual estates; even the small stream captured underground in concrete at the city limits in "A Brook in the City" retains its dark power to keep a city "from both work and sleep," the two states most necessary to the maintenance of an ordered physical and spiritual life. The bird/poet in the cage metaphor of "The Lockless Door" is, thus, a highly artificial construct, almost intrinsically ironic in the context of Frost's spatial arrangements. The walls he erects are in natural, uncontrolled landscapes that defy them to hold, so that as the drama implicit within the poetic structure unfolds formalism becomes its only containment.[28]

If Frost's perception of one's obligation to moderate appetite with control is classical, the reiterated sense of the futility of this effort predicts a modernist preoccupation with the decentered self and how one might translate that existential precariousness into language or into art. There is no condition, no state, no speaker in Frost's poetry for whom the heautocratic struggle is resolved into what would be, for the good Greek, its expected payoff in the ability to act upon and to influence others: it is by these terms emblematic that in Frost's poetry no man can persuade a woman to return to him or not to leave him, that men are reduced, as in "The Subverted Flower," to choking on words "Like a tiger at a bone," that they are brought to threaten, as in "Home Burial," "I'll follow and bring you back by force." This impotence is doubly fraught, for it signals both a social and a lyric insufficiency. Frost's unstable irony disperses the forward movements by which he claims to proceed—the "sentence sound" and the iambic surge are not sufficient to override the meanderings through which one must go to approach meaning(s). He creates a medium in which, ironically, the word takes precedence by default, rising up in all its contaminated, erotic force to suggest possibilities above and below and between the lines. He does not *need* to be "poetic" in his diction or syntax or even in his choice of subjects, and he thus protects himself from the most unmanly elements of lyric poetry; language works its own subversions on linear, forward-moving progress toward resolution. The movement is toward isolation rather than away from it, so that the discrete formal continuity of a given poem is the necessary cage for an autonomous internal conflict. The birds give a very limited, opinionated, prudential version of this reality which must be, to a large extent, supplemented by the natural correlatives for passion and appetitive uncontrol that fill the poetry. The glaring discrepancy between the uninnocent birds who know Eve's language and the elemental powers that may unmake that language—between the clock-watching birds and the gaunt beast ravaging the apple tree in "A Winter Eden"—suggests that Frost, who sees only struggle and never resolution, engages in a dialectic in which one impulse is the subversion of rational meaning to sound and form. This is an active and vigorous nihilism which suggests that "meaning" is so fluid as to be nonexistent so that arbitrarily imposed form becomes everything.

Frost's birds are, finally, at so considerable a remove from his own prosodic and tonal range that they may be seen less as direct symbols of his lyric voice than as a prosopopoeia for those who speak. The speakers, animated by Frost's voice, share only ventriloquistically in his being, as if to objectify the profound limitations of speech and language to communicate the self. They are, in effect, personifications as surely as the birds are personifications: thus the constantly shifting line between actual bird speakers (as in "The Oven Bird"), the "speaker as bird" metaphor (as in "The Lockless Door"), and the bird as symbol or correlative for the speaker (as in "Our Singing Strength" or "The Thatch" or "A Minor Bird"). Words turn men into birds—myna birds and parrots whose language is inextricably tied more to the literary past than to the lyric self—and birds into men, indiscriminately. The birds thus come to represent the rejection of traditional lyricism, begun consciously for Frost after *A Boy's Will*, as a mode that, traditionally employed, was appropriate to his poetic purposes. The Frostian overtone is wily, evasive, always potentially ironic and thus subversive of "meaning" as it resides linguistically. Only his speakers tend toward earnestness, toward the kind of articulated stolidity that one comes to perceive in the birds. As embodiments of a literary tradition (only by knowing other songs by other birds may the Oven Bird know how to frame its own unlyrical song), they are locked into thesis or antithesis, either transcendence or the denial of transcendence.

This disjunction between speaker and poet might suggest that Frost consciously obfuscates a known condition or, alternatively, that he seeks to expose an unknown and essentially unnamable condition in the nexus between two projections of self; in either case the poem uses language against itself in the service of some unarticulated state whose only encasement is the

Katherine Kearns

larger formal structure of the poem. After all, the movement from delight—pleasure, desire, *aphrodisia*—to wisdom—rationality, knowledge, *logos*—must be a careful progress between two seemingly antithetical states. The good Greek may in theory rise above desire so that wisdom *is* delight, thus becoming free to act and to rule, but in a more visceral reality the play of appetite against virile moderation produces an essentially unnamable condition of potentiality. The recurrent image of black over white throughout Frost's poetry is suggestive of the linguistic borderland in which this condition resides, for if one sees the "black branches up a snow-white trunk" as ink on paper, the full poetic meaning nonetheless resides in the calligramic cage formed in the meeting of opposites. The word does not take precedence over the background but gains its full significance only in juxtaposition. The image of the nighttime snowfield becomes endlessly evocative, as its substance resides as much in the animals buried by the sheet of snow and in the overlay of night upon it as in the snow itself. Frost's calligram of resilient prosodic bars is constructed to contain such burgeoning language, even as the cell poles may be twanged "like bow and bowstring" by the love-crazed madman. But the subversion of form and meaning are interdependent, a dynamic that can be neither completely contained nor halted.[29]

If Frost's personas are the speaking masks of one aspect of his being, his formal control is just such another mask, more stylized perhaps, but designed as well to encase the shadow self—the "real" self—in a disguise that may be seen. He would, in fact, give the oversound priority over the literally stated message available even to eye readers, so that a combination of discrete particles, not language but sound, an abstraction of "meaning," takes precedence. By handling the symbol of lyricism—the bird—over to the speakers whose assertions make up only half of the story, he approximates a modernist skepticism about the possibility and even about the value of locating oneself relative to others: the traditional lyric voice is inadequate to the task of communicating that self which is generated perpetually out of the ashes of quelled desire. Not the Oven Bird so much as the phoenix, he is like the figure in "The Bonfire" who kneels to reach into flame and then rises up out of the charred field, most potently defined at the instant of transfiguration.[30] The orgasmic moment epitomizes that most essentially oxymoronic condition, an epiphany of desire quelled, like the simultaneous victory and defeat of the man who rubs out the fire. The metaphor for lyricism is thus revealed as a completely artificial construct, a mere pretense of self-revelation as it is used to refer explicitly to a series of personas that are at best partial versions of the poet.

Frost seems to approach, in this disjunction between form and content, what Clement Greenberg defines as modernism: "The essence of modernism lies ... in the use of the characteristic methods of a discipline to criticize the discipline itself, not in order to subvert it, but in order to entrench it more firmly in its area of competence."[31] By objectifying it, Frost "criticizes" the lyric voice, a very core of poetry, while in doing so he reinforces what he perceives to be poetry's area of competence, its formal control of language, as a means of conveying a more genuine poetic truth. Greenberg would have us consider a Monet water lily: at one level it does indeed look like a water lily, but critics point to Monet's preoccupation with the "possibilities of reflection, light, color, brushwork, texture, pictorial structure, and format" as leading to the "apparent dissociation of colour and brushwork from object." What is said of Monet could almost be said of Frost: "Nature, prodded by an eye obsessed with the most naive kind of exactness, responded in the end with textures of color that could be managed on canvas only by involving the autonomous laws of the medium—which is to say that Nature became the springboard for an almost abstract art."[32] Frost asserts that the assimilation of rational meaning into sentence sounds that may reverse or alter the apparent sense ("it may even as in irony convey a meaning opposite to the words")[33] is crucial to his poetic intent. The sentence sound is itself an entity from which words may be suspended, the entirety becoming a version of truth independent of the particular word or phrase. He calls the sound of sense "the abstract vitality of our speech. It is pure sound—pure form. One who concerns himself with it more than the subject is the artist" (*Letters* 79–81). His speakers, while detailed with what might be called "the most naive kind of exactness," are not drawn for their intrinsic value, for what they themselves have to say. They become instead like the lilies, the medium through which formal elements may be elaborated; their "lyric" selves are of less value finally than the possibilities of "reflection, light, color, ... texture, pictorial structure, and format" they afford.

Lyotard defines modernism thus: "I shall call modern the art which devotes its 'little technical expertise' ... as Diderot used to say, to present the fact that the unpresentable exists. To make visible that there is something which can be conceived and which can neither be seen nor made visible."[34] Naming Frost's ambivalence about language "modernism" is one way of articulating his preoccupation with the unsaid or the unsayable, of giving, perhaps arbitrarily, a context and form to the shadow shape residing between the "speaker" and the self. It has the value, however, of suggesting, at least analogously, the distancing effects of Frost's use of dissonances within the poetry; there is an essential abstraction, a breaking of the self into planes—

of language, of prosody, of natural correlatives. Monet's paint on a canvas, Frost's black ink on white paper: in both there is a surface—laid across the lilies and across the words—that reflects what is finally a nonrepresentational; extralinguistic version of self. This perhaps is the glimmer of white beneath the narcissistic pool in "For Once, Then, Something," or it could be what Frost's women see when they look out of windows, or it could be what that stranger who wanders through the poetry knows; it is, in any event, what cannot be simply said or simply heard.

One might say in more poetic terms that Frost is entranced by the elegant paradox of the Fall, when the birds gained at once knowledge and guilt by listening all day to Eve's voice. Spoken by a woman, the words will be by definition both corrupt and arousing. Perhaps, in fact, this is the most fundamental meaning in Eve's having been the first to fill her mouth with forbidden knowledge, for it must take an intrinsically compromised creature to bring about the compromise God had in mind when he set her up for the Fall. This is the original model by which it becomes possible not only to recognize meaning but also to understand its vulnerability: to see in the very articulation of one's "knowing" its fundamentally illusory, misleading quality, its quotient of contamination. In the very beginning things could be truly named but not explained, and afterward, when it became possible to speak untruth, their names became mere disguises, at best metaphors for their variable identities. This discrepancy is, after all, what allows for and necessitates poetry, this inexorably dying generation of language. Yet the loss of innocence makes it possible to name desire—by eating the apple Adam and Eve discover appetite—and to see it as oppositional to reason.

Energized by conflict, the poet may nonetheless give way to nostalgia for a more holistic view. Frost, in the very early poem "In a Vale," from *A Boy's Will*, creates a vision of a place where language and desire are close to being the same, but it is, by implication, only the tenuous receptivity of boyhood that allows the speaker to hear and value the feminine, prerational voices.

> When I was young, we dwelt in a vale
>   By a misty fen that rang all night,
> And thus it was the maidens pale
>   I knew so well, whose garments trail
> Across the reeds to a window light.

This poem reveals an alternative vision to a world reflective of the masculine heautocratic struggle. It is an ephebian vision, predictive of the necessary limiting of sightedness in manhood and evocative of a childlike receptivity. Almost pre-fallen, this vale is a territory outside the opaque, snowbound world of silence where self is obliterated into blank whiteness and outside the world of unbridled appetite. Here the landscape is dominated by yielding mist—a veil in a vale, a tissue of air, light, and moisture. From the mist nymphs come to the speaker's windowsill. The pale maidens are flowers come to life:

> The fen had every kind of bloom,
>   And for every kind there was a face,
> And a voice that has sounded in my room
> Across the sill from the outer gloom.
>   Each came singly unto her place.

While the speaker remains in his room, he leaves his ground-floor window open, and he comes to know the maidens intimately through their nightly visitations. Personifications of femininity and of nature, born of the mist and blossoming out of the boggy earth, these maidens reveal their secrets:

> But all came every night with the mist;
>   And often they brought so much to say
> Of things of moment to which, they wist,
> One so lonely was fain to list,
>   That the stars were almost faded away

> Before the last went, heavy with dew,
>   Back to the place from which she came—
> Where the bird was before it flew,
> Where the flower was before it grew,
>   Where bird and flower were one and the same.

Unlike the speakers who direct their eyes into the dark sky, this boy is riveted to the flower nymphs while the stars fade into morning. They tell him "things of moment" to which he listens because he is lonely and young. Flowers heavy with dew, they embody a lovely sexuality, but like the man's vision in "The Generations of Men" of the girl with flowers in her lap who cannot cross the sill, they may only touch him with their voices.

These nymphs reveal the earth's natal secrets: they know of a time and place "Where bird and flower were one and the same." In this place, unlike that in which one sings in "A Line-Storm Song," the bird songs do not have to be "crushed like some wild / Easily shattered rose" so that the goldenrod may prevail: the petaled interiority of the rose—the vulnerable lyricism of the birds—does not have to be shattered by the wind and rain, which is here transformed to mist. The nymphs are incarnations of water, flowers, and birds, their trailing garments, the clinging mist, and their voices becoming petals, bird song, and the odor of flowers all intertwined. They teach the young speaker lessons that, in Frost's later poetry, are obscured by the Oven Bird's insistence that one must know "in singing not to sing," must know that the pure, undisguised lyric voice has nothing to say in a fallen, diminished world:

> And thus it is I know so well
> Why the flower has odor, the bird has song.
> You have only to ask me, and I can tell.
> No, not vainly there did I dwell,
> Nor vainly listen all the night long.

This speaker, young and receptive, predicts the duality of Frost's later speakers who can only hear human woe in birds' voices and who can use flowers only as metaphors for something else. Perceived even here as knowledge natural only to females, the maiden's secrets are yet gladly heard through a window left open to receive them. Unlike Frost's human women, who look out of windows and seek to escape, these nymphs come freely each night to salve the speaker's loneliness, and unlike the men who, like the husband of "Home Burial," "think the talk is all," this speaker is still receptive and can hear them. These voices, projections of a "female" self whose knowledge is not rational because it prefigures cause and effect, are benign and lovely. They are like the beautiful Lady North Wind of Frost's favorite childhood book, *At the Back of the North Wind*, as they teach him mysteries. And he, the poet-speaker, is the translator who puts mystery into words. He senses at once both an innocent locus of nonwords, where maidens embody flowers, dew, birds, mist, and darkness because they come from a place that is prenatal, and the erotic (fallen, guilt- and ecstasy-producing) world of names, where the ineffable emanates from the flowers called as odor and from the birds called as song.

The maidens of "In a Vale" are like the nymph in "Paul's Wife," who, delivered from her tree as a length of dry pith, rises from the water, her hair a wet helmet, and walks into the woods with Paul, enraptured, following. She goes out like a firefly when she is seen by other men, vaporized by perceptions that extinguish her unnamable state. Paul is left to be driven from place to place every time someone asks "How's the wife," because "to praise or so much as name her" is to defile her. In this later world the nymphs of "In a Vale" cannot exist, because they, like Paul's wife, cannot be spoken of "In any way the world [knows] how to speak." Frost chooses most frequently to name both the human and the poetic condition as fallen, his ironic vision epitomized in the lyric birds whose voices whimper, whisper, or shout their rational conviction that the world is a diminished, dusty place. The dewy maidens of "In a Vale" are replaced with women fleeing, like the wife of "Home Burial" for whom the husband's "words are nearly always an offense" because he doesn't "know how to speak of anything / So as to please [her]." Even the wind broadcasts the language of separation, isolation, lovelessness: "Word I was in the house alone ... Word I was in my life alone ... Word I had no one left but God," wails the speaker of "Bereft." But Frost hears other voices even when his speakers have become parrot-like in their endorsement of the diminished view. In the damp, low-lying vale where "bird and flower were one and the same" the lyric bird would know more sensual songs than the Oven Bird's. These maidens' "garments / Trail across the reeds ..." like the silken tent raised by the pole. Yet this is not an accessible world, even to the boy, who must speak only across a sill. He listens all night, every night, but he never joins them in the "misty fen," never penetrates their territory. For once naming occurs, only the scent of wholeness remains. But language, erotic, defiled, and irresistible, has the power to awaken in Frost the ambivalence of one who has known mystical voices that are, whether perceived as literal or as metaphorical, the echoes of another world beyond the rational and beyond language.

NOTES

1. Frank Lentricchia, "Lyric in the Culture of Capitalism," *American Literary History* 1, no. 1 (1989): 72. See too Richard Poirier, *Robert Frost: The Work of Knowing* (New York: Oxford Univ. Press, 1977), 38. Palgrave's *Golden Treasury* was a favorite of Frost's; see "Waiting: A field at Dusk" in *A Boy's Will*, where the speaker notes "the old worn book of old-golden song / I brought here not to read, it seems, but hold / And freshen in this air of withering sweetness."

2. Lesley Lee Francis, "A Decade of 'Stirring Times': Robert Frost and Amy Lowell," *New England Quarterly* 59, no. 4 (December 1986): 522. See too Sydney Lea, "From Sublime to Rigamorole: Relations of Frost to Wordsworth," in *Robert Frost*, ed. Harold Bloom (New York: Chelsea House, 1986), 85–110, for a discussion of Frost's ambivalent regard for Wordsworth and his resistance to "Romanticism."

3. Lawrance Thompson, *Robert Frost: The Later Years* (New York: Holt, Rinehart & Winston, 1976), 304, documents that Frost wrote this for "the woman who had been his 'devoted secretary' for more than twenty years." See Donald G. Sheehy, "(Re)Figuring

Love: Robert Frost in Crisis, 1938–42,"5 *New England Quarterly* 63, no. 2 (June 1990): 179–231, on Frost's relationship with Kathleen Morrison after the death of Elinor in 1938. A stately Elizabethan sonnet and a love poem, it also suggests a premeditated and predetermined fall from pure song to song crossed with language: "Never again would birds' song be the same. / And to do that to birds was why she came."

4. In the *Phaedo*, 85, a–b, Socrates affirms that birds do not sing when they are hungry, cold, or distressed. When swans sing before their deaths, it is because they "have prophetic powers and ... because they know the good things that await them in the unseen world, and they are happier on that day than they have ever been before."

5. See Lawrance Thompson, *Robert Frost: The Early Years, 1876–1915* (New York: Holt, Rinehart & Winston, 1966), 304: Maeterlinck's *The Blue Bird* was read to Frost by his father; Frost calls this poem "The Blue Bird to Leslie" in *Letters*, 355.

6. See Michel Foucault, *The Use of Pleasure: The History of Sexuality*, vol. 2, trans. Robert Hurley (New York: Pantheon, 1985), 82–3. While Frost claims that a poem never begins in thought but "as a lump in the throat, a sense of wrong, a homesickness, a lovesickness" (*Letters*, 199), he also holds firmly that enthusiasm must be "taken through the prism of the intellect" (*Prose*, 36). This is to subvert what he calls "sunset raving," where "It is oh's and ah's with you and no more." Lentricchia, in "The Resentments of Robert Frost," *American Literature* 62, no. 2 (June 1990): 176–7, locates Frost's contempt for "sunset raving" lyricism, which derives its energy from pretty things, in his shared contempt for what Eliot called "the Feminine in literature."

7. See too the poem immediately preceding this, "Wind and Window Flower," in which the wind is a potential lover of the flower just inside the frozen pane of glass.

8. In "A Servant to Servants" the woman is drawn to look at the lake, "Like a deep piece of some old running river / Cut short off at both ends," as the wind whips "the slow waves whiter and whiter and whiter"; this is clearly a correlative for her imminent and immanent anger/madness.

9. Thompson, *The Early Years*, 301.

10. Plato, *Symposium*, in *The Collected Dialogues*, ed. Edith Hamilton and Huntington Cairns (Princeton, N.J.: Princeton Univ. Press, 1989), 561.

11. One is drawn to think of all of the poems in which Frost pictures figures brought to the classic posture of supplication, as they find themselves in kneeling or bowing positions before a retributive or indifferent power, positions the prostrate figures themselves usually detail: "The Subverted Flower," "On Going Unnoticed," "To Earthward," "Putting in the Seed," "The Bonfire," among others, place men in positions of self-abasement, about which they speak. The dynamic in "Birches" is resonant, as it uses the erotic image of the girl on hands and knees to balance against the taut, downward-arching saplings ridden by the boy into submission.

12. In "The Thatch," the speaker, outside after a quarrel with someone upstairs (by implication, in the bedroom), finds "The world was a black invisible field. / The rain by rights was snow for cold. / The wind was another layer of mold." Once the house is abandoned, its "wind-torn thatch" lets in the rain and ends the life of the house. This living thatched house with its angry woman upstairs acts as a metonym for the speaker, who himself is windy-headed with anger. The birds living in the thatch are displaced by his sudden presence outdoors at night, and their fall into "mulch and mire," their inability to rise out of it until daylight comes and flying is "safe," is also indicative of the speaker's lyric impotence.

13. Thompson, *The Later Years*, 268.

14. An ungenerous reading of Frost's invariable undercutting of his speakers would tie in with his preoccupation with "the middle," both spatially and intellectually. Economically, he wishes to be received as a popular poet read and bought by thousands and thousands, but he achieves this at some cost (see Lentricchia, "Lyric," 63–88). See too Earl J. Wilcox, "Psyching-Out the Public and His Contemporaries: The Curious Case of Robert Frost," *McNeese Review* 31 (1984–6): 3–13. Wilcox argues that Frost is an example of what Dwight MacDonald called "Masscult": "The technicians of masscult at once degrade the public by treating it as an object ... and at the same time flatter it and pander to its taste and ideas by taking them as the criterion for reality." The public, says MacDonald, "demands a secret rebate; he must play the game—their game—..." Seen in this context, these compromised speakers of Frost's, who are so often inescapably Frost at the same time that they are not Frost, may be seen as the inevitable result of such self-abuse.

15. Poirier, *The Work of Knowing*, 86.

16. See Arthur Schopenhauer, *The World as Will and Idea*, trans. R.B. Haldane and J. Kemp (New York: Dolphin, 1961), 268–79, on music as, rather than a copy of Ideas, a copy of the will itself. See too Robert P. Morgan, "Secret Languages: The Roots of Musical Modernism," *Critical Inquiry* 10 (March 1984): 442–61, as he locates these ideas about music, articulated in philosophical terms by Schopenhauer but also widely shared in the nineteenth century, relative to painting and poetry.

17. See Lentricchia, "Resentments," for evidence of this perception of lyric as too "feminine."

18. Julia Kristeva, *Tales of Love*, trans. Leon S. Roudiez (New York: Columbia Univ. Press, 1983), 8.

19. Ibid., 8.

20. "A Masque of Reason," ll. 222–5: "Society can never think things out; / It has to see them acted out by actors, / Devoted actors at a sacrifice— / The ablest actors I can lay my hands on."

21. See Foucault, *The Use of Pleasure*, 89–91.

22. Poirier, *The Work of Knowing*, 191–2.

23. D.C. Muecke, *Irony and the Ironic* (New York: Methuen, 1970), 31.

24. Jean-François Lyotard, *The Postmodern Condition*, trans. Brian Massumi and Geoff Bennington (Minneapolis: Univ. of Minnesota Press, 1988), 22.

25. Ibid., xii.

26. See Frost on "The Lockless Door," in *Letters*, 468.

27. See Lyotard, *The Postmodern Condition*, 40, on Wittgenstein's use of the metaphor of language as "an ancient city" and his application of the paradox "How many houses or streets does it take before a town begins to be a town?" See too Frost's "Directive."

28. Maynard Mack, *The Garden and the City: Retirement and Politics in the Later Poetry of Pope, 1731–1743* (Toronto: Univ. of Toronto Press, 1969), locates Pope in a landscape of conscious artificiality, one that Romanticism would utterly displace. Yet Frost does not completely abandon markers of civilization: the "garden" is always at an advanced stage of deconstruction.

29. See Michel Foucault, *This Is Not a Pipe*, trans. James Harkness (Berkeley and Los Angeles: Univ. of California Press, 1982), 21, on the double subversion of the calligram.

30. See Norman N. Holland, "The Brain of Robert Frost," *New Literary History* 15,

no. 2 (Winter 1984): 365–85, on the identifiable sameness—the "Frostness"—of his poetic and his interpretive voices; Holland sees this continuity as Frost's identity, which is characterized by a system of inclusive dualism.

31. Lillian S. Robinson and Lise Vogel, "Modernism and History," *New Literary History* 3, no. 1 (Autumn 1971): 177.

32. Ibid., 191.

33. Thompson, *The Early Years*, 435. See too Robert Kern, "Frost and Modernism," in *On Frost: The Best from American Literature*, ed. Edwin H. Cady and Louis J. Budd (Durham, N.C.: Duke Univ. Press, 1990): 191–206.

34. Lyotard, *The Postmodern Condition*, 78.

T.S. Eliot and Hart Crane

The poems were not epicurean; still, they were innocent of public-spiritedness: they sang of private disgust and diffidence, and of people who seemed genuine because they were unattractive or weak. The author was irritated by tea parties, and not afraid to say so, with the result that his occasional "might-have-beens" rang out with the precision of a gong.... Here was a protest, and a feeble one, and the more congenial for being feeble. For what, in that world of gigantic horror, was tolerable except the slighter gestures of dissent?
—E.M. Forster on reading T.S. Eliot in 1917

By 1940 T.S. Eliot had emerged as the representative English poet of modernism. This was one of those transitions that feel natural after they have happened—that can seem to settle a reputation once and for all with a finality mysterious to readers who witnessed the struggle for fame. Of such a moment it is always fair to ask how far the climax it affords is a trick of retrospect, a shadow we mistake for a necessary part of the landscape. What if Eliot's assimilation had occurred much faster? What if it had occurred more slowly, or on a more idiosyncratic basis? Eliot's letters and occasional criticism are sown with doubt and wonder at the definitive quality of his triumph. The way a few of his poems joined with a few of his polemical essays to secure a unique place for his poetic achievement is one of those

From *Skeptical Music: Essays on Modern Poetry.* © 2001 by David Bromwich.

inspired accidents that history casts up from time to time to challenge our determinisms. Of course, this was the outcome Eliot desired all along. But the readers who first cared for his poetry must have seen the possibility of a different development.

Suppose that his poetry had been spurned in every quarter of the literary establishment for a decade or two after *The Waste Land.* What then? Eventually he might have found a place among the unassimilables, the recessive geniuses of English poetry—the company of Collins and Beddoes rather than Donne and Dryden. There would have been much justice in this. The author of *Prufrock and Other Observations* was felt by his contemporaries to be an elusive and not an imposing presence. His charm lay most of all in the relief he offered from importance. Nor did *The Waste Land* seem at first a drastic departure from the earlier sources of his appeal. It commanded respect as an experiment with voices, like "Prufrock" and the Sweeney poems. To think of it in that light may still be more pertinent than to honor it teleologically for the qualities it shares with *Ash Wednesday* and *Four Quartets.* The passing characters of the poem—Mrs. Porter, Mr. Eugenides, the Young Man Carbuncular—these figures were hardly notable for their continuous gravity. They were phantoms of a mind delicately questing after sensations, and their aim was "a new art emotion," to adapt a phrase from Eliot's criticism. Their creator appeared to be a poet averse to no stimulus, however morbid—a cautious welcomer of any experience, however drab— whose peculiarities of temperament had much to do with the dignity of his art.

Some of Eliot's essays of the period lend themselves to a similar description. "Hamlet and His Problems," now commonly read as a manifesto for dramatic objectivity, was a paradox in the vein of *The Authoress of the Odyssey,* a fit of character criticism against the character critics. Eliot's bogus primerlike title (which could be added to the books on the shelf in Beerbohm's caricature of Yeats: *Short Cuts to Mysticism, Half Hours with the Symbols, Reality: Its Cause and Cure, Hamlet and His Problems*) mocked the orderliness of his clinical tone. Even "Tradition and the Individual Talent," to a reader who weighed the chemical analogy in the second part as carefully as the axioms of culture in the first, could seem a late flower of the dandyism of Poe. These essays were, among other things, deliberate curiosities, out-of-the-way solutions to problems the reader was meant to see as in no way impersonal. The solemn reception of Eliot's criticism in the next generation, as if it had been written by a more judicious Matthew Arnold, enhanced his stature in the short run only, and on dubious terms.

I have been trying to convey the susceptible mood in which the young

Hart Crane would have approached the poetry of Eliot. But the obstacles to an adequate view of the subject have been planted by Crane as much as by Eliot. Open and impulsive as Crane's letters generally are, they give a misleading impression of this particular debt. His quotable statements of general aims and theories, which align his poetry with Eliot's, tend to take an adversarial stance when Eliot himself is in the picture. This happened, I think, in part because Crane had resolved early to write *The Bridge* as an answer to *The Waste Land.* Another motive may have been that his frequent correspondent in matters concerning Eliot was Allen Tate, a contemporary who shared Crane's advocacy of Eliot's poems but who was already, in their exchanges of letters in the 1920s, on the way to admiring Eliot as a prophet of civilization. The influence of "Gerontion" on the "Ode to the Confederate Dead" differs in character from the influence of *The Waste Land* on *The Bridge.* In the first case the relation is that of principle and illustration, in the second that of statement and counterstatement. Affinity seems a truer word than influence to describe the latter sort of kinship—a point I can bring out by comparing the early poems "La Figlia che Piange" and "My Grandmother's Love Letters."

Both poems address a feminine presence that is not quite maternal, and that is touched by erotic warmth; a presence whose memory must be appeased before the poet can venture into his own acts of love and imagination. Yet the poems exhibit, and exemplify for the sake of each poet's future, distinct uses of sympathy. Eliot's is a tenderness that will at last be detached from erotic passion, whereas Crane is seeking a temporary freedom from familial piety, earned by an intense avowal of such piety. Notwithstanding this divergence of motives, the poems share a single story and a music. The wish of the poets to serve as guardians at a scene of their former lives, protectors of something that was suffered there, is curiously blended with a self-command that makes them stand back from the scene. The result is a tone at the brink of an irony that neither poet entirely wants to formulate. The revealing point for comparison, it seems to me, is the "turn" of the poems—the place in each where the poet speaks of his seclusion from the image with which he began. In "La Figlia che Piange" that image is the glimpsed attitude of a woman at the top of a stair, holding a bunch of flowers; in "My Grandmother's Love Letters," it is a view of a nook by the corner of the roof where the letters have long been stored. Self-conscious in their bearing toward the women they write about, both poets are also safely hidden in their watching; and a sense of memory as a sheltering medium, protective for the rememberer and the image, touches with regret their knowledge of the person whose life cannot be recovered.

From this fortunate position—a voyeur but one not in search of a voyeur's pleasure—Eliot imagines a meeting with a possible consummation between the woman and a man. (The man, we are free to imagine, is the speaker himself in a different life.)

> So I would have had him leave,
> So I would have had her stand and grieve,
> So he would have left
> As the soul leaves the body torn and bruised,
> As the mind deserts the body it has used.
> I should find
> Some way incomparably light and deft,
> Some way we both should understand,
> Simple and faithless as a smile and shake of the hand.
>
> She turned away, but with the autumn weather
> Compelled my imagination many days,
> Many days and many hours:
> Her hair over her arms and her arms full of flowers.
> And I wonder how they should have been together!
> I should have lost a gesture and a pose.
> Sometimes these cogitations still amaze
> The troubled midnight and the noon's repose.

The compromised interest of the observer has much in common with the attitude of a Jamesian narrator, though even by the terms of that analogy the speaker of "La Figlia che Piange" is evasive—calling his anxiety and bewilderment "cogitations" and his shadowy desire a concern with "a gesture and a pose." He is troubled most by an intimation that the woman is morally innocent, as he somehow is not. And yet her life will be filled to a depth of experience he does not hope to share.

A larger impulse of ordinary sympathy is at work in Crane's poem. He tries—one can feel the pressure of the effort—to associate his fancies with the actual life of the woman he writes about. Yet as his ingenuity stretches to cover the distance between them, the questions his poem asks take on a careful obliqueness like Eliot's. The love that his grandmother felt seems now so far off that, if he should cross the house to retrieve her letters, each step would feel like a passage of countless years:

> Over the greatness of such space
> Steps must be gentle.

It is all hung by an invisible white hair.
It trembles as birch limbs webbing the air.

And I ask myself:

"Are your fingers long enough to play
Old keys that are but echoes:
Is the silence strong enough
To carry back the music to its source
And back to you again
As though to her?"

Yet I would lead my grandmother by the hand
Through much of what she would not understand;
And so I stumble. And the rain continues on the roof
With such a sound of gently pitying laughter.

I would, the phrase that governs the last several stanzas of Eliot's poem, is displaced by Crane to the last four lines; the entire closing montage of "La Figlia che Piange," with its surprising sudden exterior (a scene of both pathos and indifference), has been miraculously condensed. Crane has the same need to find "Some way incomparably light and deft, / Some way we both should understand" to connect person with person and present with past. Hence the difficult question he asks himself: whether he is strong enough "To carry back the music to its source / And back to you again / As though to her?" The phenomenal life of the world, which continues untroubled as before, at the ends of both of these poems may be a sign that the connection has not been achieved.

"La Figlia che Piange" and "My Grandmother's Love Letters" are linked more subtly by a seasonal counterpoint, Eliot's poem starting in spring and passing into autumn, Crane's set in an autumn that looks back on someone else's spring. There are resonances too between the sunlit and moonlit spaces in which the poems create their distinctive moods of stillness. And (the detail that feels most like conscious allusion) the separate line of "My Grandmother's Love Letters,"

It is all hung by an invisible white hair

recalls a line repeated in Eliot's opening stanza,

David Bromwich

Weave, weave the sunlight in your hair

and never returned to in the later stanzas, the weight of which nevertheless carries implicitly through the rest of Eliot's poem. The closing notes of the poems differ perhaps by a nuance of decisiveness. Eliot ends with the amazement or bemusement that was for him at this period a familiar and almost a reassuring motif: one hears it in nearly the same key at the end of the monologue "Portrait of a Lady." By contrast, the sympathy Crane had begun with deepens, as he turns from this memory to other memories.

The sense that is rich in "My Grandmother's Love Letters," of a pity that touches the poet unaccountably from a slight but charged detail of the setting, has its own precedent elsewhere in Eliot. The penultimate stanza of "Preludes" confesses:

> I am moved by fancies that are curled
> Around these images, and cling:
> The notion of some infinitely gentle
> Infinitely suffering thing.

Three further lines close "Preludes" in a vein of average irony—"Wipe your hand across your mouth, and laugh"—but "My Grandmother's Love Letters" includes the fancies as if they would do without a retraction.

"Preludes" is the poem by Eliot that seems most steadily resonant in Crane's early work. Comprising discrete impressions of a city—several perspectives, offered by a "consciousness" or "conscience" not easily distinguishable into a single person—this poem's montage tries out the shifts of tense and mood that will be more gravely performed in *The Waste Land*. It covers a matter-of-fact range, not the intensities of Tiresias, without a claim of supervening authority and without the cues of false or true guidance which would come later, with the demand of Eliot's poetry that it be read as prophetic speech.

For Crane I think the appeal of "Preludes" lay in its intuition of the city's unemphatic routine as an incitement to the poet.

> The morning comes to consciousness
> Of faint stale smells of beer
> From the sawdust-trampled street
> With all its muddy feet that press
> To early coffee-stands.
> With the other masquerades

> That time resumes,
> One thinks of all the hands
> That are raising dingy shades
> In a thousand furnished rooms.

This landscape was often in Hart Crane's mind when he wrote his shorter poems of the 1920s; hints of it appear as late as the subway entry sequence of "The Tunnel." He remembered the same passage in a sort of private joke in a letter: arrested drunk one night in 1927, "the next I knew the door crashed shut and I found myself behind the bars. I imitated Chaliapin fairly well until dawn leaked in, or rather such limited evidences of same as six o'clock whistles and the postulated press of dirty feet to early coffee stands." The casual echoes have a wider meaning. The most difficult task of Crane's poetry, as he comes close to saying elsewhere in his letters, is to connect the thought of an "infinitely gentle, infinitely suffering thing" with some surmise about the emotions proper toward the hands in those "thousand furnished rooms."

His first full response was "Chaplinesque":

> We make our meek adjustments,
> Contented with such random consolations
> As the wind deposits
> In slithered and too ample pockets.

> For we can still love the world, who find
> A famished kitten on the step, and know
> Recesses for it from the fury of the street,
> Or warm torn elbow coverts.

> We will sidestep, and to the final smirk
> Dally the doom of that inevitable thumb
> That slowly chafes its puckered index toward us,
> Facing the dull squint with what innocence
> And what surprise!

> And yet these fine collapses are not lies
> More than the pirouettes of any pliant cane;
> Our obsequies are, in a way, no enterprise.
> We can evade you, and all else but the heart:
> What blame to us if the heart live on.

The game enforces smirks; but we have seen
The moon in lonely alleys make
A grail of laughter of an empty ash can,
And through all sound of gaiety and quest
Have heard a kitten in the wilderness.

The poem answers directly with the poet's voice an experience "Preludes" reported as occurring once to someone, the experience that brought "Such a vision of the street / As the street hardly understands."

The "smirk" can seem a mystifying detail even to a reader who feels its rightness. It suggests the improbability of human contact in the city's crowds, where the "squint" looking for the main chance blots out every other concern. The tone is a good deal like "Wipe your hand across your mouth, and laugh"; and maybe for a moment this poem is testing a similar note of scorn. Then the gesture is looked at differently: "The game enforces smirks; but we have seen / The moon in lonely alleys make / A grail of laughter." The game may be the one Walt Whitman spoke of in *Song of Myself*, "Looking with side-curved head curious what will come next, / Both in and out of the game, and watching and wondering at it." Crane's mood suggests something of this poise and inquisitiveness. The kitten, a child of the city, has wandered in from outside the game, a chance embodiment of the "suffering thing." To keep it safe from the fury of the street is a charity worthy of Chaplin's tramp.

The modern artist exists to invent a shelter for the most vagrant sympathies. Crane said so in the letter to William Wright in which he also declared his interest in Chaplin:

> I am moved to put Chaplin with the poets (of today); hence the "we." In other words, he, especially in "The Kid," made me feel myself, as a poet, as being "in the same boat" with him. Poetry, the human feelings, "the kitten," is so crowded out of the humdrum, rushing, mechanical scramble of today that the man who would preserve them must duck and camouflage for dear life to keep them or keep himself from annihilation.... I have tried to express these "social sympathies" in words corresponding somewhat to the antics of the actor.

This summary brings to light the active impulse Crane speaks of missing in Eliot. But one must resist the temptation to suppose that either poet was aiming for effects the other accomplished. I doubt that Eliot, given the diffusive emotions that matter to him, would have thought of offering a setting to such lines as

> Recesses for it from the fury of the street

or

> And through all sound of gaiety and quest,

lines that are touchstones of the confidence and isolation of the man who wrote them. A certain striding eloquence seems natural to Crane, and fits with the truth he speaks to the antagonist of "Chaplinesque" (the boss or agent of the state, the character in Chaplin's films who sizes up the tramp with a lowering grimace): "We can evade you, and all else but the heart: / What blame to us if the heart live on." It is the reverse of Eliot's sentiment at the end of "Preludes": "The worlds revolve like ancient women / Gathering fuel in vacant lots." The steps of the women may look random as they cast about for bits of fuel, but a capricious determinism governs their smallest movement. At times the steps of the tramp will look no different. But "Chaplinesque" takes its buoyancy from a resolve—the mood of someone going somewhere—which the tramp asserts at irregular intervals. The forward motion is an illusion, but one that Crane brings to enchanted reality by siding with this hero.

My comments on Eliot and Crane are shaped by an aesthetic judgment as personal as any other. *Prufrock and Other Observations* and *White Buildings* seem to me among the greatest achievements of modernity, quite as original in what they accomplish as *The Waste Land* and *The Bridge*. One of the cheats of high modernist theory, abetted by Eliot in *"Ulysses,* Order, and Myth" and embraced by Crane in the conception of his longer poems, was the supposition that the virtual order of human knowledge must stand in some interesting relation to literary form. It followed that one could make the modern world systematically intelligible for art by respecting and executing the proper form of a knowledge special to art—by viewing the novel, for example, as the genre of the "transcendent homelessness of the idea" (the phrase is Lukács's, from *The Theory of the Novel*). With modernism, genre itself briefly and misleadingly became, as it had been in the eighteenth century, a master clue to the earnestness of the author's claim to represent reality. To writers like Eliot and Crane, this suggested the tactical propriety of expanding the lyric to claim again the scope of the epic. Of the pretensions of modernist poetry, none has dated so badly as this.

The Waste Land and *The Bridge* were not assisted imaginatively by the encyclopedic ambition to which they owe their conspicuous effects of structure. The miscellaneous texture of the poems is truer to their motives. A little more consistently than Eliot's early poems, *The Waste Land* divides into two separate registers for the portrayal of the city, the first reductive and satirical, the second ecstatic and agonistic—the latter, in order to be released, often seeming to require the pressure of a quotation. At any moment a detail such as "The sound of horns and motors, which shall bring / Sweeney to Mrs. Porter in the spring" may modulate to a style less easily placed:

> O City city, I can sometimes hear
> Beside a public bar in Lower Thames Street,
> The pleasant whining of a mandoline
> And a clatter and a chatter from within
> Where fishmen lounge at noon: where the walls
> Of Magnus Martyr hold
> Inexplicable splendour of Ionian white and gold.

Though the transitions of *The Bridge* are less clear-cut, part of Crane's method lies in a pattern of allusions to *The Waste Land*. This plan had emerged as early as his letter of September 11, 1927, to Otto H. Kahn, and later, piece by piece, in the echoes he found of Phlebas the Phoenician, who "Forgot the cry of gulls, and the deep sea swell / And the profit and loss"— lines that haunted him already in "For the Marriage of Faustus and Helen."

Let us turn to a kind of allusion more precisely dependent on context. Eliot in *The Waste Land*, himself looking back to Shakespeare's *Tempest*, overhears a character in "The Fire Sermon" in an unexplained trance of thought.

> While I was fishing in the dull canal
> On a winter evening round behind the gashouse
> Musing upon the king my brother's wreck
> And on the king my father's death before him....

Pondering those lines in "The River," Crane added to the Old World image of destiny the local accretions of a childhood in the American Midwest. The effect is a startling recovery and transformation:

>   Behind
> My father's cannery works I used to see

Rail-squatters ranged in nomad raillery,
The ancient men—wifeless or runaway
Hobo-trekkers that forever search
An empire wilderness of freight and rails.
Each seemed a child, like me, on a loose perch,
Holding to childhood like some termless play.
John, Jake or Charley, hopping the slow freight
—Memphis to Tallahassee—riding the rods,
Blind fists of nothing, humpty-dumpty clods.

The allegory of both poets tells of a child set loose from his moorings; but discrete elements of erotic feeling are at work in the two passages. The poet's distance from the allegory is widened by Eliot as far as possible. It is narrowed by Crane to an unembarrassed intimacy with the humble materials from which any cultural myth can be made.

The Bridge, like *The Waste Land*, is spoken by a man reluctant to conquer a landscape he imagines in the form of a woman, a landscape which itself has suffered the assault of earlier generations of men. The king of *The Waste Land* owns an inheritance that has shrunk to nothing. At its outer reach he is dimly conscious of the Thames maidens who "can connect / Nothing with nothing." The same intimation of despair is in the familiar landscape of the child Hart Crane as he watches the hobo-trekkers, but in *The Bridge* the possibility of connection is not despised:

They lurk across her, knowing her yonder breast
Snow-silvered, sumac-stained or smoky blue—
Is past the valley-sleepers, south or west.
—As I have trod the rumorous midnights, too.

The narrator of the last line is noticeably mortal, and idiosyncratic in what he confides, unlike the Tiresias of *The Waste Land*.

Tiresias was fated to endure sexual experience as a man and a woman, then punished with blindness by Hera for his report that woman's pleasure was greater, and, in compensation, rewarded with the gift of prophecy by Zeus. His self-knowledge, as the poem presents it, is a version of all knowledge. "As I have trod the rumorous midnights, too" implies a more local and personal claim. It is possible that this narrator, too, has known experience in both sexes. If so he has evidently derived feelings of potency from both. And if the word *rumorous* is a further memory of Eliot—"aetherial rumours / Revive for a moment a broken Coriolanus"—the roughs of the "empire wilderness of freight and rails" connect the memory with a different nostalgia. The paths a single echo may suggest are a consequence of disparate conceptions of poetic authority. When the speaker of "The Fire Sermon" sits down and weeps "by the waters of Leman," he imagines a fraternity shared with the lamenter of Psalms, a kind of fellowship that is possible only across time. The rail-squatters "ranged in nomad raillery" speak of a casual traffic among the traditions of the living; and American folk songs, some of them named in "The River," are a reminder of the energy of such traditions. You make a world in art, Crane seems to have believed, out of fragments knowable as parts of the world. With his submission to the sundry data of life—a gesture unmixed with contempt—the speaker of "The River" admits a fact of his personal life, namely, that he has had a childhood: something (odd as it feels to say so) that cannot be said of the narrator of *The Waste Land*. Crane is able here to discover a pathos foreign to Eliot, even in a line, *"Blind fists of nothing, humpty-dumpty clods,"* which itself has a strong foreshadowing in Eliot's "I will show you fear in a handful of dust" (as also in "other withered stumps of time"). "Blind fists of nothing" implies an energy in purposeless action that Eliot withholds from all his characters. The defeats or casualties in *The Bridge* are accepted as defeats without being accounted final. Sex is the motive of this contrast, with Eliot's plot steadily allying sexual completion and disgust—an event and a feeling that Crane may link incidentally, as he does in "National Winter Garden" and "The Tunnel," without implying that these show the working out of an invariable law.

Crane wrote several letters about *The Bridge* and *The Waste Land*. Only one of them says his purpose is the antithesis of Eliot's, and he offers the comparison in a mood of conjecture rather than assertion: "The poem, as a whole, is, I think, an affirmation of experience, and to that extent is 'positive' rather than 'negative' in the sense that *The Waste Land* is negative." Because of its use by the pragmatists James and Dewey, "experience," in the 1920s, was a word charged with specifically American associations. It was apt to serve a common argument that the individual—most of all the individual in a democracy—possessed among his inward resources a field of experiment sufficient to define an idea of freedom. Thus the potency Crane would ascribe to the Mississippi River belonged also to personal consciousness and imagination: "The River, spreading, flows—and spends your dream." Eliot's preoccupations were closer to metaphysical realism, and likely in the 1920s, as they were later, to allude with some urgency to a claim on behalf of reality. Knowledge of reality was, by definition, almost impossible to obtain, and that made the requirement of such knowledge all the more pressing. Eliot's usual metaphors when these concerns are in view—metaphors that have a source in the philosophy of F.H. Bradley—picture a realm where knowledge is complete, intelligible, and integral, yet by its nature undisclosed to individual consciousness. The nearest one can get to a sense of solidarity in experience is by imagining a sequence of identical privations, each knowing the character of the others because its contents mirror the contents of all others:

> I have heard the key
> Turn in the door once and turn once only
> We think of the key, each in his prison
> Thinking of the key, each confirms a prison.

The comfort this thought brings may be a sort of knowledge, but it is knowledge at the cost of experience, and what it confirms is a negation of freedom.

These theoretical self-definitions would have come home to Crane implicitly enough; he understood how much was at stake when he talked of "positive" and "negative." *The Waste Land* is a progress poem of a sort: it moves continuously through its series of sure-to-be-missed connections, in which every episode must prove to have been foresuffered. The structure of the poem is that of a theme and variations. The apparently chance encounters, improvised meetings, and assignations disclose themselves as versions of a single story which goes on with all the adventitious shifts of age and custom. A truth, we are invited to see, lies in wait beneath the accumulation of masks—a truth not susceptible to the inflections of personal will. There is no aspect or coloring of life that will not be known in advance to Tiresias. The progress of *The Bridge* feels just as repetitive but is harder to follow since it aims to resemble a process of growth. The poem loses what can be lost for the sake of a gain in experience; its recognitions have ceased to be an affair of the guilty living and the unburied dead:

> "Stetson!
> "You who were with me in the ships at Mylae!
> "That corpse you planted last year in your garden,
> "Has it begun to sprout?"

Eliot's style is dramatic and satirical—a choice emphasized in his splendid recording of the poem, with its dryness and air of continuous command.

Whereas, in *The Waste Land,* nothing can come of any memory that is reengaged, *The Bridge* offers another kind of memory: a meeting of eyes in which "the stubborn years gleam and atone," as the ranger's mother says in "Indiana."

It is an American hope to seek atonement through experience alone. For that reason I think Yvor Winters was right to associate *The Bridge* with *Song of Myself,* though he was wrong to suppose that this description entailed a self-evident rebuke. *The Bridge* and *Song of Myself* have the same kind of unity— of mood, texture, urgency and enterprise. Crane was conscious early of this link to Whitman, one token of which appears in "For the Marriage of Faustus and Helen." The poet presents himself in the midst of a crowd, anonymous and loitering until his name is called; the passage mingles the thought of Whitman with an echo of Eliot forgetting "the profit and loss":

> And yet, suppose some evening I forgot
> The fare and transfer, yet got by that way
> Without recall,—lost yet poised in traffic.
> Then I might find your eyes across an aisle,
> Still flickering....

The traffic makes it possible to lose oneself "without recall," shorn of a past, and yet to get by, to be on the move and somehow poised. The flickering carries a range of suggestions: of a face in back of a blind; a face suggestive by its lines, though hard to see in the glancing lights of the traffic; a face in which the eyes themselves may be blinking. The aisle seems a metaphor for the canyons dividing the façades of New York's skyscrapers, or the passage between the rows of a cinema, which in turn gives a further sense to the flickering.

In "Faustus and Helen," as in *The Bridge,* eyes know more than they are conscious of; and Crane's thought once again comes from Whitman: "Who knows, for all the distance, but I am as good as looking at you now, for all you cannot see me?" From "Prufrock" on, the eyes in Eliot's poetry are uncertain that knowledge is to be desired. His eyes alight gently but do not fix; they are cast down or averted—part of a face they help you to prepare "to meet the faces that you meet." It is fitting that Crane's most tormenting poem of love should have been a countersong to "Prufrock." There are other antithetical features of "Possessions," the title of which (with its overtones of demonic possession) works against the sense of material property or furnishings. It might have been called "Dispossessions":

Witness now this trust! the rain
That steals softly direction
And the key, ready to hand—sifting
One moment in sacrifice (the direst)
Through a thousand nights the flesh
Assaults outright for bolts that linger
Hidden,—O undirected as the sky
That through its black foam has no eyes
For this fixed stone of lust ...

Accumulate such moments to an hour:
Account the total of this trembling tabulation.
I know the screen, the distant flying taps
And stabbing medley that sways—
And the mercy, feminine, that stays
As though prepared.

And I, entering, take up the stone
As quiet as you can make a man ...
In Bleecker Street, still trenchant in a void,
Wounded by apprehensions out of speech,
I hold it up against a disk of light—
I, turning, turning on smoked forking spires,
The city's stubborn lives, desires.

Tossed on these horns, who bleeding dies,
Lacks all but piteous admissions to be spilt
Upon the page whose blind sum finally burns
Record of rage and partial appetites.
The pure possession, the inclusive cloud
Whose heart is fire shall come,—the white wind rase
All but bright stones wherein our smiling plays.

The first line ends with a pun on "tryst," and the entreaty here of a
witness or accomplice is ventured with much of Prufrock's urgency: "Oh do
not ask what is it." But this scene of turmoil has obstructions that not only
impede but chafe and penetrate; compare the lines of "Prufrock,"

It is impossible to say just what I mean!
But as if a magic lantern threw the nerves in patterns on a

screen:
Would it have been worth while

with the unreluctant answer of "Possessions":

I know the screen, the distant flying taps
And stabbing medley that sways—
And the mercy, feminine, that stays.

The contrast follows from Crane's determination to write of a desire on the
other side of satisfaction, to make a "Record of rage and partial appetites."
So the wariness of

The eyes that fix you in a formulated phrase,
And when I am formulated, sprawling on a pin,
When I am pinned and wriggling on the wall,
Then how should I begin
To spit out all the butt-ends of my days and ways?

gives way to an agonized embrace:

I, turning, turning on smoked forking spires,
The city's stubborn lives, desires.

Crane's speaker has grown old with the spent vehemence of youth, but it is
Eliot's who has the lighter step: "Prufrock" was a young man's poem about
age.
     And yet in "Possessions" the language of "Prufrock" has been so
assimilated that its ending can seem to occur the moment after "human
voices wake us and we drown." The spray of the sea, in which Prufrock's
mermaids were glimpsed, is taken up in "The pure possession, the inclusive
cloud" that marks the conquests and surrenders of the later poet, now burnt
forever into the city's memory. "Possessions" is a homosexual poem, defiantly
so. But the remarkable uncollected lyric "Legende," written when Crane was
nineteen, gives a feminine motive to the same image of erotic possession and
erasure. The woman there "has become a pathos,— / Waif of the tides"; the
poet closes by saying, "even my vision will be erased / As a cameo the waves
claim again." This sense of the good of rendering a life permanent, even as
its detail is burned away, would be constant in Crane's work: that is a reason
for the *we* of "Possessions" to imitate the Dantesque *we* of "Prufrock,"

though with a shift of emphasis. Prufrock's companion had to be knowledgeable in the ways of erotic hunger, regret, and repetition, but was largely a pretext for dramatic confidences. Crane's use of the word includes himself and his lover.

A last comparison will bring out the delicacy with which Crane could portray erotic contact as a hint of some larger acknowledgment that was never to be spoken. For his provocation he turned again to *The Waste Land* and particularly to the lines that follow the imperative "Datta":

> The awful daring of a moment's surrender
> Which an age or prudence can never retract
> By this, and this only, we have existed.

Crane's echo, at once violently explicit and curiously tacit, speaks of

> sifting
> One moment in sacrifice (the direst)
> Through a thousand nights the flesh
> Assaults outright for bolts that linger
> Hidden.

There had always been in Eliot a need to cherish the personal relation as an enigma, which by its nature belonged to a realm of untouchable grace and self-sacrifice. The anxiety of physical surrender is lest you be given something that was not yours to take: "That is not what I meant at all, / That is not it, at all." But Crane's interest is always to take everything. What survives his experience will be preserved elsewhere—it is not for him to say where—as elusive as "bright stones wherein our smiling plays." The ironic phrase at the point where memory hopes to recover something more palpable—"Accumulate such moments to an hour: / Account the total of this trembling tabulation"—suggests his view of a dry impartiality that will dispense with the work of recovery. For the idea of counting such moments is bound to be false; they are really one moment "that stays / As though prepared."

I have been discussing Crane's poetry and his temperament and personal traits as if these things were plainly related. Yet he is one of those poets who can persuade many readers much of the time that his poetry has shed any empirical relation to a life. One might tell a convincing story about his writing in which the ordinary elements, including the feelings he had for other writers, almost vanished. He would appear then as a romantic hero, uneasily committed in his early years to the "tremorous" moments he invoked in "Legend"—the first poem and in many ways the signature of *White Buildings*—but gravitating at last to a poetry unconfined by chance encounters with the actual world. No poet has written many poems outside those limits. Coleridge did it in "Kubla Khan," and Swinburne in "At a Month's End." Crane may have felt he was crossing a similar threshold when he wrote "Voyages VI." It is something to be the kind of writer for whom such a thought is possible.

On this view of his career, its fable of initiation is "Passage." For, like no other poem by Crane, "Passage" signals a break from experience. But what is impressive is how far even there the landscapes of Eliot, his cadences, and his imaginative predicament become for Crane a prophecy of what he himself must and must not become. In the allegory of the poem, the author is challenged to account for his life by an unnamed figure of admonition. The presence of such a figure is an artistic given—his life from the start has been a scene of risk. "Dangerously the summer burned / (I had joined the entrainments of the wind)," he declares, translating *entraînement*, a rapture or enthusiasm. The inquest continues as the weight of the landscape intensifies:

> The shadows of boulders lengthened my back:
> In the bronze gongs of my cheeks
> The rain dried without odour.
>
> "It is not long, it is not long;
> See where the red and black
> Vine-stanchioned valleys—": but the wind
> Died speaking through the ages that you know
> And hug, chimney-sooted heart of man!
> So was I turned about and back, much as your smoke
> Compiles a too well-known biography.

As in "Emblems of Conduct"—where we are told, of any present moment in art, "By that time summer and smoke were past"—smoke is a figure for a life whose pathos can be captured in a story. The Crane of "Passage" was turning away from such stories, as Eliot, at the end of *The Waste Land*, had done in the hope of subduing his inheritance. But there is no such hope and no acceptance in "Passage": its pledge is to master a fate that will elude any witness or historian of conduct. The poem bequeaths the poet to desires without a possessor, desires harbored and acted upon, to which writing will be a weak secondary clue. *Your* smoke—the possessive pronoun is impersonal, its grammar that of Hamlet's "There are more things in heaven and earth, Horatio, / Than are dreamt of in your philosophy." More is at stake in a life than the smoke that tells the story will ever compile.

Here is his source in Eliot:

> What are the roots that clutch, what branches grow
> Out of this stony rubbish? Son of man,
> You cannot say, or guess, for you know only
> A heap of broken images, where the sun beats,
> And the dead tree gives no shelter, the cricket no relief,
> And the dry stone no sound of water. Only
> There is shadow under this red rock,
> (Come in under the shadow of this red rock),
> And I will show you something different from either
> Your shadow at morning striding behind you
> Or your shadow at evening rising to meet you;
> I will show you fear in a handful of dust.

The passage, from "The Burial of the Dead," offers the first sign that the dread of *The Waste Land* has a metaphysical dimension. That poem ends with a gesture of reserve that commits the poet to an ordering of life, however provisional; a gesture honorable in its humility, when considered beside the fear and apathy the poem as a whole has described. At the end of "Passages" Crane, too, breaking one spell to cast another, faces a barren sea from the land's end where memory has set him down. It is here that he asks:

> What fountains did I hear? what icy speeches?
> Memory, committed to the page, had broke.

He may yet be released into a life more intoxicating than anything memory could yield.

What that life will be the man who prays for it "cannot say, or guess," not because he has ceased to exist, but because the thing he will be is unwritten. Crane lived to make few examples of the poetry that here beckons to him. After "Voyages VI" one can count "The Dance" and perhaps "O Carib Isle!" as efforts of an unexampled pressure of purpose. These are poems of agony—"I could not pluck the arrows from my side"—a record of suffering that testifies against the healing of the sufferer:

> Let not the pilgrim see himself again
> For slow evisceration bound like those huge terrapin
> Each daybreak on the wharf, their brine-caked eyes;
> —Spiked, overturned; such thunder in their strain!

But from the first there was another order of poetry that mattered to Crane, and that represents him as faithfully. An agnostic naturalism persisted from "Repose of Rivers" to "The Broken Tower." As one looks back on that span of work, its dominant note comes, one cannot fail to see, not just from the city but from the city of Eliot. What is true of "Chaplinesque" and "Possessions" is also true of "Recitative" and "To Brooklyn Bridge" and "The Tunnel." To say these poems were achieved in dialogue would be to assert too little for the poems and too little for both poets. Crane wrote poetry of a kind unimaginable without Eliot; and the accomplishment of Eliot feels somehow larger in this light.

1996

LOUIS L. MARTZ

H.D.:
Set Free to Prophesy

H.D. is the last of the great generation born in the 1880s to receive due recognition. Pound, Joyce, Eliot, Lawrence all received early acclaim—notoriety at least, if not their just due; and William Carlos Williams, after the publication of *Paterson's* first four books, soon found his poetry admired in terms that equal the acclaim won long before by his bitterly resented rival Eliot. But H.D. had to wait until the 1970s before her true stature could be widely recognized. Why has H.D. thus lagged behind?

It is not simply because after the appearance of her first volume she became fixed, delimited, by the label *Imagiste* that Pound gave her in 1912, when he sent her early poems to Harriet Monroe for publication in *Poetry*. Pound, of course, never meant to trap her in this way; two years later he was publishing her famous "Oread" in the first issue of *Blast* as an example of "Vorticist" poetry. And indeed "H.D. Vorticist" would have been a better description of her early poetry, with its swirling, dynamic power: the sort of turbulent force that Henri Gaudier-Brzeska described in his own sculptural definition of "Vortex": "Plastic Soul is intensity of life bursting the plane."[1] This restless movement, the constant surging of intense vitality, lies at the center of H.D.'s early poetry, and thus the static, lapidary, crystalline implications usually carried by the word *imagism* could never contain the strength of H.D.'s muse.[2]

From *Many Gods and Many Voices: The Role of the Prophet in English and American Modernism*.
© 1998 by the Curators of the University of Missouri.

Why, then, did the term cling to her poetry? Partly because H.D. continued to support the movement after Pound had given it over to Amy Lowell; partly too because the critical and poetical currents of the 1920s and 1930s, under the influence of Eliot and Pound and T.E. Hulme, were violently reacting against romanticism and were insisting upon the need for terse, compact poetry, rich in imagistic inference but spare in abstraction and exclamation. Thus the concentrated imagery of poems such as "Pear Tree" or "Sea Rose" seemed to represent her essence, and her passionate protest against the "Sheltered Garden" could be overlooked, along with some of the longer poems in her first volume, *Sea Garden* (1916), that show her reaching beyond Imagism toward the development of a prophetic voice more akin to Shelley than to Pound or Eliot. Her stance as prophetess has of course been widely recognized, especially by Susan Stanford Friedman in her classic book of 1981.[3] Here I wish to explore the development of this prophetic voice throughout her career.

Her early poem "Sea Gods," for example, protests against contemporary tendencies to deny the supernatural:

> They say you are twisted by the sea,
> you are cut apart
> by wave-break upon wave-break,
> that you are misshapen by the sharp rocks,
> broken by the rasp and after-rasp.

But in the second section of the poem she pays tribute to the sea gods by gifts of violets of every kind, violets as the symbols of love. And then the third section concludes in a style of ritual, liturgical repetition that foreshadows the style of "The Dancer" in the 1930s:

> For you will come,
> you will yet haunt men in ships,
> you will trail across the fringe of strait
> and circle the jagged rocks.
> You will trail across the rocks
> and wash them with your salt ...
>
> For you will come,
> you will come,
>
> you will answer our taut hearts,

you will break the lie of men's thoughts,
and cherish and shelter us.[4]

Such a style is far removed from the terse style recommended by Pound in his famous "Don'ts" for Imagists.[5] Other longer poems in *Sea Garden* seem to defy Pound's demand for "economy of words" and his warning, "Go in fear of abstractions." In poems such as "The Cliff Temple" and the poem that concludes the volume, "Cities," we can feel the poet reaching toward some sort of prophetic vision that needs a style of exhortation and exclamation, where repetition of phrases serves to enforce the expression of a need or a hope:

> Is our task the less sweet
> that the larvae still sleep in their cells?
> Or crawl out to attack our frail strength ...
>
> Though they sleep or wake to torment
> and wish to displace our old cells—
> thin rare gold—
> that their larvae grow fat—
> is our task the less sweet—
> Though we wander about,
> find no honey of flowers in this waste,
> is our task the less sweet—
>
> who recall the old splendour,
> await the new beauty of cities? (*CP*, 41)

This prophetic sense of the decline of civilization along with a mission to redeem is more strongly enforced in the ten-page poem "The Tribute," published in the *Egoist* in 1916—the same year in which *Sea Garden* appeared. Using a Greek setting, the poem fiercely attacks the decay of values in contemporary society in time of war, using throughout a technique of repeating whole lines and phrases with liturgical, ritual effect:

> Squalor spreads its hideous length
> through the carts and the asses' feet,
> squalor coils and reopens
> and creeps under barrow
> and heap of refuse ...

Squalor spreads its hideous length
through the carts and the asses' feet—
squalor has entered and taken our songs ...

Squalor spreads its hideous length
through the carts and the asses' feet,
squalor coils and draws back ...
with no voice to rebuke—
for the boys have gone out of the city,
the songs withered black on their lips. (*CP*, 59–60)

All gods have been banished from the city except the war god, as "the people gather to cry for revenge, / to chant their hymns and to praise / the god of the lance." But now the words of rebuke are arising, led by the prophetic speaker, accompanied by the voices of "a few old men" and "a few sad women" and "a few lads" who cry out, praying to the gods of nature to redeem the city from its hate:

O spirit of simples and roots
O gods of the plants of the earth—

O god of the simples and grasses,
we cry to you now from our hearts,
O heal us—bring balm for our sickness,
return and soothe us with bark
and hemlock and feverwort....

Return—look again on our city,
though the people cry through the streets,
though they hail another,
have pity—return to our gates ... (*CP*, 63–64)

This appeal to the healing powers of nature continues through the ninth strophe of this attempted ode, but then in the last two sections the speaker turns toward a defense of "beauty"—an abstract beauty never defined, though it is something that can never be destroyed despite the violence of wartime emotions:

Could beauty be caught and hurt
they had done her to death with their sneers
in ages and ages past

And then the poem abruptly ends with what seems to be a tribute to the creative achievement of the "boys" before they were sent to their destruction:

> Could beauty be beaten out,—
> O youth the cities have sent
> to strike at each other's strength,
> it is you who have kept her alight. (*CP*, 68)

The poem is hardly successful, although it shows a prophetic spirit struggling for release into larger forms of poetry, such as the choruses from Greek tragedy that H.D. was at this time publishing—examples that encouraged her to pursue this ritual mode of utterance in her own verse.

H.D. was in fact at this very time writing long, much more powerful poems: the sequence that in her typescript she calls "poems of *The Islands* series"—dating from 1916 or 1917.[6] These poems all deal with the anguish of a deserted woman, an Ariadne on Naxos, as in "The Islands":

> What are the islands to me
> if you are lost,
> what is Paros to me
> if your eyes draw back,
> what is Milos
> if you take fright of beauty,
> terrible, tortuous, isolated,
> a barren rock? (*CP*, 127)

The story is told at length in the triad preserved in her typescript: "Amaranth," "Eros," and "Envy," poems that leave no doubt that the sequence arises from the infidelities of her husband, Richard Aldington. "The Islands" was published in 1920, but the triad was never published complete during H.D.'s lifetime, although in *Heliodora* (1924) she published truncated versions of these poems under the guise of adaptations of fragments from Sappho—but carefully separated and with all references to a male lover removed.[7] In her volume of 1924, following the truncated version of "Eros" she placed a poem that might be taken to conclude "The Islands" series: "Toward the Piraeus." The title, referring to the port of Athens, suggests a poem written or conceived during the curative voyage to Greece in 1920, as the poet ponders the disaster recorded in the "Amaranth" triad. The poem opens with a prologue that fiercely denounces the weakness of modern men, compared with the heroic Greeks:

Slay with your eyes, Greek,
men over the face of the earth,
slay with your eyes, the host,
puny, passionless, weak.

The first section of the poem proper then conveys a complex view of the destructive yet creative power that her unfaithful lover has exerted upon her:

You would have broken my wings,
but the very fact that you knew
I had wings, set some seal
on my bitter heart, my heart
broke and fluttered and sang.

The second section then shows the source of the inner strength that has enabled her to survive this betrayal: it is her prophetic power, the power displayed by the prophetess at the oracle of Delphi:

I loved you:
men have writ and women have said
they loved,
but as the Pythoness stands by the altar,
intense and may not move,

till the fumes pass over
and may not falter or break,
till the priest has caught the words
that mar or make
a deme or a ravaged town:

so I, though my knees tremble,
my heart break,
must note the rumbling,
heed only the shuddering
down in the fissure beneath the rock
of the temple floor;

must wait and watch
and may not turn nor move,
nor break from my trance to speak

so slight, so sweet,
so simple a word as love.

Something deeper, something more mysterious than this love sustains her: a sense that some greater destiny awaits her. And so at the close she is able to utter a fair and balanced judgment of their troubles, with the perception that the cause of the disaster might be found in her own nature, which had to guard her poetical and her sexual qualities against the power of a soldier-husband and a fellow poet:

> It was not chastity that made me wild, but fear
> that my weapon, tempered in different heat,
> was over-matched by yours, and your hand
> skilled to wield death-blows, might break
>
> With the slightest turn—no ill will meant—
> my own lesser, yet still somewhat fine-wrought,
> fiery-tempered, delicate, over-passionate steel. (*CP,* 175–79)

The prophetic stance of the Pythoness is not often found again in the poems that H.D. published during the 1920s, though sometimes, as in "Demeter" or "Cassandra," it powerfully appears. It is not until *Red Roses for Bronze* (1931) that H.D. showed persistent attempts to strike the prophetic stance, in poems that carry the technique of repetition to an extreme, first in translations from the choruses of Greek tragedy, as in this version from *The Bacchae:*

> O which of the gifts of the gods
> is the best gift?
>
> this,
> this,
> this,
> this;
> escape from the power of the hunting pack,
> and to know that wisdom is best
> and beauty
> sheer holiness.
>
> Hard,
> hard it is to wake the gods,

> but once awake,
> hard,
> hard,
> hard is the lot
> of the ignorant man ... (*CP*, 227)

This effort to achieve something like the ritual effect of a Greek chorus apparently led to the same technique in her own independent "Choros Sequence: from *Morpheus*":

> I live,
> I live,
> I live,
> you give me that:
> this gift of ecstasy
> is rarer,
> dearer
> than any monstrous pearl
> from tropic water;
> I live,
> I live,
> I live ... (*CP*, 263)

In an earlier essay I said, "This is pitiful, grasping for a response the words cannot command." But I agree with Gary Burnett's view that this "pattern is so pervasive and so carefully pursued" that the above "characterization of it seems inadequate."[8] It would be better to say that this pervasive technique is a manifestation of H.D.'s effort to create the effect of "the Pythoness" standing by the altar, intense and trembling, waiting for a message from below the temple floor. The technique is not successful in many poems in this volume because it is simply too obvious; but where it is restrained, as in "In the Rain," "Chance Meeting," or, significantly, "Trance," the poems work. Perhaps it was H.D.'s own dissatisfaction with *Red Roses for Bronze* that led her to include near the close her "Epitaph"; but we must note that this is immediately followed by a concluding poem, "The Mysteries: Renaissance Choros," a controlled and successful poem, with the word *Renaissance* suggesting both a new era of culture and a time for personal rebirth under the power of the religious faith and figure represented in the "voice" that speaks out of the dark turbulence of the opening section: "peace / be still"— the words of Christ that calm the storm at sea (Mark 4:39). The poem continues with allusions to the Gospels, especially to the parables, combining these with allusions to the pagan mystery cults as the "voice" concludes:

> The mysteries remain,
> I keep the same
> cycle of seed-time
> and of sun and rain;
> Demeter in the grass
> I multiply,
> renew and bless
> Iacchus in the vine....
>
> *I keep the law,*
> *I hold the mysteries true,*
> *I am the vine,*
> *the branches, you*
> *and you.* (*CP*, 305)

This concluding poem of 1931 is closely linked, both in style and in subject, with the poem "Magician" (Christ is called a "magician" in the second section of "The Mysteries"), published in an obscure magazine (*Seed*) in January 1933, two months before H.D. began her treatments with Freud. This poem is spoken in the person of a disciple of Christ who has heard his words and witnessed his miracles, and who now places reliance, not upon the symbols of the Crucifixion, but upon the images of nature that appear in the parables: nature as a channel toward the divine. Both the ending of *Red Roses for Bronze* and "Magician" show that H.D. had not utterly lost her creative powers when she sought help from Freud. She was capable of writing well, and Freud seems to have realized that her condition did not require the sort of deep analysis that would occupy years. A few months of advice would, and did, suffice to bring forth an immense surge of creative power, represented in "The Dancer" triad and in the completion of her long-contemplated version of the *Ion* of Euripides, published in 1937.

What was it that Freud helped her to discover? The first part of her *Tribute to Freud, Writing on the Wall*, provides the clue in the vision, or hallucination, that gives this part its title. The vision consists of three pictures.

> The first was head and shoulders, three-quarter face, no marked features, a stencil or stamp of a soldier or airman.... It was a

silhouette cut of light, not shadow, and so impersonal it might have been anyone, of almost any country. And yet there was a distinctly familiar line about the head with the visored cap; immediately it was *somebody* unidentified indeed, yet suggesting a question—dead brother? lost friend?[9]

One thinks at once of Aldington, a soldier at the time of her anguish at his infidelity. The second picture is "the conventional outline of a goblet or cup"—symbol of the female. Do these two images suggest her bisexuality, the "two loves separate" that she describes in her poem about Freud?

The third picture is the most important and given the longest description. It is a "three-legged" image in perspective: "none other than our old friend, the tripod of classic Delphi ... this venerated object of the cult of the sun god, symbol of poetry and prophecy" (*TTF*, 46). Delphi is then emphasized a few pages later, as she concentrates her attention on these pictures, saying, "it seems now possible that the mechanism of their projection (from within or from without) had something to do with, or in some way was related to, my feelings for the shrine at Delphi" (*TTF*, 49). The "idea of Delphi has always touched me very deeply," she adds, recalling that she had said to her friend Bryher (Winifred Ellerman), while recovering from her 1919 illness, "If I could only feel that I could walk the sacred way to Delphi, I know I would get well." In section 36 she clarifies the meaning of this picture, beginning with the thought that "all through time, there had been a tradition of warnings or messages from another world or another state of being." Delphi, she reminds us, "was the shrine of the Prophet and Musician, the inspiration of artists and the patron of physicians." Then she applies the meaning of Delphi to her own situation. "Religion, art, and medicine, through the later ages, became separated; they grow further apart from day to day." But now for herself, under the ministrations of this "blameless physician," Sigmund Freud, the three are growing together, as her third picture indicates: "These three working together, to form a new vehicle of expression or a new form of thinking or of living, might be symbolized by the tripod, the third of the images on the wall before me" (*TTF*, 50–51).

The tripod, she explains, "was the symbol of prophecy, prophetic utterance of occult or hidden knowledge; the Priestess or Pythoness of Delphi sat on the tripod while she pronounced her verse couplets, the famous Delphic utterances which it was said could be read two ways." ("Verse couplets": is this perhaps one reason for adopting the form of couplets for her wartime *Trilogy*, a form not at all characteristic of her earlier poems? "The Pythian pronounces," she declares in the opening poem of the *Trilogy*, the prologue written in tercets, after which all is written in couplets.)[10]

Now in section 36 we come to the most revealing utterance:

We can read my writing,[11] the fact that there was writing, in two ways or in more than two ways. We can read or translate it as a suppressed desire for forbidden 'signs and wonders,' breaking bounds, a suppressed desire to be a Prophetess, to be important anyway, megalomania they call it—a hidden desire to 'found a new religion' which the Professor ferreted out in the later Moses picture. Or this writing-on-the-wall is merely an extension of the artist's mind, a *picture* or an illustrated poem, taken out of the actual dream or daydream content and projected from within ... (*TTF*, 51)

The "Moses picture" is the vision dealt with in section 25, the dream of "the Princess" who descends the stairs to find a baby "in the water beside me," in a "shallow basket or ark or box or boat." It is an image drawn from the Doré Bible, an illustration of the finding of Moses.

The Professor and I discuss this picture. He asks if it is I, the Dreamer, who am the baby in the reed basket? I don't think I am.... The Professor thinks there is a child Miriam, half concealed in the rushes; do I remember? I half remember. Am I, perhaps, the child Miriam? Or am I, after all, in my fantasy, the baby? Do I wish myself, in the deepest unconscious or subconscious layers of my being, to be the founder of a new religion? (*TTF*, 37)

Is it this "new religion" that, as she says in her poem to "The Master," Freud has "set me free / to prophesy?" If so, of what does this "religion" consist? It would include, first of all, the Greek elements represented in her earlier poems and also in some of the poems that apparently derive from the 1930s, "Delphi" and "Dodona," where she seeks the elusive presences of Apollo and Zeus. It would include, eminently, the declaration of female equality and power represented in her eloquent poem "The Dancer," published in 1935 and perhaps based on her memories of a performance by Isadora Duncan, whose Greek and erotic modes of dancing seem to lie behind the poem. The use of the Greek term for "rose" or "red"—*rhodo*—in repeated addresses to

"Rhododendron" and "Rhodocleia" may relate to the well-known reputation of Isadora as a "Red" after her stay in Moscow in 1920. In American performances after this visit, in defiance of those who denounced her, "Red" sympathies, she wore a red tunic and flourished a red scarf.[12] It was perhaps her return from Moscow that led H.D. to open the poem thus:

> I came far,
> you came far,
> both from strange cities,
> I from the west,
> You from the east ... (*CP*, 440)[13]

Isadora's revolutionary spirit and her free forms of dancing ("I worship nature, / you are nature" H.D. says at the end of the poem's first strophe) seem to express what H.D. celebrates in this poem, seeing the dancer as a true messenger of Apollo, who says to her:

> "you are my arrow,
> my flame;
> I have sent you into the world;
> beside you,
> men may name
> no other;
> you will never die;
>
> nor this one,
> whom you see not,
> sitting, sullen and silent,
> this poet." (*CP*, 445)

But the poet does not remain silent: in the next strophe she flings forth her plea:

> O chaste Aphrodite,
>
> let us-be wild and free.
> let us retain integrity,
> intensity,
> taut as the bow

the Pythian strings
to slay sorrow. (*CP*, 446)

The assertion of female integrity is closely related to her sessions with Freud, as she makes clear by including an even more fervent celebration of the Dancer in the middle of her poem to "The Master," with its erotic allusion to "red" and "rose":

there is purple flower
between her marble, her birch-tree white
thighs,
or there is a red flower

there is a rose flower
parted wide,
as her limbs fling wide in dance
ecstatic
Aphrodite,
there is a frail lavender flower
hidden in grass;

O God, what is it,
this flower
that in itself had power over the whole earth?
for she needs no man,

herself
is that dart and pulse of the male,
hands, feet, thighs,
herself perfect. (*CP*, 456)

This, then, is yet another element in her "new religion." But there is a more inclusive message in her prophecy, as set forth in the one volume of poetry that H.D. published between 1931 and 1944: her version of the *Ion* of Euripides, published at last in 1937, after years of pondering the play. Here the poetry is constantly interspersed with a prose commentary that is indeed inseparable from the verse, for the prose makes plain the prophetic purpose behind her choice of this particular drama—one she had worked with even during the years of World War I.

Ion is a drama that deals with the reconciliation of Apollo with Athene: the god of poetry and the goddess of wisdom combine to ensure the future of Athens, city of Ion, son of Kreousa by Apollo, and thus ensure the beginning of a great new era, Ionian culture, after a time of sterility, doubt, hatred, and attempted murder. The message to the modern world is this: it can happen again, as H.D. explains when she writes here of "the woman who is queen [Kreousa] and almost goddess, who now in her joy wishes to be nothing but the mother of Ion; the mother, if she but knew it, of a new culture, of an aesthetic drive and concentrated spiritual force, not to be reckoned with, in terms of any then known values; hardly, even to-day, to be estimated at its true worth."[14] She then makes explicit the application to the world of the present time, 1937:

> Let not our hearts break before the beauty of Pallas Athené. No; she makes all things possible for us. The human mind today pleads for all; nothing is misplaced that in the end may be illuminated by the inner fire of abstract understanding; hate, love, degradation, humiliation, all, all may be examined, given due proportion and dismissed finally, in the light of the mind's vision. Today, again at a turning-point in the history of the world, the mind stands, to plead, to condone, to explain, to clarify, to illuminate; and, in the name of our magnificent heritage of that Hellenic past, each one of us is responsible to that abstract reality; silver and unattainable yet always present, that spirit again stands holding the balance between the past and the future. What now will we make of it? (*Ion*, 113)

She adds a parable: the story of how, after the Persians had burned Athene's temple on the Acropolis and reduced her sacred olive tree to a charred stump, one devotee had climbed the Acropolis and found this:

> Close to the root of the blackened, ancient stump, a frail silver shoot was clearly discernible, chiselled as it were, against that blackened wood; incredibly frail, incredibly silver, it reached toward the light. Pallas Athené, then, was not dead. Her spirit spoke quietly, a very simple message....
> Today? Yesterday? Greek time is like all Greek miracles. Years gain no permanence nor impermanence by a line of curious numbers; numerically 1920, 1922 and again (each time, spring) 1932, we touched the stem of a frail sapling, an olive-tree, growing against the egg-shell marble walls of the Erechtheum. (*Ion*, 115)

That she had indeed touched the olive tree is proved by the eloquent poetical finale that follows. Thus the voice of the prophet, though often bitter in denunciation, is ultimately optimistic: the prophet believes that her people, at least part of her people, can be saved—a remnant that can lead to a great renewal.

The prophetic voice in *Ion*, released by Freud's ministrations, may be closely related to another remarkable poem that seems to come from this same era: "A Dead Priestess Speaks," the title poem of a collection of pieces mostly datable from the 1930s, which H.D. arranged and sent over to Norman Pearson, with a letter that helps to explain their meaning. On March 16, 1949, she wrote to Pearson: "Now I have had typed, a series of poems. I do not 'place' them, except as milestones on my way.... I call this series, *A Dead Priestess Speaks*. That is the title of the first poem and rather describes my own feelings."[15]

The title poem is the most significant and the richest of this group. Exactly when it was written we cannot say. Since most of the other poems are datable from the 1930s, one might assume that this one also comes from that era, but its range and depth, and one reference to "a new war" after she has spoken of an older war, would seem to suggest that the poem may at least have been retouched as it became the title piece for this series. In any case the reference to the Priestess as Delia of Miletus associates the poem closely with H.D. in person, for Delia Alton was a favorite pen name, while Miletus is the place where she came to be cured by the Master in her poem addressed to Freud:

> when I travelled to Miletus
> to get wisdom,
> I left all else behind ...
> "every gesture is wisdom,"
> he taught;
> "nothing is lost,"
> he said;
> I went late to bed
> or early,
>
> I caught the dream
> and rose dreaming,
> and we wrought philosophy on the dream content,
> I was content.... (*CP*, 451)

(Note the rich pun on "content.") Delia of Miletus: why Miletus? It was the greatest of all Greek cities at one time, standing on the Turkish shore of the Aegean Sea, home of the earliest Greek philosophers, the pre-Socratics: where else would one go to seek the sources of wisdom? It was also a city famous for poets, one of which claimed to be a direct disciple of Homer. And it was the birthplace of one of the earliest female intellectuals in recorded history—the famous Aspasia, noted for her learning, her wit, and her beauty. But more important, it was the city that sponsored the nearby temple of Apollo at Didyma, one of the largest shrines ever built in the Greek world, famous for the words of its prophetess. Yes, H.D. knew all the resources of that word *Miletus.*

So Delia of Miletus becomes a priestess who speaks wisdom, but it is a wisdom understood only by her deepest inner self, not by the outside world, which sees her as a pure, beneficent, and dignified figure, but does not know the anguished inner self. Even when they glimpse what they would call her eccentricities, such as her refusal to write about war, they misunderstand:

> I answered circumspectly,
> claiming no
> virtue
> that helped the wounded
> and no fire
> that sung of battle ended,
>
> then they said,
> ah she is modest, she is purposeful,
> and nominated for the Herald's place,
> one
> Delia of Miletus. (*CP*, 372)

And when they learn that she has gone into the wild wood at night to gather strange herbs and fruit, they see only the outward effects of her times of inward anger, bitterness, and despair.

> tasting leaf and root,
> I thought at times of poison,
> hoped that I
> might lie deep in the tangle,
> tasting the hemlock

blossom,
and so die;

but I came home,
and the last archon saw
me reach the door, at dawn;
I did not even care what he might say ...

I waited for the crowd to mutter filth
and stone me from the altar,
but the new archon cried,
fresh honour to Miletus,
to Delia of Miletus who has found
a new brew of bay.... (*CP,* 374)

They do not know the anguish and the exaltation of the inner self that lies
beneath the Imagist; they do not know *me,*

me, whom no man yet found,
only the forest-god
of the wet moss,
of the deep underground,
or of the dry rock
parching to the moon ... (*CP,* 370)

They do not know that within her calm demeanor she has been pursued by a god:

how was it I,
who walked so circumspectly, yet was caught
in the arms of an angry lover,
who said,
late,

late,
I waited too long for you, Delia,
I will devour you,
love you into flame,

O late
my love,

my bride
Delia of Miletus. (*CP,* 376)

They do not know the prophet within the priestess, for this lover, though no doubt he had his human counterparts, is surely here the god of poetry and prophecy—Apollo.

Gary Burnett has argued that this poem represents an answer to D.H. Lawrence,[16] and in a sense this may be so, for Lawrence had spoken sarcastically of her "virtue" and her "spiritual" being.[17] But this poem, and others, such as "Eurydice," "Toward the Piraeus," and the "Amaranth" triad, do not derive their power from the identification of any single person who may have been the poem's point of origin. As Sandra Gilbert and Susan Gubar say, such poems as these transcend their local origins by showing how the speakers "struggle with roles to which they have been consigned because of the male poet's 'glance.'" "While H.D. brooded upon Pound's or Lawrence's mastery in the first two decades of her long career, she confronted the empowering glamour and the painful frigidity brought about by her absorption with her male peers and by her dread that artistry itself somehow required ruthless strategies of objectification."[18] The struggle of woman to assert her independent integrity in the face of male misunderstanding, betrayal, or demand for submission underlies her entire career, reaching a climax in *Trilogy* and *Helen in Egypt*.

Freud and her poems of the 1930s thus led the way toward *Trilogy,* her long wartime work completed in December 1944—the best original poetry of her career.[19] *Trilogy* is sometimes called epic, but I wonder whether this is the right term. This work, like the later *Helen in Egypt,* seems rather to belong to the genre of prophecy, because it consists of a sequence of short lyric or meditative utterances, presenting a series of voices and visions amid the ruins of bombed London, where H.D. spent those wartime years. The first part, *The Walls Do Not Fall* (composed in 1942, published in 1944), presents a series of experiments in responding to the danger and the bravery of the scene, a sequence firmly grounded at beginning and end in the actual experience of the bombing:

pressure on heart, lungs, the brain
about to burst its brittle case ...

the bone-frame was made for
no such shock knit within terror,
yet the skeleton stood up to it ...

But the question remains: "we passed the flame: we wonder / what saved us? what for?" (*CP,* 510–11).

Already the opening section has begun its tacit answer to that question, as, in accord with the dedication, "for Karnack 1923 / from London 1942," the poem equates the opening of an Egyptian tomb with the "opening" of churches and other buildings by the bombs:

> there, as here, ruin opens
> the tomb, the temple; enter,
> there as here, there are no doors:
>
> the shrine lies open to the sky ... (*CP,* 509)

So too an opening happens in the mind, under the impact of disaster:

> ruin everywhere, yet as the fallen roof
> leaves the sealed room
> open to the air,
>
> so, through our desolation,
> thoughts stir, inspiration stalks us
> through gloom:
>
> unaware, Spirit announces the Presence;
> shivering overtakes us,
> as of old, Samuel:
>
> trembling at a known street-corner,
> we know not nor are known;
> the Pythian pronounces— (*CP,* 509–10)

(The body of the poem is written in "Pythian" couplets, as I noted earlier, but of course H.D. was well aware that biblical poetry was also composed in couplets; as with Samuel and the Pythian, two traditions merge.)

The fourth section presents this opening in yet another way: reverting to her old Imagist technique, she picks up the image of "that craftsman, / the shellfish" and makes it represent the tough integrity of the artist, saying, "I sense my own limit"—and yet know "the pull / of the tide."

> be firm in your own small, static, limited

> orbit and the shark-jaws
> of outer circumstance
>
> will spit you forth:
> be indigestible, hard, ungiving,
>
> so that, living within,
> you beget, self-out-of-self,
>
> selfless,
>
> that pearl-of-great-price.

This is only a beginning. From here she moves out to remember the meaning of "Mercury, Hermes, Thoth," inventors and patrons of the Word. And then, "when the shingles hissed / in the rain of incendiary," a voice speaks louder than the "whirr and roar in the high air" (*CP*, 520), and she has her vision and dream where "Ra, Osiris, *Amen* appeared / in a spacious, bare meetinghouse"—in Philadelphia or in Bethlehem, Pennsylvania:

> yet he was not out of place
> but perfectly at home
>
> in that eighteenth-century
> simplicity and grace ... (*CP*, 523)

As in Freud's study, all religions are blending into one in her mind, though critics, she knows, will complain that "Depth of the sub-conscious spews forth / too many incongruent monsters" (*CP*, 534). Nevertheless, through wordplay and all her other poetic devices, like them or not, her aim is to

> recover the secret of Isis,
> which is: there was One
>
> in the beginning, Creator,
> Fosterer, Begetter, the Same-forever
>
> in the papyrus-swamp
> in the Judean meadow. (*CP*, 541)

This is all preliminary: the secret is not yet found; the quest must continue, as the wordplay upon the name *Osiris* in sections 40–42 makes plain. "Osiris equates O-sir-is or O Sire is":

> O Sire, is this the path?
> over sedge, over dune grass,
>
> silently
> sledge-runners pass.
>
> O Sire, is this the waste?...
>
> drawn to the temple gate, O, Sire,
> is this union at last? (*CP,* 540, 542)

The answer now comes in the second part, *Tribute to the Angels* (composed in 1944, published in 1945), a sequence wholly unified and sustained, moving forward confidently under the guidance of Hermes Trismegistus, inventor of language, father of alchemy, founder of Egyptian culture; and with the support of the Book of Revelation, in which she boldly and wittily finds her role as prophet justified:

> *I John saw. I testify;*
> *if any man shall add*
> *God shall add unto him the plagues,*
> *but he that sat upon the throne* said,
>
> *I make all things new.* (*CP,* 548–49)

H.D. is remembering how the author of the Book of Revelation emerges in his own voice at the very end: "For I testify unto every man that heareth the words of the prophecy of this book, If any man shall add unto these things, God shall add unto him the plagues that are written in this book"—thus denying future prophets any function. But the poet prefers to take her stand upon the words of Jesus himself, earlier in the book: "And he that sat upon the throne said, Behold, I make all things new. And he said unto me, Write: for these words are true and faithful" (Rev. 21:5). And so, with this encouragement, she writes her own prophecy. But, as Susan Gubar points out, her prophecy of hope and redemption is utterly different from "the severity and punishing cruelty of John's apocalypse." "While John sings the praises of seven angels whose seven golden bowls pour out the wrath of God upon the earth, H.D. calls on seven angels whose presence in war-torn London is a testament to the promise of rebirth that her bowl holds."[20]

She writes because she has been privileged to witness an apocalyptic scene of war in the heavens such as no earlier generation had seen, and more than this, she has watched with all the others who

> with unbowed head, watched
> and though unaware, worshipped
>
> and knew not that they worshipped
> and that they were
>
> that which they worshipped ... (*CP,* 551)

That is, the very spirit "of strength, endurance, anger / in their hearts." Out of all this her visions appear: "where the red-death fell / ... the lane is empty but the levelled wall / is purple as with purple spread / upon an altar"—but this is not the sacrifice of blood: "this is the flowering of the rood, / this is the flowering of the reed" (*CP,* 551). Thus in her wordplay the rod of Aaron and the cross of Christ are merged; the reed that struck Christ merges with the reed of the Nile earlier mentioned, with overtones of music and of poetry. Now the poetry shows an alchemical change, as "a word most bitter, *marah*," changes into "mer, mere, mère, mater, Maia, Mary, / Star of the Sea, / Mother," and this star changes into "Venus, Aphrodite, Astarte, / star of the east, / star of the west" (*CP,* 552–53), as the crucible of the mind creates a jewel

> green-white, opalescent,
>
> with under-layer of changing blue,
> with rose-vein; a white agate
>
> with a pulse uncooled that beats yet,
> faint blue-violet;
>
> it lives, it breathes,
> it gives off—fragrance? (*CP,* 554)

It is an image that suggests a concentration of creative power in a mind prepared to realize the miracle happening in the outer world, which now in May (Maia) is re-creating itself in the same subtle hues:

> tell me, in what other place
>
> will you find the may flowering
> mulberry and rose-purple?
>
> tell me, in what other city
> will you find the may-tree
>
> so delicate, green-white, opalescent
> like our jewel in the crucible?
> . . . .
> the outer precincts and the squares
> are fragrant ... (CP, 557)

Thus inner world and outer world share in this power of re-creation.

In this spirit of discovery the first half of the sequence reaches a climax as she crosses a "charred portico," enters "a house through a wall," and then sees "the tree flowering; / it was an ordinary tree / in an old garden-square"—a tree "burnt and stricken to the heart," yet flowering. This was actual, "it was not a dream / yet it was vision, / it was a sign":

> a half-burnt-out apple-tree
> blossoming;
>
> this is the flowering of the rood,
> this is the flowering of the wood ... (CP, 558–61)

But now the dream follows, to create a higher climax, out of a dream interpreted in ways that she had learned from Freud to trust. Instead of one of the seven angels of the poem, "the Lady herself" has appeared (CP, 564). But who was this Lady? Was she the Virgin Mary, as painted in the Renaissance with all her grace and glory and "damask and figured brocade"?

> We have seen her
> the world over

Our Lady of the Goldfinch,
Our Lady of the Candelabra,

Our Lady of the Pomegranate,
Our Lady of the Chair ... (*CP*, 564)

And so on for twenty-three couplets of affectionate detail, only to conclude:
"But none of these, none of these / suggest her as I saw her," though she had
something of the pagan and "gracious friendliness" of the "marble sea-maids
in Venice / who climb the altar-stair / at *Santa Maria dei Miracoli*" (*CP*, 566).
This joyous, teasing mood is something rare in H.D., and it continues in its
tantalizing way. Her "veils were *white as snow*," to use the language of Christ's
transfiguration, but in fact she bore "none of her usual attributes; / the Child
was not with her" (*CP*, 566–67). So then it was not Mary. But who then?

she must have been pleased with us,
for she looked so kindly at us

under her drift of veils,
and she carried a book.

This is a trap for the academic interpreter, whom she now proceeds to
parody:

Ah (you say), this is Holy Wisdom,
Santa Sophia, the SS of the *Sanctus Spiritus* ...

she brings the Book of Life, obviously. (*CP*, 568–69)

And so on and so on. But now the poet intervenes.

she is the Vestal
from the days of Numa,

she carries over the cult
of the *Bona Dea* ...

This is a cult of which the Virgin Mary is perhaps a descendant, in her
beneficent and redemptive function. But she has another dimension:

she carries a book but it is not
the tome of the ancient wisdom,

the pages, I imagine, are the blank pages
of the unwritten volume of the new ...

she is Psyche, the butterfly,
out of the cocoon. (*CP,* 570)

She is the creative consciousness of the prophetic voice, represented by this poet, writing amid ruin, but reaching out toward the future, predicting its redemption, exulting in the victory of life over death.

The redemptive quality of the female presence is continued in the third part, *The Flowering of the Rod* (composed in 1944, published in 1945), where the poet creates a new fable of redemption by her story of how Mary Magdalen gained from Kaspar, one of the Magi, the alabaster jar from which she anointed the feet of Christ. The fable places great emphasis upon the radiance of "her extraordinary hair," which, the reader knows, she used to dry the feet of Christ. Thus the Magdalen stands forth as a figure that is both sensuous and spiritual, with the fragrance from the ointment in the jar suggesting the same combination of sensuous and spiritual experience.[21] This is a tale, as the opening sections make clear, that reaches out now to cover all the "smouldering cities" of Europe—not only London, but other "broken" cities that need renewal, in other lands. It is a universal myth of forgiveness and healing, a parable like that of the grain of mustard seed:

> *the least of all seeds*
> that grows branches
>
> where the birds rest;
> it is that flowering balm,
>
> it is heal-all,
> everlasting;
>
> *it is the greatest among herbs*
> *and becometh a tree.* (*CP,* 585)

This is told in a manner that in places resembles a children's story—but then one remembers that it is a Christmas tale, as the date at the end reminds us: "December 18–31, 1944."

Her use of the myth of Isis in the *Trilogy* leads on to the central image (or *Eidolon*, as she calls it) of her longest and most difficult poem, *Helen in Egypt*, published in the year of her death, 1961, but completed during the early 1950s. It is a work of intermingled prose and poetry, like her version of the *Ion* of Euripides. But here the prose sometimes presents a special problem, for it often does not so much interpret the action of the poetry as question and trouble it.

Feeling this effect, I once searched in H.D.'s manuscripts and correspondence to find some evidence that the placing of these prose "captions" at the head of each poem was not H.D.'s conception. But it was. After the poetical sequence was complete, H.D. deliberately composed them to go with each poem, and she directed their placement. In a letter to Norman Pearson from Lugano on November 26, 1955, she says:

> I have the captions, the captions for the recording gave me this idea—and I think you will find that this whole set (no repeats from recording-captions) does hold the poems together, explain the at-times difficult 'philosophy' and put some of the mythological matter on the map. I am sure that you will like the set. I have asked Miss Woolford to leave broad white space between each numbered caption, so that the pages can be cut and each caption mounted BEFORE the poem, on a page facing the same, as for later printer.[22]

So there the captions are, and their presence creates a different work from the purely poetical sequence that she originally composed. We are not at liberty to ignore them. The question is: how do they function?

We may find an answer by remembering how often the prophetic writings of the Bible, as in the Books of Isaiah or Jeremiah, intermingle poetry and prose, with the effect that the prose creates a setting, or an explanation, for the poem that follows. I do not mean to say that H.D. consciously modeled her work on the writings of the biblical prophets, although she knew those writings well. I mean only to suggest that this analogy offers perhaps a key to the *kind* of work she was writing, and thus a key to the way in which we might deal with her intermingling of poetry and prose, here as well as in *Ion*.

First of all, we might regard *Helen in Egypt* as belonging to the genre of prophecy. If we grant this we can perhaps see more clearly how the various voices in the poem work—including the prose voices. As the example of the Hebrew prophets indicates, it is the role of the prophet to hear voices and to speak forth the words of those voices. The very word *prophet*, in Greek (as I have noted earlier), means "one who speaks for another"—for God, for the gods, or for other human beings.

From the opening poem in *Helen in Egypt*, H.D.'s Helen speaks with the voice of a prophet, saying "in this Amen-temple" (the temple of Amen-Ra, or Zeus-Ammon, in Egypt) she hears the "voices" of "the hosts / surging beneath the Walls" of Troy, voices that cry

> *O Helen, Helen, Daemon that thou art,*
>
> *we will be done forever*
> *with this charm, this evil philtre,*
> *this curse of Aphrodite;*
>
> so they fought, forgetting women,
> hero to hero, sworn brother and lover,
> and cursing Helen through eternity[23]

But the next poem presents a voice of redemption, as Helen says,

> Alas, my brothers,
> Helen did not walk
> upon the ramparts,
>
> she whom you cursed
> was but the phantom and the shadow thrown
> of a reflection;
>
> you are forgiven for I know my own,
> and God for his own purpose
> wills it so, that I
>
> stricken, forsaken draw to me,
> through magic greater than the trial of arms,
> your own invincible, unchallenged Sire ... (*H*, 5)

The poem is based on the alternate myth of Helen that Euripides used in his play on this subject and that Richard Strauss used for his opera *The*

Egyptian Helen, which H.D. may have seen. Here the story says that Helen never was in Troy, but that the gods sent there a phantom of Helen, while the true Helen was transported by Zeus to Egypt, where, after the war, she was reunited with Menelaus, or in H.D.'s version, with Achilles:

> Had they met before? Perhaps. Achilles was one of the princely suitors for her hand, at the court of her earthly father, Tyndareus of Sparta. But this Helen is not to be recognized by earthly splendour nor this Achilles by accoutrements of valour. It is the lost legions that have conditioned their encounter, and "the sea-enchantment in his eyes."

> How did we know each other?
> was it the sea-enchantment in his eyes
> of Thetis, his sea-mother? (*H*, 7)

In that phrase "the sea-enchantment in his eyes" we meet in both the prose and the poetry the leading phrase and symbol of the work, for Thetis will, as the sequence proceeds, be merged with Aphrodite, also born of the sea, and with Isis, called in the prose "the Egyptian Aphrodite" (*H*, 15). Helen herself is in the latter part of the work transformed into a living symbol of all these goddesses: the love of Achilles for Helen, then, suggests a way of redeeming the war-torn world, as the voice of Helen has said very early in the poem:

> it was God's plan
> to melt the icy fortress of the soul,
> and free the man;

> God's plan is other than the priests disclose;
> I did not know why
> (in dream or in trance)

> God had summoned me hither,
> until I saw the dim outline
> grown clearer,

> as the new Mortal,
> shedding his glory,
> limped slowly across the sand. (*H*, 10)

All this is quite in accord with the dual meaning of the work that H.D. suggested later on in the letter to Norman Pearson just cited. There she says that her poem has both "exoteric" meaning related to "all war-problems ... as well as being strictly INNER and esoteric and personal." That is to say, the imagery of war suggests the problems raised by war for all mankind down through the ages, along with the personal problems that such wars inevitably cause for individual lives, and caused, as we know, for H.D. herself, witness of two wars. Helen has taken within herself the sufferings of the whole war-stricken world:

> mine, the great spread of wings,
> the thousand sails,
> the thousand feathered darts
>
> that sped them home,
> mine, the one dart in the Achilles-heel,
> the thousand-and-one, mine. (*H*, 25)

To say that Helen speaks throughout as the prophet or priestess of Isis would be to sum up the meaning of the work; for Isis, that benevolent, creative goddess, was known throughout the Mediterranean world as the "Goddess of many names." For H.D., in this poem, her name is Helen.[24]

NOTES

1. Ezra Pound, *Gaudier-Brzeska*, 21.
2. See Cyrena N. Pondrom, "H.D. and the Origins of Imagism."
3. *Psyche Reborn: The Emergence of H.D.*, esp. 74–75. Like everyone who has written on H.D. in recent years, I am deeply indebted to the insights contained in this book, especially with regard to *Trilogy* and *Helen in Egypt*. For an account of H.D. as a poet pursuing a quest for transcendence and redemption throughout her career, see the important but neglected study by Angela DiPace Fritz, *Thought and Vision: A Critical Reading of H.D.'s Poetry*. For H.D. as "a visionary poet" see Alicia Ostriker, "The Poet as Heroine: Learning to Read H.D." At a June 1996 conference in Orono, Maine, Ostriker demonstrated the continuance of the tradition of Hebrew prophecy by drawing a parallel between Allen Ginsberg and the prophet Jeremiah.
4. H.D., *Collected Poems 1912–1944*, ed. Louis L. Martz, 29–31. Quotations from H.D.'s poetry up through *Trilogy* are taken from this edition, hereafter cited as *CP*.
5. Pound, *Literary Essays*, 3–5.
6. The typescript is in the H.D. Archive of the Beinecke Library, Yale University; see the introduction to *CP*, xiv.
7. For an account of these changes see the introduction and notes to *CP*, xiv–xviii,

617–18. An interpretation of these changes has been given by Elizabeth Dodd in *The Veiled Mirror and the Woman Poet: H.D., Louise Bogan, Elizabeth Bishop, and Louise Glück*, 57–70.

8. Introduction to *CP*, xxiii; Burnett, *H.D. between Image and Epic: The Mysteries of Her Poetics*, 104.

9. *Tribute to Freud: Writing on the Wall, Advent*, 45–46; hereafter cited as *TTF*.

10. The relation of H.D.'s couplets (a "marked divergence from the style of H.D.'s earlier verse") to the couplets of the Pythian has been noted by Sandra M. Gilbert and Susan Gubar in *No Man's Land: The Place of the Woman Writer in the Twentieth Century*, 3:192.

11. The phrase "my writing" refers directly to the "writing on the wall," but it may well be taken to describe H.D.'s own writing.

12. For an account of her notorious performance as a "Red" in Boston see Irma Duncan and Allan Ross Macdougall, *Isadora Duncan's Russian Days and Her Last Years in France* (London: Gollancz, 1929), 164–65. The color red pursued Isadora even at her death, when her red shawl became entangled in the wheel of that Bugatti. In "The Dancer" H.D. presents herself as a witness of an actual performance: could this possibly have been the famous "Roses from the South" for which we have detailed choreographical directions? (See the recent volume by Nadia Chilkovsky Nahumck, *Isadora Duncan: The Dances* [Washington, D.C.: National Museum of Women in the Arts, 1994], 391–405). If this were so, the dance might provide another reason for the prefix "rhodo." In the reprise of the Dancer in the next poem of this triad, "The Master," H.D. gives (*CP*, 456) a more precise description of the "rhododendron" dance: "she leaps from rock to rock / (it was only a small circle for her dance) / and the hills dance, / she conjures the hills; /rhododendrons / awake." In this reprise the Dancer is three times addressed as "Rhodocleia" at the close; the name is evidently derived from the Greek ???os, meaning "fame" or "glory": "red fame," "rose glory." To see the Dancer as Isadora would complete the triad with another famous figure, to match the allusions to Freud and Lawrence in the two subsequent poems. In *CP* I suggested that the Dancer might be the actress-ballerina Anny Ahlers (*CP*, xxviii, 614 n. 15). But I now think this identification is unlikely, except as the early death of Anny Ahlers in 1933 may have precipitated a memory of Isadora.

13. In this opening H.D. seems to be using the word *strange* in the old sense of "foreign," "situated outside one's own land" (*OED*). These two Americans have come together (in Paris?) from "strange cities" (London, Moscow). Then at the outset of the second section she adds: "I am now from the city / of thinkers, of wisdom-makers." Is this the "Miletus" in which she met with Freud? The whole poem sounds like a backward projection, an experience relived in the present. For H.D.'s powers of projection see Adalaide Morris, "The Concept of Projection: H.D.'s Visionary Powers." In *Feminist Studies* 7 (1981): 407–16, Rachel Blau DuPlessis and Susan Stanford Friedman published "The Master," followed by their essay, "'Woman Is Perfect': H.D.'s Debate with Freud."

14. *Ion: A Play after Euripides*, rev. John Walsh, 112; hereafter cited as *Ion*.

15. H.D.–Pearson Correspondence, H.D. Archive, Beinecke Library, Yale University. *CP* (367–439) gives the whole group in H.D.'s arrangement. It is a series that moves from Greek themes through overtly personal poems of love and friendship to the final poem, "Magician" (originally entitled "Master"). (See introduction to *CP*, xxiv–xxvi.)

16. *H.D. between Image and Epic*, chap. 9.

17. See below, p. 118–19.

18. Gilbert and Gubar, *No Man's Land*, 3:180.

19. The following commentary on *Trilogy* is substantially the same as the commentary that appeared in the introduction to *CP*, but with a stronger emphasis on the prophetic voice. With this theme the commentary is distinct from, though related to, the many important interpretations of *Trilogy* that have appeared in the last two decades, many of them written from the standpoint of psychiatric theory, as in the studies of Dianne Chisholm, Susan Edmunds, Claire Buck, and Deborah Kelly Kloepfer listed in the bibliography. For a study of *Trilogy* from a related point of view see Donna Krolik Hollenberg, *H.D.: The Poetics of Childbirth and Creativity*. For a reading of *Trilogy* in the context of Pre-Raphaelite and Decadent views of woman, see Cassandra Laity, *H.D. and the Victorian Fin de Siècle*, chap. 7. See also the studies by Albert Gelpi and Adalaide Morris listed in the bibliography.

20. Susan Gubar, "The Echoing Spell of H.D.'s *Trilogy*," *Signets*, 307.

21. Susan Schweik, in *A Gulf So Deeply Cut: American Women Poets and the Second World War*, has given an eloquent account of the imagery of myrrh and the figure of the Magdalen in the third part of *Trilogy*; see her chap. 9, "Myrrh to Myrrh: H.D., War, and Biblical Narrative."

22. H.D.–Pearson Correspondence, H.D. Archive.

23. *Helen in Egypt*, 4; hereafter cited as *H*.

24. For detailed interpretations of the poem see the studies by Albert Gelpi, Dianne Chisholm, Susan Edmunds, Susan Stanford Friedman, Donna Krolik Hollenberg, and Deborah Kelly Kloepfer listed in the bibliography.

ANITA PATTERSON

Jazz, Realism, and the Modernist Lyric: The Poetry of Langston Hughes

In 1940 Richard Wright, praising Langston Hughes's contribution to the development of modern American literature, observed that Hughes's "realistic position" had become the "dominant outlook of all those Negro writers who have something to say."[1] Nineteen years later James Baldwin faulted Hughes for failing to follow through consistently on the artistic premises laid out in his early verse. The problem with his unsuccessful poems, Baldwin said, was that they "take refuge, finally, in a fake simplicity in order to avoid the very difficult simplicity of experience." In succumbing to the idiomatic demands of a sociological perspective—the pressure, that is, to "hold the experience outside him"—they did not fulfill an essential criterion of Baldwin's realism, namely, the evocation of a point of view that stands "within the experience and outside it at the same time." To argue his point, Baldwin cited the last line of a jazz poem by Hughes called "Dream Boogie," which first appeared as part of *Montage of a Dream Deferred* in 1951. "Hughes," said Baldwin, "knows the bitter truth behind these hieroglyphics, what they are designed to protect, what they are designed to convey. But he has not forced them into the realm of art where their meaning would become clear and overwhelming. 'Hey, pop! / Re-bop! / Mop!' conveys much more on Lenox Avenue than it does in this book, which is not the way it ought to be."[2]

The main criticism Baldwin raises against jazz poems like "Dream

From *Modern Language Quarterly*, Vol 61, No. 4 (December 2000). © 2000 University of Washington.

Boogie" is that they do not offer a clearly recognizable, accurate record of experience that calls attention to their embeddedness in history. Such summary judgment has hampered further exploration of how Hughes's jazz poetics contributed to twentieth-century realism or to the development of the modernist lyric.

This essay situates Hughes's jazz poetics within the arc of his entire career to show how modernist experiments in poems like "Dream Boogie" are in keeping with his earlier attempts at lyric realism. I will focus on two main ideas. The first is that Hughes's poems challenge the critical distinction between "realism" and the "avant-garde": even his simplest, most documentary, and most historically engaged poems evince a characteristically modernist preoccupation with the figurative implications of form. Second, Hughes's realist approach to the lyric offers a fresh perspective on some central tendencies in transatlantic modernism: his repudiation of racial separatism, his interest in the relationship between poetry and American music, and his experiments with a jazz poetics are, in many ways, comparable to the critique of romantic cultural nationalism undertaken by Ezra Pound, Hart Crane, T.S. Eliot, and other modernists writing in the aftermath of the Great War. The convergence between Hughes's techniques and those of the American avant-garde highlights the importance of metonymic style, and of the historical knowledge that underlies the impulse toward formal experiment and improvisation, as a relatively neglected feature of the modernist lyric.

It is by now almost a commonplace to say that Hughes revised and extended the populist angle of vision explored in the previous decade by Edwin Arlington Robinson, Vachel Lindsay, Carl Sandburg, and others. But we have yet to understand the series of formal experiments he executed within the lyric that show his engagement with questions shared by his high modernist contemporaries.

REALISM AND FORM IN HUGHES'S POETRY

As a rubric, realism has been subject to heated debate and casual dismissal in the history of American criticism. "American realism virtually has no school; its most dominating and influential advocate, William Dean Howells, often seems to ride along in a strange vacuum, nearly unheeded in his continual insistence on the proprieties of the everyday, stable characterization, and moral certainty, while almost every other important author of the period simply refused, on these terms, to become a realist."[3] Whereas in Europe the great period of realism occurred throughout the second half of the

nineteenth century, in North America the movement emerged in full force
only with Howells's advocacy in the nineties.[4]

Partly in response to Erich Auerbach's *Mimesis*, theoretical descriptions
of realism in modern American fiction have proliferated in recent decades.[5]
Yet little sustained, systematic analysis has been done on the formal
development of realism in the modern lyric.[6] Such neglect may be explained
in part by the fact that the realist movement was long excluded from accounts
of twentieth-century American poetry, because it was considered formally
without interest—a servile, transparent copying of the world.[7] *The New
Princeton Encyclopedia of Poetry and Poetics*, for example, defines realism solely
in contradistinction to the intensified perception, densely metaphorical style,
and artificiality of the lyric and adds that, "in a general sense, realistic poetry
may result from any down-to-earth opposition to what seem artificial rules
of versification or arbitrary restrictions on matter or diction.... The precepts
of realism are often considered inimical to the spirit of lyric poetry."[8]

The latent critical bias against realism was memorably addressed by
Georg Lukács, who in the late 1950s offered a surprising and useful
theoretical reappraisal that paid special attention to formal issues. In *The
Meaning of Contemporary Realism* Lukács arrived at a description of literary
realism that helped readers bracket ideological content and focus instead on
innovations in language and method. One objection he raised to current
critical approaches to realism was that the political message of literature was
fast becoming the overriding preoccupation of reviewers; as a result, literary
standards were falling precipitously.[9] Another pressing concern was that
modernist tastes in the 1920s had led critics to neglect works that exhibited
the traditional mimetic techniques of realism. Criticism, according to
Lukács, was hindered by the unexamined belief that realism was always, by
definition, antithetical to modernism:

> Let us begin by examining two prejudices. The first is typical of
> much present-day bourgeois criticism. It is contained in the
> proposition that the literature of "modernism," of the *avant-
> garde*, is the essentially modern literature. The traditional
> techniques of realism, these critics assert, are inadequate, because
> too superficial, to deal with the realities of our age. (13)

Hughes's poems raise questions about stultifying critical binarisms that
for years have pitted modern realism against modernist antirealism, tradition
against the avant-garde, political content against artistic form. As a poet,
Hughes constantly tries to illustrate how formal qualities may assist an act of

engaged social criticism. Instead of using words that deceive us into seeing
only their "transparency" and make us believe that we are taking an
unmediated look through a windowpane to a world outside the poem,
Hughes offers historical knowledge by directing our attention to his careful
arrangement of words on the page. His style often dramatizes how language
shapes the poem's social perspectives.

"Flight," which first appeared in the June 1930 issue of *Opportunity*,
demonstrates how Hughes's realist poetics meets modernist formal
expectations. The poem is set in a swamp, during the postemancipation
period: a black man, accused of raping a white woman, is trying to escape
from a lynch mob. The pursuit of hounds recalls the history of slavery and
suggests that rituals of racial violence in the South continued, and even
escalated, after emancipation. Hughes's speaker assumes two points of view:
observer and victim. The poem begins by giving the victim, who initially
occupies the same position as the reader, the impossible task of stepping in
mud without leaving tracks:

> Plant your toes in the cool swamp mud.
> Step and leave no track.
> Hurry, sweating runner!
> The hounds are at your back.
>
> *No I didn't touch her*
> *White flesh ain't for me.*
>
> Hurry! Black boy, hurry!
> They'll swing you to a tree.[10]

In "Flight" Hughes uses a short lyric form to present a splintered
aspect of a reality too vast and horrifying to comprehend in its entirety.
Instead the speaker describes, analyzes, and orders a tragic, swiftly unfolding
moment. The lyric evokes a tension between Hughes's artistic suspension of
time and the time-bound social realities that are the subject of his poem. But
despite his reliance on the temporal restrictions of the genre, Hughes refuses
to rest content with the familiar consolations of lyric transcendence and
disengagement. Distrustful of such forced integrities and closures, he builds
in a narrative structure that implies a larger, sociohistorical context, giving
disquieting openness to the exigencies that lend the poem shape and
significance.

The reign of terror in the wake of emancipation generated the special conditions in which modern African American poetry emerged. In the postbellum South slavery was replaced by other forms of racial subjection: indentured servitude, black codes, the contract system, vagrancy statutes, and lynching.[11] Between 1900 and 1930 massive numbers of African Americans fled the rural South and traveled to northern cities like Chicago, Detroit, and New York. During the time that Hughes wrote, many of his contemporaries started the long process of coming to grips with his lyric's main subject, namely, the violent causes of this exodus, now known as the "Great Migration."[12] "Flight" documents how, for many southern freedmen, migration had become more than a necessary socioeconomic resource; it was a way of life, a means of preserving their safety, sanity, and dignity.

In "Flight," however, realist verisimilitude coexists with modernist formal innovation. In this respect Hughes's style fits an essential criterion that Hugo Friedrich proposes for the modernist lyric.[13] The preoccupation with expressive freedom makes sense inasmuch as the plight of the lynched man described in "Flight" forces us to question a fundamental tenet of nineteenth-century realism: that a realist work should depict a form of social life in which the individual can act with "autonomous motivation" (Preminger and Brogan, 1016).

The guiding metaphor in the poem's title also works to correct popular misconceptions of the causes of the Great Migration, misconceptions exacerbated by the constant use of the trope in journalistic analyses by Hughes's black contemporaries. In *Opportunity*, the same journal in which Hughes's poem appeared, Charles S. Johnson asked, "How much is migration a flight from persecution?"[14] Black public intellectuals such as Alain Locke, portraying the social formation of the "New Negro" in 1925, tried to play down the violent causes of migration by using the image of "deliberate flight" to suggest that African Americans were engaged in a mythic, quintessentially American quest for opportunity.[15]

Lynching was, in certain respects, similar to the experience that the Great War offered transatlantic modernists, since its moral horrors spurred Hughes and other African American poets to discover formalist freedoms that were wholly new. But although Hughes's passion for freedom resembles that of the avant-garde, his practices as a modern lyricist are distinctive insofar as they dramatize his effort to bridge a cultural divide between a folkloric African American tradition that is largely oral and the privileged arena of "literature." Thus the lyric's opening line may be read as an apt allegory of Hughes's predicament as a modern African American poet. It compares his effort to fashion enduring metrical feet that fit the rhythms of an oral tradition with a fleeing man's attempt to "plant" his "toes" in the mud.

Because self-referentiality penetrates a privileged arena, there is also the suggestion of trespass: the poet's act is described in terms that bring to mind a man in flight, a man accused of rape. Hughes's exhilarating discovery of freedom through formal modes of expression—metaphors rich in ambiguity, the distancing effects and pleasures of rhyme and writerly italicization, the metrical swing of his verse—is counterpointed by an awareness that such freedom implicates him in the history he relates. Hughes's use of italics, for example, makes the victim's words echo, as if lifted from a realist novel about a lynching that was written for a mass audience.[16] The device reminds us that, by adopting the lyric as his preferred genre, Hughes has aligned himself with other avant-garde artists in refusing to satisfy the raging market demand for sensationalist fiction that exacerbated a mass audience's tendency toward escapism. Even as his poem resists such a flight from reality, however, Hughes also insists on his freedom as an artist: the freedom, that is, to work continually at formal experimentation and to transcend the all-determining, muddy historical contingencies that fatally distort perception.

Hughes's gesture toward modernist innovation—his veiled reference to an avant-garde flight from verisimilitude—ultimately serves the ends of his realism, insofar as it raises the reader's awareness of the post-emancipation context of the lyric. The violent historical developments that caused the Great Migration and spurred Hughes's engagement with formal questions are linked to the rhythmic cadences of "Flight" by the verb *swing*, at the end of the poem: the neat succession of rhythms that fall ("Hurry! Black boy, hurry!") and rise again ("They'll swing you to a tree") ominously dramatizes the swinging motion of the hanged man's body.

"Flight" questions familiar definitions of literary realism, as well as the idea that Hughes's realist commitments foreclose the possibility of modernism. At the same time that he tries to document the violent conditions that shaped the emergence of modern African American poetry, Hughes also invites us to consider how, and why, the poet's manipulation of his medium expresses artistic freedom from the contingencies he depicts. In the end he shows us that the nineteenth-century realist goal of transparent verisimilitude is unattainable in the modern lyric. Such figurative complexity highlights a modernist tendency in Hughes's realism.

"THE WEARY BLUES":
HUGHES'S CRITIQUE OF BLACK CULTURAL NATIONALISM

To confer shape on what Eliot described as the "immense panorama of futility and anarchy which is contemporary history," Hughes turned not to classical myths but to a poetics of migration that had been used to impose order on and give significance to the traumatic postemancipation experience of African Americans, and that figured in many ballads, reels, and blues and ragtime songs Hughes remembered hearing during his childhood in Lawrence, Kansas.[17] A great deal has already been said about the "modernity" of African American music and, in particular, about the centrality of the blues to Hughes's lyric practice.[18] Arnold Rampersad's suggestion that the blues poems in *Fine Clothes to the Jew* are some of Hughes's most important works has prompted a critical reassessment of his project and legacy.[19] There is, however, much to be learned about how his blues and jazz poetics fit in the development of the modernist lyric, both in the United States and in Europe, and, conversely, how his engagement with modernism contributed to his technique as a realist poet.

In his autobiography Hughes, appealing to the strength, humor, and "rooted power" of the blues, tries to change the derogatory view of folk culture that prevailed among the African American middle class and Euro-Americans.[20] Ralph Ellison once described the blues as a "chronicle of personal catastrophe expressed lyrically," a mode of remembrance that keeps the experience alive and also transcends it, "not by the consolations of philosophy, but by squeezing from it a near-tragic, near-comic lyricism."[21] The artistic possibilities of traditional blues are examined in "Red Clay Blues," a poem Hughes wrote in collaboration with Richard Wright. The lyric states, with eloquent simplicity, a near-tragic vision of history that is tempered by a strong belief in the sanctity of knowledge. The first premise of the opening stanza is that "knowing" history means knowing what it feels like to long for the red clay of Georgia:

> I miss that red clay, Lawd, I
> Need to feel it in my shoes.
> Says miss that red clay, Lawd, I
> Need to feel it in my shoes.
> I want to get to Georgia cause I
> Got them red clay blues.
> (*CP,* 212)

These lines suggest, with remarkable precision, the transition from spiritual to blues, and from sacred to secular idioms, that took place during the late nineteenth century. For instance, the syntax subsumes the act of praying in an ornamental cadence ("Lawd") designed to enhance the expression of personal, daily needs. Despite the starkly conventional form, the lyric's style affirms the individuality of both speaker and poet. The line breaks rhythmically emphasize the importance of human desire and possession ("miss," "need," "want," "got"), Hughes's unabashed embrace of the oral tradition and a vernacular blues syntax ("Says miss that red clay"), and the metrical freedom discovered through repeated pronominal self-naming ("I").

Hughes broke new ground in his poetry, partly because he saw that his engagement with canonical texts and his interest in traditional English and American prosody would provide a much-needed, clarifying distance from the rich but potentially formulaic idioms he borrowed from African American folk culture. Ellison made a comment that seems to encapsulate Hughes's efforts to establish a critical, intellectual perspective on the folk tradition as a poetic resource:

> The Negro American writer is also an heir of the human experience which is literature, and this might well be more important to him than his living folk tradition. For me, at least ... the stability of the Negro American folk tradition became precious as a result of an act of literary discovery.... For those who are able to translate its meanings into wider, more precise vocabularies it has much to offer indeed.[22]

Hughes was well aware that, as a poet, he needed to come to terms with the fundamental difference between blues language and poetic language. Despite his devotion to the traditional African American folk idiom, in a number of poems written during the 1920s he took a serious look at the artistic costs and devastating emotional consequences of the strict expressive constraints imposed by the blues.

In "The Weary Blues," first published in 1925, Hughes expresses his desire to encounter the idiomatic options raised by the blues as possibilities that he was free to choose, not as habitual motions that he was compelled to reiterate. The blues song has been framed by the mediating perspective of the lyric speaker, who describes the "moan" of the "poor piano." In contrast to the speaker, who tries to put the meaning of the music into words, the blues player conveys his feelings not so much with words as with the "lazy sway" of his body:[23]

> Droning a drowsy syncopated tune,
> Rocking back and forth to a mellow croon,
>   I heard a Negro play.

Down on Lenox Avenue the other night
By the pale dull pallor of an old gas light
   He did a lazy sway....
   He did a lazy sway....
To the tune o' those Weary Blues.
With his ebony hands on each ivory key
He made that poor piano moan with melody.
   O Blues!
Swaying to and fro on his rickety stool
He played that sad raggy tune like a musical fool.
   Sweet Blues!
Coming from a black man's soul.
  . . . .
Thump, thump, thump, went his foot on the floor.
He played a few chords then he sang some more—
   "I got the Weary Blues
   And I can't be satisfied.
   Got the Weary Blues
   And can't be satisfied—
   I ain't happy no mo'
   And I wish that I had died."
And far into the night he crooned that tune.
The stars went out and so did the moon.
The singer stopped playing and went to bed
While the Weary Blues echoed through his head.
He slept like a rock or a man that's dead.
                           (*CP*, 50)

    Hughes expected many readers to think that poems such as "The Weary Blues" were not about anything more than a piano player playing blues. In fact, he often invited and validated such interpretations.[24] The poem may be seen to enact, however, a renunciation of metaphor—a despairing gesture suggesting that imaginative dreamlike escapes from the "outer" world do nothing to change social conditions. In another poem the romantic images of the stars and moon going out would be richly evocative and metaphorical, signifying unfulfilled desire or desolation over a dream deferred. But here their figurative weight is offset by a context that leads us to believe that Hughes merely wants to indicate the passage of time. The latent metaphorical meaning of his idiom is suppressed. Whereas in "Flight" Hughes acknowledges his passion for figuration as a mode of transcendence, in this lyric he dramatizes how having the blues may undermine a poet's belief in the modernist freedom to trope. The stars and moon going out and the player going to bed illustrate the action of lulling metaphorical language to the dead sleep of verisimilitude.

In "The Weary Blues" Hughes implies that the conventional blues idiom is so compelling, and so limited, as to threaten his imaginative freedom. In addition, the mechanical objects that occupy the poem's setting—the gas light, the rickety stool, the piano parts, and so on—evoke another modern development that imperils artistic freedom. Like many of his contemporaries, both in the United States and abroad, Hughes was aware of the cultural crisis caused by mechanization. In 1933 F.R. Leavis, quoting H.G. Wells, would vividly condemn the "vast and increasing inattention" resulting from new forms of mechanical reproduction: "The machine ... has brought about changes in habit and the circumstances of life at a rate for which we have no parallel....When we consider, for instance, the processes of mass-production and standardisation in the form represented by the Press, it becomes obviously of sinister significance that they should be accompanied by a process of levelling-down." Two years before Hughes published "The Weary Blues," Eliot warned against the insidious effects of gramophones, motorcars, loudspeakers, and cinemas in which the mind was "lulled by continuous senseless music and continuous action too rapid ... to act upon."[25]

Hughes's concern about the leveling-down effects of technology, which are barely hinted at in "The Weary Blues," becomes a point of focus in "Summer Night," which first appeared in the December 1925 issue of *Crisis*. Like the typist in Eliot's *Waste Land*, who paces about her room, her brain allowing only a "half-formed thought," and who "smoothes her hair with automatic hand" as she puts a record on the gramophone, Hughes's lyric speaker is left virtually without words once the player piano, the Victrola, and the other "sounds" of Harlem fall silent in the still night.[26] He can only toss restlessly, muttering ineffective generalities:

> The sounds
> Of the Harlem night
> Drop one by one into stillness.
> The last player-piano is closed.
> The last victrola ceases with the
> "Jazz-Boy Blues."
> The last crying baby sleeps
> And the night becomes

Still as a whispering heartbeat.
I toss
Without rest in the darkness,
Weary as the tired night,
My soul
Empty as the silence,
Empty with a vague,
Aching emptiness,
Desiring,
Needing someone,
Something. (*CP*, 59)

The passage demonstrates the high stakes of Hughes's project as a poet who deals in words, and it implies his effort, as Pound might say, to "modernize" his perspective by distancing himself from the nonverbal expressiveness of the blues.

Together, "Summer Night" and "The Weary Blues" scrutinize the view that the blues is an essentially "black" musical emotion that can never be individuated for Euro-American readers. By raising this question, Hughes anticipates Paul Gilroy's proposition, in his recent study of music and the black diaspora, that a "topos of unsayability"—a habitual invocation of truths that cannot be put into words—lies at the heart of black musical culture.[27]

Gilroy's discussion follows in large part from W.E.B. DuBois's analysis of African American spirituals in *The Souls of Black Folk*. DuBois was one of the first to notice that many things were conventionally left unsaid in the folk lyrics. Such "omissions and silences," and the lack of reference to social conditions, testify to the violent subjugation of enslavement and reflect the "shadow of fear" that hung over the slaves. DuBois concludes that, in this crucial respect, the folk idiom imposed constraints on "allowable thought" and confined poetry "for the most part to single or double lines":

Over the inner thoughts of the slaves and their relations one with another the shadow of fear ever hung, so that we get but glimpses here and there, and also with them, eloquent omissions and silences. Mother and child are sung, but seldom father; fugitive and weary wanderer call for pity and affection, but there is little of wooing and wedding; the rocks and the mountains are well known, but home is unknown.... Of deep successful love there is ominous silence.... [The] rhythm of the songs, and the limitations of allowable thought, confined the poetry for the most part to

single or double lines, and they seldom were expanded to
quatrains or longer tales.[28]

Gilroy argues that the "topos of unsayability" is an outgrowth of the
experience of slavery, and no doubt DuBois and Hughes would agree. But
whereas Gilroy celebrates this topos, which can be used "to challenge the
privileged conceptions of both language and writing as preeminent
expressions of human consciousness" (74), Hughes considered it part of the
debilitating legacy of slavery and was deeply concerned about the "silences"
that structure thought and expression in the blues. True, in the short lyric
"Hey!" Hughes jokes about the curious effects of unsayability by drawing our
attention to the alluring ambiguity of the blues singer's sustained note, "hey":

> Sun's a settin',
> This is what I'm gonna sing.
> Sun's a settin',
> This is what I'm gonna sing:
> I feels de blues a comin',
> Wonder what de blues'll bring?
> (*CP*, 112)

But Hughes also understood how severely limiting such a convention was. In
"The Weary Blues" he suggests that unsayability cannot be a topos so long as
it is forced on African Americans by the memory of "racial terror" (Gilroy, 74).

As we have seen, the stylistic complexity of many of the poems Hughes
wrote during the 1920s and early 1930s creates a clarifying perspective on the
folk tradition and distances him from racial separatist explanations of culture.[29]
Although Hughes was noted as one of the first poets to celebrate the beauty of
the blues as an American art form, he was not a "black nationalist," in Amiri
Baraka's sense of the term.[30] In *Blues People: Negro Music in White America*
(1963) Baraka began to advance a separatist line of argument:

> Blues as an autonomous music had been in a sense inviolable.
> There was no clear way into it ... except as concomitant with what
> seems to me to be the peculiar social, cultural, economic, and
> emotional experience of a black man in America.... The materials
> of blues were not available to the white American.... It was as if
> these materials were secret and obscure, and blues a kind of
> ethno-historic rite as basic as blood.[31]

Forty years before the Black Arts movement Hughes was writing poems that examined the tragic implications of racial separatist logic. As "The Weary Blues" shows, it would have been impossible for him to write completely in accordance with the verbal constraints of the folk tradition: to do so would have resulted in an endlessly mechanical recapitulation of the racial terror of slavery. Viewed in these terms, Hughes's repudiation of racialist ideas about culture in poems written during the 1920s anticipates the positions he explored in his so-called radical poetry, written between 1932 and 1938.[32]

HUGHES AND THE MODERNIST CRITIQUE OF ROMANTIC NATIONALISM

Hughes's resistance to separatist descriptions of African American culture is, in certain respects, strikingly similar to the critique of romantic nationalism undertaken by many of his modernist contemporaries, both in the United States and in Europe. D.H. Lawrence, T.S. Eliot, Ezra Pound, Wallace Stevens, Hart Crane, and others wrote poems in which they tried to come to terms with the difficult necessity of cross-cultural identification. Many of these poems centered on the changing nature of musical experience and the devastating, far-reaching consequences of European nationalism that culminated in the Great War.

An early draft of Lawrence's "Piano," which first appeared in *New Poems* in 1918, explores how the speaker's response to Hungarian music reflects the historical causes of the war. Like Hughes, Lawrence tried to show how traces of history were ceaselessly echoed in nineteenth-century musical forms. But whereas Hughes was primarily concerned with illustrating the American legacy of racial violence that shaped musical forms such as swing and the blues, Lawrence confronted the legacy of romanticism in Europe:

> Somewhere beneath that piano's superb sleek black
> Must hide my mother's piano, little and brown, with the back
> That stood close to the wall, and the front's faded silk, both torn,
> And the keys with little hollows, that my mother's fingers had worn.

> Softly, in the shadows, a woman is singing to me
> Quietly, through the years I have crept back to see
> A child sitting under the piano, in the boom of the shaking strings
> Pressing the little poised feet of the mother who smiles as she sings.

> The full throated woman has chosen a winning, living song
> And surely the heart that is in me must belong

To the old Sunday evenings, when darkness wandered outside
And hymns gleamed on our warm lips, as we watched mother's
    fingers glide.

Or this is my sister at home in the old front room
Singing love's first surprised gladness, alone in the gloom.
She will start when she sees me, and blushing, spread out her hands
To cover my mouth's raillery, till I'm bound in her shame's heart
    spun bands

A woman is singing me a wild Hungarian air
And her arms, and her bosom, and the whole of her soul is bare,
And the great black piano is clamouring as my mother's never could
    clamour
And my mother's tunes are devoured of this music's ravaging
    glamour.[33]

"Piano" is as much about the creative hunger to absorb different
cultural influences, and the threat it poses to the cherished individuality of
regions, as it is about the fateful vying for dominance among the major
European powers in the decades preceding the Great War. The "wild
Hungarian air" (a phrase Lawrence omitted in the final version of the poem)
recalls the intensification of European nationalist rivalries during this
period.[34] The poem is built on a perceived contrast between, on the one
hand, the speaker's present experience of the "clamouring" sound of a sleek
black concert hall piano and a song that bares a woman's soul to the public;
and, on the other, his secretly erotic childhood memories of his mother and
sister performing hymns and love songs at home. By searching for hidden
continuities between the raging, devouring glamour associated with
Hungarian music and the speaker's fond memories of British middle-class
musical culture, Lawrence discloses the speaker's painful ambivalence toward
the sentiment awakened in him by the song.[35]

"Piano" also refers, more broadly, to the changing of European musical
experience and sensibility from the early nineteenth to the early twentieth
century. Concert life and musical tastes were dramatically transformed in the
Allied countries during and after the Great War. Fewer keyboard battle
pieces, for example, were written then than at the height of romantic
nationalism during the nineteenth century, and composers began to turn
their attention to serious vocal and orchestral laments. In the Allied
countries there was a growing tendency to ban concert performances of

German music; in England, France, and America musicians were encouraged to perform the works of "native" composers.[36] In the first half of the nineteenth century chamber music had gradually been moved out of domestic spaces and salons into public performance halls. "Personality," observes James H. Johnson, "thrust itself to center stage in the romantic decades."[37]

Lawrence and Hughes both questioned popular notions of racial authenticity in music. Like Hughes's "Weary Blues," Lawrence's "Piano" expresses ambivalence toward the expressive and perceptual constraints of the "polarization" of peoples in "particular localit[ies]."[38] Hughes was concerned to stand, as it were, both inside and outside the blues and figuratively to imply his own motives for moving away from the rich but ultimately constraining formulas of traditional blues lyrics. Lawrence's stance is similar, insofar as his speaker affirms, with great affection, the distinctive musical heritages of nations while he conveys the horrifying irony that such seemingly benign cultural distinctions would, in the end, be used as a justification for war. By upholding both the distinctiveness and the universality of musical experience, both poets suggest that music, in the words of Theodor Adorno, "more than any other artistic medium, expresses the national principle's antinomies" (quoted in Gilroy, 72).

Hughes's technically self-conscious approach to realism in the lyric, his prosodic resistance to separatist paradigms, and his interest in the history and irreducible hybridity of African American culture are aspects of his lyric practice that he shared with his American modernist contemporaries. Pound's 1920 poem *Hugh Selwyn Mauberley*, for example, may be said to anticipate Hughes's "Weary Blues," since it also confronts the problem of realism in the lyric. Although Pound keeps references to social setting and details to a bare minimum in the poem, his interest in finding a modern poetic equivalent to Henry James's realism is evident in a 1922 letter to Felix Schelling, in which Pound calls his poem "an attempt to condense the James novel."[39] Moreover, like Hughes, Pound uses the image of a piano to explore how modern art has come dangerously close to the mass-produced conformity, planned obsolescence, and rapid replacement associated with fashion. The pianola metonymically represents the forces of mass production:

The tea-rose tea-gown, etc.
supplants the mousseline of Cos,
The pianola "replaces"
Sappho's barbitos.[40]

Another American modernist, Hart Crane, examined how the violent history that gave rise to African American music ultimately shaped the imagery and cadence of his own idiom:

> "what do you want? getting weak on the links?
> fandaddle daddy don't ask for change—IS THIS
> FOURTEENTH? it's half past six she said—if
> you don't like my gate why did you
> swing on it, why *didja*
> swing on it
> anyhow—"
>
> And somehow anyhow swing—
>
> The phonographs of hades in the brain
> Are tunnels that re-wind themselves, and love
> A burnt match skating in a urinal—
> Somewhere above Fourteenth TAKE THE EXPRESS
> To brush some new presentiment of pain—[41]

In 1948, in *The Auroras of Autumn*, Wallace Stevens vividly probed the sources of his ambivalent love of and animosity toward primitivist decadence: the mind's eye first summons up a festive scene of "negresses" dancing and then suddenly becomes cruelly analytic, mocking the whole party for their brutish disorderliness:

> The father fetches negresses to dance,
> Among the children, like curious ripenesses
> Of pattern in the dance's ripening.
>
> For these the musicians make insidious tones,
> Clawing the sing-song of their instruments.
> The children laugh and jangle a tinny time.
> .   .   .   .
> What festival? This loud, disordered mooch?
> These hospitaliers? These brute-like guests?[42]

Of Hughes's modernist contemporaries, however, the poet whose interest in realism, racial cross-identification, and American music comes closest to his own is not Pound, Crane, or Stevens but Eliot. In many of the early poems collected in the leather-bound notebook begun in 1909—some, such as "Opera," "First Caprice in North Cambridge," and "The Burnt Dancer," which were unpublished until 1996, and others, such as "Rhapsody on a Windy Night" and "Portrait of a Lady," which appeared in *Prufrock and Other Observations* in 1917—Eliot shares Hughes's preoccupation with realism and the analogy between musical and poetic forms.[43] But whereas Hughes's poems more often than not call attention to the African American folk origins of the blues as an American musical form, Eliot takes the occasion of these early poems to explore the hybrid European origins of modern American music by adapting the idea of the "caprice" or the "rhapsody": pieces that were written out, not improvised, most likely for the piano.

In *The Dialect of Modernism* Michael North offers a groundbreaking, provocative analysis of how Eliot adapted techniques such as linguistic mimicry and racial masquerade to make the language new and to resist institutional forces of standardization. In 1921 Eliot "was laboring to put his knowledge of black music to work in *The Waste Land*, which contained at one time references to a number of rag and minstrel songs."[44] The musical allusions cut from the final text are of particular interest, since many of them—for example, Eliot's reference to a song ("I'm proud of all the Irish blood that's in me") from a musical play called *Fifty Miles from Boston* and his adaptation of lines from minstrel shows ("By the Watermelon Vine," "My Evaline," and "The Cubanola Glide")—cryptically encode the composite regional landscapes and irreducibly hybrid cultures evoked by American popular music.[45]

Eliot's fascination with ragtime is best understood in light of his effort to understand the idea of "purity" in poetry, that is, the peculiar effect of works that direct the reader's attention primarily to style and virtually exclude consideration of their subject matter. In "From Poe to Valéry," for example, he discusses poems in which words have been chosen for the right sounds while the poet has been deliberately "irresponsible" toward their meaning.[46] In "The Music of Poetry" Eliot singles out Edward Lear's "non-sense verse," whose reader is moved by the music and enjoys, again, a "feeling of irresponsibility towards the sense." In these instances, however, the source of enjoyment is not a "vacuity of sense," or the poet's total escape from meaningful representation. Rather, Lear's "non-sense ... is a parody of sense, and that is the sense of it."[47]

In *The Waste Land* Eliot illustrates the rich senses of nonsense by alluding to a popular ragtime song that hit the charts in 1912, called "That Shakespearian Rag":

That Shakespearian rag,—
Most intelligent, very elegant,
That old classical drag,
Has the proper stuff, the line "Lay on Macduff,"
Desdemona was the colored pet,
Romeo loved his Juliet—
And they were some lovers, you can bet, and yet,
I know if they were here today,
They'd Grizzly Bear in a diff'rent way,
And you'd hear old Hamlet say,
"To be or not to be,"
That Shakespearian Rag.[48]

Eliot adapted lines from the original chorus by adding the "O O O O" and a syncopated syllable in "Shakespeherian" (McElderry, 185–6):

O O O O that Shakespeherian Rag—
It's so elegant
So intelligent
"What shall I do now? What shall I do?"
                                                        (*WL*, 57)

The poem's miming of ragtime gives both the speaker and the reader a brief reprieve from the burdensome duty to convey meaning truthfully. But the "vacuity of sense" brought about by the repetition of the apostrophe "O"— a repetition that reduces the trope, quite literally, to a series of zeroes on the page—also signals the tragic lack of continuity, as well as a tragic lack of engagement with the sense of Shakespeare's vibrant words, evidenced by American popular music. Eliot's allusion to ragtime, followed by the listless, bored, near-hysterical line "What shall I do now? What shall I do?" evokes apocalyptic dread. The passage implies that, taken to an extreme, such fleeting moments of enjoyable irresponsibility toward sense may promote an increasingly automated, vast inattention in American society. By pursuing the analogies between music and poetry in *The Waste Land*, Eliot's "Shakespeherian Rag" responds stylistically to conditions that imperiled artistic freedom and anticipated Hughes's experiments with a jazz poetics.[49]

The Waste Land calls attention to the danger of popular ragtime songs, in which words have been torn away from their traditional contexts. In "The Music of Poetry," however, Eliot proposes that nonsense verse also has profoundly restorative powers, as in Lear's work. "*The Jumblies*," for example, "is a poem of adventure, and of nostalgia for the romance of foreign voyage and exploration; *The Yongy-Bongy Bo* and *The Dong with a Luminous Nose* are poems of unrequited passion—'blues' in fact. We enjoy the music, which is of a high order, and we enjoy the feeling of irresponsibility towards the sense" (*PP,* 21). In "Fragment of an Agon," part of the unfinished jazz play *Sweeney Agonistes,* Eliot illustrates the poetic vitality and beauty of nonsense. The poem includes the following text, adapted from a popular song written by the African American poet James Weldon Johnson, called "Under the Bamboo Tree":

> *Under the bamboo*
> *Bamboo bamboo*
> *Under the bamboo tree*
> *Two live as one*
> *One live as two*
> *Two live as three*
> *Under the bam*
> *Under the boo*
> *Under the bamboo tree.*
>
>   *Where the breadfruit fall*
> *And the penguin call*
> *And the sound is the sound of the sea*
> *Under the bam*
> *Under the boo*
> *Under the bamboo tree.*
>
>   *Where the Gauguin maids*
> *In the banyan shades*
> *Wear palmleaf drapery*
> *Under the bam*
> *Under the boo*
> *Under the bamboo tree.*[50]

That the other personages in the play are ludicrous, materialistic, and superficial does not suggest that Eliot's allusion to Johnson's lyric "imprisons the song once again in the minstrel tradition" (North, 88).[51] The sense of adventure and the nostalgia for exotic romance that Eliot identifies in Lear's poems are beautifully highlighted in the passage he borrows from Johnson's artful rendering of the African American vernacular.[52] The enjoyable irresponsibility toward sense that the poem dramatizes enhances the meaning: it is a poem of "unrequited passion—'blues' in fact." The provocatively playful nonsense of "Two live as one / One live as two / Two live as three" expresses the speaker's yearning to transform the social fragmentation of American society and hints at Eliot's deeper motive for incorporating Johnson's lyric. Two poets—one Euro-American, the other African American—in effect "live as one" in Eliot's poem and intimately share a sensibility embodied by the blues. The poem's outlook is hopeful and forward-looking: after all, as Eliot has shown, the hope of perpetuating any given culture lies in the creative action of exchanging ideas and influences with others.[53]

CONCLUSION: JAZZ AND MODERN REALISM

Many, if not all, of Hughes's late jazz poems highlight the freedom of improvisation and formal innovation. In "The Trumpet Player: 57th Street," published in 1947, the freedom of choice Hughes himself exercises in creating a metonymic style opens new expressive possibilities.[54] The lyric not only educates the reader to hear his writing as trumpetlike, an instrument with voiced inflection and phrasing. It also dramatically illustrates the advantages of metonymy:

> The Negro
> With the trumpet at his lips
> Has dark moons of weariness
> Beneath his eyes
> Where the smoldering memory
> Of slave ships
> Blazed to the crack of whips
> About his thighs.
> . . . . .
> The music
> From the trumpet at his lips
> Is honey
> Mixed with liquid fire.
> The rhythm
> From the trumpet at his lips
> Is ecstasy
> Distilled from old desire—

The Negro
With the trumpet at his lips
Whose jacket
Has a *fine* one-button roll,
Does not know
Upon what riff the music slips
Its hypodermic needle
To his soul. (*CP*, 338)

Even as the lyric speaker refers to the uses of metaphor in describing the "ecstasy / Distilled from old desire" expressed in the trumpet's rhythm, he ends up showing us the profound artistic satisfactions and referential range of metonymy, the depiction of the body's surface and the temporal and spatial relatedness of everyday objects in the room. As an expression of weariness, traces of a personal and collective history of oppression, the "thump, thump, thump" of "The Weary Blues" is here inscribed on the body as "dark moons of weariness" beneath the trumpet player's eyes. The relatively obscure meaning of the moon going out as an image of thwarted desire and a dream deferred in "The Weary Blues" is considered and then freely cast off in "The Trumpet Player" in favor of hybrid tropes that hover somewhere between metonymy and metaphor:

Desire
That is longing for the moon
Where the moonlight's but a spotlight
In his eyes,
Desire
That is longing for the sea
Where the sea's a bar-glass
Sucker size. (*CP*, 338)

Like a held chord, the romantic, sentimental idiom of "longing for the moon" is sustained and, at the same time, transmuted into a "spotlight / In his eyes." As an evocation of desire, the sea is condensed into a "bar-glass, / Sucker size."

Insofar as Hughes's later poems mime the improvisatory action of jazz to discover emancipatory techniques, they are stylistically similar to works written by the American avant-gardes of the interwar period. In *Spring and All*, for example, William Carlos Williams praises the freedoms of improvisation, while he laments the dangers of incomprehensibility:

The Improvisations—coming at a time when I was trying to
   remain firm
at great cost—I had recourse to the expedient of letting life go
completely in order to live in the world of my choice....
   The virtue of the improvisations is their placement in a world of
new values—
                              their fault is their dislocation of
sense, often complete.[55]

The convergence between Hughes's techniques and those of Williams, Eliot,
and others discloses the historical knowledge that informs the impulse
toward formal experiment and improvisation in the modernist lyric.
   At the beginning of this essay we saw Baldwin criticize Hughes's late
jazz poem, "Dream Boogie," for falling short of the standards of realism. I
want to conclude by suggesting that, Baldwin's criticisms notwithstanding,
the spirit of formal innovation in "Dream Boogie" is entirely in keeping with
Hughes's earlier realism in poems such as "Flight."
   "Dream Boogie" is far more modernist than "Flight," since it manifests
a sustained, figurative effort to move away from the realist duties of
verisimilitude. It avoids familiar reference to historical contexts; it twists
away from language toward abstract sequences of sound; and it brings us into
a discursive world in which speech and perception have been broken down
into fragments. Insofar as the speaker touches on realities, his treatment of
them is almost wholly nondescriptive:

>   Good morning, daddy!
>   Ain't you heard
>   The boogie-woogie rumble
>   Of a dream deferred?
>   Listen closely:
>   "You'll hear their feet
>   Beating out and beating out a—
>
>   *You think*
>   *It's a happy beat?*
>
>   Listen to it closely:
>   Ain't you heard
>   something underneath
>   like a—

What did I say?

Sure,
I'm happy!
Take it away!
    Hey, pop!
    Re-bop!
    Mop!

    Y-e-a-h! (*CP*, 388)

Like many works written by his avant-garde contemporaries, Hughes's poem is not designed to meet our interpretive expectations; it contains no meaning that, as Eliot says, would readily satisfy a "habit" of the reader (*UP*, 151). According to Eliot, modern poems are sometimes intended primarily to amplify the reader's experience of the intensity of feeling that results from the poet's movement toward ideas at the "frontiers of consciousness," where meanings have not yet been put into words. In "The Music of Poetry" he writes: "We can be deeply stirred by hearing the recitation of a poem in a language of which we understand no word.... If, as we are aware, only a part of the meaning can be conveyed by paraphrase, that is because the poet is occupied with frontiers of consciousness beyond which words fail, though meanings still exist" (*PP*, 22).

In "Dream Boogie" Hughes's idiom is modernist in Eliot's sense: the lyric's form embodies an effort to move beyond the frontiers of social consciousness and expression. The line breaks; the arrangement of words on the page, flush left and flush right; and the use of italics are stylistic elements that show the ambivalence and animosity of an African American speaker trying to explain the meaning of the music to a Euro-American listener. The rhetorical question "*You think / It's a happy beat?*" has the visual effect of stretching, tonally inflecting, and thereby extending the meaning of the trope to include its own correct response. The poem pauses, calling attention to its own act of figuration and to the poet's act of writing. Hughes's modernist predilection for experimental forms that allegorize the struggle for and against verisimilitude, and his constant awareness of the constraints of language as an artistic medium, is central to his practice as a realist poet.

Although "Dream Boogie" is modernist insofar as it illustrates an effort to escape from historical referentiality and refuses to state explicitly the bitter social truths encoded in what Baldwin calls the "hieroglyphics" of

African American music, it also remains anchored in the particularities of its own time and place, since it is essentially about the dangers posed to American society as a whole when these truths are not brought to light in the realm of art. The speaker's ambivalence toward the project of meaningful representation makes sense only when we realize that the poem takes on a subject that Adorno systematically elaborated in his celebrated diatribe against the popular culture industry: the poem figuratively suggests a deplorable lack of conscious perception on the part of many Euro-Americans who considered themselves avid jazz fans.

Like Adorno, Hughes in "Dream Boogie" suggests that too many people who listened to jazz did not hear the seriousness of its emotional message and were not aware of the violent historical conditions out of which the impulse to formal innovation emerged. Instead many Americans regarded jazz merely as a pleasant background for conversation or a happy accompaniment to dancing.[56] The italicized question addressed to the Euro-American reader marks a crucial transition from the lyric's effort to mime violence (that is, from its performance of a nonrepresentational, violent motion of beating measured feet) to an all-out confrontation with meanings on the verge of verbal explicitness. The italics themselves highlight the social and emotional pressure exerted on the speaker when he tries to say that the historical implications of jazz as an art form—a form rooted in the traumatic postemancipation history of lynching and migration—were anything but happy; they express the speaker's frustration at the listener's inability to hear the social and emotional truths conveyed by the music.[57]

Hughes's experiments with realism in the lyric help us question the distinction between realism and the avant-garde in accounts of transatlantic modernism. Like Eliot, Crane, Stevens, and other twentieth-century American poets, Hughes demonstrated that certain modernist styles were created in response to historical conditions and addressed the danger posed by modernity to artistic freedom. Leo Bersani once said that "the realistic novel gives us an image of social fragmentation contained within the order of significant form—and it thereby suggests that the chaotic fragments are somehow socially viable and morally redeemable" (quoted in Anesko, 83), and this claim also seems an apt description of Hughes's poetic evocation of jazz. Insofar as his lyrics transcend frontiers of consciousness and culture, they fulfill a cherished criterion of modernism, in turn, serves the moral ends of realism by allowing him to encompass, order, and preserve fragments of history.

NOTES

1. Wright, "The Big Sea," in *Langston Hughes: Critical Perspectives Past and Present*, ed. Henry Louis Gates Jr. and K.A. Appiah (New York: Amistad, 1993), 21. Comparing Hughes to Theodore Dreiser, Wright observed that both writers undertook the crucial task of "freeing American literary expression from the restrictions of Puritanism" (21).

2. Baldwin, "Sermons and Blues," review of *Selected Poems*, by Langston Hughes, *New York Times Book Review*, 29 March 1959, 6.

3. Eric J. Sundquist, ed., *American Realism: New Essays* (Baltimore, Md.: Johns Hopkins University Press, 1982), 4.

4. Louis Budd, "The American Background," in *The Cambridge Companion to American Realism and Naturalism: Howells to London*, ed. Donald Pizer (Cambridge: Cambridge University Press, 1995), 21–46. The concept of realism surfaced again in the 1920s, when a generation of journalists—H.L. Mencken, John Macy, Van Wyck Brooks, Ludwig Lewisohn, Lewis Mumford, and Randolph Bourne, to name a few—probed the social purpose of literature and lavished praise on previously neglected artists, such as Mark Twain, Stephen Crane, and the late Howells, who had been critical of America's social and economic values. In 1930 Vernon Louis Parrington published *The Beginnings of Critical Realism in America: 1860–1920*, an influential analysis that roundly criticized writers who were too committed to narrowly "belletristic" aspects of literature. Parrington was, in turn, condemned to obscurity by critics like Lionel Trilling, who sharply criticized his literary nationalism and his insistence that literature should appeal to a popular constituency. More recently, at least since the publication of Warner Berthoff's *Ferment of Realism: American Literature, 1884–1919* in 1965, a number of revisionary studies have explored the social construction of American realism: Sundquist; Amy Kaplan, *The Social Construction of American Realism* (Chicago: University of Chicago Press, 1988); and Michael Anesko, "Recent Critical Approaches," in Pizer, 77–94.

5. Auerbach, *Mimesis: The Representation of Reality in Western Literature*, trans. Willard R. Trask (Princeton, N.J.: Princeton University Press, 1953). Auerbach's helpful, systematic account of the emergence of modern realist fiction identifies four criteria of realism as a literary method: detailed description of everyday occurrences; serious treatment of "socially inferior groups" as subject matter for existential representation (491); belief in the capacity of language to reveal truths about the phenomenal world; and portrayal of the individual's destiny in both a particular social hierarchy and a broader historical context.

6. In a useful account of the diverse approaches undertaken by modern American poets, Cary Nelson discusses "partly forgotten poetry—including black poetry, poetry by women, the poetry of popular song, and the poetry of social mass movements—thereby giving those texts new connotations appropriate to our time" (*Repression and Recovery: Modern American Poetry and the Politics of Cultural Memory, 1910–1945* [Madison: University of Wisconsin Press, 1989], 22–3). But his study is primarily historical: he gives no extended formal analyses and—aside from remarking that "traditional forms continued to do vital cultural work" throughout the modern period (23)—tells us little about the poetics of realism.

7. See Jonathan Arac, "Rhetoric and Realism; or, Marxism, Deconstruction, and the Novel," in *Criticism without Boundaries: Directions and Crosscurrents in Postmodern Critical*

Theory, ed. Joseph A. Buttigieg (Notre Dame, Ind.: University of Notre Dame Press, 1987), 161.

8. Alex Preminger and T.V.F. Brogan, eds., *The New Princeton Encyclopedia of Poetry and Poetics* (Princeton, N.J.: Princeton University Press, 1993), 1016.

9. "If every mediocre product of socialist realism is to be hailed as a masterpiece," Lukács writes, "confusion will be worse confounded. My *tertium datur* is an objective critical appraisal of the very real innovations which we owe to socialist realism. In exposing literary mediocrity, and criticizing theoretical dogmatism, I am trying to ensure that the creative aspects of this new realism will be more clearly understood" (*The Meaning of Contemporary Realism*, trans. John Mander and Necke Mander [London: Merlin, 1963], 11).

10. *The Collected Poems of Langston Hughes*, ed. Arnold Rampersad and David Roessel (New York: Knopf, 1994), 127; hereafter cited as *CP*.

11. See Saidiya V. Hartman, *Scenes of Subjection: Terror, Slavery, and Self-Making in Nineteenth-Century America* (New York: Oxford University Press, 1997).

12. See, e.g., W.E.B. DuBois, *The Philadelphia Negro: A Social Study* (1899; rpt. New York: Schocken, 1967); Carter G. Woodson, *A Century of Negro Migration* (1918; rpt. New York: Russell and Russell, 1969); Emmett J. Scott, *Negro Migration during the War* (1920; rpt. New York: Arno, 1969); Louise Kennedy, *The Negro Peasant Turns Cityward: Effects of Recent Migrations to Northern Cities* (New York: Columbia University Press; London: King and Son, 1930); E. Franklin Frazier, *The Negro Family in Chicago* (Chicago: University of Chicago Press, 1932); St. Clair Drake and Horace R. Cayton, *Black Metropolis: A Study of Negro Life in a Northern City* (1945; rpt. New York: Harcourt, Brace and World, 1962); and Gunnar Myrdal, *An American Dilemma: The Negro Problem and Modern Democracy*, 2 vols. (1945; rpt. New York: Harper and Row, 1962). For a useful overview of the vast literature on the Great Migration see Joe Trotter, "Black Migration in Historical Perspective: A Review of the Literature," in *The Great Migration in Historical Perspective: New Dimensions of Race, Class, and Gender*, ed. Joe William Trotter Jr. (Bloomington: Indiana University Press, 1991), 1–21.

13. Friedrich argues, on the evidence of poems by Baudelaire, Rimbaud, Mallarmé, and others, that "modern poetry, in its dissonances, is obeying a law of its style. And this law ... is, in turn, obeying the historical situation of the modern mind, which, because of the excessive imperiling of its freedom, has an excessive passion for freedom" (*The Structure of Modern Poetry: From the Mid-Nineteenth to the Mid-Twentieth Century*, trans. Joachim Neugroschel [Evanston, Ill.: Northwestern University Press, 1974], 168). Cf. Paul de Man's claim that a definitively "modern" poet must reject the burdensome assumption that artists convey meaning, since it poses a limit on expressive freedom and denies "the conception of language as the act of an autonomous self" ("Lyric and Modernity," in *Blindness and Insight: Essays in the Rhetoric of Contemporary Criticism* [Minneapolis: University of Minnesota Press, 1971], 171).

14. Johnson, "How Much Is Migration a Flight from Persecution?" *Opportunity*, September 1923, 272–5.

15. Whereas in 1930 Hughes used the image of flight ironically, juxtaposing the poem's title with the closing image of a hanged black man swinging in a tree, in 1925 Locke had used a similar image to mythologize the modernizing effects of migration: "The wash and rush of this human tide on the beach line of the northern city centers is to be explained primarily in terms of a new vision of opportunity, of social and economic

freedom.... With each successive wave of it, the movement of the Negro becomes more and more a mass movement toward the larger and the more democratic chance—in the Negro's case a deliberate flight not only from countryside to city, but from medieval America to modern" ("The New Negro," in *The New Negro* [New York: Atheneum, 1992], 6).

16. Hughes did not use these italics until 1949, when the poem appeared in the collection *One-Way Ticket*. But he did use quotation marks in 1931, when it was published in *Dear Lovely Death*.

17. "'Ulysses,' Order, and Myth," in *Selected Prose of T.S. Eliot*, ed. Frank Kermode (New York: Harcourt Brace Jovanovich, 1975), 177. For a discussion of Hughes's early exposure to black music see Steven Tracy, "To the Tune of Those Weary Blues," in Gates, 69–93. Tracy observes that during his childhood (from about 1902 to 1915) Hughes would have heard ballads, reels, and the "crude blues" of an older man like Henry Thomas; that the blues shouter Big Joe Turner led blues singers through the streets of Kansas City during the late 1910s and early 1920s; and that, although early blues was often accompanied by crude homemade instruments, orchestral-type blues was already emerging during the 1910s.

18. For a discussion of Hughes's folk sources and references to blues structure, themes, and imagery, and for a useful bibliography on jazz and blues, see Steven Tracy, *Langston Hughes and the Blues* (Urbana: University of Illinois Press, 1988). For other insights into Hughes's use of the blues idiom see Patricia E. Bonner, "Cryin' the Jazzy Blues and Livin' Blue Jazz: Analyzing the Blues and Jazz Poetry of Langston Hughes," *West Georgia College Review* 20 (1990): 15–28; Patricia Johns and Walter Farrell, "How Langston Hughes Used the Blues," *Melus* 6 (1979): 55–63; and Edward E. Waldron, "The Blues Poetry of Langston Hughes," *Negro American Literature Forum* 5 (1971): 140–9.

19. Rampersad insists that we take a revisionary look at Hughes's aesthetic as having been shaped by his recognition of a link between poetry and black music; he claims that *Fine Clothes to the Jew*, Hughes's least successful volume, marks the height of his creative originality ("Hughes's *Fine Clothes to the Jew*," in Gates, 54). Rampersad's monumental biography of Hughes, as well as his and Roessel's recent edition of the *Collected Poems*, has also contributed to the renewed interest in Hughes's poetry. For an illuminating review of the *Collected Poems* that characterizes Hughes's poems in light of four main attributes—his poetics of "announced ... [but] cryptic reciprocity," his "idiosyncrasy of personal identity," his inveterate sociality, and his humorous irony—see Helen Vendler, "The Unweary Blues," *New Republic*, 6 March 1995, 37–42.

20. "I tried," Hughes observes, "to write poems like the songs they sang on Seventh Street—gay songs, because you had to be gay or die; sad songs, because you couldn't help being sad sometimes. But gay or sad, you kept on living and you kept on going.... Like the waves of the sea coming one after another, always one after another, like the earth moving around the sun, night, day—night, day-night, day—forever, so is the undertow of Black music with its rhythm that never betrays you, its strength like the beat of the human heart, its humor, and its rooted power" (*The Big Sea*, 2d ed. [New York: Hill and Wang, 1993], 215).

21. Quoted in Shelby Steele, "The Content of His Character," *New Republic*, 1 March 1999, 30.

22. Ellison, *Shadow and Act* (New York: Vintage, 1995), 58–9.

23. R. Baxter Miller argues that the blues performance in "The Weary Blues"

dramatizes several actions, including black self-affirmation, a remaking of the black self-image, and Hughes's transcendence of racial stereotypes through lyric discourse (*The Art and Imagination of Langston Hughes* [Lexington: University Press of Kentucky, 1989], 55). My discussion suggests, on the contrary, that the figurative complexity of Hughes's poem helps him arrive at a clarifying, critical perspective on the folk tradition.

24. Hughes remarked that "it was a poem about a working man who sang the blues all night and then went to bed and slept like a rock. That was all" (*Big Sea*, 215).

25. Leavis, "Mass Civilization and Minority Culture," in *For Continuity* (Cambridge: Minority, 1933), 16–8; Eliot, "Marie Lloyd," in *Selected Essays* (New York: Harcourt, Brace and World, 1960), 407. "In an interesting essay in the volume of *Essays on the Depopulation of Melanesia*," Eliot writes, "the psychologist W.H.R. Rivers adduced evidence which has led him to believe that the natives of that unfortunate archipelago are dying out principally for the reason that 'Civilization' forced upon them has deprived them of all interest in life. They are dying from pure boredom. When every theatre has been replaced by 100 cinemas, when every musical instrument has been replaced by 100 gramophones, when every horse has been replaced by 100 cheap motor cars, when electrical ingenuity has made it possible for every child to hear its bedtime stories from a loud-speaker, when applied science has done everything possible with the materials on this earth to make life as interesting as possible, it will not be surprising if the population of the entire civilized world rapidly follows the fate of the Melanesians" (407–8).

26. Eliot, *The Waste Land*, in *Collected Poems, 1909–1962* (New York: Harcourt Brace, 1963), 62; hereafter cited as *WL*.

27. "The question of racial terror," Gilroy suggests, "always remains in view when these modernisms are discussed because their imaginative proximity to terror is their inaugural experience.... Though they were unspeakable, these terrors were not inexpressible, and ... residual traces of their necessarily painful expression still contribute to historical memories inscribed and incorporated into the volatile core of Afro-Atlantic cultural creation.... The topos of unsayability produced from the slaves' experiences of racial terror ... can be used to challenge the privileged conceptions of both language and writing as preeminent expressions of human consciousness" (*The Black Atlantic: Modernity and Double Consciousness* [Cambridge, Mass.: Harvard University Press, 1993], 73–4).

28. DuBois, *The Souls of Black Folk*, in *Writings*, ed. Nathan Huggins (New York: Library of America, 1986), 542–3.

29. In "The Negro Artist and the Racial Mountain," a polemical essay published in the *Nation* in 1926, Hughes emphasizes his "racial individuality" as a poet. But even here he implies that knowledge of traditional prosody would have helped him acquire an interpretive, distanced perspective on folk resources: the African American artist, he says, must learn to "interest himself in *interpreting* the beauty of his own people" (*Within the Circle: An Anthology of African American Literary Criticism from the Harlem Renaissance to the Present*, ed. Angelyn Mitchell [Durham, N.C.: Duke University Press, 1994], 55–6).

30. In the 1960s Baraka advocated a racial separatist approach to African American music. Many of his essays written in 1965, for example, affirm nineteenth-century racialist ideas of black manifest destiny and propose the formation of a black nation through a cultural consciousness flowing from the soul of the artist: "The Black Man must realize himself as Black. And idealize and aspire to that ... The Black Artist's role in America is to aid the destruction of America as we know it" (*Home: Social Essays* [New York: Morrow, 1966], 248, 252).

31. Although at this point in his career Baraka's position is not entirely separatist, insofar as he concedes that the blues can be "appreciated" by non-African Americans, what comes across here is the inaccessibility of the blues to a Euro-American audience (*The Leroi Jones/Amiri Baraka Reader*, ed. William J. Harris [New York: Thunder's Mouth, 1991], 37).

32. For a discussion of Hughes's repudiation of racial separatist accounts of African American culture during the 1930s see Anthony Dawahare, "Langston Hughes's Radical Poetry and the End of Race," *Melus* 23, no. 3 (1998): 21–41.

33. Lawrence, *Complete Poems*, ed. Vivian de Sola Pinto and Warren Roberts (New York: Penguin, 1994), 943.

34. For a discussion of the themes and figurative resources used to remember, mythologize, and represent the war see Paul Fussell, *The Great War and Modern Memory* (New York: Oxford University Press, 1975).

35. In the final, frequently anthologized version of the poem, the speaker recognizes that the sentiments inspired by the "insidious mastery" of music betray him even as he helplessly yields to them, "till the heart of me weeps to belong / To the old Sunday evenings at home" (Lawrence, *Complete Poems*, 148).

36. Ben Arnold, *Music and War: A Research and Information Guide* (New York: Garland, 1993), 135. Arnold writes that "the concert life naturally changed, particularly in the Allied countries, where German music had been so widespread. In Great Britain, all German music was at first banned outright.... Musicians performed more music by native composers in France, England, and America than before the war" (135). See also Barbara L. Tischler, "World War I and the Challenge of 100% Americanism," in *An American Music: The Search for an American Musical Identity* (New York: Oxford University Press, 1986), 68–91.

37. Johnson, *Listening in Paris: A Cultural History* (Berkeley: University of California Press, 1995), 267.

38. Lawrence's statement sheds some light on "Piano": "Every people is polarized in some particular locality, which is home, the homeland.... The Island of Great Britain had a wonderful terrestrial magnetism or polarity of its own, which made the British people. For the moment, this polarity seems to be breaking. Can England die? And what if England dies?" (*Studies in Classic American Literature* [New York: Doubleday, 1953], 16).

39. *The Letters of Ezra Pound, 1907–1941*, ed. D.D. Paige (New York: Harcourt Brace, 1950), 180.

40. Pound, *Diptych Rome-London* (New York: New Directions, 1994), 40.

41. *The Bridge*, in *The Complete Poems of Hart Crane*, ed. Marc Simon (New York: Liveright, 1993), 98–9.

42. *The Auroras of Autumn*, in *The Collected Poems of Wallace Stevens* (New York: Vintage, 1982), 415. Helen Vendler suggests that "the source of the disgust for the father-impresario seems to be Stevens' revulsion against that deliberate primitivism of his own ... which sets itself to conjure up negresses, guitarists, and the 'unherded herds' of ox-like freed men, all in a vain attempt to reproduce on an ignorant and one-stringed instrument the sophisticated chaos of the self" (*On Extended Wings: Wallace Stevens' Longer Poems* [Cambridge, Mass.: Harvard University Press, 1969], 252).

43. Eliot, *Inventions of the March Hare: Poems, 1909–1917*, ed. Christopher Ricks (New York: Harcourt Brace, 1996), 13, 17, 62.

44. North, *The Dialect of Modernism: Race, Language, and Twentieth-Century Literature* (New York: Oxford University Press, 1994), 10.

424 Anita Patterson

45. Eliot, *The Waste Land: A Facsimile and Transcript of the Original Drafts Including the Annotations of Ezra Pound*, ed. Valerie Eliot (San Diego: Harcourt Brace, 1994), 125 nn. 2–3.

46. Eliot, "From Poe to Valéry," in *To Criticize the Critic, and Other Writings* (London: Faber and Faber, 1965), 32.

47. Eliot, "The Music of Poetry," in *On Poetry and Poets* (New York: Farrar, Straus and Cudahy, 1957), 21; hereafter cited as *PP*.

48. Quoted in Bruce McElderry, "Eliot's Shakespeherian Rag," *American Quarterly* 9 (1957): 185.

49. For a discussion of Eliot's pursuit of analogies between musical and poetic procedures, which situates his engagement with symbolism within the context of Stravinsky's *Shakespeare Songs* and works by other twentieth-century composers, see James Anderson Winn, *Unsuspected Eloquence: A History of the Relations between Poetry and Music* (New Haven, Conn.: Yale University Press, 1981), 295–9.

50. Eliot, "Fragment of an Agon," in *Collected Poems, 1909–1962*, 119–20.

51. Referring to the nature of his "experiment" in writing *Sweeney Agonistes*, Eliot recalled: "I once designed, and drafted a couple of scenes, of a verse play. My intention was to have one character whose sensibility and intelligence should be on the plane of the most sensitive and intelligent members of the audience; his speeches should be addressed to them as much as the other personages in the play—or rather, should be addressed to the latter, who were to be material, literal-minded and visionless, with the consciousness of being overheard by the former. There was to be an understanding between this protagonist and a small number of the audience, while the rest of the audience would share the responses of the other characters in the play. Perhaps this is all too deliberate, but one must experiment as one can" (*The Use of Poetry and the Use of Criticism: Studies in the Relation of Criticism to Poetry in England* [London: Faber and Faber, 1933], 153–4; hereafter cited as *UP*).

52. Henry Louis Gates Jr. observes, "We are forced to wonder aloud where in dialect poetry, with the notable exception of Sterling Brown, a black poet used his medium as effectively as did Eliot in *Sweeney Agonistes*" (*Figures in Black: Words, Signs, and the "Racial" Self* [New York: Oxford University Press, 1987], 289 n. 17).

53. See, e.g., Eliot, *Notes towards the Definition of Culture* (London: Faber and Faber, 1948), 121; and Eliot, "The Social Function of Poetry," in *PP*, 13.

54. In *Allegories of Reading: Figural Language in Rousseau, Nietzsche, Rilke, and Proust* (New Haven, Conn.: Yale University Press, 1979), Paul de Man argues that the link between metonymy and its referent is contingent and accidental; thus reliance on metonymic fragments of social reality is problematic. Although Hughes is aware that the reader may not understand the historical context of the trope, his poems repeatedly affirm that the meaning of African American experience, in certain instances, may be shared by readers from different social worlds and cultural backgrounds. His insistence on metonymy as a mainstay of his realist poetics is an assertion of his right to creative freedom of expression, even at the risk of incomprehensibility.

55. *Spring and All*, in *The Collected Poems of William Carlos Williams*, ed. A. Walton Litz and Christopher MacGowan, vol. 1 (New York: New Directions, 1986), 203.

56. Theodor Adorno, "Fetish Character in Music and Regression of Listening," in *The Essential Frankfurt School Reader*, ed. Andrew Arato and Eike Gebhardt (New York: Continuum, 1982), 288.

57. Babette Deutsch wrote that the poems in *Montage of a Dream Deferred* suffered "from a will to shock the reader, who is apt to respond coldly to such obvious devices" ("Waste Land of Harlem," *New York Times Book Review*, 6 May 1951, 23).

BONNIE COSTELLO

Moore's America

A PLACE FOR THE GENUINE

Marianne Moore is most familiar to readers as the poet of armored animals, creatures who defy our efforts to entail them. Moore is also a distinctive poet of places—and they are similarly elusive. Writing in the midst of the Progressive era's rugged individualism, she offers a posture of humility toward the wilderness. Moore's sense of the frame and the flux emerges in "A Grave" (CP, 49), which describes a seascape in Maine. Like Stevens, she knows her eccentricity and suspects a perspective that claims the center:

> Man looking into the sea,
> taking the view from those who have as much right to it as
>   you have to it yourself,
> it is human nature to stand in the middle of a thing,
> but you cannot stand in the middle of this

Landscape has an explicit political and moral implication for Moore, as well as the aesthetic and ontological implication it has for Stevens. Ultimately, no human has a "right" to the "view." Moore shows how unyielding nature is and how little it resembles us, except as a counterimage of our imperial stance. "The firs stand in a procession, each with an emerald turkey-foot at

From *Shifting Ground: Reinventing Landscape in Modern American Poetry.* © 2003 by the President and Fellows of Harvard College.

427

the top, / reserved as their contours, saying nothing." The view we would take will ultimately take us into its flux:

> the sea is a collector, quick to return a rapacious look.
> There are others besides you who have worn that look—
> whose expression is no longer a protest; the fish no
>   longer investigate them
> for their bones have not lasted.

Landscape, that prospective gaze, in which man dominates over the scene, must submit to the reciprocal gaze of nature, and ultimately to the indifferent turning away of death. Yet within this sense of the frame and of the flux, Moore does create a landscape, one in which nature is compared to itself, and we to nature. For one does not, in Moore, know the thing in itself, the "colorless primitive" of Stevens' "anti-master man." "A Grave" (CP, 49) is another "landscape with boat," but without the balcony view. The animal perspective is featured. Trees have turkey feet, birds "swim through the air at top speed, emitting cat-calls," "the blades of [our] oars / moving together like the feet of water-spiders." This is a scene full of movement and transience, representing us in our mortal, not our imperial state. One cannot "take" a view, one can only give it, and give up the ghost. Anthropomorphism proves a figure of death itself:

> The wrinkles progress among themselves in a phalanx—
>   beautiful under networks of foam,
> and fade breathlessly while the sea rustles in and out of the seaweed

Moore is famous for her menagerie, but her ideal of poetry puts the animal "in the middle" of a landscape. In Frost, the American landscape is converted to a version of the pastoral that reveals its fictional and fleeting character. In Stevens, landscape is a meditative space in which the shapes made by the imagination respond to the pressure of reality. Moore's landscapes celebrate the principle of the wild within the frame. Her landscapes, like her poems, emerge from "raw material" both natural and cultural. Landscape provides Moore the medium for her fullest exploration of America, both its society and its geography. Far more than Frost or Stevens, she draws on the patterns and images others have made, and creates a landscape of these. In particular, her "imaginary gardens with real toads in them" stand in contrast to the hard and soft pastorals that have sometimes stood in for an American sense of place. In the first part of this chapter I discuss Moore's sense of the frame as it arises in her refusal to yield to the lure of the shallow image, the illusion that America is a toad-free, prelapsarian garden.

In acknowledging the frame Moore shows humility about the imaginative appropriation of the object, and indicates a world that language cannot capture. She reveals anxiety about her own and her culture's tendency to become absorbed in the shorthand substitutes for experience, the reductions, simulations, and facile myths, the quick "takes" that convert experience to commodity and distract us from the rigors of reality. The war against the facile constructions of reality must be fought on both sides, of course, since the artist traffics in illusions. The way to salvation for this devout poet is through instruments arising from the fall. In "The Jerboa" (CP, 10–15), for instance, Moore's Depression-era poem of "too much" and the revelation of "abundance" in adversity, we see this ambivalence played out. The poem begins by enumerating the vain luxuries of ancient culture, then moves to praise a simple desert rat who thrives in poverty. What appears at first to be a nature/culture binary turns into something more complex than the praise of animal abstemiousness over human wastefulness. Western civilization presents a contrast: Roman and Egyptian mimicry and distortion, on the one hand, and Hebrew redemption of illusion in the service of divine purpose, on the other. Moore portrays a flawed imperialism that would vainly fix its image on the world with a resourceful mimicry that would draw the landscape into a higher purpose than itself. Pharaoh is ultimately at the mercy of the flooding landscape, over which he ostensibly stands master, whereas exiled Jacob, in the inhospitable desert, makes a pillow of the stones. The colossal imitation of a pine-cone in front of the Vatican may be "contrived," distorting the scale of nature, but Jacob's theft of Esau's birthright, through a trick of illusion ("cudgel staff / in claw-hand") is in line with nature's own work of camouflage. The jerboa "honors the sand by assuming its color." And so the poet's images must serve creation's grace rather than plunder it. Similarly, in surveying the American landscape and culture, Moore will try to sort out "serviceable" illusions, pierced with inner light, from those that skim reality for easy gratification and gain. As we will see in later poems, Moore's meditation on modes of inhabiting landscape entails a reflection as well on racial history. In this poem it enters through the landscape of the African desert, arising as an aside, but establishing the connection between race and place.

Moore's America is a place of constant change and accelerating speed, and she seems just as ambivalent about that quality as she is about the uses of illusion. On the one hand, she enjoys the entrepreneurial energy of American technology and business, and incorporates images of its creative momentum. Nature does not stay still, nor should man. Moore's own poems are structured syntactically, and through imagistic leaps, to catch that sense of speed. William Carlos Williams called her poem "Marriage" an "anthology in rapid transit." On the other hand, American speed is often combined with a sense of rapacity and hurry, a desire for quick takes and facile generalizations. Williams' own landscape poem "Spring and All" presents some of this same conflict—how do we see the dynamic life of nature unfurling when we are speeding by in our car? How can the sense of motion be reconciled with the desire for accuracy? Moore had a vivid feeling for the continent she had crossed by train, as she puts it in "People's Surroundings" (CP, 55), on "straight lines over such great distances as one finds in Utah and in Texas / where people do not have to be told / that a good brake is as important as a good motor." Must we choose between nature's dynamism and culture's momentum? Moore's poems attempt to integrate the world's motions with her own.

Moore's fascination with nature's "fluctuating charm" (CP, 180) and its elusive swiftness sets her against the human impulse to fix it in shallow simulations. Reality is always quicker than our grasp. She admires the swiftness of the ostrich in "He 'Digesteth Harde Yron,'" the quicksilver of the plumet basilisk, the "kangaroo speed" of the jerboa, which defeat our desire to turn nature into still life. Her landscapes, similarly, refuse to stay still within our frames. The appropriate response is not speed of possession, the plunder of time and space, but speed of transformation, "conscientious inconsistency" (134), in which the mind, "enchanted" by its object, adopts its iridescent changes.

That flux affects human affairs as well, and underlies Moore's sense of history and modernity. America's benign myths of origin stand in paradoxical relation to technological mastery through increasing speed and efficiency. America is an unfinished landscape, or a series of landscapes on the site we call America. Our origins do not establish an ultimate dominion, or even set a process in motion since beginnings are contested. Far more explicitly than in Frost or Stevens, then, Moore's temporality reveals the historical dimensions of landscape, and the impact of landscape on history. In the second part of this chapter I take up Moore's representations of American history in relation to place—her emphasis on history as process rather than image, on nature as condition and reflection of history rather than a ground of historical meaning or a proof of dominion. She critiques the tendency to convert historical sites to "sights," spaces of merely touristic collection and facile narrative, static displays rather than scenes of evolutionary struggle and contingency.

AMERICAN VERSIONS OF PASTORAL

Moore's famous remark about poetry applies as well to her view of America:

I, too, dislike it.
    Reading it, however, with a perfect contempt for it,
            one discovers in
    it, after all, a place for the genuine.
                                            (CP, 36)

But what is the genuine? Could place itself provide the sense of the genuine, an authentic connection to nature? Moore's "genuine" surprisingly evades the model of American naturalness, the always-future past of the "first idea" in which materiality and meaning are perfectly joined as "nature's nation." Moore's America, whatever original nature it may retain, is a dense network of imaginary gardens, some quite materially imposed on the landscape. If nature is not simply aligned with the genuine, neither is culture simply aligned with the artificial. But America *is* intricately bound up with landscape and geography. The task of the poet is not to create nostalgic myths of contact and presence, but to make a place within this modern condition for a lived relation to the world.

Moore knew America's landscape in modern terms, through its commercial and technological advances, its conquest of time and space, through the language of advertising and the images of fashion and entertainment. These were for her as much a part of the landscape as were the mountains and rivers that suggested to English settlers an untainted Eden. As she shows in "People's Surroundings," Moore knew America as well in its local and domestic arrangements, in the diversity of its styles, "the deal table compact with the wall," Shaker simplicity as well as the "Sèvres china and the fireplace dogs" (CP, 55) of Gilded Age extravagance. She admired efficiency and durability, as well as the ingenuity that could produce a "paper so thin that 'one thousand four hundred and twenty pages make one inch,'" but she noted with implicit distaste the flair for mass production with its "vast indestructible necropolis / of composite Yawman-Erbe separable units" (55). The idea of the genuine in America could not be reduced to single species, and would have to accommodate a dense and various life, in which nature and culture were inextricably bound together. But there were two tendencies of American life that inhibited the genuine: derivativeness and rapacity. Rapacity has the tendency to destroy what it is trying to possess. Derivatives are simulations that bypass experience and present themselves as the real thing.

America's anxiety about "the genuine" set in early, of course. The country is continually "awakening" from the slumber of derivativeness. Emerson complains in 1836 that "the foregoing generations beheld God and nature face to face: we, through their eyes. Why should not we also enjoy an original relation to the universe?" (*Nature*, 1).[1] Moore was herself a persistent critic of her culture's tendency, as she writes in "Poetry," to "become so derivative that it has become unintelligible" (CP, 267), unable to awaken genuine response ("eyes that can dilate, hair that can rise if it must" [266]). Moore and her generation also worried about a citified and suburbanized American society eschewing its rural and fundamentalist past and living, as Frank Lloyd Wright complained, by imitation "spread wide and thin over the vast surface of the continent" (quoted in Bogan, 1). But America could hardly sustain the idea of the genuine on pre-industrial terms. That "pioneer unprefunctoriness," as Moore called it in "Love in America" (240), must find a modern tenor. To be an American, she quoted Henry James as saying, is "not just to glow belligerently with one's country" (Moore, *Complete Prose*, 321). But civilizing America was not simply a matter of suppressing its wildness and imposing models of elegance and civility. On the contrary, America's uncouth and unbridled spirit was not as large a problem as its tendency to rely on received ideas and images.

I want to approach the subject of Moore's America by way of a 1920 poem called "England" (CP, 46–47) which reveals the relation of landscape to language. England merits the title only as the first word of the poem, not as the last word in good taste. As Moore conducts her Cook's tour of European excellence, she parodies the tendency to identify geography with specific cultural traits. The gravitational center of this poem is America, and while the avowed theme of the poem is that "excellence" knows no boundaries, the agenda of the poem is patriotic (though assertively non-nationalistic). Moore is wary of America's tendency to adopt chauvinistically the very identification with nature and the primitive that has driven intellectuals to Europe and encouraged Continental haughtiness toward the uncivilized American scene:

> and America where there
> is the little old ramshackle victoria in the south,
> where cigars are smoked on the street in the north;
> where there are no proof-readers, no silkworms, no digressions;
>
> the wild man's land; grassless, linksless, languageless country
>   in which letters are written
> not in Spanish, not in Greek, not in Latin, not in shorthand,

but in plain American which cats and dogs can read!
the letter *a* in psalm and calm when
pronounced with the sound of *a* in candle, is very noticeable, but
why should continents of misapprehension
have to be accounted for by the fact?

...

the flower and fruit of all that noted superiority—
if not stumbled upon in America,
must one imagine that it is not there?
It has never been confined to one locality.

America is a continent, able to encompass all the narrower attributes of
foreign locals. America as a "locality" is marked by regional diversity that
resists reduction to singular traits. America can embrace both a "little old
ramshackle victoria" of slow Southern gentility (in contrast to high-speed
living on the highways going West) and a cigar-smoking vulgarity of the
modern, industrial North. Moore begins by echoing the Europhiles'
complaint about America's lack of refinement (it is as languageless as it is
linksless), but she hints of enjoyment in the qualities deplored by outsiders.
America is a place "where there are no proofreaders, no silkworms, no
digressions" (too much of a hurry). It is "the wild man's land." But if America
is for some characterized by the lack of nuance and cultural refinement, for
others it is about straightforward naturalness where "letters are written" "in
plain American which cats and dogs can read!" This is an extreme version of
pastoral, a wish to identify culture with nature and thus to claim cultural
innocence against European decadence. In defense against England's
preemptive claims, Americans celebrated their originality. Such a theme of
American "naturalness" is illogical on any terms, disdainful or patriotic.
Turning the bizarre but colorful expression "raining cats and dogs" in on
itself, Moore parodies America's notoriety as "nature's nation"; she
nevertheless celebrates America's idiomatic vitality. It is not, in fact, a
languageless country. Moore's own language is anything but plain; it is full of
digressions (and obsessively proofread). Yet she shows the same affection that
Frost showed for the forceful conclusion, homely aphorism, and inventive
idiom of American speech.

A lively debate was going on at the time this poem was written about
whether there was such a thing as an "American language." H.L. Mencken, a
critic of English hegemony but also of American dullness ("no business ever
foundered through underestimating the American intelligence," he quipped),

scrutinized the idea of America as a "languageless country" and explored the
truth and misprision in the notion that America had merely bastardized the
mother tongue (American language as counterfeit English). It is clear that
Moore had read Mencken's *The American Language*, first published in 1919,
before writing "England" (1920). The question of the genuine has particular
relevance here, as the English evoked the concept in order to abhor all things
American, especially its "stolen" language. Mencken identified an American
language that was something more divergent than a derivative of English; it
was an entire new "stream." While the English expressed abhorrence of
American "expectoration" in the "pure well of English undefiled," Mencken
celebrated the fecundity and class and regional diversity of a new language—
the autonomy of America's new idiom. The book begins by documenting
English snobbery about Americanisms, with the first four chapters entitled
"The Earliest Alarms," "The English Attack," "American 'Barbarisms,'" and
"The English Attitude Today." Moore asks concerning "all that noted
superiority" (recognized in the world abroad): "if not stumbled upon in
America, / must one imagine that it is not there?" She may be remembering
a long passage Mencken quotes from Sydney Smith, which begins: "In the
four quarters of the globe, who reads an American book? Or goes to an
American play? Or looks at an American picture or statue? What does the
world yet owe to American physicians or surgeons ... ?" (18). In referring to
America as a "languageless country," Moore may be recalling Mencken's
quotation from Coleridge: "the Americans presented the extraordinary
anomaly of a people without a language" (3). Moore admits that "the letter *a*
in psalm and calm when / pronounced with the sound of *a* in candle, is very
noticeable," and hardly music to the ear trained on the King's English. (She is
recalling Mencken's examples of how the English revile American sounds:
"missionary becomes mission*a*ry, angel, *a*ngel, danger, d*a*nger, etc.") But why
should this mere accident of linguistic history become a summary of national
character? With Mencken, Moore rejects a notion of "natural" English, some
pure, undeveloping "well" of undefiled words. "The genuine" in language has
little to do with purity of origin. The emergence of American speech, like the
endless transformation of the landscape, was a sign of vitality in use. The link
between language and landscape here is important. Moore identifies the
dynamic, evolutionary character of culture with the diversity of nature and
dynamism of the landscape. At the same time, by connecting language to
landscape she reminds us that it is constructed as well as organic, that it
operates as a sign as well as a signified.

If Moore challenged European superiority with a call to American
creativity and diversity, she was also wary of how the myth of the American

primitive might legitimate American habits of plunder. Affectation and rapacity might seem opposite vices (the one of civilization, the other of savagery), but they are related in that both foreclose experience, and thus "the genuine." As the world becomes something to price and consume rather than to experience and praise, purchasable simulations and traces of reality supplant elusive, recalcitrant actuality. The transformation of nature into marketplace is a fact of modernity, but the poet's role is not in sales (it may be in R&D). Of course poets traffic in representations. So Moore had to negotiate a space for her art that was not incriminated by the case against the fake, the simulated, the derivative—the case she herself was making about the culture at large. Her reality would be a confluence of presences, images, and uses that make up the changing phenomenal world.

America, Ezra Pound complained, was a "half-savage country," and Moore may well be echoing his phrase when she writes, in "New York" (CP, 54), of a "savage's romance." The Progressive era was beckoning America to an out-of-date "romance"—a glamorous master narrative—of the unconquered wilderness and inexhaustible resources. The unruliness of this land, its expanse, its ingenuity, its untamed splendor, stimulated the imagination. Those growing up in America at the turn of the century indulged a taste for Cooper's 1826 romance *The Last of the Mohicans*, with its noble savages. "The hunter, like the savage whose place he filled, seemed to select among the blind signs of the wild route, with a species of instinct, seldom abating his speed, and never pausing to deliberate" (116). But as the hunter displaces the savage, so the consumer displaces the hunter in our cultural logic. The savages are the consumers as much as the objects of romantic fantasy. Is the "New York" of the title and first line the modern city, Moore's new home, or the "wilderness" of the Catskills and the Adirondacks, the site of American nostalgia for origin? The tone of the word "savage" is as ambiguous as its referent and grammatical function. Moore had taught "savages" at the Carlisle Indian School the "civilized" skills of commercial accounting and stenography, and much of her poetry pays tribute to the civilized behavior of so-called primitives. How civilized is a culture that annexes land as it "needs the space for commerce," that has appropriated wildly within the last century? The commercial lust and reckless exploitation of resources exhibited by an urban culture that can only imagine the landscape in terms of its desire for consumption, can indeed seem savage. Moore's imagery demonstrates how fashion culture has adopted the very ways of the savage. New York City is "peopled with foxes," its population parading the streets in pelts and wrapping themselves in "tepees of ermine." Moore's reversible phrase—the "savage's romance"—replaces the oppositional rhetoric of nature and culture with a reciprocal one. In this way Moore's ambiguous reference to "New York" anticipates and complicates William Cronon's view of Chicago as "nature's metropolis." The links between city and country are intricate and not all one-way. But a reciprocity requires distance as well as association. Moore's poetry maximizes proximity verbally, but then works to reestablish distance, to remind the reader that our images are not reality. The consumer's America is a warehouse for the fur trade "dotted with deer-skins" and "picardels of beaver-skin." New York commercial culture literally skins reality for material goods and self-aggrandizing images, forgetting nature's otherness. And yet it would be too simple to read the poem as the shame of culture against the tragic glory of nature. Nature can be appreciated as well as plundered in the name of culture, may indeed require the lens of culture to be seen at all. In this sense the proximity can be useful. Moore likely admires the imagination of the writer she quotes from *Field and Stream* who compares a fawn's markings to "satin needlework [that] in a single color may carry a varied pattern." He has not appropriated nature for art but rather has appreciated the art of nature. Moore's note tells us that the fawn was "discovered in a thicket and brought to the hotel." Whatever ambivalence she may have felt about this transplantation, she knows it is within culture that its markings can be seen. Moore was a devoted museum visitor, and most of her knowledge of nature comes from books, films, and exhibits. She had climbed Mt. Rainier, but in turning to write about it in "An Octopus" she does not transcribe her experience so much as collect and assemble various representations of it. The "contact" sought by Thoreau and revived by Muir remained elusive; the search for authentic experience must acknowledge the fact of mediation.

These inversions of value and attribution—the savage look of fashion, the refinement of nature—bring the two worlds of "New York" into close proximity through the power of imagination, just as they exist in close association through the power of commerce, in the first, long, embedded sentence of the poem. But in the next sentence Moore works to reestablish distance, to separate the two worlds of consumer and consumed, pointing toward a "wilderness" beyond quick acquisition. Moore is perhaps thinking of her own journey, not from the old center of the wholesale fur trade, St. Louis, to the new one, New York, but her more recent migration, from Carlisle, Pennsylvania, near Pittsburgh and the "conjunction of the Monongahela and the Allegheny," to Manhattan, when she asserts:

> It is a far cry from the "queen full of jewels"
> and the beau with the muff,

from the gilt coach shaped like a perfume-bottle,
to the conjunction of the Monongahela and the Allegheny,
and the scholastic philosophy of the wilderness.

Romance takes on a new tenor here, evoking the glass slipper and the silk rather than the leatherstocking. But the conjunction of the Monongahela and the Allegheny rivers is not a romance but a locality existing a "far cry" from the images of adventure and plunder proliferating in the brains and bowels of the culture and disseminated through postcards of "Niagara Falls, the calico horses and the war canoe." (Moore's family owned an old landscape painting representing the scene of this conjunction of rivers, leading out into the open west.) But she knows all too well that, thanks to the New York barons Carnegie and Frick, industrial Pittsburgh has grown up on this site. What does Moore mean by wilderness here? Not, it seems, what John Muir praised and William McKibben mourns. This is a new kind of wilderness, one of man and nature together; we can no longer map reality into neat binaries of city and country, where the city is "near" and the wilderness "far." Even when culture is geographically close to the landscape, however, it remains distant, other. Places must be distinguished from their representations. There is a dense geography and human history behind a "dime novel exterior." The effete "beau with the muff" and the perfume-bottle-shaped coach might be signs of urban decadence. But Teddy Roosevelt–neo-primitives, bred on urban luxury but seeking in nature a cure for the malaise of culture, who borrowed images of masculine prowess from the backwoods "atmosphere of ingenuity," are not so different. Their barehanded, anti-modern conquest of nature, of "the otter, the beaver, the puma skins / without shooting irons or dogs" was a weekend affair, not a real encounter with the wilderness. Nature is still object, not other. The wealth of the American landscape, celebrated by Henry James in *The American Scene*, cannot be reduced to "natural resources," to items for conspicuous consumption, gratuitous adventure, or even raw necessity.

This anaphora, "it is not," becomes a structure for the *via negativa* (a practice of showing distaste) like a negative map by which Moore can "make a place for the genuine," asserting distance from the simulacra of New York. The practice of reading and writing New York involves resistance, "contempt" for the quick captions. For the wilderness is its own "scholastic philosophy," equal in elusiveness to the works of Aquinas and Duns Scotus with which Moore was familiar, and equal, as well, to the wilderness of Henry James's prose, which she quotes at the end of the poem: "It is not the plunder, / but 'accessibility to experience.'" One would not think of scholastic philosophy as being accessible. But access is not ownership and experience is not simplicity. Moore's poem imitates this rigor in its suspended syntax, which takes in increasingly complex clauses, full of conceptually demanding details. In the end Moore does reduce the wilderness to a phrase, but it is a phrase that points beyond itself to a depth and density that cannot be fathomed. The poem, like scholastic philosophy, becomes its own wilderness (rather than an image of the wilderness) in the concatenation of phrases. And here we return to the paradox that initiates the poem. For if one aim of "New York" is to establish the distance between nature's wealth and culture's desire, another aim is to refuse the opposition of nature and culture. The wilderness and scholastic philosophy, like real toads and imaginary gardens, become enfolded in a denser reality, a greater wilderness, which is always near and accessible, but also remote, requiring no special charter or protection from the accretions of commerce. One need not travel to the Adirondacks or the Catskills to visit it. This reality, the subject of all Moore's poems, is minutely particular, but "has never been confined to one locality." It can be experienced or ignored; it cannot be occupied.

In "New York" Moore largely "stands outside and laughs" when confronted with the wilderness, as she wrote in her first version of the poem. In "An Octopus" (CP, 71–76) she has at heart our getting lost. While "New York" catalogued the modes of plunder, "An Octopus" tries to convey the immediate experience of the wilderness. It does so, paradoxically, by drawing attention to our mediations. Moore presents a reality that is never circumscribed, which cannot be reduced to an image or a use, and cannot be mastered by a single perspective. She does not so much describe reality as give us an analogous experience in language. She draws a map in order to get us lost. "An Octopus" may well have been inspired by a map—an aerial map, "deceptively reserved and flat," of Mt. Rainier and its eight-armed glacier, included in a park pamphlet. But disorientation is the rule in the expedition that follows the title. The relation of land and sea becomes ambiguous; the poem compares the lowest point of the continent—the life of the sea—to the highest. There are no stable coordinates here:

> an octopus
> of ice. Deceptively reserved and flat,
> it lies "in grandeur and in mass"
> beneath a sea of shifting snow-dunes;

The map can only lie in trying to configure the "grandeur" in which the glacier "lies." And the passage goes on to suggest a distinction between this elusive reality and the frames we put on it:

> dots of cyclamen-red and maroon on its clearly defined pseudo-podia
> made of glass that will bend—a much needed invention—
> comprising twenty-eight ice-fields from fifty to five hundred feet thick,
> of unimagined delicacy.

Thus begins a six-page descriptive poem, piling up different languages, nomenclature of the sea, flora, human anatomy, technology, geology, every line of which bears close reading, but which pulls us along in the momentum of its syntax. Here we have radically different regions of nature compared— the cyclamen flower evoked at the site of the ocean creature, the octopus, fuses the flora of Mt. Rainier and the fauna of the underwater world. For whom and by whom is the "pseudo-podia" "clearly defined"? What is clear when we impose the category of a "foot" on either an ice field or an octopus? Mt. Rainier, the poem suggests, cannot be charted; that does not mean it cannot be experienced. Like an octopus the reality spreads out in all directions, and the safe distance of metaphoric abstraction yields to mind-boggling shifts of scale and scene, exuberant lists, densely textured, proliferating images of power and delicacy, that come as close as any modern poem to the American sublime, that aesthetic triumph over mapping. The ambition of the poem, in its accreted quotation, its disarming metaphors and strained syntax, its radical parataxis, its shifts in scale and perspective, is to develop our regard for what is beyond our power to circumscribe, to quantify, and to sell off.

In 1922 Moore visited her brother, stationed near Seattle, and together they made an expedition to Mt. Rainier, which only two decades before, in 1899, had become a national park. Like so many of her contemporaries, then, she had rushed to acquire the wilderness experience, on the "game preserve" of the American Eden. But Moore's poem is not a spontaneous overflow of powerful feeling. She does not indulge in naïve realism or frontier fantasies—old myths of American priorism, of the wilderness within unleashed by the wilderness without. She does not come "face to face" with original nature. The landscape has been heavily intercepted by a collage of maps and field guides, by human interpretation and representation; it cannot be known independent of these constructions. Moore's way, then, to the American sublime is by heightening rather than suppressing the mediations. Nature has little to do with the wilderness that is legally chartered and protected by park rules and regulations, the wilderness simulation that

William Cronon has documented in "The Trouble with Wilderness." But the poet can evoke a recalcitrant reality through various frames and signposts, one that subsumes us in its power and exceeds our knowledge in its "capacity for fact." Its "neatness of finish" defies the finish of any pictorial frame. The glacier and park at Mt. Rainier become emblematic of this elusive reality, a bounded nature exhibiting nature's boundlessness. The poem is constructed out of quotations from the park manual, along with a wide variety of sources including the *London Illustrated News* (sea world), Baxter's *Saints' Everlasting* (spiritual world), and a conversation overheard at the circus (social world). We may apply here Gertrude Stein's remark about the landscapes of America: "I like a view, but I like to put my back to it." Moore does not invite us to take the view of Mt. Rainier; it cannot be "taken." A site cannot be fixed as a sight. What the imagination can do is give us something. Moore creates a distinctly textual reality in collage form that provides an analogy (rather than a simulation) to the wilderness experience it evokes, a rhetorical sublime to suggest a natural sublime. Reference to language, and even self-reference, as well as pictorial representation, overlap. The diagrammatic reality, the "glassy octopus symmetrically pointed," turns into a fearful symmetry which "receives one under winds that tear the snow to bits / and hurl it like a sandblast / sheering off twigs and loose bark from the trees ... is 'tree' the word for these things / flat on the ground like veins?" The attention to flatness again functions doubly here: to challenge our notion of the relation of the word "tree" with its vertical association to this austere, faceted reality, this incredible height that flattens all other features; and also to remind us that our own "smooth" "flat" maps are not the textured reality they point to. This octopus knocks the map out of our hands, and the trees themselves, "flattened mats of branches shrunk in trying to escape," are a little like our own feeble efforts to escape nature's magnitude by mapping it. Put another way, we may try to flatten, or map, Mt. Rainier, but in fact it flattens all our efforts. The sense that we have turned Mt. Rainier into a theme park for "those who lived in hotels but who now live in camps—who prefer to" contends with the image that we and our maps are just part of the fauna of the place.

Man's will to map the world by coordinating it to his own body, Moore emphasizes, finds its match in nature's power to deceive. The glacier dotted with flowers looks like the "pseudo-podia" of the cephalopod, which is itself footlike only to bipeds. And we don't even seem to know our hands from our feet. The "Goat's Mirror ... that lady*finger*like depression in the shape of the left human *foot*" (italics mine) "prejudices you in favor of itself before you have had time to see the others." The maps we make send us in circles:

"Completing a circle, you have been deceived into thinking you have progressed." The octopus on the aerial map is "deceptively reserved and flat," but the real one has the "concentric crushing rigor of the python," and obeys a vaster geometry than ours. The Indian ponies in the landscape are "hard to discern" among the birch trees, ferns, lily pads, and other enumerated flora. Nature may play the prickly host—we are "met by the polite needles of the larches"—but only to elude us. Maps give us a false sense of security too. This glacier is an active volcano and produces an avalanche at the end. Its "reserve" is temporary. Moore is fully aware, in quoting the promotional rhetoric of the park administration, that nature's intention is a human fiction. But our plunder and presumption are more than matched by its mysterious geologic presence that can alchemically transmute verdure into onyx, and that displays spruce trees with the eerie legacy of an American royal family "each like the shadow of the one beside it." Nature is continually erasing the images that it projects; the storm "obliterates the shadows of the fir trees." Man's fraudulence turns on itself as he witnesses miracles he "dare not speak [of] at home for fear of being viewed as an impostor."

Moore takes nature off the map, then, but she knows she has put it in a theater. To remind us of this, a curtain falls at the end of the poem, an avalanche to image the blank page: "a curtain of powdered snow launched like a waterfall." Ultimately this is not a poem about Mt. Rainier. Like other modernist texts, it is presentational rather than representational, and Mt. Rainier itself becomes enfolded in the dense fabric of a poem that is about nothing less than the earth and our institutional and imaginative relationship to it, enacting rather than describing that relationship. We cannot "know nature," in Thoreau's phrase, except through the kaleidoscope of our landscapes. Hence the poem is a compilation of quotations and allusions rather than a first-hand account, like Thoreau's description of Mt. Katahdin or Muir's description of Yosemite. Thoreau's "Contact! Contact!" like Emerson's "original relation to nature" is an elusive ideal, but not just because of modern development. Man has not ruined nature; nature has absorbed man. Indeed, humans become part of the "fauna" of the scene at Mt. Rainier—the mountain guide and the hotel keeper are among the "diversity of creatures" who make their home in this place. While they and the tourists they draw are constructing "Mt. Rainier," then, Mt. Rainier is encompassing them.

As Patricia Willis and John Slatin have shown, Moore's poem asks us to recall *Paradise Lost* and to acknowledge that we have forfeited that "power that Adam had," the power of naming, and of original sight. This allusion has specific relevance to the tradition of the American sublime, of course, and the myth of America as the unfallen Eden. The paintings of Albert Bierstadt and Frederic Church suggested immanence and transparence. Moore's poem acknowledges mediation from the outset, dashing any illusion of an American Adam who might establish an innocent civilization in harmony with nature. Moore's poem insists that there is no easy turning back. A return to nature is not a return to innocence. Rainier has been framed and structured by man; the wilderness, as we conceive it, is a construction. But Moore creates another kind of sublime in returning elusive power to the object—a sublime beyond us, not ourselves.[2] This thrilling encounter with place is intercepted repeatedly by the comic presence of tourists who are "happy seeing nothing," and businessmen "who require 365 holidays a year." The sense that we have turned Mt. Rainier into a theme park for tourists enamored of the pseudo-rigors of outdoor life contends with proliferating details and jolts to our orientation that the contemplation of this place provokes.

"New York" and "An Octopus" critique the rough pastoral of American wilderness discourse and suggest a sublime reality that cannot be reduced to an image or a tag. "The Steeple Jack" (CP, 5–7), written about a decade later, considers the soft pastoral, exposing the dangers that lie within Arcadia. Not only wilderness parks, but also resort towns were a growing phenomenon of the new century. Empson's definition of pastoral as "a partial world depicted as a whole world" suits this poem, in which enumerated flowers display gardens containing much of the predatory animal kingdom (foxglove, tiger lily, spiderwort, snapdragon), without threat, and in which "there are cats, not cobras, to keep down the rats." In this temperate zone we have "the tropics at first hand" without the threat of exotic serpent life, except on fashionable snakeskin shoes. Moore delights in the harmonious blends of the natural and human worlds and values retreat from the centers of modern life. But she is no Norman Rockwell. She brings her urbanity with her, reminding us at every turn that we are not in paradise, that place cannot return our innocence, and that indeed the pastoral world, if we forget the artifice that makes it, may be more dangerous than any other.

Moore was certainly aware of a different role for herself as she wrote "The Steeple Jack." The poet of "New York" and "An Octopus" was publishing in obscure avant-garde magazines (*Others* and *Broom*). She did not cater to a "public out of sympathy with neatness" (CP, 76). Her audience was the New York avant-garde, out of sympathy with the genteel tradition of literary pastoral. But as winner of the Dial Award and editor of *The Dial*, she had become an arbiter of taste rather than its critic, and her audience had widened. Exhausted from her editorship, and from attending to her mother's weakening health, perhaps also retreating from the frenzy of Manhattan brought on by the stock market crash, Moore decided at the end of 1929 to seek a quieter existence in what was at that time still a suburban milieu. Brooklyn had only been annexed to New York City for thirty years when Moore moved there, and it retained an outsider identity. Here Moore returned to the writing of poetry, making significant changes in her style. The poems became more musical, the syntax more relaxed, the pleasures more accommodating. Rhyme enters the work more conspicuously than before, knitting the voice into pleasant sonic patterns. Moore's own language supplants quotation, and its tone is more ingratiating. Had she dropped her vigilance against the temptations of the glossy phrase or the gilded image? Had she succumbed to parochial pieties and surface harmonies? How, Moore asks, might one be "at home" in such a place, open to its genuine satisfactions, without mistaking it for the world? This home differs from the one in the poem "Dock Rats," which she wrote upon moving to Manhattan in 1918; that was a site of transitions, of comings and goings, this, of complacencies and moral slumber. But Moore's poem reminds us that we are "not native" in Arcadia.

Particularly at issue, for this artist who liked elegance "of which the source is not bravado," was how to reconcile aesthetic coherence and moral incoherence. From the beginning of "The Steeple Jack" (CP, 5) she does this by emphasizing artifice, by drawing attention to the frame:

> Dürer would have seen a reason for living
>   in a town like this, with eight stranded whales
> to look at; with the sweet sea air coming into your house
> on a fine day, from water etched
>   with waves as formal as the scales
> on a fish.

Moore conceived a composite place, part Maine resort (she had summered on Monhegan Island) and part residential borough (the steeple jack she names—C.J. Poole—actually worked in Brooklyn, and some of the images, like the stranded whales, are taken from local newspaper accounts). The constructed scene displays the abundance and variety of nature, with all its extremes, refined into pattern and harmony—what the classical writers called *discordia concors*. Pastoral is a form of still life, concealing history and temporality and engaging in illusions of timelessness. The seagulls flying back and forth over the town clock erase time in their shuttle. The "etched" water will not flow. No work goes on in this eclogue, though there are "fishnets arranged to dry." Virgil would have seen a reason for living in a town like this. But Moore's scene is inscribed with *et in arcadia ego*—"I too am in arcadia," says the real toad in the imaginary garden. Our sins wash up like Leviathan on the beach. As Susan Stewart has suggested in *On Longing*, in the modern system of objects, the gigantic is often a metaphor for the abstract authority of the state and the collective public life. If the notion applies here, the stranded whales provide a troubling allegory. Yet this is not a bleak poem, nor is its assertion that "it could not be dangerous to be living in a town like this" entirely insincere. It celebrates the perennial abundance of nature and delight in sensory orders, and the pleasure of things "ambition cannot buy or take away." In another sense hope is affirmed—a hero is present, a student, an artist—and their ideals survive their human habitation.

"About suffering they were never wrong, / The Old Masters. How well they understood / Its human position," wrote W.H. Auden in "Musée des Beaux Arts" (*Selected Poems*, 79). He was looking at some paintings by Breughel, particularly "Landscape with the Fall of Icarus," in which one can barely perceive, in an otherwise placid agrarian scene, the fallen Icarus sinking into the sea. Auden admired Moore's poetry (adopting her syllabics) and knew her "Steeple Jack" well, so perhaps he took some inspiration from this poem as he struggled with the tension between aesthetic pleasure and moral vigilance. Moore places her perspective close to that of another Old Master, Dürer (she had written about him for *The Dial*, mentioning his travel to see a stranded whale). Her view is thus one of a perceptive outsider. To be "not native" to the pastoral myth of place can give one a privileged view, a heightened sensitivity to both its pleasures and its faults. Like Dürer, she is attracted to the extraordinary (eight stranded whales, a twenty-five-pound lobster), and like him, she creates a painstaking but understated formal (etched) order. (The gulls flying over the clock in ones and twos and threes almost image the carefully counted syllables in these matching, sonorous, unaccented stanzas.) But also like Dürer, Moore brings a moral (and religious) sensibility to this scene. To look at eight stranded whales with a feeling for suffering is to go beyond the thrill of spectacle or merely aesthetic response. Surely the "sweet air" is tainted by the moral, not to mention the physical, odor of their displacement, though we tend to hold our noses. From the outset, then, Moore creates a tension between the delight in designing picturesque surfaces and the moral compunction to expose a corruption beneath them, a tension between pastoral and parable.

Whereas "An Octopus" was aimed at getting you lost (the poem disorients you immediately: "an octopus / of ice"), "The Steeple Jack" seems to want to make you feel at home. Nature is close but does not consume us; technology is close but does not control us.

> One by one in two's and three's, the seagulls keep
>   flying back and forth over the town clock,
> or sailing around the lighthouse without moving their wings—
> rising steadily with a slight
>   quiver of the body—or flock
> mewing where
>
> a sea the purple of the peacock's neck is
>   paled to greenish azure as Dürer changed
> the pine green of the Tyrol to peacock blue and guinea
> gray.

Easy passage here between the human and natural worlds characterizes the pastoral. Moore goes on to note the hospitable character of the climate (again, in contrast to the forbidding Mt. Rainier), which favors a rich variety of flowers, the fog enhancing, rather than obstructing, their lush growth. But the mention of the fog serves as well to remind us that appearances are unreliable—the unsaid is as important as the said in Moore's method of understatement. Moore has put us on alert. And soon enough, a storm encroaches on the placid scene.

> The
>
> whirlwind fife-and-drum of the storm bends the salt
>   marsh grass, disturbs stars in the sky and the
> star on the steeple; it is a privilege to see so
> much confusion.

This is written off as more charming Americana, nothing to get ruffled about, but its "fife and drum" may also recall a revolutionary struggle and sacrifice that we forget at our peril. Pastoral is the forgetting of time, but our well-being was achieved in history and can be undone by history. Moore harbors a special fondness for "the student / named Ambrose [...] / with his not native books and hat" who appears in stanza 8, because he is not complacently parochial, does not take this partial world for a whole world. Ambrose is not the shepherd-insider of the pastoral world, through whom we imagine a life of harmony. That is, he knows not to mistake this retreat for America, and knows that small-town life is not an escape from the corruptions that plague America. Named for a Saint, and the embodiment of Emerson's American scholar, he appreciates the charms of this place while recognizing its imperfections and the artifice behind its placid surfaces. From the distance of the hillside he can delight that "there is nothing that ambition can buy or take away," yet he knows that such ambitious buying and selling drives American life, so recently shaken to its foundations. Here is a respite from Wall Street, not a cure for it. If *he* appreciates locality for itself, rather than for its speculative value as souvenir or natural resource, still, the *place* is not innocent. Ambrose conducts us to the pitch of the church, which, while it is part of the overall picturesque charm of the place, is "not true."

This has been from the beginning a poem about *seeing*. Dürer's stylized gaze conducted us through the first part of the poem, with its etched water, its play of scale, and its enhanced colors. But as the poem turns to Ambrose for direction, a transition occurs. The body enters the scene, since Ambrose, unlike Dürer, is in it. From his hilltop prospect he can miniaturize the world and make it a kind of souvenir (memorizing the antique-sugar-bowl-shaped summerhouse, the mechanical boats), but he must finally surrender the toy-like scenery and confront what has hitherto been disguised by fog. The decorative palette of the poem now turns to stark and unambiguous black, white, and red. Humans, in various social positions, enter the poem, and so does a worker: the steeple jack of the poem's title, the moral counterpart of the artist, placing danger signs even as he "gilds." We are reminded that what is seen has been made, and with that recognition danger and sin become explicit. The "not true" has exposed not just fiction, but falsehood and corruption.

There are other prospective inhabitants of this hitherto empty town, "waifs, children, animals, prisoners, / and presidents," escaping "sin driven senators," all of them creatures who are vulnerable or corrupt. These "simple people" do not ensure the innocence we cling to as a legacy of American small-town life. Rather, this is a place where presidents (Coolidge was in office) evade their responsibilities, choosing not to see or think about the evil in their midst, and thus serving its ends. As Moore turns to the institution of the church, she locates the worst form of hypocrisy (whitewash) exactly where there should be none. But as a pious Presbyterian, she believes that all human institutions are erected in hope, not in innocence. The church may be most susceptible to corruption because presumed most innocent. The columns of the church, supports for a frail humanity, are "made solider by whitewash" (thus to appearances only, and not reliable at all). The steeple jack, the very figure assigned to correct the collapsing steeple, is himself only human and thus a sinner. (We recall Jonathan Edwards' "Sinners in the Hands of an Angry God" in this image of a spider spinning a thread. The indelibly "etched" scene of the artist now becomes as fragile as a web. Ingenious man is not really in control at all, but a sinner hung by God over the pit of Hell.) The steeple jack wears the colors of Satan and "gilds" the star that "stands for hope." Hope is misplaced, it seems, when it is invested in human institutions, whether they be stock exchanges, places of worship, or small-town societies. Yet this is not a sermon in the tradition of Jonathan Edwards, but a pastoral in the tradition of Andrew Marvell. The poet delights in a world arrayed for sensual pleasure and relaxation, a world of densely varied vegetation, with "cat-tails, flags, blueberries and spiderwort, / striped grass, lichens, sunflowers, asters, daisies" (and so on for several stanzas, some two-thirds of which had been cut to make this still copious version) and charming human structures—"a schoolhouse, a post-office in a / store, fish-houses, hen-houses, a three-masted schooner on / the stocks." Moore's lists are little societies—one notices the relative modesty of this list of dwellings (where a schoolhouse gets no higher grammatically than a fishhouse, where a grand schooner, like a beached whale, sits on stocks), in contrast with the verbal and visual plenitude of the gardens. Still, man and nature do achieve a kind of harmony in this place, at least in moments of detached meditation, when history is pressed into the background. But this poem was included in a collection of three entitled "Part of a Novel, Part of a Poem, Part of a Play," and one feels strongly that a story (narrative is the end of pastoral) is about to begin.

Whether she is dealing with city or wilderness, sublime or pastoral landscapes, then, Moore's America becomes a place for the genuine when she reveals the frames that create "people's surroundings." Because these environments are made as well as inhabited, they do not offer places of permanence or grounds of origin. What is true of her animal poems is true of her landscapes—nature, as it relates to human beings, is embedded in history.

LANDSCAPE AND HISTORY

These investigations of contemporary America's myths about itself led Moore increasingly to inquire into American historical origins, especially as embedded in our sense of place. American ideology reveals a resistance to the idea that "nature's nation" should be subject to history at all. How could a culture grounded in innocent nature be anything but permanent? An incarnate culture does not *evolve;* it is truth revealed. History, for Americans, was becoming a commodity, something we could collect to enhance our image and permit our complacency about the present. By emphasizing historical place we create the illusion that our origins are natural and inevitable, and that historical meaning is a static set of images. But Moore's poetry insists that all human institutions are subject to the contingencies of historical process. And all landscapes are historical, shaped and marked by the human history that has traversed them. She responds, particularly, to the tendency of Americans to convert historical sites to tourist "sights," flattening history with received, abridged images. When history becomes a sight, an object of tourist consumption or national myth, it flattens out. Moore seeks to return a certain depth to history by discovering from the surface its dense network of meanings. Historical sites speak not so much of a sanctified, living heritage as of the profundity of the historical process itself. History is not heroic narrative or divine fiat but a set of contingencies, "what has come about" (CP, 109) in the mingling of human intentions with nature's ways. History is the opposite of still life. Moore is a descriptive, not a narrative poet. But description in her work resists mythic formations. Again, she makes a place for the genuine by reading with a certain contempt.

The triad of poems called "Part of a Novel, Part of a Poem, Part of a Play" included, besides "The Steeple Jack," "The Student" and "The Hero," two poems that examine American distinction without succumbing to American bravado. "The Hero" in particular (CP, 8–9) speaks to this difference between luminous sites and superficial sights. The hero is listed among those variously "at home" in the seaside town of "The Steeple Jack," and it is clear that Moore invests some hope in his presence. But for him to be "at home" is not to be complacent or provincial, but on alert. And he is not a conventional hero of bold feats and reckless courage. Theodore Roosevelt went looking for danger. This hero "shrinks" and does not like "deviating headstones / and uncertainty." Moore's personal hero was George Washington, whom she mimicked with her tricorn hat and cape. But while the popular image saw him crossing the Rubicon, Moore might remember that his strategy was retreat. Washington was, as she said of the hero of another poem, "hindered to succeed." "The hero" here is an appropriate heir to Washington, a type of the Christian soldier "that covets nothing that he has let go." But he is not a "natural," at least not a biological or social, heir to Washington, since his embodiment in this poem is African-American. He is not interested at all in surfaces, the thrilling surfaces of the romantic wilderness or the charming surfaces of seaside retreats. He is intent on "the rock crystal thing to see," "brimming with inner light." In this inward relation toward place and its meaning, he is "at home" even though his racial origin stands continents away. The hero's foil is the "fearless sightseeing hobo" (who is implicitly not at home), the hobo of contemporary tourism; she checks off her list of sights and domesticates historical meaning. "What's this, what's that," she asks, demanding of history that it be named and pinpointed, rather than contemplated.

In an understated fashion, while presenting a contemporary image, Moore introduces here the major struggles of our heritage, the "deeds of war," as Frost called them in "The Gift Outright." These connect us to the land: the revolution and founding of a nation, and the civil war and near foundering of a nation, which continues in a struggle for racial justice. These are parts of the historical landscape that the sightseeing hobo cannot penetrate. For this obnoxious woman, such transforming events are nothing but a collection of monuments. This "hero"—never named—is merely a "frock coated Negro," a park attendant at a national cemetery (Williamsburg) dressed in revolutionary costume. He is invisible to the tourist, part of the background. She addresses her question ("where's Martha buried?") not to this informed guide but to "the man she's with," so unheroic as to have no other designation in the poem. Yet the guide has a "sense of human dignity and reverence for mystery" which his visitor lacks. Ignored by the tourist, probably because he is black, he nevertheless provides the information required: "Gen-ral Washington / there; his lady, here." He is more authentic in his response than she is in her question, though he is "speaking / as if in a play," on the stage of history. The guide has a historical imagination rather than a tourist's curiosity, and sees with an inner light. We might recall that the 1930s, when this poem was written, was a dormant period in the struggle for civil rights. A complacent attitude toward Jim Crow laws prevailed. Many of Moore's poems of this period feature the unheralded heroism and nobility of the black race. There may be some racialism in this attitude, as Cristanne Miller has pointed out (128–166), but it stands as a direct retort to the racism of the time. "Standing in the shadow of the willow," his figure acknowledges that the past is not a "sight" but a mystery that continues to inform the present.

Throughout her poetry Moore sustained an admiration for the natural world that reckoned with the story of humans in it. This is perhaps most apparent in Moore's poems of the South. Moore's visits to her brother in Virginia inspired three poems in the 1930s, "Smooth-Gnarled Crepe Myrtle," "Bird-Witted," and "Virginia Britannia." Together they form a sort of updated "Notes on the State of Virginia." "Virginia Britannia" (CP, 107–111) looks at landscape through the lens of history and vice versa, more than one hundred and fifty years after Jefferson's account, and more than three hundred years after the Jamestown settlement. It aims for a different kind of seeing than "sight seeing." And it engages in a different kind of historical imagination than that encouraged by Williamsburg pageantry. With the inclusion of this 1935 poem, the title of Moore's subsequent volume, *What Are Years* (1941), takes on a particular American emphasis, expressing not only lyric's traditional meditation on mortality, but a study of history and its meaning as well. The poem has a special implication when considered not only in the light of continued racism at home, but also surging, racialist nationalisms abroad, where nature is used to mask the sinister purposes of power.

"England" had been concerned with a contemporary situation in which America was seen as rough and backward, inferior to all things "abroad." "Virginia Britannia" looks back at the earliest efforts to impose European culture on American land. What was allegorical in Stevens, the question of the relationship between the soil and man's intelligence, becomes in Moore a literal meditation on New World settlement. The poem exposes the provisional and contingent character of dominion, undermining imperial attitudes through the selection and arrangement of details. Neither dominion nor incarnation, but rather adaptability, intermixture, mimicry, and mutability prove the strongest traits in the history of this landscape. The land is not, finally, ours, but we are "the land's" in the sense that landscape determines history as much as history determines landscape.

"Virginia Britannia" starts very much as "The Steeple Jack" does, scanning the scene for curiosities, gathering impressions. Here the poet begins with the broad prospect, the anticipatory sweep of dominion, then moves in to complicating detail and anecdote. But while the language is paratactic and mimics a tourist brochure, Moore wanders away from the official tour, observing the overlooked and what has been much looked at but not properly seen. Jamestown was situated on a narrow sandbar linked to the mainland of Virginia. The poem opens with an approach, in present tense, which simulates the approach of the first European visitors to the tidewater. But the Virginia that Moore beholds is no Virgin Land: the new world has seen an old dominion come and go; historical process quickly imposes itself on landscape. This nature has been "known" by many and for a long time—by man and by animal, the wild and tame of each species, though by none in its totality.

> Pale sand edges England's Old
>   Dominion. The air is soft, warm, hot
>   above the cedar-dotted emerald shore
>   known to the red-bird, the red-coated musketeer,

the trumpet-flower, the cavalier,
the parson, and the wild parishioner. A deer-
track in the church-floor
brick, and a fine pavement tomb with engraved top, remain.
The now tremendous vine-encompassed hackberry
starred with the ivy-flower,
shades the tall tower;
And a great sinner lyeth here under the sycamore.

The sense of manifest destiny in "Dominion" is immediately qualified by "Old" and "edges." "Pale" initiates a vocabulary of color that will later scrutinize racial attitudes throughout the poem; "pale sand," in the context of the whole, suggests the white man's presumption of natural dominion in this place. But the colors remain primarily aesthetic here. In presenting "red bird" next to the "red coat," aesthetically equalizing nature and man, Moore deliberately delays reference to "red skin," which appears in stanza 10, though the Indian presence in this place is central to its history, beginning in stanza 2. Perhaps Moore knew that "red skin" was itself a convention, based not on the natural pigmentation of the Amerindian but on his bear-grease decorative paint, which the earliest European visitors mistook for racial essence. What is "natural" and what is "cultural" or man-made collide and overlap one another from the outset, belying presumptions of dominion. The Earthly Paradise of imperialist lore, with its "soft, warm" air and lush, welcoming flora and fauna must give way to the truth of a "hot" climate where "unEnglish insect sounds" suggest not just aesthetic diversity but a relentless struggle against malaria. "Care" has formed the roses, but also the "yew" in the poem; suffering underlies but does not consecrate dominion. When Moore later remarks on the "outdoor tea-table, ... the French mull dress with the Madeira- / vine-accompanied edge" and other "luxuries," she is struck by how paradoxically "stark" they seem "when compared with what the colonists / found here"—a far from nurturing environment met a far from godly invader. The material "glory" of these Old Dominion grounds is itself now only a replica of a hard-won, genteel past, the unlikely outgrowth of a morally and physically rough frontier whose conquest is less than certain or heroic.

The past is written into the face of the present, not as its original and enduring glory but as a conglomeration. The juxtapositions of human and natural inhabitants work here as leveling parody ("the trumpet flower, the cavalier"), especially as the man/nature opposition of the list influences the "parson/wild parishioner" pairing. (The lineation makes us read "the wild parishioner" as "a deer," since he has wandered into the church; but of course the wild parishioner is also the colonial himself, that "great sinner.") From here it is but a deer-step into the church; all boundaries are permeable. The accident of the hoof print claims as much posterity as the careful engraving. Nature itself inscribes this struggle for dominion as the vine encompasses the "tremendous" hackberry that now "shades" the "tall tower." Moore's later imagining of the "strangler figs choking / a banyan" dispels the myth of nature's innocence. The struggle for dominion is natural and nature is neutral, co-present with man, and available to model man's moral life in its graces and faults. Moore expropriates and diverts the pious rhetoric of the past. As the eye moves from the landscape's "edge" to its presumed human center, we encounter a grave: "A great sinner lyeth here" is a period quotation, but the spiritual accounting takes on new direction as the words share church walls with "tobacco crop records." Here is a land of "cotton mouth snakes" and "cotton fields," of "wolf design" on Lawrence pottery, a land far from Eden and still in need of grace. Even Jefferson's picturesque curving brick wall is "serpentine."

The great sinner "awaits a joyful resurrection" (presuming election), but a complex history intervenes, as Moore makes the transition from the subversion of the nature/culture hierarchy to challenge the dominion of one race over another. It is clear in this poem that the Indian represents culture, not nature—he is not "all brawn and animality." Moore introduces the story of Captain Smith, Christopher Newport, and Powhatan, compressing much American lore into a stanza's worth of anecdotal fragments (such as a tourist might gather, but only an artist could meaningfully arrange). The founders are not predestined leaders but "odd" figures, reminding us that all norms are embedded in history. Indeed, the term "odd" and its more flattering companion "rare" recur throughout the poem and become the primary descriptive adjectives for the phenomena of this place from the modern point of view:

> We-re-wo
> co-mo-co's fur crown could be no
> odder than we were, with ostrich, Latin motto,
> and small gold horse-shoe:
> arms for an able sting-ray-hampered pioneer—
> painted as a Turk, it seems—continuously
>   exciting Captain Smith
>   who, patient with
> his inferiors, was a pugnacious equal, and to

Powhatan as unflattering
as grateful. Rare Indian, crowned by
Christopher Newport!

(CP, 107)

Moore alludes here to Smith's unconventional leadership and love of
adventure. Captain Smith was an Englishman who joined Hungarians in
fighting the Turks, beheading three before being taken as slave and later
escaping, only to be poisoned by a sting-ray he lived to consume; his motto
was *vincere est vivere*, to vanquish is to live. But this fetishized coat of arms
has become an emblem of audacity. Moore also conveys Powhatan's pride,
who, when offered a coronation as emperor of Indian tribes and vassal to the
English king, replied "I also am a king and this is my land," instead giving his
fur crown and cloak to Christopher Newport, who returned with them to
England. (Moore probably saw them in the Ashmolean Museum when she
visited Oxford as a young woman.) Odd perhaps is Pocahantas with a bird-
claw earring, but even odder her cross-dressing as an English lady. History
exposes the truth of exchange over the presumption of dominion, where the
English spout Latin mottoes and paint themselves as Turks, endlessly
posturing and naming counties after English lords while adopting Indian
names for rivers, sporting French finery, and importing Andalusian flowers.
Assertive identity defeats itself in acts of appropriative mimicry.

A garden is not only an aesthetic arrangement, it is a language, by
which historical cultures express their desires and social arrangements
(splendor, pride, in the language of flowers). Moore's gardens are eccentric
allegorical spaces. Here the poem borders the garden with the human
story—the stanza form slides one into the other without transition. History
shapes nature just as nature shapes history. The long lists of flora and fauna
convey the convergence and struggle of these disparate cultures. Moore
records that struggle in her own thematic shaping, the index of scent and size
("dwarf" and "gigantic" recur in the description of plants), but especially, as
we saw in the opening passage, in the vocabulary of color. The green
propriety of the sculptured boxwoods established by the English colony and
their uniformly "white roses" asserted against "unEnglish" (malarial) "insect
sounds" nevertheless have tough stems, "thick as Daniel Boone's grapevine,"
a sign of their adaptation to the challenging American soil.

The "jet-black pansies" and "African violet" mark the presence of the
Negro "established"—as the euphemism goes—on the banks of the
Chickahominy. "Established" like imported plants, not willing humans, in
this post-lapsarian garden, they nevertheless become integral to the

emergence of civilized life in Virginia. Moore relishes the image of the black
pansy "overpowering" the lesser flora. And in their later resistance blacks are
indeed "inadvertent ally and best enemy of tyranny" in a society still, in the
thirties, far from righteous. The color of the mockingbird, we are told three
times, is "gray," and as "terse Virginian" he is emblem of the confederacy, the
assertion of an old South still resentful of the Emancipation that requires it
to pay wages to the Negro it employs for gain. (In an earlier version Moore
referred to these sharecropper landlords ironically as "the bothered by wages
new savages," again checking the presumption of civil community where
behavior is in fact barbaric.) We are invited to "observe" the mockingbird,
standing blind on a pillar of cupidity. But the mocking bird is also a reminder,
as John Slatin has pointed out (208–252), that America is about mimicry
more than originality. The primary "native" trait is "endless imitation." The
"terse Virginian" adopts the call "of whippoorwill or lark or katydid" in his
pursuit of their nests and eggs. He is a figure for a culture "that did not see"
the world beyond its own interests, but at the same time absorbed the traits
of that world, becoming something else.

    As in "England," language is an important feature of dynamic national
identity, and language impresses itself especially on geography. Language in
this poem develops as nature does, absorbing local and imported words to
establish a diverse sense of place. Language is integral to historical process
and leaves its mark on the "narrow tongue of land that Jamestown was," not
only in the linguistic mix of place names, but in a legacy of contending
doctrines. The rival mottoes of colonizers—*vincere est vivere*—and
colonials—"don't tread on me" (spoken, Moore reminds us, by a snake)—
lead to the wisdom through suffering of the "black idiom" which sees us
"advancin' backward in a circle," repeating ourselves through time rather
than progressing. "Colonizing" is a way of saying "taking what we please."
And in removing the euphemism, Moore subverts dominion.

    Moore's own language works against "dominion" through a stanza
pattern that overrides syntax and creates a contrapuntal rhythm through
heavily hyphenated adjectives. These absorb rather than enhance assertion.
The dense imagery, the propulsion of the list, the quick juxtapositions,
submerge hierarchies and preferences in the aesthetic pleasure of sensory
overload and the overall sense of *discordia concors*. Moore does not "cradle"
"priorities" as the colonists did. She can afford more equanimity. The
intricate rhyme scheme (a twelve-line stanza including a triple rhyme in the
middle, a couplet in the penultimate lines, and a rhyme between lines 3 and
12) gives the poem "an elegance of which the source is not bravado." The art
of the poem is to draw our attention to an aesthetic order rather than a

cultural hegemony or a single-minded critique. The aesthetic order of the poem does not whitewash moral incoherence, but it shows equanimity in its attention to details, reordering the site to describe the rich entanglement of nature and human purposes that has brought us where we are.

The poem that began with an approach to the "pale sand" of Virginia's shores closes with a receding view of the "darkening filigree" of the live oak's boughs. Naïve claims to dominance give way to this elegant entwining, itself yielding to the day's decline. Moore turns visionary at the end of the poem, but she first locates spirit in the minute particularity of the sparrow's "ecstatic burst of joy." This precisely identified "caraway-seed- / spotted sparrow" that "wakes up seven minutes sooner than the lark" may offer a hope more explicable to the religious Moore than it was to Hardy in "The Darkling Thrush." The sparrow also reminds us of mortality and heralds the finale:

> The live oak's darkening filigree
>   of undulating boughs, the etched
> solidity of a cypress indivisible
>   from the now aged English hackberry,
>   become with lost identity,
>   part of the ground, as sunset flames increasingly
> against the leaf-chiseled
>   blackening ridge of green; while clouds, expanding above
>   the town's assertiveness, dwarf it, dwarf arrogance
>   that can misunderstand
>   importance; and
> are to the child an intimation of what glory is.

This "indivisible" is not yet the achievement of liberty and justice for all, or a Wordsworthian memory of celestial glory. Throughout the poem Moore has presented Virginia as a hodgepodge, an "inconsistent flower bed," despite the passion for monoculture of those who thought they held "dominion" over it. The natural cypress and the hackberry, like the historical Indian and the colonist, and indeed nature and man together, become "indivisible" because intertwined in a continual struggle for dominance and survival. And as mutability and mortality rule all living orders and entities, they "become with lost identity, / part of the ground." The imagery of this poem has been structured on a principle of incongruity and intermixture. The "etched solidity" of historical memory and even of nature becomes a fading outline. Here all colors darken, and all proportions are dwarfed. John Slatin is undoubtedly correct to hear Wordsworth in these lines, and thus an intimation of immortality, but the focus of the poem is not on immortality. The expanding clouds suggest the absorptive power of change; the mini-conflagration of the sunset at the end of the poem reminds us not only of God's power dwarfing man's, but perhaps also of the tragic history of the South, the consequence of arrogant dominion. History tells a story not just of origins but of convergences and disappearances, of forces that thought to dominate but ultimately had to succumb, identities absorbed that were once imposed.

Moore revisited the subject of Jamestown in 1957, after a U.S. Air Force celebration of the 350th anniversary of the Jamestown landing. "Enough: Jamestown 1607–1957" (CP, 185–187) retains a frankness, in the midst of cold war ideology, about America's origins: "Marriage, tobacco, and slavery, / initiated liberty." The poem repeats the story of the failed colony, its starvation, the subjugation of Indians, the craving for quick wealth that resulted in neglect of husbandry and pervasive death. Again she contrasts a cultivated garden, lush and seductive to the contemporary visitor, to the unforgiving conditions of early Virginians, whose colony "did not flower," who were not heroic but "tested until so unnatural / that one became a cannibal." But ultimately Moore does not pass judgment on the past ("who knows what is good") and finds room to endorse the celebration. America's origins are "partial proof" that must be renewed by "present faith" in the yet-unrealized ideals of the nation.

For Moore the genuine is historical; it cannot be held in place. Landscapes are framed and mediated, subject to both human and natural flux. But a place can be made for the genuine even in a world that is increasingly mediated and abstracted. That is perhaps why the attitude of contempt must accompany all efforts to represent it. Moore's America is an ongoing project that has no telos; a confluence of presences, images, and uses makes up the phenomenal world. We keep making and unmaking landscapes on the site we call America. Rather than exalt an ideal of what America once was, she expresses an idea of what it might be, "home to a diversity of creatures," not a collection of icons, slogans, and national attributes, not a "dime novel exterior," but a land remarkable for "accessibility to experience."

NOTES

1. Elisa New begins her important book *The Line's Eye* by putting aside this Emerson essay and attending, instead, to his "Experience." But Moore, a great admirer of Emerson, did not distinguish these phases of his work. Many of the precepts that Emerson enumerates in "Nature" are central to Moore's emblematic poetry, and it is the advent of

modernism and her own originality, rather than a shift in Emerson, that accounts for her differences from "Nature." Furthermore, as Sharon Cameron has pointed out, even "Experience" retains much of the old imperial Emerson; his "impersonal" is easily identified with the transcendental, empowered self. Moore's impersonal functions very differently, toward the effect of humility, not transcendence.

2. For a thoughtful reconciliation of the aesthetic of the sublime with environmental values, see Christopher Hitt's "Toward an Ecological Sublime" in *Ecocriticism*, a special issue of *New Literary History*.

Chronology

1868	Edgar Lee Masters is born in Garnett, Kansas.
1869	Edwin Arlington Robinson is born on December 22 in Gardiner, Maine.
1872	Paul Laurence Dunbar is born on June 27 in Dayton Ohio.
1874	Robert Lee Frost is born in San Francisco on March 26.
1878	Carl August Sandburg is born January 6 in Galesburg, Illinois.
1879	Wallace Stevens is born on October 2 in Reading Pennsylvania. Nicholas Vachel Lindsay is born in Springfield, Illinois on November 10.
1883	William Carlos Williams is born in Rutherford, New Jersey on September 17.
1884	Sara Teasdale is born in St. Louis, Missouri on August 8.
1885	Elinor Hoyt Wylie is born September 7 in Somerville, New Jersey. Ezra Pound is born October 30 in Hailey, Idaho.
1887	Robinson Jeffers is born in Pittsburgh, Pennsylvania on January 10. Marianne Moore is born November 15 in Kirkwood, Missouri.
1888	John Crowe Ransom is born in Pulaski, Tennessee on April 30. H.D. (Hilda Doolittle) is born September 10 in Bethlehem, Pennsylvania. T.S. Eliot is born September 26 in St. Louis, Missouri.

1889	Conrad Aiken is born in Savannah, Georgia on August 5.
1892	Edna St. Vincent Millay is born in Rockland, Maine on February 22.
1894	E.E. Cummings is born on October 14 in Cambridge, Massachusetts.
1899	Hart Crane is born in Garrettsville, Ohio. Allen Tate is born November 19 in Winchester, Kentucky.
1900	Sigmund Freud: *The Interpretation of Dreams*. Death of Friedrich Nietzche.
1902	Langston Hughes is born February 1 in Joplin, Missouri. William James: *The Varieties of Religious Experience*. Edwin Arlington Robinson: *Captain Craig and Other Poems*.
1903	Countee Cullen is born March 30. Death of Herbert Spencer. Ford Motor Company founded. Wright brothers make first successful flight.
1904	Russo-Japanese War begins. Academy of Arts and Letters founded. Max Weber: *The Protestant Ethic and the Birth of Capitalism*.
1905	Alfred Stieglitz opens "291" in New York.
1906	Death of Paul Laurence Dunbar.
1907	William James: *Pragmatism*. Picasso: *Les Demoiselles d'Avignon*. Sara Teasdale: *Sonnets to Duse and Other Poems*. Cubist Exhibition in Paris.
1908	Gertrude Stein: *Three Lives*.
1909	Ezra Pound: *Personae*. Gertrude Stein: *Three Lives*. Gustave Mahler: *Symphony No. 9*. William Carlos Williams: *Poems*.
1911	Triangle Shirtwaist Company Fire in New York. Ezra Pound: *Canzoni*. Sara Teasdale: *Helen of Troy and Other Poems*.
1912	Marcel Duchamp: *Nude Descending a Staircase*. *Poetry* magazine founded in Chicago. Amy Lowell: *A Dome of Many-Colored Glass*.
1913	Robert Frost: *A Boy's Will*. Marcel Proust: *Swann's Way*. Marcel Duchamp's *Nude Descending a Staircase* exhibited at the Armory in New York.
1914	Robert Frost: *North of Boston*. World War I begins. Ezra Pound (ed.): *Des Imagistes*. Amy Lowell: *Sword Blades and Poppy Seeds*. *Blast* founded.
1915	Edgar Lee Masters: *Spoon River Anthology*.

1916	Carl Sandburg: *Chicago Poems*. Amy Lowell: *Men, Women, and Ghosts*. James Joyce: *A Portrait of the Artist as a Young Man*. Robert Frost: *Mountain Interval*. H.D.: *Sea Garden*. Edwin Arlington Robinson: *The Man Against the Sky*.
1917	T.S. Eliot: *Prufrock and Other Observations*. The United States enters World War I. Ezra Pound: *Lustra and Other Poems*. Edna St. Vincent Millay: *Renascence and Other Poems*. William Carlos Williams: *Al Que Quiere!*
1918	Charles Reznikoff: *Rhythms*. Paul Klee: *Gartenplan*.
1919	Versailles Treaty is signed. Sherwood Anderson: *Winesburg, Ohio*. T.S. Eliot: "Tradition and the Individual Talent." John Crowe Ransom: *Poems About God*.
1920	Prohibition goes into effect. 19th Amendment allows women to vote. Henri Matisse: *L'Odalisque*. Ezra Pound: *Hugh Selwyn Mauberley*. T.S. Eliot: *The Sacred Wood*.
1921	Albert Einstein lectures in New York. Charles Chaplin: *The Kid*. Marianne Moore: *Poems*.
1922	T.S. Eliot: *The Waste Land*. James Joyce: *Ulysses*. Eugene O'Neill: *The Hairy Ape*.
1923	Wallace Stevens: *Harmonium*. William Carlos Williams: *Spring and All*. Jean Toomer: *Cane*. E.E. Cummings: *Tulips and Chimneys*. Robert Frost wins the first of his four Pulitzer Prizes for *New Hampshire*. Edna St. Vincent Millay: *Ballad of the Harp-Weaver*. Louise Bogan: *Body of This Death*. Mina Loy: *Lunar Baedecker*.
1924	H.D.: *Heliodora and Other Poems*. T.S. Eliot: *Sweeney Agonistes*. Sergei Eisenstein: *Battleship Potemkin*. Archibald MacLeish: *The Happy Marriage*. Marianne Moore: *Observations*. John Crowe Ransom: *Chills and Fever*.
1925	F. Scott Fitzgerald: *The Great Gatsby*. Harold Ross founds *The New Yorker*. T.S. Eliot: *The Hollow Men*. E.E. Cummings: *XLI Poems*. Alain Locke: *The New Negro: An Anthology*. William Carlos Williams: *In the American Grain*. Death of Elinor Hoyt Wylie.
1926	Hart Crane: *White Buildings*. Langston Hughes: *The Weary Blues*. Ernest Hemingway: *The Sun Also Rises*. E.E. Cummings: *Is 5*. Marianne Moore becomes editor of *The Dial*. Laura Riding Jackson: *The Close Chaplet*.

1927   Charles Lindbergh makes solo flight over the Atlantic
              Ocean. Martin Heidegger: *Being and Time*. Langston
              Hughes: *Fine Clothes to the Jew*. Robinson Jeffers: *The
              Woman at Point Sur*.
1928   Robert Frost: *West-Running Brook*. W.B. Yeats: *The Tower*.
              D.H. Lawrence: *Lady Chatterly's Lover*. Nella Larsen:
              Quicksand. Allen Tate: *Mr. Pope and Other Poems*.
1929   William Faulkner: *The Sound and the Fury*. Stock market
              crash initiates the Great Depression. Museum of Modern
              Art opens in New York. Louise Bogan: *Dark Summer*.
1930   Hart Crane: *The Bridge*. Empire State Building erected in
              New York. T.S. Eliot: *Ash Wednesday*. Ezra Pound: *A Draft
              of XXX Cantos*. W.H. Auden: *Poems*.
1931   E.E. Cummings: *ViVa*. Langston Hughes: *Dear Lovely
              Death*. Laura Riding Jackson: *Laura and Francisca*. John
              Crowe Ransom: *God Without Thunder*. Death of Nicholas
              Vachel Lindsay.
1932   Death of Hart Crane. Ernest Hemingway: *Death in the
              Afternoon*. Aldous Huxley: *Brave New World*. Robinson
              Jeffers: *Thurso's Landing*.
1933   Gertrude Stein: *Autobiography of Alice B. Toklas*. T.S. Eliot:
              The Use of Poetry and the Use of Criticism. John Brooks
              Wheelright: *Rock and Shell*. Death of Sara Teasdale.
1934   Ezra Pound: *ABC of Reading*. T.S. Eliot: *After Strange Gods*.
              George Oppen: *Discrete Series*. Charles Reznikoff: *Jerusalem*.
1935   T.S. Eliot: *Murder in the Cathedral*. Salvador Dali: *Giraffe on
              Fire*. Marianne Moore: *Selected Poems*. Walter Benjamin:
              "The Work of Art in the Age of Mechanical Reproduction."
              Wallace Stevens: *Ideas of Order*. William Carlos Williams:
              An Early Martyr. Robinson Jeffers: *Solstice and Other Poems*.
              Muriel Rukeyser: *Theory of Flight*. Death of Edwin
              Arlington Robinson.
1936   Robert Frost: *A Further Range*. Piet Mondrian: *Composition
              in Red and Blue*. Spanish Civil War begis. Charlie Chaplin:
              Modern Times. Allen Tate: *The Mediterranean and Other
              Poems*.
1937   Pablo Picasso: *Guernica*. J.R.R. Tolkien: *The Hobbit*.
              Wallace Stevens: *The Man with the Blue Guitar*. Louise
              Bogan: *The Sleeping Fury*.

1938   E.E. Cummings: *Collected Poems*. Adolf Hitler assumes command of the German Army.

1939   James Joyce: *Finnegan's Wake*. Outbreak of World War II. John Steinbeck: *The Grapes of Wrath*. T.S. Eliot: *Family Reunion*. Muriel Rukeyser: *A Turning Wind*.

1940   Paris occupied by the Germans. Richard Wright: *Native Son*. Langston Hughes: *The Big Sea*. Randall Jarrell: *The Rage for the Lost Penny*.

1941   Japanese attack Pearl Harbor. Orson Welles: *Citizen Kane*. William Carlos Williams: *Broken Span*. Edward Hopper: *Nighthawks*. Marianne Moore: *What Are Years?* Theodore Roethke: *Open House*.

1942   Robert Frost: *A Witness Tree*. Wallace Stevens: *Parts of a World*. Randall Jarrell: *Blood for a Stranger*. Robert Penn Warren: *Eleven Poems on the Same Theme*.

1943   Weldon Kees: *The Last Man*.

1944   T.S. Eliot: *Four Quartets*. H.D.: *The Walls Do Not Fall*. William Carlos Williams: *The Wedge*. W.H. Auden: *For the Time Being* and *The Sea and the Mirror*. Robert Lowell: *Land of Unlikeness*. Marianne Moore: *Nevertheless*.

1945   Atomic bomb dropped on Hiroshima. World War II ends. Robert Frost: *A Masque of Reason*. H.D.: *Tribute to the Angels*. Gwendolyn Brooks: *A Street in Bronzeville*.

1946   Robert Penn Warren: *All the King's Men*. H.D.: *The Flowering of the Rod*. Robert Lowell: *Lord Weary's Castle*. Death of Countee Cullen.

1947   Tennessee Williams: *A Streetcar Named Desire*. Robert Frost: *Steeple Bush*. Wallace Stevens: *Transport to Summer*.

1948   T.S. Eliot wins the Nobel Prize for Literature. Ezra Pound: *The Pisan Cantos*. Theodore Roethke: *The Lost Son*.

1949   Arthur Miller: *Death of a Salesman*. T.S. Eliot: *The Cocktail Party*.

1950   The United States attacks Korea. Jackson Pollock: *Lavender Mist*. Robert Lowell: *The Mills and the Kavanaughs*. Deaths of Edgar Lee Masters and Edna St. Vincent Millay.

1951   Marianne Moore wins the Pulitzer Prize and the National Book Award for her *Collected Poems*. Wallace Stevens: *The Necessary Angel*. Langston Hughes: *Montage of a Dream Deferred*. James Merrill: *First Poems*.

1952	Ralph Ellison: *Invisible Man*. Willem de Kooning: *Woman and Bicycle*. Archibald MacLeish: *Collected Poems*. W.S. Merwin: *A Mask for Janus*. Frank O'Hara: *A City Winter and Other Poems*.
1953:	Randall Jarrell: *Poetry and the Age*. Charles Olson: *In Cold Hell, in Thicket*. Robert Penn Warren: *Brother to Dragons*.
1954	Wallace Stevens: *Collected Poems*. William Carlos Williams: *The Desert Music*.
1955	Ezra Pound: *Rock Drill*. Allen Ginsberg: *Howl*. Randall Jarrell: *Selected Poems*. A.R. Ammons: *Ommateum*. Death of Wallace Stevens.
1956	John Ashbery: *Some Trees*.
1957	Samuel Beckett: *Endgame*.
1959	Robert Lowell: *Life Studies*.
1960	Charles Olson: *The Maximus Poems*.
1961	Death of H.D. Ezra Pound: *Thrones*.
1962	John Frankenheimer: *The Manchurian Candidate*. Deaths of Robinson Jeffers, William Faulkner, and E.E. Cummings. Robert Frost: *In the Clearing*. William Carlos Williams: *Pictures from Brueghel*.
1963	Deaths of Robert Lee Frost and William Carlos Williams.
1964	Ernest Hemingway: *A Moveable Feast*. Frank O'Hara: *Lunch Poems*. Theodore Roethke: *The Far Field*.
1965	Malcolm X assassinated. George Oppen: *This in Which*. Death of T.S. Eliot.
1966	Thomas Pynchon: *The Crying of Lot 49*. Gwendolyn Brooks: *We Real Cool*. James Merrill: *Nights and Days*. Robert Penn Warren: *Selected Poems: New and Old, 1923-1966*. Robert Hayden: *Selected Poems*.
1967	Deaths of Langston Hughes, Dorothy Parker, and Carl August Sandburg. Marianne Moore: *Complete Poems*. W.S. Merwin: *The Lice*.
1968	Martin Luther King assassinated. First manned landing on the moon. Louise Bogan: *The Blue Estuaries 1923-1968*. Death of Yvor Winters.
1970	Death of Louise Bogan.
1972	Deaths of Ezra Pound, Marianne Moore, and Edmund Wilson.

Contributors

HAROLD BLOOM is Sterling Professor of the Humanities at Yale University. He is the author of over 20 books, including *Shelley's Mythmaking* (1959), *The Visionary Company* (1961), *Blake's Apocalypse* (1963), *Yeats* (1970), *A Map of Misreading* (1975), *Kabbalah and Criticism* (1975), *Agon: Toward a Theory of Revisionism* (1982), *The American Religion* (1992), *The Western Canon* (1994), and *Omens of Millennium: The Gnosis of Angels, Dreams, and Resurrection* (1996). *The Anxiety of Influence* (1973) sets forth Professor Bloom's provocative theory of the literary relationships between the great writers and their predecessors. His most recent books include *Shakespeare: The Invention of the Human* (1998), a 1998 National Book Award finalist, *How to Read and Why* (2000), *Genius: A Mosaic of One Hundred Exemplary Creative Minds* (2002), *Hamlet: Poem Unlimited* (2003), and *Where Shall Wisdom be Found* (2004). In 1999, Professor Bloom received the prestigious American Academy of Arts and Letters Gold Medal for Criticism, and in 2002 he received the Catalonia International Prize.

KENNETH BURKE (1897–1993) taught at Princeton University, the University of Chicago, Harvard University, and Dartmouth College during his long and distinguished career as a man of letters. His works include *A Grammar of Motives*, *Counter-Statement*, *A Rhetoric of Motives*, and *Language As Symbolic Action*.

HUGH KENNER (1923–2003) taught English at Johns Hopkins University and the University of Georgia. His many books include *The Pound Era, The Stoic Comedians, The Counterfeiters,* and *A Homemade World.*

ALAN TRACHTENBERG has taught at Pennsylvania State University and at Yale University. He has written *The Incorporation of Amerca: Culture and Society in the Gilded Age* and *Reading American Photographs: Images as History, Matthew Brady to Evans Walker.*

THOMAS R. WHITAKER is Emeritus Professor of English at Yale University. His books include *Fields of Play in Modern Drama* and *Mirrors of Our Playing,* as well as studies of Yeats and Williams.

HELEN HENNESSEY VENDLER teaches at Harvard University. Her many books include studies of Yeats, Stevens, Herbert, Keats, Heaney, and Shakespeare's sonnets. Her most recent work is *Coming of Age as a Poet.*

ROBERT LANGBAUM has taught English at the University of Virginia. His works include *The Modern Spirit, The Mysteries of Identity,* and *The Poetry of Experience.*

RICHARD POIRIER is Professor Emeritus of English at Rutgers University. He is the Editor of *Raritan Quarterly.* In addition to *Robert Frost: The Work of Knowing,* he is the author of *The Performing Self, A World Elsewhere, Poetry and Pragmatism,* and *Trying it Out in America.*

JAMES E. MILLER, JR. is Helen A. Regenstein Professor Emeritus of English at the University of Chicago. His books include *T.S. Eliot's Personal Wasteland, The American Quest for a Supreme Fiction: Whitman's Legacy in the Personal Epic,* and *Leaves of Grass: America's Lyric-Epic of Self and Democracy.*

ELEANOR COOK is Professor of English at the University of Toronto. She is the author of *Poetry, Word-Play, and Word-War in Wallace Stevens* and *Against Coercion: Games Poets Play.*

EDWARD HIRSCH teaches at the University of Houston. He is the author of five books of poetry, and he writes frequently about poetry for *American Poetry Review* and *The New Yorker.*

LANGDON HAMMER is Professor of English at Yale University. He is the author of *Hart Crane and Allen Tate: Janus-Faced Modernism* and co-editor of *O My Land, My Friends: The Selected Letters of Hart Crane*. Currently he is at work on a biography of James Merrill.

KATHERINE KEARNS has taught at New York University and Yale University. She is the author of *Robert Frost and the Poetics of Appetite*, *Nineteenth-century Literary Realism*, and *Psychoanalysis, Historiography, and Feminist Theory*.

DAVID BROMWICH is Housum Professor of English at Yale University. His books include *Hazlitt: The Mind of the Critic, Disowned by Memory: Wordsworth's Poetry of the 1790s, A Choice of Inheritance: Self and Community from Edmund Burke to Robert Frost*, and *Skeptical Music*.

LOUIS L. MARTZ has taught English at Yale University. His books include *From Renaissance to Baroque, Thomas More: The Search for the Inner Man*, and most recently, *Many Gods and Many Voices: The Role of the Prophet in English and American Modernism*.

ANITA PATTERSON is Associate Professor of English at Boston University. She is the author of *From Emerson to King: Democracy, Race, and the Politics of Protest*. Her many essays on American literature have appeared in a variety of journals and reviews, including *The Journal of Commonwealth Literature, Modern Language Quarterly, Salmagundi*, and *The Massachusetts Review*.

BONNIE COSTELLO is Professor English at Boston University. She is the author of *Marianne Moore: Imaginary Possessions, Elizabeth Bishop: Questions of Mastery*, and *Shifting Ground: Reinventing Landscape in Modern American Poetry*. She has also written on the poetry of John Ashbery, Wallace Stevens, Jorie Graham, Amy Clampitt, and Charles Wright.

Bibliography

Alexander, Michael. *The Poetic Achievement of Ezra Pound*. Berkeley: University of California Press, 1979.

Bagby, George F. *Frost and the Book of Nature*. Knoxville: University of Tennessee Press, 1993.

Baker, Houston A. *Modernism and the Harlem Renaissance*. Chicago: University of Chicago Press, 1987.

Baker, Peter. *Obdurate Brilliance: Exteriority and the Modern Long Poem*. Gainesville: University of Florida Press, 1991.

Bernstein, Michael. *The Tale of the Tribe: Ezra Pound and the Modern Verse Epic*. Princeton: Princeton University Press, 1980.

Blackmur, R. P. *Form and Value in Modern Poetry*. Garden City: Doubleday, 1957.

Bloom, Harold. *Agon: Towards a Theory of Revisionism*. New York: Oxford University Press, 1982.

———. *Figures of Capable Imagination*. New York: Seabury Press, 1976.

———. *Poetry and Repression*. New Haven: Yale University Press, 1976.

———. *Wallace Stevens: The Poems of Our Climate*. Ithaca, NY: Cornell University Press, 1977.

Boroff, Marie. *Language and the Poet: Verbal Artistry in Frost, Stevens, and Moore*. Chicago: University of Chicago Press, 1979.

Breslin, James E.B. *William Carlos Williams*. New York: Oxford University Press, 1970.

Bridgman, Richard. *Gertrude Stein in Pieces*. New York: Oxford University Press, 1970.

Bromwich, David. *A Choice of Inheritance: Self and Community from Edmund Burke to Robert Frost*. Cambridge, MA: Harvard University Press, 1989.

———. *Skeptical Music*. Chicago: University of Chicago Press, 2001.

Bush, Ronald. *T.S. Eliot: A Study in Character and Style*. New York: Oxford University Press, 1984.

———. *The Genesis of Ezra Pound's Cantos*. Princeton: Princeton University Press, 1976.

Casillio, Robert. *The Genealogy of Demons: Anti-Semitism, Fascism, and the Myths of Ezra Pound*. Evanston: Northwestern University Press, 1988.

Cohen, Milton A. *Poet and Painter: The Aesthetics of E.E. Cummings's Early Work*. Detroit: Wayne State University Press, 1987.

Cook, Eleanor. *Poetry, Word-Play, and Word-War in Wallace Stevens*. Princeton: Princeton University Press, 1988.

Costello, Bonnie: *Marianne Moore: Imaginary Possessions*. Cambridge, MA: Harvard University Press, 1981.

Crawford, Robert. *The Savage and the City in the Work of T.S. Eliot*. Oxford: Clarendon Press, 1987.

DiBattista, Maria and Lucy McDiarmid, eds. *High and Low Moderns: Literature and Culture 1889–1939*. New York: Oxford University Press, 1996.

Dijkstra, Bram. *The Hieroglyphics of a New Speech: Cubism, Stieglitz and the Early Poetry of William Carlos Williams*. Princeton: Princeton University Press, 1969.

Donoghue, Denis. *Connoisseurs of Chaos: Ideas of Order in Modern American Poetry*. New York: Macmillan, 1965.

DuPlessis, Rachel Blau. *H.D.: The Career of that Struggle*. Brighton: Harvester, 1986.

Edelman, Lee. *Transmemberment of Song: Hart Crane's Anatomies of Rhetoric and Desire*. Stanford: Stanford University Press, 1987.

Filreis, Alan. *Modernism from Right to Left: Wallace Stevens, the Thirties, and Literary Radicalism*. Cambridge: Cambridge University Press, 1994.

Kermode, Frank. *Wallace Stevens*. London: Oliver and Boyd, 1960.

Friedman, Norman. *e.e. cummings: the art of his poetry*. Baltimore: Johns Hopkins Press, 1960.

Fussell, Paul. *The Great War and Modern Memory*. New York: Oxford University Press, 1975.

Gelpi, Albert, ed. *Wallace Stevens and the Poetics of Modernism*. New York: Cambridge University Press, 1985.

Gilbert, Sandra, and Susan Gubar. *No Man's Land*. 3 vols. New Haven: Yale University Press, 1988–1994.

Gordon, Lydnall. *Eliot's Early Years*. Oxford: Oxford University Press, 1977.

———. *Eliot's New Life*. Oxford: Oxford University Press, 1988.

Gross, Harvey. *Sound and Form in Modern Poetry: A Study of Prosody from Thomas Hardy to Robert Lowell*. Ann Arbor: University of Michigan Press, 1964.

Guest, Barbara. *Herself Defined: The Poet H.D. and Her World*. Garden City: Doubleday, 1984.

Hammer, Langdon. *Janus-Faced Modernism: Hart Crane and Allen Tate*. Princeton: Princeton University Press, 1993.

Jarrell, Randall. *Poetry and the Age*. New York: Knopf, 1953.

Julius, Anthony. *T.S. Eliot, Anti-Semitism, and Literary Form*. Cambridge: Cambridge University Press, 1995.

Kalaidjian, Wlater. *American Culture Between the Wars: Revisionary Modernism and Postmodern Critique*. New York: Columbia University Press, 1993.

Kalstone, David. *Becoming a Poet: Elizabeth Bishop with Marianne Moore and Robert Lowell*. Ed. Robert Hemenway. New York: Farrar Straus and Giroux, 1989.

Keller, Lynn. *Re-making it New: Contemporary American Poetry and the Modernist Tradition*. New York: Cambridge University Press, 1987.

Kenner, Hugh. *The Pound Era*. Berkeley: University of California Press, 1971.

Lane, Gary. *I Am: A Study of E.E. Cummings' Poems*. Lawrence: The University Press of Kansas, 1976.

Latham, Edward Connery, ed. *The Poetry of Robert Frost*. New York: Holt, Rinehart & Winston, 1969.

Leavell, Linda. *Marianne Moore and the Visual Arts: Prismatic Color*. Baton Rouge: Louisiana State University Press, 1995.

Lentricchia, Frank. *Ariel and the Police: Michel Foucault, William James, Wallace Stevens*. Brighton: Harvester Wheatsheaf, 1988.

———. *Modernist Quartet*. Cambridge: Cambridge University Press, 1994.

Litz, A. Walton. *Introspective Voyager: The Poetic Development of Wallace Stevens*. New York: Oxford University Press, 1972.

———, ed. *Eliot in His Time*. Princeton: Princeton University Press, 1973.

Longenbach, James. *Modernist Poetics of History*. Princeton: Princeton University Press, 1987.

———. *Stone Cottage: Pound, Yeats, and Modernism*. New York: Oxford University Press, 1988.

———. *Wallace Stevens: The Plain Sense of Things*. New York: Oxford University Press, 1991.

Materer, Timothy. *Vortex: Pound, Eliot, and Lewis*. Ithaca, NY: Cornell University Press, 1979.

MacLeod, Glen. *Wallace Stevens and Modern Art: From the Armory Show to Abstract Expressionism*. New Haven: Yale University Press, 1993.

McDiarmid, Lucy. *Saving Civilization: Yeats, Eliot, and Auden Between the Wars*. Cambridge: Cambridge University Press, 1984.

Miller, Cristanne. *Marianne Moore: Questions of Authority*. Cambridge, MA: Harvard University Press, 1995.

Miller, J. Hillis. *The Linguistic Moment: From Wordsworth to Stevens*. Princeton: Princeton University Press, 1985.

———. *Poets of Reality*. Cambridge, MA: Harvard University Press, 1966.

Nelson, Cary. *Repression and Recovery: Modern American Poetry and the Politics of Cultural Memory, 1910–1945*. Madison: University of Wisconsin Press, 1989.

North, Michael. *The Political Aesthetic of Yeats, Eliot, and Pound*. Cambridge: Cambridge University Press, 1991.

Pack, Robert. *Belief and Uncertainty in the Poetry of Robert Frost*. Hanover: Middlebury College Press, 2003.

Parisi, Joseph. *Marianne Moore: The Art of a Modernist*. Ann Arbor: University of Michigan Research Press, 1987.

Pearce, Roy Harvey. *The Continuity of American Poetry*. Princeton: Princeton University Press, 1961.

Perloff, Marjorie. *The Dance of the Intellect: Studies in the Pound Tradition*. Cambridge: Cambridge University Press, 1985.

———. *The Poetry of Indeterminacy: Rimbaud to Cage*. Princeton: Princeton University Press, 1981.

Poirier, Richard. *Poetry and Pragmatism*. London: Faber and Faber, 1992.

———. *Robert Frost: The Work of Knowing*. New York: Oxford University Press, 1977.

Pritchard, William. *Robert Frost: A Literary Life*. Oxford University Press, 1984.

Quartermain, Peter. *Disjunctive Poetics: From Gertrude Stein and Louis Zukofsky to Susan Howe*. New York: Cambridge University Press, 1992.

Rainey, Lawrence. *Ezra Pound and the Monument of Culture: Text, History, and the Malatesta Cantos.* Chicago: University of Chicago Press, 1991.

Ricks, Christopher. *T.S. Eliot and Prejudice.* Berkeley: University of California Press, 1988.

Riddel, Joseph. *The Clairvoyant Eye: The Poetry and Poetics of Wallace Stevens.* Baton Rouge: Louisiana State University Press, 1965.

Ruddick, Lisa. *Reading Gertrude Stein: Body, Text, Gnosis.* Ithaca: Cornell University Press, 1990.

Schwartz, Sanford. *The Matrix of Modernism: Pound, Eliot and Early Twentieth-Century Thought.* Princeton: Princeton University Press, 1985.

Sigg, Eric. *The American T.S. Eliot: A Study of the Early Writings.* New York: Cambridge University Press, 1989.

Slatin, Myles. *The Savage's Romance: The Poetry of Marianne Moore.* University Park: Pennsylvania State University Press, 1986.

Stewart, John L. *The Burden of Time: The Fugitives and Agrarians.* Princeton: Princeton University Press, 1965.

Stock, Noel *The Life of Ezra Pound.* New York: Pantheon, 1970.

Tate, Allen. *The Man of Letters in the Modern World: Selected Essays, 1928–1955.* New York: Meridian Books, 1955.

Trachtenberg, Alan. *The Brooklyn Bridge, Fact and Symbol.* New York: Oxford University Press, 1965.

Vendler, Helen. *On Extended Wings: Wallace Stevens' Longer Poems.* Cambridge, MA: Harvard University Press, 1969.

———. *Part of Nature, Part of Us: Modern American Poets.* Cambridge, MA: Harvard University Press, 1980.

Wagner, Linda Welsheimer. *The Poems of William Carlos Williams.* Middletown: Wesleyan University Press, 1964.

Walker, Cheryl. *Masks Outrageous and Austere: Culture, Psyche, and Persona in Modern Women Poets.* Bloomington: University of Indiana Press, 1991.

Weaver, Mike. *William Carlos Williams: The American Background.* Cambridge: Cambridge University Press, 1971.

Whitaker, Thomas R. *William Carlos Williams.* New York: Twayne, 1968.

Witmeyer, Hugh. *The Poetry of Ezra Pound.* Berkeley: University of California Press, 1981.

Yingling, Thomas. *Hart Crane and the Homosexual Text.* Chicago: University of Chicago Press, 1990.

Acknowledgments

"Motives and Motifs in the Poetry of Marianne Moore" by Kenneth Burke from *A Grammar of Motives*. © 1969 by The Regents of the University of California. Reprinted by permission.

"Mauberley" by Hugh Kenner from *The Poetry of Ezra Pound*. © 1968 by New Directions Publishing Corp. Reprinted by permission of New Directions Publishing Corp.

"The Shadow of a Myth" by Alan Trachtenberg from *Brooklyn Bridge: Fact and Symbol*. © 1965 by Alan Trachtenberg. Reprinted by permission.

"Open to the Weather" by Thomas R. Whitaker from *William Carlos Williams*. © 1968 by Twayne Publishers, Inc. Reprinted by permission of The Gale Group.

"Douceurs, Tristesses" by Helen Vendler from *On Extended Wings: Wallace Stevens' Longer Poems*. © 1969 by the President and Fellows of Harvard College. Reprinted by permission.

"New Modes of Characterization in *The Waste Land*" by Robert Langbaum from *Eliot in His Time*, ed. A. Walton Litz. © 1973 by Princeton University Press. Reprinted by permission of Princeton University Press.

"Soundings for Home" by Richard Poirier from *Robert Frost: The Work of Knowing*. © 1977 by Oxford University Press, Inc. Reprinted by permission.

"How Shall I Be Mirror to This Modernity: William Carlos Williams's 'Paterson'" by James E. Miller, Jr. from *The American Quest for a Supreme Fiction: Whitman's Legacy in the Personal Epic*. © 1979 by the University of Chicago. Reprinted by permission.

"Late Poems: Places, Common and Other" by Eleanor Cook from *Poetry, Word-Play, and Word-War in Wallace Stevens*. © 1988 by Princeton University Press. Reprinted by permission of Princeton University Press.

"Helmet of Fire: American Poetry in the 1920s" by Edward Hirsch from *A Profile of Twentieth-Century American Poetry*, ed. Jack Myers and David Wojahn. © 1991 by the Board of Trustees, Southern Illinois University. Reprinted by permission.

"Siena Mi Fe'; Disfecemi Maremma" by Ezra Pound from *Personae*. © 1926 by Ezra Pound. Reprinted by permission of New Directions Publishing Corporation.

"Spring and All" by William Carlos Williams from *Collected Poems: 1909–1939*, Vol. 1. © 1938 by New Directions Publishing Corporation. Reprinted by permission of New Directions Publishing Corporation.

"Poetry" of Marianne Moore from *The Collected Poems of Marianne Moore*. © 1935 by Marianne Moore; renewed © 1963 by Marianne Moore and T.S. Eliot. Reprinted by permission of Scribner, an imprint of Simon & Schuster Adult Publishing Group.

The Complete Poems and Selected Letters and Prose of Hart Crane by Hart Crane, ed. Brom Weber. © 1933, 1958, 1966 by Liveright Publishing Corporation. © 1962 by Brom Weber. Used by permission of Liveright Publishing Corporation.

"Dice of Drowned Men's Bones" by Langdon Hammer from *Hart Crane and Allen Tate: Janus-Faced Modernism*. © 1993 by Princeton University Press. Reprinted by permission of Princeton University Press.

"Lyricism: At the Back of the North Wind" by Katherine Kearns from *Robert Frost and the Poetics of Appetite*. © 1994 by Cambridge University Press. Reprinted by permission.

"T.S. Eliot and Hart Crane" by David Bromwich from *Skeptical Music: Essays on Modern Poetry*. © 2001 by David Bromwich. Reprinted by permission.

"H.D.: Set Free to Prophecy" by Louis L. Martz from *Many Gods and Many Voices: The Role of the Prophet in English and American Modernism*. © 1998 by The Curators of the University of Missouri. Reprinted by permission of the University of Missouri Press.

"Jazz, Realism, and the Modernist Lyric: The Poetry of Langston Hughes" by Anita Patterson from *Modern Language Quarterly* 61, no. 4 (December 2000): 651–682. © 2000 by the University of Washington. Reprinted by permission of Duke University Press.

"Moore's America" by Bonnie Costello from *Shifting Ground: Reinventing Landscape in Modern American Poetry*. © 2003 by the President and Fellows of Harvard College. Reprinted by permission.

Index

1, 7, 11, 14, 19, 21, 25, 82, 50, 111, 143, 167, 195, 23 3, 253, 281, 343, 395, 427